AF682495

NATIONAL SECURITY AND INTERNATIONAL ECONOMIC LAW

This book offers a timely and insightful exploration of security exceptions in international trade and investment law, focusing on the growing tension between national security measures and global economic stability. Through in-depth analysis and case studies of major global players, it uncovers how current practices are shaping international trade governance. The book examines the challenges posed by overly broad or narrow security exceptions, proposes practical reforms to improve legal clarity, and suggests ways to enhance cooperation between international organizations like the World Trade Organization (WTO) and the United Nations (UN). Aimed at policymakers, legal professionals, and scholars, this book provides valuable recommendations to help navigate the evolving landscape of global trade, offering concrete solutions to balance national security concerns with the need for economic cooperation.

OLGA HRYNKIV is an international law scholar with a background in legal practice. She is the author of multiple academic articles and book chapters on international economic law and legal challenges in digitalizing critical infrastructure and advancing energy transition. She obtained her PhD (cum laude) from Tilburg University, where she was honored with the PhD Dissertation Prize.

CAMBRIDGE INTERNATIONAL TRADE AND ECONOMIC LAW

Series Editors

Professor Lorand Bartels
University of Cambridge

Professor Thomas Cottier
University of Berne

Professor Tomer Broude
Hebrew University of Jerusalem

Professor Andrea K. Bjorklund
McGill University, Montréal

Processes of economic regionalisation and globalisation have intensified over the last decades, accompanied by increases in the regulation of international trade and economics at the levels of international, regional and national laws. At the same time, significant challenges have arisen with respect to economic liberalization, rule-based systems of trade and investment, and their political and social impacts. The subject matter of this series is international economic law, in this contemporary context. Its core is the regulation of international trade, investment, finance and cognate areas such as intellectual property and competition policy. The series publishes books on related regulatory areas, in particular human rights, labour, environment and culture, as well as sustainable development. These areas are horizontally interconnected and vertically linked at the international, regional and national levels. The series also includes works on governance, dealing with the structure and operation of international organisations related to the field of international economic law, and the way they interact with other subjects of international and national law. The series aims to include excellent legal doctrinal treatises, as well as cutting-edge interdisciplinary works that engage law and the social sciences and humanities.

Books in the Series

National Security and International Economic Law: Restoring Balance
Olga Hrynkiv

International Financial Institutions and Sustainable Development: Lawmaking and Accountability
Johanna Aleria P. Lorenzo

The Making of an International Investment Facilitation Framework: Legal, Political and Economics Perspectives
Axel Berger and Manjiao Chi

International Economic Law in the Era of Datafication
Shin-yi Peng

Causation in the Law of the World Trade Organization: An Econometric Approach
Catherine Gascoigne

The European Union and International Investment Law Reform: Between Aspirations and Reality
Ivana Damjanovic

Agricultural Domestic Support under the WTO: Experience and Prospects
Lars Brink and David Orden

Capital Controls and International Economic Law
Bryan Mercurio

The Law and Practice of Global ICT Standardization
Olia Kanevskaia Whitaker

Between Market Economy and State Capitalism: China's State-Owned Enterprises and the World Trading System
Henry S. Gao and Weihuan Zhou

New Asian Regionalism in International Economic Law
Pasha L. Hsieh

Essential Interoperability Standards: Interfacing Intellectual Property and Competition in International Economic Law
Simon Brinsmead

Digital Services in International Trade Law
Ines Willemyns

Law and Politics on Export Restrictions: WTO and Beyond
Chien-Huei Wu

Energy in International Trade Law: Concepts, Regulation and Changing Markets
Anna-Alexandra Marhold

Shareholders' Claims for Reflective Loss in International Investment Law
Lukas Vanhonnaeker

Transparency in the WTO SPS and TBT Agreements: The Real Jewel in the Crown
Marianna B. Karttunen

Preferential Services Liberalization: The Case of the European Union and Federal States
Johanna Jacobsson

Emerging Powers in International Economic Law: Cooperation, Competition and Transformation
Sonia E. Rolland and David M. Trubek

Commitments and Flexibilities in the WTO Agreement on Subsidies and Countervailing Measures
José Guilherme Moreno Caiado

The Return of the Home State to Investor-State Disputes: Bringing Back Diplomatic Protection?
Rodrigo Polanco

Industrial Policy and the World Trade Organization: Between Legal Constraints and Flexibilities
Sherzod Shadikhodjaev

The Public International Law of Trade in Legal Services
David Collins

The Prudential Carve-Out for Financial Services: Rationale and Practice in the GATS and Preferential Trade Agreements
Carlo Maria Cantore

Preferential Services Liberalization: The Case of the European Union and Federal States
Johanna Jacobsson

Judicial Acts and Investment Treaty Arbitration
Berk Demirkol

Distributive Justice and World Trade Law: A Political Theory of International Trade Regulation
Oisin Suttle

Freedom of Transit and Access to Gas Pipeline Networks under WTO Law
Vitalily Pogoretskyy

Reclaiming Development in the World Trading System, 2nd edition
Yong-Shik Lee

Developing Countries and Preferential Services Trade
Charlotte Sieber-Gasser

Establishing Judicial Authority in International Economic Law Edited by
Joanna Jemielniak, Laura Nielsen and Henrik Palmer Olsen

WTO Dispute Settlement and the TRIPS Agreement: Applying Intellectual Property Standards in a Trade Law Framework
Matthew Kennedy

Trade, Investment, Innovation and Their Impact on Access to Medicines: An Asian Perspective
Locknie Hsu

The WTO and International Investment Law: Converging Systems
Jürgen Kurtz

The Law, Economics and Politics of International Standardisation Edited by
Panagiotis Delimatsis

Export Restrictions on Critical Minerals and Metals: Testing the Adequacy of WTO Disciplines
Ilaria Espa

Optimal Regulation and the Law of International Trade: The Interface between the Right to Regulate and WTO Law
Boris Rigod

The Social Foundations of World Trade: Norms, Community, and Constitution
Sungjoon Cho

Public Participation and Legitimacy in the WTO
Yves Bonzon

The Challenge of Safeguards in the WTO
Fernando Piérola

General Interests of Host States in International Investment Law Edited by Giorgio Sacerdoti, with Pia Acconci, Mara Valenti and Anna De Luca

WTO Disciplines on Subsidies and Countervailing Measures: Balancing Policy Space and Legal Constraints
Dominic Coppens

The Law of Development Cooperation: A Comparative Analysis of the World Bank, the EU and Germany
Philipp Dann

Liberalizing International Trade after Doha: Multilateral, Plurilateral, Regional, and Unilateral Initiatives
David A. Gantz

Domestic Judicial Review of Trade Remedies: Experiences of the Most Active WTO Members Edited by
Müslüm Yilmaz

The Relevant Market in International Economic Law: A Comparative Antitrust and GATT Analysis
Christian A. Melischek

International Organizations in WTO Dispute Settlement: How Much Institutional Sensitivity?
Marina Foltea

Public Services and International Trade Liberalization: Human Rights and Gender Implications
Barnali Choudhury

The Law and Politics of WTO Waivers: Stability and Flexibility in Public International Law
Isabel Feichtner

African Regional Trade Agreements as Legal Regimes
James Thuo Gathii

Processes and Production Methods (PPMs) in WTO Law: Interfacing Trade and Social Goals
Christiane R. Conrad

Non-Discrimination in International Trade in Services: 'Likeness' in WTO/GATS
Nicolas F. Diebold

The Law, Economics and Politics of Retaliation in WTO Dispute Settlement
Edited by Chad P. Bown and Joost Pauwelyn

The Multilateralization of International Investment Law
Stephan W. Schill

Trade Policy Flexibility and Enforcement in the WTO: A Law and Economics Analysis
Simon A. B. Schropp

NATIONAL SECURITY AND INTERNATIONAL ECONOMIC LAW

Restoring Balance

OLGA HRYNKIV
Tilburg University

CAMBRIDGE
UNIVERSITY PRESS

CAMBRIDGE
UNIVERSITY PRESS

Shaftesbury Road, Cambridge CB2 8EA, United Kingdom

One Liberty Plaza, 20th Floor, New York, NY 10006, USA

477 Williamstown Road, Port Melbourne, VIC 3207, Australia

314–321, 3rd Floor, Plot 3, Splendor Forum, Jasola District Centre, New Delhi – 110025, India

Cambridge University Press is part of Cambridge University Press & Assessment, a department of the University of Cambridge.

We share the University's mission to contribute to society through the pursuit of education, learning and research at the highest international levels of excellence.

www.cambridge.org
Information on this title: www.cambridge.org/9781009649070

DOI: 10.1017/9781009649124

© Olga Hrynkiv 2026

This publication is in copyright. Subject to statutory exception and to the provisions of relevant collective licensing agreements, no reproduction of any part may take place without the written permission of Cambridge University Press & Assessment.

When citing this work, please include a reference to the DOI 10.1017/9781009649124

First published 2026

Cover image: Abstract Geometric Shapes. Black and Blue Circles with Spray Brush Strokes Illustration on Gray Background / oxygen / Collection: Moment / Getty Images

A catalogue record for this publication is available from the British Library

Library of Congress Cataloging-in-Publication Data
Names: Hrynkiv, Olga author
Title: National security and international economic law : restoring balance / Olga Hrynkiv, Tilburg University.
Description: Cambridge, United Kingdom ; New York, NY : Cambridge University Press, 2026. | Series: Cambridge international trade and economic law | Includes index.
Identifiers: LCCN 2025034449 (print) | LCCN 2025034450 (ebook) | ISBN 9781009649070 hardback | ISBN 9781009649100 paperback | ISBN 9781009649124 ebook
Subjects: LCSH: World Trade Organization | Foreign trade regulation – International cooperation | Investments, Foreign (International law) | Security, International – Economic aspects | National security – Law and legislation | Economic stabilization
Classification: LCC K3943 .H79 2026 (print) | LCC K3943 (ebook) | DDC 343.08/7–dc23/eng/20250731
LC record available at https://lccn.loc.gov/2025034449
LC ebook record available at https://lccn.loc.gov/2025034450

ISBN 978-1-009-64907-0 Hardback

Cambridge University Press & Assessment has no responsibility for the persistence or accuracy of URLs for external or third-party internet websites referred to in this publication and does not guarantee that any content on such websites is, or will remain, accurate or appropriate.

For EU product safety concerns, contact us at Calle de José Abascal, 56, 1°, 28003 Madrid, Spain, or email eugpsr@cambridge.org

To my husband Joris and our daughter Stella who showed me
the true essence of balance

CONTENTS

ACKNOWLEDGMENTS

This book stems from years of learning, unlearning, and relearning about the interplay between international trade, international law, and geopolitics. The idea for it began forming in 2017 while I was still in my home country, Ukraine. At that time, I worked as a trade lawyer, grappling with the complexities of economic sanctions and export controls. It was also then that the World Trade Organization had to make its first-ever ruling on a national security exception in the case Ukraine brought against Russia.

In 2018, I met Panos Delimatsis, who shares my passion for international trade law and whose career achievements have inspired me to conduct my doctoral research at Tilburg University under his supervision. Little did I know that within four years, Russia would launch a full-scale invasion of my home country, causing massive casualties and destruction. This war led many, including myself, to question the role and purpose of international law. It also underscored the urgent need to revisit the link between international trade and national security, a task I undertake in this book.

This book would not have been possible without the mentorship, brainstorming sessions, and unwavering support of Panos Delimatsis in every step of my research. I also had the privilege of working with amazing colleagues at the Tilburg Institute for Law, Technology, and Society, the Tilburg Law and Economics Center, and the Fletcher School of Law and Diplomacy. Their intellectual prowess, openness, and collaborative spirit inspired me to continue my journey in academia and eventually complete and publish this book. I am especially grateful to Joel Trachtman, who profoundly influenced the trajectory of my research. Finally, I am grateful to the anonymous reviewers for their feedback and valuable comments on my book proposal.

TABLE OF CASES

PCIJ/ICJ

Affaire du Lac Lanoux (France v Espagne) (1957) ICJ.
Alleged Violations of the 1955 Treaty of Amity, Economic Relations, and Consular Rights (Iran v US) (2021) ICJ.
Case concerning certain German Interests in Polish Upper Silesia (Germany v Poland) (1926) PCIJ.
Case Concerning Certain Questions on Mutual Assistance in Criminal Matters (Djibouti v France) (2008) ICJ.
Case Concerning Military and Paramilitary Activities in and against Nicaragua (Nicaragua v US) (1986) ICJ.
Corfu Channel (United Kingdom of Great Britain and Northern Ireland v Albania) (1949) ICJ.
Gabčíkovo – Nagymaros Project (Hungary/Slovakia) (1997) ICJ.
Oil Platforms (Iran v US) (1996) ICJ.
US Diplomatic and Consular Staff in Tehran (US v Iran) (1980) ICJ.

GATT/WTO PANELS AND APPELLATE BODY

Argentina – Measures Affecting the Importation of Goods (January 15, 2015) Appellate Body WT/DS438/AB/R, WT/DS444/AB/R, WT/DS445/AB/R.
Brazil – Measures Affecting Imports of Retreaded Tyres (December 3, 2007) Appellate Body WT/DS332/AB/R.
Canada – Continued Suspension of Obligations in the EC – Hormones Dispute (October 16, 2008) Appellate Body WT/DS321/AB/R.
Chile – Taxes on Alcoholic Beverages (December 13, 1999) Appellate Body WT/DS87/AB/R WT/DS110/AB/R.
China – Measures Affecting Trading Rights and Distribution Services for Certain Publications and Audiovisual Entertainment Products (December 21, 2009) Appellate Body WT/DS363/AB/R.
China – Measures Related to the Exportation of Rare Earths, Tungsten and Molybdenum (August 7, 2014) Appellate Body WT/DS431/AB/R WT/DS432/AB/R WT/DS433/AB/R.

China – Measures Related to the Exportation of Various Raw Materials (January 30, 2012) Appellate Body WT/DS394/16 WT/DS395/15 WT/DS398/14.

Colombia – Anti-Dumping Duties on Frozen Fries from Belgium, Germany and the Netherlands (December 21, 2022) Art 25 Arbitration Report WT/DS591/ARB25.

Colombia – Measures Relating to the Importation of Textiles, Apparel and Footwear (June 7, 2016) Appellate Body WT/DS461/AB/R.

EC – Customs Classification of Certain Computer Equipment (June 5, 1998) Appellate Body WT/DS62/AB/R.

EC – Measures Affecting and Asbestos-Containing Products (March 12, 2001) Appellate Body WT/DS135/AB/R.

EC – Measures Affecting the Approval and Marketing of Biotech Products (September 29, 2006) WTO Panel WT/DS291/R, WT/DS292/R, WT/DS293/R.

EC – Measures Prohibiting the Importation and Marketing of Seal Products (May 22, 2014) Appellate Body WT/DS400/AB/R WT/DS401/AB/R.

EC – Protection of Trademarks and Geographical Indications for Agricultural Products and Foodstuffs (March 15, 2005) WTO Panel WT/DS290/R.

EU and Its Member States – Certain Measures Relating to the Energy Sector (August 10, 2018) WTO Panel WT/DS476/R.

Indonesia – Safeguard on Certain Iron or Steel Products (August 15, 2018) Appellate Body WT/DS490/AB/R; WT/DS496/AB/R.

Korea – Measures Affecting Imports of Fresh, Chilled and Frozen Beef (December 11, 2000) Appellate Body WT/DS161/AB/R WT/DS169/AB/R.

Mexico – Anti-Dumping Investigation of High Fructose Corn Syrup (HFCS) from the US (October 22, 2001) Appellate Body WT/DS132/AB/RW.

Russia – Measures Concerning Traffic in Transit (April 5, 2019) WTO Panel WT/DS512/R, WT/DS512/R/Add.1.

Russia – Measures on the Importation of Live Pigs, Pork and Other Pig Products from the European Union (February 23, 2017) Appellate Body WT/DS475/AB/R.

Saudi Arabia – Measures Concerning the Protection of Intellectual Property Rights (June 16, 2020) WTO Panel WT/DS567/R, WT/DS567/R/Add.1.

US – Certain Measures on Steel and Aluminium Products (China) (December 9, 2022) WTO Panel WT/DS544/R, WT/DS544/R/Add.1.

US – Certain Measures on Steel and Aluminium Products (Norway) (December 9, 2022) WTO Panel WT/DS552/R.

US – Certain Measures on Steel and Aluminium Products (Switzerland) (December 9, 2022) WTO Panel WT/DS556/R.

US – Certain Measures on Steel and Aluminium Products (Turkey) (December 9, 2022) WTO Panel WT/DS564/R.

US – Continued Dumping and Subsidy Offset Act of 2000 (January 16, 2003) Appellate Body WT/DS217/AB/R WT/DS234/AB/R.

US – Import Prohibition of Certain Shrimp and Shrimp Products (October 12, 1998) Appellate Body WT/DS58/AB/R.

US – Measures Affecting Imports of Woven Wool Shirts and Blouses from India (April 25, 1997) Appellate Body WT/DS33/AB/R.

US – Measures Affecting the Cross-Border Supply of Gambling and Betting Services (April 7, 2005) Appellate Body WT/DS285/AB/R.

US – Origin Marking Requirement (December 21, 2022) WTO Panel Report WT/DS597/R, WT/DS597/R/Add.1.

US – Standards for Reformulated and Conventional Gasoline (April 29, 1996) Appellate Body WT/DS2/AB/R.

US – Tariff Measures on Certain Goods from China (September 15, 2020) WTO Panel WT/DS543/R.

US – Trade Measures Affecting Nicaragua (October 13, 1986) GATT Panel L/6053.

INVESTMENT TRIBUNALS

Angel Samuel Seda and others v Republic of Colombia (June 27, 2024) ICSID Case No ARB/19/6.

Bear Creek Mining Corporation v Republic of Peru (2017) ICSID Case No ARB/14/21.

Bundesgericht 4A 65–2018 – Deutsche Telekom AG v The Republic of India (2018) PCA Case No 2014–10.

Canfor et al v US (Consolidated) (September 7, 2005) NAFTA Tribunal.

CC/Devas (Mauritius) Ltd v Republic of India (2016) PCA Case No 2013–09.

Chevron Corp v Ecuador (2008) PCA Case No 34877.

CMS Gas Transmission Co v Argentine Republic (2005) ICSID Case No ARB/01/8.

Continental Casualty Co v Argentine Republic (2008) ICSID Case No Arb/03/9.

Copper Mesa Mining Corporation v Republic of Ecuador (2016) PCA No 2012–2.

Deutsche Telekom AG v Republic of India (2017) PCA Case No 2014–10.

Eco Oro Minerals Corp v Republic of Colombia (2021) ICSID Case No ARB/16/41.

El Paso Energy International Company v Argentine Republic (2011) ICSID Case No ARB/03/15.

Enron Corporation v Argentine Republic (2007) ICSID Case No ARB/01/3.

LG&E Energy Corp LG&E Capital Corp and LG&E International, Inc v Argentine Republic (2007) ICSID Case No ARB/02/1.

Marvin Feldman v Mexico (2002) NAFTA Tribunal ARB(AF)/99/1.

Michael Anthony Lee-Chin v Dominican Republic (October 6, 2023) ICSID Case No UNCT/18/3.

Mobil Exploration and Development Inc Suc Argentina and Mobil Argentina SA v Argentine Republic (2013) ICSID Case No ARB/04/16.

Novenergia II – Energy & Environment (SCA), SICAR v Kingdom Of Spain (2018) SCC Case No V2015/063.

Rompetrol Group NY v Romania (2013) ICSID Case No ARB/06/3.

Sempra Energy International v Argentine Republic (2007) ICSID Case No ARB/02/16.

White Industries Australia Limited v The Republic of India (2011) UNCITRAL Arbitration.

EUROPEAN COURTS

Case C-273/97 Angela Maria Sirdar v The Army Board and Secretary of State for Defence [1999] EU:C:1999:246.
Case C-54/99 Association Eglise de scientologie de Paris and Scientology International Reserves Trust v The Prime Minister [2000] EU:C:2000:124.
Case C-548/09 P Bank Melli Iran v Council [2011] EU:C:2011:735.
Case C-124/20 Bank Melli Iran v Telekom Deutschland GmbH [2021] EU:C:2021:1035.
Case C-72/83 Campus Oil Limited and others v Minister for Industry and Energy and others [1984] EU:C:1984:256.
Case C-176/03 Commission v Council [2005] EU:C:2005:542.
Case C-200/13 P Council of the European Union v Bank Saderat Iran [2016] EU:C:2016:284.
Case C-833/19 P Council of the European Union v Hamas [2021] EU:C:2021:950.
Case C-440/14 P National Iranian Oil Company v Council [2016] EU:C:2016:128.
Case T-228/02 Organization des Modjahedines du Peuple d'Iran v Council [2006] EU:T:2006:384.
Case C-155/07 Parliament v Council (EIB Guarantees) [2008] EU:C:2008:605.
Case T-256/07 People's Mojahedin Organization of Iran v Council [2008] EU:T:2008:461.
Case C-72/15 PJSC Rosneft Oil Company v Her Majesty's Treasury and Others [2017] EU:C:2017:236.
Case C-741/19 République de Moldavie v Komstroy LLC [2021] EU:C:2021:655.
Case C-36/75 Rutili v Minister for the Interior [1975] EU:C:1975:137.
Case C-45/15 P Safa Nicu Sepahan Co v Council of the European Union [2017] EU:C:2017:402.
Case C-284/16 Slowakische Republik v Achmea BV [2018] EU:C:2018:158.
Joined Cases C-402/05 P and C-415/05 P Yassin Abdullah Kadi and Al Barakaat International Foundation v Council of the European Union and Commission of the European Communities [2008] EU:C:2008:461.
Case C-300/11 ZZ v Secretary of State for the Home Department [2013] EU:C:2013:363.

NATIONAL COURTS

Chinese Courts

Interpretation of the Supreme People's Court on the Application of the Administrative Procedure Law of the People's Republic of China (2018).

Dutch Courts

Case No C-09–529140-HA ZA 17–315 (November 14, 2018) Rechtbank Den Haag ECLI:NL:RBDHA:2018:15532.

Indian Courts

AK Kaul & Anr v Union of India & Anr (1995) AIR 1403, (1995) SCC (4).
Ananta Hari v State of West Bengal (1972) AIR 1256, (1972) SCC (1) 580.

Russian Courts

EAEU Court Advisory Opinion No CE-2–2/2–17-BK (October 30, 2017) (in Russian) www.alta.ru/tamdoc/17a00017/.
Resolution No F05-14552/2018 of the Arbitration Court of the Moscow District in case No A40-72889/2018 (August 12, 2019).

US Courts

Am Inst for Intl Steel, Inc v US No 2019–1727 (Fed Cir 2020).
Citizens to Preserve Overton Park, Inc v Volpe 401 US 402, 415, 91 S Ct 814, 28 L Ed 2d 136 (1971).
Haig v Agee 453 US 280, 307 (1981).
Hamdi v Rumsfeld 542 US 507, 530 (2004).
Islamic Am Relief Agency v Gonzales 477 F 3d (DC Cir 2007).
Kadi v Geithner 42 F Supp 3d 1 (DDC 2012).
Kolovrat v Oregon 366 US 187, 194 (1961).
Marland v Trump, Civil Action No 20–4597 (2020).
Motor Vehicle Mfrs v State Farm Mutual Automobile Ins Co 463 US 29 (1983).
TikTok Inc v Trump, Civil Action No 1:20-cv-02658 (CJN) (2020).
US v Tajideen Criminal Case No 17–46 (RBW) (2018).
US WeChat Users Alliance v Trump 488 F Supp 3d 912 (ND Cal 2020).
Zarmach Oil Servs v US Dept of the Treasury 750 F Supp 2d 150 (DDC 2010).

TABLE OF TREATIES

Charter of the United Nations (1945).

Convention, Regulations, and Rules of the International Centre for Settlement of Investment Disputes (2003).

Draft Articles on Responsibility of States for Internationally Wrongful Acts adopted by the International Law Commission (with commentaries) (2001).

Friendship, Commerce, and Navigation Treaty between the United States of America and the Netherlands (1956).

Friendship, Commerce, and Navigation Treaty between the United States of America and Nicaragua (1956).

Marrakesh Agreement Establishing the World Trade Organization (April 15, 1994).

Rules on the Taking of Evidence in International Arbitration adopted by the International Bar Association (2010).

Standard Draft Friendship, Commerce, and Navigation treaty (1945).

Treaty of Amity Economic Relations and Consular Rights between the US and Iran (1955).

Treaty on European Union (1992), entered into force November 1, 1993.

Vienna Convention on the Law of Treaties (1969), entered into force January 27, 1980.

TABLE OF LEGISLATION

US LEGISLATION

Countering America's Adversaries through Sanctions Act, Pub L No 115–44 (August 2, 2017).

Exon-Florio Amendment, 50 USC app 2170 (1988).

Foreign Investment and National Security Act (2007).

Foreign Investment Risk Review Modernization Act (2018).

International Emergency Economic Powers Act codified at 50 USC § 1701ff (1977).

National Security Strategy of the US, The White House (December 2017).

National Security Strategy of the US, The White House (October 2022).

Presidential Decree No 520 on the Application of Special Economic Measures in the Financial and Fuel and Energy Sectors related to the Unfriendly Actions of Certain Foreign States and International Organizations (August 5, 2022).

Presidential Memoranda, 'Ceasing U.S. Participation in the JCPOA and Taking Additional Action to Counter Iran's Malign Influence and Deny Iran all Paths to a Nuclear Weapon' (May 8, 2018) https://trumpwhitehouse.archives.gov/presidential-actions/ceasing-u-s-participation-jcpoa-taking-additional-action-counter-irans-malign-influence-deny-iran-paths-nuclear-weapon/.

Protecting Europe's Energy Security Act of 2019 HR3206 116th Congress (2019–20).

Text – HR4346 – 117th Congress (2021–2022): Supreme Court Security Funding Act of 2022 (August 9, 2022)

Unlawful Activities (Prevention) Act (1967).

Unlawful Activities (Prevention) Amendment Act No 3 (2013).

US Commerce Department Identification of Prohibited Transactions to implement EO 13942 and address the Threat posed by TikTok and the National Emergency with respect to the Information and Communications Technology and Services Supply Chain 85 FR 60061 (September 24, 2020).

US Department of the Treasury Directive 4 under EO 14024 on Prohibitions Related to Transactions Involving the Central Bank of the Russian Federation, the National Wealth Fund of the Russian Federation, and the Ministry of Finance of the Russian Federation 87 FR 32303 (February 28, 2022).

US Notification G/MA/QR/N/USA/5/Add.3 from March 21, 2022 to the Committee on Market Access.

US President EO on Addressing United States Investments in Certain National Security Technologies and Products in Countries of Concern (August 9, 2023).
US President EO Regarding the Proposed Acquisition of United States Steel Corporation by Nippon Steel Corporation (January 3, 2025).
US President EO 12170 on Blocking Iranian Government Property 44 FR 65729 (November 14, 1979).
US President EO 12513 on Prohibiting Trade and Certain Other Transactions involving Nicaragua 50 FR 18629 3 CFR 1985 Comp (May 1, 1985).
US President EO 12532 on Prohibiting Trade and Certain Other Transactions involving South Africa 50 FR 36861 3 CFR 1985 Comp (September 9, 1985).
US President EO 13047 on Prohibiting New Investment in Burma Federal Register Vol 62 No 99 (May 20, 1997).
US President EO 13405 on Blocking Property of Certain Persons Undermining Democratic Processes or Institutions in Belarus Federal Register Vol 71 No 118 (June 16, 2006).
US President EO 13413 on Blocking Property of Certain Persons Contributing to the Conflict in the Democratic Republic of the Congo Federal Register Vol 71 No 210 (October 27, 2006).
US President EO 13466 on Continuing Certain Restrictions with respect to North Korea and North Korean Nationals Federal Register Vol 73 No 125 (June 26, 2008).
US President EO 13536 on Blocking Property of Certain Persons Contributing to the Conflict in Somalia Federal Register Vol 75 No 72 (April 12, 2010).
US President EO 13661 on Blocking Property of Additional Persons Contributing to the Situation in Ukraine Federal Register Vol 79 No 53 (March 16, 2014).
US President EO 13692 on Blocking Property and Suspending Entry of Certain Persons Contributing to the Situation in Venezuela Federal Register Vol 80 No 47 (March 8, 2015).
US President EO 13712 on Blocking Property of Certain Persons Contributing to the Situation in Burundi Federal Register Vol 80 No 227 (November 22, 2015).
US President EO 13808 on Imposing Additional Sanctions with respect to the Situation in Venezuela Federal Register Vol 82 No 166 (August 24, 2017).
US President EO 13818 on Blocking the Property of Persons Involved in Serious Human Rights Abuse or Corruption Federal Register Vol 82 No 246 (December 20, 2017).
US President EO 13848 on Imposing Certain Sanctions in the Event of Foreign Interference in a US Election Federal Register Vol 83 No 179 (September 12, 2018).
US President EO 13873 on Securing the Information and Communications Technology and Services Supply Chain 84 FR 22689 (May 15, 2019).
US President EO 13882 on Blocking Property and Suspending Entry of Certain Persons Contributing to the Situation in Mali Federal Register Vol 84 No 146 (July 26, 2019).
US President EO 13894 on Blocking Property and Suspending Entry of Certain Persons Contributing to the Situation in Syria Federal Register Vol 84 No 201 (October 14, 2019).

US President EO 13936 on The President's Executive Order on Hong Kong Normalization Federal Register Vol 85 No 138 (July 14, 2020).

US President EO 13942 on Addressing the Threat posed by TikTok, and Taking Additional Steps to address the National Emergency with respect to the Information and Communications Technology and Services Supply Chain 85 FR 48637 (August 6, 2020).

US President EO 13943 Addressing the Threat Posed by WeChat, and Taking Additional Steps to Address the National Emergency with respect to the Information and Communications Technology and Services Supply Chain 85 FR 48641 (August 6, 2020).

US President EO 14014 on Blocking Property with respect to the Situation in Burma Federal Register Vol 86 No 28 (February 10, 2021).

US President EO 14017 on America's Supply Chains 86 FR 11849 (February 24, 2021).

US President EO 14024 on Blocking Property with respect to Specified Harmful Foreign Activities of the Government of the Russian Federation Federal Register Vol 86 No 73 (April 15, 2021).

US President EO 14066 on Prohibiting Certain Imports and New Investments with respect to Continued Russian Federation Efforts to Undermine the Sovereignty and Territorial Integrity of Ukraine Federal Register Vol 87 No 47 (March 8, 2022).

US President EO 14083 on Ensuring Robust Consideration of Evolving National Security Risks by the Committee on Foreign Investment in the United States 87 FR 57369 (September 15, 2022).

US President EO 14193 on Imposing Duties to Address the Flow of Illicit Drugs Across Our Northern Border Federal Register (February 1, 2025).

US President EO 14194 on Imposing Duties to Address the Situation at Our Southern Border Federal Register (February 1, 2025).

US President EO 14195 on Imposing Duties to Address the Synthetic Opioid Supply Chain in the People's Republic of China Federal Register (February 1, 2025).

US Presidential Proclamation 9704 on Adjusting Imports of Aluminum into the US 83 FR 51 (February 1, 2021).

US Presidential Proclamation 9705 on Adjusting Imports of Steel into the US 83 FR 11625 (March 8, 2018).

US Trade Representative, USMCA, CA-US Side Letter on 232 Process https://ustr.gov/sites/default/files/files/agreements/FTA/USMCA/Text/CA-US_Side_Letter_on_232_Process.pdf.

US Trade Representative, USMCA, MX-US Side Letter on 232 https://ustr.gov/sites/default/files/files/agreements/FTA/USMCA/Text/MX-US_Side_Letter_on_232.pdf.

US Trade Representative, USMCA, MX-US Side Letter on 232 Dispute Resolution https://ustr.gov/sites/default/files/files/agreements/FTA/USMCA/Text/MX-US_Side_Letter_on_232_Dispute_Settlement.pdf.

US Trade Representative, USMCA, MX-US Side Letter on 232 Process https://ustr.gov/sites/default/files/files/agreements/FTA/USMCA/Text/MX-US_Side_Letter_on_232_Process.pdf.

US Trade Representative, USMCA, Side Letter Text on 232 CA-US Response https://ustr.gov/sites/default/files/files/agreements/FTA/USMCA/Text/Side_Letter_Text_on_232_CA-US_Response.pdf.

EU LAW AND REGULATIONS

Commission Delegated Regulation (EU) 2018/1100 of January 6, 2018, Amending the Annex to Council Regulation (EC) 2271/96 Protecting against the Effects of Extra-Territorial Application of Legislation Adopted by a Third Country, and Actions Based Thereon or Resulting therefrom (2018) OJ L 1991.

Common Position of October 28, 1996 defined by the Council on the basis of Article J.2 of TEU, on Burma/Myanmar (1996) OJ L 287 (no longer in force); Council Decision (CFSP) 2021/639 of April 19, 2021 amending Decision 2013/184/CFSP concerning Restrictive Measures in view of the Situation in Myanmar/Burma (2021) OJ L 132I.

Council Common Position 2004/661/CFSP of September 24, 2004 concerning Restrictive Measures against Certain Officials of Belarus (2004) OJ L 301.

Council Common Position 2006/276/CFSP of April 10, 2006 concerning Restrictive Measures against Certain Officials of Belarus and Repealing Common Position 2004/661/CFSP (2006) OJ L 101.

Council Decision (CFSP) 2018/1544 of October 15, 2018 concerning Restrictive Measures against the Proliferation and Use of Chemical Weapons (2018) ST/11936/2018/INIT OJ L 259.

Council Decision (CFSP) 2020/1127 of July 30, 2020 amending Decision (CFSP) 2019/797 concerning Restrictive Measures against Cyber-Attacks Threatening the Union or its Member States (July 30, 2020) L 246/12.

Council Decision (CFSP) 2022/335 amending Decision 2014/512/CFSP concerning Restrictive Measures in view of Russia's Actions Destabilising the Situation in Ukraine (February 28, 2022) OJ L 57.

Council Decision 2013/184/CFSP of April 22, 2013 concerning Restrictive Measures in view of the Situation in Myanmar/Burma (2013) OJ L 111.

Council for Trade in Goods, Procedures to Enhance Transparency and Strengthen Notification Requirements Under WTO Agreements (June 25, 2021) JOB/GC/204/Rev5 JOB/CTG/14/Rev5.

Council of the EU, Basic Principles on the Use of Restrictive Measures (Sanctions) (June 7, 2004) 10198/1/04 REV 1.

Council of the EU, EU Best Practices for the Effective Implementation of Restrictive Measures (June 27, 2022) 10572/22.

Council of the EU, Guidelines on Implementation and Evaluation of Restrictive Measures (Sanctions) in the framework of CFSP (May 4, 2018) 5664/18.

Council Regulation (EC) 2271/96 of November 22, 1996, Protecting Against the Effects of the Extra-Territorial Application of Legislation Adopted by a Third Country, and Actions Based Thereon or Resulting Therefrom, 1996 OJ L 309.

Council Regulation (EU) 2022/879 of June 3, 2022 amending Regulation (EU) No 833/2014 concerning Restrictive Measures in view of Russia's Actions Destabilising the Situation in Ukraine (2022) OJ L 153.

Directorate General of Foreign Trade, Notification of ITC (HS), 2022 – Schedule –1 (Import Policy) (February 9, 2022) Notification No 39/2015–2020.

European Commission, Communication from the Commission Guidance to the Member States concerning Foreign Direct Investment and Free Movement of Capital from Third Countries, and the Protection of Europe's Strategic Assets, ahead of the Application of Regulation (EU) 2019/452 (FDI Screening Regulation) 2020/C 99 I/01 [2020] OJ C 99I.

European Commission, Communication from the Commission to the European Parliament, the Council, the European Economic and Social Committee and the Committee of the Regions (October 18, 2022) COM(2022) 548 final.

European Commission, Communication from the Commission to the European Parliament, the European Council, the Council, the European Economic and Social Committee and the Committee of the Regions on the EU Security Union Strategy (July 24, 2020) COM/2020/605 final.

European Commission, Report from the Commission to the European Parliament and the Council. First Annual Report on the Screening of Foreign Direct Investments into the Union (2021) COM(2021) 714 final.

European Commission, Report from the Commission to the European Parliament and the Council. Second Annual Report on the Screening of Foreign Direct Investments into the Union (2022) COM(2022) 433 final.

European Commission, Joint Communication to the European Parliament, the European Council and the Council on European Economic Security Strategy (June 20, 2023) JOIN(2023)20 final.

European Commission, Memo on European Economic Security (January 24, 2024).

European Parliament resolution of October 24, 2019 on the Turkish Military Operation in Northeast Syria and its Consequences (2019/2886(RSP)).

Proposal for a Regulation of the European Parliament and of the Council on a Framework for the Free Flow of Non-Personal Data in the EU – Analysis of the Final Compromise Text with a View to Agreement (June 25, 2018) 2017/0228 (COD).

Proposal for a Regulation of the European Parliament and of the Council on the Protection of the Union and its Member States from Economic Coercion by Third Countries (December 8, 2021) COM/2021/775 final.

Regulation (EU) 2019/452 of the European Parliament and of the Council of March 19, 2019 Establishing a Framework for the Screening of Foreign Direct Investments into the Union (2019) OJ L 79I.

Regulation (EU) No 1219/2012 of the European Parliament and of the Council (December 12, 2012) Establishing Transitional Arrangements for Bilateral Investment Agreements between the Member States and Third Countries [2012] OJ L 351.

LEGISLATION OF BRAZIL

Brazil's Decree of the President No 85.064 (August 26, 1980).
Brazil's Law 6.634 (May 2, 1979).
Decree of the President of Brazil No 6703 (December 18, 2008).

LEGISLATION OF THE RUSSIAN FEDERATION

Decree of the Government of the Russian Federation No 456 on the conclusion of agreements between the Government of the Russian Federation and the governments of foreign states on the encouragement and mutual protection of investments (with amendments and additions) (June 9, 2001).
Decree of the President of the Russian Federation No 100 on Implementation of Special Economic Measures in the Area of External Relations to Ensure National Security of the Russian Federation (March 8, 2022).
Decree of the President of the Russian Federation No 252 on Russian Countersanctions against Individuals and Entities of the Countries which have imposed Sanctions on Russia (May 3, 2022).
Decree of the President of the Russian Federation No 400 on the National Security Strategy of the Russian Federation (July 2, 2021).
Decree of the President of the Russian Federation No 592 on Implementation of Special Economic Measures in Connection with Inimical Actions of Ukraine in relation to Russian Citizens and Legal Entities (as amended) (October 22, 2018).
Decree of the President of the Russian Federation No 683 on the National Security Strategy of the Russian Federation (December 31, 2015).
Decree of the President of the Russian Federation on Measures to Ensure National Security of the Russian Federation and the Protection of Citizens of the Russian Federation against Criminal and Other Illegal Acts and on the Application of Special Economic Measures Against the Turkish Republic (November 28, 2015).
Executive Order of the President of the Russian Federation No 79 (February 28, 2022).
Executive Order of the President of the Russian Federation No 81 (March 1, 2022).
Federal Law No 127-FZ on Measures of Impact (Counteraction) on Unfriendly Actions of the US and Other Foreign States (June 4, 2018).
Federal Law No 136-FZ (July 28, 2001).
Federal Law No 160-FZ on Foreign Investments in the Russian Federation (July 9, 1999).
Federal Law No 165-FZ (July 5, 2017).
Federal Law No 171-FZ On the Incorporation of Amendments to the Arbitrazh Procedure Code of the Russian Federation in Order to Protect the Rights of Natural Persons and Legal Entities in Connection with Restrictive Measures Imposed by a Foreign State, an Association and/or Union of States, and/or a Governmental (Intergovernmental) Institution of a Foreign State or Association and/or Union of States (June 8, 2020).

Federal Law No 281-FZ on Special Economic Measures (December 30, 2006).
Federal Law No 57-FZ (April 2, 2008).
Federal Law No 92-FZ (April 15, 2022).
Federal Law on (Counteracting) Measures in response to the Unfriendly Actions of the US and Other Foreign States (June 4, 2018).
Federal Law on Mass Media No 2124–1 as amended (2014).
General Approaches to the Conclusion of International Agreements of the Russian Federation on the Promotion and Protection of Investments approved by the Resolution of the Government of the Russian Federation No 992 (September 30, 2016).
Law on Closed Administrative Territorial Zones established under the Law on Closed Administrative-Territorial Zones No 3297–1 as amended (2018).

LEGISLATION OF INDIA

Government of India, Ministry of Home Affairs, CTCR Division, Order on Procedure for Implementation of Section 51A of the Unlawful Activities (Prevention) Act, 1967 File No 14014/01/2019/CFT (March 14, 2019).
Governmental Order No 1716–83 on Ban on the Import into Russia of Goods Produced in Ukraine or Transported through its Territory (December 29, 2018).
Governmental Order No 460–25 on Ban on the Import into Russia of Goods Produced in Ukraine or Transported through its Territory (April 18, 2019).
Information Technology Act (2000).
National Security Strategy (Hooda Report), Indian National Congress (March 2019) https://manifesto.inc.in/pdf/national_security_strategy_gen_hooda.pdf.
New Foreign Trade Policy (2015–20).

LEGISLATION OF CHINA

Anti-Foreign Sanctions Law (2021).
Circular of the General Office of the State Council on the Establishment of the Security Review System for Mergers and Acquisitions of Domestic Enterprises by Foreign Investors (2011).
Interim Provisions on Matters Relevant to the Implementation of the System for Security Review of Acquisition of Domestic Enterprises by Foreign Investors, Announce No 8 (March 2011).
Interim Provisions on Mergers and Acquisitions of Domestic Enterprises by Foreign Investors (2006).
Law of the People's Republic of China on Safeguarding National Security in the Hong Kong Special Administrative Region, applied to the HKSAR (June 30, 2020).
National People's Congress, The Foreign Investment Law of the People's Republic of China (March 15, 2019).

National Security Law of the People's Republic of China, 12th National People's Congress (July 1, 2015).

Provisions of the Ministry of Commerce on Implementing a Security Review System for Mergers and Acquisitions of Domestic Enterprises by Foreign Investors, Announce No 53 (September 2011).

Special Administrative Measures (Negative List) for Foreign Investment Access (2021 edn) www.china-briefing.com/news/chinas-foreign-investment-negative-list-2021-edition-english-version/.

LEGISLATION OF SOUTH AFRICA

Competition Amendment Act, 2018, Act No 18 of 2018, Government Gazette Vol 644 No 175 (February 14, 2019).

White Paper on National Defence for the Republic of South Africa (May 1996) www.files.ethz.ch/isn/155722/SouthAfrica1996.pdf.

TABLE OF OFFICIAL AND POLICY DOCUMENTS

Arrangements for Effective Cooperation with Other Intergovernmental Organizations: Relations between the WTO and the United Nations (November 15, 1995) WT/GC/W/10.

Communication from Sweden, *Sweden – Import Restrictions on Certain Footwear* (November 17, 1975) L/4250 1 https://docs.wto.org/gattdocs/q/GG/L4399/4250.PDF.

Communication from the US, 'Reflections from the United States on the Handling of Disputes Involving Essential Security Measures' (December 11, 2024) JOB/DSB/10.

Communication from the US in *US – Certain Measures on Steel and Aluminium Products (China)* (April 17, 2018) WT/DS544/2.

Communication from the US in *US – Certain Measures on Steel and Aluminium Products (EU)* (April 17, 2018) WT/DS548/14.

DSB, Minutes of Meeting held in the Centre William Rappard on July 29, 2020 (October 14, 2020) WT/DSB/M/443. Regarding *Japan – Measures related to the Exportation of Products and Technology to Korea* (DS590).

GATT Council, Minutes of Meeting held on May 29, 1985, C/M/188 www.wto.org/gatt_docs/English/SULPDF/91150029.pdf.

Decision Concerning Article XXI of the General Agreement (December 2, 1982) L/5426 www.wto.org/gatt_docs/english/SULPDF/91000212.pdf.

General Council, Draft Decision on Procedures to Enhance Transparency and Strengthen Notification Requirements under WTO Agreements (June 25, 2021) JOB/GC/204/Rev.5 JOB/CTG/14/Rev.5.

Draft Decision on Procedures to Enhance Transparency and Strengthen Notification Requirements under WTO Agreements (April 28, 2022) JOB/GC/204/Rev.9 JOB/CTG/14/Rev.9.

ICJ, Legality of the Threat or Use of Nuclear Weapons, Advisory Opinion (1996) ICJ Rep 226.

Joint Statement Initiative on Electronic Commerce (July 26, 2024) INF/ECOM/87 https://docs.wto.org/dol2fe/Pages/SS/directdoc.aspx?filename=q:/INF/ECOM/87.pdf&Open=True.

Message from the US President transmitting NAFTA, Statement of Administrative Action and Requiring Supporting Statements (1993) HRDoc 103–159.

Message from the US President transmitting the Treaty between the US and the Republic of Kazakhstan concerning the Reciprocal Encouragement and Protection of Investment, signed at Washington on May 19, 1992 https://2009-2017.state.gov/e/eb/ifd/43294.htm.

Message from the US President transmitting the Treaty between the US and the Republic of Moldova concerning the Reciprocal Encouragement and Protection of Investment, signed at Washington on April 21, 1993 https://2001-2009.state.gov/documents/organization/43578.pdf.

Message from the US President transmitting the Treaty between the US and the Republic of Armenia concerning the Reciprocal Encouragement and Protection of Investment, signed at Washington on September 23, 1992 https://2001-2009.state.gov/documents/organization/43477.pdf.

Message from the US President transmitting the Treaty between the US and Ukraine concerning the Encouragement and Reciprocal Protection of Investment, signed at Washington on March 4, 1994 https://2009-2017.state.gov/e/eb/ifd/43366.htm.

Message from the US President transmitting the Treaty between the US and the Government of the State of Bahrain concerning the Encouragement and Reciprocal Protection of Investment, signed at Washington on September 29, 1999 https://2009-2017.state.gov/e/eb/ifd/43236.htm.

Message from the US President transmitting Treaty between the Government of the US and the Government of the Republic of El Salvador concerning the Encouragement and Reciprocal Protection of Investment signed at San Salvador on March 10, 1999 www.sice.oas.org/Investment/BITSbyCountry/BITs/US_ElSalvador_e.asp.

Nicaragua – Measures Affecting Imports from Honduras and Colombia (January 20, 2000) WT/DS188/1; WT/DS201/1 G/L/387 S/L/85; WT/DSB/COM/5/Rev1.

Note by the Secretariat, *US – the Cuban Liberty and Democratic Solidarity Act*, Lapse of the Authority for Establishment of the Panel (April 24, 1998) WT/DS38/6 https://docs.wto.org/dol2fe/Pages/SS/directdoc.aspx?filename=Q:/WT/DS/38-6.pdf&Open=True.

Replies of the EU to Questions from the Panel in *US – Certain Measures on Steel and Aluminium Products (EU)* (February 14, 2020) in DS548 (settled in 2022) https://trade.ec.europa.eu/doclib/docs/2020/may/tradoc_158757.doc.pdf.

Second Session of the Preparatory Committee of the UN Conference on Trade and Employment: Verbatim Report. Eleventh Meeting of the Tariff Agreement Committee Held on Friday, September 5, 1947 at 2.30 pm in the Palais des Nations, Geneva (September 5, 1947) E/PC/T/TAC/PV/11 www.wto.org/gatt_docs/English/SULPDF/90260038.pdf.

Statement by HE Ambassador Dr Zhang Xiangchen at the WTO General Council Meeting regarding *US – Certain Measures on Steel and Aluminium Products (China)* (May 18, 2018) http://wto.mofcom.gov.cn/article/newsupdates/201805/20180502741686.shtml.

Statement by US Ambassador María L Pagán on the WTO E-Commerce Joint Statement Initiative (July 26, 2024) https://geneva.usmission.gov/2024/07/26/state

ment-by-ambassador-maria-l-pagan-on-the-wto-e-commerce-joint-statement-initiative/.

Third Session – Reply by the Vice Chairman of the US Delegation, Mr John W Evans, to the Speech by the Head of the Czechoslovak Delegation under Item 14 on the Agenda (June 2, 1949) GATT/CP3/38 https://docs.wto.org/gattdocs/q/GG/GATTCP3/38.PDF.

Third Session – Statement by the Head of the Czechoslovak Delegation, Mr Zdeněk Augenthaler, to Item 14 of Agenda (CP3/2/Rev2) (May 30, 1949) GATT/CP3/33 www.wto.org/Gatt_docs/English/SULPDF/90320183.pdf.

Third Session – Summary Record of the Twenty-Second Meeting CP3/SR22 – II/28 (June 8, 1949) www.sice.oas.org/dispute/gatt/49expres.asp.

TPR Mechanism as amended by the General Council (Revision, effective as of January 1, 2019).

Trade Restrictions Affecting Argentina applied for Non-Economic Reasons (May 18, 1982) Communication to the Members of GATT Council L/5319.

Trade Restrictions Affecting Argentina Applied for Non-Economic Reasons (April 30, 1982) GATT Communication L/5317.

UN – Economic and Social Council, Preparatory Committee of the UN Conference on Trade and Employment, Final Act of the UN Conference on Trade and Employment and Related Documents (April 1948) www.wto.org/english/docs_e/legal_e/havana_e.pdf.

UN General Assembly, Climate Change and its Possible Security Implications, Resolution adopted by the General Assembly (September 11, 2009) A/64/350.

Creation of a Global Culture of Cybersecurity and the Protection of Critical Information Infrastructures, Resolution Adopted by the General Assembly (December 23, 2003) A/RES/58/199.

Declaration of Solidarity of the United Nations in the Face of the Challenges posed by the Coronavirus Disease 2019 (COVID-19), Resolution Adopted by the General Assembly (March 27, 2020) A/74/L.51.

Resolution 377 (V) Uniting for Peace adopted at the 294th Plenary Meeting of the UN General Assembly (November 3, 1950).

The Human Right to a Clean, Healthy and Sustainable Environment, Resolution Adopted by the General Assembly (August 1, 2022) A/RES/76/300.

UN Security Council, Resolution 1373 (September 28, 2001) S/RES/1373 (2001).

WTO, Multi-Party Interim Appeal Arbitration Arrangement Pursuant to Article 25 of the DSU (April 30, 2020) Job/DSB/1/Add.12.

ABBREVIATIONS

5G	5th Generation of Wireless Mobile Telecommunications Technology
AA	association agreement
AI	artificial intelligence
APTA	Asia Pacific Trade Agreement
ARSIWA	Articles on Responsibility of States for Internationally Wrongful Acts
ASEAN	Association of Southeast Asian Nations
BIT	bilateral investment treaty
BRICS	Brazil, Russia, India, China, South Africa
CAATSA	Countering America's Adversaries through Sanctions Act
CAFTA-DR	Dominican Republic-Central America – US Free Trade Agreement
CBA	carbon border adjustment
CCP	common commercial policy
CECA	Comprehensive Economic Cooperation Agreement
CECPA	Comprehensive Economic Cooperation and Partnership Agreement
CEPA	Comprehensive Economic Partnership Agreement
CETA	Comprehensive Economic and Trade Agreement
CFIA	Cooperation and Facilitation Investment Agreement
CFSP	common foreign and security policy
CIS	Commonwealth of Independent States
CJEU	Court of Justice of the European Union
DSB	dispute settlement body
DSS	dispute settlement system
DSU	dispute settlement understanding
EAEU	Eurasian Economic Union
EC	European Community
ECJ	European Court of Justice
ECTA	Economic Cooperation and Trade Agreement
ECtHR	European Court of Human Rights
EEC	European Economic Community
eg	for example
EPA	partnership and cooperation agreement
EPCA	enhanced partnership and cooperation agreement

EU	European Union
FCN	friendship, commerce, navigation
FDI	foreign direct investment
FTA	free trade agreement
FTC	free trade commission
GATS	General Agreement on Trade in Services
GATT	General Agreement on Tariffs and Trade
GPA	Agreement on Government Procurement
GSTP	Agreement on Global System of Trade Preferences among Developing Countries
ICJ	International Court of Justice
ICSID	International Centre for Settlement of Investment Disputes
i.e.	id est
IEEPA	International Emergency Economic Powers Act
IIA	international investment agreement
ILC	International Law Commission
ISM	investment screening mechanism
IT	information technology
ITO	International Trade Organization
JCPOA	Joint Comprehensive Plan of Action
MERCOSUR	Southern Common Market
MFN	most-favored nation
MOFCOM	Ministry of Commerce in China
NAFTA	North American Free Trade Agreement
NDRC	National Development and Reform Commission
NSL	national security law
NSS	national security strategy
OECD	Organisation for Economic Co-operation and Development
PCA	Permanent Court of Arbitration
PEESA	Protecting Europe's Energy Security Act
RCEP	Regional Comprehensive Economic Partnership Agreement
RTA	regional trade agreement
RTAA	Reciprocal Trade Agreements Act
SACU	Southern African Customs Union
SADC	Southern African Community
SAFTA	South Asia Free Trade Area
SDGT	specially designated global terrorist
SPS	sanitary and phytosanitary
SOE	state-owned enterprise
TBT	technical barriers to trade
TEU	Treaty on the European Union
TFEU	Treaty on the Functioning of the European Union

TPR	Trade Policy Review
TRIMs	Agreement on Trade-Related Investment Measures
TRIPs	Agreement on Trade-Related Aspects of Intellectual Property Rights
UAE	United Arab Emirates
UAPA	Unlawful Activities (Prevention) Act
UEL	unreliable entity list
UK	United Kingdom
UN	United Nations
US	United States of America
USMCA	United States – Mexico – Canada Agreement
VCLT	Vienna Convention on the Law of Treaties
WMD	weapons of mass destruction
WTO	World Trade Organization

1

Introduction

States' leaders and scholars in international affairs,[1] political science,[2] and law[3] have frequently addressed national security threats posed by wars, armed conflicts, terrorism, and espionage. In 1937, Cordell Hull, the Secretary of State in the United States of America (US), declared that "enduring peace and the welfare of nations are indissolubly connected with . . . the maximum practicable degree of freedom in international trade."[4] His firm belief in the linkage of trade and peace gave the US an ideological direction during the negotiations of international agreements in the 1940s.[5] It was based on the conviction that deeper economic integration would mitigate conflicts between nations[6] and, therefore, would serve to protect their national security interests.

Yet, in recent years, national security rhetoric has gained particular prominence, partly due to the geo-economic and geopolitical developments that have raised the stakes of international competition and new forms of economic warfare.[7] The importance of emerging technology has surpassed the role of pure military power.[8] The strategic rivalry between

1 See eg Chris C Demchak, *Wars of Disruption and Resilience: Cybered Conflict, Power, and National Security* (UGA Press 2011).

2 See eg Arnold Wolfers, '"National Security" as an Ambiguous Symbol' (1952) 67(4) Political Science Q 481.

3 See eg Shin-Yi Peng, 'Cybersecurity Threats and the WTO National Security Exceptions' (2015) 18 J Intl Econ L 449.

4 Douglas A Irwin, Petros C Mavroidis, and Alan O Sykes, *The Genesis of GATT* (CUP 2008) 10.

5 Ibid 11.

6 J Benton Heath, 'The New National Security Challenge to the Economic Order' (2020) 129 Yale LJ 1020, 1047–1048.

7 Juan Carlos Zarate, *Treasury's War: The Unleashing of a New Era of Financial Warfare* (1st ed., PublicAffairs 2013) 385.

8 Joel Slawotsky, 'National Security Exception in an Era of Hegemonic Rivalry: Emerging Impacts on Trade and Investment' in Julien Chaisse and others (eds.), *Handbook of International Investment Law and Policy* (Springer Nature Singapore Pte Ltd 2019) 4 https://link.springer.com/referenceworkentry/10.1007%2F978-981-13-5744-2_2-1.

the US and China is spiraling into a multilayered world conflict, culminating in significant efforts by the US government to restrain China's development of technologies critical for its technological and military advancement.[9] Furthermore, the international system has faced unprecedented challenges related to cybersecurity, climate change, supply chain crisis, and migration flows. As these developments unfold, economic interdependence is no longer viewed as a guarantee for growing prosperity and stability in the global order but as a source of possible threats to national security.[10] While such concerns have provoked reforms and strategic policies, by attempting to restore their sense of security, states at times enlarge insecurity in the global economy.

Since World War II, the reduced perception of direct military threats and a strategic economic perspective have driven the US to prioritize long-term economic considerations in its foreign policy decision-making.[11] The US has led a course of increasing multilateralism, through bodies such as the United Nations (UN), the Bretton Woods institutions,[12] and the intended predecessor of the World Trade Organization (WTO) – the failed International Trade Organization (ITO) – designed to tackle global issues.[13] The multilateral trading system that emerged in the General Agreement on Tariffs and Trade (GATT) (1947)[14] was further endorsed and expanded in the WTO agreements under the lead of the US. Yet, over time, US policymakers have started to view the WTO as ineffective in promoting trade liberalization and disciplining the trade and industrial policies of new members, such as China.[15]

[9] See more chapter 3, section 3.1.2.

[10] Wolfgang Weiss, 'Interpreting Essential Security Exceptions in WTO Law in View of Economic Security Interests' in Wolfgang Weiß and Cornelia Furculita (eds.), *Global Politics and EU Trade Policy* (Springer International Publishing 2020) 258–259.

[11] Antonio F Perez, 'To Judge between the Nations: Post Cold War Transformations in National Security and Separation of Powers-Beating Nuclear Swords into Plowshares in an Imperfectly Competitive World' (1997) 20 Hastings Intl & Comp L Rev 331, 410.

[12] Richard Peet and others, *Unholy Trinity: The IMF, World Bank and WTO* (SIRD 2003) 148.

[13] Richard Toye, 'Developing Multilateralism: The Havana Charter and the Fight for the International Trade Organization, 1947–1948' (2003) 25(2) The Intl History Rev 282, 286.

[14] GATT (Geneva, October 30, 1947) 55 UNTS 187, provisionally entered into force on January 1, 1948 (hereafter GATT (1947)), superseded by Final Act Embodying the Results of the Uruguay Round of Multilateral Trade Negotiations (Marrakesh, Morocco, April 15, 1994) 1867 UNTS 14, 33 ILM 1143, entered into force on January 1, 1995 (hereafter GATT (1994)).

[15] Stephen Kirchner, 'From "China Shock" to Deglobalisation Shock: China's WTO Accession and US Economic Engagement 20 Years on' (January 2022) US Studies Centre at the University of Sydney 19.

Starting in 2016, President Trump united widespread domestic discontent over increasing economic dislocation, precariousness, and inequality within the US with growing concern about the US's hegemonic decline amid the rise of China.[16] The US manifested its increasing dissatisfaction with the current multilateral trade order through a nationalist unilateralism that explicitly frames the economic security of the US as a matter of national security.[17] Among others, the US attempts to minimize risks to its national security by restricting trade with China, exceeding tariff bindings, and shifting the production of certain critical goods, such as in high-tech areas, from the countries it considers unfriendly back to the US ("reshoring") or to the countries it considers trustworthy ("friend-shoring").[18] In early 2025, President Trump's proposal to acquire Greenland and a renewed push to impose tariffs on Mexico, Canada, and China further underscored how his administration increasingly links national security with the economic interests of the US to boost its competitiveness. Notably, the US's "reshoring" and "friend-shoring" strategies that subordinate trade to foreign policy and national security might significantly impact future bilateral and regional trade negotiations with the US and global efficiency.[19]

Because of its history, proclaimed values, and objectives, the European Union (EU) has never been comfortable with national security and unilateralism.[20] Having been founded on security concerns,[21] the EU aims to provide peace and stability in Europe by linking economic cooperation, anti-terrorism, migration, cyberspace, and protection of human rights with EU security issues, thereby manifesting an example of collective

16 Kristen Hopewell, 'Trump & Trade: The Crisis in the Multilateral Trading System' (2020) 26(2) New Political Economy 271, 280.

17 Ibid 274.

18 Hung Tran, 'Decoupling/Reshoring Versus Dual Circulation: Competing Strategies for Security & Influence' (Atlantic Council Geoeconomics Center, April 2021) www.atlanticcouncil.org/wp-content/uploads/2021/04/Decoupling_Reshoring_versus_Dual_Circulation.pdf.

19 See more Robert Wolfe, 'Is Using Trade Policy for Foreign Policy a "SNO Job"? On Linkage, Friend-Shoring and the Challenges for Multilateralism' (2022) Robert Schuman Centre for Advanced Studies Research Paper No RSC 2022/74 https://cadmus.eui.eu/bitstream/handle/1814/75067/RSC_WP_2022_74.pdf?sequence=1.

20 Bernard O'Connor, 'European Union: Is the EU Becoming More Unilateralist?' (NCTM Studio Legale, August 29, 2018) www.mondaq.com/export-controls-trade-investment-sanctions/731312/is-the-eu-becoming-more-unilateralist.

21 Maya Swisa, 'Future Stability in the European Union: Realism, Constructivism, and Institutionalism' (2011) Claremont-UC Undergraduate Research Conference on the European Union 125, 129.

securitization.[22] Multilateralism has been acknowledged as one of the critical features of European institutions and EU member states since the beginning of the European integration process.[23] In some instances, the EU reverts to unilateral measures, portraying it not as a disengagement with multilateralism but rather as the need to make progress where it cannot be achieved through multilateral institutions.[24] Given that in the area of Common Foreign and Security Policy (CFSP), the EU generally works by consensus, EU member states can block any excessive unilateral actions and thus prevent the advancement by the EU of a more power-based strategy.[25] Yet, a backlash against multilateralism because of Brexit, rising Euroscepticism, the war in Ukraine, and the increasing use of economic coercion by other states inevitably impacts the EU and transforms its idea of multilateralism and economic security architecture.[26]

The hegemony of traditional powers, such as the US and European states, seems to be becoming less significant in dealing with emerging and reemerging security threats, at least in economic terms.[27] The international arena is rapidly turning into a multipolar system where a growing role is played by emerging powers,[28] such as Brazil, Russia, India, China, and South Africa (BRICS).[29] BRICS, countries with very

[22] James Sperling and Mark Webber, 'The European Union, Security Governance and Collective Securitization' (2019) 42(2) West Eur Politics 228, 247.

[23] Luk Van Langenhove, Tania Felicio, and Isabella Torta 'The EU's Preferences for Multilateralism: A SWOT Analysis of EU/UN Relations' (2006) O-2006/21 UNU-CRIS 1, 7.

[24] Jan Wouters and Vineet Hegde, 'Reform of Global Trade Governance: The Role of the European Union' (2022) 44(5) J of European Integration 715, 724. See also Bernard O'Connor, 'European Union: Is the EU Becoming More Unilateralist?' (NCTM Studio Legale, August 29, 2018) www.mondaq.com/export-controls-trade-investment-sanctions/731312/is-the-eu-becoming-more-unilateralist.

[25] Stephen Woolcock, 'The Role of the European Union in the International Trade and Investment Order' (2019) 26(1) J of Constitutional Law in Eastern and Central Europe 1, 3.

[26] Matthew Bevington and Anand Menon, 'Implications of Brexit for the UK and the EU: The Knowns and the Unknowns' in Helen Wallace, Nikos Koutsiaras, and George Pagoulatos (eds.), *Europe's Transformations: Essays in Honour of Loukas Tsoukalis* (OUP 2021) 170, 175.

[27] Bartolome T Carvajal, 'American Unilateralism v European Multilateralism: The World Is Watching' (*Vocal Europe*, July 26, 2018) www.vocaleurope.eu/american-unilateralism-vs-european-multilateralism-the-world-is-watching/.

[28] Ibid.

[29] The acronym BRIC (later BRICS) denotes rising awareness of the growing importance of these big emerging markets. See Leslie Elliott Armijo, 'The BRICs Countries (Brazil, Russia, India, and China) as Analytical Category: Mirage or Insight?' (2007) 31 Asian Perspective 7, 8.

different social systems and approaches to economic management, joined the WTO and entered into many investment agreements with binding dispute resolution, purporting to play by the same economic rules as the US and the other major economic players. All five possess a range of economic, military, and political resources; some capacity to contribute to the production of international order, regionally or globally; and some degree of internal cohesion and power for successful unilateral actions.[30] They are harnessing their nonmilitary power to challenge US global hegemony through soft balancing, including the formation of limited diplomatic coalitions, especially at the UN.[31] Furthermore, China and Russia show their readiness to use war, armed conflict, coercive diplomacy, economic measures, and cyberattacks to become, at minimum, a regional hegemon en route to potentially becoming a global superpower. BRICS have grounds to be wary of existing liberal order largely created by the US since it usually favors the previously established power distribution.[32]

The role of geo-economic calculations in national economic agendas, economic coercion, the securitization of national economic interests, the weakening of the WTO, and noninstitutionalized bilateral and unilateral initiatives have led some academic commentators to argue about the emergence of a "new geo-economic order."[33] In this new order, international trade rules might serve states' foreign policies, where the WTO is merely an instrument to be used by members whenever convenient.[34]

Yet, WTO members have not returned to the same situation they were in during the Cold War. In a globalized world, national security depends on flows of capital, data, goods, and people, which renders traditional territory-based foreign and security policies ineffective.[35] While hostility is back, no actual alternative political configuration is on

[30] PS Vivek, 'India's Public Policy Issues and Challenges & BRICS' in Gustavo Lins Ribeiro (ed.), *Social, Political and Cultural Challenges of the BRICS* (Langaa RPCIG 2015) 103.

[31] Oluwaseun Tella, 'South Africa in BRICS: The Regional Power's Soft Power and Soft Balancing' (2017) 44(3) Politikon 387, 389.

[32] Wolfgang Weiss, 'Interpreting Essential Security Exceptions in WTO Law in View of Economic Security Interests' in Wolfgang Weiß and Cornelia Furculita (eds.), *Global Politics and EU Trade Policy* (Springer International Publishing 2020) 258.

[33] Anthea Roberts, Henrique Choer Moraes, and Victor Ferguson, 'Toward a Geoeconomic Order in International Trade and Investment' (2019) 22(4) J Intl Econ L 655, 655.

[34] Daniel Chee King Chow, 'United States Unilateralism and the World Trade Organization' (2019) 37 BU Int'l LJ 1, 29.

[35] Sören Scholvin and others, 'Conclusion' in Mikael Wigell, Sören Scholvin, and Mika Aaltola (eds.), *Geo-Economics and Power Politics in the 21st Century: The Revival of Economic Statecraft* (Routledge 2018) 220.

offer.[36] Most WTO members seem to choose to pursue their own interests through unilateral measures while still purporting to some extent to act in the pursuit of superficially accepted but, at times, ill-defined multilateral values. The existence of a rules-based international order is not taken for granted since a world from which any notions of multilateral values and global security disappear will be one of global instability.[37] WTO members still seem to see the benefits of multilateralism and abiding by international rules, even if that does not prevent them from using or, at times, misusing those rules for the "wrong" reasons.

Ultimately, unilateralism can be attributed not only to the premeditated and deliberate undermining of the entire multilateral system of rules but also to the temporal dimension of the social, economic, and political state of affairs envisaged by such rules, the ambiguity and indeterminacy of treaty language, or limitations on the capacity of the participating states to carry out their responsibilities.[38] The core question remains how identifiable standards, clear accountability, and effective retaliatory remedy in case of the application of unilateral measures might be able to boost the cooperative, integrative purposes of the multilateral trading system, thereby contributing to international peace and security in the long run.

1.1 What Are Security Exceptions and Their Current Challenges?

The global economic order and the concept of security are deeply intertwined.[39] The UN Security Council has a broad authority to call upon the UN members to take measures for maintaining or restoring international peace and security, including the complete or partial interruption of economic relations.[40] States can also decide unilaterally to restrict trade relations or prohibit foreign investments for national

36 Antonios Tzanakopoulos, 'We Who Are Not as Others' in Robin Geiß and Nils Melzer (eds.), *The Oxford Handbook of the International Law of Global Security* (OUP 2021) http://opil.ouplaw.com/view/10.1093/law/9780198827276.001.0001/law-9780198827276.

37 Elizabeth Wilmshurst, 'The Use of Force' in Robin Geiß and Nils Melzer (eds.), *The Oxford Handbook of the International Law of Global Security* (OUP 2021) http://opil.ouplaw.com/view/10.1093/law/9780198827276.001.0001/law-9780198827276.

38 Abram Chayes and Antonia Handler Chayes, *The New Sovereignty: Compliance with International Regulatory Agreements* (HUP 1996) 10.

39 J Benton Heath, 'The New National Security Challenge to the Economic Order' (2020) 129 Yale LJ 1020, 1024.

40 Article 41 of the Charter of the UN (October 24, 1945) 1 UNTS XVI www.refworld.org/docid/3ae6b3930.html (hereafter the UN Charter).

security reasons. Absent any treaty exceptions, such measures might violate states' numerous commitments under international economic law. To illustrate, Russia's restrictions on traffic in transit across the Ukraine–Russia border imposed different treatment depending on the origin of the goods[41] and thus could be found in breach of Russia's core commitments under WTO agreements, including the principles of most favored nations (MFN) and national treatment.[42] In the same vein, investment restrictions (such as Colombia's seizure of the property of US investors in the interests of national security[43]) can violate the principles of MFN and national treatment (such as under the US–Colombia Trade Promotion Agreement (TPA) (2006)). Such restrictions can also run afoul of the guarantee to foreign investors against expropriation without compensation and the principles of fair and equitable treatment and full protection and security.[44]

States have always strived to preserve maximum discretion in taking unilateral trade actions whenever they consider that their national security interests are at stake (hereafter the Security Measures).[45] For this purpose, most trade and more recent investment agreements incorporate national security exceptions legitimizing the unilateral derogation from contracting parties' commitments in the interests of national security (hereafter the Security Exceptions).[46]

For many years, WTO members tried to limit invoking Security Exceptions before international adjudicators. Then, starting in 2017, several WTO panels were established after respondents declared that they considered the challenged measures necessary to protect their essential security interests.[47] States claim to be using Security

41 *Russia – Measures Concerning Traffic in Transit* (April 5, 2019) WTO Panel Report WT/DS512/R [2.1].

42 See eg Articles I and III GATT (1994).

43 *Angel Samuel Seda and others v Republic of Colombia* (June 27, 2024) ICSID Case No ARB/19/6 Award.

44 See eg paragraphs 3, 4, 5, and 7 of Article 10 of US–Colombia TPA (2006).

45 For the avoidance of doubt, this research refers to a measure as a Security Measure because of its national security objectives irrespective of whether such a measure can be justified under treaty-based Security Exceptions or not.

46 See eg Article XXI GATT (1994), Article XIV*bis* of General Agreement on Trade in Services (GATS), Article 73 of the Agreement on Trade-Related Aspects of Intellectual Property Rights (TRIPs), Article 10.8.3 of the Technical Barriers to Trade (TBT) Agreement, Article III:1 of the Agreement on Government Procurement (GPA) (2012).

47 Geraldo Vidigal, 'WTO Adjudication and the Security Exception: Something Old, Something New, Something Borrowed – Something Blue?' (2019) 46(3) Legal Issues of Economic Integration 203, 203.

Measures to pursue various policy objectives, such as to fight armed conflicts, ensure cybersecurity, and advance human rights, but they also use them to urge counterparties to engage in trade negotiations, targeting competitors who are arguably using unfair trade practices and protecting domestic producers. In the interests of national security, the US introduced additional tariffs on imports of steel and aluminum products because existing import flows were adversely affecting its domestic industries;[48] the United Arab Emirates (UAE) imposed trade embargoes against Qatar for allegedly providing support to their regional arch-enemy Iran and armed opposition groups;[49] and Russia adopted transit restrictions that excluded Ukrainian exporters from the key markets in Central Asia and the Caucasus with the escalation of the Russia–Ukraine conflict.[50] In response to Russia's invasion of Ukraine, several WTO members, such as the US and the EU, have adopted "unprecedented" economic sanctions, which have included sanctioning Russia's central bank and restricting its access to the dollar-dominated global financial system.[51] Some countries also withdrew MFN treatment in trade relations with Russia, relying on WTO Security Exceptions.[52] The US took the stance that Security Exceptions under international trade law are nonjusticiable, which is consistent with the US Presidential administration's position that the national security actions of the President are not subject to adjudicatory review.[53] Disregarding adverse rulings by the WTO panels, the US emphasizes

[48] See eg US Presidential Proclamation 9704 on Adjusting Imports of Aluminum into the US 83 FR 51 (February 1, 2021); US Presidential Proclamation 9705 on Adjusting Imports of Steel into the US 83 FR 11625 (March 8, 2018).

[49] Circular of the Saudi Ministry of Culture and Information and the General Commission of Audio and Visual Media from June 19, 2017 in *Saudi Arabia – Measures Concerning the Protection of Intellectual Property Rights* (June 16, 2020) WTO Panel Report WT/DS567/R [2.47].

[50] Resolution of the Government of the Russian Federation No 842 on Amendments to the Resolutions of the Government of the Russian Federation dated August 7, 2014 No 778 and dated July 31, 2015 No 774 (August 13, 2015) in *Russia – Measures Concerning Traffic in Transit* (April 5, 2019) WTO Panel Report WT/DS512/R [7.1].

[51] See eg US Department of the Treasury Directive 4 under EO 14024 on Prohibitions Related to Transactions Involving the Central Bank of the Russian Federation, the National Wealth Fund of the Russian Federation, and the Ministry of Finance of the Russian Federation 87 FR 32303 (February 28, 2022) that expands restrictions on Russian state-controlled financial instructions under the April 2021 EO 14024. See more chapter 3, sections 3.1.2 and 3.1.3.

[52] Inu Manak, 'Suspend Russia's Trade Benefits, For Now' (Council on Foreign Affairs, March 3, 2022) www.cfr.org/article/suspend-russias-trade-benefits-now.

[53] See more chapter 3.

that "the WTO has no authority to second-guess the ability of a WTO Member to respond to a wide-range of threats to its security."[54]

In addition, with the rise of emerging economies (such as China and Brazil) and developments in cutting-edge technologies, such as computer microchips, artificial intelligence (AI), quantum, and machine learning, many countries are increasingly tightening restrictions on foreign direct investment (FDI), based on national security concerns.[55] The concerns are particularly related to the FDI of state-owned enterprises (SOEs) and sovereign wealth funds due to suspicions that these investments may prioritize geopolitical objectives over purely market-driven strategies.[56]

National security is a compelling concept and tool that can be potentially borderless and inherently dangerous, primarily because of its unspecified, subjective nature. Some degree of indeterminacy is inevitable in any body of rules.[57] However, the costs of such indeterminacy diminish legal uncertainty and can undermine the effect of international rules on contracting parties and society in general.[58] Indeterminate normative standards make it harder to know what is expected from the players of the trading system and, consequently, make it easier to justify any non-compliance with international rules. This lack of clarity elevates the risk that, in this world of increased competitiveness and global interdependence, the invokers of Security Exceptions might be more eager than ever to conclude that they are always right and can resort to the exceptions whenever it favors their economic agendas and strategic interests to do so.[59]

54 Office of the US Trade Representative, Statement from USTR Spokesperson Adam Hodge (Press Release, December 9, 2022) https://ustr.gov/about-us/policy-offices/press-office/press-releases/2022/december/statement-ustr-spokesperson-adam-hodge?s=03. See also Office of the US Trade Representative, Statement from USTR Spokesperson Adam Hodge (Press Release, December 21, 2022) https://mailchi.mp/394146669449/statement-from-ustr-spokesperson-adam-hodge?s=09.

55 Anastasia Ufimtseva, 'The Rise of Foreign Direct Investment Regulation In Investment-Recipient Countries' (2020) 11(2) Global Policy 222, 223.

56 See more Panos Delimatsis and Olga Hrynkiv, 'Sovereign Investors and National Security Exceptions in WTO and Investment Law' in P Delimatsis, G Dimitropoulos, and A Gourgourinis (eds.), *State Capitalism and International Investment Law* (Hart Publishing 2023) 236.

57 Ian Hurd, *How to Do Things with International Law* (Princeton UP 2017) 32.

58 Thomas Cottier, 'The Legitimacy of WTO Law' in Linda Yueh (ed.), *The Law and Economics of Globalisation: New Challenges for a World in Flux* (Edward Elgar Publishing 2009) 18.

59 Wesley A Cann, 'Creating Standards and Accountability for the Use of the WTO Security Exception: Reducing the Role of Power-Based Relations and Establishing a New Balance between Sovereignty and Multilateralism' (2001) 26 Yale J Intl L 413, 416.

To a great extent, the international community is left at a crossroads. If Security Exceptions are drafted and interpreted too narrowly, there is a risk that they will not cover essential emerging security threats, including cyber threats, the vulnerability of critical infrastructure, the expansion of the list of critical minerals, climate change, and states' legitimate geo-economic concerns. If, however, Security Exceptions are drafted and interpreted too broadly, they can allow anything under the sun, making states' international commitments meaningless.

1.2 Deconstructing Security Exceptions: Research Approach and Layout

Most of the literature on national security defense in international law used to focus on the initial choice and design of Security Exceptions.[60] With the rise of geo-economic statecraft and national security discourse, several scholars have attempted to shed light on the history and legal developments in Security Exception clauses incorporated in WTO agreements,[61] other trade agreements,[62] or investment treaties,[63] suggesting different approaches to interpreting the multivocal concepts of "security interests" and "emergency in international relations." Yet, relatively little attention is devoted to the relationships between different Security Exception clauses under international trade and investment treaty regimes. The emergence of new national security concerns and the frequent reliance of WTO members on previously intact Security

[60] See eg Alan Alexandroff and Rajeev Sharma, 'The National Security Provision: GATT Article XXI' in Patrick Macrory, Arthur Appleton, and Michael Plummer (eds.), *The World Trade Organization: Legal, Economic, and Political Analysis* (Springer Science Business Media Inc 2005); Andrew Emmerson, 'Conceptualizing Security Exceptions: Legal Doctrine or Political Excuse' (2010) 11 J Intl Econ L 135.

[61] See eg Mona Paulsen, 'Trade Multilateralism and U.S. National Security: The Making of GATT Security Exception' (2020) 41 Mich J Intl L 109; Mona Paulsen, Kamal Saggi, and Petros Mavroidis, 'The National Security Exception at the WTO: Should It Just Be a Matter of When Members Can Avail of It? What About How?' (2024) 23(3) World Trade Review 271.

[62] See eg Ji Yeong Yoo and Dukgeun Ahn, 'Security Exceptions in the WTO System: Bridge or Bottle-Neck for Trade and Security?' (2016) 19(2) J Intl Econ L 417; Gian Franco Chianale, 'The General and Security Exceptions in the European Union's Free Trade Agreements' in Denise Prévost, Iveta Alexovičová, and Jens Hillebrand Pohl (eds.), *Restoring Trust in Trade: Liber Amicorum in Honour of Peter Van den Bossche* (Hart Publishing 2019).

[63] See eg Mantilla Blanco Sebastián and Alexander Pehl, National Security Exceptions in International Trade and Investment Agreements: Justiciability and Standards of Review (Springer 2020).

Exceptions under international economic law have also provoked no shortage of proposals for reforms.[64] While they all provide insightful attempts to overcome some of the most compelling problems arising from the invocation of Security Exceptions, many deal with isolated questions and focus either on introducing the rebalancing mechanisms to international agreements,[65] strengthening the WTO institutional requirements,[66] bilateral and plurilateral bargaining,[67] or domestic policy.[68] Only several scholars have recently attempted to discuss trade governance and economic security more comprehensively, offering proposals on how to systematically address members' security concerns, not just through international adjudication, but also by considering the role of other international mechanisms, such as enhancing transparency, fostering dialogue, reforming WTO rules that address members' noneconomic objectives, or creating new mechanisms for their economic security goals.[69]

Notably, until recently, the discourse has been more inclined to emphasize the need for international oversight of the use of Security Exceptions to ensure necessary checks against abusive overuse of national security claims,[70] underestimating the question of whether current international mechanisms leave states with enough regulatory space to deal with ever-evolving threats to their national security interests, including cyberwars,

[64] See eg Simon Lester and Huan Zhu, 'A Proposal for Rebalancing to Deal with National Security Trade Restrictions' (2019) 42 Fordham Intl LJ 1451; J Benton Heath, 'The New National Security Challenge to the Economic Order' (2020) 129 Yale LJ 1020; Gregory Shaffer, 'Governing the Interface of U.S.-China Trade Relations' (2021) 115(4) Am J Intl L 622.

[65] See eg Simon Lester and Huan Zhu, 'A Proposal for Rebalancing to Deal with National Security Trade Restrictions' (2019) 42 Fordham Intl LJ 1451.

[66] See eg Peter Van den Bossche and Sarah Akpofure, 'The Use and Abuse of the National Security Exception under Article XXI(b)(iii) of GATT (1994)' in Chia-Jui Cheng (ed.), *A New Global Economic Order: New Challenges to International Trade Law* (Brill Nijhoff 2021).

[67] See eg Gregory Shaffer, 'Governing the Interface of U.S.-China Trade Relations' (2021) 115(4) Am J Intl L 622.

[68] See eg Yong-Shik Lee, 'Weaponizing International Trade in Political Disputes: Issues Under International Economic Law and Systemic Risks' (2022) 56(3) JWT 405.

[69] See eg Mona Paulsen, 'The Past, Present, and Potential of Economic Security' (2025) 50 Yale J Intl L 222; Bernard Hoekman, Petros Mavroidis, and Douglas R Nelson, 'Non-Economic Objectives, Globalisation, and Multilateral Trade Cooperation' (*CEPR*, September 11, 2023) https://cepr.org/voxeu/columns/non-economic-objectives-globalisation-and-multilateral-trade-cooperation; Harlan Cohen, 'Toward Best Practices for Trade-Security Measures' (2024) 27(1) J Intl Econ L 93.

[70] See eg Michael J Hahn, 'Vital Interests and the Law of GATT: An Analysis of GATT's Security Exception' (1991) 12 Mich J Intl L 558, 617.

developments in AI, climate change, pandemics, and geo-economic competition. It has been separately discussed whether specific trade-restrictive measures related to the consequences of economic crisis,[71] cyber attacks,[72] or climate change[73] fall within the scope of existing Security Exceptions, yet less attention has been devoted to the development of an encompassing study analyzing how far states could be willing to and should be allowed to push the boundaries of Security Exceptions in international law in the future in light of emerging and reemerging threats to national and international security.

This book attempts to broaden the horizons for descriptive and normative inquiry by advancing a comprehensive doctrinal work that examines and compares the evolution of the role of Security Exceptions under different treaty regimes and its implications for current debates over emerging threats to national security. To this end, the book collects and systematizes the relevant rules and jurisprudence under international trade and investment dispute resolution systems and clarifies the factors and grounds that have been determinative in upholding the Security Exception. It also provides an in-depth examination of how key principles of international economic law are reflected and applied in the fields of international trade law and investment law. It compares the relevant findings under the selected systems from both a procedural and substantive perspective, highlights the underlying commonalities and discrepancies, and rationalizes these to the extent possible. This comparative approach serves as a tool to contribute to a better and more sustainable future pathway, allowing states to be more conscious about adopting the best features of WTO law and customizing resulting flexibilities to address the unique institutional context of investment law. It also contributes to developing a consistent, coherent approach to the concept of national security in international law and to the drafting and interpretation of Security Exceptions, providing greater certainty for the future invocation and adjudication of security matters.

Different from other scholarly work, this book starts from the premise that the evolving geo-economic and geopolitical environment is

[71] See eg Lizzie Knight and Tania Voon, 'The Evolution of National Security at the Interface between Domestic and International Investment Law and Policy: The Role of China' (2020) 21(1) J World Investment & Trade 104, 109.

[72] See eg Shin-yi Peng, 'Cybersecurity Threats and the WTO National Security Exceptions' (2015) 18 J Intl Econ L 449, 469–478.

[73] See eg Felicity Deane, 'The WTO, the National Security Exception and Climate Change' (2012) 2 Carbon & Climate L Rev 149, 155–157.

challenging to judge if one focuses only on the compliance of different Security Measures with the current international legal framework and the case-by-case interpretation of highly volatile concepts under international economic agreements. Although this research is grounded in international law and focuses on legal instruments, it considers the diverse security interests of different states. This approach distinguishes it from formalist legal perspectives, which tend to remain skeptical of emerging security claims.

Furthermore, this book assumes that WTO members will be given the most space for dialogue if they admit that some national security questions are more prone to stricter regulation than others. It advances the idea that the dialogue between states over a revised approach toward Security Exceptions might start with drawing a line between conventional security measures, for which there is an ex ante agreement among all WTO members to justify extreme responses, and other security matters that might arise in the future or that are of concern for some contracting parties but where the agreement between all contracting parties over their urgency has not yet been reached. This research particularly seeks to explore how a coherent framework for international adjudication, the revised language of Security Exceptions, the involvement of the UN, the requirement of trade compensation, and specific procedural conditions for invoking the exceptions taken together can incentivize cooperation between governments and help strengthen trade and investment legalism where needed while leaving other national security issues to domestic politics and diplomacy.

All this considered, this book aims to answer the overarching normative question of how to achieve the balance between states' autonomy to adopt Security Measures and binding international law. To answer this question, this book first examines the extent to which the policy objectives of different WTO members are securitized. Second, the book explores how Security Exception clauses under different treaty regimes strike a balance between national autonomy to adopt Security Measures and states' international responsibilities. Third, it discusses what role international adjudicators and other institutions involved in governing economic and security policies play in interpreting or implementing this balance. Finally, the book suggests how international law should be better equipped to provide an optimal level of coherence and control while addressing states' security concerns, including by reforming Security Exceptions and the procedural and institutional requirements for their application on multilateral, regional, and/or bilateral levels.

Admittedly, the avenue of inquiry is far from exhausted. This book does not provide a comprehensive and exclusive account of how renegotiated Security Exceptions could work, much less an infallible means of resolving all questions about the role of national security concerns for international economic law in the future. As states' national security concerns evolve and as each government strives to build a techno-resilient national economy, some of the analysis undertaken in this book may be overtaken by new developments. The contribution of this book is in mapping out the potential direction of these developments, drawing on existing scholarship and practices to provide a foundation for future discussions.

In particular, this book draws on several scholarly discourses in the course of establishing its claims. While the research is primarily conducted from a legal perspective, the issues it discusses derive from the geo-economic statecraft and the national security discourse and, therefore, cannot be holistically analyzed without the interdisciplinary approach looking into unilateral measures from the perspective of international relations, economics, and political science.

The descriptive part of this book focuses on the decades-long interplay between the initial design of Security Exceptions, their subsequent invocation by states, and their reshaping by courts asked to rule on purported abuses. This book uses the case studies of the US, the EU, and BRICS countries. These WTO members are selected by virtue of their economic and political power, their importance in global supply chains, and their roles in the transformation of the global order. This book initially examines the application of Security Measures by selected jurisdictions. It explores how different domestic authorities manage the national security risks arising from economic interaction by comparing the legislative framework and the practice of using economic statecraft in selected jurisdictions. In order to sharpen and reify the issues, this book compares the measures that the US, the EU, and BRICS could use in response to a broader range of threats to their security interests beyond the "traditional" national security activities limited to military and defense matters. Such measures include economic sanctions and investment screening mechanisms. While a fully-fledged comparative analysis between courts or between domestic authorities of the US, the EU, and BRICS is beyond the goal of this research, not in the least because of the challenging character of such a task, this book compares the responsibilities and discretion of domestic authorities of the US, the EU, and BRICS in the application of economic measures and examines the possibility of a review of their decisions.

Further, the book examines regional trade agreements (RTAs)[74] and investment treaties (often referred to as bilateral investment treaties or BITs) (hereafter RTAs and BITs, together the Regional Agreements) entered into by the US, the EU, and BRICS and attempts to determine the extent to which the differences in the language of their Security Exception clauses affect the standard of review of their Security Measures. The limitations of such analysis stem from the research design and the selection of Regional Agreements. This book looks into the RTAs of the US, the EU, and BRICS that have been notified to the WTO before 2023.[75] Given that the US, the EU, and BRICS have been or have become capital-exporting states that usually initiate negotiations of investment agreements based on their model or prototype treaties,[76] whenever available, this research analyses model BITs developed by the respective WTO members.[77] In particular, it attempts to identify the exception clauses in the analyzed model agreements that incorporate security-related terms and to examine whether the US, the EU, and BRICS have followed the approach of their model agreements to drafting such exception clauses while negotiating BITs with specific counterparties.

Different from other scholarly works, this book not only discusses the domestic practice on the application of Security Measures or analyses particular Security Exceptions under international trade or investment agreements and WTO/IIA case law. It also discusses the convergence of the approaches under international trade and investment regimes, engages with the literature that builds the bridge between the WTO and the UN, and examines the substantive field of security studies and selected theories of international relations. Given this, the normative part of this book is twofold.

First, based on the current debates in international economic law, it discusses how to make the standard of review of Security Exceptions by

[74] RTAs in the WTO are understood as any reciprocal trade agreement between two or more WTO members, not necessarily belonging to the same region. See Peter Van den Bossche and Werner Zdouc, *The Law and Policy of the World Trade Organization. Text, Cases, and Materials* (5th ed., CUP 2022) 730–731.

[75] The RTA-IS database provides information on RTAs in force that have been notified, or for which an early announcement has been made, to the WTO https://rtais.wto.org/UI/PublicMaintainRTAHome.aspx.

[76] Jeswald W Salacuse, 'BIT by BIT: The Growth of Bilateral Investment Treaties and Their Impact on Foreign Investment in Developing Countries' (1990) 24 Intl L 655, 662.

[77] This research largely relies on the information about concluded investment treaties, model BITs, and their texts provided by the Investment Policy Hub of the UNCTAD https://investmentpolicy.unctad.org/international-investment-agreements.

adjudicators more coherent. To this end, it draws upon the underlying principles and concepts of international law and refers to the literature discussing the legal meaning of Security Exceptions and the approaches to their adjudication, highlighting the ambiguities and criticisms in applying Security Exceptions to emerging and reemerging threats to economic security.

Second, this book explores how additional legal and policy tools might enable Security Exception clauses to accommodate the competing demands of national security and legality. Such research is based on a solid theoretical foundation built upon the economic contract theory, the theories of international relations, such as realism, institutionalism, and constructivism, and the recently reemerged concept of "securitization" advanced by the Copenhagen School of security studies. It attempts to contemplate transparent and sophisticated procedures for the review of Security Measures that leave room for the appreciation of the state's interests to push the boundaries of Security Exceptions without undermining the international treaty regime. Among others, it explores the possibility of improving the cooperation between the WTO and the UN and introducing alternative to adjudication institutional means of allowing states to rely on the treaty exceptions without leading to their abuse, such as a better exchange of information between governments, notification requirements, and rebalancing mechanisms.

This book proceeds as follows. Chapter 2 discusses the theories and concepts relevant to this research. In particular, it seeks to construct the chain that links trade and security-related issues arising from the application of Security Measures by clarifying the concept of national security to be used for this research, revisiting the current role of international organizations in balancing free trade and national security, that is, the UN and the WTO, and finally contemplating the decision to incorporate Security Exceptions into international economic agreements or the decision to adopt Security Measures through the lenses of economic contract theory, the theories of international relations, such as realism, institutionalism, and constructivism, and the concept of securitization.

Chapter 3 outlines the national legal frameworks for applying Security Measures by the US, the EU, and BRICS in order to understand the level of securitization of their policy objectives. It focuses on the measures that are or can be applied by the US, the EU, and BRICS in pursuit of their national (regional) security interests and, thus, potentially subjected to Security Exceptions under international law. Specifically, this chapter discusses the practice of application of economic sanctions and investment screening mechanisms in those jurisdictions.

Chapter 4 examines the diversity of practice in drafting Security Exceptions under the international economic agreements entered into by the US, the EU, and BRICS. The first section discusses RTAs, and the second section examines BITs and investment chapters in RTAs. The chapter compares the texts of the Security Exceptions used by the US, the EU, and BRICS, identifies to what extent the texts of the analyzed agreements differ from the WTO agreements, and examines how such differences affect the approaches of the US, the EU, and BRICS to the application of Security Exceptions and their interpretation by international and domestic adjudicative bodies. Ultimately, it concludes whether and why different WTO members have different approaches to drafting Security Exceptions under WTO agreements and in their Regional Agreements.

Chapter 5 examines whether and to what extent WTO members can be accountable for applying Security Measures before international adjudicators and how the invocation of Security Exceptions can impact the international courts' or tribunals' proceedings. The idea of balancing free trade and national security is bound to substantiate itself in a compression of the right to sovereignty, which can be assessed through the good faith review or the use of a necessity test. The investigation of the meaning and mechanisms of these tests and the scope of discretion that should be granted to the decisions of WTO members in their national security matters allows for establishing the framework for reviewing Security Exceptions.

Chapter 6 proposes a coherent approach to the review of Security Exceptions under international trade and investment agreements by international adjudicators. The contribution of this chapter is twofold. First, it examines whether the clarification of the scope of the existing Security Exception clauses and their coherent application by international adjudicators under both regimes could help restrain the securitization of states' trade and investment policies. Second, and conversely, it aims to draw some conclusions about the extent to which existing Security Exception clauses provide sufficient policy space for WTO members to protect their national interests.

Chapter 7 discusses legal and policy options for reforming Security Exceptions through implementing substantive and procedural mechanisms to maximize joint gains from international trade and investment and the protection of the national security interests of WTO members. In particular, relying on the theories and concepts relevant to this book and the conducted comparative research, this chapter attempts to reconsider the role of Security Exception clauses in international economic law and contemplates additional institutional responses to remedy the current flaws in their interpretation and application. What is needed, and what this book seeks to provide, is an analytic perspective for assessing when more restraint on the application of Security Measures is desirable and when it is not.

Chapter 8, the final chapter, concludes and discusses future directions.

2

Relevant Theories and Concepts

This chapter aims to clarify the concept of national security to be used for the purposes of this research (section 2.1). Notably, even if technically a situation may qualify as a national security issue, it remains unclear whether, in practice, it will suffice to trigger the application of the relevant Security Exception clause under a specific treaty.[1] To this end, this chapter further provides an overview of international rules relating to the protection of national security interests under international trade and investment regimes and discusses the limitations of the scope of this research (section 2.2). It further discusses the current role of the UN and the WTO in balancing free trade and national security (section 3.3) and explores the existing challenges in interpreting and applying Security Exceptions under WTO law, focusing on the normative questions these challenges bring to light (section 2.4). In addition, this chapter compares and contrasts the role of Security Exceptions in international economic agreements from the perspective of different theories of regulatory policy and economic relations that examine state sovereignty, interstate relations, and economic incentives (section 2.5). Finally, it concludes (section 2.6).

2.1 The Concept of National Security

Marked under different terms, such as "essential security interests,"[2] "national security,"[3] "public security,"[4] "homeland security,"[5] and

[1] Catharine Titi, *The Right to Regulate in International Investment Law* (Nomos 2014) 84.

[2] See eg Article XXI GATT (1994), Article XIV*bis* GATS.

[3] See eg Articles 2.2, 2.10, 5.4, and 5.7 of TBT Agreement, and Article III:1 of the Revised Agreement on GPA (2012).

[4] See eg Article 36 of the Treaty on the Functioning of the EU (TFEU).

[5] There is no distinction between national security and homeland security. See Martin J Alperen, *Foundations of Homeland Security: Law and Policy* (2nd ed., Wiley 2017) 3.

"international peace and security,"[6] the concept of security has always been an organizing principle of the global order.[7] The literature on international relations also frequently uses the terms "globalized security,"[8] "regional security,"[9] or "transnational security."[10] Albeit possessing a well-defined meaning in our daily lives, the interpretation of the term "security" depends on the prevailing historical and political fabric. Ultimately, no matter which adjective is used (if any), the concept of security implies some degree of protection of specific values previously acquired.[11] The question remains which values are to be protected, from which kind of threats, and by which means.

2.1.1 Evolution of the Concept of National Security from the Cold War until Today

The term "national security" entered the legal lexicon of the US with the passage of the 1947 National Security Act.[12] Similarly, it started being used by the other states to define their national political strategies.[13] At the beginning of the Cold War in the 1940s, Morgenthau suggested an approach to interpreting national security, stating that "national security must be defined as the integrity of the national territory and its institutions."[14] It followed that for half a century, from 1940 to 1990, national security focused on providing defenses against military attacks to preserve state sovereignty.[15]

[6] See eg Article 1 of the UN Charter; Article XXI GATT (1994).

[7] Catharine Titi, *The Right to Regulate in International Investment Law* (Nomos 2014) 78–79.

[8] See eg Alun Gibbs, 'Public Foundation as the Striving for Security' in Massimo Fichera and Jens Kremer (eds.), *Law and Security in Europe: Reconsidering the Security Constitution* (Intersentia 2013) 113.

[9] See eg Gregory J Moore, *North Korean Nuclear Operationality: Regional Security and Nonproliferation* (John Hopkins University 2013) 5.

[10] See eg Ersel Aydinli (ed.), *Emerging Transnational (In)security Governance: A Statist-Transnationalist Approach* (Routledge 2010) 1.

[11] Arnold Wolfers, '"National Security" as an Ambiguous Symbol' (1952) 67(4) Political Science Q 481, 484.

[12] National Security Act (1947) Public Law 235 61 STAT. 496 (July 26, 1947).

[13] See eg Alan G Stolberg, *How Nation-States Craft National Security Strategy Documents* (Strategic Studies Institute US Army War College 2012).

[14] Simon Dalby, 'Security, Intelligence, the National Interest and the Global Environment' (1995) 10 Intelligence and National Security 175, 175.

[15] Donald N Zillman, 'Energy Trade and the National Security Exception to GATT' (1994) 12(1) J Energy & Natural Resources Law 117, 124.

With the end of the Cold War, a new era dawned on international politics, particularly states' national security policies. The older problem of East–West conflict during the Cold War, featuring various types of Soviet military threats, has been reduced dramatically.[16] The nature of sovereignty has changed with the blurring of the lines between domestic and foreign issues,[17] prompting states to reconsider their understanding of national interests and how prevailing ideologies and institutional structures can affect their pursuit of those interests.[18]

In the 1990s, Mathews highlighted the need to broaden the definition of national security to include, in particular, the issues of availability of resources, the protection of the environment, and demographic challenges.[19] As mentioned by Kennedy,

> the definition of national security ... ought to refer instead to those sources, those underpinnings of long-term national strength in the state and power of our manufacturing, investment in science and technology, of educational skills, all of which ultimately the Armed Forces and defense policy of this country have to rest upon.[20]

National security has transformed from a largely state-to-state paradigm into a multifaceted notion that addresses a range of threats, including nonmilitary or nonhuman, such as economic crises, cyber threats, infectious disease, climate change, transnational crime, and corruption.[21] Economic coercion and constraints have started to play a more significant role than military coercion in the current trade and regulatory realms.[22] Unprecedented economic and technological challenges have resulted in a "new way of wars" through cyber warfare, devaluating currencies, and industrial policies promoting specific high-tech

[16] National Academy of Engineering and others, 'Finding Common Ground: US Export Controls in a Changed Global Environment' (National Academies Press 1991) 43.

[17] Margaret P Karns and others, *International Organizations: The Politics and Processes of Global Governance* (3rd ed., Lynne Rienner Publishers 2015) 1.

[18] Anthea Roberts, Henrique Choer Moraes, and Victor Ferguson, 'Toward a Geoeconomic Order in International Trade and Investment' (2019) 22(4) J Intl Econ L 655, 676.

[19] Jessica Tuchman Mathews, 'Redefining Security' (1989) 68 Foreign Affairs 162, 162.

[20] Donald N Zillman, 'Energy Trade and the National Security Exception to GATT' (1994) 12(1) J Energy & Natural Resources Law 117, 126.

[21] Margaret P Karns and others, *International Organizations: The Politics and Processes of Global Governance* (3rd ed., Lynne Rienner Publishers 2015) 577.

[22] Gregory C Shaffer, 'Power, Governance and the WTO: A Comparative Institutional Approach' in Michael Barnett and Bud Duvall (eds.), *Power in Global Governance* (CUP 2005) 133.

sectors,[23] making the separation between security threats and economic issues even more difficult. Consequently, in contemporary legal and political theory, the concept of national security should be understood as encompassing a wider range of issues, from a narrow focus on military threats to broader concerns with security in all aspects of public life,[24] which suggests that even failures in the education sector can pose a threat to national security.[25]

Against this background, in addition to addressing concerns directly related to "traditional" national security activities (e.g. military and defense matters), the notion of "national security" among the US, the EU, and BRICS increasingly encompasses the protection of other areas that have been gradually making their way onto the security agendas of these nations.[26] For one, economic security has emerged as an important strategic priority for their governments and regulators. Economic security can include certain aspects of trade and investment that directly impact a state's ability to defend itself, such as the reliability of supplies of military equipment.[27] In addition, economic security has often been referred to in terms of "security of supply," such as the security of supply of oil, energy, and some rare minerals and specialized technologies.[28] To illustrate, the EU's Economic Security Strategy (2023) (the ES Strategy) highlights four risk areas for the EU economic security: "the resilience of supply chains, including energy security," "risks to the physical and cyber-security of critical infrastructure," "risks related to technology

23 See eg US President EO 13873 on Securing the Information and Communications Technology and Services Supply Chain 84 FR 22689 (May 15, 2019).

24 J Benton Heath, 'The New National Security Challenge to the Economic Order' (2020) 129 Yale LJ 1020, 1096.

25 Massimo Fichera, 'Security Issues as an Existential Threat to the Community' in Massimo Fichera and Jens Kremer (eds.), *Law and Security in Europe: Reconsidering the Security Constitution* (Intersentia 2013) 90.

26 National Security Strategy of the US, The White House (October 2022); European Commission, Communication from the Commission to the European Parliament, the European Council, the Council, the European Economic and Social Committee and the Committee of the Regions on the EU Security Union Strategy (July 24, 2020) COM/2020/605 final; Decree of the President of Brazil No 6703 (December 18, 2008); Decree of the President of the Russian Federation No 400 on the National Security Strategy of the Russian Federation (July 2, 2021); India's National Security Strategy (Hooda Report), Indian National Congress (March 2019); National Security Law of the People's Republic of China, 12th National People's Congress (July 1, 2015); White Paper on National Defence for the Republic of South Africa (May 1996).

27 Vincent Cable, 'What Is International Economic Security?' (1995) 71(2) Intl Affairs 305, 306.

28 Ibid.

security and technology leakage," and "risks of weaponization of economic dependencies or economic coercion."[29] According to the ES Strategy, certain listed risks "could also go so far as to threaten national security in certain circumstances," for example, in cases of dual-use technology leakage.[30] Since 2017, the US National Security Strategy expressly stipulates that economic security is national security.[31] The BRICS also define their national security in rather economic terms,[32] additionally raising the critical issue of the extent to which geo-economic objectives and the protection of domestic industries are included in "national security." The geo-economic position of such states and the fear that relatively poor economic performance might undermine their military capacity could also prompt extraordinary responses.

Furthermore, the questions around the understanding of economic security as a part of the state's national security arise while dealing with investments in strategic industries or unhindered supply chains to exchange necessary supplies, such as face masks, and for addressing the COVID-19 pandemic, or overcoming the consequences of the rising sea levels caused by climate change.[33] By the same token, cyber threats from the dramatically increasing number of attacks against critical infrastructures significantly affect states' economies,[34] making the US, the EU, and BRICS view cybersecurity as one of their security concerns.[35] Environmental security, and

[29] The ES Strategy (2023), Part 2. See more Isabella Morgott, 'Strategic Security in the Digital Age: The EU's Deep Dive into Critical Technologies' (*Inline*, October 27, 2023) www.inlinepolicy.com/blog/eu_critical_technology.

[30] The ES Strategy (2023), Part 2.

[31] National Security Strategy of the US, The White House (December 2017) 17.

[32] Decree of the President of Brazil No 6703 (December 18, 2008); Decree of the President of the Russian Federation No 400 on the National Security Strategy of the Russian Federation (July 2, 2021); India's National Security Strategy (Hooda Report), Indian National Congress (March 2019); National Security Law of the People's Republic of China, 12th National People's Congress (July 1, 2015); White Paper on National Defence for the Republic of South Africa (May 1996).

[33] Denise Lu and Christopher Flavelle, 'Rising Seas Will Erase More Cities by 2050, New Research Shows' *The New York Times* (October 29, 2019) www.nytimes.com/interactive/2019/10/29/climate/coastal-cities-underwater.html.

[34] Julian Jang-Jaccard and Surya Nepal, 'A Survey of Emerging Threats in Cybersecurity' (2014) 80 Special Issue on Dependable and Secure Computing 973, 973.

[35] National Security Strategy of the US, The White House (October 2022); European Commission, Communication from the Commission to the European Parliament, the European Council, the Council, the European Economic and Social Committee and the Committee of the Regions on the EU Security Union Strategy (July 24, 2020) COM/2020/605 final; Decree of the President of Brazil No 6703 (December 18, 2008); Decree of the President of the Russian Federation No 400 on the National Security Strategy of the Russian Federation (July 2, 2021); India's National Security Strategy (Hooda Report),

climate change specifically, has made it to the security agendas of the US, the EU, Russia, India, China, and South Africa.[36] The protection of public health has also been expressly acknowledged in the US.[37] Other WTO members refer to the threats caused by diseases and pandemics and their consequences, though in different terms.[38] The US, the EU, and BRICS view cybersecurity as one of their security concerns.[39]

The securitization of different spheres of life in the US, the EU, and BRICS suggests that their regulators might adopt extraordinary measures, including those of an economic nature, to protect various national interests, even if such measures run afoul of their international commitments, and then attempt to justify them under Security Exceptions. This poses a risk that when WTO members do not feel restrained in using Security Measures, modern national security demands could undermine

Indian National Congress (March 2019); National Security Law of the People's Republic of China, 12th National People's Congress (July 1, 2015); White Paper on National Defence for the Republic of South Africa (May 1996).

[36] National Security Strategy of the US, The White House (October 2022); European Commission, Communication from the Commission to the European Parliament, the European Council, the Council, the European Economic and Social Committee and the Committee of the Regions on the EU Security Union Strategy (July 24, 2020) COM/2020/605 final; Decree of the President of the Russian Federation No 400 on the National Security Strategy of the Russian Federation (July 2, 2021); India's National Security Strategy (Hooda Report), Indian National Congress (March 2019); National Security Law of the People's Republic of China, 12th National People's Congress (July 1, 2015); White Paper on National Defence for the Republic of South Africa (May 1996).

[37] National Security Strategy of the US, The White House (October 2022).

[38] European Commission, Communication from the Commission to the European Parliament, the European Council, the Council, the European Economic and Social Committee and the Committee of the Regions on the EU Security Union Strategy (July 24, 2020) COM/2020/605 final; Decree of the President of Brazil No 6703 (December 18, 2008); Decree of the President of the Russian Federation No 400 on the National Security Strategy of the Russian Federation (July 2, 2021); India's National Security Strategy (Hooda Report), Indian National Congress (March 2019); National Security Law of the People's Republic of China, 12th National People's Congress (July 1, 2015); White Paper on National Defence for the Republic of South Africa (May 1996).

[39] National Security Strategy of the US, The White House (October 2022); European Commission, Communication from the Commission to the European Parliament, the European Council, the Council, the European Economic and Social Committee and the Committee of the Regions on the EU Security Union Strategy (July 24, 2020) COM/2020/605 final; Decree of the President of Brazil No 6703 (December 18, 2008); Decree of the President of the Russian Federation No 400 on the National Security Strategy of the Russian Federation (July 2, 2021); India's National Security Strategy (Hooda Report), Indian National Congress (March 2019); National Security Law of the People's Republic of China, 12th National People's Congress (July 1, 2015); White Paper on National Defence for the Republic of South Africa (May 1996).

states' legal responsibilities and the vitality of the international economic order. The question of whether existing Security Exceptions under international trade and investment regimes could potentially cover such a broad range of national security concerns is central to this research.[40]

2.1.2 *Difference between Concepts of National Security and International Security*

While national security has been generally described as the ability of a state to cater to the protection and defense of its citizens and its institutions, international security, global security, or transnational security evolved from the demands that no national security apparatus can handle on its own and that, as such, call for the cooperation of states.[41] Therefore, unlike national security, international security denotes the interdependence of states concerning their security relations.[42]

Threats facing international security include not only direct violence between states but also other threats that bring about state instability.[43] The global financial crisis, the breakdown of transatlantic solidarity over Iraq, the consequences of global warming, and others were directly or indirectly related to the new era of globalization.[44] These challenges call for concerted international action because no state could successfully address them alone.[45] However, not all human, environmental, and other security problems are necessarily of concern to international security.[46] To illustrate, few would argue that gang warfare in the US constitutes an international security concern. At the same time, the terrorist attacks of 9/11 urged policymakers worldwide to declare transnational terrorism a threat to international security.[47]

40 See more chapter 6.

41 Segun Osisanya, 'National Security versus Global Security' UN Chronicle www.un.org/en/chronicle/article/national-security-versus-global-security.

42 David A Baldwin, 'The Concept of Security' (1997) 23 Rev Intl Stud 5, 26.

43 C Elisabeth St Jean, 'The Changing Nature of "International Security": The Need for an Integrated Definition' (2007) 8 Graduate J Intl Affairs 22, 31.

44 Robert Hutchings, 'The United States and the Emerging Global Security Agenda' in Luis Peral (ed.), *Global Security in a Multipolar World* (2009) (EUISS 2009) 103.

45 Ibid.

46 C Elisabeth St Jean, 'The Changing Nature of "International Security": The Need for an Integrated Definition' (2007) 8 Graduate J Intl Affairs 22, 30.

47 UN Security Council, Resolution 1373 (September 28, 2001) S/RES/1373 (2001).

The UN's stated objective is to maintain international peace and security, which requires eliminating, reducing, or managing any threats to the peace.[48] Various documents and policy papers have also been developed on a regional level to deal with security concerns. In particular, the Organization for Security and Co-operation (OSCE) in Europe recognized that "threats to security and stability in the OSCE region are today more likely to arise as negative, destabilizing consequences of developments that cut across the politico-military, economic and environmental and human dimensions, than from any major armed conflict."[49] National views on international or "external" threats to the state are developed along the same lines when the global dimension of major problems becomes apparent.[50]

The foregoing suggests that the concept of international security can be defined as encompassing any threat, referent object, or response, so long as it affects or might potentially affect the global system or it involves the international community either through direct violence between states or through other kinds of instability.[51] When the UN, or any regional organization, decides to mitigate a rising problem, it is because it views it as an international or regional security threat, regardless of whether it originated as an internal problem of a particular state. Consequently, it is plausible to say that the difference between international and national security lies in the geographical impact of the threat and the nature of the response to such a threat rather than in the type of threat (such as military or environmental) or its origin (such as a conflict between states or within a state).

2.2 Linkage between National Security and International Economic Law

International law does not include an implicit, open-ended Security Exception that applies across all treaties.[52] Customary international law provides the exceptions related to the law of reprisal or a fundamental

[48] Article 1 of the UN Charter.

[49] OSCE Strategy to Address Threats to Security and Stability in the Twenty-First Century [3] www.osce.org/mc/17504?download=true.

[50] Luis Peral, 'Conclusion' in Luis Peral (ed.), *Global Security in a Multipolar World* (EUISS 2009) 121.

[51] C Elisabeth St Jean, 'The Changing Nature of "International Security": The Need for an Integrated Definition' (2007) 8 Graduate J Intl Affairs 22, 32.

[52] Susan Rose-Ackerman and Benjamin Billa, 'Treaties and National Security' (2008) 40(2) NYU J Intl L & Pol 437, 439.

change of circumstances codified in the Vienna Convention on the Law of Treaties (VCLT)[53] or the doctrines of self-defense and necessity under the Articles on the Responsibility of States for Internationally Wrongful Acts (ARSIWA) adopted by the International Law Commission (ILC).[54] Neither the VCLT nor the ARSIWA includes a Security Exception. Thus, such an exception can only be derived from the specific treaty in question.

The GATT Article XXI-type Security Exception clause was first developed for the ITO Charter. Albeit intended to operate alongside the Bretton Woods institutions, the ITO never saw the light of day.[55] With the demise of the ITO Charter, only the Security Exception clause incorporated in Article XXI GATT (1947) and further transmitted into the GATT (1994) has survived until today. Since the creation of the WTO in 1995, trade rules have been expanded to cover other areas, including trade in services and intellectual property. The WTO agreements regulating these areas include an almost identical text of the Security Exception clause. In particular, with only slight modifications, the Security Exception clause was incorporated in the GATS, the TRIPs Agreement, and the GPA. Article XXI (Security Exceptions) of the GATT (1994) comprises three separate exceptions. The first exception, prescribed in subparagraph (a) of Article XXI, refers only to disclosing information. The third exception, specified in subparagraph (c) of Article XXI, allows a contracting party/member to take any action in pursuance of its obligations under the UN Charter to maintain international peace and security. This exception refers to Chapter VII of the UN Charter allowing the UN Security Council to decide on measures not involving the use of armed force to maintain or restore international peace and security, including complete or partial interruption of economic relations and rail, sea, air, postal, telegraphic, radio, and other means of communication, and the severance of diplomatic relations.[56] The UN members are required to abide by the decisions of the UN Security Council. Furthermore, in the event of a conflict between the obligations of the UN members under the UN Charter and their obligations under any other international agreement, including the WTO agreements, the

[53] Articles 60 and 62 of VCLT.

[54] Articles 21 and 25 of ARSIWA.

[55] Richard Peet and others, *Unholy Trinity: The IMF, World Bank and WTO* (SIRD 2003) 148.

[56] Article 41 of the UN Charter.

obligations under the UN Charter shall prevail.[57] Therefore, subparagraph (c) of Article XXI merely recognized the overriding obligation of the UN members under the UN Charter.

For the most part, GATT contracting parties, and later WTO members, tried to profit from the ambiguity of the second exception under subparagraph (b) of Article XXI.[58] In particular, the debates focused on the words "it considers necessary," which can be regarded as the textual hallmark of a "self-judging" clause, and on the lack of proper definition of "essential security interests" and a measure "taken in time of war or other emergency in international relations" under Article XXI(b)(iii) GATT (1994). This book is restricted to the effects of subparagraph (b) of Article XXI GATT (1994) (and respective Security Exception clauses under Regional Agreements). Yet, this research discusses some of the questions arising from the application of subparagraphs (a) and (c), where it is relevant for a better understanding of the scope and limits of subparagraph (b).

RTAs often use similar text of Security Exceptions (precisely, the equivalent of subparagraph (b) of Article XXI GATT (1994), as incorporated in the WTO agreements). Nevertheless, some agreements appear to be pushing the boundaries for the exercise of Security Exceptions to expressly enable a wider variety of actions that may be inconsistent with the rules of the underlying agreements. The specific language of Security Exception clauses under different agreements will be further analyzed.[59]

The investment regime has developed based on a different political economy and logic than trade agreements, which has affected the approach to incorporating Security Exceptions in earlier International Investment Agreements (IIAs). For one, states generally have fewer interests in restricting foreign investments than foreign imports, partly because foreign investments can promote domestic employment, national economic growth, and technology.[60] After failing to create a comprehensive multilateral set of investment rules and in response to the growing opposition of developing countries to foreign investment, capital-exporting countries decided to protect their respective interests in

[57] Ibid Article 103.

[58] Tania Voon, 'The Security Exception in WTO Law: Entering a New Era' (2019) 113 AJIL Unbound 45, 48.

[59] See chapter 4.

[60] Joel P Trachtman, *The Future of International Law: Global Government* (CUP 2013) 213.

foreign investments by entering into BITs.[61] Such agreements sought to create a basic legal framework to regulate investments by nationals of one country in the territory of the other country, known as the host state.[62] By providing treaty-based protection, BITs were supposed to act as a "signaling device" to foreign investors about particular state intentions and an amiable investment environment.[63] This signaling role of BITs has been even more critical in countries with high regulatory risks that foreign investment is exposed to, particularly BRICS.

The pro-investor partly explains why most BITs, at least until the 1990s, lacked the appropriate general or security exceptions.[64] However, exception clauses are just one way to balance state sovereignty and investor rights in IIAs. The structural differences between international trade and investment agreements, including their context, object, and purpose, and the nature and sources of substantive obligations, could also explain the lack of exception clauses in earlier IIAs.[65] For example, the parties to IIAs can ensure the regulatory autonomy to take measures in the interests of national security or other public policy objectives by limiting the general scope of application of the treaty as a whole or by clarifying the scope of application of the specific obligations, particularly regarding the obligation to compensate in case of expropriation.[66]

As a matter of newer treaty practice, state parties have become more eager to prioritize the insertion of exceptions to substantive obligations and, in some cases, explicitly model these new exceptions on the WTO law.[67] Such a move illustrates the changes in states' understanding of

[61] Thomas Eilmansberger, 'Bilateral Investment Treaties and EU Law' (2009) 46(2) CMLR 383, 384.

[62] Rudolf Dolzer and Christoph Schreuer, *Principles of International Investment Law* (OUP 2012) 1.

[63] Prabhash Ranjan, 'Comparing Investment Provisions in India's FTAs with India's Stand-Alone BITs Contributing to the Evolution of New Indian BIT Practice' (2015) 16 J World Investment & Trade 899, 928.

[64] Sungjoon Cho and Jürgen Kurtz, 'Convergence and Divergence in International Economic Law and Politics' (2018) EJIL 29(1) 169, 186.

[65] Bradly J Condon, 'Treaty Structure and Public Interest Regulation in International Economic Law' (2014) 17 J Int'l Econ L 333, 350–351.

[66] See eg Andrew Newcombe, 'The Use of General Exceptions in IIAs: Increasing Legitimacy or Uncertainty' in Armand De Mestral and Céline Lévesque (eds.), *Improving International Investment Agreements* (Routledge 2013) 267–83. See more on police power doctrine in chapter 6, section 6.1.

[67] Sungjoon Cho and Jürgen Kurtz, 'Convergence and Divergence in International Economic Law and Politics' (2018) 29(1) EJIL 169, 189.

investment treaties and the exceptions thereunder.[68] Furthermore, in the last two decades, there has been some progress in integrating trade and investment rules in trade agreements, in particular, in the GATT (1994) and Agreement on Trade-Related Investment Measures (TRIMs Agreement) in the WTO but also RTAs, starting with the North American Free Trade Agreement (NAFTA) (1992) (now US–Mexico–Canada Agreement, or USMCA), which have included investment chapters with preestablishment market access provisions.[69] Today, combining trade and investment rules in one agreement is more common.[70] Such an interplay between trade and investment regimes, further complicated by cross-cutting exceptions, leads to an increasingly complex and, at times, overlapping network of rights and obligations.[71]

Trends in the drafting techniques for Security Exceptions followed by the US, the EU, and BRICS in their Regional Agreements could result in the application of more subjective or more objective standards of review of Security Measures.[72] Thus, the use of different language and construction in relation to security defenses might affect both the extent to which the contracting parties exercise their discretion to restrict trade or investment in the interests of national security and the approach to the legality of such measures under international law.

2.3 Reconciling Pieces of Security Governance: The UN and the WTO

The UN is the central piece of global security governance,[73] while the WTO is a central site for global governance of the multilateral trading

[68] Armand de Mestral and Lukas Vanhonnaeker, 'Exception Clauses in Mega-Regionals (International Investment Protection and Trade Agreements)' in Thilo Rensmann (ed.), *Mega-Regional Trade Agreements* (Springer International Publishing 2017) 83.

[69] Debra Steger, 'International Trade and Investment: Towards a Common Regime?' in Roberto Echandi and Sauvé Pierre (eds.), *Prospects in International Investment Law and Policy: World Trade Forum* (CUP 2013) 157.

[70] Joost Pauwelyn, ' The Re-Convergence of International Trade and Investment Law: Causes, Questions, and Reform' (2014) 108 Proceedings of the ASIL Annual Meeting 255, 255.

[71] Ibid 257.

[72] See more chapter 4.

[73] In this sense, security governance is understood as a bundle of policies that may individually or jointly encourage or discourage collective or unilateral actions. See Emil J Kirchner and James Sperling (eds.), *National Security Cultures: Patterns of Global Governance* (Taylor & Francis Group 2010) 1.

system.[74] The UN Security Council is the primary legitimizer of actions initiated to deal with threats and aggression.[75] In this mindset, the UN Security Council has the task of determining the existence of a threat and deciding what measures should be taken to maintain or restore international peace and security.[76] Reasonably carrying this idea forward, if nonconventional trade issues reach the WTO, they could also be transferred to the UN Security Council or UN specialized agencies with the mandate and expertise to deal with security issues.[77]

Understanding the role of the UN and the WTO in security governance starts with the nature and design of both organizations. The WTO was designed to cope with growing problems of international interdependence and globalization by using legal tools.[78] At the same time, the UN Charter affirms that the Security Council is a political rather than a legal organ and that it responds to threats to international peace and security instead of violations of international law.[79] Thus, the UN and the WTO have taken different niches in the international order.

As a practical matter, the goals of the two organizations can be difficult to differentiate. Chapter IX of the UN Charter states that the UN shall promote, among others, higher standards of living, full employment, and conditions of economic and social progress and development. Similarly, the Preamble of Marrakesh Agreement Establishing the WTO specifies that the ultimate objectives of the WTO are "to raise standards of living, ensuring full employment and a large and steadily growing volume of real income and effective collective demand, and the expansion of the trade in production of goods and services."[80] In other words, the declarations of both

[74] Supachai Panitchpakdi, 'The WTO, Global Governance and Development' in Gary P Sampson (ed.), *WTO and Global Governance: Future Directions* (UNUP 2008) 187.

[75] Margaret P Karns and others, *International Organizations: The Politics and Processes of Global Governance* (3rd ed., Lynne Rienner Publishers 2015) 109.

[76] Article 39 of the UN Charter.

[77] Gary P Sampson, 'Introduction and Overview Future Directions' in Gary P Sampson (ed.), *WTO and Global Governance: Future Directions* (UNUP 2008) 15.

[78] John H Jackson, *Sovereignty, the WTO and Changing Fundamentals of International Law* (CUP 2006) 131.

[79] Ian Hurd, *How to Do Things with International Law* (Princeton UP 2017) 40.

[80] Marrakesh Agreement Establishing the World Trade Organization (April 15, 1994), The Legal Texts: The Results of the Uruguay Round of Multilateral Trade Negotiations 4 (1999) 1867 UNTS 154, 33 ILM 1144 (1994) (hereafter Marrakesh Agreement).

organizations seem to overlap. Therefore, even though the UN and the WTO were designed to deal with different challenges by using different means, the policies of one organization might influence the policies of the other.[81]

The WTO's origins lie within the UN.[82] While negotiating and drafting the Security Exception clause for the Charter of the ITO – the intended predecessor of the WTO – the contracting parties discussed that the ITO should have the capacity to act upon economic measures taken for political reasons only where the UN did not or would not involve itself.[83] At the same time, GATT's practice confirms that GATT contracting parties distinguished between economic and political goals, and some of them viewed the former as within the mandate of the GATT and the latter as outside it.[84] In *US – Trade Measures Affecting Nicaragua*, where the Security Exception clause was invoked under the GATT (1947), some states also held that trade measures for non-economic reasons could only be justified if authorized by a decision from the UN Security Council.[85] Accordingly, "in the absence of such a decision or resolution, there was a serious risk that such measures might be [] arbitrary and would undermine the multilateral trading system."[86]

Admittedly, since its creation in 1995, the WTO has increasingly faced matters that only have a limited connection with trade. Major policy issues such as precaution, the environment, biodiversity, labor standards, and climate change could drift toward the WTO "not by design but by default," even if the WTO dispute settlement system (DSS) is not necessarily adequately equipped to deal with the emerging controversies and tensions that they generate.[87] Nothing in the WTO

81 Saba L Mollaian, 'Does Trade Equal Peace? The Role of the WTO in International Peace' (2019) 46(1) Legal Issues of Economic Integration 77, 80.

82 Richard Peet and others, *Unholy Trinity: The IMF, World Bank and WTO* (SIRD 2003) 27.

83 David D Knoll, 'The Impact of Security Concerns upon International Economic Law' (1984) 11(3) Intl Econ L 567, 605.

84 In *EC – Falkland Islands* (1982), the GATT Council met to address the dispute, with delegates from thirty-seven countries expressing an opinion on the matter. Twenty countries described the trade embargo as falling within the inherent right of the contracting parties and beyond GATT's competence. See Roger P Alford, 'The Self-Judging WTO Security Exception' (2011) Utah L Rev 697, 711.

85 GATT Council, Minutes of Meeting held on May 29, 1985, C/M/188 www.wto.org/gatt_docs/English/SULPDF/91150029.pdf.

86 *Regarding Case Concerning Military and Paramilitary Activities in and against Nicaragua (Nicaragua v US)* (June 27, 1986) ICJ Rep Merits.

87 Bert Koenders, 'Enhancing the Role of the WTO in Global Governance' in Gary P Sampson (ed.), *WTO and Global Governance: Future Directions* (UNUP 2008) 84.

agreements suggests that the questions arising from the invocation of Security Exceptions should be deferred to the UN or any other organization. Given that social norms and political issues are inextricably linked with the global economic system, their integration into all aspects of economic policymaking can ensure that markets are open and efficient but also fair and just.[88] In *China – Raw Materials*, for example, the Appellate Body recognizes that the WTO agreements reflect "the balance struck by WTO Members between trade and non-trade-related concerns."[89] To that end, it is plausible to state that the WTO's ability to serve as a global trade governor that manages international economic interdependence between its members relies on its success in recognizing and reinforcing other policy goals while promoting trade liberalization, including the ones related to the protection of the security of its members.[90]

Even though the WTO agreements do not identify the relationship between the WTO and other international organizations concerning Security Measures,[91] they still envisage some links with the UN, even without expressly referring to the UN instruments. For one, Article XXI(b) GATT (1994) might require the review of the existence of an emergency in international relations that pertains to the UN's competence on security matters. Given that disregarding the security implications of trade measures or trade implications of Security Measures might lead to failed policies in each area, stronger ties between the UN and the WTO on the review of Security Exceptions might be essential for a better understanding of the scope of Security Exceptions under the WTO agreements.

[88] Ernst-Ulrich Petersmann, 'WTO Negotiators and Academics Analyse the Doha Development Round of the WTO' in Ernst-Ulrich Petersmann and James Harrison (eds.), *Reforming the World Trading System: Legitimacy, Efficiency, and Democratic Governance* (International Economic Law Series OUP 2005) 528.

[89] *China – Measures Related to the Exportation of Various Raw Materials* (January 30, 2012) Appellate Body Report WT/DS394/16 WT/DS395/15 WT/DS398/14 [306].

[90] Daniel C Esty, 'Governing at the Trade: Environment Interface' in Gary P Sampson (ed.), *WTO and Global Governance: Future Directions* (UNUP 2008) 116.

[91] Article XXVI GATS only mentions that the General Council shall make appropriate arrangements for consultation and cooperation with the UN and its specialized agencies concerned with services. Likewise, Article XXXVI GATT (1994) states that there is a need for appropriate collaboration between the contracting parties, other intergovernmental bodies, and the organs and agencies of the UN system, whose activities relate to the trade and economic development of less-developed countries.

2.4 The History of the Application of Security Exceptions under WTO Law

GATT contracting parties and later WTO members attempted to justify their measures based on national security considerations in a limited number of cases before 2017. Only on infrequent occasions did they expressly invoke Article XXI GATT (1947) and later GATT (1994).[92] The Security Exceptions regained momentum under WTO law after Russia, the US, and Saudi Arabia invoked Article XXI(b) GATT (1994) to justify multiple trade restrictions relying on their national security interests. Such disputes demonstrate the different views of WTO members on the interpretation and application of WTO-style Security Exceptions and the problems arising from compliance with adverse panel rulings on members' national security defense.

2.4.1 Application of Security Exceptions before 2017

Until recently, none of the cases invoking Article XXI(b) had been conclusively resolved either by a panel or in the practice of GATT contracting parties/WTO members,[93] in part because the governments tried to resolve any disagreements involving the application of trade restrictions through diplomatic rather than institutional procedures.[94] Only one case has reached the level of a formalized dispute settlement – *US – Trade Measures Affecting Nicaragua*, even though, in the end, the terms of reference precluded the panel from ruling on the nature of Security Exceptions.[95] The other disputes invoking the security defense were invoked mostly in relation to bona fide military conflicts and resolved through negotiations, remaining to be significant for what has not happened rather than for what has happened.[96] GATT contracting parties informally perceived abuse of the security defense in the case of *Sweden – Import Restrictions on Certain Footwear* and persuaded Sweden

[92] Roger P Alford, 'The Self-Judging WTO Security Exception' (2011) 3 Utah L Rev 697, 699.

[93] Dapo Akande and Sope Williams, 'International Adjudication on National Security Issues: What Role for the WTO?' (2003) 43 Virginia J Intl L 365, 373.

[94] Gabrielle Marceau, *A History of Law and Lawyers in GATT/WTO: The Development of the Rule of Law in the Multilateral Trading System* (CUP 2015) 12.

[95] Hannes L Schloemann and Stefan Ohlhoff, 'Constitutionalization and Dispute Settlement in the WTO: National Security as an Issue of Competence' (1999) 93 Am J Intl L 424, 435.

[96] See eg *US – Issue of Export Licenses* (1949); *Sweden – Import Restrictions on Certain Footwear* (1975); *EC – Falkland Islands* (1982).

to withdraw its trade-restrictive measures.[97] However, neither the GATT (1947) Council nor, up until recently, the WTO had presented a formal position on the matter.

The initial reluctance to invoke Security Exceptions could be explained for two principal reasons. First, from the very beginning, the GATT (1947) was essentially an agreement between the states of the Western bloc of the Cold War interested in maintaining the economic and political stability of the bloc.[98] Thus, GATT contracting parties had little initiative to impose trade-restrictive measures on each other. Second, it can be argued that the GATT (1947) had neither the capacity nor legitimacy to interpret or rule over Security Exceptions.[99] The GATT (1947) was designed as a provisional agreement without a developed institutional framework and only limited provisions on dispute resolution.[100] All GATT legal obligations were qualified by provisional application, and there was no procedure for interpreting the agreement.[101] Even though the GATT (1947) managed to develop over time into a de facto organization, "by calling each other 'Contracting Parties' rather than 'Members' and referring to decisions of the GATT as those of 'the Contracting Parties' acting collectively they preserved the legal reality that no true organization existed."[102]

The DSS of the GATT (1947) was intended to maintain the negotiated balance of trade concessions rather than to secure free trade or enforce trade sanctions for violations of GATT obligations.[103] The system was based on a culture of diplomacy rather than a formalized procedure which was feasible in part due to the small number of participants in the agreement: a limited number of people were engaged in dispute settlement, and most of them knew each other; a time framework for setting a dispute gave each interested party as much time as necessary to

97 Peter Lindsay, 'The Ambiguity of GATT Article XXI: Subtle Success or Rampant Failure' (2003) 52 Duke LJ 1277, 1303.

98 Ji Yeong Yoo and Dukgeun Ahn, 'Security Exceptions in the WTO System: Bridge or Bottle-Neck for Trade and Security?' (2016) 19(2) J Intl Econ L 417, 430.

99 Robert E Hudec, *GATT Legal System and World Trade Diplomacy* (2nd ed., Butterworth Legal 1990) 77.

100 Joseph Conti, *Between Law and Diplomacy: The Social Contexts of Disputing at the World Trade Organization* (SUP 2011) 27.

101 Robert E Hudec, *GATT Legal System and World Trade Diplomacy* (2nd ed., Butterworth Legal 1990) 58.

102 Antonio F Perez, 'WTO and UN Law: Institutional Comity in National Security' (1998) 23 Yale J Intl L 301, 308.

103 Joseph Conti, *Between Law and Diplomacy: The Social Contexts of Disputing at the World Trade Organization* (SUP 2011) 28.

ensure that the matter was ultimately settled.[104] Different from a traditional adjudicating procedure, the key aim of the old GATT DSS was to find a solution mutually beneficial for disputing parties rather than to provide an exhaustive legal analysis of the legal rules and apply them to the facts of a specific case to determine who was right and who was wrong.[105] Therefore, the GATT panel was not an actual "panel" in the sense this word is used today. As suggested by Cann and Wesley, under such circumstances, allowing the GATT (1947) to deal with politically sensitive issues would not only introduce an element of unpredictability but would redefine and politicize the nature of the GATT (1947) in a way that would be unacceptable to many contracting parties.[106] Ultimately, any politically controversial ruling might have prompted any unsatisfied contracting party to abandon the GATT (1947), which could undermine all the efforts of its creators to build up global trade cooperation.[107]

Against this background, the contracting parties did not view the invocation of Article XXI GATT (1947) as a remedy or a real foreign policy tool aimed to justify the violation of their GATT (1947) commitments but rather as a defense of last resort to be used to induce the other contracting parties to further negotiations.

Even though, over the years, the GATT (1947) managed to develop the features that made it look and work much like any other international organization,[108] it was only with the formation of the WTO, and the creation of the new WTO dispute settlement process, that a multilateral trading system gained a formal international organization.[109] This resulted in two crucial novelties: the creation of the dispute settlement mechanism and the transformation of the trading system from a limited bargain among the most powerful trade players to the institution granted a "law-creating power." The latter has been established in particular by

[104] Gabrielle Marceau, *A History of Law and Lawyers in GATT/WTO: The Development of the Rule of Law in the Multilateral Trading System* (CUP 2015) 66.

[105] Ibid.

[106] Wesley A Cann, 'Creating Standards and Accountability for the Use of the WTO Security Exception: Reducing the Role of Power-Based Relations and Establishing a New Balance between Sovereignty and Multilateralism' (2001) 26 Yale J Intl L 413, 417–419.

[107] Ji Yeong Yoo and Dukgeun Ahn, 'Security Exceptions in the WTO System: Bridge or Bottle-Neck for Trade and Security?' (2016) 19(2) J Intl Econ L 417, 432.

[108] Ingo Venzke, *How Interpretation Makes International Law: On Semantic Change and Normative Twists* (OUP 2012) 148.

[109] Gabrielle Marceau, *A History of Law and Lawyers in GATT/WTO: The Development of the Rule of Law in the Multilateral Trading System* (CUP 2015) 4.

the provisions on the WTO DSS, where the WTO panels and the Appellate Body were granted the authority to determine the values underlying the WTO agreements in the context of resolving particular disputes between members.[110]

Therefore, the argument that the GATT (1994) has a meaning different from the GATT (1947) despite their identical language seems more persuasive if one takes the view that, from an institutional standpoint, the WTO "represents both the continuation of GATT and a departure from the informal status of previous GATT procedures."[111] Nevertheless, for a long time, WTO members seemed to continue following the assumptions from the pre-WTO era that Security Exceptions should be narrowly construed and rarely invoked.[112]

Notably, the threat to "essential security interests" has always been in the eye of the beholder, differing from case to case and from state to state. Any contracting party/WTO member invoking Security Exceptions generally argued that it was for a sole judge to decide whether or not a disputable measure was necessary to protect its security interests[113] and that a GATT/WTO panel could not or should not be established to consider a dispute.[114] The other contracting parties of the GATT (1947) participating in discussions and proceedings rarely have expressed strong opinions on the interpretation of Security Exceptions.[115] This is not surprising given that all the statements of the governments' representatives were made in a politically charged atmosphere. The representatives were often reluctant to elaborate on whether the legal prerequisites for the invocation of Security Exceptions had been met, mainly because their

110 Dan Sarooshi, 'Transfers of Powers to International Organizations' in Dan Sarooshi (ed.), *International Organizations and their Exercise of Sovereign Powers* (OUP 2007) 78.

111 Antonio F Perez, 'WTO and UN Law: Institutional Comity in National Security' (1998) 23 Yale J Intl L 301, 331.

112 Petros C Mavroidis, *The Regulation of International Trade: GATT and the WTO Agreements on Trade in Goods* (Vol. 1, MIT Press 2016) 480–487.

113 Particularly, the continuous position of the US was that a GATT system was limited to trade law, and the national security exception was "a separate legal realm" rather than a part of that system. See Hannes L Schloemann and Stefan Ohlhoff, 'Constitutionalization and Dispute Settlement in the WTO: National Security as an Issue of Competence' (1999) 93 Am J Intl L 424, 438. See more chapter 5, section 5.1.

114 This was the case when there was no automatic right to have a panel to consider disputes between contracting parties. See Dapo Akande and Sope Williams, 'International Adjudication on National Security Issues: What Role for the WTO?' (2003) 43 Virginia J Intl L 365, 374.

115 Dapo Akande and Sope Williams, 'International Adjudication on National Security Issues: What Role for the WTO?' (2003) 43 Virginia J Intl L 365, 374.

statements could have consequences for future disputes. Thus, the governments might have been willing to leave the politically sensitive issues ambiguous so as to be able to rely on the Security Exceptions in other cases where it would be more beneficial for them.

The differences in approach to the interpretation of Security Exceptions call into question the value of the economic autonomy of different contracting parties/WTO members within the GATT (1947) and later the WTO.[116] The cases where a security defense was invoked in the past primarily relate to situations where Security Measures were adopted to condemn, influence, or change the policy of the targeting states – such as Argentina's occupation of the Falkland Islands or the Nicaraguan government's aggressive activities in Central America – or as a response to the escalated crisis. In line with the realists' assumptions, the possession of power allows a state to pursue its self-interest more actively, including by adopting Security Measures.[117] In this respect, the ambiguity of Security Exceptions could have been entirely satisfactory for trade players, such as the US, who had the initiative to impose trade-restrictive measures against their counterparties with the aim to establish or reiterate the rules of the game that better suited their national interests. By doing so, they were able to preserve the freedom to invoke the security defense whenever they considered it necessary. Since any trade-restrictive measures inevitably influence the market of both an imposing state and a state against which the measures are applied, developing states have had fewer, if any, reasons and incentives to resort to Security Measures against their counterparties.[118]

2.4.2 *Brave New World after 2017*

Since China and Russia have become WTO members, a wider and deeper spectrum of economic exchange among more diverse states within the WTO has further confused the relationship between trade and security.[119] As confirmed by state practice after 2017, the ideas that

[116] Dan Sarooshi, 'Transfers of Powers to International Organizations' in Dan Sarooshi (ed.), *International Organizations and their Exercise of Sovereign Powers* (OUP 2007) 81.

[117] See more on realism in chapter 2, section 2.5.2.

[118] Wesley A Cann, 'Creating Standards and Accountability for the Use of the WTO Security Exception: Reducing the Role of Power-Based Relations and Establishing a New Balance between Sovereignty and Multilateralism' (2001) 26 Yale J Intl L 413, 419.

[119] Ji Yeong Yoo and Dukgeun Ahn, 'Security Exceptions in the WTO System: Bridge or Bottle-Neck for Trade and Security?' (2016) 19(2) J Intl Econ L 417, 436. See more on constructivism in chapter 2, section 2.5.4.

drove the creation of the multilateral trade order are no longer sufficient to prevent WTO members from more actively attempting to interpret the ambiguous Security Exceptions in their own favor. The willingness of certain governments to address domestic political or economic concerns as a national security issue is not anymore off the table.[120]

Facing competing narratives and strategic politics, the WTO panels have to do their best to reach a balanced and defensible position on the meaning of the Security Exception clauses under the WTO agreements. The first-panel report to examine the issue in *Russia – Traffic in Transit* was adopted in April 2019 without appeal.[121] The second-panel report concerns the dispute brought by Qatar, alleging breaches of the GATT, GATS, and TRIPs Agreement in the context of coercive attempts at economic isolation imposed by Saudi Arabia.[122] Qatar further restored ties with Saudi Arabia and decided to suspend the appeal proceedings, leaving the panel report in this dispute unadopted.[123]

Further, the US invoked Security Exceptions in quite a few WTO disputes. First, the US relied on GATT Security Exceptions to justify tariffs imposed on steel and aluminum imports from several trading partners pursuant to Section 232 of the Trade Expansion Act.[124] Several of these disputes with the US, such as the ones brought before the WTO by the EU,[125] Canada,[126] and Mexico,[127] were eventually

[120] Communication from the US in *US – Certain Measures on Steel and Aluminium Products (China)* (April 17, 2018) WT/DS544/2.

[121] *Russia – Measures Concerning Traffic in Transit* (April 5, 2019) WTO Panel Report WT/DS512/R.

[122] *Saudi Arabia – Measures Concerning the Protection of Intellectual Property Rights* (June 16, 2020) WTO Panel Report WT/DS567/R.

[123] Although unadopted panel reports have no formal legal status in the GATT or WTO system, the reasoning contained in an unadopted panel report can nevertheless provide useful guidance to a panel or the Appellate Body in a subsequent case involving the same legal question. See WTO, 'Legal Status of Adopted/Unadopted Reports in other Disputes' www.wto.org/english/tratop_e/dispu_e/disp_settlement_cbt_e/c7s2p1_e.htm.

[124] See eg Communication from the US in *US – Certain Measures on Steel and Aluminium Products (EU)* (April 17, 2018) WT/DS548/14 (settled in 2022) and *Association Eglise de scientologie de Paris and Scientology International Reserves Trust v The Prime Minister* [2000] ECJ I-01335 [17]. Communication from the US in *US – Certain Measures on Steel and Aluminium Products (China)* (April 17, 2018) WT/DS544/2.

[125] *US – Certain Measures on Steel and Aluminium Products (EU)* DS548 (settled in 2022).

[126] *US – Certain Measures on Steel and Aluminium Products (Canada)* DS550 (settled in 2019).

[127] *US – Certain Measures on Steel and Aluminium Products (Mexico)* DS551 (settled in 2019).

settled. Second, the US invoked Security Exceptions in the dispute with Hong Kong, China concerning the US origin marking requirement "Made in China" for the goods from Hong Kong, China.[128] Third, the US can also be expected to invoke a Security Exception in the WTO proceedings initiated by China over the sweeping US export controls.[129] Among the challenged export controls are the measures adopted in October 2022, arguably aiming to weaken China's semiconductor industry advancement.[130]

Finally, in addition to the US, Japan referred to Security Exceptions under Article XXI GATT (1994) in the dispute with South Korea over the export ban on dual-use goods.[131] Given Japan's initial statement that it views "dialogue as the best way of resolving this matter rather than dispute settlement,"[132] it is not surprising that this dispute was eventually settled by the parties without the issuance of the panel ruling.[133]

The Security Exception clause, unamended since 1947, does not reflect the transitions in geopolitical and geo-economic contexts. Therefore, even though it is plausible to state that, with the creation of the WTO, political concerns no longer automatically incentivize the members to forgo their trade interests, the fundamental problem remains of how to transform the WTO into a framework of global rules that can accommodate the coexistence of several different and in many instances incompatible political and economic systems: China's state capitalism versus market economies in the west; developed versus developing countries; and democratic versus nondemocratic

128 *US – Origin Marking Requirement* (December 21, 2022) WTO Panel Report WT/DS597/R.

129 Edward White, Demetri Sevastopulo, and Eleanor Olcott, 'China Hits back at US Chip Sanctions with WTO Dispute' *FT* (December 13, 2022) www.ft.com/content/4eaedee4-5267-4e3a-b9da-5d2bb6f356ee.

130 'Commerce Implements New Export Controls on Advanced Computing and Semiconductor Manufacturing Items to the People's Republic of China (PRC)' (Press Release of Bureau of Industry and Security, October 7, 2022) www.bis.doc.gov/index.php/documents/about-bis/newsroom/press-releases/3158-2022-10-07-bis-press-release-advanced-computing-and-semiconductor-manufacturing-controls-final/file.

131 DSB, Minutes of Meeting held in the Centre William Rappard on July 29, 2020 (October 14, 2020) WT/DSB/M/443 15. Regarding *Japan – Measures related to the Exportation of Products and Technology to Korea* (DS590).

132 WTO, 'DS590: Japan – Measures Related to the Exportation of Products and Technology to Korea' (*WTO News*, July 29, 2020) www.wto.org/english/news_e/news20_e/dsb_29jul20_e.htm.

133 *Japan – Measures related to the Exportation of Products and Technology to Korea* DS590 (settled in 2023).

regimes. Ultimately, the legality of the invocation of Security Exceptions in different cases remains contentious, which partially stems from the language and structure of Security Exception clauses, but also different approaches of WTO members to implementing Security Measures. These considerations will be further raised in the chapters to follow.

2.5 Theoretical Foundations of Security Exceptions

The ability to regulate within its own borders is a core feature of each sovereign state. The precise level of regulation is specific to every government and can vary depending on its risk attitude and the nation's wealth.[134] It implies that in the absence of any international commitments, states are free to choose with whom they wish to trade[135] and from which countries they wish to attract investment.

Yet, the right to regulate also includes the decision to enter into international agreements and undertake trade and investment commitments that change the permissible limits of states' subsequent regulations. States enter international agreements to achieve particular objectives, such as to foster cooperation in international trade or attract foreign investments, keeping in mind that, under certain conditions, such objectives might be surpassed by other goals, such as the need to protect national security.

The architectural challenge emerges from the attempt to balance these competing interests. The international trading system and investment law reinforce such a delicate balance by embedding the right to regulate as the power of a sovereign state to adopt trade and investment restrictions for public welfare purposes. For example, treaty exceptions in specific areas, such as Security Exceptions, have been construed to reflect it.[136] It would be false to assume that states always blindly seek to maximize their right to regulate under international economic agreements. Instead, they seek an optimal level of flexibility that allows them to satisfy their urgent needs when necessary but also to rely on the reciprocal binding commitments of their counterparties. On this view, the right

[134] Boris Rigod, *Optimal Regulation and the Law of International Trade: The Interface between the Right to Regulate and WTO Law* (CUP 2015) 50.

[135] See eg Hersch Lauterpacht, 'Boycott in International Relations' (1933) 14 Brit YB Intl L 125.

[136] Vera Korzun, 'The Right to Regulate in Investor-State Arbitration: Slicing and Dicing Regulatory Carve-outs' (2017) 50 Vand J Transnatl L 355, 388.

to regulate changes its meaning depending on the context of the public policy debates and the provision of an international agreement in which it is manifested.[137]

The complexities of today's international economic law and the high dissatisfaction of some WTO members toward trade and investment instruments and dispute settlement, in particular, might encourage WTO members to reconsider the balance between their right to regulate in the interests of national security and the binding law. The WTO is an example of how power and law are complementary: WTO rules reflect the collective self-interest of powerful states, and their power helps enforce those rules.[138] The shifts in economic power and trade flows might prompt some members to exploit the loopholes of the international trade regime, for example, by adopting illegitimate Security Measures. Similarly, the discussion over the legitimacy of Security Measures under the regional and bilateral regimes reveals the complexity of the relationship between different international actors in the pursuit of power, security, stability, and cooperation. This discussion fits into a broader debate about the role of different forces driving and motivating actors within the international economic order and the constraints imposed on those actors by the nature of the system itself.

To understand the decision of why and how WTO members enter international commitments and the underlying logic of escape clauses, such as Security Exceptions, this section initially draws on the economic contract theory developed for private contracting.[139] Further, it provides a short overview of central theories of international relations: realism, institutionalism, and constructivism. Realism has been considered a dominant theory of international relations for a long time[140] and has contributed to explaining the reasons for conflicts among states. It might remain relevant for those sections of the international system where community norms and shared beliefs are insignificant. Yet, for the rest, new concepts

[137] Ibid 380. See also Maria Weimer, 'Reconciling Regulatory Space with External Accountability through WTO Adjudication: Trade, Environment and Development' (2017) 30 Leiden J Intl L 901, 903.

[138] Mark Wu, 'Rethinking the Temporary Breach Puzzle: A Window on the Future of International Trade Conflicts' (2015) 40 Yale J Intl L 95, 152–153.

[139] Anne Van Aaken, 'International Investment Law between Commitment and Flexibility: A Contract Theory Analysis' (2009) 12 J Intl Econ L 507, 519.

[140] Andrew Emmerson, 'Conceptualizing Security Exceptions: Legal Doctrine or Political Excuse' (2008) 11 J Intl Econ L 135, 139.

would be needed to give a different context to how and why states interact on a global scale.[141] In particular, institutionalism helps better understand the worldwide setting dominated by international institutions, such as the WTO, and their antecedent agreements. Concurrently, the approach of constructivism can better explain the evolution of state sovereignty as a central theme in international relations. Each of these theories provides a contrasting view on the international trade order and the limits of the state's right to regulate, which helps further analyze and reevaluate the approaches to the nature and effectiveness of Security Exceptions under international economic law. Finally, this section discusses the concepts and ideas advanced by the securitization "theory," which, among others, offers a means of comprehending what makes something a security issue in international relations.[142]

2.5.1 *Economic Contract Theory*

Parties can be expected to participate in the agreement only if the expected costs of the performance of their commitments do not exceed the expected benefits.[143] Yet, practically every contract is incomplete. No contracting party fully knows the nature and impact of future contingencies at the time of its conclusion, nor the possible actions that its contracting party might undertake during the entire life span of a contract. If circumstances change, the costs and benefits of the contractual performance also change.[144] When the benefits of breaching an agreement exceed the costs of complying with an agreement, it might be in society's interest to encourage breach, which in economic terms is a "first-best" outcome.[145] In this case, the system governing the agreement should allow a party to deviate from its obligations,[146] in other words, to encourage an "efficient breach."

141 Ian Hurd, 'Legitimacy and Authority in International Politics' (1999) 53 Intl Org 379, 404.
142 James Sperling and Mark Webber, 'The European Union, Security Governance and Collective Securitization' (2019) 42(2) West Eur Politics 228, 238.
143 Anne Van Aaken, 'International Investment Law between Commitment and Flexibility: A Contract Theory Analysis' (2009) 12 J Intl Econ L 507, 509.
144 Alan Schwartz and Robert E Scott, 'Contract Theory and the Limits of Contract Law' (2003) 113(3) Yale LJ 541, 547–548.
145 Joel P Trachtman, *The Economic Structure of International Law* (HUP 2008) 259.
146 Richard Morrison, 'Efficient Breach of International Agreements' (1997) 23 Denv J Intl L & Poly 183, 183.

The availability of such an "escape" raises a moral hazard problem, given that it allows a respondent to shift the costs of the performance of its obligations on its counterparty. The tort and contract law in the US addresses this problem by requiring a party who decides not to perform the contract in order to protect its interests to compensate for the actual harm caused to its contracting party by non-performance.[147] Alternatively, to prevent abuse, a respondent can be precluded from relying on the escape clause if it contributed to the condition that changed the costs and benefits of its contractual performance.[148]

Contractual clauses that excuse performance under contingencies can range from force majeure to economic necessity.[149] Noperformance under force majeure and in the case of economic necessity is caused by different situations and might be subjected to different contractual consequences.[150] In the case of economic necessity, a respondent can choose whether to adopt the measures that are in breach of its treaty commitments or choose another course of action, which admittedly, in some cases, could be more detrimental to its interests than the nonperformance. Thus, the nonperformance is a voluntary decision of a responding party to save its costs by transferring them to another party. In the case of force majeure, a respondent has no option to perform its obligations because of external force other than a complainant. While the compensation requirement can be a valuable tool to mitigate the consequences of a moral hazard problem where the contingencies allow a party to choose between performance and nonperformance, it cannot incentivize a party to perform the contract where the performance is not possible. Thus, the contractual consequences for noperformance in the case of force majeure and economic necessity could be different.

International trade agreements[151] and investment treaties[152] are also examples of incomplete contracting. The negotiators of international

[147] Alan O Sykes, 'Economic "Necessity" in International Law' (2015) 109(2) Am J Intl L 296, 298.

[148] For example, a party cannot rely on the escape clause where its counterparty's act is compelled by coercion or duress.

[149] Eric A Posner and Alan O Sykes, 'Efficient Breach of International Law: Optimal Remedies, "Legalized Noncompliance," and Related Issues' (2011) 110(2) Mich L Rev 243, 257.

[150] Alan O Sykes, 'Economic "Necessity" in International Law' (2015) 109(2) Am J Intl L 296, 298.

[151] WTO, 'Trade Policy Commitments and Contingency Measures' (2009) World Trade Report 28 www.wto.org/english/res_e/publications_e/wtr09_e.htm.

[152] Anne Van Aaken, 'International Investment Law between Commitment and Flexibility: A Contract Theory Analysis' (2009) 12 J Intl Econ L 507.

agreements, like the parties to private contracts, enter the bargain with uncertainty about the future, such as the possible changes in economic conditions or the strength of domestic interest groups. For these reasons, the drafters are expected to include mechanisms for adjusting the bargain when required. An optimal level of contract incompleteness can be achieved when the parties negotiate until the expected benefit of adding the provisions equals the transaction cost of agreeing on them.[153] In the realm of international economic agreements, an optimal level of incompleteness would allow the contracting parties to balance the profits from international trade or investment liberalization with the interests in other areas where states are unwilling to compromise. On this view, it can be argued that by giving contracting parties discretion in unusual circumstances that change the costs and benefits of the contractual performance, similar to private contracting, the treaty exceptions secure deeper treaty commitments at the time of negotiations and thereby raise the expected gains.[154] Thus, from a strictly economic point of view, each government has a legitimate reason to abandon its obligations negotiated under the WTO or other trade or investment agreements when it has to deal with such unforeseen contingencies that make previous commitments inefficient. The safeguard measures under WTO law are one example.[155]

As things stand now, Security Exceptions under international economic agreements can potentially be invoked where a responding state claims that the performance of the obligations is not possible without undermining its national security but also that the benefits of ensuring its essential interests are higher than the compliance with the contractual commitments.[156] The allocation of risk for nonperformance in both scenarios depends on how the parties drafted their agreement for such future contingencies.

Contract theory distinguishes between precise and vague terms, or rules and standards, with rules being established more specifically in advance and standards delegating more discretion to adjudicative bodies.[157] Typically, rules are more costly than standards to create,

[153] Tae J Park, *Incomplete International Investment Agreements* (Edward Elgar Publishing 2022) 68–69.

[154] Robert E Scott and Paul B Stephan, *The Limits of Leviathan: Contract Theory and the Enforcement of International Law* (CUP 2006) 61–62.

[155] See more chapter 7, section 7.2.5.

[156] See more chapter 4.

[157] Anne Van Aaken, 'International Investment Law between Commitment and Flexibility: A Contract Theory Analysis' (2009) 12 J Intl Econ L 507, 519.

while standards are more costly to interpret at a later stage when deciding how to act or how to apply the standards to past conduct.[158] Thus, the distinction between rules and standards commonly derives from the decision to give the law its content ex ante or ex post.[159] The cost-benefit analysis favors the creation of standards when the rule makers cannot be efficient at specifying ex ante all of the details of the treatment of particular cases and where the rate of change of circumstances over time may benefit from a more remarkable ability of adjudicators to adjust.[160] However, the inclusion of such flexibilities makes it harder to ensure the performance of the contract and, therefore, creates more opportunities for nonperformance.[161]

Existing international economic agreements address the situation where a contracting party adopts a Security Measure in response to an unforeseen threat to its national security in two different ways.

On the one hand, Security Exception clauses grant a wide standard-like flexibility in determining the legality of security concerns by incorporating open-ended terms and conditions. When a standard applies to a measure, the party who wants to behave strategically must ask how a court will later interpret the standard.[162] For example, the question arises of how a court or tribunal would engage in a balancing test in order to determine the necessity of a Security Measure. In this case, the possibility of adjudicating national security disputes and reviewing whether the agreed preconditions for the invocation of Security Exceptions are met acts as insurance against the risk of opportunistic behavior by either party.

On the other hand, certain agreements expressly limit the intensity of adjudicatory review of national security disputes by incorporating self-judging wording to Security Exceptions, such as "it considers necessary," or purporting to exclude their review completely.[163] Theoretically, the parties should still be able to achieve efficient trade and investment flow under such agreements when they can account for reputation costs, the

[158] Louis Kaplow, 'Rules versus Standards: An Economic Analysis' (1992) 42 Duke LJ 557, 557.

[159] Ibid 559.

[160] Joel P Trachtman, *The Economic Structure of International Law* (HUP 2008) 215–216.

[161] Kenneth W Abbott and Duncan Snidal, 'Hard & Soft Law in International Governance' (2000) 54 Intl Org 421, 446.

[162] Alan Schwartz and Robert E Scott, 'Contract Theory and the Limits of Contract Law' (2003) 113(3) Yale LJ 541, 603.

[163] Caroline Henckels, 'Permission to Act: The Legal Character of General and Security Exceptions in International Trade and Investment Law' (2020) 69(3) International and Comparative Law Q 557, 564.

prospect of future relations, the principle of reciprocity, or other informal means of contract enforcement.[164] By relying on self-restraint in the application of Security Measures and on diplomatic routes for solving any disputes arising from security concerns outside contractual DSS, such an approach to drafting Security Exceptions not only grants contracting parties desired flexibility in the timing and manner of any response but also enables them to address any perceived concerns over national sovereignty and security, with the belief that the system of self-checks against an abusive overuse of Security Exceptions claims should work as long as both parties benefit from the performance under the agreement. On the flip side, because such Security Exceptions confer considerable discretion on parties, they open more room for impermissible behavior; this can include efforts to evade performance in pursuit of opportunistic goals or attempts to force a renegotiation of a contract's terms by imposing costs on one's contractual partner.[165] The vaguer legal standard gives a party more incentive to resolve doubts about the application of Security Exceptions in its own favor.[166]

Unlike private contracts that generally use standardized language having definite legal meaning, or at least meaning that is easily ascertained according to widely accepted characteristics,[167] the real meaning of the terms in international treaties may be disguised with diplomatic language so that its wording is indicative only of what it does not mean.[168] This concern is especially relevant to interstate relationships because of the absence of a comprehensive body of customary or other general law that can be applied to supply missing terms to incomplete treaties.[169] Thus, contracting parties usually face the difficult task of writing a contract that is optimal not only from an ex ante perspective, encouraging the parties to invest in the contractual relationship at the time of the conclusion of the contract, but also from an ex post perspective so that it still maximizes the values of contractual performance after

164 Robert E Scott and Paul B Stephan, *The Limits of Leviathan: Contract Theory and the Enforcement of International Law* (CUP 2006) 82.

165 Anne Van Aaken, 'Smart Flexibility Clauses in International Investment Treaties and Sustainable Development: A Functional View' (2013) 15 J World Investment & Trade 827, 838.

166 Alan Schwartz and Robert E Scott, 'Contract Theory and the Limits of Contract Law' (2003) 113(3) Yale LJ 541, 603.

167 BS Chimni, *International Law and World Order: A Critique of Contemporary Approaches* (2nd ed., CUP 2017) 79.

168 Ibid.

169 Joel P Trachtman, *The Economic Structure of International Law* (HUP 2008) 174.

all future uncertainties have been resolved.[170] If there is too much flexibility in international economic agreements, the value of the commitment is undermined.[171] If, however, there is too little flexibility, states may refuse to make essential commitments or may quickly abandon their responsibilities.[172]

Given the rise of new national security concerns and higher risks of parties' opportunism, states can be expected to change their course and search for the approaches to drafting Security Exceptions beyond the discussed models. Contracting parties should be able to create an optimal contract that can mandate different legal consequences for unforeseen contingencies (good faith) and opportunistic behavior (bad faith) and encourage efficient use of Security Exceptions.[173] The risk that a contracting party might act in bad faith raises the cost of entering into the contract, potentially making the cost of negotiations too high.[174] Thus, at least in some cases, states might be required to change their approach to drafting Security Exceptions in order to enter into contractual relations in the first place.[175] The compensation requirement borrowed from tort and contract law can be seen as one of the ways to incentivize the states to use Security Exceptions more efficiently.

2.5.2 Realism, Anarchy, and Struggle for Power

Realism begins with the assumption that states are the primary actors in international relations.[176] Due to the lack of a global government analogous to the state, the international environment is anarchic by nature.[177] States under anarchy behave as "rational egoists"[178] and calculate their

[170] Anne Van Aaken, 'International Investment Law between Commitment and Flexibility: A Contract Theory Analysis' (2009) 12 J Intl Econ L 507, 516.

[171] WTO, 'Trade Policy Commitments and Contingency Measures' (2009) World Trade Report 19 www.wto.org/english/res_e/publications_e/wtr09_e.htm.

[172] Ibid.

[173] Anne Van Aaken, 'International Investment Law between Commitment and Flexibility: A Contract Theory Analysis' (2009) 12 J Intl Econ L 507, 519.

[174] Curtis J Mahoney, 'Treaties as Contracts: Textualism, Contract Theory, and the Interpretation of Treaties' (2007) 116 Yale LJ 824, 850.

[175] See more the NAFTA negotiations chapter 4, sections 4.1.1 and 4.2.1.

[176] Philp M Nichols, 'Realism, Liberalism, Values, and the World Trade Organization' (2014) 17 U Pa. J Intl L 851, 874.

[177] Duncan SA Bell, 'Anarchy, Power and Death: Contemporary Political Realism as Ideology' (2002) 7 J Political Ideologies 221, 228.

[178] Nathan A Canestaro, 'Realism and Transnationalism: Competing Visions for International Security' (2007) 25(1) Boston U Intl LJ 113, 120.

interests in terms of power or in terms of their interest defined as power.[179] In such a world of the "war of every one against every one,"[180] states decide for themselves whether and when to use coercion (military or economic).[181] Fighting for power turns international politics into a struggle for power,[182] where states seek to survive under anarchy by maximizing their relative gains.[183] From this perspective, power is the currency of the international system,[184] while any attempt at restricting the state's sovereignty through international law is doomed to fail.[185]

States use their foreign policy as a tool to effectively enhance national power.[186] In particular, states enter into international treaties and create international institutions provided that they are in line with their interests, defined in terms of power, which constrains the feasible bargaining space and affects the transaction costs of making international commitments.[187] More powerful players have advantages in negotiating favorable terms in international agreements. They can force the other states to adopt their rules of the game,[188] including the specific conditions for applying Security Exceptions. Moreover, they can change the meaning of international rules and exceptions.[189] As a result, international rules largely reflect the preferences of the most powerful states in the system.[190] The rules and institutions might bring some degree of order to

[179] Hans J Morgenthau, *Politics among Nations: The Struggle for Power and Peace* (Knopf 1948) 13.

[180] Thomas Hobbes, *Leviathan* (first published 1651, OUP 1998) 86.

[181] Stephen A Kocs, 'Explaining the Strategic Behavior of States: International Law as System Structure' (1994) 38(4) Intl Studies Q 535, 536.

[182] Hans J Morgenthau, *Politics among Nations: The Struggle for Power and Peace* (Knopf 1948) 13.

[183] Michael E Brown and others, *The Perils of Anarchy: Contemporary Realism and International Security International Security Readers* (MIT Press 1995) 85.

[184] Anne-Marie Slaughter, 'International Law in a World of Liberal States' (1995) 6 Eur J Intl L 503, 507.

[185] Kristoffer Lidén and Henrik Syse, 'The Politics of Peace and Law: Realism, Internationalism, and the Cosmopolitan Challenge' in CM Bailliet (eds.), *Research Handbook on International Law and Peace* (Edward Elgar Publishing 2019) 30.

[186] Shirley V Scott, 'International Law as Ideology: Theorizing the Relationship between International Law and International Politics' (1994) 5 EJIL 313, 314.

[187] Robert O Keohane, 'International Institutions: Two Approaches' (1988) 32(4) Intl Studies Q 379, 387.

[188] Mitsuo Matsushita and others, *The World Trade Organization: Law, Practice, and Policy* (3rd edn, OUP 2015) 8.

[189] Ibid.

Ian Hurd, *How to Do Things with International Law* (Princeton UP 2017) 38.

[190] Robert O Keohane, 'International Institutions: Two Approaches' (1988) 32(4) Intl Studies Q 379, 387.

relations among states.[191] Furthermore, the perception of a common threat can lead to collective actions, which explains, for example, a swift, coordinated response by the US and the EU to Russia's invasion of Ukraine in 2022.[192] Still, such examples only reflect strategic maneuvers in the states' struggle for survival and cannot themselves transform the anarchic nature of interstate relations.[193] Thus, when there is a shift in power distribution among contracting parties, no legal authority or prior agreement can be expected to prevent states from disregarding their international obligations to increase relative gains.[194]

On these premises, the evolution of the GATT into the WTO was feasible only because it served the strategic interests of powerful nations, such as the US and the members of the European Community (EC) (now the EU), leaving little choice for other states not to join due to the risk of losing their trade attractiveness.[195] Any shift in the distribution of power within the WTO can prompt its members to rebalance the organization to better reflect their current perceived interests. In particular, in the absence of an overarching authority that can enforce international trade commitments and due to rising concerns over national power and security,[196] some members might adopt unilateral measures to stabilize their position in the global order[197] or to gain control over the policies of another nation[198] by, for

[191] Stephen A Kocs, 'Explaining the Strategic Behavior of States: International Law as System Structure' (1994) 38(4) Intl Studies Q 535, 537.

[192] Stephen M Walt and Renée Belfer, 'An International Relations Theory Guide to the War in Ukraine' (*Foreign Policy*, March 8, 2022) https://foreignpolicy.com/2022/03/08/an-international-relations-theory-guide-to-ukraines-war/.

[193] Kristoffer Lidén and Henrik Syse, 'The Politics of Peace and Law: Realism, Internationalism, and the Cosmopolitan Challenge' in CM Bailliet (eds.), *Research Handbook on International Law and Peace* (Edward Elgar Publishing 2019) 42.

[194] Beth Ann Simmons, 'Compliance with International Agreements' (1998) 1 Annual Rev of Political Science 75, 79.

[195] Anvar Rahmetov, 'Is WTO Reform Feasible? Lessons from Political Science Research,' Summary of Prof Manfred Elsig's speech at the April 3, 2019 Trade Lecture Sessions www.wti.org/institute/news/589/is-wto-reform-feasible-lessons-from-political-science-research/.

[196] Robert Powell, 'Anarchy in International Relations Theory: The Neorealist-Neoliberal Debate' (1994) 48 Intl Org 313, 330; Ian Hurd, *How to Do Things with International Law* (Princeton UP 2017) 132.

[197] Wolfgang Weiss, 'Interpreting Essential Security Exceptions in WTO Law in View of Economic Security Interests' in Wolfgang Weiß and Cornelia Furculita (eds.), *Global Politics and EU Trade Policy* (Springer International Publishing 2020) 258.

[198] Hans J Morgenthau, *Politics among Nations: The Struggle for Power and Peace* (Knopf 1948) 15.

example, withholding trade concessions until their trading partners lower their barriers first, even if it runs afoul of their international commitments.

Realists place national interests over collective interests and national security over collective security and international commitments.[199] Security Exceptions reaffirm the priority of national interests over international obligations. Schmitt has contended that the state is the primary juristic reality that remains above legal form and that the state is "he who makes the exception."[200] From Schmitt's perspective, a state seems to be the one who decides when and under which circumstances to invoke Security Exceptions in international trade and investment agreements. If states' relative gains from the international agreement are lower than those of potential enemies, or competitors, such states have the incentive to renegotiate terms with their partners or to limit their cooperation,[201] for example, by adopting Security Measures. In this vein, Security Measures have their roots in deep concerns over the position of certain states in global trade and their capacity to maintain relative power in the global order.[202]

All this considered, states' reluctance to prioritize common political and economic goals and further economic cooperation over relative gains leaves the door open for sweeping application, inconsistent interpretation of international norms, and overreliance on Security Exceptions and other similar exceptions. Following the line that those are sovereign states who have the authority to define their essential security interests and when to invoke them, international law has no effective tools to restrain such behavior.

2.5.3 *Institutionalism's Restraints of Realism*

Accepting the realists' claims about the anarchy of the international system, institutionalists assert that state sovereignty is not absolute but can be mitigated through "rules, norms, principles and decision-making

199 Nigel D White, *Advanced Introduction to International Conflict and Security Law* (Edward Elgar 2014) 5.

200 Carl Schmitt, *Political Theology: Four Chapters on the Concept of Sovereignty* 5 (George Schwab tr., Halliday Lithograph 1988) 5, 21–23, 30–35.

201 Peter Liberman, 'Trading with the Enemy: Security and Relative Economic Gains' (1996) 21(1) International Security 147, 150–155.

202 Wolfgang Weiss, 'Interpreting Essential Security Exceptions in WTO Law in View of Economic Security Interests' in Wolfgang Weiß and Cornelia Furculita (eds.), *Global Politics and EU Trade Policy* (Springer International Publishing 2020) 259.

procedures."[203] States are motivated to comply with legal rules and norms because they do not want to undermine the international legal order, whose credibility is in their own interest.[204] By focusing on absolute gains[205] and providing evidence of its existence via international institutions,[206] institutionalists believe that the presence of international institutions modifies the anarchic environment and induces states to cooperate over their long-term common interests, even if this goes against their short-term interests.[207] For one, institutions legitimize or delegitimize different kinds of behavior and enhance the value of a state's reputation for respecting its international commitments.[208] They also diminish mistrust by providing a flow of information and facilitating complex negotiations between states. A good reputation for cooperation can affect the continued interaction of a state with other actors, which makes governments consider their reputational costs of non-compliance with international law whenever evaluating the possible benefits of a breach.[209] Finally, institutions promote enforcement and sanction actors if they display noncooperative behavior and, with this, create additional foundations for long-term, stable patterns of cooperative interaction.[210] Thus, even though international institutions cannot resolve conflicts of interest or stop great powers' fights, they can facilitate more effective collective responses when the interests of different states align.[211] The UN's efforts in safeguarding international security serve as one example of this.

[203] Anne-Marie Slaughter and others, 'International Law and International Relations Theory: A New Generation of Interdisciplinary Scholarship' (1998) 92(3) Am J Intl L 367, 390.

[204] Bernhard Zangl and others, 'Between Law and Politics: Explaining International Dispute Settlement Behavior' (2012) 18 Eur J Intl Relations 369, 372.

[205] Robert Powell, 'Absolute and Relative Gains in International Relations Theory' (1991) 85(4) The American Political Science Rev 1303, 1303.

[206] Charles L Glaser, 'A Flawed Framework: Why the Liberal International Order Concept Is Misguided' (2019) 43(4) Intl Security 51, 61.

[207] Bernhard Zangl and others, 'Between Law and Politics: Explaining International Dispute Settlement Behavior' (2012) 18 Eur J Intl Relations 369, 372.

[208] Kenneth W Abbott and Duncan Snidal, 'Why States Act through Formal International Organizations' (1998) 42(1) J Conflict Resolution 3, 26–27.

[209] Rachel Brewster, 'Reputation in International Relations and International Law Theory' in Jeffrey L Dunoff and Mark A Pollack (eds.), *Interdisciplinary Perspectives on International Law and International Relations: The State of the Art* (CUP 2013) 540–541.

[210] Denise de Buck and Madeleine O Hosli, 'Traditional Theories of International Relations' in Madeleine O Hosli and Joren Selleslaghs (eds.), *The Changing Global Order: Challenges and Prospects* (Springer International Publishing 2020) 13.

[211] Stephen M Walt and Renée Belfer, 'An International Relations Theory Guide to the War in Ukraine' (*Foreign Policy*, March 8, 2022) https://foreignpolicy.com/2022/03/08/an-international-relations-theory-guide-to-ukraines-war/.

International institutions, regimes, treaties, agreements, and protocols cover diverse realms, including security and arms control, global trade, the environment, human rights, and political relations.[212] Some of these domains might narrowly reflect the interests of the most powerful states. However, most still represent the outcomes of negotiations (even if not necessarily equal ones) based on a much broader set of interests.[213] Furthermore, where the legal order provides for third-party dispute resolution, legal rules and institutions can empower less powerful states despite being biased in favor of more powerful ones.[214] In light of this, international rules and institutions have a more complex and contingent relationship with the rise and fall of state power than realists assume.[215]

Trading nations understand that profits arise from the pursuit of free trade, which hinges on shared commitments to international trade rules and their enforcement.[216] The pursuit of free trade requires all states to be bound by "some minimum requirements of international law" without any exceptions.[217] In particular, the establishment of the GATT (1947) and, further, the WTO represents the most notable effort to multilateralize trade interaction and to limit the exercise of unilateral discretion ever undertaken.[218] International trade law can be viewed as following a top-down model, with the WTO at the apex and its members below on an equal plane, all subject to the jurisdiction of the WTO.[219] The WTO agreements tend to emphasize the need for cooperation and the principle of sovereign equality.

Unilateral measures can still be justified under international trade arrangements when necessary to protect important societal objectives. For example, states make an effort to reserve at least part of their

212 John G Ikenberry, 'Why the Liberal World Order Will Survive' (2018) 32(1) Ethics & Intl Affairs 17, 20.
213 Ibid.
214 Gregory C Shaffer, *Emerging Powers and the World Trading System: The Past and Future of International Economic Law* (CUP 2021) 7.
215 John G Ikenberry, 'Why the Liberal World Order Will Survive' (2018) 32(1) Ethics & Intl Affairs 17, 20.
216 Mitsuo Matsushita and others, *The World Trade Organization: Law, Practice, and Policy* (3rd ed., OUP 2015) 7.
217 Henry Schermers, 'Different Aspects of Sovereignty' in Gerard Kreijen and others (eds.), *State, Sovereignty, and International Governance* (OUP 2002) 192.
218 Wesley A Cann, 'Creating Standards and Accountability for the Use of the WTO Security Exception: Reducing the Role of Power-Based Relations and Establishing a New Balance between Sovereignty and Multilateralism' (2001) 26 Yale J Intl L 413, 436.
219 Daniel Chee King Chow, 'United States Unilateralism and the World Trade Organization' (2019) 37 BU Int'l LJ 1, 29–30.

sovereign rights over the most sensitive areas, such as national security. Taken too far and without suitable safeguards, such flexibilities in the trade rules could be left open to abuse for protectionist aims[220] and thus shall be treated under WTO law with extreme caution.

The high level of trade between states is expected to give the states little incentive to abuse Security Exceptions since that might disrupt trust between the members and cancel the profits of trade. Thus, it is the nature and benefits of the international trading system that should be able to prevent states from violating their commitments and abusing exception clauses, even in the absence of official adjudication. In addition, Security Exceptions are not left to the complete discretion of state power since they are embedded into legally binding texts and generally open to challenge before an independent adjudicator.[221] The WTO's legal process restrains politically motivated invocation of Security Exceptions since the legitimacy of any such invocation is to be determined within the system.[222] On these premises, Security Exceptions should be interpreted to allow for limited derogation from undertaken trade obligations when states' national security interests are at stake.

Yet, international agreements frequently do not provide determinate answers to all questions that can arise from their application. Either their language cannot capture meaning with precision, or the drafters do not foresee many possible applications, let alone their contextual settings. Together with the changes in economic, technological, and scientific conditions and political circumstances, all these factors can produce a zone of ambiguity within which it is difficult to precisely say what is permitted and what is forbidden under international law.[223] By viewing international regimes as universal regulators and safety mechanisms in the case of rising tensions and focusing less on the economic dimension of international relations, institutionalism remains vulnerable in explaining some of those future contingencies.[224] Where states' interests diverge, power politics promoted by realists is likely to

[220] Philip Joseph Wells, 'Unilateralism and Protectionism in the World Trade Organization: The Interpretation of the Chapeau within GATT Article XX' (2014) 13(3) J Intl Trade Law and Policy 222, 229.
[221] Kamal Saggi and Halis Murat Yildiz, 'Bilateralism, Multilateralism, and the Quest for Global Free Trade' (2010) 81 J Intl Econ 26, 26.
[222] Ibid.
[223] Ibid.
[224] Boris Ananyev, 'Sanctions in IR: Understanding, Defining, Studying' (2019) 14(3) Intl Org Research J 136, 142.

continue to dominate.[225] Thus, if abused, a unilateral approach to trade policies could fundamentally shift the global trading system toward one based on power rather than on rules, which would undermine efforts at global governance and cooperation.

2.5.4 *State of Constructivism and Embedded Liberalism*

Constructivists have a more normative vision of international politics and acknowledge the possibility of its transformation from a realist existence to a more cooperative globalist phenomenon.[226] States' varying identities and beliefs oppose the simplistic notions of rationality under which states pursue simply power, according to realism.[227] Not just power and self-interest but ideas, values, identities, and norms are the main parameters for states' behavior.[228] Institutions such as international organizations may not only offer formal rules of interstate interaction but also shape states' behavior.[229] The gradual acquisition and development of shared norms may be learned and gradually seen as valuable by mutual interaction.[230] From this perspective, constructivists seek to dispute the idea that anarchy and sovereignty are fixed conditions of world politics. Instead, they emphasize that national interests and national security can be better assured through cooperation rather than conflict.[231]

Applying the constructivist approach to the international trade regime, Ruggie describes the institutional reconstruction after World War II as an "intersubjective framework of meaning."[232] From the

[225] Deborah Z Cass, *The Constitutionalization of the World Trade Organization: Legitimacy, Democracy, and Community* (OUP 2005) 71–72.

[226] James Wakefield, *Giovanni Gentile and the State of Contemporary Constructivism: A Study of Actual Idealist Moral Theory* (Andrews UK Ltd 2015) 11 https://ebookcentral.proquest.com/lib/uvtilburg-ebooks/detail.action?docID=2030503.

[227] Anne-Marie Slaughter and Hale Thomas, 'International Relations, Principal Theories' in *Max Planck Encyclopedia of Public International Law* (OUP 2013) [21].

[228] Jutta Brunnee and Stephen J Toope, 'Constructivism and International Law' in Jeffrey L Dunoff and Mark A Pollack (eds.), *Interdisciplinary Perspectives on International Law and International Relations: The State of the Art* (CUP 2013) 121.

[229] Alexander Wendt, 'Anarchy Is What States Make of It: The Social Construction of Power Politics' (1992) 46 Intl Org 391, 394.

[230] Jutta Brunnee and Stephen J Toope, 'Constructivism and International Law' in Jeffrey L Dunoff and Mark A Pollack (eds.), *Interdisciplinary Perspectives on International Law and International Relations: The State of the Art* (CUP 2013) 120.

[231] Oisin Suttle, *Distributive Justice and World Trade Law: A Political Theory of International Trade Regulation* (CUP 2017) 120.

[232] John Gerard Ruggie, 'International Regimes, Transactions, and Change: Embedded Liberalism in the Postwar Economic Order' (1982) 36 Intl Org 379, 380.

perspective of constructivism, the WTO's procedures, doctrines, rights, and obligations organize its membership in society.[233] The commitment to the WTO agreements and procedures and institutional setups provided under the WTO agreements progressively transforms a WTO member's identity constructed from traditional sovereignty.[234] It allows for constructing the identity of members committed to trade liberalization and multilateralism, which would give up on their international commitments only in sporadic cases. States' participation in the international trade regime makes them develop a sense of obligation that promotes long-term cooperation and valuable predictability. When a WTO member violates its international commitments, it deviates from the collective understanding of the law and thus bears the burden of providing legal justifications for its violation.[235] WTO members might feel compelled to provide such justification for both interest and identity-related reasons.[236]

Using Ruggie's idea of "embedded liberalism" aimed to achieve "a form of multilateralism that is compatible with the requirements of domestic stability,"[237] various WTO agreements allow for the intervention of domestic politics in certain situations to protect national interests.[238] The "embedded liberalism" model of the GATT (1947)[239] was established for a broader societal acceptance of the trade regime by allowing contracting parties to politically adjust their engagement with the system in times of pressure, for example, through resorting to national security claims.[240] The greater the uncertainty that state leaders face about their ability to maintain domestic compliance with international agreements, the more likely agreements are to contain broadly

233 Andrew Emmerson, 'Conceptualizing Security Exceptions: Legal Doctrine or Political Excuse' (2008) 11 J Intl Econ L 135, 151.

234 Ibid 152.

235 Jutta Brunnee and Stephen J Toope, 'Constructivism and International Law' in Jeffrey L Dunoff and Mark A Pollack (eds.), *Interdisciplinary Perspectives on International Law and International Relations: The State of the Art* (CUP 2013) 132.

236 Ibid.

237 John Gerard Ruggie, 'International Regimes, Transactions, and Change: Embedded Liberalism in the Postwar Economic Order' (1982) 36 Intl Org 379, 399.

238 Sungjoon Cho and Jürgen Kurtz, 'Convergence and Divergence in International Economic Law and Politics' (2018) 29(1) EJIL 169, 175.

239 Ruggie's idea of "embedded liberalism" was further developed and nuanced in "policy space theory." See Timothy Meyer, 'The Political Economy of WTO Exceptions' (2022) 99 Washington U L Rev 1299, 1318.

240 Sungjoon Cho and Jürgen Kurtz, 'Convergence and Divergence in International Economic Law and Politics' (2018) 29(1) EJIL 169, 198.

drafted flexibilities for potential future contingencies.[241] Stated this way, Security Exceptions can be viewed as a kind of "safety valve" that, while undermining the authority of the undertaken responsibilities in certain areas,[242] can help secure deeper commitments for a more extended period.

It follows from this perspective that Security Exceptions are designed not to support the anarchy of international relations but rather to mitigate the anarchic consequence of the realist premise and contribute to bringing order and allocation of tasks between states.[243] They embody the interrelation between multilateralism and the quest for domestic stability, reflecting the shared legitimacy of a set of social objectives of the post-war order.[244]

Current geopolitical and geo-economic developments may signal a more superficial shift in the instruments and institutions of the existing order and the need to recognize emerging threats to states' security interests to maintain the more profound continuity of the system at the level of normative commitment and functional logic.[245] The attempts of certain WTO members to politicize Security Exceptions and invoke them to justify the measures with potentially mixed motives[246] indicate the deficiency in the work of the international trading system and its inability to fully affect members' behavior and identity. In particular, it can be argued that not all members seem to perceive the system as being as solid and efficient as it used to be and thus they try to satisfy their interests by boosting domestic initiatives and, in some instances, regional cooperation.

If a state perceives the values of the others as too different, even alien, it will probably compete with them, while if the state perceives that the others share its values, it is much more probable that the state will cooperate with

[241] B Peter Rosendorff and Helen V Milner, 'The Optimal Design of International Trade Institutions: Uncertainty and Escape' (2001) 55(4) Intl Org 829, 831.

[242] WTO, 'Trade Policy Commitments and Contingency Measures' (2009) World Trade Report 26 www.wto.org/english/res_e/publications_e/wtr09_e.htm.

[243] Andrew Emmerson, 'Conceptualizing Security Exceptions: Legal Doctrine or Political Excuse' (2008) 11 J Intl Econ L 135, 152.

[244] John Gerard Ruggie, 'International Regimes, Transactions, and Change: Embedded Liberalism in the Postwar Economic Order' (1982) 36 Intl Org 379, 398.

[245] Andrew Lang, 'Protectionism's Many Faces' (2020) 44 Yale J Intl L Online 54, 55 https://cpb-us-w2.wpmucdn.com/campuspress.yale.edu/dist/8/1581/files/2019/02/6_Lang_YJIL-Symposium_Protectionisms-Many-Faces_12.07.18-2nrcl0m.pdf.

[246] For the purposes of this research, the measures with mixed motives are understood as the measures that pursue a permitted goal potentially covered by Security Exceptions while simultaneously seeking to achieve the other public policy objective, to protect domestic industry, or to weaken the economy of a counterparty.

them. Thus, the behavior of the WTO members can be changed by gradually transforming the international trade order to better accommodate the interests of very different states and groups. Whether and how this transformation is possible largely depends on how the WTO members perceive the international trading system, their role in it, their potential benefits from participation, and how the WTO can interact with current domestic political realities to prevent actors' opportunistic behavior.

2.5.5 Security Exceptions as Restraints on Securitization

The concept of securitization offers a means of comprehending what makes something a security issue in international relations.[247] It postulates that national security is a speech act rather than necessarily an objective condition.[248] In other words, elites and/or those in a position to make their voices heard (securitizing agents) may define any issue as a security issue by claiming that there is an existential threat to an object that is being threatened and needs to be protected (referent object).[249] In most cases, however, it is not the speech act itself but a process of speech articulations over time that creates a threat text that turns sequentially into securitization.[250]

In essence, the notion of securitization is seen as a synthesis of realism and constructivism that looks at power and identity. In particular, the specificity of security in the work of the Copenhagen School is supported by an understanding of the politics of hostility and emergency, the focus on existential threats as the essence of security, and the definition of securitization as placing an issue beyond normal politics.[251] Yet, the securitization theory takes a different understanding of causality and breaks out of the positivistic assertion that an explanation can only be objective.[252] It has a close affinity with constructivism, particularly with the works that examine the role of language, the status of practice, and the

[247] James Sperling and Mark Webber, 'The European Union, Security Governance and Collective Securitization' (2019) 42(2) West Eur Politics 228, 238.

[248] Biljana Vankovska, 'Dealing with COVID-19 in the European Periphery: Between Securitization and "Gaslighting"' (2020) 7(1) J Global Faultlines 71, 74.

[249] Ibid.

[250] Holger Stritzel, 'Towards a Theory of Securitization: Copenhagen and Beyond' (2007) 13(3) Eur J Intl Relations 357, 377.

[251] Michael C Williams, 'Words, Images, Enemies: Securitization and International Politics' (2003) 47(4) Intl Studies Q 511, 515.

[252] Stefano Guzzini, 'Securitization as a Causal Mechanism' (2011) 42 Security Dialogue 329, 338.

power of argument in world politics.[253] It concerns security practices as specific forms of social construction and securitization as a particular kind of social accomplishment.[254]

Securitization might advance new global or national issues to the level of existential security threats. Once securitizing agents securitize an issue, then normal means and actions can be replaced by security concerns, which justifies the adoption of extraordinary protection measures designed to deal with security threats.[255] Thus, the key idea underlying securitization is that the issue is claimed to be of such prominence, urgency, or exceptionality that it cannot be handled within the normal political and institutional processes.[256] Such prominence, urgency, and exceptionality enable those authorized to address the issue to use whatever extraordinary means they deem most appropriate, even if such means go beyond the established rules and procedures.[257] Extraordinary protection measures need not always include force but can incorporate alternative actions such as trade restrictions.[258] To illustrate, the securitization of Chinese telecommunications companies in the US started in 2010 and further escalated when the Trump administration took office in 2016 and started a "trade war" with China.[259] The EU's foreign policy discourses and actions have also undergone a drastic shift since the 2010s, demonstrating tangible signs of collective securitization moves toward China.[260] Another example is the securitization of climate change in India and China and its implications for interstate disputes in the Asian region.[261]

253 Thierry Balzacq, Sarah Léonard, and Jan Ruzicka, '"Securitization" Revisited: Theory and Cases' (2016) 30(4) Intl Relations 494, 496.

254 Michael C Williams, 'Words, Images, Enemies: Securitization and International Politics' (2003) 47(4) Intl Studies Q 511, 514.

255 Biljana Vankovska, 'Dealing with COVID-19 in the European Periphery: Between Securitization and "Gaslighting"' (2020) 7(1) J Global Faultlines 71, 74.

256 Jens Kremer, 'Exception, Protection and Securitization: Security Mindsets in Law' in Massimo Fichera and Jens Kremer (eds.), *Law and Security in Europe: Reconsidering the Security Constitution* (Intersentia 2013) 19.

257 Thierry Balzacq, Sarah Léonard, and Jan Ruzicka, '"Securitization" Revisited: Theory and Cases' (2016) 30(4) International Relations 494, 495.

258 Sabine Hirschauer, *The Securitization of Rape: Women, War and Sexual Violence* (Palgrave Macmillan 2014) 27.

259 Karsten Friis and Olav Lysne, 'Huawei, 5G and Security: Technological Limitations and Political Responses' (2021) 52(5) Development and Change 1174, 1177–1179.

260 Xuechen Chen and Xinchuchu Gao, 'Analysing the EU's Collective Securitisation Moves towards China' (2022) 20 Asia Eur J 195, 212.

261 See more Anjan Kumar Sahu and Surinder Mohan, 'From Securitization to Security Complex: Climate Change, Water Security and the India–China Relations' (2022) 59(2) Intl Politics 320.

On the one hand, the legitimate possibility of taking exceptional measures in extraordinary times makes states more reluctant to violate their international commitments under normal circumstances.[262] It follows that by legitimizing trade and investment restrictions in response to states' security concerns, Security Exceptions allow for securing states' commitments to international trade and an open investment climate in ordinary times. On the other hand, securitization results from "a complex repertoire of causes" that occurs between an influential set of events and their impact on interactions (e.g. between securitizing actors and the audience) and includes the factors that reinforce or discourage such securitization.[263] States' officials might decide to securitize the issue for different reasons: to draw attention to the particular importance of the topic or to enlarge the policy space for taking emergency actions.[264] Populists might also strategically employ securitization practices to advance their domestic political agenda, as in the case of migration.[265] In this sense, leaving states with broad flexibility to justify any Security Measure under international law might encourage further securitization, making political power the central tool used to enforce a state's interest.[266] To avoid such implications, any given securitized interest of a state should not automatically be considered legitimate.

The process of securitization itself has some limits. For the process of securitization to be successful, apart from the speech act alone, the audience must accept the issue positioning so that emergency measures are legitimized.[267] Depending on the situation, the audience might include public opinion or state elites.[268] What exactly constitutes the

262 Krzysztof J Pelc, *Making and Bending International Rules: The Design of Exceptions and Escape Clauses in Trade Law* (CUP 2016) 5.

263 Thierry Balzacq, 'The Three Faces of Securitization: Political Agency, Audience and Context' (2005) 11(2) European J of Intl Relations 171, 193.

264 Geraldo Vidigal and Stephan W Schill, 'International Economic Law and the Securitization of Policy Objectives: Risks of a Schmittean Exception' (2021) 48(2) Legal Issues of Economic Integration 109, 116–117.

265 See more Patrick Müller and Charlott Gebauer, 'Austria and the Global Compact on Migration: The "Populist Securitization" of Foreign Policy' (2021) 19 Comp Eur Polit 760.

266 Krzysztof J Pelc, Making and Bending International Rules: The Design of Exceptions and Escape Clauses in Trade Law (CUP 2016) 5.

267 Andrew Stephen Campion, 'From CNOOC to Huawei: Securitization, the China Threat, and Critical Infrastructure' (2020) 28(1) Asian J Political Science 47, 49–51.

268 Jens Kremer, 'Exception, Protection and Securitization: Security Mindsets in Law' in Massimo Fichera and Jens Kremer (eds.), *Law and Security in Europe: Reconsidering the Security Constitution* (Intersentia 2013) 21.

audience's acceptance or approval of the securitizing act has given rise to many discussions.[269] In particular, it is still debatable whether, for an issue to be regarded as securitized, the audience must agree that the issue raises security concerns, approve the proposed remedy, or potentially both.[270]

Furthermore, based on just war theory (in which a test has been developed to determine the morality of war), Floyd suggests an objective test that makes it possible to determine the moral tightness of securitization and thus democratize the securitization process.[271] Floyd supports the view that just war theory has been incorporated into war-making as a fundamental constraint on when and how wars are fought and, therefore, has helped democratize war-making insofar as citizens that are well versed in the ideas of a just war can and repeatedly do hold decisionmakers accountable for their actions.[272] Accordingly, all this could hold for a just securitization theory. In particular, Floyd proposes three criteria for determining the moral tightness of securitization: (1) there must be an objective existential threat; (2) the referent object of security must be morally legitimate; and (3) the security response must be appropriate to the threat in question.[273]

It can be argued that the moral tightness of securitization taken from a just war theory should be embodied in the concept of Security Exceptions under international law. While a specific test applicable to the review of Security Measures in each particular case might vary from treaty to treaty, trade and investment agreements should ensure that: the language of security can be accepted only in those cases where there exist objective existential threats to a state's security interest, such an interest is morally legitimate, and the response to the threat is appropriate under the circumstances. This also means that where Security Exceptions are expressly excluded from any adjudication, international law and politics are expected to design other tools that differentiate between the need to protect states' legitimate security objectives and the opportunistic securitization of other policy goals.

269 Thierry Balzacq, Sarah Léonard, and Jan Ruzicka, '"Securitization" Revisited: Theory and Cases' (2016) 30(4) Intl Relations 494, 499–500.

270 Ibid 520.

271 Rita Floyd, 'Can Securitization Theory Be Used in Normative Analysis? Towards a Just Securitization Theory' (2011) 42(4–5) Security Dialogue 427, 429–430.

272 Ibid 430.

273 428.

2.6 Conclusion

The UN's and the WTO's history and common objectives supply a basis for inferring the need to allocate responsibility and clear boundaries to the types of security issues that the two organizations can review. Unlike the other noneconomic areas, the very controversial issues arising from the application of Security Measures – particularly the level of discretion the states want to preserve while defining national security matters – require a specific approach to determining the institutional mandate to review the legality of such measures. The inquiry undertaken in the remainder of this book analyses, among others, whether and in which cases the issues related to states' national security fall within the scope of the WTO mandate and how this should influence the standard of review of Security Exceptions and the possible need for stronger cooperation between the UN and the WTO dealing with such matters.[274] Notably, even though the national security landscape has evolved since GATT's adoption and might require updated tools for its regulation, international trade remains an essential pillar in promoting international and national security.[275]

The concept of national security is fluid in part due to its evolving nature and subjective determination by each of the WTO members, which implies that new concerns falling within the ambit of national security continue to emerge.[276] For the purposes of this book, the concept of national security will be defined broadly to cover each and every case where the US, the EU, or any of BRICS have relied on, or can be expected to rely on, their national security interests to justify the application of unilateral measures. Such an approach to national security is rather holistic. It opens room for a better understanding of the dilemmas of global economic order and state sovereignty and the possibility of reaching a "shared understanding of what is considered a threat" to national security.[277] At the same time, the fact that the language of Security Exceptions varies across agreements suggests that irrespective of the approach to the definition of the concept of national security, there is no uniform doctrine of national security that applies to all treaties and

[274] See more chapters 6 and 7.

[275] Scott Lincicome and Alfredo Carrillo Obregon, 'The (Updated) Case for Free Trade' (2022) Policy Analysis No 925 Cato Institute 8.

[276] Catharine Titi, *The Right to Regulate in International Investment Law* (Nomos 2014) 79.

[277] Nigel D White, *Advanced Introduction to International Conflict and Security Law* (Elgar 2014) 6.

that any Security Exception must be given form within the agreement in question.[278]

Finally, analyzing Security Exceptions from the perspective of different theories confirms that the concept of Security Exceptions can change its meaning depending on the lens of social, political, and economic contexts they are being looked through. At one end of the spectrum lies realism, which supports the idea of the enduring nature of anarchy and states' fairly fixed concerns for security. It follows that states will be willing to invoke Security Exceptions and circumvent their international responsibilities whenever they expect to gain an advantage in economic, military, or political terms. At the other end lies constructivism, which assumes that international institutions and norms can change states' identities. Constructivism asserts that international cooperation can shape the ideas and interests of all actors. States can be expected to subordinate the multilateral trading system to domestic priorities only when it is necessary for domestic stability or when the actions of other actors run afoul of shared ideas and interests. Yet, the reasons for joining international agreements and living up to the expectations of other actors should tame excessive reliance on Security Exceptions. Furthermore, international agreements should remain relevant even in exceptional situations when states need to respond to national security concerns.

Between the two extremes of realism and constructivism is institutionalism. From the perspective of institutionalism, states will obey international rules and institutions to the extent they promote states' values and allow participants to achieve mutually beneficial gains. When this is not the case, and when there are no sufficient reputational incentives not to abuse discretion accorded pursuant to Security Exceptions, states might explore the loopholes to disregard some of their trade commitments. While open trade and investment policies aim to achieve absolute gains, security concerns of certain states can lead only to relative gains, in which case power-based politics affects the decisions of domestic authorities about the type of measure to be applied.

In a similar vein, from the standpoint of economic contract theory, Security Exceptions reflect a compromise between the state's interest in sustaining cooperation and the interest in shifting the terms of the contract to their own advantage in the case of unforeseen future contingencies. On this view, states can be expected to resort to Security

[278] Susan Rose-Ackerman and Benjamin Billa, 'Treaties and National Security' (2008) 40(2) NYU J Intl L & Pol 437, 443.

Exceptions whenever the benefit from suspending performance under the agreement rises above the costs of compliance.

Each theory alone cannot sufficiently explain the recent developments in the trade policies of different WTO members, yet it accounts for part of the story. They offer comprehensive insight into how to delineate the scope of a national security defense and which legal provisions for dealing with Security Measures provide WTO members with adequate incentives for performing their treaty commitments, thereby creating the basis for the normative and evaluative questions of this book in the chapters to follow.

3

Security Measures in Domestic Law and Practice

Beginning in 2017 with the first national security dispute before the WTO and crystallizing in 2018 with the US's adoption of weaponized tariffs, an increasing number of WTO members are expanding on their national security interests and seeing competition for technological leadership and geopolitical hegemony as a risk to their national security.[1] Economic power can be more consequential than military power in the pursuit of strategic goals.[2] In particular, while adopting new economic sanctions and heightening screening requirements for foreign investments, WTO members seem to steer what Wesley describes as the "securitization of economic policy and economization of strategic policy."[3] Notably, because of different economic and political structures, some WTO members might be more predisposed to such securitization and economization than others.

As governments decide which measures to take in response to national security threats, they are faced with a trade-off between the interest in preserving open trade and attracting investment with the duty to protect security interests. Such a trade-off is complicated further by the difference in the magnitude of national security threats. To illustrate, the backlash against FDI from certain countries or prohibitions on trade with certain counterparties might be driven by the need to protect national interests during war or other armed conflict, to prevent an increase in the military and technology capacity of competitors, or to address emerging security concerns, such as a risk of a cyberattack. Different threats might require different responses on domestic levels.

[1] See also chapter 2, section 2.4.

[2] Sören Scholvin and others, 'Conclusion' in Mikael Wigell, Sören Scholvin, and Mika Aaltola (eds.), *Geo-Economics and Power Politics in the 21st Century: The Revival of Economic Statecraft* (Routledge 2018) 221.

[3] Anthea Roberts, Henrique Choer Moraes, and Victor Ferguson, 'Toward a Geoeconomic Order in International Trade and Investment' (2019) 22(4) J Intl Econ L 655, 655; Michael Wesley, 'Australia and the Rise of Geoeconomics' (*The Centre of Gravity Series*, November 2016) http://bellschool.anu.edu.au/sites/default/files/uploads/2017-05/australia_and_the_rise_of_geoeconomics.pdf.

From the perspective of geo-economics, the expansion of economic measures can be explained by the decision to prioritize the promotion and defense of national interests, subjecting efficiency considerations and a market-driven logic to pursuing security and strategic goals.[4] Such economic measures can also be seen as bargaining instruments between states, adopted to incite change in the policies of other governments by exploiting their dependence on trade and investment[5] or as tools of coercive diplomacy used as an alternative to, or a substitute for, war.[6] Finally, the increase in unilateral economic measures can signal a power-based approach to international relations, leading to an imbalance between national sovereignty and the spirit of multilateral economic governance.[7]

Against this background, this chapter focuses on the areas in which the US, the EU, and BRICS (hereafter Selected WTO Members) adopt economic sanctions (section 3.1) and investment screening measures (section 3.2), relying on the need to protect their security interests. In particular, it aims at exploring whether or not – and under what conditions – the US, the EU, and BRICS impose such measures to protect their economic security and respond to emerging security concerns, based on the analysis of the relevant law, regulations, and practice primarily as of 2023. Finally, this chapter attempts to distill the list of policy objectives where excessive claims of security threats by Selected WTO Members may inappropriately undermine their existing commitments in international trade and investment agreements and discusses the system of checks and balances under domestic law that is designed to prevent the abusive invocation of such security claims (section 3.3).

3.1 Economic Sanctions

The term "sanctions" remains controversial. The ILC even labeled it as "imprecise," while pointing out that Article 41 of the UN Charter refers

[4] See eg Anthea Roberts, Henrique Choer Moraes, and Victor Ferguson, 'Toward a Geoeconomic Order in International Trade and Investment' (2019) 22(4) J Intl Econ L 655.

[5] R Harrison Wagner, 'Economic Interdependence, Bargaining Power, and Political Influence' (1988) 42(3) Intl Organization 461, 463.

[6] See eg Natalino Ronzitti, 'Sanctions as Instruments of Coercive Diplomacy: An International Law Perspective' in Natalino Ronzitti (ed.), *Coercive Diplomacy, Sanctions and International Law* (Brill 2016).

[7] Wesley A Cann, 'Creating Standards and Accountability for the Use of the WTO Security Exception: Reducing the Role of Power-Based Relations and Establishing a New Balance between Sovereignty and Multilateralism' (2001) 26 Yale J Intl L 413, 414.

to "measures" rather than "sanctions."[8] A sanction in international affairs generally means a penalty imposed against a state to force it to comply with international law or to alter its policy in another way.[9] The focus of this section is economic sanctions, which can be defined broadly to include the use of, or threat to use, "measures of an economic – as contrasted with diplomatic or military – character taken to induce [a target state] to change some policy or practices or even its governmental structure."[10] For the avoidance of doubt, this definition of economic sanctions includes the pursuit of both political and economic goals. Since sanctions with economic goals can equally have political consequences for a target's foreign relations, such an approach explains a broader range of coercive bargaining situations in international relations,[11] which is essential for understanding the nature of economic sanctions labeled as Security Measures.

Economic sanctions have characterized the conflict in and between societies in one form or another throughout history, even in Ancient Rome.[12] However, the use of sanctions during peacetime was not generally adopted until the 1920s following the enactment of the League of Nations Covenant, which authorized sanctions against countries that had committed military aggression against other states.[13] As states have grown economically more interdependent, economic concerns have become more relevant than military concerns for achieving and sustaining national security.[14] In particular, since World War II, economic sanctions have become a standard and common policy tool by which several developed states address issues, by targeting nations that they disagree with.[15]

8 Natalino Ronzitti, 'Sanctions as Instruments of Coercive Diplomacy: An International Law Perspective' in Natalino Ronzitti (ed.), *Coercive Diplomacy, Sanctions and International Law* (Brill 2016) 9.

9 Geoff Simons, *Imposing Economic Sanctions: Legal Remedy or Genocidal Tool?* (Pluto Press 1999) 9.

10 Natalino Ronzitti, 'Sanctions as Instruments of Coercive Diplomacy: An International Law Perspective' in Natalino Ronzitti (ed.), *Coercive Diplomacy, Sanctions and International Law* (Brill 2016) 2.

11 A Drury, *Economic Sanctions and Presidential Decisions: Models of Political Rationality* (Palgrave Macmillan 2005) 14–16.

12 Geoff Simons, *Imposing Economic Sanctions: Legal Remedy or Genocidal Tool?* (Pluto Press 1999) 11–12.

13 Kern Alexander, *Economic Sanctions: Law and Public Policy* (Palgrave Macmillan 2009) 9.

14 Mikael Wigell, Sören Scholvin, and Mika Aaltola, 'Conclusion' in Mikael Wigell, Sören Scholvin, and Mika Aaltola (eds.), *Geo-Economics and Power Politics in the 21st Century: The Revival of Economic Statecraft* (Routledge 2018) 221.

15 Lance Davis and Stanley Engerman, 'History Lessons Sanctions: Neither War nor Peace' (2003) 17(2) J Economic Perspectives 187, 190.

Given the elasticity of the concept of national security and the fact that the operative meaning of national security might vary for any given state and/or regional/international organization depending on its approach and understanding of this concept in particular circumstances,[16] many sanctions regimes that are in place today can directly or indirectly relate to the objective of protecting the national security interests of the state applying those economic sanctions. This research will focus on the areas that go beyond the trade in arms and ammunition and trade restrictions that are normally covered by export control regimes to understand how far states can push the notion of national security on the domestic level by securitizing additional policy objectives.

Some WTO members naturally have a bigger appetite for imposing unilateral economic sanctions than others; hence, some sanctions regimes are more aggressive and far-reaching than others. Economic sanctions power derives from the ability to deny access to a sought-after economy or international currency credibly.[17] Thus, in the past, the countries imposing sanctions had almost always been more prominent and economically and militarily powerful than the target country.[18] However, nowadays, more countries have started to develop unilateral sanctions programs "symptomatically" in response to sanctions or other foreign conduct against them or other countries (e.g. Ukraine, Singapore, Switzerland, and the Bahamas).[19] WTO members that support and proclaim multilateralism in their official documents also choose to apply unilateral sanctions in response to particular threats to their national interests, and this could be viewed either as an example of "selective multilateralism" or as proof of the revisionist mood of the WTO members targeted by sanctions.

Notably, a distinction should be made between the cases where there is a broad multilateral consensus to impose sanctions in response to the actions of a particular country (such as the sanctions against Russia because of its war in Ukraine) and the cases where a country or a group of countries impose sanctions purely because of their national or regional

[16] Chapter 2, section 2.1.

[17] Andrew Rennemo, 'How China Joined the Sanctions Game' *The Diplomat* (February 8, 2021) https://thediplomat.com/2021/02/how-china-joined-the-sanctions-game/.

[18] Lance Davis and Stanley Engerman, 'History Lessons. Sanctions: Neither War nor Peace' (2003) 17(2) J Economic Perspectives 187, 191.

[19] Minami Funakoshi, Hugh Lawson, and Kannaki Deka, 'Tracking Sanctions against Russia' *Reuters* (March 9, 2022, updated July 7, 2022) www.reuters.com/graphics/UKRAINE-CRISIS/SANCTIONS/byvrjenzmve.

concerns (such as the US–China trade war). States can be expected to continue adopting economic sanctions without a broad multilateral consensus only when they are politically and economically powerful to do so. Furthermore, the war in Ukraine, the threat to food security, and the uncertainty around natural gas will play a major role in the future of economic warfare, catalyzing domestic reforms and potential changes to the vision of economic sanctions in international law and politics.

This section is drafted with certain assumptions and limitations. Unlike in the US and the EU, unilateral economic sanctions have not been a popular foreign policy tool for BRICS. Until recently, the reference to "sanctions" has not been used in BRICS domestic regulations. Nevertheless, Russia, India, and China have, in fact, extended the practice of unilaterally restricting access to their domestic market for products from specific countries, at least in part intending to influence the political and economic situation of some of their "problematic" neighbors. Furthermore, all three countries have started to develop a more robust legal framework for applying economic sanctions, which creates prerequisites for a potential shift from defensive to more proactive geo-economic strategies. This section does not assume that all the restrictive measures of Russia, India, and China discussed below were applied to promote foreign policy and/or national security objectives. Acknowledging that the nature of some of the discussed restrictive measures is problematic (not least because the proper procedure for their application was not correctly followed), labeling such measures as sanctions is open to dispute. For the avoidance of doubt, such measures are called "economic sanctions" only for the purposes of this research and without any intention to contest their nature under domestic regulations.

Furthermore, domestic legislation labels economic sanctions differently. In some instances, they are referred to as "countersanctions" or "countermeasures." Under the law of state responsibility, it is possible for states to unilaterally maintain lawful sanctions that are applied in response to an allegedly unlawful act of the target state, even if the sanctions are themselves prima facie illegal, as long as they meet the criteria for lawful countermeasures.[20] The commentary to the ARSIWA defines countermeasures as "a feature of a decentralized system by

[20] Daniel H Joyner, 'International Legal Limits on the Ability of States to Lawfully Impose International Economic/Financial Sanctions' in Ali Z Marossi and Marisa R Bassett (eds.), *Economic Sanctions under International Law: Unilateralism, Multilateralism, Legitimacy, and Consequences* (Springer Asser Press 2015) 90.

which injured states may seek to vindicate their rights and to restore the legal relationship with the responsible state which has been ruptured by the internationally wrongful act."[21] Countermeasures are also named "legitimate reprisals" or, more generally, measures of "self-protection" or "self-help,"[22] which can be resorted to only if the target state has committed an internationally wrongful act and certain other conditions are met.[23]

Discussions have arisen around the potential qualification of some unilateral sanctions as countermeasures or "third-party countermeasures,"[24] as well as the possible overlap of Security Exceptions with the rules on countermeasures.[25] In particular, it can be argued that if a measure cannot be justified under the WTO Security Exceptions and thus is found to be in breach of WTO commitments, the justification of such a measure as a countermeasure under public international law would not be recognized in the WTO law.[26] Arguments for the opposite also exist. To illustrate, the EU anti-coercion instrument seems to take the view that if a measure is recognized as a countermeasure under public international law, it would no longer be considered illegal under WTO law.[27] Nevertheless, for the purposes of this research, unilateral sanctions are distinguished from countermeasures under the ARSIWA. The scope of this section is limited to analysis of the sanctions regime grounded in the domestic legislation of the US, the EU, and BRICS and thus does not attempt to discuss whether and under which circumstances unilateral sanctions comply with the rules on countermeasures under international law.

[21] ILC, 'Draft Articles on Responsibility of States for Internationally Wrongful Acts, with Commentaries' (UN 2001) 128.

[22] Ibid 75.

[23] Natalino Ronzitti, 'Sanctions as Instruments of Coercive Diplomacy: An International Law Perspective' in Natalino Ronzitti (ed.), *Coercive Diplomacy, Sanctions and International Law* (Brill 2016) 11.

[24] See eg Martin Dawidowicz, *Third-Party Countermeasures in International Law* (CUP 2017).

[25] See eg Danae Azaria, 'Trade Countermeasures for Breaches of International Law Outside the WTO' (2022) 71(2) ICLQ 389.

[26] Gabrielle Marceau and Julian Wyatt, 'Dispute Settlement Regimes Intermingled: Regional Trade Agreements and the WTO' (2010) 1 JIDS 67, 74. See also Freya Baetens and Marco Bronckers, 'The EU's Anti-Coercion Instrument: A Big Stick for Big Targets' (*EJIL:Talk!*, January 19, 2022) www.ejiltalk.org/the-eus-anti-coercion-instrument-a-big-stick-for-big-targets/.

[27] Proposal for a Regulation of the European Parliament and of the Council on the Protection of the Union and Its Member States from Economic Coercion by Third Countries (December 8, 2021) COM/2021/775 final.

3.1.1 *The US Approach*

For decades, the US has used sanctions as a foreign policy tool against its most dangerous adversaries to signal rebuke and condemn their specific policies or activities.[28] Each decision to impose economic sanctions is based on foreign, domestic, and cognitive biases of the US decision-makers, constrained by the state of the US economy and the level of trade relations with a target.[29] Over the past years, economic sanctions have become tools of first resort and even central strategies of the US in dealing with its most demanding national security challenges.[30]

3.1.1.1 Legal Framework for Application of Economic Sanctions

Under the US Constitution, all authority to regulate trade between the US states themselves and between the US and foreign countries, including imposing economic sanctions and enacting any laws to carry out this authority, rests with Congress.[31] However, Congress has delegated the power and discretion to impose economic sanctions to the US President acting through the executive branch.[32] Congress's delegation of such authority to the President would seem to fit the policy objective of promoting the efficient exercise of foreign policy since authorizing the President as an executive agent of the legislature to design and implement sanctions can be a measure to promote the foreign policy of Congress and national security objectives.[33]

Under statutory regulations, the US President enjoys a broad authority to impose sanctions in response to national security or foreign policy concerns. To illustrate, the Trading with the Enemy Act (1917) and the

[28] Elizabeth Rosenberg, 'Assessing the Use of Sanctions in Addressing National Security and Foreign Policy Challenges. Testimony before the HFSC Subcommittee on National Security' (CHAS, May 15, 2019) 2 www.cnas.org/publications/congressional-testimony/assessing-the-use-of-sanctions-in-addressing-national-security-and-foreign-policy-challenges.

[29] A Drury, *Economic Sanctions and Presidential Decisions: Models of Political Rationality* (Palgrave Macmillan 2005) 178–180.

[30] US Congress House, Committee on Foreign Affairs, 'Sanctions and Financial Pressure: Major National Security Tools' Hearing Before the Committee on Foreign Affairs, House of Representatives, One Hundred Fifteenth Congress, Second Session (Publishing Office, January 10, 2018) www.govinfo.gov/content/pkg/CHRG-115hhrg28178/html/CHRG-115hhrg28178.htm.

[31] Kern Alexander, *Economic Sanctions: Law and Public Policy* (Palgrave Macmillan 2009) 97.

[32] Ibid.

[33] Ibid.

International Emergency Economic Powers Act (IEEPA) (1977) enable the President to prohibit some or all trade and financial transactions with foreign countries, groups, or individuals.[34] In addition to this far-reaching authority, the US President can undertake other sanctions-like measures, as they are, for example, authorized under the Countering America's Adversaries through Sanctions Act (CAATSA) (2017) and the Protecting Europe's Energy Security Act (PEESA) (2019). Ever since 1977, contemporary US sanctions have largely fallen under the IEEPA.[35]

The IEEPA is intended to deal with "any unusual and extraordinary threat, which has its source in whole or substantial part outside the United States, to the national security, foreign policy or economy of the United States."[36] The IEEPA does not attempt to specify what could constitute a threat to the national security of the US, which could be explained by the fact that the list of possible threats and the concept of national security itself have constantly been developing and changing over time. The IEEPA also does not define "unusual" and "extraordinary" threats to the US's national security, foreign policy, or economy. In the markup of the IEEPA, Fred Bergsten, then-Assistant Secretary for International Affairs in the Department of the Treasury, praised the requirement that a national emergency for the purposes of IEEPA should be "based on an unusual and extraordinary threat" because such a language "emphasizes that such powers should be available only in true emergencies."[37] Thus, a President's declaration of a national emergency must be confined "to a specific set of circumstances which constitutes a real emergency, and for no other purpose."[38] If the President determines that such a threat exists, they have the discretion to declare a national emergency under the National Emergency Act (NEA),[39] and only then can they impose economic and financial sanctions in accordance with the IEEPA.

The President typically launches the process of imposing sanctions by issuing an executive order (EO) that declares a national emergency. The EOs invoking the IEEPA generally indicate in response to which actions/

[34] Gary Clyde Hufbauer and others, *Economic Sanctions Reconsidered* (3rd ed., Peterson Institute for International Economics 2009) 133.

[35] IEEPA codified at 50 USC § 1701ff.

[36] Ibid.

[37] Congressional Research Service, 'International Emergency Economic Powers Act: Origins, Evolution, and Use' (updated July 14, 2020) CRS Report 44 https://sgp.fas.org/crs/natsec/R45618.pdf.

[38] *US v Tajideen* (2018) Criminal Case No 17–46 (RBW) 6.

[39] IEEPA codified at 50 USC § 1701ff.

events a national emergency is invoked and whether such actions/events constitute a threat to the US national security, foreign policy, or economy. In many cases, EOs do not separate between the threat to national security, the threat to foreign policy, and the threat to the economy of the US but rather declare that the particular actions/events constitute "an unusual and extraordinary threat to the national security, foreign policy and economy of the United States." To illustrate, the US President found a threat to the national security, foreign policy, and economy of the US in a vast range of cases, including the Iran hostage crisis (EO 12170),[40] the regional conflict regarding Yugoslavia (Serbia and Montenegro) (EO 12808),[41] the human rights abuse and corruption (Global Magnitsky Human Rights Accountability Act) (EO 13818),[42] the unrestricted acquisition or use of the Information and Communications Technology and Services Supply Chain (although the EO does not identify any particular entity, it is widely interpreted to target a telecommunication giant, China's Huawei Technologies Co (Huawei)) (EO 13873),[43] the harmful foreign activities of Russia, including efforts to undermine elections in the US, cyber-enabled activities against the US, and disrespecting the territorial integrity of other states (EO 14024),[44] the situation concerning Hong Kong, including recent actions taken by China to undermine Hong Kong's autonomy (EO 13936),[45] and illegal immigration and unchecked drug trafficking from Mexico and China (EO 14194[46] and EO 14195[47]).

At the same time, in some instances, the President's EOs specify that the actions/events constitute "an unusual and extraordinary threat to the national security and foreign policy of the United States," without

[40] US President EO 12170 on Blocking Iranian Government Property 44 FR 65729 (November 14, 1979).

[41] US President EO 13808 on Imposing Additional Sanctions with respect to the Situation in Venezuela Federal Register Vol 82 No 166 (August 24, 2017).

[42] US President EO 13818 on Blocking the Property of Persons Involved in Serious Human Rights Abuse or Corruption Federal Register Vol 82 No 246 (December 20, 2017).

[43] US President EO 13873 on Securing the Information and Communications Technology and Services Supply Chain 84 FR 22689 (May 15, 2019).

[44] US President EO 14024 on Blocking Property with respect to Specified Harmful Foreign Activities of the Government of the Russian Federation Federal Register Vol 86 No 73 (April 15, 2021).

[45] US President EO 13936 on The President's Executive Order on Hong Kong Normalization Federal Register Vol 85 No 138 (July 14, 2020).

[46] US President EO 14194 on Imposing Duties to Address the Situation at Our Southern Border Federal Register (February 1, 2025).

[47] US President EO 14195 on Imposing Duties to Address the Synthetic Opioid Supply Chain in the People's Republic of China Federal Register (February 1, 2025).

mentioning the threat to the US economy, for example the Nicaraguan government's aggressive activities in Central America in the 1980s (EO 12513),[48] the military government in Burma (EO 13047),[49] the actions undermining democracy in Belarus in 2006 (EO 13405);[50] weapons proliferation in North Korea (EO 13466),[51] the deterioration of the security situation and the persistence of violence in Somalia, acts of piracy and armed robbery at sea off the coast of Somalia (EO 13536),[52] the actions and policies of Russia with respect to Ukraine (EO 13661),[53] terrorism, narcotics trafficking, trafficking in persons, human rights abuses, hostage-taking, and attacks against civilians and international security forces in Mali (EO 13882),[54] the Venezuela's human rights violations (EO 13692),[55] the situation in Burundi, which has been marked by the killing of and violence against civilians, unrest, the incitement of imminent violence, and significant political repression (EO 13712),[56] the foreign interference in the US elections (EO 13848),[57] the actions by Turkey to conduct a military offense into northeast Syria (EO 13894),[58] the coup in Burma (EO 14014),[59] Russian efforts to undermine the sovereignty and territorial integrity of Ukraine (EO 14066),[60]

[48] US President EO 12513 on Prohibiting Trade and Certain Other Transactions involving Nicaragua 50 FR 18629 3 CFR 1985 Comp (May 1, 1985).

[49] US President EO 13047 on Prohibiting New Investment in Burma Federal Register Vol 62 No 99 (May 20, 1997).

[50] US President EO 13405 on Blocking Property of Certain Persons Undermining Democratic Processes or Institutions in Belarus Federal Register Vol 71 No 118 (June 16, 2006).

[51] US President EO 13466 on Continuing Certain Restrictions with respect to North Korea and North Korean Nationals Federal Register Vol 73 No 125 (June 26, 2008).

[52] US President EO 13536 on Blocking Property of Certain Persons Contributing to the Conflict in Somalia Federal Register Vol 75 No 72 (April 12, 2010).

[53] US President EO 13661 on Blocking Property of Additional Persons Contributing to the Situation in Ukraine Federal Register Vol 79 No 53 (March 16, 2014).

[54] US President EO 13882 on Blocking Property and Suspending Entry of Certain Persons Contributing to the Situation in Mali Federal Register Vol 84 No 146 (July 26, 2019).

[55] US President EO 13692 on Blocking Property and Suspending Entry of Certain Persons Contributing to the Situation in Venezuela Federal Register Vol 80 No 47 (March 8, 2015).

[56] US President EO 13712 on Blocking Property of Certain Persons Contributing to the Situation in Burundi Federal Register Vol 80 No 227 (November 22, 2015).

[57] US President EO 13848 on Imposing Certain Sanctions in the Event of Foreign Interference in a US Election Federal Register Vol 83 No 179 (September 12, 2018).

[58] US President EO 13894 on Blocking Property and Suspending Entry of Certain Persons Contributing to the Situation in Syria Federal Register Vol 84 No 201 (October 14, 2019).

[59] US President EO 14014 on Blocking Property with respect to the Situation in Burma Federal Register Vol 86 No 28 (February 10, 2021).

[60] US President EO 14066 on Prohibiting Certain Imports and New Investments with respect to Continued Russian Federation Efforts to Undermine the Sovereignty and Territorial Integrity of Ukraine Federal Register Vol 87 No 47 (March 8, 2022).

and the flow of illicit drugs from Canada (EO 14193).[61] Furthermore, in a couple of instances, EOs expressly state that the actions/events constitute "an unusual and extraordinary threat to the foreign policy of the United States," such as the policies and actions of the government of South Africa (e.g. apartheid) (EO 12532)[62] and the regional instability due to widespread violence and atrocities in Congo (EO 13413).[63]

Thus, while in practice, it might be challenging to determine how a specific situation is labeled in each particular case, the analysis of the EOs declaring a national emergency demonstrates that certain actions/events are interpreted as constituting a threat to the US national security but not to the US economy, that is to say, military intervention, the persistence of violence, acts of piracy and other actions undermining democracy in third countries, weapons proliferation, terrorism, narcotics trafficking, trafficking in persons, and human rights violations, thereby confirming that US national security interests and the interests of the US economy constitute two separate grounds for declaring a national emergency and subsequently imposing economic sanctions under the IEEPA.

At the same time, in some cases, the President's acts clarify that the measures are adopted to protect US national security specifically. To illustrate, EO 13942 (TikTok EO) issued in 2020 expressly states that "the United States must take aggressive action against the owners of TikTok to protect [US] national security," as further discussed in section 3.1.1.2.[64] EO 14017 directed a review of critical US supply chains to ensure the US access to the components it needs to be a global leader in manufacturing, which is important "to support national and economic security" of the US.[65] EO 14024, adopted in 2021, states that Russia's "harmful foreign activities," including efforts to undermine free and fair democratic elections and institutions, malicious cyber activities (including the recent SolarWinds incident),

[61] US President EO 14193 on Imposing Duties to Address the Flow of Illicit Drugs Across Our Northern Border Federal Register (February 1, 2025).

[62] US President EO 12532 on Prohibiting Trade and Certain Other Transactions involving South Africa 50 FR 36861 3 CFR 1985 Comp (September 9, 1985).

[63] US President EO 13413 on Blocking Property of Certain Persons Contributing to the Conflict in the Democratic Republic of the Congo Federal Register Vol 71 No 210 (October 27, 2006).

[64] US President EO 13942 on Addressing the Threat posed by TikTok, and Taking Additional Steps to address the National Emergency with respect to the Information and Communications Technology and Services Supply Chain 85 FR 48637 (August 6, 2020).

[65] US President EO 14017 on America's Supply Chains 86 FR 11849 (February 24, 2021).

transnational corruption, targeting of dissidents and journalists, undermining national security and violating the territorial integrity of states, "undermine security in countries and regions important to United States national security."[66] In 2018, the US withdrew from the Joint Comprehensive Plan of Action (JCPOA) (i.e. the nuclear deal under which the US and EU had agreed to lift their nuclear-related sanctions programs in return for the restriction of Iran's nuclear activity) and reimposed several sanctions against Iran, among others, "to ensure the safety and security of the United States and the American people."[67] It can be distilled from such acts that the US perceives a broad range of threats to its national security, from conventional nuclear-related threats and threats caused by armed conflicts to cyberspace activities and the need to protect human rights.

Ultimately, the President has broad discretion to impose and waive the application of sanctions in the interest of national security. Given multiple complexities and nuances in the situations in which the US adopts economic sanctions, it is not surprising that the President often relies on various grounds and various objectives to use its national emergency powers. Nevertheless, the practice of applying economic sanctions demonstrates that the President is inclined to refer to national security in response to a wide range of threats and that the national security and economic interests of the US are, at least in some cases, closely connected. Such an approach is confirmed by the preference of the US to incorporate broadly drafted Security Exceptions under RTAs and the attempts to present the matters of economic security as national security concerns before international trade fora.[68]

3.1.1.2 Court Review of US Sanctions

US lower courts are split over the judicial review of the President's statutory powers. Yet, they appear to have grown more reluctant to apply the political question doctrine in the US foreign affairs context, ultimately deciding that lawsuits involving foreign affairs or national security issues

[66] US President EO 14024 on Blocking Property with respect to Specified Harmful Foreign Activities of the Government of the Russian Federation Federal Register Vol 86 No 73 (April 15, 2021).

[67] Presidential Memoranda, 'Ceasing U.S. Participation in the JCPOA and Taking Additional Action to Counter Iran's Malign Influence and Deny Iran all Paths to a Nuclear Weapon' (May 8, 2018) https://trumpwhitehouse.archives.gov/presidential-actions/ceasing-u-s-participation-jcpoa-taking-additional-action-counter-irans-malign-influence-deny-iran-paths-nuclear-weapon/.

[68] See more chapter 4, section 4.1.1.

are reviewable or justiciable.[69] It is generally acknowledged that "no governmental interest is more compelling than the security of the Nation."[70] Yet, US judges have also acknowledged that

> as critical as the Government's interest may be in detaining those who pose an immediate threat to the national security of the United States during ongoing international conflict, history and common sense teach us that an unchecked system of detention carries the potential to become a means for oppression and abuse of others who do not present that sort of threat.[71]

As the practice demonstrates, US courts generally review requests of the persons subject to US economic sanctions and other interested parties to overturn designations, asset freezes, or sanctions provisions.[72] The US government is also growing reluctant to invoke jurisdictional defense on national security grounds,[73] even though it emphasizes that the measures based on national security concerns are subject to limited scrutiny.[74]

Recent court rulings enjoining enforcement of the restrictions targeting TikTok (a video-sharing social networking service owned by Chinese company ByteDance) also confirm the limits of the President's sweeping powers to impose economic sanctions under the IEEPA.[75] On May 15, 2019, President Trump issued EO 13873, which declared a national emergency under the IEEPA and the NEA concerning "an unusual and extraordinary threat to the national security, foreign policy and economy

[69] Alexander F Cohen and Joseph Ravitch, 'Economic Sanctions, Domestic Deprivations, and the Just Compensation Clause: Enforcing the Fifth Amendment in the Foreign Affairs Context' (1988) 13 Yale J Intl L 146, 155.

[70] *Haig v Agee* 453 US 280, 307 (1981) (quoting *Aptheker v Secretary of State* 378 US 500, 509 (1964)) 31.

[71] *Hamdi v Rumsfeld* 542 US 507, 530 Opinion of J O'Connor (2004) 23.

[72] See eg *Kadi v Geithner* 42 F Supp 3d 1 (DDC 2012).

[73] See eg *Am Inst for Intl Steel, Inc v US* No 2019–1727 (Fed Cir 2020); *US WeChat Users Alliance v Trump*, 488 F Supp 3d 912 (ND Cal 2020).

[74] See eg *US WeChat Users Alliance v Trump*, 488 F Supp 3d 912 (ND Cal 2020).

[75] In August 2020, President Trump issued an EO imposing restrictions on US persons' activities involving TikTok (which relied on the earlier authority of the 2019 EO 13873 declaring a national emergency with respect to the threat related to the Information and Communications Technology and Services Supply Chain). The EO did not specify the precise scope of the restrictions – that was later circulated in prohibitions published by the Department of Commerce in September 2020. See US President EO 13873 on Securing the Information and Communications Technology and Services Supply Chain 84 FR 22689 (May 15, 2019).

of the United States" posed by foreign adversaries.[76] Citing EO 13873 and pursuant to his authority under the IEEPA, President Trump issued EO 13942 (TikTok EO) on August 6, 2020, naming TikTok a threat to the "national security, foreign policy, and economy of the United States" because of its foreign ownership and the company's ability to "automatically capture[] vast swaths of information from its users."[77] President Trump identified a risk that China could use TikTok to "access ... Americans' personal information for blackmail, and conduct corporate espionage" or "for disinformation campaigns that benefit [China], such as when TikTok videos spread debunked conspiracy theories about the origins of the 2019 Novel Coronavirus."[78] Accordingly, "the United States must take aggressive action against the owners of TikTok to protect [US] national security."[79] On September 18, 2020, the Secretary of Commerce published a list of six prohibited transactions shortly revised and republished.[80] TikTok itself,[81] as well as a group of TikTok content creators,[82] filed the lawsuits alleging, among others, that the imposed restrictions exceed the President's and Secretary's authority under the IEEPA.

Both the US District Court for the District of Columbia and the US District Court for the Eastern District of Pennsylvania upheld that even though the ultimate purpose of the TikTok restrictions is to protect the US national security by preventing China from accessing that data and

[76] For example, unrestricted acquisition or use in the US of information and communications technology or services designed, developed, manufactured, or supplied by persons owned by, controlled by, or subject to the jurisdiction or direction of foreign adversaries augments the ability of foreign adversaries to create and exploit vulnerabilities in information and communications technology or services, with potentially catastrophic effects. See US President EO 13873 on Securing the Information and Communications Technology and Services Supply Chain 84 FR 22689 (May 15, 2019).

[77] US President EO 13873 on Securing the Information and Communications Technology and Services Supply Chain 84 FR 22689 (May 15, 2019).

[78] US President EO 13942 on Addressing the Threat posed by TikTok, and Taking Additional Steps to address the National Emergency with respect to the Information and Communications Technology and Services Supply Chain 85 FR 48637 (August 6, 2020).

[79] Ibid.

[80] US Commerce Department Identification of Prohibited Transactions to implement EO 13942 and address the Threat posed by TikTok and the National Emergency with respect to the Information and Communications Technology and Services Supply Chain 85 FR 60061 (September 24, 2020).

[81] *TikTok Inc v Trump*, Civil Action No 1:20-cv-02658 (CJN) (September 27, 2020).

[82] *Marland v Trump*, Civil Action No 20-4597 (October 30, 2020).

skewing content on TikTok, the restrictions unduly infringe upon personal communications and are related to the importation or exportation of information or informational materials, which makes them run afoul of the IEEPA.[83] Consequently, the US District Courts confirmed the likelihood of the plaintiffs' success on the merits and granted apreliminary injunction against the TikTok restrictions.[84]

In a similar vein, the US users of the messaging, social media, and mobile payment app WeChat challenged EO 13943, which prohibited certain transactions with WeChat, given that "the spread in the United States of mobile applications developed and owned by companies in the People's Republic of China (China) continues to threaten the national security, foreign policy, and economy of the United States."[85] The US District Court for California found that "[t]he prohibited transactions burden substantially more speech than is necessary to serve the government's significant interest in national security, especially given the lack of substitute channels for communication."[86] Subsequently, President Biden rescinded the relevant executive orders, and the lawsuits were further dismissed.[87]

Even though the US court practice suggests that the objective of protection of the US national security is not a talisman shielding a governmental policy against judicial review, the US courts generally

83 The IEEPA contains two express limitations relevant here: the "authority granted to the President . . . does not include the authority to regulate or prohibit, directly or indirectly" either (a) the importation or exportation of "information or informational materials," or (b) "personal communication[s], which do[] not involve a transfer of anything of value." 50 USC § 1702(b)(1).

84 The injunction was granted on the basis that the IEEPA explicitly excludes the authority to regulate the importation or exportation of information or informational materials, or personal communications, which do not involve a transfer of anything of value. In April 2024, the US President signed a bill that included the Protecting Americans from Foreign Adversary Controlled Applications Act (PAFACAA), among other policies. PAFACAA appears to bypass some of the constraints imposed on the President by the existing US legislative framework, as highlighted by the discussed TikTok litigation. See more Paolo Mazzotti, 'PAFACAA: "TikTok Ban" or New Milestone in US Economic Security Law?' (*CELIS Blog*, August 2024) www.celis.institute/celis-blog/the-protecting-americans-from-foreign-adversary-controlled-applications-act-pafacaa-tiktok-ban-or-new-milestone-in-us-economic-security-law/.

85 US President EO 13943 Addressing the Threat Posed by WeChat, and Taking Additional Steps to Address the National Emergency with respect to the Information and Communications Technology and Services Supply Chain 85 FR 48641 (August 6, 2020).

86 *US WeChat Users Alliance v Trump* 488 F Supp 3d 912 (ND Cal 2020) [927].

87 Christopher A Casey and others, 'The International Emergency Economic Powers Act: Origins, Evolution, and Use' (March 25, 2022) Congressional Research Service 45.

continue to apply the narrow standard of review concerning designation decisions,[88] and the high margin of deference when matters of foreign policy and national security are concerned.[89] In *Kadi v Geithner*, Kadi, a citizen and permanent resident of Saudi Arabia, challenged the decision of the Office of Foreign Assets Control (OFAC) to designate him as a "specially designated global terrorist" (SDGT).[90] Finding the challenge to the agency's decision as arbitrary and capricious, the Court highlighted that courts are particularly mindful that their review is highly deferential when matters of foreign policy and national security are concerned.[91] The Court reiterated several considerations, including that "a highly deferential review applies" to the examination of an SDGT designation,[92] that the "scope of review under the 'arbitrary and capricious' standard is narrow, and a court is not to substitute its judgment for that of the agency,"[93] that the agency's decisions are entitled to a "presumption of regularity,"[94] meaning that the government's officials "have properly discharged their official duties," and that "inquiry into the facts is to be searching and careful, the ultimate standard of review is a narrow one."[95] In the end, the Court ruled against Kadi's challenge to his listing in the US. In that respect, this ruling contradicts Kadi's partial victories in litigation outside the US, as will be further discussed.

[88] The ordinary mechanism that the US courts use for balancing serious competing interests, and for determining the procedures that are necessary to ensure that a citizen is not "deprived of life, liberty, or property, without due process of law" is generally the test articulated in *Mathews v Eldridge*. It dictates that the process due in any given instance is determined by weighing "the private interest that will be affected by the official action" against the Government's asserted interest, "including the function involved" and the burdens the Government would face in providing greater process. The Mathews calculus then contemplates a judicious balancing of these concerns, through an analysis of "the risk of an erroneous deprivation" of the private interest if the process were reduced and the "probable value, if any, of additional or substitute procedural safeguards." See *Hamdi v Rumsfeld* 542 US 507, 530 Opinion of J O'Connor (2004) 21–22.

[89] *Zarmach Oil Servs v US Dept of the Treasury* 750 F Supp.2d 150, 155 DDC (2010).

[90] *Kadi v Geithner* 42 F Supp 3d 1 (DDC 2012).

[91] "[O]ur review – in an area at the intersection of national security, foreign policy, and administrative law – is extremely deferential." See *Islamic Am Relief Agency v Gonzales* 477 F 3d (DC Cir 2007).

[92] *Islamic Am Relief Agency v Gonzales* 477 F 3d (DC Cir 2007).

[93] *Motor Vehicle Mfrs v State Farm Mutual Automobile Ins Co* 463 US 29 (1983).

[94] *Citizens to Preserve Overton Park, Inc v Volpe* 401 US 402, 415, 91 S Ct 814, 28 L Ed 2d 136 (1971).

[95] Ibid.

3.1.2 *The EU Approach*

Like the US, the EU is increasing the use of economic sanctions, or "restrictive measures," as they are referred to in the EU documents. The EU prefers to employ the term "restrictive measures" over the term "sanctions" in the comments to the acts.[96] For the purposes of this section, the terms "EU economic sanctions" and "EU restrictive measures" are used interchangeably.[97]

3.1.2.1 Legal Framework for Application of Economic Sanctions

The EU sanctions regime demonstrates how states can use regional institutions to coordinate the application of economic sanctions based on a set of common principles and values.[98] The TEU includes restrictive measures as one of the tools to pursue the CFSP goals.[99] Restrictive measures implemented within the CFSP must be consistent with the CFSP objectives, as set out in Article 21 of TEU including the objectives to "safeguard [EU] values, fundamental interests, security, independence and integrity," and/or "preserve peace, prevent conflicts and strengthen international security, in accordance with the purposes and principles of the United Nations Charter, with the principles of the Helsinki Final Act and with the aims of the Charter of Paris, including those relating to external borders." The procedures for adopting unilateral or autonomous economic sanctions by the EU are complex, reflecting the institutional and legal architecture of the EU and the allocation of

[96] Natalino Ronzitti, 'Sanctions as Instruments of Coercive Diplomacy: An International Law Perspective' in Natalino Ronzitti (ed.), *Coercive Diplomacy, Sanctions and International Law* (Brill 2016) 16.

[97] The Treaty of Rome (1957) already implied that members of the EC could coordinate their trade policies to produce the effects of economic sanctions. However, the Treaty of Rome had no express authority providing for a Community competence in economic sanctions. Thus, it was only from 1992 with the Maastricht Treaty that the EU started to impose unilateral, or autonomous, economic sanctions. See Kern Alexander, *Economic Sanctions: Law and Public Policy* (Palgrave Macmillan 2009) 128.

[98] Kern Alexander, *Economic Sanctions: Law and Public Policy* (Palgrave Macmillan 2009) 2.

[99] Article 2(4) of TFEU has conferred on the EU the competence to define and implement the CFSP. Articles 3–6 of TFEU, however, do not clarify the nature of this competence and do not include the CFSP as either EU exclusive or shared competence. In any case, it has always been clear that the CFSP is not an exclusive competence. See Piet Eeckhout, *EU External Relations Law* (2nd ed., OUP 2012) 167.

competences between the EU and EU member states on matters of the CFSP.[100]

The EU Security Union Strategy for 2020–25 specifies that "tailored and effective restrictive measures could be explored to counter hybrid threats."[101] The Basic Principles on the Use of Restrictive Measures (Sanctions) (hereafter the Basic Principles) highlight that the EU can impose restrictive measures autonomously whenever "necessary" to meet the objectives of the EU.[102] It reiterates that the EU restrictive measures should be adopted in supporting efforts to fight terrorism and prevent the proliferation of weapons of mass destruction (WMD), and "uphold respect for human rights, democracy, the rule of law, and good governance."[103] Guidelines on Implementation and Evaluation of Restrictive Measures (Sanctions) in the Framework of the CFSP (hereafter the Guidelines) specify that "restrictive measures do not have an economic motivation."[104] This is an important clarification that narrows down the list of circumstances under which restrictive measures can be applied.

The contexts in which the EU imposes sanctions are diverse. In the past, the EU generally preferred to impose sanctions in conflict-related situations, that is, violent conflicts (as in Sudan or Yugoslavia) or post-conflict situations (as in Indonesia or Yugoslavia), and was less likely to use these in

[100] Thomas Biersteker and Clara Portela, 'EU Sanctions in Context: Three Types' (EU Institute for Security Studies, July 2015) www.iss.europa.eu/sites/default/files/EUISSFiles/Brief_26_EU_sanctions.pdf.

[101] European Commission, Communication from the Commission to the European Parliament, the European Council, the Council, the European Economic and Social Committee and the Committee of the Regions on the EU Security Union Strategy (July 24, 2020) COM/2020/605 final.

[102] The Basic Principles were approved in June 2004 by the Political and Security Committee to address a request by the Council to develop a policy framework for more effective use of sanctions. This document expressed in clear terms the willingness of the EU to use sanctions as a key instrument of its foreign policy and, for the first time, designed a strategy for the use of sanctions. See Marco Gestri, 'Sanctions Imposed by the European Union: Legal and Institutional Aspects' in Natalino Ronzitti (ed.), *Coercive Diplomacy, Sanctions and International Law* (Brill 2016) 72.

[103] Council of the EU, Basic Principles on the Use of Restrictive Measures (Sanctions) (June 7, 2004) 10198/1/04 REV 1.

[104] Council of the EU, Guidelines on Implementation and Evaluation of Restrictive Measures (Sanctions) in the framework of the CFSP (May 4, 2018) 5664/18 [5].

Guidelines were approved in 2003 and updated in 2005, 2009, 2012, and 2017. They contain definitions and directives on how to design and implement restrictive measures, as well as important information with regard to the different types of restrictions that can be imposed and how to measure their effectiveness.

peacetime.[105] This remains true today. The EU practice also demonstrates that the sanctions are most often adopted to promote democracy and human rights, sustain post-crisis transitional arrangements, and uphold nonproliferation regimes. Such an approach is not surprising given that the EU constitutional framework under Article 21 of TEU embeds the specific role of the EU on the international scene to advance in the wider world "democracy, the rule of law, the universality and indivisibility of human rights and fundamental freedoms, respect for human dignity, the principles of equality and solidarity, and respect for the principles of the United Nations Charter and international law." It can be challenging to determine in which contexts the EU decides to impose restrictive measures specifically to protect its security interests instead of pursuing other common objectives. Given the broad scope of the definition of threats to the EU security interests,[106] the objectives of restrictive measures can often directly or indirectly relate to the protection of EU security. Direct security-related objectives can include deterring an ongoing conflict or alleged support of terrorism, dealing with post-conflict situations, and nonproliferation of WMD, while indirect security-related objectives can encompass the obstruction of democracy and human rights.[107]

Notably, in the cases where the EU and the US imposed unilateral sanctions in response to the same actions and policies of third countries, the US seemed to be keener than the EU to call such measures a response to the threat to its security and rely on domestic procedures for their implementation designed to deal with national security matters. To illustrate, in 2006, in response to the flawed democratic election and subsequent arrests and detention of independent political activists in Belarus, President Bush conferred that such actions and policies of certain members of the government of Belarus and other related persons "constitute an unusual and extraordinary threat to the national security and foreign policy" of the US.[108] The EU also condemned the situation in

[105] Clara Portela, 'Where and Why Does the EU Impose Sanctions?' (2005) 3(17) Politique Européenne 83, 97.

[106] European Commission, Communication from the Commission to the European Parliament, the European Council, the Council, the European Economic and Social Committee and the Committee of the Regions on the EU Security Union Strategy (July 24, 2020) COM/2020/605 final.

[107] Clara Portela, 'Where and Why Does the EU Impose Sanctions?' (2005) 3(17) Politique Européenne 83, 92.

[108] US President EO 13405 on Blocking Property of Certain Persons Undermining Democratic Processes or Institutions in Belarus Federal Register Vol 71 No 118 (June 16, 2006).

Belarus and adopted trade-restrictive measures primarily aligned with the US sanctions, yet without mentioning that the situation in Belarus constituted a threat to EU security interests or that the trade-restrictive measures against Belarus' officials were necessary for the protection of EU security.[109] Instead, the EU documents heavily relied on the concern about the deterioration of democracy, the rule of law, and human rights in Belarus, as well as the obstruction of justice.[110] Similarly, the US expressly called the military coup and the serious human rights violations in the Myanmar/Burma coup in 2021 to "constitute an unusual and extraordinary threat to [US] national security and foreign policy."[111] While imposing trade-restrictive measures in response to the same threats, the EU did not refer to protecting its security interests[112] but highlighted the need to promote progress toward democratization and human rights in Myanmar/Burma.[113]

In some recent official documents imposing restrictive measures, the EU explicitly mentions that certain situations threaten EU security.[114] To illustrate, the EU expressed its concern at the rise of malicious behavior in cyberspace that undermines the EU's integrity, security, and economic competitiveness, with the eventual risk of conflict.[115] In June 2017, the EU stepped up its response by establishing a Framework for a Joint EU Diplomatic Response to Malicious Cyber Activities (Cyber Diplomacy Toolbox).[116] Sanctions are one of the options available in the EU's Cyber

[109] Council Common Position 2006/276/CFSP of April 10, 2006 concerning Restrictive Measures against Certain Officials of Belarus and Repealing Common Position 2004/661/CFSP (2006) OJ L 101. No longer in force.

[110] Council Common Position 2004/661/CFSP of September 24, 2004 concerning Restrictive Measures against Certain Officials of Belarus (2004) OJ L 301. No longer in force.

[111] US President EO 14014 on Blocking Property with respect to the Situation in Burma Federal Register Vol 86 No 28 (February 10, 2021).

[112] Council Decision 2013/184/CFSP of April 22, 2013 concerning Restrictive Measures in view of the Situation in Myanmar/Burma (2013) OJ L 111.

[113] Common Position of October 28, 1996 defined by the Council on the basis of Article J.2 of TEU, on Burma/Myanmar (1996) OJ L 287 (no longer in force); Council Decision (CFSP) 2021/639 of April 19, 2021 amending Decision 2013/184/CFSP concerning Restrictive Measures in view of the Situation in Myanmar/Burma (2021) OJ L 132I.

[114] Francesco Giumelli, Fabian Hoffmann, and Anna Książczaková, 'The When, What, Where and Why of European Union Sanctions' (2021) 30(1) Eur Security 1, 2.

[115] The Council of the EU, 'Cyber-Attacks: Council is now Able to Impose Sanctions' (Press Release, May 17, 2019) www.consilium.europa.eu/en/press/press-releases/2019/05/17/cyber-attacks-council-is-now-able-to-impose-sanctions/.

[116] The Council of the EU, 'Cyber Attacks: EU Ready to Respond with a Range of Measures, including Sanctions' (Press Release, June 19, 2017) www.consilium.europa.eu/en/press/press-releases/2017/06/19/cyber-diplomacy-toolbox/.

Diplomacy Toolbox to prevent, deter, and respond to malicious cyber activities directed against the EU or its member states. According to the most recent EU Best Practices for the Effective Implementation of Restrictive Measures, "[w]ith this regime, the EU is equipped with a further tool to strengthen its resilience and its ability to protect the integrity and security of the EU."[117]

In 2020, within the framework of the Cyber Diplomacy Toolbox, the Council decided to impose restrictive measures against specific entities and individuals that were responsible for or were involved in various cyberattacks, in part to protect the security interests of the EU.[118] The EU foreign affairs chief Josep Borrell stated that the sanctions were part of the EU's response to "promote international security and stability in cyberspace."[119] Thus, the sanctions were seen as threatening international security rather than EU security, confirming the role of the EU as an international peacekeeper. The EU also suspended the broadcasting activities of several Russian state-owned outlets in June 2022 as a part of the bundle of measures imposed in response to Russia's invasion of Ukraine. The Council Regulation indicates that continuous and concerted propaganda actions have been channeled through these outlets, which "constitute a significant and direct threat to the Union's public order and security."[120]

Furthermore, in a couple of other instances, the EU documents were drafted in a way that it remains unclear whether they refer to the protection of EU security interests or international security. To illustrate, in 2018, the EU introduced the sanctions regime in response to the repeated

[117] Council of the EU, EU Best Practices for the Effective Implementation of Restrictive Measures (June 27, 2022) 10572/22 [115].

[118] The Council of the EU, 'EU imposes the First-Ever Sanctions against Cyber-Attacks' (Press Release, July 30, 2020) www.consilium.europa.eu/en/press/press-releases/2020/07/30/eu-imposes-the-first-ever-sanctions-against-cyber-attacks/; Council Decision (CFSP) 2020/1127 of July 30, 2020 amending Decision (CFSP) 2019/797 concerning Restrictive Measures against Cyber-Attacks Threatening the Union or its Member States (July 30, 2020) L 246/12.

[119] Council of the EU, 'Declaration by the High Representative Josep Borrell on behalf of the EU: European Union Response to Promote International Security and Stability in Cyberspace' (Press Release, July 30, 2020) www.consilium.europa.eu/en/press/press-releases/2020/07/30/declaration-by-the-high-representative-josep-borrell-on-behalf-of-the-eu-european-union-response-to-promote-international-security-and-stability-in-cyberspace/.

[120] Council Regulation (EU) 2022/879 of June 3, 2022 amending Regulation (EU) No 833/2014 concerning Restrictive Measures in view of Russia's Actions Destabilising the Situation in Ukraine (2022) OJ L 153 [9]–[10].

use of chemical weapons in Syria, marking a pressing new security challenge and raising concerns about the erosion of the taboo on chemical weapons use. The European Council concluded that "the use of chemical weapons, including any toxic chemicals as weapons under any circumstances, is completely unacceptable, must be systematically and rigorously condemned and constitutes a security threat to us all."[121] Similarly, the European Parliament, in its resolution, strongly condemned the unilateral Turkish military intervention in northeast Syria and stated that the further escalation and destabilization in the region presented, both for the region itself and the EU, increasing security risks.[122] The Council's decision in response to the military aggression against Ukraine in 2022 has introduced new restrictive measures against Russia given that "[b]y its illegal military actions, Russia is . . . undermining European and global security and stability."[123]

Thus, similarly to the US, because of the complexity and versatility of the situations in which the EU decides to imply economic sanctions, it is difficult to differentiate between cases where the EU imposes restrictive measures in response to threats to the EU security interests and cases where the EU responds to the threats to other common objectives that are rather not connected to its security. The EU practice illustrates that the adoption of EU restrictive measures can be directly connected to the protection of EU security but only in limited instances that are generally related to the prevention of the proliferation of WMD, human rights violations, use of chemical weapons, military intervention in other countries, and protection of cyberspace. Unlike the US, the EU seems to stay more reserved in labeling the situation as a threat to its security and prefers to refer in its sanctions documents to more universal objectives, such as the protection of international peace and security. At least until recently, EU Security Measures could be expected to be more limited in scope, given that economic motives for EU's economic sanctions were not generally recognized. Such an approach corresponds with the

[121] Council Decision (CFSP) 2018/1544 of October 15, 2018 concerning Restrictive Measures against the Proliferation and Use of Chemical Weapons (2018) ST/11936/2018/INIT OJ L 259.

[122] European Parliament resolution of October 24, 2019 on the Turkish Military Operation in Northeast Syria and its Consequences (2019/2886(RSP)).

[123] Preamble of the Council Decision (CFSP) 2022/335 amending Decision 2014/512/CFSP concerning Restrictive Measures in view of Russia's Actions Destabilising the Situation in Ukraine (February 28, 2022) OJ L 57 [4].

preference of the EU to include narrowly drafted WTO-like Security Exceptions in its RTAs.[124]

Yet, the EU has taken steps to revisit its economic security architecture in response to the recent geopolitical developments. In 2018, following the reimposition of US economic sanctions against Iran, the EU amended its blocking statute to compel EU persons not to comply with US measures.[125] The EU blocking statute was initially adopted in 1996 to neutralize the US economic sanctions against Cuba, Iran, and Libya.[126] The European Commission has also designed an anti-coercion instrument that allows the EU to impose economic countermeasures in response to third-country coercion.[127] Such an instrument should be able to deter offensive actions by other states when all other options had failed to secure Europe's resilience.[128]

3.1.2.2 Review of EU Sanctions by CJEU

Clarifying the extent of the court's jurisdiction to review and interpret restrictive measures imposed by the Council, the ECJ confirmed that it had no jurisdiction to review the Council's decisions imposing measures of general application (i.e. nontargeted measures that apply objectively to predetermined situations and produce legal effects concerning categories of persons in a general and abstract manner).[129] At the same time, the Court of Justice of the EU (CJEU)[130] has been conducting

[124] See more chapter 4, section 4.1.2.

[125] Commission Delegated Regulation (EU) 2018/1100 of January 6, 2018, Amending the Annex to Council Regulation (EC) 2271/96 Protecting against the Effects of Extra-Territorial Application of Legislation Adopted by a Third Country, and Actions Based Thereon or Resulting therefrom (2018) OJ L 1991. See the clarification on the scope and content of the blocking statute in the practice of CJEU, eg Case C-124/20 *Bank Melli Iran v Telekom Deutschland GmbH* [2021] EU:C:2021:1035.

[126] Council Regulation (EC) 2271/96 of November 22, 1996, Protecting Against the Effects of the Extra-Territorial Application of Legislation Adopted by a Third Country, and Actions Based Thereon or Resulting Therefrom, 1996 OJ L 309 1.

[127] European Parliament, 'Proposed Anti-Coercion Instrument' (Briefing, June 16, 2022) www.europarl.europa.eu/thinktank/en/document/EPRS_BRI(2022)729299.

[128] See eg Jonathan Hackenbroich and Pawel Zerka, 'Measured Response: How to Design a European Instrument against Economic Coercion' (ECFE, June 23, 2021) https://ecfr.eu/publication/measured-response-how-to-design-a-european-instrument-against-economic-coercion/.

[129] Case C-72/15 *PJSC Rosneft Oil Company v Her Majesty's Treasury and Others* [2017] EU:C:2017:236 [98]–[99].

[130] For the purpose of this research, CJEU means either Court of Justice (or European Court of Justice (ECJ)) or General Court of the EU.

a judicial review of hundreds of targeted sanctions adopted to advance the CFSP.[131]

The ECJ has jurisdiction to consider the challenges to economic sanctions against natural and legal persons based on non-conformity with fundamental and procedural rights, even where the measures in question originate from the decisions of the UN Security Council concerning the protection of international peace and security, as it was found in *Kadi I* and *Kadi II* judgments (Kadi Judgments).[132] It follows from the Kadi Judgments that considerations relating to international peace and security may not, as such, exclude the decisions imposing restrictive measures from judicial review.[133] Notably, the ECJ acknowledged that although it is for EU member states to ensure their internal and external security, the mere fact that a decision concerns state security does not exclude the application of the EU law.[134]

For the purposes of this research, the Kadi Judgments, specifically *Kadi II*, are important to understand the scope of review of the measures adopted for the protection of security interests. In the UN Security Council, Kadi was identified as a possible supporter of Al-Qaida and therefore subjected to sanctions.[135] The EU transposed the UN sanctions resolution by a regulation that Kadi then challenged before the ECJ. In the first instance, the ECJ refused to review the EU regulation because this would constitute a review of the measure of the UN Security Council. In its judgment on appeal, the ECJ, nevertheless, reviewed the lawfulness of the EU regulation transposing the UN sanctions resolution arguing that all EU measures must be compatible with fundamental rights since the protection of fundamental rights forms part of the very foundations of the EU legal order.[136]

131 See eg Case T-256/07 *People's Mojahedin Organization of Iran v Council* [2008] EU:T:2008:461; Case C-548/09 P *Bank Melli Iran v Council* [2011] EU:C:2011:735; Case C-200/13 P *Council of the European Union v Bank Saderat Iran* [2016] EU:C:2016:284. See more Elena Chachko, 'Revisiting Judicial Review in Foreign Affairs' (2020) 43 Fordham Intl LJ 1273.

132 Joined Cases C-402/05 P and C-415/05 P *Yassin Abdullah Kadi and Al Barakaat International Foundation v Council of the European Union and Commission of the European Communities* [2008] EU:C:2008:461.

133 See also Case C-45/15 P *Safa Nicu Sepahan Co v Council of the European Union* [2017] EU:C:2017:402 [105].

134 Case C-300/11 *ZZ v Secretary of State for the Home Department* [2013] EU:C:2013:363 [38].

135 Juliane Kokott and Christoph Sobotta, 'The Kadi Case – Constitutional Core Values and International Law – Finding the Balance' (2012) 23 Eur J Intl L 1015, 1020.

136 Joined Cases C-402/05 P and C-415/05 P *Yassin Abdullah Kadi and Al Barakaat International Foundation v Council of the European Union and Commission of the European Communities* [2008] EU:C:2008:461 [290].

The ECJ ruling in *Kadi II* was appealed due to an error in law while applying an excessive level of judicial scrutiny.[137] However, the appeals were dismissed.[138] Confirming the previous findings, the ECJ ruled that it "must . . . ensure the review, in principle the full review, of the lawfulness of all Union acts in the light of the fundamental rights forming an integral part of the European Union legal order."[139] The General Court reaffirmed an applicant's rights of defense and, in particular, the need for the Council to provide a sufficient statement of reasons when implementing restrictive measures in the following cases.[140]

As regards the question of whether the adoption of the restrictive measures is necessary for the protection of EU security interests and the maintenance of peace and international security, the ECJ confirmed that "the Council has a broad discretion in areas which involve the making by that institution of political, economic and social choices, and in which it is called upon to undertake complex assessments."[141] In *Council of the European Union v Bank Saderat Iran*, the ECJ also reaffirmed that decisions aimed at protecting peace and security fall within the Council's margin of appreciation.[142] Yet, on multiple occasions, the ECJ reviewed the procedural aspects of the Council's decisions and the need for the Council to provide a sufficient statement of reasons when implementing restrictive measures.[143]

3.1.3 The Approach of Russia

Russia's Federal Law on Special Economic Measures (2006) establishes the legal basis for adopting economic measures when the circumstances require immediate reaction "to an internationally illegal act or unfriendly

137 Koen Lenaerts, 'The Kadi Saga and the Rule of Law within the EU' (2014) 67 SMU L Rev 707, 712.

138 Ibid.

139 Joined Cases C-402/05 P and C-415/05 P *Yassin Abdullah Kadi and Al Barakaat International Foundation v Council of the European Union and Commission of the European Communities* [2008] EU:C:2008:461 [283]–[285].

140 Case T-256/07 *People's Mojahedin Organization of Iran v Council* [2008] EU:T:2008:461.

141 Case C-440/14 P *National Iranian Oil Company* v *Council* [2016] EU:C:2016:128 [77].

142 Case C-200/13 P *Council of the European Union v Bank Saderat Iran* [2016] EU:C:2016:284 [93].

143 See eg Case T-228/02 *Organization des Modjahedines du Peuple d'Iran v Council* [2006] EU:T:2006:384 [117]; Joined Cases C-402/05 P and C-415/05 P *Yassin Abdullah Kadi and Al Barakaat International Foundation v Council of the European Union and Commission of the European Communities* [2008] EU:C:2008:461 [283]–[285]; Case C-833/19 P *Council of the European Union v Hamas* [2021] EU:C:2021:950 [41]–[85].

action of a foreign state or its bodies and officials," posing a threat "to the interests and security of Russia," or violating the rights and freedoms of its citizens.[144] Russia's legislation does not label its unilateral measures against other countries as sanctions. Given that Russia claims to adopt such measures in response to sanctions against it, Russia calls them "countersanctions" or "certain special economic measures." For the purposes of this research, the measures adopted by Russia are referred to as special economic measures, economic sanctions, or countersanctions interchangeably. However, it should be highlighted that the question of whether such measures constitute countermeasures under international law is outside the purview of this section.

Initially, in 2014, several countries imposed unilateral measures on Russia as a reaction to Russia's annexation of Crimea and involvement in the armed conflict in southern and eastern Ukraine.[145] Russia retaliated against such sanctions by adopting restrictive measures against specific individuals without even publishing the list of names of the sanctioned persons.[146] The Russian government revealed the names of the banned persons only after several EU politicians were denied entry to Russia on arrival.[147] Furthermore, in August 2014, Russia "imposed import bans on specified agricultural products, raw materials, and food originating from countries that had imposed sanctions against it," including the US and EU member states (hereafter the Agricultural Embargo).[148] Russia also imposed restrictions on the transit of goods through its territory. These transit restrictions were among those challenged by Ukraine before the WTO in *Russia – Traffic in Transit.*

At first glance, it might be argued that Russia's special economic measures are generally imposed out of geopolitical motives, not because of economic considerations.[149] However, the motives for some of

[144] Federal Law No 281-FZ on Special Economic Measures (December 30, 2006).

[145] Paulina Pospieszna, Joanna Skrzypczyńska, and Beata Stępień, 'Hitting Two Birds with One Stone: How Russian Countersanctions Intertwined Political and Economic Goals' (2020) 53(2) PS: Political Science & Politics 243, 243.

[146] Martin Russell, 'Sanctions over Ukraine. Impact on Russia' (EPRS Briefing, March 2016) www.europarl.europa.eu/EPRS/EPRS-Briefing-579084-Sanctions-over-Ukraine-impact-Russia-FINAL.pdf.

[147] Ibid.

[148] European Commission, 'Russian Import Ban on EU Products' https://ec.europa.eu/food/horizontal-topics/international-affairs/eu-russia-sps-issues/russian-import-ban-eu-products_en.

[149] Matěj Bělín and Jan Hanousek, 'Making Sanctions Bite: The EU–Russian Sanctions of 2014' (*VOX EU*, April 29, 2019) https://voxeu.org/article/making-sanctions-bite-eu-russian-sanctions-2014.

Russia's special economic measures were not straightforward. In particular, the Agricultural Embargo was presented as a special economic measure to protect Russia's security. Although the embargo was adopted in retaliation to the sanctions, it was framed as a positive and necessary policy for Russia's development and growth: "[s]anctions or no, we have taken this path and will not deviate from it."[150]

Some researchers argue that the Agricultural Embargo facilitated Russia's protectionist policy already implemented before Russia's special economic measures were introduced.[151] Arguably, such measures aimed to ensure Russia's long-term self-sufficiency in the food sector and benefit domestic producers and exporters by subsidizing local production.[152] Russia has a long history of banning agricultural imports over alleged food safety concerns.[153] To illustrate, alleged import restrictions on live pigs and their genetic material, pork, and certain other pig products from the EU as a whole, as well as from four EU member states: Estonia, Latvia, Lithuania, and Poland, were subject to review by the WTO in *Russia – Pigs (EU)*.[154] Russia tried to justify the ban based on concerns related to African swine fever. Nevertheless, the WTO panel found, and the Appellate Body confirmed, that the ban was illegal.[155] Notably, in December 2017, Russia reported that it had implemented the rulings and recommendations of the WTO DSB in *Russia – Pigs (EU)* dispute and opened the import of live pigs, fresh pork, and other pig products.[156] However, due to the almost simultaneous introduction of the Agricultural Embargo concerning pork imports, actual imports of pigs from the EU to Russia remain banned.[157] As a result of Russia's

[150] Alexandra Hofer, 'All the World's a Stage, and Sanctions the Merely Props: An Interactional Account of Sender-Target Dynamics in the Ukrainian Crisis' (2021) 28 Intl Peacekeeping 259, 275.

[151] Paulina Pospieszna, Joanna Skrzypczyńska, and Beata Stępień, 'Hitting Two Birds with One Stone: How Russian Countersanctions Intertwined Political and Economic Goals' (2020) 53(2) PS: Political Science & Politics 243, 244.

[152] Ibid.

[153] Martin Russell, 'Sanctions over Ukraine. Impact on Russia' (Briefing EPRS, March 2016) 4 www.europarl.europa.eu/EPRS/EPRS-Briefing-579084-Sanctions-over-Ukraine-impact-Russia-FINAL.pdf.

[154] *Russia – Measures on the Importation of Live Pigs, Pork and Other Pig Products from the European Union* (February 23, 2017) Appellate Body Report WT/DS475/AB/R.

[155] Ibid.

[156] *Russia – Measures on the Importation of Live Pigs, Pork and Other Pig Products from the European Union* (December 13, 2017) Communication from Russia Doc No 17-6863.

[157] 'Russia Complies with WTO Requirements to Open Pork Imports from Europe' (*IZ.RU*, December 6, 2017) https://iz.ru/679773/2017-12-06/rf-podchinilas-trebovaniiam-vto-otkryt-import-svininy-iz-evropy.

special economic measures in 2014, agriculture became one of Russia's few economic sectors to grow in 2015, arguably benefiting from the reduced competition with the EU and other sanctioned partners.[158] This suggests that Russia's special economic measures, at least in part, were implemented with some economic considerations. Since the Agricultural Embargo was presented as a special economic measure to protect Russia's security, it can also be seen as a confirmation that Russia's security interests can be understood in rather economic terms and intertwined with Russia's domestic economic policies.

As the conflict between Russia and Western countries escalated, Russia decided to strengthen its legislative framework for the adoption of trade restrictions. In 2018, it adopted Law on Measures (Countermeasures) against Unfriendly Actions of the US and Other Foreign Countries[159] (hereafter the Law on Countermeasures) and Law on the Introduction of Special Economic Measures in connection with the Unfriendly Actions of Ukraine against Russian Citizens and Legal Entities[160] aimed at protecting the interests and security of the Russian Federation and its sovereignty and territorial integrity, as well as the rights and freedoms of the citizens of the Russian Federation from unfriendly actions. The laws do not provide a straightforward definition of "unfriendly actions." Article 1(1) of the Law on Countermeasures only states that unfriendly actions may occur through the imposition of political or economic sanctions against Russia and/or Russian citizens and/or Russian legal entities but also may take the form of other actions "threatening the territorial integrity of Russia or aimed at economic and political destabilization of Russia" (unofficial translation).[161] The first economic measures under the new framework laws on special economic measures were imposed on Ukraine, including the prohibition on the import of a variety of Ukrainian goods, for example certain agricultural products, raw materials, food, spirits, construction materials, furniture, turbines,

[158] Martin Russell, 'Sanctions over Ukraine. Impact on Russia' (Briefing EPRS, March 2016) 10 www.europarl.europa.eu/EPRS/EPRS-Briefing-579084-Sanctions-over-Ukraine-impact-Russia-FINAL.pdf.

[159] Federal Law No 127-FZ on Measures of Impact (Counteraction) on Unfriendly Actions of the US and Other Foreign States (June 4, 2018).

[160] Decree of the President of the Russian Federation No 592 on Implementation of Special Economic Measures in Connection with Inimical Actions of Ukraine in relation to Russian Citizens and Legal Entities (as amended) (October 22, 2018).

[161] Federal Law on (Counteracting) Measures in response to the Unfriendly Actions of the US and Other Foreign States (June 4, 2018).

agricultural machinery, electrical conductors,[162] but also oil and oil products, certain engineering products, light industry goods, and metalwork products.[163]

In 2022, Russia introduced further "countermeasures" in response to the Western sanctions over its invasion of Ukraine. Among others, it prohibited the import and export of products and raw materials from the country "in order to ensure the security of the Russian Federation and the uninterrupted functioning of the industry."[164] Relying on the need to protect the "national interests of the Russian Federation," the government subjected real estate sale and purchase transactions with foreign individuals and companies affiliated with "unfriendly" states (i.e. the states that imposed or joined an extraordinary set of coordinated economic sanctions against Russia, including the US and EU member states) to special permits.[165] The Russian government also introduced a legal framework for blocking sanctions against it.[166] Russia's energy coercion, including cutting gas supplies to European countries, is the latest example of how Russia weaponizes trade and uses energy exports as an instrument of strategic leverage.[167] Russia also restricted certain transactions for foreign persons in the financial, fuel, and energy sectors.[168]

Notably, Russian courts were granted exclusive jurisdiction over disputes involving Russian individuals and legal entities subject to Western sanctions and foreign legal entities affected by such sanctions.[169] It means

[162] Governmental Order No 1716-83 on Ban on the Import into Russia of Goods Produced in Ukraine or Transported through its Territory (December 29, 2018).

[163] Governmental Order No 460-25 on Ban on the Import into Russia of Goods Produced in Ukraine or Transported through its Territory (April 18, 2019).

[164] Decree of the President of the Russian Federation No 100 on Implementation of Special Economic Measures in the Area of External Relations to Ensure National Security of the Russian Federation (March 8, 2022).

[165] Executive Order of the President of the Russian Federation No 79 (February 28, 2022); Executive Order of the President of the Russian Federation No 81 (March 1, 2022).

[166] Decree of the President of the Russian Federation No 252 on Russian Countersanctions against Individuals and Entities of the Countries which have imposed Sanctions on Russia (May 3, 2022).

[167] Pjotr Sauer, 'Russia Will Not Resume Gas Supplies to Europe until Sanctions Lifted, Says Moscow' *The Guardian* (September 5, 2022) www.theguardian.com/world/2022/sep/05/russia-will-not-resume-gas-supplies-to-europe-until-sanctions-lifted-says-moscow.

[168] Presidential Decree No 520 on the Application of Special Economic Measures in the Financial and Fuel and Energy Sectors related to the Unfriendly Actions of Certain Foreign States and International Organizations (August 5, 2022).

[169] Federal Law No 171-FZ On the Incorporation of Amendments to the Arbitrazh Procedure Code of the Russian Federation in Order to Protect the Rights of Natural Persons and Legal Entities in Connection with Restrictive Measures Imposed by

that the mere fact that such Russian entities are subject to any sanctions should be enough to render a foreign jurisdiction or arbitration clause unenforceable in Russia.

At the same time, nothing in Russia's legislation suggests that Russia implies that the protection of its security interests includes the protection of its economic interests. Russia's Regional Agreements generally expressly restrict the protection of the parties' essential security interests under Security Exceptions to military and defense matters and the situations of war and international emergencies, similar to the WTO agreements, which suggests that at least in its relationships with other countries, Russia prefers to use a narrow definition of national security which does not expressly cover its economic interests.[170] Yet, this has not prevented Russia from claiming in the *Russia – Traffic in Transit* dispute that narrowly drafted Security Exceptions under Article XXI GATT (1994) are nonreviewable.[171] The WTO panel avoided consideration of the motivations of Russia to impose trade restrictions on specific goods rather than a complete embargo, which leaves the question of their economic dimension open.[172]

3.1.4 *The Approach of India*

On multiple occasions, India has argued that coercive measures are unlikely to help resolve differences between the states.[173] At the same time, India has complied with the UN Security Council sanctions resolutions but also implemented unilateral restrictions on imports or exports in response to undesirable actions or criticism by neighboring countries.

Indian legislation grants the central government[174] (more specifically, the Directorate General of Foreign Trade) a broad authority to prohibit,

a Foreign State, an Association and/or Union of States, and/or a Governmental (Intergovernmental) Institution of a Foreign State or Association and/or Union of States (June 8, 2020).

170 See more chapter 4, section 4.1.4.

171 *Russia – Measures Concerning Traffic in Transit* (April 5, 2019) WTO Panel Report WT/DS512/R/Add.1, ANNEX C – 3 [47].

172 See more chapter 6, section 6.3.

173 Felix Hett and Moshe Wien (eds), Between Principles and Pragmatism Perspectives on the Ukraine Crisis from Brazil, India, China and South Africa (Friedrich Ebert Stiftung, May 2015) 6 https://library.fes.de/pdf-files/id-moe/11354.pdf.

174 The central government means the union government created by the constitution of India as the legislative, executive, and judicial authority of the union of twenty-eight states and seven union territories, collectively called the Republic of India.

restrict, or otherwise regulate the import and export of goods. In particular, the Foreign Trade Policy 2015–20, extended to 31 March 2023, states that exports and imports are "free," except when they are regulated by way of "prohibition," "restriction," or exclusive trading. Restrictions and prohibitions on export and import can be imposed, where necessary, for different purposes, including the protection of trade of fissionable material or material from which they are derived; or the prevention of traffic in arms, ammunition, and implements of war.[175] Nothing in the Foreign Trade Policy mentions other security-related objectives.

The central government can also restrict trade with other countries by imposing "digital" restrictions. Section 69A of the Information Technology Act (IT Act) (2000), read with the relevant provisions of the Information Technology Rules (IT Rules) (2009), allows the central government to block public access to an intermediary "in the interest of sovereignty and integrity of India, defence of India, security of the State, friendly relations with foreign States or public order or for preventing incitement to the commission of any cognisable offence relating to above."[176] The Supreme Court of India emphasized the distinction between the security of the state and the maintenance of public order and has observed that only serious and aggravated forms of public order can be calculated to endanger the state's security.[177] After considering the earlier decisions on the question of the meaning of the expressions, "law and order," "public order," and "security of the State," the Supreme Court of India also observed that "one has to imagine three concentric circles: Law and order represents the largest circle within which is the next circle representing public order and the smallest circle represents the security of the State."[178] Thus, accordingly, the security of the state in India should be understood as limited to the most severe threats.

In addition, India also adopts restrictions against nonstate actors. The Unlawful Activities (Prevention) Act (UAPA) (1967) serves as a platform under which India has sanctioned illegal entities, terrorist organizations, and individuals. The UAPA was developed as an anti-terrorism law.[179] In

175 India New Foreign Trade Policy (2015–20).
176 IT Act (2000).
177 Ibid.
178 *Ananta Hari v State of West Bengal* [1972] AIR 1256, [1972] SCC (1) 580, 5 relying on the case *Madhu Limave v Sub-Divisional Magistrate, Monghyr and Ors* [1966] 1 SCR 709 (2), [1970] 3 SCR 746.
179 Deepali Bhandari and Deeksha Pokhriyal, 'The Continuing Threat of India's Unlawful Activities Prevention Act to Free Speech' (*Jurist*, June 2, 2020) www.jurist.org/commentary/2020/06/bhandari-pokhriyal-uapa-free-speech/.

particular, it allows the central government to freeze the assets and other economic resources, prevent entry into or transit through the territory, and prevent the direct or indirect supply, sale, or transfer of arms and ammunition to particular individuals or entities. India has been relying on the provisions of the UAPA to implement UN Security Council sanctions resolutions and adopt unilateral measures against terrorists.[180]

Remarkably, while defining the terrorist act, the UAPA refers, among others, to "any act with intent to threaten or likely to threaten the unity, integrity, security, economic security, or sovereignty of India."[181] Thus, the UAPA differentiates between "economic security" and "security." The term "economic security" was added to the UAPA together with other amendments in 2012[182] and is stated to include "financial, monetary and fiscal stability, security of means of production and distribution, food security, livelihood security, energy security, ecological and environmental security."[183] The UAPA does not define the term "security." However, the presence of the reference to "economic security" delimits and limits the scope of the term "security" since the two are drafted as different legal grounds. Given a broad definition of "economic security," the term "security" seems to be more aligned with a traditional definition of national security interests related to, among others, defense and military matters.

India does not have a consolidated list of sanctions. Under the UAPA, the central government should notify a list of individuals, groups, and organizations that are suspected of being or that are classified as terrorist organizations.[184] The list has to be periodically amended. Furthermore, unlike the US or the EU, India has not always officially specified the reasons for and the aims of its restrictive measures. Therefore, it might be difficult to understand in which cases India adopts the measures to protect its national security and what exactly it considers to be a threat to its security.

Pakistan has continuously been deemed a threat to India's interests,[185] in particular, because of territorial disputes over the Kashmir region since

180 Government of India, Ministry of Home Affairs, CTCR Division, Order on Procedure for Implementation of Section 51A of the Unlawful Activities (Prevention) Act, 1967 File No 14014/01/2019/CFT (March 14, 2019).

181 Ibid.

182 Unlawful Activities (Prevention) Amendment Act No 3 (2013).

183 Unlawful Activities (Prevention) Act (1967).

184 Ibid.

185 Ambika Khanna, 'Devising an Indian policy on Sanctions for Pakistan' *Gateway House* (April 30, 2020) www.gatewayhouse.in/indian-policy-sanctions-pakistan/; India's

1947.[186] This suggests that the measures related to the relationship between India and Pakistan have been at least in part taken to protect India's security. To illustrate, in February 2019, India withdrew the MFN status granted to Pakistan after the Pulwama attack in Kashmir.[187] Bilateral trade between India and Pakistan stood at quite a low point, which means that the withdrawal of MFN status could not seriously impact trade between the two countries.[188] Such a decision can be yet considered a unilateral restrictive measure adopted by India for foreign policy and potential security motives.

Furthermore, starting in 2019, there was pressure on India's government to toughen its sanctions regime and consider imposing unilateral sanctions on Pakistan.[189] The first steps were to strengthen the extant of the UAPA to allow for the specific and targeted imposition of unilateral sanctions.[190] The most fundamental of these changes empower the central government to designate individuals as terrorists, merely if it believes so, leaving little to no recourse for them to protest their designation.[191]

In January 2020, the Directorate General of Foreign Trade issued Notification No 39/2015-2020, amending the import policy of refined palm oil and refined palmolein from "free" to "restricted."[192] This notification applies to imports from all countries.[193] However, such a move primarily hit Malaysia, the main supplier to India of refined palm oil and

National Security Strategy (Hooda Report), Indian National Congress 23 https://manifesto.inc.in/pdf/national_security_strategy_gen_hooda.pdf.

186 Kelly Buchanan, 'FALQs: Article 370 and the Removal of Jammu and Kashmir's Special Status' (Library of Congress, October 3, 2019) https://blogs.loc.gov/law/2019/10/falqs-article-370-and-the-removal-of-jammu-and-kashmirs-special-status/.

187 'Pulwama Terror Attack: India withdraws Most Favoured Nation' *The Times of India* (February 15, 2019) https://timesofindia.indiatimes.com/india/pulwama-attack-india-withdraws-mnf-status-from-pakistan/articleshow/68004450.cms.

188 Mahua Venkatesh, 'India's Withdrawal of MFN Status for Pakistan Has More to Do with Diplomacy Than Trade' *The Print* (February 15, 2019) https://theprint.in/theprint-essential/indias-withdrawal-of-mfn-status-for-pakistan-has-more-to-do-with-diplomacy-than-trade/193442/.

189 Ambika Khanna, 'Can Sanctions Solve the Pakistan Problem' *Gateway House* (April 30, 2020) www.gatewayhouse.in/sanctions-pakistan/.

190 Nitika Khaitan, 'The UAPA amendments: What it Really Means' *Hindustan Times* (August 9, 2019) www.hindustantimes.com/analysis/the-uapa-amendments-what-it-really-means/story-9gOsDNk1syqxyYd0iFeHDN.html.

191 Ibid.

192 Ministry of Commerce and Industry, 'Buying of Palm Oil from Malaysia' (PIB Delhi, February 7, 2020) www.pib.gov.in/PressReleseDetailm.aspx?PRID=1602417.

193 Ibid.

palmolein.[194] India's government and industry sources confirmed that the government was seeking to target Malaysia after the criticism of India by Malaysian Prime Minister Mahathir Mohamad, who had said that India "invaded and occupied" Kashmir.[195]

Besides, India's recent initiatives aimed at self-reliance in digital technologies and the development of an independent digital economy[196] have also been strengthened with "digital sanctions." During the ongoing border tensions between India and China in eastern Ladakh (a part of the larger Kashmir region), the Ministry of Electronics and Information Technology of India (MEITY) issued a notification on June 29, 2020 and announced its decision to disallow the usage in India of fifty-nine applications, among them, popular mobile and nonmobile internet-enabled services having Chinese origins, including applications like TikTok, CamScanner, Shareit, UC Browser, Club Factory, and Xender.[197] The MEITY notification stated that the actions were taken under Section 69A of the IT Act, read with the relevant provisions of the IT Rules 2009, since, based on the information available with MEITY, the banned applications were involved in activities which were prejudicial "to the sovereignty, integrity, defense, and security of India."[198] In particular, the banned applications were said to be indulging in stealth and transmission of users' data in an unauthorized manner to servers outside of India and were generally violative of Indian data privacy norms. Accordingly, "[t]he compilation of these data, its mining and profiling by elements hostile to national security and defense of India, which ultimately impinges upon the sovereignty and integrity of India, is a matter of profound and immediate concern which requires emergency measures."[199]

In 2021, invoking cybersecurity concerns and the need to limit access to sensitive data, India also adopted a de facto import ban on power

194 'Government Imposes Restriction on Palm Oil Import after Malaysia's Criticism of PM Modi's Action on Kashmir, CAA' *Business Today* (January 9, 2020) /www.businesstoday.in/current/economy-politics/govt-imposes-restriction-on-palm-oil-import-after-malaysia-criticism-of-pm-modi-action-on-kashmir-caa/story/393445.html.

195 Ibid.

196 Neha Mishra, 'India: Leading or Thwarting Data Governance and Digital Trade?' (*Hinrich Foundation*, August 10, 2021) www.hinrichfoundation.com/research/article/digital/india-leading-or-thwarting-data-governance-and-digital-trade/.

197 Ministry of Electronics and IT, 'Government Bans 59 Mobile Apps which are Prejudicial to Sovereignty and Integrity of India, Defence of India, Security of State and Public Order' (PIB Delhi, June 29, 2020) https://pib.gov.in/PressReleasePage.aspx?PRID=1635206.

198 Ibid.

199 Ibid.

equipment from China[200] and began 5G trials excluding Chinese technology.[201] In February 2022, the Directorate General of Foreign Trade issued Notification No 39/2015-2020, announcing the ban on the import of drones, thereby shutting down a growing market for China's SZ DJI Technology Co, the leading drone maker in the world.[202] Given the nature and design of such measures targeting China, they seem to be at least in part aimed at promoting India's domestic industry rather than grounded purely on cybersecurity concerns.[203]

Consequently, the central government in India has broad authority to restrict trade with other countries or adopt targeted sanctions against companies and individuals in national security interests. In practice, however, India does not often refer to the objective of protecting its national security interests while adopting trade restrictions. The possible connection to security objectives discussed above usually derives from the geopolitical background of particular situations and the nature of the measures applied rather than based on the analysis of specific sanctions documents. Any disproportionate measures, including those adopted in national security interests, are, in principle, subject to judicial review in India,[204] yet the court practice on this issue is limited and not unambiguous.[205]

Given that India also prefers to incorporate in its trade agreements the Security Exceptions limited to specific situations such as military or defense matters, situations of war, or other emergencies, in line with the WTO agreements, it can be suggested that India prefers to use a narrow definition of national security dealing with its counterparties.[206] The recent example of using "digital sanctions" by India seems to

[200] Sankalp Phartiyal, 'India Holds up Wireless Approvals for China-Made Devices, Delaying Launches' *Reuters* (May 7, 2021) www.reuters.com/business/media-telecom/exclusive-india-holds-up-wireless-approvals-china-made-devices-delaying-launches-2021-05-07/.

[201] Ministry of Communications, 'Telecom Department Gives go-ahead for 5G Technology and Spectrum Trials' (Press Release, May 4, 2021) www.pib.gov.in/PressReleasePage.aspx?PRID=1715927.

[202] Directorate General of Foreign Trade, Notification of ITC (HS), 2022 – Schedule –1 (Import Policy) (February 9, 2022) Notification No 39/2015-2020.

[203] Matthew P Goodman, Matthew Reynolds, and Julianne Fittipaldi, 'Economic Security in Emerging Markets' (*CSIS Briefs*, May 2022) 4 https://csis-website-prod.s3.amazonaws.com/s3fs-public/publication/220517_Goodman_Economic_Security.pdf?5RvPqxIMcJNgIl0fb2V3rYd0MKL.HTr.

[204] See eg *AK Kaul & Anr v Union of India & Anr* (1995) AIR 1403, (1995) SCC (4) 73.

[205] See eg Mayur Suresh, 'The Slow Erosion of Fundamental Rights: How Romila Thapar v Union of India Highlights what is Wrong with the UAPA' (2019) 3(2) Indian L Rev 212.

[206] See more chapter 4, section 4.1.5.

challenge this assumption. Thus, it remains to be seen how the region's situation, particularly India's relationship with China, will influence India's further practice of applying unilateral measures.

3.1.5 The Approach of China

China used to oppose sanctions, in part for ideological reasons.[207] However, with China's economy growing rapidly since the 1980s, its economic leverage has dramatically increased, thereby expanding its capacity to adopt economic sanctions to affect other states' policies.[208] As China grew economically more powerful, so did its diplomatic power because its role in international trade became central.[209] Thus, Chinese strategists started to explore new ways to deploy China's own economic might for strategic benefit.[210]

Until recently, China has reverted to vague threats, variation in leadership visits, control of the media and state-owned enterprises, selective application of domestic regulations, and other informal measures rather than formal economic sanctions. Different from the US and the EU, which publicly announced the adoption of economic sanctions to achieve particular national security or foreign policy goals, China used to publicly deny that its economic measures were aimed at achieving any political objectives.[211] This allowed China to plausibly have greater flexibility to escalate and de-escalate the conflict if necessary.

To illustrate, Taiwan is the most sensitive issue in China's foreign relations. In January 2010, China threatened sanctions on US companies that would sell arms to Taiwan. China claimed that by selling arms to Taiwan (by US companies), the US had "damaged China's national security."[212] Even

207 Andrew Rennemo, 'How China Joined the Sanctions Game' *The Diplomat* (February 8, 2021) https://thediplomat.com/2021/02/how-china-joined-the-sanctions-game/.

208 Tong Zhao, 'Sanction Experience and Sanction Behavior: An Analysis of Chinese Perception and Behavior on Economic Sanctions' (2010) 16(3) Contemporary Politics 263, 272.

209 Nikolay Anguelov, *Economic Sanctions v Soft Power: Lessons from North Korea, Myanmar, and the Middle East* (Palgrave Macmillan 2015) 142.

210 Peter Harrell, Elizabeth Rosenberg, and Edoardo Saravalle, 'China's Use of Coercive Economic Measures' (Center for a New American Security, June 2018) 5 https://s3.us-east-1.amazonaws.com/files.cnas.org/documents/China_Use_FINAL-1.pdf?mtime=20180604161240&focal=none.

211 Christina Lai, 'Acting One Way and Talking Another: China's Coercive Economic Diplomacy in East Asia and Beyond' (2018) 31(2) The Pacific Rev 169, 170.

212 China Threatens US Firms with Sanctions over Taiwan Arms (*RIA Novostiat*, January 30, 2010) http://en.rian.ru/world/20100130/157723449.html.

though China did not apply any sanctions against the US in 2010, the sales of arms to Taiwan by US companies decreased,[213] suggesting that the sole threat had an effect of a sanction. In 2021, China disallowed imports of Lithuanian products after the Lithuanian government approved the establishment of a representative office under the name of "Taiwan."[214] Such cases confirm the pattern of behavior where China uses economic coercion to signal to the international community and the Chinese public that it would not tolerate any foreign interference in its affairs. Poh also analyzed eight cases of unilateral Chinese sanctions between 2008 and 2017 against France, the US, Japan, Norway, the Philippines, Vietnam, Taiwan, and South Korea to conclude that such measures were signaling a political dispute rather than aimed to affect trade and investment between China and its target significantly.[215] China's restriction on rare earth minerals exports to Japan in 2010 is an exception. It can be argued that such measures were aimed to advantage Chinese electronics manufacturers compared with foreign rivals and thus were at least in part economically motivated.[216] Japan collaborated with the US and the EU on a WTO case against China on the matter, which the challengers won in 2014.[217]

Yet, since 2020, China has started formalizing some of its coercive economic measures. In accordance with the Foreign Trade Law and the NSL, it has established the Unreliable Entity List (UEL), under which restrictive measures might be imposed on designated foreign entities, including companies, other organizations, or individuals, for activities that are contrary to China's national interest.[218] On September 19, 2020, upon approval of the State Council, China's Ministry of Commerce (MOFCOM) released the Provisions on the UEL.[219] According to this, foreign entities may be designated in the UEL for their conduct in

[213] Ibid.

[214] Tsugami Toshiya, 'Three Things to Know About China's "Economic Security"' (*Nippon*, March 7, 2022) www.nippon.com/en/in-depth/a07902/.

[215] Angela Poh, *Sanctions with Chinese Characteristics: Rhetoric and Restraint in China's Diplomacy* (Amsterdam UP 2021) 191–217.

[216] Jost Wübbeke, 'China's Rare Earth Industry and End-Use: Supply Security and Innovation' in Ryan David Kiggins (ed.), *The Political Economy of Rare Earth Elements: Rising Powers and Technological Change* (Palgrave Macmillan UK 2015) 27.

[217] See more *China – Measures Related to the Exportation of Rare Earths, Tungsten and Molybdenum* (August 7, 2014) Appellate Body Report WT/DS431/AB/R WT/DS432/AB/R WT/DS433/AB/R.

[218] Laney Zhang, 'China: Government Releases Provisions on Unreliable Entity List Regime' (Library of Congress, October 9, 2020) www.loc.gov/law/foreign-news/article/china-government-releases-provisions-on-unreliable-entity-list-regime/.

[219] Ibid.

international economic, trade, and other related activities that are, among others, endangering China's national sovereignty, security, or development interests.[220] China's UEL regime shares the features of the economic sanctions, even though the MOFCOM has indicated that the UEL regime is not intended to target any particular country.[221] It can still be argued that the UEL is a direct response to increasing tensions in the US–China relationship, especially given that China first announced the UEL in May 2019, namely at the height of its trade dispute with the US and that the criteria for designation are formulated broad enough to include actions taken in response to the US economic sanctions against China.[222]

In addition, in response to the increased use of "secondary" economic sanctions[223] by the US, MOFCOM created a framework for "blocking" foreign sanctions against Chinese interests through the Rules on Counteracting Unjustified Extraterritorial Application of Foreign Legislation and Other Measures in January 2021 (hereafter the Blocking Rules).[224] The Blocking Rules were formulated in accordance with the NSL and aimed to (among others) counteract the impact on Chinese companies and citizens caused by the unjustified extraterritorial application of foreign legislation and other relevant measures. When seeking to determine whether there was an unjustified extraterritorial application of a foreign measure, its potential impact on China's national sovereignty, security and development interests, and other factors shall be considered. The issuance of the Blocking Rules signals that the Chinese government is making efforts to tackle various restrictions targeting China, relying, among others, on protecting China's security interests.

Finally, China decided to strengthen its legal "toolbox" for dealing with challenges and preventing risks concerning sanctions against it by

[220] Ibid.

[221] Ibid.

[222] Qingxiu Bu, 'China's Blocking Mechanism: The Unreliable Entity List' (2020) 19(3) J Intl Trade Law and Policy 159, 159.

[223] The US applies both "primary sanctions" and "secondary sanctions." US primary sanctions generally apply to transactions and/or entities that involve a "nexus to US jurisdiction." See Tom Ruys and Cedric Ryngaert, 'Secondary Sanctions: A Weapon out of Control? The International Legality of, and European Responses to, US Secondary Sanctions' (2020) BYIL 1, 4.

[224] Laney Zhang, 'China: Government Releases Provisions on Unreliable Entity List Regime' (Library of Congress, October 9, 2020) www.loc.gov/law/foreign-news/article/china-government-releases-provisions-on-unreliable-entity-list-regime/.

adopting the Anti-Foreign Sanctions Law.[225] The Anti-Foreign Sanctions Law is designed to "safeguard China's national sovereignty, security, and development interests."[226] According to Gao, the Anti-Foreign Sanctions Law significantly adds teeth to China's previous legislation because two measures – the UEL for foreign businesses and its blocking statute – were both "departmental rules which are much lower in the legislative hierarchy."[227] Thus, the adoption of the Anti-Foreign Sanctions Law demonstrates the importance that China attaches to the issue of its national security and signals to the rest of the world, especially the US, that China is serious about protecting its national interests.

In 2020 and 2021, China decided to sanction certain US companies and individuals involved in US arms sales to Taiwan and nongovernmental organizations involved in the turmoil in Hong Kong.[228] In response to the EU and US sanctions on individual Chinese officials and a Chinese entity based on findings of human rights violations in Xinjiang, China's Ministry of Foreign Affairs of China also announced new sanctions against specific individuals. The official English-language notices explained that the sanctioned persons and entities were deemed to have "severely harmed China's sovereignty and interests, and maliciously spread lies and disinformation."[229] From the limited announced enforcement cases under the Anti-Foreign Sanctions Law, it can be distilled that the Chinese government has taken actions against several US citizens (most of whom are US politicians), one US entity, and two US military contractors, that is, Raytheon Company and Lockheed Martin Space Systems Company for their weapon sales to the Taiwan Region.[230]

[225] Wang Jiangyu, 'An Offensive Defense: China's Anti-Foreign Sanctions Law' *Beijing Review* (June 18, 2021) www.bjreview.com/Opinion/Voice/202106/t20210618_800250032.html.

[226] Chinese Anti-Foreign Sanctions Law (2021).

[227] 'Could Business be Caught in the Crossfire of China's 'Legal Battle with the West?' *AP News* (June 9, 2021) https://apnews.com/article/china-933c947665ca463b85b4dd9375ceb18f.

[228] Laney Zhang, 'China: Government Releases Provisions on Unreliable Entity List Regime' (Library of Congress, October 9, 2020) www.loc.gov/law/foreign-news/article/china-government-releases-provisions-on-unreliable-entity-list-regime/.

[229] Nathan Bush and Ray Xu, 'China's Expanding Economic Sanctions Regime' (DLA Piper, March 31, 2021) www.dlapiper.com/en/romania/insights/publications/2021/03/chinas-expanding-economic-sanctions-regime/.

[230] Ministry of the Foreign Affairs of the People's Republic of China, 'Foreign Ministry Spokesperson Wang Wenbin's Regular Press Conference' (February 21, 2022) www.fmprc.gov.cn/mfa_eng/xwfw_665399/s2510_665401/2511_665403/202202/t20220221_10644075.html. See also 'Anti-Foreign Sanction Law what MNCs Need to Know about' (Dentons, March 31, 2022) www.dentons.com.

Notably, decisions of a national security review are not subject to administrative reconsideration or judicial review in China. The Supreme People's Court (SPC) clarified the scope of judicial review of governmental actions in the 2018 SPC Interpretation (hereafter the Interpretation). The Interpretation sets out national security among the categories of exclusions from review, all of which had been gray areas where judges made inconsistent decisions, such as public or national security investigations pursuant to the criminal procedure law.[231] Furthermore, in *HKSAR v Lai Chee Ying* (2021), the Court also ruled that it had no jurisdiction to review the controversial Law of the People's Republic of China on Safeguarding National Security in the Hong Kong Special Administrative Region.[232]

Thus, the developments in the Chinese sanctions policy highlight that the Chinese government has a broad authority to impose economic sanctions against other states (but also entities and individuals) in response to foreign conduct that might impact its national interests. It can be argued that China has been shifting from a defensive to a more proactive strategy, as evidenced by China's engagement in multilateral, regional, and bilateral affairs, as well as domestic regulatory developments on sanctions, export control, and retaliatory measures.[233] Formally, such mechanisms remind the "blocking" strategies of the EU (including the amendment of a blocking statute and the development of an anti-coercion mechanism adopted to mitigate the impact of foreign sanctions). In practice, however, sanctions with Chinese characteristics can be more far-reaching and grounded on economic rather than security motives, at least given the broad scope of discretion granted to the Chinese government and the lack of adequate checks and controls on its exercise.

Should the question of whether such measures comply with China's international commitments arise, it is necessary to note that most of China's RTAs limit the application of Security Exceptions to military and defense matters, situations of war, and other emergencies in international relations, but also the protection of critical public infrastructure, such as

231 Interpretation of the Supreme People's Court on the Application of the Administrative Procedure Law of the People's Republic of China (2018).

232 The Law of the People's Republic of China on Safeguarding National Security in the Hong Kong Special Administrative Region, applied to the HKSAR (June 30, 2020).

233 Weihuan Zhou, Huiqin Jiang, and Zhe Chen, 'Trade v Security: Recent Developments of Global Trade Rules and China's Policy and Regulatory Responses from Defensive to Proactive' (2022) World Trade Rev 1, 19.

communication infrastructure.[234] This suggests that China tries to preserve more regulatory space for actions in the areas vital for its national interests in a more specific and regulated way than including a broadly drafted exception clause.[235] The unwillingness to officially acknowledge the breach of its international commitments might partially explain why China used to have a preference for informal restrictive measures in the past and why it remains careful with imposing unilateral sanctions today, treating them as a defense tool rather than a typical foreign policy response. Notably, China projects itself as a keen supporter of the WTO, while in parallel, it aims to end the US and European dominance in the WTO by building institutions and transnational economic ties and using soft power.[236] More developments on the matter can follow depending on China's economic progress, the increase of its trade and technology leverage, and the outcomes of its ongoing geopolitical and trade conflicts with other states.

3.1.6 *Weaponization of Trade*

Economic sanctions have long been an important foreign policy tool for the US and the EU. Russia, India, and China used to apply restrictive measures against their contracting parties in specific areas and sectors, arguably where they believed they had more economic leverage to affect a target country's market or send the proper political signal. Yet, the pressure that the Western sanctions put on Russia because of its war in Ukraine, the disputes with China over Hong Kong,[237] the trade tension between China and the US,[238] the disputes with India over Kashmir,[239] and the competition for technological leadership seem to have prompted Russia, India, and China to expand their sanction policies and to develop more specific sanctions regulations, in particular as a tit-for-tat step in the interstate power game. Such developments in states' sanction practices indicate the shift in the expectations about the identity of

[234] See more chapter 4, section 4.1.6.

[235] Chapter 4, sections 4.1.6 and 4.2.6.

[236] Gregory Shaffer and Gao Henry, 'A New Chinese Economic Order?' (2020) 23(3) J Intl Econ L 607, 612.

[237] See *US – Origin Marking Requirements* DS597.

[238] See eg *US – Certain Measures on Steel and Aluminium Products (China)* (December 9, 2022) WTO Panel Report WT/DS544/R.

[239] See eg Hilal Mir, 'Kashmir Situation Likely to Deteriorate in 2021: Report' (AA, February 23, 2021) www.aa.com.tr/en/asia-pacific/kashmir-situation-likely-to-deteriorate-in-2021-report/2153865.

sanctioners and their motives for sanction implementation. They also signal a shift in the understanding of the identity of selected targets and of how the restrictions on trade with them can contribute to protecting states' national interests, including security interests. To this end, the US and the EU, which have extensive experience in sanctioning smaller countries, are still about to experience the effects of severe trade-restrictive measures against significant economies, such as China and Russia. Thus, many more questions and disputes might arise regarding the application of economic sanctions worldwide and the compliance of such measures with states' international commitments.

The differences between the EU approach and the approach of other WTO members to implementing economic sanctions derive from the nature of the EU as a multilateral organization and the institutionalization of its comprehensive concept of threats to its common values and interests, including security interests, which promises to clash with the single-mindedness of other Selected WTO Members in pursuing their national objectives.

The EU practice confirms that the adoption of restrictive measures within the EU is limited to specific situations, generally related to armed conflicts, preventing the proliferation of WMD, upholding respect for human rights, democracy, the rule of law, and good governance, and protecting cyberspace. The EU does not often ground the adoption of economic sanctions on the need to protect its security interests, even though some of its official acts indicate that the objectives of the EU sanctions can directly or indirectly contribute to the EU's security.

In essence, the utilization of restrictive measures should contribute to "the consolidation of the autonomy, capability, and coherence/cohesion of the EU as an international actor."[240] This partially explains why the EU prefers to apply economic sanctions to pursue more universally recognized objectives, including protecting international peace and security, and attempts to be more specific about the reasons for and objectives of utilizing trade restrictions against other countries. This can also explain why the EU expressly states in its documents that unilateral sanctions cannot serve economic motives, in line with Article 21 of TEU.

At the same time, the other Selected WTO Members seem to be silent on the question of economic motives of sanctions or even expressly rely on the protection of their national economies or economic security as a ground

[240] Francesco Giumelli, Fabian Hoffmann, and Anna Książczaková, 'The When, What, Where and Why of European Union Sanctions' (2021) 30(1) Eur Security 1, 2.

for applying trade restrictions. To illustrate, the US regulatory framework does not prevent the US President from imposing sanctions to pursue national economic interests. The IEEPA differentiates between the threat to US national security, the threat to US foreign policy, and the threat to the US economy as separate grounds for declaring a national emergency and subsequently imposing economic sanctions. However, in practice, many situations in which the US President imposed economic sanctions were labeled as a threat to US foreign policy, national security, and the economy, making it impossible to draw a line between these different concepts. Respective domestic legal frameworks in the US, India, Russia, and China generally grant their presidents or governments broad powers to impose unilateral measures. They do not ensure that economic sanctions exclude economic considerations or hybrid motives. This exacerbates competitive and confrontational behavior and can lead to interstate disputes over the legitimacy of the restrictive measures of these members aimed at achieving foreign policy and national security objectives.

Notably, the US is generally open about intertwining its interests in protecting national security and the economy. As its practice demonstrates, it is ready to push the boundaries of Security Exceptions to justify its trade restrictions on both WTO and RTA levels.[241] The return of Trump's Administration in 2025 has further reignited concerns about the possibility of new far-reaching trade restrictions from the US on national security grounds. At the same time, India, Russia, and China remain reluctant to recognize the economic objectives, and sometimes even political motives, of their trade restrictions. Given the opacity of the objectives of certain sanctions policies and their contradictory nature, these WTO members can still be expected to invoke Security Exceptions under WTO agreements or RTAs, claiming the objective to protect their national security but "smuggling" in a measure designed to pursue economic motives, such as protecting the domestic market or a specific industry. To illustrate, Indian strategic trade controls in the technology sector aimed at China, China's ban on rare earth mineral exports to Japan, and Russia's decision to restrict trade in agriculture in response to Western sanctions seem to have both protectionist and national security motives. Yet, different from the US, the preference of India, Russia, and China to draft Security Exceptions in their RTAs in a narrower manner[242] could also signal that instead of invoking

[241] Chapter 2, section 2.4.2; chapter 4, section 4.1.1.
[242] Chapter 4, sections 4.1.4, 4.1.5, and 4.1.6.

Security Exceptions, they would be prepared to revert to other means to justify similar policies.

3.2 Investment Screening

Despite the advantages of globalization and the free flow of FDI, states have concerns that unconditional openness to FDI would make them more vulnerable, especially in the rapidly changing geopolitical environment and intensified systemic competition between the states of the Atlantic West and the emerging economies.[243] Genuine concerns arise from the possibility that FDI can make a host state dependent on a foreign supplier of goods or services in areas crucial to its normal functioning, or can imply the transfer of technology or expertise to a foreign entity that another state could deploy, or can introduce the capability for surveillance or sabotage into the provision of certain services or goods.[244] Notably, the WTO agreements do not cover FDI-related issues. Therefore, WTO members are well within their rights to restrict the flow of FDI into their territories in the interests of national security. Specific limitations on such investment restrictions can be found in IIAs adopted on bilateral or regional levels.

Restrictions on FDI are generally aimed at the investment pre-establishment phase. Some IIAs provide market access guarantees, allowing foreign investment from a home country to enter the market of a host country, for example MFN and national treatment principles. FDI restrictions at the investment pre-establishment phase could potentially be found to be in breach of such IIAs. In addition, since the perception of states' security concerns is related to FDI changes, certain foreign investments might be prohibited in the host country during the post-establishment stage. Such measures can violate not only MFN and national treatment principles but also obligations not to expropriate without compensation, "fair and equitable treatment," and "full protection and security."

Under different conditions, FDI could, in principle, affect specific sectors of state activity that are directly relevant to military and defense

[243] OECD Secretariat, 'Transparency, Predictability and Accountability for Investment Screening Mechanisms' (OECD, May 27, 2021) [2] www.oecd.org/daf/inv/investment-policy/2009-Guidelines-webinar-May-2021-background-note.pdf.

[244] Carlos Esplugues Mota, 'A More Targeted Approach to Foreign Direct Investment: The Establishment of Screening Systems on National Security Grounds' (2018) 15 Braz J Intl L 440, 444–445.

security.[245] In particular, national security concerns could originate from: the risk of the dominance of the supply chain in specific strategic sectors; foreign surveillance; economic espionage; and the movement of weapons and soldiers. However, it is only since the beginning of the twentieth century that this question has received broad attention among investment policymakers.[246] In particular, UNCTAD identified at least twenty instances of planned foreign takeovers with a value exceeding $50 million that were blocked or withdrawn for national security reasons from 2016 to September 2019.[247] Ultimately, the COVID-19 pandemic has been critical in severely affecting global value chains.[248] In particular, the outbreak of COVID-19 has exposed the risks of reliance on foreign markets for various crucial products and raised concerns that important assets can now be acquired at depressed prices. The fears of "opportunistic takeovers" by foreign investors have encouraged more WTO members to tighten FDI screening mechanisms to protect their health sector and industries in other sectors considered particularly important in the crisis[249] or severely affected by the crisis, especially in the context of depreciated value.

For the most part, policy attention on the unlimited flow of FDI has resulted in reforms or in the introduction of acquisition- and ownership-related policies to safeguard countries' security interests (most often in the form of market access measures, the maintenance of state monopolies, equity limitations, and investment screening mechanisms (ISMs)), allowing governments to prohibit the implementation of specific foreign investment proposals, to require their unwinding, or to impose

245 Martin Nettesheim, 'Screening for What Threat: Preserving "Public Order and Security," Securing Reciprocity in International Trade, or Supporting Certain Social, Environmental, or Industrial Policies?' in Steffen Hindelang and Andreas Moberg (eds.), *YSEC Yearbook of Socio-Economic Constitutions 2020: A Common European Law on Investment Screening (CELIS)* (Springer International Publishing 2021) 484.

246 Frederic Wehrlé and Joachim Pohl, 'Investment Policies Related to National Security: A Survey of Country Practices' (2016) 2016/02 OECD Working Papers on International Investment, OECD Publishing 10.

247 UNCTAD, 'National Security-Related Screening Mechanisms for Foreign Investment. An Analysis of Recent Policy Developments' (December 2019) 2 https://unctad.org/system/files/official-document/diaepcbinf2019d7_en.pdf.

248 Byeongho Lim and others, 'Impacts of Reverse Global Value Chain (GVC) Factors on Global Trade and Energy Market' (2021) 14 Energies 1 https://doi.org/10.3390/en14123417.

249 Christine Zhenwei Qiang and others, 'Foreign Direct Investment and Global Value Chains in the Wake of COVID-19: Preparing for the New Normal' (*World Bank Blogs*, May 22, 2020) https://blogs.worldbank.org/psd/foreign-direct-investment-and-global-value-chains-wake-covid-19-preparing-new-normal.

mitigation measures.[250] ISMs, for the purposes of this section, refer to the requirements under the host state's law that foreign investors attain approval before (or concurrently with) making a new investment.[251] Even though most ISMs apply to a new transaction involving FDI, the legislation of some states allows for a retrospective screening of FDI that has already been established in a host state.[252] ISMs based on national security grounds are becoming increasingly popular nowadays,[253] making their analysis especially important for understanding the national security concerns of different WTO members in the area of FDI.

Most states use two distinct approaches to identify which investments subject to their policies are related to national security. The first approach is to set specific rules for investment in certain sensitive sectors, such as real estate, telecommunications, or energy infrastructure.[254] The second approach refers to threats to national security in general. Accordingly, whether an individual transaction raises national security threats and is subject to investment review can be deduced from the state's definition of national security.[255] Yet, in practicc, instead of defining "national security interests" that can trigger an investment review, states tend to offer a vague "clarifying definition" or include a potential illustrative list of "threats to national security," such as investments from foreign countries that do not respect democracy and the rule of law.[256]

While the discussion over national security reviews is mainly related to inward investment, the screening (or other mechanisms of selection) of outward investment also exists. For example, the Chinese government has devised an internal vetting system for SOEs that become eligible to

250 OECD Secretariat, 'Transparency, Predictability and Accountability for Investment Screening Mechanisms' (OECD, May 27, 2021) [7] www.oecd.org/daf/inv/investment-policy/2009-Guidelines-webinar-May-2021-background-note.pdf.

251 Jonathan Bonnitcha, 'The Return of Investment Screening as a Policy Tool' (IISD, December 19, 2020) www.iisd.org/itn/en/2020/12/19/the-return-of-investment-screening-as-a-policy-tool-jonathan-bonnitcha/.

252 For example, in the US. See more Tania Voon and Dean Merriman, 'Incoming: How International Investment Law Constrains Foreign Investment Screening' (2023) 24 J World Investment & Trade 75.

253 Carlos Esplugues Mota, 'A More Targeted Approach to Foreign Direct Investment: The Establishment of Screening Systems on National Security Grounds' (2018) 15 Braz J Intl L 440, 455.

254 Mikko Rajavuori and Kaisa Huhta, 'Investment Screening: Implications for the Energy Sector and Energy Security' (2020) 144 Energy Policy 1, 3.

255 Frederic Wehrlé and Joachim Pohl, 'Investment Policies Related to National Security: A Survey of Country Practices' (2016) 2016/02 OECD Working Papers on International Investment, OECD Publishing 19.

256 Ibid 20–21.

invest in projects abroad.[257] In the same vein, with diplomatic tensions between the US and China continuing, the US is considering additional tools to safeguard national security, including the review of investments that US-based businesses make in China and other countries of concern.[258] For example, the US has made it more difficult for US semiconductor companies to invest in China.[259] Furthermore, in 2023, the US started to control certain types of outbound investments in sectors like microelectronics, quantum information technologies, and artificial intelligence in "countries of concern," including China.[260] Since these investments could potentially threaten US national security, they will either need to comply with specific notification rules or will be prohibited. The EU also considers examining additional tools necessary for outbound investment control.[261] This research, however, focuses on screening mechanisms for inward investment only. Furthermore, in addition to the national security review, states generally subject cross-border transactions involving FDI to competition review,[262] which goes beyond the scope of this chapter.

3.2.1 The US Approach

The US is both the world's largest foreign direct investor and the largest beneficiary of FDI.[263] The US ISMs have faced a constant shift in national

[257] Georgios Dimitropoulos, 'National Security: The Role of Investment Screening Mechanisms' in Julien Chaisse and others (eds.), *Handbook of International Investment Law and Policy* (Springer Nature Singapore Pte Ltd 2019) 11 https://ssrn.com/abstract=3538735.

[258] Thilo Hanemann and others, 'National Committee on U.S. China Relations, An Outbound Investment Screening Regime for the United States?' (2022) Report by the US–China Investment Project 21 https://rhg.com/wp-content/uploads/2022/01/RHG_TWS_2022_US-Outbound-Investment.pdf.

[259] Text – HR4346 – 117th Congress (2021–2022): Supreme Court Security Funding Act of 2022 (August 9, 2022) Congress.gov.

[260] US President EO on Addressing United States Investments in Certain National Security Technologies and Products in Countries of Concern (August 9, 2023).

[261] European Commission, Communication from the Commission to the European Parliament, the Council, the European Economic and Social Committee and the Committee of the Regions (October 18, 2022) COM(2022) 548 final 8.

[262] Felix I Lessambo, *Mergers in the Global Markets: A Comparative Approach to the Competition and National Security Laws among the US, EU, and China* (Springer International Publishing 2020) 4.

[263] OECD, Foreign Direct Investment Statistics: Data, Analysis and Forecasts www.oecd.org/investment/statistics.htm#:~:text=Top%20recipients%20of%20FDI%20inflows,Kingdom%20(USD%2036%20billion).

security perceptions of the US and the global economic order, with the growing rise of economies like China and state-led entities playing an increasingly active role in the global markets.[264] In 1988, the Exon-Florio Amendment allowed the President to block foreign acquisitions posing national security risks without first declaring an emergency.[265] The amendment was claimed to be motivated by Japan's acquisitions of certain US companies that could supposedly challenge the US economic leadership.[266] The Defense Production Act (1950), the statutory cornerstone of ISMs, was further modified by the Foreign Investment and National Security Act (FINSA) (2007).[267] Such a shift was pushed by the Dubai Ports World controversy when the Dubai-based, state-owned firm planned to acquire control of primary US port operations, which was believed to increase the risk of a terrorist attack on the US.[268]

The FINSA expanded the legal meaning of "national security" to include critical infrastructure and required the Committee on Foreign Investment in the US (CFIUS) (responsible for conducting a national security review) to investigate all foreign investment deals in which the overseas entity is owned or controlled by a foreign power. In particular, the FINSA allows the President, acting through the CFIUS, to review and investigate certain transactions whereby a foreign person acquires control over a US business to determine the impact of these transactions on US national security.[269] The FINSA indicates that "national security" encompasses issues relating to "homeland security" and "critical infrastructure."[270] It understands "critical infrastructure" as "systems and assets, whether physical or virtual, so vital to the United States that the incapacity or destruction of such systems or assets would have a debilitating impact on national security."[271] The President and the CFIUS are granted the authority to review any "covered transaction," broadly defined as "any transaction that is proposed or pending after

[264] Wei Yin, 'A Comparison of the US and EU Regulatory Responses to China's State Capitalism: Implication, Issue and Direction' (2020) 19(1) Asia Europe Journal: Studies on Common Policy Challenges 1, 5.

[265] Ibid.

[266] Ibid.

[267] Foreign Investment and National Security Act (2007).

[268] Council on Foreign Relations, 'Foreign Investment and U.S. National Security' (August 28, 2018) www.cfr.org/backgrounder/foreign-investment-and-us-national-security.

[269] Foreign Investment and National Security Act (2007).

[270] Ibid.

[271] Ibid.

August 23, 1988, by or with any foreign person, which could result in control of a US business by a foreign person."[272]

The CFIUS reviews focus on genuine national security concerns a covered transaction raises, not on other national interests.[273] In particular, the CFIUS has to identify all national security considerations (i.e. facts and circumstances that have potential national security implications) to assess whether the transaction poses a national security risk.[274] Section 721(f) of the Defense Production Act (1950), as amended by the FINSA, provides an illustrative list of factors for consideration by the CFIUS and the President in determining whether a transaction poses a national security risk, including, among others, the potential effects of the transaction on the US international technological leadership in areas affecting US national security, the potential national security-related effects on US critical technologies and US critical infrastructure, such as significant energy assets, and whether the transaction "could result in the control of a US business by a foreign government or by an entity controlled by or acting on behalf of a foreign government."[275] The list is quite detailed and comprehensive and is phrased in a comprehensive manner referring to the "potential effects" of the transaction, which indicates that the drafters of the FINSA took a holistic approach to define the potential threats to US national security. Notably, the list does not focus only on the areas relevant to the military and defense capacity of the US but also on energy and digital security and the availability of critical resources.

As of 2008, some covered transactions have been found by the CFIUS to present national security considerations because they involve infrastructure that may constitute US critical infrastructure, including significant energy assets; they were related to the US businesses' production of certain types of advanced technologies, including the ones engaged in the design and production of semiconductors, the production or supply of goods and services involving cryptography, data protection, and internet security.[276] The transactions involving US businesses that could

[272] Ibid.

[273] Office of Investment Security, Guidance Concerning the National Security Review Conducted by the Committee on Foreign Investment in the US Federal Register Vol 73 No 236 (December 8, 2008).

[274] Ibid.

[275] Foreign Investment and National Security Act (2007).

[276] Office of Investment Security, Guidance Concerning the National Security Review Conducted by the Committee on Foreign Investment in the US Federal Register Vol 73 No 236 (December 8, 2008).

significantly and directly affect the US financial system have also accounted for several covered transactions reviewed by the CFIUS that have presented national security considerations.[277]

The Foreign Investment Risk Review Modernization Act (FIRRMA) (2018) has broadened the jurisdiction of the CFIUS over FDIs related to critical technology, critical infrastructure, specific real estate, and sensitive personal data.[278] The FIRRMA grants the President the power to deny, approve, or condition such investment. Unlike the FINSA, the FIRRMA did not arise out of a particular crisis but rather gradually emerged from a growing frustration with the foreign policy of particular states and highly public transactions that highlighted CFIUS' concerns.[279] The initial worries over suspecting the motives of the investments from the Organization of the Petroleum Exporting Countries (including Iran, Iraq, Kuwait, Saudi Arabia, and Venezuela)[280] have been replaced by skepticism over Chinese and Russian "economic espionage" and trade secret theft in the US.[281] Law scholars commonly agree that the FIRRMA was "born out of the nexus of increased fear regarding China's growing strategic and economic clout and the potential loss of American technology supremacy" and thus was "clearly directed at China."[282]

The 2018 reform of the CFIUS review has demonstrated that the concept of national security in the US has expanded to include the preservation of the national security innovation base, critical infrastructure, emerging technologies, and protection of US citizen data.[283] "In determining whether a proposed transaction presents [US] national security concerns," the CFIUS considers factors regarding (i) the "threat"

[277] Ibid.

[278] Section 1703 of the Foreign Investment Risk Review Modernization Act (2018).

[279] Jayden R Barrington, 'CFIUS Reform: Fear and FIRRMA, an Inefficient and Insufficient Expansion of Foreign Direct Investment Oversight' (2019) 21 Transactions: Tenn J Bus L 77, 103.

[280] Greta Lichtenbaum and David J Ribner, 'Foreign Investment Screening in the USA' in S Hindelang and A Moberg (eds.), *YSEC Yearbook of Socio-Economic Constitutions 2020: A Common European Law on Investment Screening (CELIS)* (Springer International Publishing 2021) 364 https://link-springer-com.tilburguniversity.idm.oclc.org/content/pdf/10.1007%2F16495_2020_7.pdf.

[281] Jayden R Barrington, 'CFIUS Reform: Fear and FIRRMA, an Inefficient and Insufficient Expansion of Foreign Direct Investment Oversight' (2019) 21 Transactions: Tenn J Bus L 77, 103.

[282] Keyan Lai, 'National Security and FDI Policy Ambiguity: A Commentary' (2021) 4(4) J Intl Business Policy https://doi.org/10.1057/s42214-020-00087-1.

[283] Foreign Investment Risk Review Modernization Act (2018).

posed by the foreign investors, such as the investor's nationality/country of origin; and (ii) "the 'vulnerability' of the targeted assets, including the potential effects on [US] technological leadership, domestic production of national defense requirements, critical infrastructure, and critical technologies."[284] By expanding CFIUS's jurisdiction to include all technological and industrial areas, the FIRRMA implicitly acknowledges that the US superiority in these areas cannot be left up to the market; the drafters of the FIRRMA seem to believe that these critical areas must be protected from being acquired by foreign entities, even if the transactions occur in a free market.[285]

Before 2017, the US Presidents formally blocked three FDIs on national security grounds: the acquisition by the Chinese National Aero-Technology Import and Export Corporation of MAMCO Manufacturing, a US-based supplier of aerospace parts, the acquisition by the Chinese-owned Ralls Corporation of a wind farm project in Oregon close to a US military facility, and the acquisition by the Chinese Fujian Grand Chip Investment Fund of the US assets of Aixtron, a Germany-based semiconductor company.[286] In 2017, as the US government has placed greater emphasis on economic security as a critical element of national security, President Trump blocked two high-profile deals: the acquisition by Canyon Bridge Capital Partners of Lattice Semiconductor Corp, a US semiconductor company, and the acquisition of Qualcomm, a US semiconductor and telecommunication equipment company, by Broadcom.[287] In 2020, he also compelled ByteDance, the owner of TikTok, to divest its stake in Musical.ly and Beijing Shiji Information Technology Co Ltd to divest its interests in StayNTouch Inc.[288] In 2024, President Biden blocked the acquisition of real estate operating as a cryptocurrency mining facility near Francis

[284] Greta Lichtenbaum and David J Ribner, 'Foreign Investment Screening in the USA' in S Hindelang and A Moberg (eds.), *YSEC Yearbook of Socio-Economic Constitutions 2020* (Springer 2021) 369 https://link-springer-com.tilburguniversity.idm.oclc.org/content/pdf/10.1007%2F16495_2020_7.pdf.

[285] Rachel H Boyd, 'FIRRMA: "Buy American" Products, or Bye American Progress?' (2019) 19(2) Wake Forest J Bus & IPL 103, 110.

[286] Council on Foreign Relations, 'Foreign Investment and U.S. National Security' (August 28, 2018) www.cfr.org/backgrounder/foreign-investment-and-us-national-security.

[287] Congressional Research Service, 'Committee on Foreign Investment in the United States (CFIUS)' (updated December 9, 2024) CRS Report https://crsreports.congress.gov/product/pdf/IF/IF10177.

[288] Ibid.

E Warren Air Force Base.[289] More recently, in 2025, he blocked the acquisition of US Steel by Nippon Steel on national security grounds, marking the only transaction among those mentioned above without ties to Chinese ownership or influence.[290]

Apart from these decisions by the US President, many other investments, especially those proposed by the Chinese companies, were objected to because of national security considerations, particularly certain transactions proposed by the telecommunication giant Huawei, a Chinese company leading in the development of the 5G.[291] The CFIUS raised objections over Huawei's proposed investment in US network security company 3Com (Computer Communication Compatibility) in 2008 and the investment in mobile communications companies Wire and Motorola in 2010, citing suspected ongoing ties between Huawei's founder and CEO Ren Zhengfei and Chinese military and intelligence agencies, charges that Huawei vehemently denies.[292] In 2011, the CFIUS advised Huawei to withdraw its already completed acquisition of the cloud computing assets of 3Leaf Systems or face a divestiture order from President Obama.[293] A congressional panel warned that Chinese telecommunication equipment makers Huawei and ZTE Corporation posed a security threat to the US and recommended that these two companies be barred from US mergers and acquisitions.[294] After adopting the FIRRMA, expanding the concept of national security, and giving the CFIUS a vaguer mandate to maintain US technological supremacy, the technology war against Chines companies only escalated. The CFIUS forced the divestiture of interests of Chinese companies from PatientsLikeMe (patient-network and research platform), Grindr (gay dating app), and StayNTouch, Inc (a US company providing mobile technology and property-management systems for hotels), as well as opened an investigation into the short-video app TikTok, acquired by China's ByteDance.[295]

289 Ibid.

290 US President EO Regarding the Proposed Acquisition of United States Steel Corporation by Nippon Steel Corporation (January 3, 2025).

291 Huawei – Building a Fully Connected, Intelligent World www.huawei.com/en/.

292 Scott M Flicker and Dana M Parsons, 'Huawei – CFIUS Redux: Now It Gets Interesting' (*Paul Hastings*, March 31, 2011) 1 https://webstorage.paulhastings.com/Documents/PDFs/1868.pdf.

293 Stephanie Kirchgaessner and Kathrin Hille, 'Huawei in Challenge to US' *FT* (February 15, 2011) www.ft.com/content/f7d582f0-393a-11e0-97ca-00144feabdc0.

294 Baban Hasnat, 'US National Security and Foreign Direct Investment' (2015) 57(3) Thunderbird Intl Business Rev 185, 188.

295 Roslyn Layton, 'Why Is U.S. Policy Tough On Huawei And TikTok But Not Lenovo?' *Forbes* (June 26, 2020) www.forbes.com/sites/roslynlayton/2020/06/26/why-is-us-policy-tough-on-huawei-and-tiktok-but-not-lenovo/.

In 2022, EO 14083 was adopted to sharpen the current US ISMs, especially targeting the transactions with FDIs "involving foreign adversaries or other countries of special concern," which could "actually present an unacceptable risk to United States national security due to the legal environment, intentions, or capabilities of the foreign person, including foreign governments involved in the transaction."[296] In particular, the CFIUS was empowered to consider additional national security factors, such as technological leadership (in such areas as microelectronics, AI, and climate adaptation technologies), industry investment trends, cyber-enabled activities, supply chain dependency, and risks to personal data. For the first time in the CFIUS's history, the President expressly directed the CFIUS to focus on such critical factors in its review of security risks arising from inbound investment, thereby highlighting the President's view on the importance of certain areas for US national security. As discussed before, the CFIUS has already been intensely focused on supply chains and critical technologies, especially with respect to Chinese FDIs. Janet Yellen, the US Secretary of the Treasury and chair of the CFIUS, noted that EO 14083 "reaffirms CFIUS's mission to protect America's technological leadership and the security of [US] citizens' sensitive data from emerging threats."[297]

All this suggests that the US is increasingly focused on Chinese investment trends[298] and perceives China as its geopolitical rival.[299] The US has also sought to convince its allies and trading partners to adopt similar positions concerning their ISMs.[300] Chinese investment in sensitive sectors could arguably lead to espionage, US technology making its way into Chinese armament, and situations of dependence where investment creates political leverage, with politicians self-censoring their criticism of

[296] US President EO 14083 on Ensuring Robust Consideration of Evolving National Security Risks by the Committee on Foreign Investment in the United States 87 FR 57369 (September 15, 2022).

[297] Statement by Secretary of the Treasury Janet L Yellen on President Biden's Executive Order on the Committee on Foreign Investment in the United States, US Department of the Treasury (September 15, 2022) https://home.treasury.gov/news/press-releases/jy0951.

[298] Edward M Graham and David Marchick, *US National Security and Foreign Direct Investment* (Peterson Institute for International Economics 2006) 102.

[299] Wei Yin, 'A Comparison of the US and EU Regulatory Responses to China's State Capitalism: Implication, Issue and Direction' (2020) 19(1) Asia Europe Journal: Studies on Common Policy Challenges 1, 20.

[300] Jason Jacobs, 'Tiptoeing the Line between National Security and Protectionism: A Comparative Approach to Foreign Direct Investment Screening in the United States and European Union' (2019) 47(2) Intl J Legal Information 105, 106.

Chinese policies.[301] At the same time, the US concern about the threats to national security posed by Chinese FDIs can also be understood as reflecting the frustration because of a deteriorating competitive advantage of the US, a fear of changing network of power relations between nations, and the desire to formulate FDI policy that could protect the US long-term national interest.[302] All these concerns resulted in China being the number one home country for investment deals reviewed by the CFIUS and blocked by the President since 2011.[303] The US attack on China using economic sanctions and strict ISMs on national security grounds could be compared with the US backlash against Japanese investment in the 1980s, widely recognized as the outcome of the rising power in Japan being considered a military threat to US national security.[304] The recent developments thus demonstrate that the US attempts to deploy the same means to protect its military and now economic might. Notably, Presidential determinations and actions related to investment screening are not subject to judicial review under US law.[305]

3.2.2 The EU Approach

While the EU has historically maintained an open mindset toward foreign investors, the trends and policies of emerging FDI providers, such as China, have cast doubt on the effectiveness of the decentralized and fragmented system of FDI screening in the EU – in use only by some EU member states.[306] The difficulty in striking a balance between FDI openness and security concerns in the EU has been compounded by the complexity of the EU system of allocation of powers: on the one hand, after the Lisbon Treaty, the EU has exclusive competence in the field of

[301] Wei Yin, 'A Comparison of the US and EU Regulatory Responses to China's State Capitalism: Implication, Issue and Direction' (2020) 19(1) Asia Europe Journal: Studies on Common Policy Challenges 1, 15.

[302] Keyan Lai, 'National Security and FDI Policy Ambiguity: A Commentary' (2021) 4(4) J Intl Business Policy https://doi.org/10.1057/s42214-020-00087-1.

[303] Brandice Canes-Wrone, Lauren Mattioli, and Sophie Meunier, 'Foreign Direct Investment Screening and Congressional Backlash Politics in the United States' (2020) 22(4) The British J Politics and Intl Relations 666, 670.

[304] Keyan Lai, 'National Security and FDI Policy Ambiguity: A Commentary' (2021) 4(4) J Intl Business Policy https://doi.org/10.1057/s42214-020-00087-1.

[305] The Exon-Florio Amendment, 50 USC app 2170 (1988).

[306] European Parliament, EU Framework for FDI Screening (Briefing, April 2019) www.europarl.europa.eu/RegData/etudes/BRIE/2018/614667/EPRS_BRI%282018%29614667_EN.pdf.

the Common Commercial Policy (CCP), including the FDIs (Article 207(1) of TFEU) while, on the other hand, the member states are sovereign in restricting or prohibiting FDI for national security reasons according to Article 4(2) of TFEU. The strong connection of the member states' screening mechanisms with the protection of their national security interests, which is outside the purview of the EU competence, may explain why member states insisted that the FDI Screening Regulation leaves them the decision on the factors considered during the investment screening.[307]

In addition to mentioning the broad criteria of security and public order, the FDI Screening Regulation provides a list of factors for EU member states to consider while making a final screening decision.[308] According to Article 4(1) of the FDI Screening Regulation, when screening FDI, the member states and the European Commission "may consider" the potential effects on, among other things, critical infrastructure, critical technologies and dual-use items, access to sensitive information, or the freedom and pluralism of the media.[309] It reflects the trend for expanding the material and personal scope of investment screening by incorporating a comprehensive and non-exhaustive set of factors that may be considered during the FDI screening.

In addition, the FDI Screening Regulation contains a provision for investments with a specific EU dimension. If an investment is likely to affect projects or programs of EU interest, as listed in the FDI Screening Regulation, the European Commission may issue an opinion on whether the investment constitutes a threat to public security or order.[310] In particular, this includes projects and programs involving substantial

[307] Regulation (EU) 2019/452 of the European Parliament and of the Council of March 19, 2019 Establishing a Framework for the Screening of Foreign Direct Investments into the Union (2019) OJ L 79I. On the EU framework. See also Olga Hrynkiv and Saskia Lavrijssen, 'Foreign Investments and Energy Transition in the Netherlands: Balancing Economic and Security Interests' (2024) 42(1) JLCOM 1.

[308] European Commission, Communication from the Commission Guidance to the Member States concerning Foreign Direct Investment and Free Movement of Capital from Third Countries, and the Protection of Europe's Strategic Assets, ahead of the Application of Regulation (EU) 2019/452 (FDI Screening Regulation) 2020/C 99 I/01 [2020] OJ C 99I, Annex Part 1.

[309] Wolf Zwartkruis and Bas de Jong, 'The EU Regulation on Screening of Foreign Direct Investment: A Game Changer?' (2020) 31(3) Eur Bus L Rev 447, 463.

[310] Thomas Verellen, 'When Integration by Stealth Meets Public Security: The EU Foreign Direct Investment Screening Regulation' (2021) 48(2) Legal Issues of Economic Integration 19, 26.

EU funding or established by the EU law regarding critical infrastructure, critical technologies, or critical inputs.[311]

Notably, the FDI Screening Regulation neither establishes screening at the EU level nor fully harmonizes screening procedures at the member state level; rather, it aims to coordinate the domestic procedures used by EU member states.[312] Since the FDI Screening Regulation does not harmonize and "does not further define the level of protection of security and public order," the member states are "still, in principle, free to determine the requirements of public order and public security in the light of their national needs."[313] Yet, even though EU member states are free to perform FDI screening based on domestic legislation when determining whether a cross-border transaction with a third country is likely to affect their national security, they have to be ready to justify their restrictions in the interests of their national security based on valid reasons, especially if they go beyond the guiding factors proposed in the FDI Screening Regulation.

The legislative and policy developments in the EU are compatible with the current investment screening practice in the US.[314] To illustrate, the determination of security concerns in both members can derive from the nationality of an investor.[315] In 2018, for example, the FDIs from China to Europe fell by as much as 70 percent compared to the previous record year.[316] It can also be suggested that the policy goals outlined in the FDI Screening Regulation align with the US goals outlined in the FIRRMA concerning Chinese investment practices in particular.[317] The

311 Article 8(3) of the FDI Screening Regulation.

312 Georgios Dimitropoulos, 'National Security: The Role of Investment Screening Mechanisms' in Julien Chaisse and others (eds.), *Handbook of International Investment Law and Policy* (Springer Nature Singapore Pte Ltd 2019) 13 https://ssrn.com/abstract=3538735.

313 Andreas Moberg and Steffen Hindelang, 'The Art of Casting Political Dissent in Law: The EU's Framework for the Screening of Foreign Direct Investment' (2020) 57(5) CMLR 1427, 1452.

314 Mikko Rajavuori and Kaisa Huhta, 'Investment Screening: Implications for the Energy Sector and Energy Security' (2020) 144 Energy Policy 1, 4.

315 Manisha Reuter, 'Responding to the China Challenge: The State of Play on Investment Screening in Europe' (*ECFR (blog)*, November 27, 2020) https://ecfr.eu/article/responding-to-the-china-challenge-the-state-of-play-on-investment-screening-in-europe/.

316 Tobias Gehrke, 'Redefining the EU-China Economic Partnership: Beyond Reciprocity Lies Strategy' (Security Policy Brief, February 2019) www.egmontinstitute.be/content/uploads/2019/02/SPB-Gehrke-Final.pdf?type=pdf.

317 Jason Jacobs, 'Tiptoeing the Line between National Security and Protectionism: A Comparative Approach to Foreign Direct Investment Screening in the United States and European Union' (2019) 47(2) Intl J Legal Information 105, 114.

resistance to Chinese investments is not only influenced by fear of loss of competitive strength but even more by the concern that China is competing in an unequal and nonreciprocal manner. In particular, it has been argued that Chinese and EU companies do not only compete directly but that Chinese companies benefit from different forms of support and protection provided by Chinese state intervention.[318]

However, there are also critical differences between the EU and the US measures. The most striking one is the lack of the Commission's power under the FDI Screening Regulation to suspend or block investments.[319] The European Commission may only provide nonbinding opinions that the member states are required to consider.[320]

One of the first transactions screened after the adoption of the FDI Screening Regulation was the blockage by the Italian Council of Ministers of the sale of 70 percent of Milan-based LPE to the Chinese company Shenzhen Investment Holdings Co in March 2021.[321] Since Chinese investment in critical European infrastructure has traditionally received most of the attention, with risks of excessive leverage sometimes mentioned, it is prominent that the first screening case leaked to the public also concerns high technology and the semiconductor sector.[322] The first annual report on the investment screening in the EU after the adoption of the FDI Screening Regulation highlights that the EU and its members "remain very open to FDI, intervening only in a tiny proportion of cases to address deals likely to affect security or public order."[323] Accordingly, a significant number of cases notified by member states during this period involved one or more factors for consideration listed in the FDI Screening Regulation, including critical infrastructure, technology, and dual-use items, access to sensitive information, and possible government's ownership or control of, or influence over, the foreign

[318] Wolf Zwartkruis and Bas de Jong, 'The EU Regulation on Screening of Foreign Direct Investment: A Game Changer?' (2020) 31(3) Eur Bus L Rev 447, 451.

[319] Jason Jacobs, 'Tiptoeing the Line between National Security and Protectionism: A Comparative Approach to Foreign Direct Investment Screening in the United States and European Union' (2019) 47(2) IJLI 105, 116.

[320] Ibid 115.

[321] Mathieu Duchâtel, 'The New Landscape of Investment Screening in Europe' (*Institut Montaigne*, June 21, 2021) www.institutmontaigne.org/en/blog/new-landscape-investment-screening-europe.

[322] Ibid.

[323] European Commission, Report from the Commission to the European Parliament and the Council. First Annual Report on the Screening of Foreign Direct Investments into the Union (2021) COM(2021) 714 final 11.

investor.[324] Both the first and second annual reports on investment screening in the EU stipulate that most notifications for screening concerned the manufacturing sector, encompassing critical infrastructures and/or technologies, ICT, and wholesale and retail, with the top three countries of origin of investors among notified FDI cases being the US, the UK, and China.[325]

An accelerating "trade war" between the US and China for control over semiconductors impacts the EU and its member states. In the aftermath of the US draconian restrictions on trade with China in the autumn of 2022,[326] national security concerns about potential Chinese control over critical European infrastructure prompted Germany to block a sale of a chip factory to a Chinese-related company.[327] Similar concerns have been raised in other EU member states, such as the Netherlands.[328] Such developments highlight the importance of digital sovereignty and supply chain security for EU member states. As the rivalry between the US and China escalates, the EU is caught in the middle.[329] On the one hand, the EU and the US share common concerns about the threat posed by a range of Chinese non-market policies and practices and have committed to work together on exploring policy tools to address such concerns.[330] On the other hand, China's participation in the global economy continues to represent significant opportunities for

324 Ibid 15.

325 Ibid 12–13; European Commission, Report from the Commission to the European Parliament and the Council. Second Annual Report on the Screening of Foreign Direct Investments into the Union (2022) COM(2022) 433 final 19.

326 See more chapter 3, section 3.2.2.

327 Michelle Toh, 'The US-China Chip War is Spilling over to Europe' *CNN* (November 25, 2022) https://edition.cnn.com/2022/11/25/tech/us-china-chip-war-spillover-europe-intl-hnk/index.html.

328 'VVD'er: Kabinet moet Overname Delfts Chipbedrijfje door Nexperia Blokkeren' *FD* (December 1, 2022) (in Dutch) https://fd.nl/tech-en-innovatie/1459876/vvd-er-kabinet-moet-overname-delfts-chipbedrijfje-door-nexperia-blokkeren.

329 See more Linda Monsees and Daniel Lambach, 'Digital Sovereignty, Geopolitical Imaginaries, and the Reproduction of European Identity' (2022) 31(3) European Security 377.

330 For example, the announcement at the EU–US summit of the creation of a Trade and Technology Council specifically mentions investment screening as an area of cooperation. See Mathieu Duchâtel, 'The New Landscape of Investment Screening in Europe' (*Institut Montaigne*, June 21, 2021) www.institutmontaigne.org/en/blog/new-landscape-investment-screening-europe. See also European Commission, 'EU–US Joint Statement of the Trade and Technology Council' (Press Release, December 5, 2022) https://ec.europa.eu/commission/presscorner/detail/en/STATEMENT_22_7516.

European companies.[331] In response to a growing debate over computer microchip deals in Europe, a Chinese Foreign Ministry spokesperson Zhao Lijian invited Germany and other countries to "refrain from politicizing normal economic and trade cooperation, still less using national security as a pretext to practice protectionism."[332]

In January 2024, the EU came up with new incentives to advance the implementation of the ES Strategy, including a legislative proposal for the revision of the FDI Screening Regulation "to improve its effectiveness and efficiency" and a White Paper to identify potential security risks posed by EU outbound investment.[333] These incentives indicate the Commission's aim to enhance coordination among competent national authorities, with the goal of bolstering the effectiveness of current EU controls in sensitive areas. It remains to be seen whether forthcoming developments will lead to securitization or de-securitization of doing business with China and how that will affect the coordination of ISMs among the EU and its member states and the EU's cooperation with the US (and potentially other countries) in addressing China's industrial policies.

3.2.3 *The Approach of Brazil*

Brazil has long been a significant investment recipient.[334] Foreign ownership in Brazil of local companies is generally permitted except in sectors considered to be of strategic importance. Brazil implements investment reviews designed to protect national security interests in a narrow range of sectors, focusing on those traditionally considered national security-sensitive sectors, such as defense and related fields, real estate, and land in border areas or near strategically important facilities.[335] Furthermore, Brazilian legislation restricts foreign investments into the healthcare, mass

331 Yang Sheng and Wang Qi, 'EU Needs to 'Cooperate with China' as Concerns of Trade War with US Rise' *Global Times* (December 5, 2022) www.globaltimes.cn/page/202212/1281181.shtml.

332 Ministry of Foreign Affairs of the People's Republic of China, 'Foreign Ministry Spokesperson Zhao Lijian's Regular Press Conference' (November 9, 2022) www.fmprc.gov.cn/mfa_eng/xwfw_665399/s2510_665401/2511_665403/202211/t20221109_10891661.html.

333 European Commission, Memo on European Economic Security' (January 24, 2024) https://ec.europa.eu/commission/presscorner/detail/en/QANDA_24_364.

334 Congyan Cai and Yifei Wang, 'Introduction' in Congyan Cai, Huiping Chen, and Yifei Wang (eds.), *The BRICS in the New International Legal Order on Investment* (Brill 2020) 4.

335 'Investment Climate Statements: Brazil' (2020) www.state.gov/reports/2020-investment-climate-statements/brazil/.

media, telecommunications, aerospace, maritime, and air transport sectors, but also the automobile, renewable energy, life sciences, oil, and gas sectors.[336]

The Brazilian government relies on the concept of "national security" to limit foreign investors from acquiring areas near the international borders of Brazil, in particular, within a security zone of 150 km along its national land borders.[337] The transactions subject to approval include transfers of lands, construction of certain infrastructure, means of broadcasting, establishment, operation of certain industries, or the acquisition of rural property in the border zone.[338]

Unlike the US and the EU, Brazil imposes limits on the FDI only in a limited number of sectors and has not strengthened its ISMs in response to the recent geopolitical changes and technological developments. In part, it can be explained by the fact that Brazil is less concerned with participating in the global race for technological supremacy. In comparison with other countries, the relevance of China as a source of foreign capital to the Brazilian economy is still moderate.[339] However, it should be noted that China has become a relevant foreign investor in Brazil from 2010 onwards, mainly through SOEs investing in infrastructure – particularly in the energy sector, and this trend might continue further.[340] Ultimately, in several instances, local officials refused to sell the massive tracts of land they sought to Chinese investors.[341] Furthermore, Chinese investment in Brazil has recently started to fall, with some pointing to unfair targeting of Chinese agribusiness and even accusations of Sinophobia.[342]

[336] Ibid. See also sector-specific: healthcare (Law 13097/2015), mass media (Law 10610/2002), telecommunications (Law 12485/2011), aerospace (Law 7565/1986, Decree 6834/2009, updated by Law 12970/2014, Law 13133/2015, and Law 13319/2016), rural property (Law 5709/1971), maritime (Law 9432/1997, Decree 2256/1997), and insurance (Law 11371/2006).

[337] Law 6.634 (May 2, 1979); Decree of the President No 85.064 (August 26, 1980).

[338] See eg 'How Brazilian Restrictions on the Acquisition of Rural Land by Foreigners have an Impact on Corporate Transactions' (*Ibradim*, 2022) https://ibradim.org.br/how-brazilian-restrictions-on-the-acquisition-of-rural-land-by-foreigners-have-an-impact-on-corporate-transactions/.

[339] Pedro da Motta Veiga and Sandra Polónia Rios, 'China's FDI in Brazil: Recent Trends and Policy Debate' (Policy Center for the New South, June 25, 2019) 10 www.policycenter.ma/publications/china%E2%80%99s-fdi-brazil-recent-trends-and-policy-debate.

[340] Ibid 1.

[341] Aaron Baum, 'Investment Screening for Developing Asia' (June 10, 2020) Yale J Intl Affairs www.yalejournal.org/publications/investment-screening-for-developing-asia.

[342] Gustavo de LT Oliveira, 'Chinese Land Grabs in Brazil? Sinophobia and Foreign Investments in Brazilian Soybean Agribusiness' (2018) 15(1) Globalizations 114, 120–121.

3.2.4 The Approach of Russia

With the market changes in the 1990s, Russia "chose a path of maximum non-interference" in regulating foreign investment transactions.[343] Until 2008, there had been no special procedure for screening foreign investments; in practice, competition law clearance was used for such purposes.[344]

"The most salient case" that spurred the advancement of comprehensive regulations on foreign investment controls in Russia was the unsuccessful attempt by the German Siemens to acquire control of Russian Siloviye Mashiny, the machine-building company that produces various military equipment.[345] Some members of the Russian Parliament claimed that "the proposed transaction (if approved) would cause the loss of control of Russia over its power-plant industry, a strategic industry that safeguards the national defense of the country, its energy, and economic safety."[346] The Federal Antimonopoly Service (FAS) stated in the corresponding press release that based on the results of their analysis, "the possible positive effect of this transaction could not be fully realized" given that current legislation does not address some critical issues, including the participation of foreign companies in the production of defense goods.[347]

Stricter control over FDIs was supposed to be ensured with the Federal Law on Procedures for Foreign Investments in Companies Having Strategic Importance for National Security and Defence (hereafter the Strategic Investment Law), enumerating the categories of activities that were of "strategic significance" for ensuring the country's defense and state security.[348] The list includes, among others, the companies active in the defense sector (e.g. aviation and space, weapons and military equipment, radioactive materials, encryption, infrastructure surveillance) and media (e.g. particular television and radio broadcasting and certain publishing activities); economic entities which have a dominant position in the Russian market as well as natural monopolies; and companies operating in the natural resources sector, provided that such companies

343 Vladimir V Talanov, 'Foreign Investment Screening in Russia' in S Hindelang and A Moberg (eds.), *YSEC Yearbook of Socio-Economic Constitutions 2020* (Springer 2020) 332.

344 Ibid 334.

345 Ibid.

346 Ibid.

347 Ibid.

348 Federal Law No 57-FZ (April 2, 2008).

use subsoil plots deemed to be of federal significance. In 2022, Russia amended the list also to include the transportation of goods by sea and inland waters; and the development of an automated information system for air transportation, including the relevant databases, the IT network that ensures the system's operation, and the exercise of operator functions.[349] Notably, Russia continues to blur the line between antimonopoly control and foreign investment control, even though these two mechanisms serve different purposes and operate differently.[350]

The Law on Mass Media prescribes one of the most debated restrictions on foreign investment.[351] The new Article 19.1 prohibiting foreign states, companies, and entities from being a founder of mass media, an editorial office of Russian mass media, or a broadcasting organization was challenged before the Constitutional Court of Russia as a "disproportionate, discriminatory, and unclearly drafted restriction" of foreign investment.[352] The Constitutional Court of Russia concluded that the introduced restrictions are, in principle, "permissible under the Russian Constitution as information security forms part of national security."[353] Judge Aranovskiy, nevertheless, suggested another view in its dissenting opinion claiming that no objective "evidence of the threat to any constitutional values by foreign ownership of mass media has been placed before the Court, whereas the foreign origin of capital, persons, or ideas itself could not be an indication of threat to constitutionally protected values."[354]

In addition to the screening mechanism prescribed by the Strategic Investment Law, Russia has established a complete prohibition of foreign acquisitions in specific sectors, such as land near national borders, in seaports, and certain territories specified by federal laws.[355] Territorial restrictions on FDI are also connected to the Ministry of Defence activities. Russia includes some territories where foreign investors do not have a right to establish a legal person without special permission from the

[349] Federal Law No 92-FZ (April 15, 2022).

[350] Vladimir V Talanov, 'Foreign Investment Screening in Russia' in S Hindelang and A Moberg (eds.), *YSEC Yearbook of Socio-Economic Constitutions 2020* (Springer 2020) 336.

[351] Federal Law on Mass Media No 2124-1 as amended in 2014.

[352] Vladimir V Talanov, 'Foreign Investment Screening in Russia' in S Hindelang and A Moberg (eds.), *YSEC Yearbook of Socio-Economic Constitutions 2020* (Springer 2020) 355.

[353] Ibid.

[354] Ibid 355–366.

[355] Article 15(3) of Federal Law No 136-FZ (July 28, 2001).

state – Closed Administrative-Territorial Zones.[356] While the legislation does not expressly determine the reasons for these restrictions, some may be motivated by concerns about Russia's security interests.

The amendments to Federal Law on Foreign Investments in the Russian Federation also introduced a general (rather than sectoral) ISM.[357] It allows the Russian Prime Minister to require the prior approval of any transaction carried out by a foreign investor concerning any Russian company (not just a strategic entity) in the manner prescribed by the Strategic Investment Law.[358] The law is quite broadly worded, suggesting that such resolutions can be issued concerning virtually any transaction by a foreign investor involving any Russian entity, whether strategic or not.[359]

Consequently, the focus of ISMs in Russia is the protection of national defense and state security. Russia maintains a list of strategic activities the investment into which is subject to certain limitations. Apart from this, neither the Strategic Investment Law nor the secondary legislation establishes any specific criteria the FDI review should consider when assessing an application on national security grounds.[360] The FAS practice shows a trend for the broad application of the concept of "related business activities" to the strategic activities listed in the Strategic Investments Law. In the *Nabors/Tesco* case, for example, the FAS declared that the running casing services for drilling are a type of strategic activity since such activities constitute an integral part of technological processes for the geological study of subsurface resources or exploration and mining of mineral resources in subsoil areas of federal significance.[361] Furthermore, the Constitutional Court of Russia ruled that organizations providing oilfield services in subsoil areas of federal value are business entities of strategic importance in ensuring the country's defense and state security.[362]

[356] Law on Closed Administrative Territorial Zones established under the Law on Closed Administrative-Territorial Zones No 3297-1 as amended in 2018.

[357] Federal Law No 160-FZ on Foreign Investments in the Russian Federation (July 9, 1999).

[358] Federal Law No 165-FZ (July 5, 2017).

[359] 'Federal Antimonopoly Service Strengthens Enforcement of Foreign Investments Legislation' (White & Case, December 3, 2020) www.jdsupra.com/legalnews/foreign-direct-investment-reviews-2020-82639/.

[360] Ji Ma, 'International Investment and National Security Review' (2019) 52 Vand J Transnatl L 899, 914.

[361] Resolution No F05-14552/2018 of the Arbitration Court of the Moscow District in case No A40-72889/2018 (August 12, 2019).

[362] FAS, Constitutional Court of the Russian Federation recognized Oilfield Services in Subsoil Areas of Federal Significance as a Strategic Activity (FAS News, July 6, 2020) https://web.archive.org/web/20210814175503/http://fas.gov.ru/news/30069.

Therefore, "strategic activities" and "related business activities" can be interpreted by Russia's authorities rather broadly, especially in the oil and gas sectors.

Remarkably, in some instances, the FAS blocked the transaction though it was not related to the activities mentioned in the list. For example, in April 2013, after nine months of review, the proposed acquisition of Russian vaccine manufacturer Petrovax Pharm by Abbott Laboratories (US-based) was blocked.[363] The head of the FAS noted that this was one of the sporadic cases where it had decided to deny clearance based on national security considerations.[364] He emphasized that the Commission's decision was not against Abbott Laboratories or the US but rather represented the government's position that the production of vaccines is a strategic type of business,[365] even though it is not expressly mentioned in the Strategic Investment Law.

Finally, foreign investors are massively leaving Russia after the beginning of the war between Russia and Ukraine and the unprecedented Western sanctions targeting Russia's economy and prohibiting investments in Russia. Russia's government attempts to make investors stay, for example, by imposing a temporary ban on selling Russian assets by foreign investors.[366] It follows that current Russia's concerns are to preserve the economic benefits from existing investments and reinforce a political signal to the international community rather than restrict FDIs for economic or other strategic interests.

3.2.5 The Approach of India

Since 1991, India's liberalization of its foreign investment regulations has turned India into one of the fastest-growing destinations for FDIs.[367] Yet, India's Foreign Direct Investment Policy (FDI Policy) provides for sector-specific regulations in the form of investment caps, requirements for

363 Reuters Staff, 'Russia Rejects Abbott Laboratories' Plan to Buy Petrovax' *Reuters* (April 19, 2013) www.reuters.com/article/us-abbott-russia-idINBRE93I0GJ20130419.

364 Reuters Staff, 'Russia rejects Abbott Laboratories' plan to buy Petrovax' *Reuters* (April 19, 2013) www.reuters.com/article/us-abbott-russia-idINBRE93I0GJ20130419.

365 'Legal Overview of Foreign Investment in Russia's Strategic Sectors' (Clifford Chance, May 2014) www.cliffordchance.com/content/dam/cliffordchance/briefings/2014/05/a-legal-overview-of-foreign-investment-in-russias-strategic-sectors.pdf.

366 Meeting on Improving the Sustainability of the Development of the Russian Economy (Government News, March 1, 2022) http://government.ru/news/44677/.

367 Brent M Cardenas and Zackary R Berg, *Conditions for Foreign Direct Investments in India* (Nova Science Publishers 2010) 9.

investment, and sectors in which FDI is prohibited.[368] The FDI Policy has a limited list of prohibited sectors, including atomic energy, tobacco manufacturing, and gambling. Investments in mining, defense, print media, civil aviation, satellites, financial services, telecommunications, broadcasting, banking, private security agencies, and pharmaceuticals can be undertaken only with prior approval by the government.[369] A survey of the FDI Policies shows that more and more sectors have been opened to foreign investment in India over the years.[370] India's government has taken steps to relax restrictions on foreign investors in sectors including insurance, defense, railways, construction, and medical devices, 100 percent opening of aviation sectors, and 100 percent opening in the defense manufacturing sectors.[371]

On April 17, 2020, India's government again reviewed its FDI Policy for "curbing opportunistic takeovers/acquisitions of Indian companies due to the current COVID-19 pandemic" and decided to introduce additional control for all investments originating from countries that share land borders with India, including from Afghanistan, Bangladesh, Bhutan, China, Nepal, and Pakistan.[372] The alleged aim of the amendments was to curb opportunistic takeovers of Indian companies, especially by Chinese entities, a concern fueled by sharp corrections in equity markets in March 2020.[373] The increased scrutiny and subsequent stalling of Chinese investment proposals coincided with clashes along the India–China border and the ban on more than 100 Chinese apps for

368 Ammar Nainar, 'Building Indian States' Capacity in Monitoring FDI' (*CSIS*, November 5, 2020) www.csis.org/blogs/new-perspectives-asia/building-indian-states-capacity-monitoring-fdi.

369 RV Anuradha, 'India. Evolving Regulations on National Security and How They Impact Investments' *Mondaq* (September 17, 2018) www.mondaq.com/india/international-trade-investment/737050/evolving-regulations-on-national-security-and-how-they-impact-investments.

370 Aniruddah Rajput, *Protection of Foreign Investment in India and Investment Treaty Arbitration* (Kluwer Law International 2017) 1.

371 Xiuyan Fei, 'Investment Barriers, Investment Facilitation and the BRICS Countries' Investment Treaty Policies and Practice' in Congyan Cai, Huiping Chen, and Yifei Wang (eds.), *The BRICS in the New International Legal Order on Investment* (Brill 2020) 210.

372 Government of India, Department of Industrial Policy and Promotion, Ministry of Commerce and Industry, 'Review of Foreign Direct Investment (FDI) Policy for Curbing Opportunistic Takeovers/Acquisitions of Indian Companies due to the current COVID-19 Pandemic' (Press Note 3, April 17, 2020).

373 Pratik Datta, 'India Needs National Security Screening of FDI' *The Indian Express* (March 13, 2021) https://indianexpress.com/article/opinion/columns/india-foreign-direct-investments-rules-china-7225979/.

national security reasons.[374] Further, since 2020, a citizen of Pakistan or an entity incorporated in Pakistan can invest in sectors and activities other than defense, space, atomic energy, and sectors/activities prohibited for foreign investment only upon receiving governmental approval.[375]

3.2.6 The Approach of China

When China adopted an open-door investment policy in 1979, its FDI regime was defined by a case-by-case approval system.[376] The Chinese Foreign Equity Joint Ventures Law (1979) allowed foreigners to enter the Chinese market only upon prior approval.[377] The reasons for rejecting the transaction included concerns that the investment might "jeopardize China's sovereignty" and "not conform with the requirements of the development of China's national economy."[378] Since then, China has overhauled its policies repeatedly and complemented its initial mechanism with additional ones.[379]

The critical part of the Chinese model is state planning, including massive investment in infrastructure.[380] China's regional development strategy and urban economic restructuring policies played a key role in shaping its FDI framework.[381] As a result, in the early stages of China's

[374] Naina Bhardwaj and Melissa Cyrill, 'Chinese Investment in India: Impact of New FDI Restrictions by New Delhi' *India Briefing News* (March 5, 2021) www.india-briefing.com/news/india-rethinking-its-fdi-policy-stance-with-china-what-we-know-21824.html/.

[375] Government of India, Department of Industrial Policy and Promotion, Ministry of Commerce and Industry, 'Review of Foreign Direct Investment (FDI) Policy for Curbing Opportunistic Takeovers/Acquisitions of Indian Companies due to the Current COVID-19 Pandemic' (Press Note 3, April 17, 2020).

[376] Qingjiang Kong and Cherry Kaiyuan Chen, 'Foreign Investment Screening in China' in S Hindelang and A Moberg (eds), *YSEC Yearbook of Socio-Economic Constitutions 2020* (Springer 2020) 404, 412.

[377] Chieh Huang, 'China's Take on National Security and its Implications for the Evolution of International Economic Law' (2021) 48(2) Legal Issues of Economic Integration 119, 128.

[378] Ibid.

[379] Qingjiang Kong and Cherry Kaiyuan Chen, 'Foreign Investment Screening in China' in S Hindelang and A Moberg (eds.), *YSEC Yearbook of Socio-Economic Constitutions 2020* (Springer 2020) 412–420.

[380] Gregory C Shaffer, *Emerging Powers and the World Trading System: The Past and Future of International Economic Law* (CUP 2021) 225.

[381] Qingjiang Kong and Cherry Kaiyuan Chen, 'Foreign Investment Screening in China' in S Hindelang and A Moberg (eds.), *YSEC Yearbook of Socio-Economic Constitutions 2020* (Springer 2020) 409.

opening up, its FDI was concentrated mainly in coastal areas and labor-intensive industries.[382] Since then, China has expanded the geographic regions open to foreign investment and started linking FDIs to domestic development priorities.[383]

In 1995, China adopted the Interim Provisions on Guiding Foreign Investment (1995) (hereafter the Interim Provisions), thereby dividing market access of FDI into four categories "encouraged," "approved," "restricted," and "prohibited" investment. On the one hand, Article 7 of the Interim Provisions stipulated that a foreign investment "harming national security or impairing the public interest" or "harming the safety and usage of military facilities" should be prohibited without providing further details on the application or implementation of this rule. On the other hand, Article 19 of the Interim Provisions established that if a government agency considers that "important factors [in relation to the transaction] exist which seriously impact . . . State economic security," then the investor may be required to inform the MOFCOM of the transaction.[384] Thus, the Interim Provisions differentiate between investments that could be harmful to China's national security and public interests and investments that can impact China's economic security. Only concerns about China's national security and public interests would make the FDI prohibited. It is important to note that at that stage, the concept of national security in Chinese general legal discourse was still centered on traditional military and political concerns.[385] Thus, it is not surprising that the national security concept under the Interim Provisions also reflected such a narrow approach, which is to be separated from a broader "public interest" concern (i.e. "impairing the public interest") and China's economic security.[386]

In 2003, China adopted the Interim Provisions on Mergers and Acquisitions of Domestic Enterprises by Foreign Investors, establishing the review mechanism to manage risks to security interests posed by FDI

[382] Cheryl Xiaoning Long and Galina Hale, *Foreign Direct Investment In China: Winners And Losers* (World Scientific Publishing Company 2012) 3.

[383] Ibid.

[384] Article 19 of the Interim Provisions on Mergers and Acquisitions of Domestic Enterprises by Foreign Investors (2006).

[385] Chieh Huang, 'China's Take on National Security and its Implications for the Evolution of International Economic Law' (2021) 48(2) Legal Issues of Economic Integration 119, 122.

[386] Chieh Huang, 'China's Take on National Security and its Implications for the Evolution of International Economic Law' (2021) 48(2) Legal Issues of Economic Integration 119, 128–129.

(security review). When adopting the mechanism, the concept of national security in the Chinese legislation had developed and expanded to "major factors which seriously impact market competition, the national economy, and people's livelihood, or state economic security."[387] China's national security discourse started to include China's economic security, which can also be illustrated in the examples of the transactions attempted. In October 2005, the Carlyle Group (Carlyle), a US private equity firm, announced its intention to buy an 85 percent stake in Xugong Construction Machinery Group (Xugong). Xugong was the largest construction machinery maker in China and was under the ownership of the Xuzhou local government. The deal immediately triggered widespread concerns over national economic security (that China was selling its strategic companies too cheaply to foreign investors).[388] Arguably, for this reason, the central government had been considering its approval for a long time. After three years of waiting and making additional concessions without securing MOFCOM approval, the deal was finally abandoned.[389] Despite Carlyle's problems, not all foreign investments in China at the beginning of the twentieth century were subjected to such scrutiny. In November 2006, the acquisition by Rotary Vortex of Shineway Group, the biggest state-owned meat processor, was approved.[390] The key difference between Carlyle's and Rotary's deal seemed to be whether the target was a strategic asset in a critical sector.[391]

A formal review mechanism of FDIs was established by the Circular of the General Office of the State Council on the Establishment of the Security Review System for Mergers and Acquisitions of Domestic Enterprises by Foreign Investors in 2011 (hereafter the Circular 2011).[392] Although the

387 Ibid 129.

388 Wan Zhihong, 'Carlyle Abandons Xugong Dream' *China Daily* (July 24, 2008) www.chinadaily.com.cn/business/2008-07/24/content_6873004.htm.

389 Felix I Lessambo, Mergers in the Global Markets: A Comparative Approach to the Competition and National Security Laws among the US, EU, and China (Springer International Publishing 2020) 129.

390 Leigh Brown, Sebastian Hempel, and Lawrence Lu, 'China's National Security Screening for Foreign Acquisitions: Case Study of Blackstone and Carlyle' *Mondaq* (July 17, 2007) www.mondaq.com/china/compliance/50338/chinas-national-security-screening-for-foreign-acquisitions-case-study-of-blackstone-and-carlyle.

391 Ibid.

392 Circular 2011 was complemented by the Interim Provisions on Matters Relevant to the Implementation of the System for Security Review of Acquisition of Domestic Enterprises by Foreign Investors, Announce No 8 of March 2011 and the Provisions of the Ministry of Commerce on Implementing a Security Review System for Mergers and Acquisitions of Domestic Enterprises by Foreign Investors, Announce No 53 of September 2011.

Chinese review mechanism was primarily inspired by the CFIUS in the US, at the time of establishing the national security review mechanisms, the concept of national security in China was much more comprehensive than its US counterpart. In particular, the scope of the national security review in China covered "transactions involving important agricultural products, energy and resources, infrastructure facilities, and transportation services[,] core technologies and important equipment manufacturing enterprises."[393] The factors triggering the national security review process included the stable running of China's economy and the capacity for research and development of crucial technology.[394] Such factors went beyond China's national defense interests.[395] The publishing sector and traditional green tea sector were under control as sectors of economic or cultural importance,[396] even though they had little to do with conventional security concerns. The public interest concern, thus, had become a part of the new discourse of national security that could be understood from a broader context of China's governmental control in key sectors or "essential industries."[397]

In 2017, the Catalogue System was replaced with the negative list approach. Accordingly, restrictions on FDI in specified sectors are contained in a negative list of sectors where foreign investment is prohibited or restricted (hereafter the Negative List). Foreign investment in all other sectors enjoys national treatment in terms of establishment in China. China prohibits foreign investment in industries in the Prohibited Category while permitting foreign investment in the Restricted Category, subject to additional restrictions, such as maximum foreign shareholding limits and requirements to obtain approvals from responsible authorities (rather than making filings). Investments in media, natural resources, and the military generally fall under the Prohibited Category, while telecommunications, transportation, energy, utilities, banks, financial institutions, agriculture, and some less-sensitive media businesses generally fall under the Restricted Category.[398] The 2021 edition of the Negative List widened

393 Article 1.1 of the Circular 2011.

394 Ibid.

395 Chieh Huang, 'China's Take on National Security and its Implications for the Evolution of International Economic Law' (2021) 48(2) Legal Issues of Economic Integration 119, 130.

396 Ibid.

397 Ibid.

398 'Foreign Investment Control Heats Up: A Global Survey of Existing Regimes and Potential Significant Changes on the Horizon' (*Jonesday*, January 2018) 4 www.jonesday.com/files/upload/Foreign%20Investment%20Control%20Heats%20Up.pdf.

market access for foreign investors by removing restrictions from FDIs in automobile manufacturing and satellite television broadcast ground receiving facilities.[399] Certain entries in the Negative List are presumably motivated by concerns about national security, such as "manufacturing of weapons and ammunitions."[400]

The entry into force of the NSL in 2015 also brought changes to the system. The NSL defines two categories of security: national and economic security, highlighting that "the national security with Chinese characteristics" refers to the interconnection between economic and security.[401] The NSL not only defines what falls into China's national security concerns but also mandates the security review of "foreign investment that jeopardizes, or may jeopardize, national security," "key materials and technologies," "internet or information technology products and services," "construction projects that implicate national security," and "other major projects or events." Thus, the NSL further broadens the scope of national security rhetoric in China.

In addition, the traditional regime of FDI screening, which relied on case-by-case approval and industrial policies, has been replaced by the "pre-establishment national treatment plus negative list" approach in the new Foreign Investment Law of the People's Republic of China (2019).[402] The Foreign Investment Law in Article 35 refers to a "security review system for foreign investment" without providing much detail on its operation and scope.[403] Compared to the final enacted Foreign

[399] Special Administrative Measures (Negative List) for Foreign Investment Access (2021 ed.) www.china-briefing.com/news/chinas-foreign-investment-negative-list-2021-edition-english-version/.

[400] OECD Secretariat, 'Acquisition- and Ownership-related Policies to Safeguard Essential Security Interests. Current and Emerging Trends, Observed Designs, and Policy Practice in 62 Economies (OECD, May 2020) [413] www.oecd.org/investment/OECD-Acquisition-ownership-policies-security-May2020.pdf.

[401] Chieh Huang, 'China's Take on National Security and its Implications for the Evolution of International Economic Law' (2021) 48(2) Legal Issues of Economic Integration 119, 141.

[402] Qingjiang Kong and Cherry Kaiyuan Chen, 'Foreign Investment Screening in China' in S Hindelang and A Moberg (eds.), *YSEC Yearbook of Socio-Economic Constitutions 2020* (Springer 2020) 417.

[403] National People's Congress, The Foreign Investment Law of the People's Republic of China (March 15, 2019) Article 35. See also OECD Secretariat, 'Acquisition- and Ownership-related Policies to Safeguard Essential Security Interests. Current and Emerging Trends, Observed Designs, and Policy Practice in 62 Economies (May 2020) OECD [412] www.oecd.org/investment/OECD-Acquisition-ownership-policies-security-May2020.pdf.

Investment Law, the draft version circulated in 2015 contained much more detailed provisions on national security review. Ultimately, China seemed to prefer to keep the national security review flexible or unclear.[404]

The first case of security review under the Foreign Investment Law involved a plan of Yonghui Superstores to increase its stake in the state-backed retailer Wuhan Zhongbai Group. Jardine Matheson, the sprawling British conglomerate, held roughly a 20 percent stake in the majority of Chinese-owned Yonghui through its subsidiary Dairy Farm International.[405] It is rare for the National Development and Reform Commission (NDRC) to cite national security concerns when reviewing deals between companies in China's retail sector.[406] Nevertheless, the NDRC asked Yonghui "to file for a foreign investment security review and submit supplementary documents" in August 2019.[407] In the absence of any NDRC official statements, Chinese legal practitioners suspected that the security concern of this review was connected to the retailing industry affected by this deal, which falls under a MOFCOM list of sectors that might trigger a national security review.[408] The nontransparent operation of the NDRC, together with the vague language adopted by the Foreign Investment Law (2019), confirms the broad discretion of the Chinese government in the national security review.[409]

On December 19, 2020, the NDRC and the MOFCOM jointly issued the Measures on Security Review of Foreign Investment. Accordingly, the security review requirements apply to foreign investments in the sectors related to, among others, critical agricultural products; energy and resources, major equipment manufacturing; important infrastructures; important IT and internet/online products and services; important

[404] Chieh Huang, 'China's Take on National Security and its Implications for the Evolution of International Economic Law' (2021) 48(2) Legal Issues of Economic Integration 119, 131.

[405] Gordon Watts, 'China Moves to Close the Door on Opening-up' *Asia Times* (August 28, 2019) https://asiatimes.com/2019/08/china-moves-to-close-the-door-on-opening-up/.

[406] Ding Yi, 'Yonghui Drops Plans to Increase Stake in Chinese Retailer After National Security Probe' (*CX Tech*, December 17, 2019) www.caixinglobal.com/2019-12-17/yonghui-drops-plans-to-increase-stake-in-chinese-retailer-after-national-security-probe-101495178.html.

[407] Chieh Huang, 'China's Take on National Security and its Implications for the Evolution of International Economic Law' (2021) 48(2) Legal Issues of Economic Integration 119, 132.

[408] Ibid.

[409] Ibid 132–133.

financial services, key technologies.[410] The terms "important" and "key" are not further clarified, leaving the Chinese authority with broad discretion to decide which transactions in those areas should be restricted. The list also demonstrates that China has been particular about controlling and accessing information and media within the country and the related effect on social stability. As such, industries with a publishing or IT angle are broadly restricted or prohibited from foreign investment. To illustrate, any online business model where the operator may have access to a significant amount of personal user data is restricted from foreign investment.[411]

Consequently, two mechanisms to manage risks to China's security interests associated with FDI currently coexist. First, China has established a list of sectors/industries where foreign investment is generally prohibited (Negative List). Second, China uses a security review mechanism combining multi-sectoral and cross-sectoral approaches. It can be suggested that the focus of investment screening in China is protecting national security in critical areas and sectors, including economic security. While the US and the EU tend to be more specific about the criteria that have to be taken into account while evaluating the potential threat of the transaction to national/union security, Chinese policymakers focus on general areas when it comes to determining the catalog or list of reviewable sectors, thereby allowing a wide range of situations to be perceived as potential threats to China's national security.[412] Furthermore, different from the practice of most other Selected WTO Members, the decisions of the Chinese authorities on FDI are not publicized.[413] The second paragraph of Article 35 of the Foreign Investment Law (2019) clarifies that "the decision made upon the security review under the law shall be final," meaning there will be no relevant challenge procedure regarding the issue. In other words, there is no way to challenge or appeal the decision of the authorized bodies to restrict FDI.

410 Jenny Sheng and Chunbin Xu, 'China Publishes New Rules on National Security Review of Foreign Investment' (*JD Supra*, December 23, 2020) www.jdsupra.com/legalnews/china-publishes-new-rules-on-national-23076/.

411 Global Legal Group, 'International Comparative Legal Guides. Foreign Direct Investments Regimes. China' https://iclg.com/practice-areas/foreign-direct-investment-regimes-laws-and-regulations/china.

412 Xingxing Li, 'National Security Review in Foreign Investments: A Comparative and Critical Assessment on China and U.S. Laws and Practices' (2016) 13(1) Berkeley Business LJ 255, 283.

413 Global Legal Group, 'International Comparative Legal Guides. Foreign Direct Investments Regimes. China' https://iclg.com/practice-areas/foreign-direct-investment-regimes-laws-and-regulations/china.

3.2.7 *The Approach of South Africa*

South Africa has started to attract foreign investment as a part of the re-internationalization plan after the apartheid regime.[414] The South African government has been encouraging FDI to support the country's economic growth and stability.[415] As a result, most sectors in South Africa are generally open to FDI.

The principal law governing FDI in South Africa is the Protection of Investment Act (2015), which does not compel a review of inbound foreign investment, irrespective of the nature of the investment proposed, and merely grants South Africa's authorities the power to regulate FDI in the public interest.[416] Governmental approval is required for certain transactions involving foreign entities, particularly in the sectors such as energy, mining, banking, insurance, and defense.[417]

Recently, South Africa has also taken the direction of tightening restrictions and implementing barriers to foreign investments to protect its national security interests. In 2018, South Africa established a mechanism to manage risks to its national security interests associated with the foreign acquisition of certain enterprises under the Competition Act No 89 (1998) (hereafter the Competition Act).[418] According to Article 18A of the Competition Act, the established mechanism is institutionally and materially unrelated to merger reviews for competition purposes, despite its legislative basis in the Competition Act.[419] It adds "national security interests" to the list of factors that need to be considered in reviewing mergers involving a foreign company. In determining what constitutes national security interests, the President must take into account the potential impact

414 Richard W Roeder, Foreign Mining Investment Law: The Cases of Australia, South Africa and Colombia (Springer 2016) 28.

415 Jonas Mosia, 'When Is Foreign Direct Investment Beneficial to a Country and When Is It Not? The Case of South Africa' (2012) Economic Diplomacy Programme www.files.ethz.ch/isn/145917/saia_spb_44_mosia_20120223.pdf.

416 Stephen Kennedy-Good and others, 'COVID-19 Crisis Inspires Global Tightening of Foreign Investment Screening' Norton Rose Fulbright www.nortonrosefulbright.com/-/media/files/nrf/nrfweb/knowledge-pdfs/global-rules-on-foreign-direct-investment/global-rules-on-foreign-direct-investment–south-africa.pdf?la=en&revision=396854e5-87d4-45ab-aa1a-812b6fd978be.

417 Xiuyan Fei, 'Investment Barriers, Investment Facilitation and the BRICS Countries' Investment Treaty Policies and Practice' in Congyan Cai, Huiping Chen, and Yifei Wang (eds.), *The BRICS in the New International Legal Order on Investment* (Brill 2020) 211.

418 Competition Amendment Act, 2018, Act No 18 of 2018, Government Gazette Vol 644 No 175 (February 14, 2019).

419 Ibid [14].

of a merger transaction on the use or transfer of sensitive technology or know-how outside of South Africa; on the security of infrastructure, including processes, systems, facilities, technologies, networks, assets and services essential to the health, safety, security or economic well-being of citizens and the effective functioning of government; on the supply of critical goods or services to citizens, and the economic and social stability of South Africa.[420] This implies that South Africa considers a wide range of factors to potentially be able to jeopardize its national security and thereby confirms its understanding of the scope of national security in quite broad terms. Because of South Africa's FDI screening mechanism, controversial transactions with foreign investors reviewed on public interest grounds might face increased scrutiny on national security grounds.[421]

3.2.8 *Weaponization of Investment*

The ISMs in all Selected WTO Members have been or are planned to be subject to structural changes and sophisticated reforms, which often result in granting domestic authorities more power to restrict FDI in the interests of national security. In particular, since 2017, new FDI screening laws have been introduced in the US, the EU, India, China, and South Africa. The ISMs implemented in those WTO members reflect recent tendencies in the international economic order: the reemergence of geo-economic statecraft, the securitization of national economic interests, and geo-economic calculations in national economic agendas.

The ISMs in the US, the EU, and BRICS are far from being similar. While some still primarily rely on sector-based FDI screening (e.g. BRICS), others prefer to use cross-sectoral screening mechanisms elaborating on certain criteria when the transaction can threaten national/union security (e.g. the US and the EU).

Whichever approach states choose in order to define the scope of application of their investment policies related to national security, some areas of national economies generally seem more consensually sensitive to national security threats than others.[422] The operation of

[420] Ibid.

[421] Lerisha Naidu and Selma Matsinhe, 'South Africa: The de-Globalizing Pandemic: FDI and Preparing for the Post-COVID Reality' (*Lexology*, July 15, 2020) www.lexology.com/library/detail.aspx?g=abb50576-cd28-45d9-bdf0-1e9959a2565d.

[422] Frederic Wehrlé and Joachim Pohl, 'Investment Policies Related to National Security: A Survey of Country Practices' (2016) 02 OECD Working Papers on International Investment, OECD Publishing 22.

the critical infrastructure, including various public utilities, telecommunications, and transport sectors, and the protection of critical minerals is generally considered essential for economic development and the well-being of the population. The availability of natural resources, acquisition of land near the borders, and control over the media sector can also have a significant economic, political, and social impact on a state. Yet, these areas seem to play more important roles for some WTO members than others. The respective preferences for different approaches to ISMs can be explained by complicated domestic political and economic processes within each WTO member (including their openness to FDI, the level of self-sufficiency and economic growth, and the level of media pluralism), as well as the current geo-economic order (including the place of a WTO member in the international trading system, redistribution of global economic power, and strategic rivalry).

The US uses investment screening more proactively to contribute to the development and growth of domestic sectors and industries, specifically relevant to "technology wars." In particular, the US increasingly regards its semiconductor industry and investment in green technology as an issue of national security importance. Like the US, since 2019, the EU seems to be more vigilant and defensive in terms of protecting its technological assets. However, the US seems to act more aggressively by banning, for instance, certain Chinese firms from the market without providing clear evidence that their involvement in 5G would be harmful, while the EU is arguing for risk management in FDI and has slowly been taking steps to ensure that, for example, Chinese activity in Europe is subject to more scrutiny.[423] The choice of different approaches to addressing potential security threats posed by FDI could be attributed to many factors, including the different interests the US and the EU pursue while restricting FDI, which further confirms the subjective nature of what is considered to be regarded as national/union security in the US and the EU respectively.

New terminology used in ISM regulations highlights that Selected WTO Members generally see it as insufficient to consider only market criteria while screening foreign investments. The trend seems to be that more and more members are using ISMs as a means of export control,

[423] Ian Bond, 'Huawei, My Way or the Highway: Which Way Should the EU Turn?' (Center for European Reform, June 18, 2019) www.cer.eu/insights/huawei-my-way-or-highway-which-way-should-eu-turn.

often in conjunction with export control measures.[424] It can be argued that countries with less adaptive capabilities in the case of disruptions to the global market can be expected to use protectionist policies more vividly to shield their economies from external pressures.[425] Yet, the current practice demonstrates that the development of new technologies and emerging concerns related to them, in part because the data and technology have dual uses, make all governments feel more vulnerable and ready to rely on geopolitical and geo-economic considerations rather than economic analysis in their decision-making. It follows that domestic authorities are generally more eager, to a greater or lesser extent, to intervene in the flow of FDI in telecommunication and technology sectors using ISMs as a response and defense mechanism in dealing with perceived security threats.

The lack of shared understanding of how far the concept of national security could and should be stretched to balance the interests of a globalized world and an individual country results in systemic uncertainty and creates more opportunities for future protectionist-minded governments to block cross-border transactions that generally would not be expected by the international community to constitute a threat to a state's national security. Against the backdrop of rising nationalism around the world and the complex geo-economics among WTO members, more reforms in the area of FDI in the US, the EU, and BRICS can be expected.

What the international community would prefer to avoid is a common practice of states blocking or vetoing a cross-border transaction on national security grounds when there is no objective risk to their security interests (or when any national security risks involved can, instead, be mitigated by simply modifying the transaction) or of states regularly intervening in foreign takeovers when there are no justifiable national security concerns present. Government's involvement in cross-border transactions for the purposes of protecting national security interests might pose a risk if states decided that it was now "normal politics" to, on the one hand, selectively promote the free flow of FDI where doing so would augment their strengths but, on the other hand, protect the weaknesses of domestic economies by restricting foreign investments

[424] Olga Hrynkiv, 'Export Controls and Securitization of Economic Policy: Comparative Analysis of the Practice of the United States, the European Union, China, and Russia' (2022) 56(4) JWT 633, 642–656.

[425] David D Knoll, 'The Impact of Security Concerns upon International Economic Law' (1984) 11(3) Intl Econ L 567, 567.

under the guise of ensuring national security. Such a trend would inevitably result in costly economic, political, and diplomatic outcomes for the states involved, further undermining the legitimacy and stability of the international economic system.[426]

3.3 Conclusion

Selected WTO Members aim to safeguard their national security in different ways depending on their societal context and preferences. They adopt economic measures to protect national critical infrastructure, sectors, and processes that are vital for the functioning of the state/union; to respond to trade tension with their counterparts; to counter economic (cyber) espionage; to ensure the supply of energy and raw materials; and to prevent domestic companies in sensitive sectors from being controlled by a foreign government. Some of these are based on the rules and statutes that have existed alongside free trade norms for a long time (e.g. IEEPA in the US). In contrast, others have been adopted on the basis of new or amended domestic regulations.

Now expanded, such regulations open the door to Security Measures that can affect or change the policy of a specific state or nonstate actor and respond to emerging security concerns, plus, in some cases, ensure the availability and competitiveness of domestic products. Thus, from a rigorous analytic perspective, the mandate of national authorities in Selected WTO Members related to national security matters is not limited to what affects their military and defense capabilities. On the contrary, with rising tensions in the international trading system, and the visible return of strategic competition between major powers, global interdependence is also emerging as a national security issue and potential concern.[427] The analysis of the cases where Selected WTO Members have adopted trade or investment restrictions in the interests of their national security and where domestic legislation enables them to do so leads to some important conclusions about the use of economic measures by Selected WTO Members to shield themselves from emerging security threats and recent geopolitical and geo-economic developments.

First, all Selected WTO Members can adopt economic restrictions under respective domestic regulations to ensure their cybersecurity,

426 Ashley Thomas Lenihan, *Balancing Power without Weapons: State Intervention into Cross-Border Mergers and Acquisitions* (CUP 2018) 292.

427 Eric B Lorber and Juan C Zarate, 'National Economic Security' (*FDD*, January 14, 2021) www.fdd.org/analysis/2021/01/14/national-economic-security/.

which might comprise, among others, noninterference in election processes, the protection of personal data and private-sector trade secrets, and even technological leadership in cyberspace. By the same token, the list of their sensitive or strategic sectors is growing, covering telecommunications and technology sectors. Such concerns are not unwarranted. Data and technology can also be used for military purposes. For example, the sale of Huawei 5G infrastructure might not only facilitate espionage but also bring the threat of a shutdown of wireless services within a country.[428] Notably, neither the protection of the environment nor the need to address the consequences of climate change and pandemics is used as a justification for the analyzed economic Security Measures, despite them having made their way onto the security agendas of most Selected WTO Members. This confirms that different emerging threats have a different magnitude of concern for Selected WTO Members and thus result in different policy responses, not all of which are yet intertwined with the protection of their security interests.

Second, some domestic regulations are drafted in a way that allows for the application of economic measures in the interests of the economic security of Selected WTO Members. In particular, Russia, India, and China prefer to keep their regulatory options as broad as possible, which suggests that new concerns about their national security interests might more easily result in the application of Security Measures depending on domestic political and economic processes and the demands of a constantly evolving geo-economic order. The regulations of these WTO members have limited potential to differentiate the use of economic policy instruments to protect genuine and pressing national security concerns from the need to protect other domestic interests.

The US and the EU seek to ensure that their economic sanctions and ISMs operate as tools to protect national security and not as a means of protectionism, for example, by including specific conditions and procedural safeguards for their adoption under domestic law. The same applies to FDI regulations in Brazil and South Africa. This is not to say that the regulations of these members necessarily prevent the adoption of protectionist measures or measures with mixed motives. Yet, they limit the discretion of responsible domestic authorities to implement such measures without providing additional information or evidence proving the need to protect national security.

[428] Gregory Shaffer, 'Trade Law in a Data-Driven Economy: The Need for Modesty and Resilience' (2021) 20(3) World Trade Rev 259, 266.

It can also be argued that the prospect of judicial review incentivizes governments to develop more sophisticated procedural regularity in imposing economic measures.[429] Selected WTO Members approach the judicial review of foreign affairs and national security matters in different ways. For the same reasons that self-judging language is used within the Security Exceptions in international economic law, the measures granting authority to the US President and China's government in national security matters often limit judicial review of their decisions, thereby granting them more discretionary powers. On the contrary, a substantial number of the reviewed sanctions by the CJEU demonstrates that judicial control focused on procedural norms might be an appropriate compromise between oversight and flexibility in certain areas of national or regional security and foreign policy. Notably, the reviewed cases suggest that domestic and regional courts more readily review the cases brought by individuals, mostly on constitutional grounds and with respect to due process concerns.

Less effective checks on the actions of executive branches in national security matters can result in domestic industry groups having a greater influence on decisions to adopt Security Measures and, consequently, on the mixed motives of such measures. To this end, the lack of domestic judicial review can sharpen the trend that Security Exceptions are invoked for situations they are not well-equipped to deal with.

New regulations and implementation within WTO member states would further contribute to a better understanding of the evolving concept of national security and, potentially, economic security in the era of increasingly pervasive digitalization, developments in AI, the rising importance of new economic sectors, and threats that can easily overhaul the very foundation of modern society. In particular, more industries and sectors could be deemed strategic, more FDI could be treated as posing a risk to host states, and more prospective deals could be blocked on national security grounds. For one, the EU is in the process of reviewing its economic statecraft, which might enable it to catch up with the securitization of economic relations in the US and China.[430] Any further shifts in the current policies of Selected WTO Members will continue to shape the changes in the understanding by their respective authorities of national security threats and foreign policy targets, signaling further securitization, or potentially de-securitization, of their national interests.

[429] Elena Chachko, 'Administrative National Security' (2020) 108 Geo LJ 1063, 1135.

[430] See more Chien-Huei Wu, 'The EU's Proposed Anti-coercion Instrument: Legality and Effectiveness' (2023) 57(2) JWT 297.

4

Evolution of Security Exceptions in Trade and Investment Agreements

As in WTO agreements, many RTAs include Security Exception clauses. As a matter of newer investment treaty practice, WTO members also insert Security Exceptions in their BITs and investment chapters of RTAs (together, IIAs).[1] While Security Exceptions under RTAs and IIAs are often modeled on the WTO law, some contracting parties decide to adopt a different approach to their drafting and application.

Overlaps may occur in the operation of the separate legal systems of RTAs, on the one hand, and WTO agreements, on the other hand,[2] including in the application of Security Exceptions. The WTO case law suggests that the WTO system treats RTAs as complementary, as an exception to the principle of nondiscrimination that is allowed only when the requirements of the WTO provisions devoted to RTAs are met.[3] When involved in cases capable of simultaneously falling under the ambit of the regional and multilateral trade systems, WTO members are expected to act in good faith and to find a solution that preserves the unity of the WTO system.[4] Following this logic, if a Security Measure meets the threshold prescribed by the Security Exception under a particular RTA, it is, in principle, considered legal under that RTA. Yet, the same measure can potentially be found in breach of the state's obligations under WTO law if it does not meet the conditions of the WTO Security Exceptions.

Given that the WTO agreements have a trade-dominated perspective on FDI and only partially cover issues related to investment,[5] there is very

[1] Chapter 2, section 2.2.

[2] Gabrielle Marceau and Julian Wyatt, 'Dispute Settlement Regimes Intermingled: Regional Trade Agreements and the WTO' (2010) 1(1) JIDS 67, 93.

[3] Elisa Baroncini, 'The Relation between the Marrakesh System and Regional Trade Agreements in the WTO Case-Law' (2017) 2 Dialoghi Con Ugo Villani 835, 842.

[4] Elisa Baroncini, 'La Soluzione Delle Controversie Commerciali Tra Stati Tra Multilateralismo E Regionalismo by Laura Zoppo' (2014) 17(2) J of Intl Economic Law 473, 478.

[5] Carlos Esplugues Mota, *Foreign Investment, Strategic Assets and National Security* (Intersentia 2018) 39.

little chance for overlap between the application of Security Exceptions under the WTO agreements and that of IIAs.

The current debates predominantly focus on the self-judging character of certain Security Exceptions and the need to defer to the judgment of domestic authorities while deciding on highly volatile security issues.[6] Given this, this chapter purports to construct a tentative taxonomy of Security Exceptions based on the degree of deference that should be granted to domestic authorities under different types of Security Exception clauses:

- the exceptions that do not use any "self-judging" language, such as "it considers necessary";
- the exceptions that allow a state to take Security Measures when "it considers necessary" but prescribe additional criteria for the invocation of the exception, narrowing it down to specific situations (WTO-style exceptions);
- the exceptions that allow a state to take Security Measures when "it considers necessary" but exclude the additional criteria narrowing down the exception, thereby making any review of invocations of the exception, even a good faith review, more difficult to justify ("self-judging" exceptions); and
- the exceptions that specifically exclude any Security Measures from being subject to judicial review.

This taxonomy tracks a spectrum from the most objectively drafted exceptions, leaving less room for contracting parties' discretion, to the most broadly drafted Security Exceptions that completely exclude adjudication of Security Measures.

This chapter discusses the approaches of the US, the EU, and BRICS to incorporating and drafting Security Exception clauses in RTAs (section 4.1) and IIAs (section 4.2), with an attempt to distill their differences and commonalities (section 4.3). In particular, it focuses on the drafting techniques used by the US, the EU, and BRICS and discusses the ordinary meaning of the terms used in Regional Agreements. The preference for textualism is driven by the concern to place international trade and investment rules upon solid foundations, "incapable of being manipulated by states in pursuit of their subjective interests,"[7] and the role of textualism in the treaty interpretation under the VCLT.

6 Chapter 5, section 5.1.

7 Fuad Zarbiyev, 'A Genealogy of Textualism in Treaty Interpretation' in Andrea Bianchi, Daniel Peat, and Matthew Windsor (eds.), *Interpretation in International Law* (OUP 2015) 261.

4.1 Security Exceptions in Trade Agreements

The proliferation of Security Exception clauses in RTAs started long before the vigorous disagreement about the interpretation of Security Exceptions under WTO agreements.[8] All the recent RTAs of the US refer to the measures "[a state] considers necessary" to protect its essential security interests without narrowing it down to specific types of transactions or situations. The analysis of these RTAs suggests that such drafting techniques used by the US allow for an expansion of the scope of the measures taken for the sake of national security. At the same time, the current approach of the EU to drafting its security defense is to use the language of WTO-style Security Exceptions, sometimes in combination with a more objective language for certain exceptions. BRICS prefer to use WTO-style exceptions in some RTAs but to draft Security Exceptions more broadly in others.

On the one hand, various approaches to drafting Security Exceptions can signal the lack of consensus over the desirable scope of the security defense in international trade law. On the other hand, at least in some cases, Security Exceptions can be phrased instrumentally. The specific language of exception clauses might also depend on the bargaining power of negotiators and reflect their understanding of international law and the desirability to strengthen the undertaken trade commitments. Finally, it can be assumed that certain discrepancies in the language of Security Exceptions can be attributed to negligence rather than the drafters' intention. This, however, does not exclude that these discrepancies could be used as a basis to justify states' particular views on the interpretation of their right to security defense.

4.1.1 The US Approach

For the first time, the US postwar FCN treaties[9] included an exception for measures "necessary for protecting the essential interests."[10] In 1954, the Security Exceptions provision was the subject of extensive discussion

[8] This section refers to the RTAs listed in the RTA-IS database. This database provides information on RTAs that have been notified, or for which an early announcement was made, to the WTO https://rtais.wto.org/UI/PublicMaintainRTAHome.aspx.

[9] The FCN treaties addressed many issues, including trade and investment protection, which have later become subject to separate specialized agreements. They remain primarily of historical interest, especially concerning the issues related to the parties' understanding of their national security concerns. See John F Coyle, 'The Treaty of Friendship, Commerce and Navigation in the Modern Era' (2013) 51 Colum J Transnatl L 302, 326.

[10] Article XXV(1)(c) of Standard Draft FCN Treaty (1945).

between the US and Germany. US negotiators explained at the beginning of the discussion that no precise interpretation existed for the expression "to protect . . . essential security interests." Accordingly, "the language had been drafted in such a manner as to leave a wide area of discretion to both parties in order to allow for necessary action over an indefinite future . . . [N]o serious consequences were expected from this reservation so long as the relations between both countries remained friendly."[11] The US State Department "stressed [that] the words 'necessary' and 'essential' had been added to emphasize that the reservation was not to be invoked in a frivolous manner."[12] The German negotiators stated that they were glad to hear the last point.[13] Concerning a different clause, the German negotiators proposed to incorporate into the treaty what they described as a "subjective" test under which each party would have the sole discretion to determine whether to impose exchange controls.[14] The US negotiators objected to the addition of the phrase "it considers" on the ground that the addition of the words would make the determination "unilateral" and "in effect nullify the paragraph."[15] Thus, it can be assumed that the US did not incorporate into its FCN treaties the phrase "it considers" since it did not intend to make any of their provisions self-judging.

The FCN treaty with the Netherlands (1956) also allows for the measures, among others, "necessary to protect [a party's] essential security interests."[16] The Netherlands proposed additional language indicating that the essential security interest exception would be strictly construed so that it would not be abused. However, it was objected to by the US since it called into question the consistency of existing US laws with the treaty.[17] Ultimately, the two parties agreed on the inclusion of a paragraph in the protocol that provided the clarification sought by the Netherlands, balanced by language that the US proposed in

[11] Kenneth J Vandevelde, *The First Bilateral Investment Treaties: U.S. Postwar Friendship, Commerce, and Navigation Treaties* (OUP 2017) 514.

[12] Ibid.

[13] Ibid.

[14] Ibid 516.

[15] Ibid 522.

[16] Article XXII of FCN Treaty with the Netherlands (March 27, 1956). Based on Article XXI (1)(d) of Standard Draft FCN Treaty (1955) provided that "[t]he present Treaty shall not preclude the application of measures . . . necessary to protect [a party's] essential security interests."

[17] The Senate had accepted the existing language, and thus any change could pose an obstacle to Senate advice and consent to ratification. See Kenneth J Vandevelde, *The First Bilateral Investment Treaties: U.S. Postwar Friendship, Commerce, and Navigation Treaties* (OUP 2017) 321.

response,[18] clarifying that: "It is understood that it is not the purpose of the security reservation to create a basis for unduly prolonged departures from any provision of the Treaty. On the other hand, each Party determines, according to its own best judgment, the measures deemed necessary to protect its essential security interests."

Such a proposal demonstrates first that the US and the Netherlands did acknowledge that Security Measures can be applied only temporarily and, second, that even omitting the self-judging language in the Security Exception clause, the parties left the determination of the measures "necessary to protect essential security interests" to their domestic authorities.

The language inserted by the US into its FCN treaty with the Netherlands was similar to the language used by the US to refer to the application of various other provisions of the treaty as well. After analyzing the negotiation history of several FCN treaties, however, Vandevelde concluded that when the US used the language "according to its own best judgment," it did not mean to preclude the review of the measures but rather to allow each party to make the initial determination of whether a measure was consistent with the treaty.[19]

While examining the similarly drafted Security Exception clause under US–Nicaragua FCN Treaty (1956),[20] the International Court of Justice (ICJ) differentiated between the wording of Article XXI(b) GATT (1947) referring to the measures "[a state] considers necessary" and the respective Security Exception under the US–Nicaragua FCN Treaty referring to "necessary" measures.[21] The impact of the ICJ ruling in this dispute was to draw attention to the consequences of adding to the Security Exception clause the words "it considers necessary," as will be further discussed.

4.1.1.1 WTO-Style Exceptions

Earlier, US RTAs used the text of Security Exceptions similar to Article XXI GATT (1994), including the wording "it considers necessary." To illustrate, US–Israel Free Trade Agreement (FTA) (1985) incorporates Article XXI GATT (1994) by reference.[22] US–Jordan FTA (2000)

[18] Kenneth J Vandevelde, *The First Bilateral Investment Treaties: U.S. Postwar Friendship, Commerce, and Navigation Treaties* (OUP 2017) 321.

[19] Ibid.

[20] Article XXI of FCN Treaty between the US and the Republic of Nicaragua (January 21, 1956).

[21] *Case Concerning Military and Paramilitary Activities in and against Nicaragua (Nicaragua v US)* (June 27, 1986) ICJ Rep Merits [222].

[22] Article 7 of the Agreement on the Establishment of a Free Trade Area between the Government of Israel and the Government of the US (1985).

almost reiterates the text of Article XXI GATT (1994).[23] Security Exceptions under NAFTA (1992), the predecessor of USMCA, uses slightly different language compared to the GATT (1994).[24] Notably, the NAFTA Implementation Act (1993) specifies that the Security Exception is self-judging, "although each government would expect the provisions to be applied by the other in good faith."[25] It is unclear whether an invocation of such an exception under NAFTA in good faith was intended to be presumed or reviewed by NAFTA dispute resolution procedures.[26]

Furthermore, the NAFTA prescribes special treatment of the investment measures and the measures that restrict imports/exports of an energy or basic petrochemical good from/to another party. Investment measures are excluded from the tribunal's review.[27] The fact that the parties expressly agreed that the dispute settlement mechanism would not apply in the case of disputes with investors suggests that it would apply in other cases in disputes with other states over trade matters. At the same time, the exception related to the energy measures has no self-judging language and specifies the exact circumstances under which the security defense can be invoked to reassure that North American supplies should be considered secure in any future emergency.[28] Using a self-judging language for most Security Measures but removing it for the measures that restrict imports/exports of an energy or basic petrochemical good also suggests that the standard of review for such exceptions would differ. Yet, the NAFTA leaves these questions open.

[23] Article 12 of US–Jordan FTA (2000).

[24] First, Article 2102 (National Security) of NAFTA covers the measures "relating to the implementation of national policies or international agreements respecting the non-proliferation of nuclear weapons or other nuclear explosive devices," while GATT (1994) refers only to the measures "relating to fissionable materials or the materials from which they are derived." Second, it encompasses not only measures "relating to the traffic in arms, ammunition and implements of war" but also relating to "such traffic and transactions in other goods, materials, services and technology undertaken directly or indirectly for the purpose of supplying a military or other security establishment."

[25] Message from the US President transmitting NAFTA, Statement of Administrative Action and Requiring Supporting Statements (1993) HRDoc 103–159, 666.

[26] See eg Knoll, who doubts whether the element of good faith could be made subject to judicial review: David D Knoll, 'The Impact of Security Concerns upon International Economic Law' (1984) 11(3) Intl Econ L 567, 589.

[27] Chapter 4, section 4.2.1.

[28] Article 607 NAFTA (1992).

4.1.1.2 Toward "Self-Judging" Exceptions

The US adopted a different approach to drafting Security Exception clauses in its FTAs concluded in 2003–2005. They expand the scope of states' discretion to apply Security Measures in particular by using broad language in describing the essential security interests and omitting any specific precondition for the invocation of Security Exceptions. To illustrate, the Dominican Republic–Central America–US FTA (CAFTA–DR) signed in 2004 in Article 21.2(b) (Essential Security) refers to the measures "that [a state] considers necessary for the fulfillment of its obligations with respect to the maintenance or restoration of international peace or security, or the protection of its own essential security interests."[29] Article 21.2(b) is a combined form of Article XXI(b) and (c) GATT (1994), which, however, misses three subparagraphs of Article XXI(b). As in the case of many FCN treaties, Security Exceptions under the CAFTA–DR do not include the subparagraphs clarifying the circumstances under which the defense aimed to protect the state's essential security interests could be invoked. The CAFTA–DR has no reference to "arms, ammunition or war materials" or measures "taken in time of war or other emergency in international relations." It simply states "the protection of its own essential security interests." Furthermore, different from the FCN treaties, the CAFTA–DR refers to the measures "that [a state] considers necessary," either for "protection of its own essential security interests," similar to Article XXI(b) GATT (1994), or "fulfillment of its obligations with respect to the maintenance or restoration of international peace or security," similar to Article XXI(c) GATT (1994).

The same language of Security Exceptions has been incorporated into US–Chile FTA (2003),[30] US–Singapore FTA (2003),[31] US–Australia FTA (2004),[32] US–Bahrain FTA (2005),[33] and US–Oman FTA (2006).[34] US–Morocco FTA (2004)[35] follows the same approach. However, it specifies that:

> For greater certainty, measures that a Party considers necessary for the protection of its own essential security interests may include, inter alia, measures relating to the production of or traffic in arms, ammunition, and implements of war and to such traffic and transactions in other goods,

[29] Article 21.2 of the Dominican Republic–Central America–US FTA (CAFTA-DR) (2004).
[30] Article 23.2 of US–Chile FTA (2003).
[31] Article 21.2 of US–Singapore FTA (2003).
[32] Article 22.2 of US–Australia FTA (2004).
[33] Article 20.2 of US–Bahrain FTA (2005).
[34] Article 21.2 of US–Oman FTA (2006).
[35] Article 21.2 of US–Morocco FTA (2004).

> materials, services, and technology undertaken directly or indirectly for the purpose of supplying a military or other security establishment.

This addition resembles the circumstances under which the defense aimed to protect the state's essential security interests could be invoked under Article XXI(b)(ii) GATT (1994). However, different from the GATT (1994), the list of such circumstances is not exhaustive. It merely provides an example of cases where the parties can rely on Security Exceptions.

The US RTAs concluded in 2006–2007 also use broad language in describing the essential security interests and omit any specific precondition for the invocation of Security Exceptions. In addition, similar to the NAFTA approach, they differentiate between trade and investment provisions concerning the application of Security Measures.[36]

The most recent example of the FTA concluded by the US is the successor of NAFTA, USMCA (2018).[37] The USMCA's Security Exception clause deviates from NAFTA's approach. It is broader in scope, consistent with the US FTAs concluded in 2003–2007, as discussed above. In particular, the Security Exception clause omits specific preconditions for the invocation of the security defense.[38] Article 32.2 USMCA (2018) generally refers to the measures that "[a state] considers necessary for . . . the protection of its own essential security interests." This move could enable the US to use broad interpretations of its security interests later.[39]

The parties to USMCA have clarified specific issues regarding the application of Security Measures under Section 232 of the Trade Expansion Act. First, the US agrees that some passenger vehicles, light trucks, and auto parts from Canada and Mexico are excluded from future Section 232 Security Measures.[40] Second, the parties agree to a sixty-day consultation before the US can apply Security Measures against Canada

[36] Chapter 4, section 4.1.1.

[37] Article 32.2 USMCA (2018).

[38] Ibid Article 32.2.

[39] Tori Smith andGabriella Beaumont-Smith, 'An Analysis of the United States–Mexico–Canada Agreement' (*The Heritage Foundation*, January 28, 2019) www.heritage.org/trade/report/analysis-the-united-states-mexico-canada-agreement. See more Chapter 3, section 3.1.2.

[40] US Trade Representative, USMCA, MX-US Side Letter on 232 https://ustr.gov/sites/default/files/files/agreements/FTA/USMCA/Text/MX-US_Side_Letter_on_232.pdf; US Trade Representative, USMCA, Side Letter Text on 232 CA-US Response https://ustr.gov/sites/default/files/files/agreements/FTA/USMCA/Text/Side_Letter_Text_on_232_CA-US_Response.pdf.

or Mexico (and guarantees access levels in the case of autos).[41] Third, the US limited the ability of Canada and Mexico to dispute any potential tariffs on these items through the NAFTA and USMCA except "with respect to whether the US has excluded the number of passenger vehicles and light trucks, and the value of auto parts as set out."[42] Nevertheless, given the US position that it has broad authority to impose tariffs for national security reasons and that the USMCA's Security Exceptions shall be interpreted broadly, Canada and Mexico may find it hard to challenge US national security tariffs under the USMCA.

4.1.2 The EU Approach

4.1.2.1 Exceptions That Do Not Use "Self-Judging" Language

Most RTAs concluded by the EU (the EC at that time) from 1972–2008 differentiate between the circumstances left to EU member states to define (similar to the GATT (1947)/GATT (1994)) and those subject to objective interpretation. To illustrate, EU–Switzerland–Liechtenstein FTA (1972) in Article 21 differentiates between three types of measures:

- "which relate to trade in arms, munitions or war materials or to research, development or production indispensable for defence purposes";
- "which [the party] considers necessary to prevent the disclosure of information contrary to its essential security interests"; and
- "which [the party] considers essential to its own security in time of war or serious international tension."[43]

[41] US Trade Representative, USMCA, MX-US Side Letter on 232 Process https://ustr.gov/sites/default/files/files/agreements/FTA/USMCA/Text/MX-US_Side_Letter_on_232_Process.pdf; US Trade Representative, USMCA, CA-US Side Letter on 232 Process https://ustr.gov/sites/default/files/files/agreements/FTA/USMCA/Text/CA-US_Side_Letter_on_232_Process.pdf.

[42] US Trade Representative, USMCA, Side Letter Text on 232 CA-US Response https://ustr.gov/sites/default/files/files/agreements/FTA/USMCA/Text/Side_Letter_Text_on_232_CA-US_Response.pdf; US Trade Representative, USMCA, MX-US Side Letter on 232 Dispute Resolution https://ustr.gov/sites/default/files/files/agreements/FTA/USMCA/Text/MX-US_Side_Letter_on_232_Dispute_Settlement.pdf.

[43] Article 21 of the Agreement between the European Economic Community and the Swiss Confederation and Liechtenstein (1972). Similar approaches were used in the RTAs with Iceland (1972), Norway (1973), Syria (1977), Tunisia (1995), Israel (1995), the Faroe Islands (1996), Mexico (1997), Jordan (1997), Palestine (1997), Egypt (2001), North Macedonia (2001), Lebanon (2002), Albania (2006), Algeria (2006), Montenegro (2007), Morocco (2007), Bosnia and Herzegovina (2008), and Serbia (2008).

The EU has also established three Deep and Comprehensive Free Trade Areas with Georgia,[44] Moldova,[45] and Ukraine,[46] each of which constitutes a part of each country's EU Association Agreement (AA). The agreements with Moldova and Georgia have been modeled upon the AA with Ukraine.[47] All three AAs incorporate two separate Security Exception clauses. To illustrate, EU–Ukraine AA (2014) contains Article 143 (Security Exceptions) as part of Title IV on Trade and Trade-Related Matters and Article 472 (Measures related to essential security interests) as part of Title VII on Institutional, General and Final Provisions. Article 143 contains the WTO-like security defense allowing each party to take measures that "it considers necessary" and referring to the measures, among others, "taken in time of war or other emergency in international relations." At the same time, Article 472 follows the approach of the earlier EU RTAs. It differentiates between two ranges of circumstances under which the security defense can be invoked: (1) allowing the states to take measures that they consider necessary/essential (e.g. in times of war or other serious international tension), and (2) allowing the states to take measures that relate to the specific subject matter (e.g. trade in arms). Thus, Article 472 seems to have removed the subjective language "it considers necessary" from certain Security Exceptions, which indicates the intention of the drafters to give less room to the discretionary power of the parties in non-trade-related matters, particularly in cases of economic and sector cooperation, financial cooperation and political matters. The same approach was adopted in EU–Moldova AA (2014) and EU–Georgia AA (2014).

4.1.2.2 WTO-Style Exceptions

Security Exceptions in the recent EU RTAs predominantly use the WTO format. The EU RTAs incorporate the WTO Security Exceptions by reference[48] or use the same or very similar to the WTO Security

[44] Association Agreement between the EU and the European Atomic Energy Community and their Member States, of the one part, and Georgia, of the other part (2014).

[45] Association Agreement between the EU and the European Atomic Energy Community and their Member States, of the one part, and the Republic of Moldova, of the other part (2014).

[46] Association Agreement between the EU and Its Member States, of the one part, and Ukraine of the other part (2014).

[47] Guillaume Van der Loo, *The EU–Ukraine Association Agreement and Deep and Comprehensive Free Trade Area* (Brill 2016) 314.

[48] See eg Article 1.5 of the Agreement between the EU and Japan for an Economic Partnership (2018).

Exceptions language with only minor deviations.[49] To illustrate, EU–Canada Comprehensive Economic and Trade Agreement (CETA) (2016)[50] incorporates two types of Security Exceptions. Article 28.6 (National security) refers to the circumstances under which the security defense can be invoked as provided for in Article XXI GATT (1994) and Article XIV*bis* GATS, while Article 19.3 (Security and general exceptions) provides for an additional situation when the security defense can be invoked as it is prescribed in Article XXIII GPA (1994) (Security Exceptions) (later Article III of the revised GPA (2012) which the EU became a party to in 2014).

EU–Singapore FTA (2018)[51] has a similar approach. Compared to Article XXI(b)(iii) GATT (1994), Article 16.11 (Security Exceptions) also refers to the measures taken "to protect critical public infrastructure (this relates to communications, power or water infrastructure providing essential goods or services to the general public) from deliberate attempts to disable or disrupt it."

EU–New Zealand FTA (2022) reiterates Security Exceptions under the GATT (1994) and GATS.[52] Notably, the FTA separately prescribes the exception for public security and clarifies the application of general exceptions under Article XX GATT (1994) by specifying that they cover "environmental measures necessary to protect human and animal or plant life or health."[53] The inclusion of public security exceptions and the clarification of general exceptions arguably delimits the room for broadening the scope of Security Exceptions under EU–New Zealand FTA,[54] thus reaffirming that the EU understands a national security defense in relatively narrow terms. The same approach is adopted in EU–Chile FTA (2022).[55] Notably, both agreements broaden the WTO-style Security Exception for traffic in arms and other military- and defense-related goods by allowing the restrictions "connected to the production of ... and to such traffic and transactions in ... services and technology" for military purposes.[56] As a "chip war" between the US and China escalates, the EU seems to be willing to preserve more

[49] See eg Article 9.3 of the FTA between the EU and the Socialist Republic of Viet Nam (2020); Article 415 of EU–UK FTA & Economic Integration Agreement (2020).

[50] Article 28.6 of EU–Canada CETA (2016).

[51] Article 16.11 of the FTA between the EU and the Republic of Singapore (2018).

[52] Article 25.2 of EU–New Zealand FTA (2022).

[53] Ibid Article 25.1(2) and (3).

[54] See more Chapter 6.

[55] Article 32.2 of EU–Chile FTA (2022).

[56] Article 25.2(b)(i) of EU–New Zealand FTA (2022) and Article 32.2(b)(i) of EU–Chile FTA (2022).

policy space to take necessary measures in response to technological developments and export controls of other WTO members.[57]

The ECJ case law with respect to the trade between EU member states (intra-EU trade) sheds some light on the interpretation of the public policy and security exception. While analyzing the exception under Article 65(1)(b) of TFEU (public security exception from the free movement of capital),[58] the ECJ highlighted that such exceptions excluded purely economic interest from their scope. Article 65(1)(b) of TFEU uses broad language for the exceptions without listing the cases where public security or other policy interests can be protected but only specifying that member states can "take measures which are justified on grounds of public policy or public security." In *Eglise de Scientologie v France*, the ECJ underlined that "those derogations must not be misapplied so as, in fact, to serve purely economic ends."[59] The ECJ also referred to *Rutili v Minister for the Interior*, dealing with the expression "subject to limitations justified on the grounds of public policy, public security or public health" in Article 48 of the EEC Treaty (free movement of workers). The ECJ mentioned that Article 2 of the Council Directive No 68/360 on Freedom of Movement for Workers provides that grounds of public policy shall not be "invoked to service economic ends."[60]

At the same time, the ECJ held that maintaining sufficient domestic capacity could be justified based on the public security exception under the EU law.[61] In the *Campus Oil* case, Ireland required importers to cover a certain proportion of their needs by purchasing from a state-owned refinery in Ireland, thus discriminating against foreign products. The ECJ found such measures justifiable, explaining that even though a public security exception refers to matters of a noneconomic nature, "in the

[57] Olga Hrynkiv and Saskia Lavrijssen, 'Not Trading with the Enemy: the Case of Computer Chips' (2024) 58(1) JWT 61, 77–79.

[58] Article 65(1)(b) of TFEU allows the member states to "take measures which are justified on grounds of public policy or public security" and which do not "constitute a means of arbitrary discrimination or a disguised restriction on the free movement of capital and payments."

[59] Case C-54/99 *Association Eglise de scientologie de Paris and Scientology International Reserves Trust v The Prime Minister* [2000] EU:C:2000:124 [17].

[60] Case C-36/75 *Rutili v Minister for the Interior* [1975] EU:C:1975:137 [30].

The rationale behind this rule can be that a member state cannot rely on a derogation to justify excluding foreign nationals from its labor market simply because unemployment is high in that state and there is a political need to preserve jobs for nationals. See Catherine Barnard, *The Substantive Law of the EU. The Four Freedoms* (OUP 2007) 461.

[61] Case C-72/83 *Campus Oil Limited and others v Minister for Industry and Energy and others* [1984] EU:C:1984:256 [51].

light of the seriousness of the consequences that an interruption in supplies of petroleum products may have for a country's existence, the aim of ensuring a minimum supply of petroleum products at all times is to be regarded as transcending purely economic considerations and thus as capable of constituting an objective covered by the concept of public security."[62]

In a similar vein, it can be suggested that Security Exceptions under the RTAs concluded by the EU aim to protect the noneconomic interests of contracting parties, and they can justify the protection of parties' economic interests only in extremely rare situations. It can also be argued that the scope of restrictions on capital movements to and from non-Member States (trade with countries outside the EU) and within the EU may differ, but CJEU case law on this is limited.[63]

4.1.3 *The Approach of Brazil*

Neither the Treaty of Asunción establishing the Southern Common Market (MERCOSUR for its Spanish initials) (1991)[64] nor the Montevideo Treaty creating the Latin American Integration Association (1980)[65] mentions Security Exceptions. Only the Protocol of Montevideo on Trade in Services in MERCOSUR incorporates GATS-like Security Exceptions.[66]

Through MERCUSOR, Brazil does have a Preferential Trade Agreement with the Southern African Customs Union (SACU), India, Israel, and Egypt. These RTAs regulate only trade in goods and incorporate Article XXI GATT (1994) by reference (e.g. India,[67] Israel,[68] Egypt,[69] SACU[70]).

The Brazil–Mexico Agreement of Economic Complementation[71] has no exception clause. At the same time, the Agreement on Global System of

[62] Ibid [35].

[63] Olga Hrynkiv and Saskia Lavrijssen, 'Foreign Investments and Energy Transition in the Netherlands: Balancing Economic and Security Interests' (2024) 42(1) JLCOM 1, 30.

[64] Treaty Establishing a Common Market between Argentine Republic, the Federal Republic of Brazil, the Republic of Paraguay and the Eastern Republic of Uruguay (MERCOSUR) (1991).

[65] Treaty of Montevideo Instrument Establishing the Latin American Integration Association (ALADI) Montevideo, August 1980 (Includes Resolutions CM/1 to 7 adopted by the LAFTA Council of Ministers of Foreign Affairs).

[66] Article XIV of Montevideo Protocol on Trade in Services of MERCOSUR.

[67] Article 9 of MERCOSUR–India FTA (2004).

[68] Chapter XII, Article 1 of MERCOSUR–Israel FTA (2007).

[69] Article 22 of MERCOSUR–Egypt FTA (2010).

[70] Article 13 of MERCOSUR–SACU Partial Scope Agreement (2008).

[71] Agreement of Economic Complementation No 53 (known as ACE No 53) (2002).

Trade Preferences among Developing Countries (GSTP) (1988), to which Brazil is a party, includes a broadly drafted clause allowing for "any action which [a participant] considers necessary for the protection of its essential security interests."[72] Otherwise, Brazil has not been especially active in signing off RTAs. Thus, the above analysis sheds little light on the preferable drafting techniques used by Brazil for Security Exception clauses.

4.1.4 The Approach of Russia

4.1.4.1 Exceptions That Do Not Use "Self-Judging" Language and "Self-Judging" Exceptions

Russia is a founding member state of the Eurasian Economic Union (EAEU). The Treaty on EAEU incorporates separate Security Exception clauses related to various fields of Eurasian integration: trade in goods, trade in services, subsidies, and financial services. To illustrate, Article 29(1) of the Treaty on EAEU provides exceptions for the free movement of goods within the EAEU common market. It is a combined form of Article XX and Article XXI GATT (1994). In particular, it refers to the measures which are necessary for the protection of human life and health, public morals, and other values similar to Article XX GATT (1994), as well as to the measures which are necessary for the defense and security of the member states. Article 29 of the Treaty on EAEU refers to the measures that are necessary rather than that a party considers necessary. Besides, it includes, very similar to the chapeau of Article XX, language that mentions that the measures shall not result in unjustifiable discrimination or a disguised restriction on trade.[73] A similar provision is provided in Annex 7 Protocol on Measures for Non-tariff Regulation concerning Third Countries.[74] At the same time, Article 74(5) General Provisions includes a broad language of Security Exceptions prescribing that nothing in the section related to competition matters should be interpreted as preventing any member state from taking any measures it considers necessary for the protection of the vital interests of national defense or security of the state.[75] The clause uses self-judging language but does not prescribe the conditions under which a party can invoke it to protect its vital national defense or security interests.

72 Article 33 of GSTP (1988).

73 Treaty on the EAEU (2014).

74 See Annex 7 of the Protocol on Measures for Non-tariff Regulation with regard to Third Countries of the Treaty on the EAEU (2014) [30], [38].

75 Treaty on the EAEU (2014).

There is no established case law on the application of the security clauses within the Treaty on EAEU. Therefore, it is not easy to understand the drafters' intention for using different language for Security Exception clauses incorporated within the same agreement. In particular, it remains contentious whether omitting the phrase "it considers necessary" and adding additional preconditions for invoking the security defense similar to the chapeau of Article XX makes the scope of states' discretion in the application of the exception under Article 29 of the Treaty on EAEU narrower than the other Security Exceptions incorporated in the agreement. The only act that indirectly covers the interpretation of Article 29 of the Treaty on EAEU is the EAEU Court Advisory Opinion of October 30, 2017.[76] The EAEU Court reiterated that Article 29(1) of the Treaty on EAEU could be used only under exceptional circumstances[77] if the objective of the measure at issue responds to one of the conditions prescribed in the exception clause (including defense and security of the member states) and if the measure does not "constitute a means of arbitrary discrimination or a disguised restriction on trade between member states."[78] Remarkably, even though Article 29(1) uses language similar to Article XX GATT (1994) and refers to the measures necessary for the achievement of certain policy and security objectives, the EAEU Court did not prescribe the necessity test as a precondition for justifying the measure under the exception clause. Instead, it referred to the practice of the ECJ in *WJG Bauhuis v The Netherlands State* (Case C-46/76) and *Adriaan de Peijper* (Case C-104/75) dealing with public security and other policy exception under the EEC Treaty to confirm that the member states' discretion at the application of Article 29(1) is not absolute and the provisions of this Article should be interpreted strictly.[79] The EAEU Court did not mention any specific considerations for Security Exceptions. It remains to be seen whether the EAEU Court would use a different legal test to apply other exception clauses under the agreement, which use self-judging language and do not refer to the preconditions similar to the chapeau of Article XX GATT (1994).[80]

[76] EAEU Court Advisory Opinion No CE-2-2/2-17-BK (October 30, 2017) www.alta.ru/tamdoc/17a00017/.

[77] EAEU Court Advisory Opinion No CE-2-2/2-17-BK (October 30, 2017) [8].

[78] Ibid [6].

[79] Ibid [8].

[80] Vitaliy Slepak, 'National Security Clause: Law and Practice of European Union and Eurasia Economic Union' (2019) 1406 J Phys: Conf Ser 5 https://iopscience.iop.org/article/10.1088/1742-6596/1406/1/012002/pdf.

4.1.4.2 WTO-Style Exceptions

In most other cases, Russia's RTAs either reiterate the language of Article XXI GATT (1994)[81] or incorporate Article XXI GATT (1994) by reference.[82]

At the same time, it is not uncommon to find in Russia's RTAs the clause combining WTO-like Security Exceptions with general exceptions, with slightly different terms than the WTO agreements.[83] To illustrate, the Russia–Azerbaijan FTA (1992) in Article 11 refers to the measures that the parties consider necessary for protecting their vital interests or which are undoubtedly necessary for compliance with international agreements to which they are or intend to become parties when they related to certain goods or values.[84] Different from the WTO Security Exceptions, the Russia–Azerbaijan FTA (1992) refers to vital/essential interests rather than "essential security interests." It specifies the grounds on which the defense can be invoked. Still, unlike the GATT (1994), such grounds do not include the measures "taken in time of war or other emergency in international relations."

4.1.5 The Approach of India

4.1.5.1 WTO-Style Exceptions

Several RTAs entered into by India have replicated the WTO Security Exceptions as a default template. To illustrate, the India–Sri Lanka FTA (1998),[85] India–Chile FTA (2006),[86] and India–MERCOSUR Preferential Trade Agreement (PTA) (2004)[87] incorporate Article XXI GATT (1994) by reference. India's RTAs cover a broad range of areas, such as trade in goods, services, intellectual property, and investment, and they include

[81] See eg Article 14 of EAEU–Serbia FTA (2019).

[82] Russia has an FTA with the Commonwealth of Independent States (CIS), which includes, in addition to the EAEU members, Moldova and Tajikistan. The Treaty on a Free Trade Area between Members of the CIS incorporates Article XXI GATT (1994) by reference. The EAEU–China Economic and Trade Cooperation Agreement (2018) reiterates the language of Article XXI GATT (1994), with some minor changes.

[83] Article 11 of Russia–Turkmenistan FTA (1993), Article 12 of Russia–Georgia FTA (1994), and Article 5 of Russia–Belarus–Kazakhstan RTA (1994) adopt a similar approach and combine WTO-like Security Exceptions and general exceptions under the same clause.

[84] Russia–Azerbaijan FTA (1992).

[85] Article IV of India–Sri Lanka FTA (1998).

[86] Article XIX of India–Chile PTA (2006).

[87] Article 9 of India–MERCOSUR PTA (2004).

several Security Exception clauses applicable to the specific field of regulation. To illustrate, Chapter 2 (Trade in goods) of the India–Korea FTA (2009)[88] incorporates Article XXI GATT (1994) by reference; Chapter 6 (Trade in services) includes Article 6.15, which resembles Article XIV*bis* GATS but adds one additional circumstance for invocation of the security defense when the party considers it necessary for the protection of its essential security interests – the measures "relating to protection of critical public infrastructure for communications, power and water supply from deliberate attempts intended to disable or degrade such infrastructures" (hereafter the Exception for critical public infrastructures). Such exceptions apply if Security Measures are not "applied in a manner which would constitute a means of arbitrary or unjustifiable discrimination against the other Party, or a disguised restriction on trade in services," which resembles the chapeau of general exceptions under the GATT (1994) and the GATS and further restrict the scope of application of the respective defense. The India–Japan FTA (2011),[89] India–Malaysia Comprehensive Economic Cooperation Agreement (CECA) (2011),[90] the Chapter on Services of India–Mauritius Comprehensive Economic Cooperation and Partnership Agreement (CECPA) (2021),[91] India–Australia Economic Cooperation and Trade Agreement (ECTA) (2022),[92] and India–UAE Comprehensive Economic Partnership Agreement (CEPA) (2022)[93] also clarify that "essential security interests" include the Exception for critical public infrastructures. In addition to WTO-like grounds and the Exception for critical public infrastructure, the India–Australia ECTA (2022) defines that the "essential security interests" of its contracting parties encompass the measures "taken in time of national emergency."[94] Notably, several India's RTAs apply different rules to trade-related and investment-related Security Measures, as will be further discussed.

4.1.5.2 "Self-Judging" Exceptions

The Asia Pacific Trade Agreement (APTA) (1975) (formerly known as the Bangkok Agreement) combines general exceptions and the security

88 Article 2.9 of India–Korea FTA (2009).
89 Article 11 of India–Japan FTA (2011).
90 Article 12.2 of India–Malaysia CECA (2011).
91 Article 6.21 of India–Mauritius CECPA (2021).
92 Article 11.2 of India–Australia ECTA (2022).
93 Article 16.2 of India–UAE CEPA (2022).
94 Article 11.2 of India–Australia ECTA (2022).

defense under one clause stating that "[n]othing in this Agreement shall prevent any Participating State from taking action and adopting measures which it considers necessary for the protection of its national security, the protection of public morality, the protection of human, animal and plant life and health, and the protection of articles of artistic, historical and archaeological value."[95] The same approach is adopted in the India–Thailand FTA (2003),[96] India–Afghanistan PTA (2003),[97] and Agreement between India and the Association of Southeast Asian Nations (ASEAN) (2009).[98] Different from APTA, they use the chapeau of Article XX GATT (1994) and thus still limit the application of Security Exceptions, as well as general exceptions, to certain specific conditions.

The Chapter on Goods of India–Mauritius CECPA (2021) combines general exceptions and the security defense under one clause using self-judging language and stating that the measures thereunder shall be taken "in conformity with Articles XX and XXI GATT (1994), which are incorporated into and/or as provided in this Agreement mutatis mutandis."[99] Such wording raises significant concerns as to the intention of the parties to make the general exceptions self-judging in conflict with Article XX GATT (1994), as well as the lack of specification of security concerns falling under a broadly drafted Security Exception different from Article XXI. It can be argued that parties have agreed on different from the WTO terms of application of exceptions, and thus GATT conditions apply only to the extent they do not contradict the wording of the CECPA. Yet, the Security Measure adopted under the CECPA would arguably contradict Article XXI if it cannot be justified under one of its subparagraphs. Thus, such a drafting technique leaves many questions about drafters' intentions open.

India is also part of the South Asia Free Trade Area (SAFTA) (2004), which in Article 14 provides for a separate broadly drafted Security Exception clause stipulating that: "[n]othing in this Agreement shall be construed to prevent any Contracting State from taking action and adopting measures which it considers necessary for the protection of its national security." Furthermore, different from India's other RTAs that have chosen

95 Article 35 of APTA (1975).

96 Article 9 of India–Thailand FTA (2003).

97 Article IV of the PTA between the Republic of India and the Transitional Islamic State of Afghanistan (2003).

98 Article 10 of the Framework Agreement on Comprehensive Economic Cooperation between the Republic of India and the Association of South East Asian Nations (2009).

99 Article 2.6 of India–Mauritius CECPA (2021).

to preserve the WTO-like language of Security Exceptions incorporating the phrase "it considers necessary," the India–Nepal FTA (2008) specifies that "[n]othing in this treaty shall prevent either Contracting Party from taking any measures which may be necessary for the protection of its essential security interests or in pursuance of general international conventions."[100]

The approach of APTA and SAFTA seems to expand Security Exceptions compared to the WTO agreements. Any event not necessarily related to military or defense matters or extreme situations in the time of war can fall within its scope. Such an event can include any kind of economic and political situation. India's RTAs with Thailand, Afghanistan, and ASEAN use a similar approach. However, the incorporation of the language that reminds the chapeau requirements under Article XX GATT (1994) still limits the scope of Security Exceptions thereunder to the measures that are not applied in a manner that would constitute "a means of arbitrary or unjustifiable discrimination or a disguised restriction on trade."

4.1.6 The Approach of China

4.1.6.1 WTO-Style Exceptions

China has started to use RTAs as a new platform to open up further to the outside and speed up domestic reforms. The China–Pakistan FTA (2006) has no Security Exceptions.[101] Yet, many RTAs concluded by China use the same language of Security Exceptions as the WTO agreements. To illustrate, the China–Australia FTA (2015),[102] China–Georgia FTA (2017),[103] China–Korea FTA (2015),[104] and China–Cambodia FTA (2020)[105] incorporate Article XXI GATT (1994) and Article XIV*bis* GATS by reference. The China–Mauritius FTA (2019) reiterates the language of Article XXI GATT (1994).[106]

Yoo and Ahn question how the China–Korea FTA (2015) reproduces the WTO language of Security Exceptions. In particular, they believe that if the parties followed the WTO structure, they would expressly incorporate not only Article XXI GATT (1994) and Article XIV*bis* GATS but also Article 73

[100] Article X of India–Nepal FTA (2008).
[101] China–Pakistan FTA (2006).
[102] Article 16.3 of China–Australia FTA (2015).
[103] Article 16.3 of China–Georgia FTA (2017).
[104] Article 12.14 of China–Korea FTA (2015).
[105] Article 15.2 of China–Cambodia FTA (2020).
[106] Article 7.21 of China–Mauritius FTA (2019).

of the TRIPs Agreement. This would make sense given that the China–Korea FTA (2015) contains a relatively comprehensive Chapter 15 (Intellectual Property) and the longwinded technology rivalry between Korea and China.[107] It is questionable whether the omission of the reference to Article 73 of the TRIPs Agreement would change the availability of the security defense in case of the application of the restrictions on intellectual property by either China or Korea, given that the Security Exception clause under the China–Korea FTA (2015) (incorporating Article XXI GATT (1994) and Article XIV*bis* GATS by reference) applies to the whole agreement, including Chapter 15, and that Article 73 of the TRIPs Agreement does not broaden the scope of the security defense compared to other WTO agreements. Ultimately, different approaches to incorporating Security Exceptions in China's RTAs, even without changing their substance, can also be attributed to the drafters' negligence rather than intention.

Other China's RTAs add additional grounds for invoking the security defense. To illustrate, the China–ASEAN FTA (2004) has expanded the scope of the security defense concerning trade in goods[108] by including the measures "taken so as to protect critical communications infrastructure from deliberate attempts intended to disable or degrade such infrastructure," as well as taken in time of "other emergency in domestic [rather than international] relations."[109]

After India's withdrawal, the Regional Comprehensive Economic Partnership (RCEP) was signed by fifteen parties which account for around 30 percent of the world's population and 30 percent of the world's GDP[110] (ten ASEAN joined by ASEAN free trade agreement partners - China, Australia, Japan, New Zealand, and Korea).[111] RCEP covers different areas, including trade in goods, trade in services, e-commerce, intellectual property rights, investment, competition, and government procurement. Article 17.13 (Security Exceptions) covers the whole agreement (with the exceptions that will be further discussed) and uses language similar to Article XXI GATT (1994). Apart from the measures taken in times of war or other

107 Ji Yeong Yoo and Dukgeun Ahn, 'Security Exceptions in the WTO System: Bridge or Bottle-Neck for Trade and Security?' (2016) 19(2) J Intl Econ L 417, 437.

108 Article 13 of the Agreement on Trade in Goods of the Framework Agreement on Comprehensive Economic Co-operation between China and ASEAN (2004).

109 "(iv) action taken in time of war or other emergency in domestic or international relations."

110 Eleanor Albert, 'China Leans Into RCEP Conclusion as Win - The Diplomat' *The Diplomat* (November 19, 2020) https://thediplomat.com/2020/11/china-leans-into-rcep-conclusion-as-win/.

111 ASEAN members: Indonesia, Thailand, Malaysia, Singapore, Philippines, Vietnam, Cambodia, Brunei, Myanmar (Burma), and Laos.

emergency in international relations as prescribed in the GATT (1994), Security Exceptions also cover the measures taken in times of national emergency. Security Exceptions under Article 17.13 of RCEP (2020) expand to critical public infrastructures (whether publicly or privately owned), including communications, power, and water infrastructures. Remarkably, Article 13(b)(iii) of the China–ASEAN FTA (2004) also includes actions "taken so as to protect critical communications infrastructure from deliberate attempts intended to disable or degrade such infrastructure." Removing the intent element with "deliberate attempts intended to disable or degrade" instead of focusing on critical communications, the RCEP Security Exceptions under Article 17.13 seem to cover all critical public infrastructures. In addition, Article 10.15 of RCEP (2020) provides a specific security defense for Chapter 10 on Investments,[112] while Articles 12.14 and 12.15 provide a particular security defense for cross-border electronic commerce (Section D of Chapter 12), as discussed in section 4.1.6.2.

4.1.6.2 "Self-Judging" Exceptions and Exceptions Excluded from Review

Before signing RCEP, APTA was the only "self-judging" exception incorporated in RTAs, to which China is a party.[113] Concerning the location of computing facilities and cross-border transfer of information by electronic means, RCEP allows for "any measure that [a party] considers necessary for the protection of its essential security interests." It also expressly states that "[s]uch measures shall not be disputed by other Parties," which suggests that they shall be considered non-reviewable. Thus, the Security Exceptions under Articles 12.14 and 12.15 in the E-Commerce Chapter are far more expansive than Article 17.13 – the Security Exceptions which apply to the rest of the RCEP agreement. In addition to specific Security Exceptions, Articles 12.14 and 12.15 allow for measures related to the location of computing facilities and cross-border transfer of information through electronic means if a party deems it necessary to fulfill a legitimate public policy goal. Notably, such measures shall not be applied in a manner that would constitute "a means of arbitrary or unjustifiable discrimination or a disguised restriction on trade." Thus, RCEP differentiates between public policy and national security objectives. Even though both types of exceptions are drafted in a self-judging manner, only Security Measures are expressly "non-disputable."

[112] Chapter 4, section 4.2.6.
[113] China joined APTA in 2001.

4.1.7 The Approach of South Africa

Most RTAs concluded with South Africa regulate trade in goods and use Article XXI GATT (1994) as a default template.[114] Yet, the SACU Agreement incorporates an expansive exception stipulating that member states shall have the right to impose restrictions on imports or exports following national laws and regulations, among others, for the protection of national security.[115]

4.1.8 Toward a Common Approach?

Security Exceptions under US RTAs can be interpreted as not being restricted to military threats and, in theory, could be expanded to threats beyond those prescribed in Article XXI GATT (1994) relating to military matters, situations of war, or other emergencies. As well as including new threats, like terrorism, cybersecurity, and others deemed by the state to be "essential," they could potentially open the door to economic situations or other events determined by the US or its contracting party. Yet, in those areas where the US and/or its counterparties want to ensure that Security Measures can be applied only in limited cases or should not be reviewed by any adjudicative body (energy, investment, automotive sectors), the parties prescribe special provisions for the application of Security Exceptions.

In addition to RTAs concluded by the US, "self-judging" exceptions using the phrase "it considers necessary" without elaborating on the additional grounds for the invocation of Security Exceptions can be

[114] South Africa is a member of African Continental Free Trade Agreement (AfCFTA) which reduces intra-border taxes on 90 percent of all products traded within Africa to zero. Article 27 of the Protocol on Trade in Goods to the Agreement establishing AfCFTA mirrors Article XXI GATT (1994), while Article 16 of the Protocol on Trade in Services mirrors Article XIV*bis* GATS. South Africa also has a partial FTA with MERCUSOR and European Free Trade Association (EFTA) via SACU. Article 13 of MERCOSUR–SACU FTA (2008) replicates the WTO Security Exceptions and Article 98 of UK–SACU and Mozambique FTA (2019), while Article 24 of EFTA–SACU FTA (2006) incorporates Article XXI GATT (1994) by reference. Similarly, Article 98 of EU–Southern African Community (SADC) Economic Partnership Agreement (2016) reiterates Article XXI GATT (1994).

[115] Article 18 of SACU Agreement (2002) incorporates a very broad exception stipulating that member states shall have the right to impose restrictions on imports or exports following national laws and regulations, among others, for the protection of national security.

found in several Indian RTAs and in at least one agreement each entered into by Brazil, Russia, China, and South Africa. Thus, in some cases, the practice of these states could result in a more deferential standard of review of Security Measures while also making jurisdictional objections based on national security more plausible. Yet, most RTAs concluded by BRICS use the WTO Security Exceptions as a default template.

The EU's RTAs mostly follow the elements of Article XXI GATT (1994), using identical language (including the phrase "it considers necessary") and a similar structure. The earlier EU's RTAs removed the "self-judging" language "it considers" from certain Security Exceptions (e.g. arms trafficking) but preserved it for the measures taken in times of war, other emergency, or serious tension, which is the critical point of interpretation for the ongoing disputes before the WTO. This can be seen as evidence that the EC, later the EU, and its contracting parties always wanted to preserve more discretion in situations of war or emergencies but not necessarily for export controls.

Notably, while most RTAs include a freestanding security clause similar to the WTO agreements, some RTAs (concluded mainly by Russia and India with third parties) incorporate Security Exceptions with the other exceptions and prescribe the same preconditions for their invocation. The negotiators of the GATT (1947) wanted to differentiate between Security Exceptions and general exceptions to the trade rules. They agreed on different preconditions for the invocation of Security Exceptions and general exceptions, leaving states more flexibility for the suspension of their trade obligations in times when their national security interests were at stake.[116] Incorporating Security Exceptions and general exceptions under one umbrella implies that the drafters do not differentiate between their security interests arising from extraordinary situations and other public policy interests, thus subjecting the two to the same regulation and standard of review.

Notably, in general, RTAs of the US, the EU, and BRICS do not expressly exclude the adjudication of Security Exceptions concerning trade matters.

[116] Second Session of the Preparatory Committee of the UN Conference on Trade and Employment: Verbatim Report. Eleventh Meeting of the Tariff Agreement Committee Held on Friday, September 5, 1947 at 2.30 pm in the Palais des Nations, Geneva (September 5, 1947) E/PC/T/TAC/PV/11 [24] www.wto.org/gatt_docs/English/SULPDF/90260038.pdf.

4.2 Security Exceptions in Investment Treaties

The fundamental policy of the US toward international investment has historically been neither to promote nor to discourage inward and outward flows of capital.[117] The US has vital interests in fostering the economic benefits associated with an open investment climate.[118] However, the US also has strong interests in protecting its national security from certain FDIs.[119] The conflicting jurisprudence that had emerged from the Argentine cases on the scope of the security defense has prompted a shift in the US treaty practice. The US treaty drafters have decided to expressly ensure not only that the concept of "essential security interests" is broad and general but also that the US has broad discretion in adopting investment-related Security Measures whenever it considers it necessary. The US has tried to reach this goal using different drafting techniques: incorporating self-judging language in Security Exception clauses and/or expressly noting that Security Measures are nonreviewable.[120] In both scenarios, the US claims that Security Exceptions are totally self-judging: the position it also tries to convey to the international community concerning WTO agreements.

As in the case of RTAs, the EU appears to adhere to the WTO approach to drafting Security Exceptions in its investment treaties which can be arguably explained by a strong commitment of the EU to respect and comply with international law and the resulting preference for multilateral rather than bilateral agreements.[121] This is not the case for the BITs of individual EU member states, entered into separately from the EU before the Treaty of Lisbon amending the Treaty on the EU and the Treaty Establishing the EC (Lisbon Treaty).[122]

Brazil, India, and South Africa used BITs as a tool to attract investments in the 1990s. After started facing complaints brought by foreign investors challenging measures that they had taken in the name of public policy

[117] Carolyn J Kubota, 'Closing the Open Door to Foreign Direct Investment' (1982) 15(1) Cornell Intl LJ 121, 121.

[118] Alan P Larson and David M Marchick, 'Foreign Investment and National Security: Getting the Balance Right' (2006) Council on Foreign Relations 3.

[119] Chapter 3, section 3.2.2.

[120] See more chapter 4, section 4.1.1.

[121] See more chapter 4, section 4.1.2.

[122] Nevertheless, EU member states must take the measures necessary to eliminate incompatibilities with EU law, where they exist, contained in BITs concluded between them and third countries. Thus, it can reasonably be assumed that whenever the Security Exceptions under the respective BIT of the EU member state are invoked, the EU understanding of security matters should be taken into account. See more chapter 4, section 4.2.2.

goals, these WTO members have shifted toward investment regulations that ensure more regulatory space for state actions. This can explain the decision of these WTO members to start preserving more discretionary state power in the application of Security Measures and thus to follow the US approach to drafting Security Exceptions in their IIAs.[123]

At the same time, China and Russia do not have a strong view on incorporating Security Exceptions into their treaties. Both states remain proactive in attracting foreign investments. Their IIAs generally do not incorporate Security Exceptions or include the exceptions drafted in a more specific manner compatible with the WTO agreements. In some IIAs, they even exclude any self-judging language from the exception clauses.[124]

As will be further demonstrated, many WTO members have changed their approaches to drafting general exceptions and Security Exceptions in particular.[125] Some of them were more active in entering into IIAs in the past than now. Some of them have only recently amended their model investment treaties signaling the shift to a different drafting technique which has not yet been reflected in their actual IIAs. Thus, the total numbers of different types of Security Exceptions used by the US, the EU, and BRICS in their IIAs do not necessarily reflect their current preferences. Instead, the nuances in the approaches of the US, the EU, and BRICS and their developments based on current model treaties are further discussed in more detail in this section.

4.2.1 The US Approach

In response to the discontent over the general nature of the FCN treaties and the expansion of international commerce, the US decided to start its own BIT program.[126] In the 1980s, the US focused on preparing its First Model Treaty to serve as a basis for further negotiations with developing states.[127] Newer versions of the US Model BIT were issued by the Office

[123] See more chapter 4, sections 4.2.3, 4.2.5 and 4.2.7.

[124] See more chapter 4, sections 4.2.4 and 4.2.6.

[125] This research relies on the information about concluded IIAs provided by the Investment Policy Hub of the UNCTAD https://investmentpolicy.unctad.org/international-investment-agreements. For the avoidance of doubt, IIAs include both BITs and investment chapters of RTAs.

[126] Kenneth J Vandevelde, *The First Bilateral Investment Treaties: U.S. Postwar Friendship, Commerce, and Navigation Treaties* (OUP 2017) 383.

[127] Jeswald W Salacuse, 'BIT by BIT: The Growth of Bilateral Investment Treaties and Their Impact on Foreign Investment in Developing Countries' (1990) 24 Intl L 655, 657.

of the US Trade Representative in 1994, 1998, 2004, and 2012, incorporating directives from Congress and standards of protection from existing BITs.[128] The US has also increasingly included investment chapters in its RTAs that mirror the provisions of existing US BITs.[129] All versions of the US Model BIT include references to Security Exceptions.[130] All the US RTAs that include investment chapters/provisions also incorporate Security Exceptions provisions.[131]

4.2.1.1 Exceptions That Do Not Use "Self-Judging" Language

In January 1982, the US Trade Representative for Investment Policy announced the formulation of the First Model BIT and the commencement of negotiations toward the conclusion of investment treaties with Egypt and Panama.[132] The First Model BIT incorporates Security Exceptions along with public order exceptions.[133] The Security Exceptions provision uses a standard of essential security interests which is not further limited or defined, that is, an open-ended term. To illustrate, the First Model BIT refers to the measures "necessary in its jurisdiction for the maintenance of public order, the fulfillment of its obligations with respect to the maintenance or restoration of international peace or security, or the protection of its own essential security interests."[134] The first generation of US BITs follows this approach.[135]

Notably, similar to the postwar FCN treaties, none of the early US BITs contain the words "it considers." The US tried to argue that Security Exceptions provisions were nevertheless totally self-judging. First, in 1984, the US unsuccessfully argued this position before the ICJ concerning Security Exceptions under the FCN treaty between the US and Nicaragua

128 Jeongho Nam, 'Model BIT: An Ideal Prototype or a Tool for Efficient Breach' (2017) 48 Geo J Intl L 1275, 1282.

129 Chapter 4, section 4.1.1.

130 Investment Policy Hub of the UNCTAD https://investmentpolicy.unctad.org/international-investment-agreements/model-agreements.

131 Chapter 4, section 4.1.1.

132 Deirdre Annette Cody, 'The United States Bilateral Investment Treaties: Egypt and Panama' (1983) 13 Ga J Intl & Comp L 491, 492.

133 US Model Treaty Concerning the Reciprocal Encouragement and Protection of Investment, reprinted in (1986) 4 Intl Tax & Bus Lawyer (1984 version).

134 Ibid.

135 US–Panama BIT (1982) in Article X also states that "[t]his treaty shall not preclude the application by either Party of any and all measures necessary for the maintenance of public order, the fulfillment of its obligations with respect to the maintenance or restoration of international peace and security, or the protection of its own essential security interests." The same approach was adopted in US–Morocco BIT (1985).

(1956).[136] The Reagan Administration also reiterated the self-judging interpretation of Security Exceptions during a 1986 Senate hearing on BITs.[137] With respect to the first eight US BITs, the Senate attached the following understanding to the Security Exception clause: "either Party may take all measures necessary to deal with any unusual and extraordinary threat to its national security."[138] The Senate did not discuss how such threats were to be determined. However, the decision to subject the Security Exception clause to such understanding demonstrates that the US aimed to reserve the discretion to abstain from BITs in pursuit of foreign policy goals but only in extreme situations.

Whether Security Exceptions in the first-generation US BITs are reviewable was also an important topic of discussion in several arbitral proceedings against the backdrop of the Argentine economic crisis. Argentina invoked Security Exceptions under the US–Argentina BIT (1991) in several cases, including *Continental Casualty v Argentina*, *Enron v Argentina*, *CMS v Argentina*, *LG&E v Argentina*, *Sempra v Argentina*, *El Paso v Argentina*, and *Mobil v Argentina* (hereafter the Argentine economic crisis cases). Following the pattern of the other first-generation US BITs, the US–Argentina BIT (1991) does not use a self-judging language of Security Exceptions and does not use any reservations about their scope.[139] A key matter was whether or not a measure taken by a state in times of economic crisis could be viewed "self-judging" in the absence of the express language about it, as will be further discussed.[140]

4.2.1.2 Toward "Self-Judging" Exceptions

In the 1990s, the US treaty drafters started explicitly referencing the self-judging nature of Security Exceptions.[141] This shift began with the Protocol to the US–Russia BIT (1992) (which has never come into effect), stating that "whether a measure is taken by a Party to protect its essential

[136] Kenneth J Vandevelde, *The First Bilateral Investment Treaties: U.S. Postwar Friendship, Commerce, and Navigation Treaties* (OUP 2017) 636.
[137] Ibid.
[138] Investment Treaties with Senegal, Zaire, Morocco, Turkey, Cameroon, Bangladesh, Egypt, and Grenada S Exec Rep No 32 100th Cong 2d Sess (1988).
[139] Article XI of US–Argentina BIT (1991).
[140] See more chapter 5, section 5.1.
[141] Mantilla Blanco Sebastián and Alexander Pehl, *National Security Exceptions in International Trade and Investment Agreements: Justiciability and Standards of Review* (Springer 2020) 47.

security interests is self-judging."[142] Such wording confirms the parties' understanding that the Security Exception provision grants the parties vast discretion to decide when to impose Security Measures.

In later treaties, the language of Security Exceptions remained the same, but the letter of transmittal from the President to the Senate provided more detail.[143] In particular, several letters of transmittal state that, in the view of US drafters, Security Exceptions were self-judging despite the absence of the words "it considers" or other similar wording. To illustrate, the letter of transmittal for the US–Kazakhstan BIT (1992) suggests that the Security Exception clause is self-judging by referring to the measures "which [a party] regards as necessary for the protection of its own essential security interests."[144] It also explains that the "measures permitted by the provision on the protection of a party's essential security interests" include "security-related actions taken in time of war or national emergency; actions not arising from a state of war or national emergency must have a clear and direct relationship to the essential security interest of the Party involved."[145] The protection of essential security interests of a party mainly applies in cases where the country wants to protect itself against war, armed conflict, or national emergencies, or otherwise "have a clear and direct relationship to the essential security interest of the Party involved."[146]

142 Article 10 of US–Russia BIT (1992); Heribert Golsong, 'Russian Federation – United States: Treaty concerning the Encouragement and Reciprocal Protection of Investment' (1992) 31(4) ILM 794, 811.

143 The so-called "letters of transmittal" from the President to the Senate are submitted for information purposes only and are not legally binding. See Study Prepared for the Committee of Foreign Relations by the Congressional Research Service Library of Congress on Treaties and Other International Agreements: The Role of The United States Senate (2001) www.govinfo.gov/content/pkg/CPRT-106SPRT66922/html/CPRT-106SPRT66922.htm.

However, "when interpreting a treaty under domestic law, US courts include as relevant matters indications of US intent in making the agreement, as well as the executive branch's interpretation of the agreement's meaning." See Elizabeth McBride, 'Treaties and Other International Agreements: The Role of the United States Senate' (1985) 12(1) Government Publications Rev 79. To illustrate, in *Kolovrat v Oregon*, the court mentioned that "[w]hile courts interpret treaties for themselves, the meaning given them by the departments of government particularly charged with their negotiation and enforcement is given great weight." See *Kolovrat v Oregon* 366 US 187, 194 (1961).

144 Message from the US President transmitting the Treaty between the US and the Republic of Kazakhstan concerning the Reciprocal Encouragement and Protection of Investment, signed at Washington on May 19, 1992, Article X https://2009-2017.state.gov/e/eb/ifd/43294.htm.

145 Ibid.

146 Ibid.

The same combination of treaty language and letter-of-transmittal language is included in the other US BITs signed between 1992–1993, including the US BITs with Moldova,[147] Armenia,[148] and Ukraine.[149] Thus, around 1994, the US began to view the Security Exception clauses as self-judging or wished that they would be considered so by the other party. At the same time, the US reiterated that Security Exceptions could be invoked only in specific extreme situations and only if there was a clear and direct relationship between the measure and the essential security interest to be protected with its implementation.

The same pattern was followed in the Security Exception clauses of the Model BIT (1994). Article XIV provides that "[t]his Treaty shall not preclude a Party from applying measures necessary for the fulfilment of its obligations with respect to the maintenance or restoration of international peace or security, or the protection of its own essential security interests."[150] Under paragraph 3 of the Protocol to the BIT, the parties clarified that even though Security Exceptions shall be considered self-judging, they are to be invoked only in good faith.[151] Unlike the First Model BIT, the US Model BIT (1994) does not include public order exceptions.[152]

In 1999, US–El Salvador BIT introduced the right of a contracting party to take measures that "it considers necessary . . . for the protection of its own essential security interests."[153] The US State Department also explained that "[t]his Treaty makes explicit the implicit understanding

[147] Message from the US President transmitting the Treaty between the US and the Republic of Moldova concerning the Reciprocal Encouragement and Protection of Investment, signed at Washington on April 21, 1993, Article IX https://2001-2009.state.gov/documents/organization/43578.pdf.

[148] Message from the US President transmitting the Treaty between the US and the Republic of Armenia concerning the Reciprocal Encouragement and Protection of Investment, signed at Washington on September 23, 1992, Article X https://2001-2009.state.gov/documents/organization/43477.pdf.

[149] Message from the US President transmitting the Treaty between the US and Ukraine concerning the Encouragement and Reciprocal Protection of Investment, signed at Washington on March 4, 1994, Article IX https://2009-2017.state.gov/e/eb/ifd/43366.htm.

[150] US Model BIT (1994).

[151] Ibid.

[152] US–Honduras BIT (1995) followed this approach in Article XIV. US–Nicaragua BIT (1998) also provides in Article XIV(1) that: "This Treaty shall not preclude a Party from applying measures necessary for the fulfillment of its obligations with respect to the maintenance or restoration of international peace or security, or the protection of its own essential security interests."

[153] Article XIV of US–El Salvador BIT (1999).

that measures to protect a Party's essential security interests are self-judging in nature."[154] Yet, the State Department also added "an important caveat" that "each Party would expect the provision to be applied by the other in good faith."[155] The same approach was adopted in the US–Bahrain BIT (2001).[156] These ideas were further crystalized in the US Model BIT (2004)[157] and later the US Model BIT (2012).[158] All such BITs use a standard of essential security interests that is not further limited or defined. They are not specifying under which circumstances the exceptions can be invoked, apart from where a state considers it necessary to protect its essential security interests. Such an approach was adopted by most US BITs concluded after 1994.[159]

4.2.1.3 Exceptions Excluded from Review

The NAFTA concluded in 1992 includes a GATT-like Security Exceptions provision regarding trade and investments, which allows each contracting party to take the measures that "it considers necessary" when certain expressly stated preconditions are met.[160] At the same time, the NAFTA differentiates between trade and investment provisions concerning the reviewability of Security Measures. The NAFTA clarifies that its dispute settlement provisions do not apply where any party invokes Security Exceptions to justify its decision to prohibit or restrict the acquisition of an investment in its territory by an investor of another party or its investment.[161] Thus, the tribunal or panel shall automatically apply such "self-judging" exceptions without reviewing the investment-related measure.

[154] Message from the US President transmitting Treaty between the Government of the US and the Government of the Republic of El Salvador concerning the Encouragement and Reciprocal Protection of Investment signed at San Salvador on March 10, 1999, Article XIV www.sice.oas.org/Investment/BITSbyCountry/BITs/US_ElSalvador_e.asp.

[155] Ibid.

[156] Message from the US President transmitting the Treaty between the US and the Government of the State of Bahrain concerning the Encouragement and Reciprocal Protection of Investment, signed at Washington on September 29, 1999, Article 14 https://2009-2017.state.gov/e/eb/ifd/43236.htm.

[157] US Model BIT (2004).

[158] Ibid.

[159] US, International Investment Agreements Navigator, UNCTAD Investment Policy Hub https://investmentpolicy.unctad.org/international-investment-agreements/countries/223/united-states-of-america.

[160] Article 2102 NAFTA (1992). See also chapter 4, section 4.1.1.

[161] Article 1138 NAFTA (1992).

The negotiation history of NAFTA's investment chapter demonstrates that initially, the US, further supported by Mexico, wanted to incorporate a separate Security Exception clause for the investment matters that resembled the Security Exceptions under the US First Model BIT and that allowed for the "measures necessary for . . . the protection of [party's] own essential security interests." The proposed text also included the note stating that "[t]his provision is self-judging."[162] At the same time, Canada proposed the Security Exception clause for the whole agreement, including the investment chapter, with parts (a), (b), and (c) as in Article XXI GATT (1947). The draft clause proposed by Canada refers to the measure that a party "determines is directly related and essential to" one of the listed circumstances involving the situation of war, military or defense sectors.[163] It suggests that the invoking party should have a final word in determining its essential security interests at stake. Yet, the draft clause states that the party "shall ensure that its action or measure is that which least infringes the rights or any reasonable expectations of the other Parties under this Agreement, and is no broader in scope or duration than necessary."[164] Such a precondition resembles a least trade-restrictive alternative test under the objective necessity requirement[165] and could arguably result in a stricter review of the measure than what the WTO-style Security Exceptions imply.

The US, Canada, and Mexico have eventually reached a compromise by incorporating the WTO-style Security Exception clause for both trade and investment treaty provisions but by expressly excluding the investment-related Security Measures from the dispute settlement system. Such an approach signals the weight given to state discretion over an international authority regarding investment matters. It, nevertheless, undermines the importance the parties put on the wording "it considers necessary" added to NAFTA's Security Exceptions. Should the parties to NAFTA's negotiations consider this phrasing sufficient to make the provision nonreviewable, they would not add the clarification about the nonapplicability of dispute settlement provisions to investment-related Security Measures.

Following the approach adopted in the NAFTA, the US RTAs concluded in 2006–2007 started to differentiate between trade and

[162] Draft Treasury Annex Composite Investment (July 22, 1992) www.international.gc.ca/trade-agreements-accords-commerciaux/assets/pdfs/chap11-neg-14.pdf.
[163] Ibid.
[164] Ibid.
[165] See more chapter 5, section 5.3.2.2.

investment provisions concerning the application of Security Measures. To illustrate, US–Korea FTA signed in 2007 used the same language of Security Exceptions as the US FTAs concluded in 2003–2005, only specifying that: "For greater certainty, if a Party invokes Article 23.2 [Security Exceptions] in an arbitral proceeding initiated under Chapter Eleven (Investment) or Chapter Twenty-Two (Institutional Provisions and Dispute Settlement), the tribunal or panel hearing the matter shall find that the exception applies."[166]

The same approach was adopted in the US–Colombia TPA (2006),[167] US–Peru FTA (2006),[168] and US–Panama FTA (2007).[169] In 2022, Colombia invoked the Security Exception clause under Article 22.2(b) of US–Colombia TPA (2006). The tribunal did not agree with Colombia that the Security Exception is either "non-justiciable" or "operates to exclude a tribunal's jurisdiction."[170] Based on the ordinary meaning of the terms, the tribunal interpreted Article 22.2(b) and its footnote in a way that "the process of invocation of the [Security Exception] entails a finding of applicability by a tribunal, meaning that the provision does not apply automatically."[171] Among others, the tribunal contrasted the language of Article 22.2(b) and its footnote with the India–Singapore CECA (2005) (discussed further), which expressly stipulates that "any decision of the disputing Party taken on such security considerations shall be non-justiciable."[172] At the same time, the tribunal determined that Article 22.2(b) differs from the wording of the Security Exceptions as interpreted by the ICJ in *US – Trade Measures Affecting Nicaragua* and should instead be understood *a contrario* as a self-judging provision.[173]

A more recent example of RTA with the investment chapter concluded by the US is the successor of NAFTA, USMCA (2018).[174] The USMCA's Security Exception clause deviates from NAFTA's approach and does not include any specific rules for investment-related measures. It remains to be seen whether, in the case of a dispute, the US would attempt to exempt investment-related Security Measures in breach of USMCA provisions

166 Article 23.2 of US–Korea FTA (2007) fn 2.
167 Article 22.2 of US–Colombia TPA (2006) fn 2.
168 Article 22.2 of US–Peru FTA (2006) fn 2.
169 Article 21.2 of US–Panama FTA (2007) fn 2.
170 *Angel Samuel Seda and others v Republic of Colombia* (June 27, 2024) ICSID Case No ARB/19/6 Award [711]–[725].
171 Ibid [719].
172 Ibid [714].
173 Ibid [704].
174 Article 32.2 USMCA (2018).

from the dispute settlement procedure by relying on USMCA's Security Exceptions and asserting that such Security Exception clause is nevertheless nonreviewable.

4.2.2 *The Approaches of the EU and Its Member States*

An important phase in the historical development of IIAs began at the end of the 1950s, as the members of the EC, later the EU, undertook to negotiate bilateral treaties[175] that, unlike previous commercial agreements, dealt exclusively with foreign investment. Having lost all of its foreign investments due to its defeat in World War II, Germany led the new phase of IIAs.[176]

EU member states retained the jurisdiction over foreign investment and the capability to negotiate and conclude IIAs until 2009, when the Lisbon Treaty entered into force.[177] The Lisbon Treaty brought FDI under the ambit of the CCP, thereby transferring the competence over FDI from the EU member states to the EU. EU member states are still allowed to amend existing IIAs or conclude new IIAs with third countries, provided that the terms, conditions, and procedures set out in the EU regulations are respected.[178] In particular, to open negotiations or sign a BIT, EU member states must obtain authorization from the European Commission.[179]

The discussion over the complicated nature of the relationship between BITs concluded by the individual EU member states and the EU legal order[180] is outside the purview of this research. Instead, this research focuses on the Security Exception clauses included in the IIAs entered into by EU member states before and after the Lisbon Treaty and the Security Exception clauses included in the IIAs entered into by the

175 Martin A Weiss, CRS Report for Congress, 'The U.S. Bilateral Investment Treaty Program: An Overview' (April 24, 2007) Congressional Research Service 4.

176 Jeswald W Salacuse, 'BIT by BIT: The Growth of Bilateral Investment Treaties and Their Impact on Foreign Investment in Developing Countries' (1990) 24 Intl L 655, 657.

177 Carrie E Anderer, 'Bilateral Investment Treaties and the EU Legal Order: Implications of the Lisbon Treaty' (2010) 35(3) Brook J Intl L 851, 854; Lisbon Treaty (December 13, 2007) 2007/C 306/01.

178 Article 7 of Regulation (EU) No 1219/2012 of the European Parliament and of the Council (December 12, 2012) Establishing Transitional Arrangements for Bilateral Investment Agreements between the Member States and Third Countries [2012] OJ L 351.

179 Ibid Article 9.

180 See eg Case C-284/16 *Slowakische Republik v Achmea BV* [2018] EU:C:2018:158; Case C-741/19 *République de Moldavie v Komstroy LLC* [2021] EU:C:2021:655.

EU itself. Where necessary, this research also refers to the IIAs of member states that are not in force anymore (or will become ineffective soon) to understand the approaches to drafting techniques of Security Exception clauses adopted by such member states.

4.2.2.1 Exceptions in IIAs of EU Member States

As of October 2022, fourteen EU member states negotiated investment treaties based on their model BITs. The review of these model IIAs confirms that they have different approaches to the inclusion of Security Exceptions. The specific terminology in drafting clauses addressing the security defense also varies among agreements. Among other things, the choice of the terms in BITs might be affected by the domestic concepts used in the national legislation of the member states. As a result, instead of the term "essential security interests," other IIAs use the term "public security," for example Germany. At the same time, some treaties refer only to "security," as in the case of the BITs concluded by the Belgium–Luxemburg Economic Union. Ultimately, fourteen available model BITs of EU member states were reviewed for this research. They are divided into three categories:

- *Model BITs that do not include any reference to Security Exceptions or any other security-related exceptions*:

  Croatia Model BIT (1998), France Model BIT (2006), Greece Model BIT (2001), Denmark Model BIT (2000), Spain Model BIT (2008), and Sweden Model BIT (2002).

- *Model BITs that include Security Exceptions:*

  Finland Model BIT (2001), Czech Republic Model BIT (2016), Slovakia Model BIT (2019), and Italy Model BIT (2022).

- *Model BITs that only include other security-related exceptions (such as public security):*

  Austria Model BIT (2008), Belgium–Luxemburg Economic Union Model BIT (2019), Germany Model BIT (2008), and the Netherlands Model BIT (2019).[181]

The detailed comparison of BITs of all EU member states is outside the purview of this research. Yet, it is important to note that the EU member

[181] EU, Investment Policy Hub of the UNCTAD https://investmentpolicy.unctad.org/international-investment-agreements/groupings/28/eu-european-union-.

states that prefer to include Security Exceptions in their model BITs draft them based on the WTO law (see Finland Model BIT (2001), Czech Republic Model BIT (2016), Slovakia Model BIT (2019), and Italy Model BIT (2022)).

4.2.2.2 Exceptions in the EU IIAs

With the entering into force of the Lisbon Treaty, the EU has exclusive competence in foreign direct investment. The European Commission has indicated that it does not intend to negotiate BITs with all possible countries. Instead, it would focus on its largest trading partners like India, Canada, Russia, China, and MERCOSUR.[182] The European Commission also prefers to include investment provisions in the FTAs rather than negotiate stand-alone BITs.[183]

The EU RTAs with investment chapters/provisions generally do not incorporate any special rules for applying Security Exception clauses to investment-related Security Measures.[184] They generally use the WTO format of Security Exception clauses, sometimes differentiating between WTO-style exceptions and objectively drafted exceptions.[185] The EU–Central America FTA (2012),[186] EU–Ghana FTA (2016),[187] EU–Armenia Economic Integration Agreement (2017),[188] EU–Viet Nam FTA (2019),[189] EU–Viet Nam Investment Protection Agreement (2019),[190] the Agreement between the EU and Japan for an Economic Partnership (2018),[191] EU–Singapore Investment Protection Agreement (2018),[192] and EU–UK Free Trade Agreement & Economic Integration Agreement (2020)[193] incorporate Security Exception clauses using language similar to Article XXI of GATT and Article XIV*bis* GATS.

[182] Marc Mae, 'The Lisbon Treaty and the New EU Investment Competence' in Ross Eventon (ed.), *Reclaiming Public Interest in Europe's International Investment Policy. EU Investment Agreements in the Lisbon Treaty Era: A Reader* (Transnational Institute 2010) 13.

[183] Ibid.

[184] Chapter 4, section 4.1.2.

[185] Ibid.

[186] Article 357 of EU–Central America FTA (2012).

[187] Article 69 of EU–Ghana FTA (2016).

[188] Article 202 of EU–Armenia Economic Integration Agreement (2017).

[189] Article 9.3 of the FTA between the EU and the Socialist Republic of Viet Nam (2020).

[190] Article 4.8 of EU–Viet Nam Investment Protection Agreement (2019).

[191] Article 1.5 of the Agreement between the EU and Japan for an Economic Partnership (2018).

[192] Article 4.5 of EU–Singapore Investment Protection Agreement (2018).

[193] Article 415 of EU–UK Free Trade Agreement & Economic Integration Agreement (2020).

4.2.3 *The Approach of Brazil*

Brazil is historically known for not having any BIT in force.[194] Brazil signed fourteen traditional BITs between 1994 and 1999, which were never approved by the country's National Congress, seeing the investor-state arbitration regime as limiting states' right to regulate.[195] The traditional BITs signed but not ratified by Brazil in the 1990s generally do not incorporate Security Exceptions.[196]

Even without any BIT in force, Brazil has been more concerned about the outward flow of investments from Brazil than attracting FDIs.[197] For this purpose, Brazil developed a different model focusing not only on the protection of investors and their investments but also on promoting and facilitating productive investment: the Cooperation and Facilitation Investment Agreement (CFIA).[198] Unlike traditional BITs, the CFIA is designed to leave significantly more policy space for state actions and focuses not on protecting foreign investors but on promoting state-to-state cooperation and facilitating bilateral investments. The CFIA provides new wording to old traditional clauses inserted into BITs (e.g. when addressing national treatment and MFN treatment and expropriation), includes provisions that were alien to traditional investment agreements (e.g. articles on corporate social responsibility), and proposes new dispute resolution mechanisms focusing on amicable settlement and replacing investor-state arbitration by state-to-state arbitration.[199]

Brazil has been trying to attract foreign investments by agreeing to specific commitments under the CFIAs while, at the same time, making such obligations vague and flexible enough not to restrain its tools in

194 Brazil, International Investment Agreements Navigator, UNCTAD Investment Policy Hub https://investmentpolicy.unctad.org/international-investment-agreements/countries/27/brazil.

195 Henrique Moraes Choer and Felipe Hees, 'Breaking the BIT Mold: Brazil's Pioneering Approach to Investment Agreements' (2018) 112 Ajil Unbound 197, 198.

196 Brazil, International Investment Agreements Navigator, UNCTAD Investment Policy Hub https://investmentpolicy.unctad.org/international-investment-agreements/countries/27/brazil.

197 Henrique Moraes Choer and Felipe Hees, 'Breaking the BIT Mold: Brazil's Pioneering Approach to Investment Agreements' (2018) 112 Ajil Unbound 197, 198.

198 Catherine Titi, 'Recent Developments in International Investment Law' in Marc Bungenberg and others (eds.), *European Yearbook of International Economic Law* (Springer International Publishing 2016) 708.

199 See Natali Cinelli Moreira, 'Cooperation and Facilitation Investment Agreements in Brazil: The Path for Host State Development' (*Kluwer Arbitration Blog*, September 13, 2018) http://arbitrationblog.kluwerarbitration.com/2018/09/13/cooperation-and-facilitation-investment-agreements-in-brazil-the-path-for-host-state-development/.

dealing with domestic challenges. It can be argued that such an approach to attracting investments also affected how the Security Exceptions under the CFIA were drafted. Article 13(1) of the Model CFIA provides that "[n]othing in this Agreement shall be construed to prevent a Party from adopting or maintaining measures aimed at preserving its national security or public order, or to apply the provisions of their criminal laws or comply with its obligations regarding the maintenance of international peace and security in accordance with the provisions of the UN Charter."[200] Notably, the exception itself does not contain any self-judging language. However, Article 13(2) of the Model CFIA removes the measures adopted for either national security or public order from the scope of the dispute settlement mechanism under the CFIA.[201] This approach was followed, among others, under the Brazil–Mexico CFIA (2015),[202] Brazil–Ecuador CFIA (2019),[203] and Brazil–UAE CFIA (2019).[204]

The Brazil–India CFIA (2020) also incorporates Security Exceptions. However, it deviates from the text proposed in the Model CFIA. Article 24 contains WTO-like Security Exceptions in paragraphs (a), (b), and (c). Paragraph (b) allows for "any action which [a contracting party] considers necessary for the protection of its essential security interests."[205] Unlike the WTO agreements, it provided an illustrative rather than exclusive list of circumstances under which the exceptions could be invoked. The list includes, apart from GATT and GATS-like preconditions, the Exception for critical public infrastructure, as well as the exception for such requirements as obtaining any security clearance for any company, personnel, or equipment. The Brazil–India CFIA further guides interpreting Security Exceptions. Annex I envisages that the Security Measures shall be adopted with the intention and objective of the party imposing the measures to protect its essential security interests. Accordingly, Security Measures are nonjusticiable and shall not be open for review by an arbitral tribunal. Such drafting techniques resemble the current approach of India to drafting its BITs and investment chapters in FTAs.[206]

200 Brazil Model CFIA (2015).
201 Ibid.
202 Article 12 of Brazil–Mexico CFIA (2015).
203 Article 13 of Brazil–Ecuador CFIA (2019).
204 Article 13 of Brazil–United Arab Emirates CFIA (2019).
205 Article 24 of Brazil–India Investment Cooperation and Facilitation Treaty (2020).
206 Chapter 4, section 4.2.5.

4.2.4 The Approach of Russia

After the Soviet Union disintegrated at the end of 1991, Russia urgently sought to attract foreign investments to support its economic restructuring and recovery and quickly adopted a Model BIT that did not incorporate any Security Exceptions.[207] Different from the Model BIT, the Russia–US BIT signed in 1992 (but never ratified) includes US-style Security Exceptions.[208] Also, the Russia–Sweden BIT (1995) and Russia–Hungary BIT (1995) mention the exceptions for the purposes of the maintenance of defense, national security, and public order.[209]

In 2001, Russia adopted a new Model BIT, which sought to accommodate WTO requirements by admitting the exceptions to BIT's guaranteed national treatment. The Model BIT (2001) allowed each contracting party to use the exceptions from the national treatment of foreign investors and their investments.[210] However, it was silent about the nature of the exceptions applied against current or prospective investors and their investments, mainly whether Security Measures would fall under such an exception. Furthermore, as is the case of most analyzed jurisdictions, the text of particular treaties concluded reflects a negotiation process and often results in a different approach from the model agreement.

Faced with several expropriation claims, Russia has changed its BIT policy.[211] In 2016, Russia adopted a new Regulation on Entering into International Treaties on the Encouragement and Mutual Protection of Investments (hereafter the Regulation). The Regulation contains nonbinding guidelines for drafting and negotiating future investment protection treaties (hereafter the Guidelines). The methodology of conclusion BITs and their substantive issues have changed, signaling

207 Noah Rubins and Azizjon Nazarov, 'Investment Treaties and the Russian Federation Baiting the Bear?' (2008) 9(2) BLI 100, 103.

208 Article 10 of US–Russia BIT (1992); Heribert Golsong, 'Russian Federation – United States: Treaty concerning the Encouragement and Reciprocal Protection of Investment' (1992) 31(4) ILM 794, 811.

209 Article 3 of Russia–Sweden BIT (1995) and Article 2 of Russia–Hungary BIT (1995).

210 Decree of the Government of the Russian Federation No 456 'On the conclusion of agreements between the Government of the Russian Federation and the governments of foreign states on the encouragement and mutual protection of investments (with amendments and additions) (lost force) (unofficial translation) (June 9, 2001) http://base.garant.ru/12123282/#ixzz6fZBThXIU.

211 Aleksandr P Alekseenko, 'New Russian Model BIT and the Practice of Investment Arbitration' (2019) 16 Manchester J Intl Econ L 79, 79.

a more open approach to investment treaties.[212] This can be partially explained by Russia's shift at the time from being mainly a capital-importing state to also becoming a capital-exporting one.[213] The Guidelines prescribe that "the provisions of the Agreement shall not prevent the Parties to the Agreement from taking measures necessary to protect essential security interests relating to emergencies in international relations, including war, relating to the supply for the needs of armed forces and law enforcement agencies; relating to the supply of fissionable materials or materials from which they are derived."[214] Different from the WTO agreements, the Security Exception clause under the Guidelines does not use a self-judging language ("it considers") and is drafted in a slightly different manner. There is no known case to date where a BIT concluded by Russia would use such a language.

4.2.5 *The Approach of India*

Since 1991, India has "decided to lift its self-imposed exile and insulation from the global economy"[215] and has been signing treaties at regular intervals with a range of developed and developing nations worldwide.[216] Initially, India did not have a consistent approach to incorporating security defense. To illustrate, it contained Security Exceptions in its BITs with Germany, Russia, and the Netherlands but not in the BITs with Italy and Denmark.[217]

212 Sergey V Bakhin and Iuliia K Beketova, 'Conclusion of Bilateral Investment Treaties: New Approaches of the Russian Federation' (2017) 61(5) Pravovedenie 160, 161 (in Russian) https://pravovedenie.spbu.ru.

213 Dmitry K Labin and Alena V Soloveva, 'Russia's Foreign Investment Policy: Recent Developments and Future Trends in Terra (In)Cognita' in Congyan Cai, Huiping Chen, and Yifei Wang (eds.), *The BRICS in the New International Legal Order on Investment: Reformers or Disruptors* (Brill Nijhoff 2020) 39.

214 General Approaches to the Conclusion of International Agreements of the Russian Federation on the Promotion and Protection of Investments approved by the Resolution of the Government of the Russian Federation No 992 (September 30, 2016) (unofficial translation) https://investmentpolicy.unctad.org/international-investment-agreements/treaty-files/6009/download.

215 Prabhash Ranjan, 'India's Bilateral Investment Treaty Programme: Past, Present and Future' in Kavaljit Singh and Burghard Ilge (eds.), *Rethinking Bilateral Investment Treaties: Critical Issues and Policy Choices* (Both ENDS, Madhyam, SOMO 2016) 103.

216 India, International Investment Agreements Navigator, UNCTAD Investment Policy Hub https://investmentpolicy.unctad.org/international-investment-agreements/countries/96/india.

217 Ibid.

4.2.5.1 Exceptions That Do Not Use "Self-Judging" Language

The India Model BIT (2003) incorporated Security Exceptions that were not drafted in a self-judging manner. Article 12 allowed for "any action for the protection of party's essential security interests or in circumstances of extreme emergency in accordance with its laws normally and reasonably applied on a non-discriminatory basis." Such Security Exceptions provision is present in many current Indian BITs.[218] Notably, few Indian BITs concluded before 2015 allow deviation from the investment protection such as public order, health, and the environment or on grounds such as supporting domestic industries.[219] Yet, there are some exceptions to this approach. The Security Exceptions provision in the investment chapter of India's FTA with Japan (2011) is based on Article XIV*bis* GATS.[220] Article 11(5) and (7) also specifies additional preconditions for denying the benefits of the agreement to the investor owned or controlled by an investor or persons of a nonparty.

4.2.5.2 Exceptions Excluded from Review

India's position concerning the regulation of investments changed when it started to face challenges from foreign investors against measures taken by its government that allegedly violated investors' rights according to the terms of BITs.[221] This also affected India's position in drafting the exception clauses under IIAs.

Security Exceptions in the investment chapter of the India–Singapore CECA (2005) follow the structure of Article XXI GATT (1994) and Article XIV*bis* GATS.[222] Article 6.12(1)(b) also adds an Exception for critical public infrastructures. The parties clarified in their exchange of letters that Security Measures within the meaning of Article 6.12(1) should be understood as measures adopted with the intention and objective to protect a party's essential security interests and imposed on

[218] Model Text for the Indian Bilateral Investment Treaty https://investmentpolicy.unctad.org/international-investment-agreements/treaty-files/3560/download.

[219] James J Nedumpara, 'India's Trade and Investment Agreements: Striking a balance between Investor Protection Rights and Development Concerns' in Fabio C Morosini and Michelle Ratton Sanchez Badin (eds.), *Reconceptualizing International Investment Law from Global South* (CUP 2018) 212.

[220] Article 11 of India–Japan CEPA (2011).

[221] To illustrate, the four-million-dollar condemnation of India before an arbitral tribunal in the *White Industries Australia v India*. See *White Industries Australia Limited v The Republic of India* (November 30, 2011) UNCITRAL, Final Award www.italaw.com/sites/default/files/case-documents/ita0906.pdf.

[222] Article 6.12 of India–Singapore CECA (2005).

a nondiscriminatory basis.[223] At the same time, Article 6.12(4) of India–Singapore CECA (2005) read together with Annex 5 states that "any decision of the disputing Party taken on such security considerations shall be non-justiciable in that it shall not be open to any arbitral tribunal to review the merits of any such decision, even where the arbitral proceedings concern an assessment of any claim for damages and/or compensation, or an adjudication of any other issues referred to the tribunal." This provision clarifies that the tribunal cannot review the action of the host states, arguably not even concerning whether it was made in good faith.[224] Disputes over damages and/or compensation for a breach of a Security Exception may nevertheless be submitted to arbitration.[225] For greater clarity, Article 6.4 of the India–Singapore CECA (2005) allows foreign investors that suffer losses owing to war or other armed conflict, a state of emergency or civil disturbances in the territory of the host state to claim compensation or other settlement "no less favourable than that which that Party accords to its own investors or to investors of any non-Party." In other words, in the case of war or other armed conflicts, foreign investors can be eligible for a certain form of compensation even if India successfully invokes Security Exceptions. Yet, since Security Exceptions are considered nonjusticiable, arbitrators would not be able to review the merits of such claims beyond deciding on damages and/or compensation and its amount. A similar approach was adopted in the India–South Korea FTA (2009)[226] and India–Malaysia CECA (2011).[227] Yet, different from the India–Singapore CECA (2005) and India–South Korea FTA (2009), India–Malaysia CECA (2011) does not clarify whether disputes over damages and/or compensation due to Security Measures may be submitted to arbitration.

Eventually, India created a new model investment agreement stating that Security Exceptions are nonreviewable. While maintaining a more traditional investment treaty template, a new model treaty attempted to enlarge India's policy space and protect the country against future legal challenges.[228] India framed a new Model BIT in 2015, moving to

[223] Ibid Annex 4 (Security Exceptions for Investment).

[224] Prabhash Ranjan, 'Non-Precluded Measures in Indian International Investment Agreements and India's Regulatory Power as a Host Nation' (2012) 2 Asian J Intl L 21, 42.

[225] Annex 5 (Non-Justiciability of Security Exceptions) of India–Singapore CECA (2005).

[226] Annexes 10-B and 10-C of India–Korea FTA (2009).

[227] Annexes 12-1 and 12-2 of India–Malaysia CECA (2011).

[228] Fabio C Morosini and Michelle Ratton Sanchez Badin, 'Reconceptualizing International Investment Law from Global South: An Introduction' in Fabio C Morosini and Michelle

a somewhat protectionist approach to FDIs.[229] The Model BIT (2015) has more exceptions to investor protections than protections themselves.[230] It narrows down the definition of investment needed to qualify for BIT protection, completely omits the fair and equitable treatment standard and a clause on legitimate expectations, limits the liability for a host state, and raises the bar required to bring a claim under the BIT.[231] Since adopting the Model BIT (2015), India has unilaterally terminated sixty-six BITs between 2016 and 2019, including some BITs with European countries, sending negative signals to the global investor community.[232]

In addition to general exceptions, the Model BIT (2015) incorporates WTO-like Security Exceptions with paragraphs a, b, and c. Paragraph b allows for "any action which [a contracting party] considers necessary for the protection of its essential security interests."[233] It further provides an illustrative rather than exclusive list of circumstances under which the exceptions could be invoked, including GATT and GATS-like preconditions, the Exception for critical public infrastructure, and the exception regarding obtaining any security clearance. It further guides the interpretation of Security Exceptions. Each contracting party must inform the other party to the fullest extent possible of Security Measures.[234] Annex I envisages that such measures shall be applied with the intention and objective of the Party imposing the measures to protect its essential security interests; they shall be imposed on a nondiscriminatory basis and may be found in specifically approved regulations of each contracting party. It also establishes that Security Measures are not subject to review by the arbitral tribunal. In other words, unlike the Model BIT (2003), the Model BIT (2015) confirms that the Security Exception clause is nonreviewable. Such drafting techniques remind of the approach of the

Ratton Sanchez Badin (eds.), *Reconceptualizing International Investment Law from Global South* (CUP 2018) 19–20.

229 Model Text for the Indian Bilateral Investment Treaty https://investmentpolicy.unctad.org/international-investment-agreements/treaty-files/3560/download.

230 Nilanjan Sen and Amarendu Nandy, 'What Ails India's Model BIT?' *BusinessLine* (June 28, 2020) www.thehindubusinessline.com/opinion/what-ails-indias-model-bit/article31939413.ece.

231 Abhishek Dwivedi, 'India's Flawed Approach to Bilateral Investment Treaties' *The Diplomat* (December 4, 2020) https://thediplomat.com/2020/12/indias-flawed-approach-to-bilateral-investment-treaties/.

232 India, International Investment Agreements Navigator, UNCTAD Investment Policy Hub https://investmentpolicy.unctad.org/international-investment-agreements/countries/96/india.

233 Article 33(1) of the Model Text for the Indian Bilateral Investment Treaty.

234 Ibid Article 33(2).

India–Singapore CECA (2007), India–South Korea FTA (2009), and India–Malaysia CECA (2011) discussed above. Similar to the India–Malaysia CECA (2011), it remains unclear whether disputes over damages and/or compensation due to Security Measures may be submitted to arbitration, given that the decision of a party to adopt a Security Measure is not subject to review.

There could be multiple reasons for a change in India's drafting techniques over time, including India's shift to a more protectionist approach concerning foreign investments and the desire to broaden policy space and the ability to regulate investment-related matters. In addition, India's success in insisting on non-reviewable Security Exception clauses during BITs negotiations can signal its intention to become a "rule-maker" regarding investment agreements.

4.2.6 *The Approach of China*

China is the top recipient of foreign direct investments among emerging markets and the second-largest exporter of foreign direct investments globally, after the US.[235] China has been negotiating stand-alone BITs since the end of the 1990s.[236] In 2013, China launched a new development strategy to develop connectivity and cooperation across parts of Africa, Asia, and Europe – the Belt and Road Initiative, and continued to invest in Western countries.[237] Yet, after reaching a record level in 2016, Chinese FDI began to decline worldwide.[238] The existence of multiple outdated BITs and the engagement of Chinese investors with the host states with high political risks demonstrates the pragmatism of Chinese investment policies that use political and other means to advance investments.[239] While not all of the transactions blocked or suspended

[235] Fabio C Morosini and Michelle Ratton Sanchez Badin, 'Reconceptualizing International Investment Law from Global South: An Introduction' in Fabio C Morosini and Michelle Ratton Sanchez Badin (eds.), *Reconceptualizing International Investment Law from Global South* (CUP 2018) 16.

[236] Haiyan Zhang and Daniel Van Den Bulcke, 'China's Direct Investment in the European Union: A New Regulatory Challenge?' (2014) 12 Asia Eur J 159, 172.

[237] Carlos Alexandre Lobo and Vitor Rozenthal, 'The New Protectionism Era: Its Effects on M&A Transactions Globally and in Brazil' (*IBA*, 2021) www.ibanet.org/article/7585c6ae-c97f-40d3-b2b5-6d0bd3efa653.

[238] Ibid.

[239] Vivienne Bath, 'The South and Alternative Models of Trade and Investment Regulation: Chinese Investment and Approaches to International Investment Agreements' in Fabio C Morosini and Michelle Ratton Sanchez Badin (eds.), *Reconceptualizing International Investment Law from Global South* (CUP 2018) 84.

"by reasons of national security" have involved Chinese investors, many high-profile Chinese deals in the West have been blocked over the last few years.[240] This affects China's approach to drafting and negotiating investment agreements.

China has not been considered a dominant norm maker concerning key investment clauses.[241] To date, China has not adopted any Model BIT. Its treaty program historically did not contain a reference to Security Exceptions. However, certain BITs, including the BITs with Finland and Germany, incorporate security-related exceptions. To illustrate, the China–Finland BIT (2004) provides that "[n]othing in this Agreement precludes the host Contracting Party from taking necessary action in abnormal circumstances for the protection of its essential security interests or in circumstances of extreme emergency in accordance with its laws applied on a non-discriminatory basis."[242] The BIT with Germany (2003) prescribes that "[m]easures that have to be taken for reasons of public security and order, public health or morality shall not be deemed "treatment less favorable."[243]

4.2.6.1 Exceptions That Do Not Use "Self-Judging" Language

Several IIAs concluded by China use a broad standard of national security yet exclude any self-judging language. To illustrate, the China–Colombia BIT (2008) provides that nothing in the agreement shall "prevent a Party from adopting or maintaining measures intended to preserve public order including measures to protect the essential security interests of the State."[244] The agreement clarifies that such measures are also subject to specific preconditions that remind the chapeau of Article XX GATT (1994) and are subject to review by an arbitral tribunal.

4.2.6.2 WTO-Style Exceptions

Since 1998, China has also negotiated treaties that contain comprehensive investment provisions in its RTAs. The China–South Korea FTA in Article 12.14 includes Security Exceptions for the Chapter on

[240] Carlos Alexandre Lobo and Vitor Rozenthal, 'The New Protectionism Era: Its Effects on M&A Transactions Globally and in Brazil' (*IBA*, 2021) www.ibanet.org/article/7585c6ae-c97f-40d3-b2b5-6d0bd3efa653.

[241] Heng Wang, 'The RCEP and Its Investment Rules: Learning from Past Chinese FTAs' (2017) 3(2) The Chinese J Global Governance 160, 174.

[242] Article 3 of China–Finland BIT (2004).

[243] Ad Article 3 of China–Germany BIT (2003).

[244] Article 12 of China–Colombia BIT (2008).

Investment. It consists of two parts: part A resembles Article XXI(b), and part b corresponds to Article XXI(c) GATT (1994).[245] Part (b), however, uses different from GATT grounds for the security defense. In particular, it refers explicitly not only to the measures taken in times of war but also taken in times of armed conflict and not only to the measures taken in times of other emergencies in international relations but also taken in times of other emergencies in the party invoking the defense (domestic relations). Article 12.14 also expressly stipulates that the party shall not use a such measure to avoid its obligations under the Chapter.

Article 17 of the Agreement on Investment of China–ASEAN FTA (2004)[246] uses the language of Security Exceptions, similar to Article XXI GATT (1994). However, it clarifies that the list of grounds for the exercise of the security defense is not exhaustive. It also includes actions "taken so as to protect critical communications infrastructure from deliberate attempts intended to disable or degrade such infrastructure" and refers not only to actions "taken in time of war or other emergency in international relations" but also to the actions taken in time of other emergencies in domestic relations.[247] Following the EU approach to drafting Security Exceptions, the China–EU Comprehensive Agreement on Investment (2021) follows the WTO approach.

4.2.6.3 Exceptions Excluded from Review

Aiming to create an enabling investment environment in the region, the RCEP signed in November 2020 contains provisions on the protection, liberalization, promotion, and facilitation of investments, which upgrade existing ASEAN RTAs. Article 10.15 of the Investment Chapter of RCEP provides a specific Security Exception clause applicable to the investment chapter only and allows for the measures that "[a party] considers necessary for ... the protection of its own essential security interests." Article 10.15 does not further limit the invocation of the security defense to specific circumstances. Thus, it can be suggested that this Article provides a more expansive basis for the security defense, especially in the context of the emergence of laws across several RCEP members on the enhanced security scrutiny of investments. Remarkably, the general exceptions under Article 17.12 of RCEP cover the investment chapter

245 China–Korea FTA (2015).

246 Agreement on Investment of the Framework Agreement on Comprehensive Economic Co-operation between China and ASEAN (2002).

247 "(iv) action taken in time of war or other emergency in domestic or international relations."

and do not prescribe different rules for the application to investment-related matters. That demonstrates that the agreement does not prescribe specific treatment for the investment-restrictive measures based on the general exceptions but differentiates between investment and other measures if the security defense is considered.

RCEP is an exception from China's general approach to allow for the review of investment-related Security Measures. It has differentiated between investment and other matters under the agreement using a broad notion of the security defense in the case of the application of investment-related measures. RCEP is unique in several aspects: first, it is the only mega FTA in which China is involved, and second, China appears to be more flexible in negotiations with ASEAN than other partners, and ASEAN led the RCEP negotiations.[248] This can partially explain why China agreed to use a different approach to the Security Exceptions in RCEP. It remains to be seen in the subsequent practice of China participating in Regional Agreements whether this is a one-time deviation or a shift in the tactic.

4.2.7 The Approach of South Africa

In 1994–1998, South Africa concluded several BITs, mainly with European countries,[249] as a diplomatic signal confirming that South Africa reentered the international community after years of isolation under apartheid.[250] All the BITs between South Africa and European countries do not include Security Exceptions.[251] The same applies to the South Africa Model BIT (1998).

Since the assessment of BITs brought out several inconsistencies with South Africa's post-apartheid Constitution transformation agenda,[252]

[248] Heng Wang, 'The RCEP and Its Investment Rules: Learning from Past Chinese FTAs' (2017) 3(2) The Chinese J Global Governance 160, 177.

[249] Xavier Carim, 'International Investment Agreements and Africa's Structural Transformation: A Perspective from South Africa' in Kavaljit Singh and Burghard Ilge (eds.), *Rethinking Bilateral Investment Treaties: Critical Issues and Policy Choices* (Both ENDS, Madhyam, SOMO 2016) 59.

[250] Ibid.

[251] Only South Africa–Germany BIT incorporates the public security and order exception in its non-discrimination clause. Article 3.

[252] Xavier Carim, 'International Investment Agreements and Africa's Structural Transformation: A Perspective from South Africa' in Kavaljit Singh and Burghard Ilge (eds.), *Rethinking Bilateral Investment Treaties: Critical Issues and Policy Choices* (Both ENDS, Madhyam, SOMO 2016) 60.

South Africa decided to review its investment regulatory framework. It aimed to redress the legacy of apartheid rule, as a result of which some of the lands where foreign investment projects were located were forcibly taken away from the South African community without compensation.[253]

After foreign investors brought claims against South Africa challenging its measures to implement the post-apartheid Constitution transformation agenda and in view of the risk of other similar claims, the government had to reconsider its approach to investment regulation.[254] In April 2010, South Africa decided to enter into BITs in the future only in compelling economic and political circumstances; and review all early BITs signed shortly after the democratic transition in 1994, meaning to be terminated and possibly renegotiated based on a new Model BIT.[255] The empowerment of historically disadvantaged groups has affected the government's shift from treaty-based investment protection to investment protection by national law, which leaves more room for domestic politics.[256] Throughout 2012 and 2013, South Africa formally notified those European countries with which it had BITs about their termination and focused on developing a new Model BIT on a regional level to rebalance investor rights and states' regulatory space.[257]

South Africa has participated in a new SADS Model BIT (2012), which, among others, limits the definition of investment/investor, excludes fair and equitable treatment to foreign investors, and replaces investor-state dispute settlement with South African courts. It incorporates Security Exceptions under Article 25.5, stating that "[n]othing in this Agreement shall apply to a State Party's measures that it considers necessary for the

[253] Fabio C Morosini and Michelle Ratton Sanchez Badin, 'Reconceptualizing International Investment Law from Global South: An Introduction' in Fabio C Morosini and Michelle Ratton Sanchez Badin (eds.), *Reconceptualizing International Investment Law from Global South* (CUP 2018) 20.

[254] Ibid 21.

[255] Xavier Carim, 'International Investment Agreements and Africa's Structural Transformation: A Perspective from South Africa' in Kavaljit Singh and Burghard Ilge (eds.), *Rethinking Bilateral Investment Treaties: Critical Issues and Policy Choices* (Both ENDS, Madhyam, SOMO 2016) 61.

[256] Malebakeng Agnes Forere, 'The New South African Protection of Investment Act: Striking a Balance between Attraction of FDI and Redressing the Apartheid Legacies' in Fabio C Morosini and Michelle Ratton Sanchez Badin (eds.), *Reconceptualizing International Investment Law from Global South* (CUP 2018) 263, 281.

[257] Xavier Carim, 'International Investment Agreements and Africa's Structural Transformation: A Perspective from South Africa' in Kavaljit Singh and Burghard Ilge (eds.), *Rethinking Bilateral Investment Treaties: Critical Issues and Policy Choices* (Both ENDS, Madhyam, SOMO 2016) 62.

fulfilment of its obligations with respect to the maintenance or restoration of international peace or security, or the protection of its national security interests."[258] Article 25.6 also incorporates the Security Exception concerning furnishing or allowing access to any information, the disclosure of which a contracting party determines to be contrary to its national security interests (similar to subparagraph a of Article XXI of GATT).[259] The SADC Model BIT asserts in the commentary to Article 25 that "[t]he exclusions relating to national security are inspired by the US Model BIT and subsequent US treaties. They are self-executing here, meaning that as soon as a State declares this exception, it is binding and not subject to arbitral review. This removes the review of this issue from any dispute settlement process. This self-executing approach is seen in the US treaties."[260] Therefore, South Africa and other SADC Members have chosen to follow the US approach to Security Exceptions and have confirmed the self-judging nature of Security Exception clauses.

South Africa has not entered into any BIT after 2012. It remains to be seen whether newly renegotiated investment treaties with European countries, if successful, would follow the approach of the SADC Model BIT and adopt a broad language of Security Exception clauses.

4.2.8 Toward a Common Approach?

Even though US BITs take different approaches to the drafting of Security Exception clauses, the US has always tried to argue that when interpreting Security Exception clauses they should be deemed "self-judging." The US intended to preserve a greater regulatory discretion concerning investment and to circumscribe the discretion of arbitral tribunals should its regulation be challenged. Irrespective of the drafting techniques used, the US reserved the claim that it could invoke Security Exceptions whenever its essential security interests were at stake, even if that was not expressly mentioned in the agreement. Nevertheless, the drafting and negotiation history of the US BITs also demonstrates that the US expected states generally to enjoy a presumption of acting in good faith, including while taking the measures under exception clauses, which are regarded as "self-judging." Thus, despite excluding Security Exceptions from tribunal review, the US did not have grounds for

[258] SADC Model Bilateral Investment Treaty Template with Commentary (2012).
[259] Ibid.
[260] Ibid.

believing that it could implement any measure in breach of its treaty commitments to justify its policy goals.

The analysis of the texts of the model BITs and IIAs concluded by EU member states with other countries demonstrates that EU member states have different approaches to the inclusion of Security Exceptions in their BITs, while the EU itself tends to follow the WTO approach. Many factors might contribute to the differences in approach among EU member states to security defense clauses, including the choice for the contracting parties, the discrepancy in the bargaining power of the contracting parties, the nature of the commitments under the respective BITs, membership in the EC, or later the EU. Ultimately, those BITs of EU member states that include Security Exception clauses still rely on the WTO model.

A shift toward nonreviewable Security Exceptions in investment security-related matters is the perspective of the US, recently joined by Brazil, India, and South Africa. It might open the door to a range of national interests potentially falling under the exceptions, such as measures adopted to protect national food security, which has been an increasing challenge for all three states. The other WTO members whose practice was analyzed for the purposes of this research allow adjudicators to interpret and apply the operative components of the Security Exceptions under their investment treaties. Russia's latest practice is to recommend excluding any self-judging language from Security Exception clauses. China's IIAs generally either do not include Security Exceptions or expressly incorporate specific conditions for the invocation of such exceptions, which preclude their use in a broad range of circumstances. The RCEP entered by China is an exception; it follows the US approach to Security Exceptions and incorporates a broadly drafted security defense clause that excludes investment-related Security Measures from adjudicative review.

4.3 Conclusion

The taxonomy of Security Exceptions suggested in this chapter leads to several important conclusions. First, having been economically powerful, capital-exporting WTO members since the birth of multilateral trade and investment regimes, the US and the EU have a clear preference for one type of exception over the other. The approach of the US, however, clashes with the EU approach. Recently, the US either prefers to use "self-judging" exceptions in its RTAs or expressly excludes investment-related Security

Measures from adjudicatory review, thus signaling its need to preserve the broadest policy space in adopting Security Measures. On the contrary, the EU prefers to adhere to the WTO approach to drafting and interpreting Security Exceptions in its Regional Agreements regarding both trade and investment matters. This is not surprising given that Article 21 of the Treaty on the European Union (TEU) sets out that "[t]he Union's action on the international scene shall be guided by the principles which have inspired its own creation, development and enlargement, and which it seeks to advance in the wider world" and that the EU shall work for a high degree of cooperation in all fields of international relations in order to, among other things, "promote an international system based on stronger multilateral cooperation and good global governance." Because of this, it can be argued that the EU's preference to follow the WTO approach to the drafting of Security Exceptions derives from a solid commitment to respect and comply with international law and the resulting preference for multilateralism.

The approaches taken by BRICS, most of which have only just started being capital-exporting countries participating in a range of regional and bilateral initiatives, differ depending on the contracting parties and domestic political and economic developments; this does not always allow for identifying a strong preference for one approach over the other. Yet, as recent practice demonstrates, their agreements commonly exclude Security Measures from adjudicative review in the case of an investment dispute but not a trade dispute. Similar to the US, the current practice of Brazil, India, and South Africa follows a trend of their model investment treaties expressly excluding the review of investment-related Security Measures. Notably, while broadly drafted Security Exceptions that use self-judging language can be found in addition to US RTAs, in India's RTAs – and, more as an exception than a rule, in some RTAs entered into by Brazil, Russia, China, and South Africa – none of the examined trade agreements expressly excluded the review of Security Measures. The difference in the treatment of trade and investment matters can be attributed to many factors, including the different attitudes of WTO members to the openness of their respective markets to foreign investors.[261] Nevertheless, the creation of a comprehensive multilateral set of trade rules under the WTO and the greater reluctance of WTO members to deviate from them seems to allow for more consistent approaches among WTO members to trade-related exceptions.

261 See more chapter 3, section 3.2.

Second, in addition to the inclusion or exclusion of "self-judging" language or the express exclusion of adjudicatory review altogether, Security Exceptions differ in terms of the additional criteria for their invocation that narrow them down to specific situations. While many Regional Agreements incorporate preconditions similar to those in Article XXI GATT (1994), such as "relating to fissionable materials," others add additional grounds for invoking the security defense, such as the protection of critical infrastructure or the existence of a domestic emergency (e.g. the EU, China, and India). According to Anuradha, such articulation appears to be a more precise and transparent strategy than having open-ended Security Exception clauses.[262]

It can be argued that the WTO members with the broadest expectations about the scope of Security Exceptions, such as the US in its Regional Agreements, might be those keenest to invoke the exceptions whenever they are willing to protect their state interests. In contrast, those WTO members who construe Security Exceptions more narrowly and acknowledge that the exceptions are judicially reviewable, such as the EU, are signaling that they might not be inclined to invoke a security defense. Trade cooperation between WTO members with different approaches to understanding Security Exceptions could be unstable and unpredictable. Even if such members agree to choose one of the reviewed approaches to drafting Security Exceptions in their Regional Agreement, the party that wants to preserve more discretion in national security questions may prefer its interpretation of such Security Exceptions regardless of the wording of Security Exception clauses incorporated in the agreement.

Ultimately, opting for one of the described drafting techniques for incorporating security defenses might still lead to the same result: the parties will apply Security Measures when they consider such measures to fall within the scope of Security Exceptions based on their interpretation. Such an approach can lead to systematic challenges in the current global trading system, such as further market fragmentation, undermining the existential need for international regulation of trade.

The WTO is arguably more capable of addressing these issues than regional or bilateral agreements. It could leverage its institutional authority to interpret Security Exceptions within WTO agreements, determining what constitutes a security defense. This would allow the WTO to

[262] RV Anuradha, 'Petrificus Totalus: The Spell of National Security!' (2018) 13 Asian J WTO & BLI Health Law and Policy 311, 328.

balance trade and national security for its members while maintaining a consistent approach to the application of Security Measures worldwide. To follow such a rationale would mean that using WTO-style Security Exceptions in Regional Agreements is a safer and more secure way for the international community.

At the same time, it cannot be excluded that those who want to have more discretion in invoking Security Exceptions might prefer their broader interpretation even in multilateral agreements. Therefore, in light of renewed debates over the scope of Security Exceptions under the GATT (1994), it remains unclear whether the existing WTO approach to Security Exceptions is likely to remain dominant in the RTAs adopted by the EU and BRICS and whether it can ensure better stability of a rules-based trading system. Moreover, a recent trend toward the exclusion of review of Security Measures under the IIAs of the US, Brazil, India, and South Africa suggests that the approach of WTO members to trade restrictions and investment restrictions adopted to protect national security might continue to diverge.

5

Framework for Review of Security Exceptions

The correct approach to reviewing Security Exceptions begins with distinguishing between the authority to define and the authority to interpret.[1] The authority to define the threat to national security and the necessity of the response pertains to the questions of the state's sovereignty and remains the function of domestic authorities. Conversely, the authority to interpret international agreements generally rests with international courts and tribunals as long as the contracting states have explicitly accepted their jurisdiction. Following this line, the debate over the "self-judging" nature of Security Exceptions highlights the underlying tension between states as masters of treaties and adjudicators as their interpreters.

The approach to interpreting Security Exceptions cannot be reasonably satisfied with the rudimentary tools of state power outside any treaty regime. Instead, it draws on the well-established rules of customary public international law primarily reflected in the provisions of the VCLT.[2] While treaty interpretation involves identifying the actual meaning of the provision and, thus, the substantive obligations incumbent on the state, the standard of review refers to the scope and intensity of the review exercised by the adjudicator.[3] In the international context, the standard of review is defined as "the nature and intensity of review by court or tribunal of decisions taken by governmental authority."[4] Thus, the standard of review is employed to distribute powers among international and domestic institutions. The principles of treaty interpretation

[1] Hannes L Schloemann and Stefan Ohlhoff, 'Constitutionalization and Dispute Settlement in the WTO: National Security as an Issue of Competence' (1999) 93 Am J Intl L 424, 426.

[2] Michael J Hahn, 'Vital Interests and the Law of GATT: An Analysis of GATT's Security Exception' (1991) 12 Mich J Intl L 558, 564.

[3] Johannes Hendrik Fahner, *Judicial Deference in International Adjudication: A Comparative Analysis* (Hart 2020) 130.

[4] Lukasz Gruszczynski and Wouter Werner, 'Introduction' in Lukasz Gruszczynski and Wouter Werner (eds.), *Deference in International Courts and Tribunals: Standard of Review and Margin of Appreciation* (OUP 2014) 2.

determine how these powers should be applied to a specific treaty commitment.[5] Notably, the standard of review does not replace treaty interpretation, meaning that it does not alter the applicable law.[6]

Being drafted as standard-type norms that use open-ended terms and, at times, expressly refer to the discretion of contracting parties to decide on specific issues,[7] Security Exceptions may be interpreted according to competing legal principles, the application of which reflects a variety of value-laden choices.[8] By choosing a proper standard of review for Security Exceptions, international adjudicators should be able to navigate between the states' prerogative to adopt Security Measures and the obligation to comply with undertaken commitments to free trade and investment liberalization. The process of interpretation often requires adjudicators to balance competing interests and values.[9] Yet, the difficulty of such a balancing exercise in national security disputes lies in an inherent trade-off between state sovereignty in protecting national security and undertaken international commitments. The dichotomy between the definition of national security defenses as given by national governments and their interpretation by international adjudicators raises the question of the extent to which adjudicators should limit state sovereignty by enforcing international law. Answering this question might require a nuanced and sensitive approach to distributing powers among international and domestic institutions.

This chapter aims to establish a framework for reviewing Security Exceptions that would balance the competing regulatory objectives and policies of WTO members. It proceeds in four parts. First, it examines whether states should generally be accountable for applying Security Measures before international adjudicators (section 5.1). Second, it discusses how the invocation of Security Exceptions impacts the international court's or tribunal's powers (section 5.2). Third, this chapter examines how international adjudicators can reconcile international cooperation with the state's occasional preference for unilateralism within cooperative regimes

[5] Johannes Hendrik Fahner, 'In Dubio Mitius: Advancing Clarity and Modesty in Treaty Interpretation' (2021) 32(3) EJIL 835, 858–859.

[6] Valentina Vadi, *Proportionality, Reasonableness and Standards of Review in International Investment Law and Arbitration* (Edward Elgar Publishing 2018) 190.

[7] Chapter 2, section 2.5.1 and chapter 4.

[8] David D Knoll, 'The Impact of Security Concerns upon International Economic Law' (1984) 11(3) Intl Econ L 567, 583.

[9] Mads Andenas and Stefan Zleptnig, 'The Rule of Law and Proportionality in WTO Law' in Wenhua Shan, Penelope Simons, and Dalvinder Singh (eds.), *Redefining Sovereignty in International Economic Law* (Hart Publishing 2008) 191.

by balancing states' international commitments and the need to respond to national security concerns (section 5.3). Finally, this chapter concludes (section 5.4).

5.1 Jurisdiction and Justiciability

The jurisdiction of international courts and tribunals over a dispute differs from the justiciability of a particular matter.[10] As the Oxford Dictionary puts it, "jurisdiction" means "exercise of judicial authority, or of the functions of a judge or legal tribunal, power of administering law or justice" or "the extent or range of judicial or administrative power."[11] "Justiciable" means "amenable to jurisdiction," "liable to be tried in a court of justice."[12] Based on these definitions, "jurisdiction" determines whether an adjudicator has the authority to hear a dispute conferred upon it by law, while "justiciable" refers to how appropriate it is that an adjudicator determines the matter. If an adjudicator does not have jurisdiction to make determinations, then the question of justiciability does not arise.[13] For example, in *Russia – Traffic in Transit*, the US used the term "jurisdiction" to refer to the ability of the panel to organize and hear a dispute according to the DSU, and it used the term "justiciability" to refer to "the ability of the panel to make findings and provide a recommendation to the DSB."[14] Yet, the distinction between jurisdiction and justiciability is complicated by the fact that sometimes these terms appear to be used interchangeably.[15]

"Justiciable" or "justiciability" is not often mentioned in legal documents. "Nonjusticiability" is a familiar, albeit contentious, feature in some domestic legal systems envisaging that some disputes are inappropriate for settlement by a court.[16] Its core is concerned with the separation of powers doctrine, whereby the judicial system is designed to be an

[10] Ariel L Bendor, 'Are There Any Limits to Justiciability – The Jurisprudential and Constitutional Controversy in Light of the Israeli and American Experience' (1997) 7 Ind Intl & Comp L Rev 311, 317.

[11] Lesley Brown (ed.), *The New Shorter Oxford English Dictionary on Historical Principles* (OUP 1993) 1465.

[12] Ibid 1466.

[13] Dominic McGoldrick, 'The Boundaries of Justiciability' (2010) 59(4) ICLQ 981, 983.

[14] *Russia – Measures Concerning Traffic in Transit* (April 5, 2019) WTO Panel Report Annex D – 10 Executive Summary of the Arguments of the US WT/DS512/R/Add.1 [29].

[15] Dominic McGoldrick, 'The Boundaries of Justiciability' (2010) 59(4) ICLQ 981, 983.

[16] Anna John, 'Inarticulate and Unconscious: Non-Justiciability before the International Court of Justice' (2021) 20 LPICT 77, 77.

apolitical branch that cannot take over the executive branch's powers.[17] Among others, "justiciable" or "justiciability" are vaguely used in domestic administrative law to describe controversies removed from the jurisdiction of domestic courts and entrusted to administrative authorities.[18] In the US, for example, the issue of justiciability is dealt with primarily within the context of the "political question" doctrine, which limits the adjudication of matters, such as foreign relations and national security, that are generally within the responsibility of other governmental authorities.[19]

5.1.1 *Security Exceptions in ICJ Case Law*

The Statute of the ICJ contains no mention of political disputes, yet Article 36(2) of the Statute refers to the Court's jurisdiction over "legal disputes." Article 36(3) of the UN Charter also raises the referral of "legal disputes" to the ICJ.[20] Neither the Statute nor the Charter defines a "legal dispute." The reasons for the inclusion of the word "legal" are unclear. At the same time, the ICJ has explicitly rejected the notion that some disputes before it are nonjusticiable because of their political nature.[21] In *US v Iran*, the ICJ stressed that "[l]egal disputes between sovereign states by their very nature are likely to occur in political contexts, and often form only one element in a wider and long-standing political dispute between the states concerned."[22] The ICJ further rejected the view that "because a legal dispute submitted to the Court is only one aspect of a political dispute, the Court should decline to resolve for the parties the legal questions at issue between them."[23] Accordingly, if the ICJ were to decline to adjudicate a case for this reason, "[i]t would impose a far-reaching and unwarranted restriction upon the role of the Court in the peaceful solution of international disputes."[24]

In *Djibouti v France*, the ICJ has reviewed a self-judging clause incorporated in Article 2(c) of the Mutual Assistance Convention stating that

17 Ibid 78.

18 Hersch Lauterpacht, 'The Doctrine of Non-Justiciable Disputes in International Law' (1928) 24 Economica 277, 277.

19 Ariel L Bendor, 'Are There Any Limits to Justiciability: The Jurisprudential and Constitutional Controversy in Light of the Israeli and American Experience' (1997) 7 Ind Intl & Comp L Rev 311, 312.

20 Article 36(3) of the UN Charter.

21 Ibid 107.

22 *US Diplomatic and Consular Staff in Tehran (US v Iran)* (May 24, 1980) ICJ Rep [37].

23 Ibid.

24 Ibid.

assistance in criminal proceedings "may be refused . . . if the requested state considers that the execution of the request is likely to prejudice its sovereignty, its security, its ordre public or other of its essential interests."[25] France refused to provide the required documents to Djibouti, relying on this clause.[26] Notwithstanding the self-judging wording, the ICJ nevertheless found that it had jurisdiction to hear the dispute and considered the dispute justiciable and thus subject to judicial review.[27]

In the *Nicaragua v US* case, the ICJ considered claims brought by Nicaragua against the US for violations of the 1956 FCN Treaty permitting either signatory to take action necessary to protect its essential security interests.[28] The ICJ recalled that "the Court has never shied away from a case brought before it merely because it had political implications" and ruled that it had jurisdiction in the case based on either Article 36 of the Statute of the ICJ (i.e. compulsory jurisdiction) or the 1956 FCN Treaty.[29] The ICJ further differentiated between the wording of Article XXI(b) GATT (1947) and the wording of the Security Exception clause under the 1956 FCN Treaty, which referred to "necessary" measures rather than those "considered [by a state] to be necessary."[30] The ICJ thus attributed the significance of the treaty's wording and the definitions of the terms under the exception clause.

In *Oil Platforms*, the US invoked the Security Exception clause under Article XX(1)(d)) of the Treaty of Amity with Iran justifying the measures necessary to protect the US's essential security interests.[31] Initially, the US had argued in its written pleadings that the court had no jurisdiction to consider the case where Security Exception was invoked.[32] However, during the oral pleadings, the US accepted that the proper interpretation of the Security Exception was a matter of the merits

25 *Case Concerning Certain Questions on Mutual Assistance in Criminal Matters (Djibouti v France)* (June 4, 2008) ICJ Rep [135].

26 Ibid.

27 Ibid [140].

28 FCN Treaty between the US and Nicaragua (1956).

29 *Case Concerning Military and Paramilitary Activities in and against Nicaragua (Nicaragua v US)* (November 26, 1984) ICJ Rep Jurisdiction of the Court and Admissibility of the Application [96].

30 Ibid [222].

31 The Treaty of Amity Economic Relations and Consular Rights between the US and Iran (August 15, 1955).

32 Dapo Akande and Sope Williams, 'International Adjudication on National Security Issues: What Role for the WTO?' (2003) 43 Virginia J Intl L 365, 380.

phase.[33] In interpreting the scope of Article XX, the ICJ turned to the general international law on the use of force, reasoning that "[i]n the present case, the question of whether measures taken were 'necessary' overlaps with the question of their validity as acts of self-defence."[34] It concluded that if the uncontested uses of force by the US could be justified as acts of self-defense, they equally would amount to measures necessary to ensure their essential security interests.[35] These concepts were thus treated, in essence, as synonymous by the ICJ.

The US also relied on the Security Exception under the Treaty of Amity in another dispute with Iran, claiming that its sanctions against Iran were non-justifiable since they were, among others, "relating to fissionable materials" and were necessary to protect the US "essential security interests."[36] The ICJ has recalled *Oil Platforms*, where it had found that Article XX, paragraph 1(d) of the Treaty of Amity does not restrict its jurisdiction.[37] According to the ICJ, the analysis of the Security Exception would raise the question of the existence of the claimed "essential security interests" and might require an assessment of the reasonableness and necessity of US sanctions in so far as they affected the obligations under the Treaty of Amity.[38] Eventually, the ICJ differentiated between the standard of review applied in its judgment in the *Djibouti v France* case, where the applicable treaty used a self-judging language ("it considers"), and the objectively drafted Security Exception under the Treaty of Amity to find that it was for the US to demonstrate that its trade restrictions were "a measure necessary to protect its essential security interests," and that the US "has not convincingly demonstrated that this was so."[39] Thus, the ICJ did not uphold the US national security defense.[40]

These cases indicate that even where a state considers itself to be a sole judge as to what constitutes a threat to its national security and what kind of measures could be applied to protect its national security interests, the ICJ generally recognizes that the invocation of Security Exceptions does

[33] Ibid.
[34] *Oil Platforms* (*Iran v US*) (November 6, 2003) ICJ Rep Merits [43].
[35] Ibid [40]–[44].
[36] *Alleged Violations of the 1955 Treaty of Amity, Economic Relations, and Consular Rights (Iran v US)* (February 3, 2021) ICJ Rep [103].
[37] Ibid [109].
[38] Ibid [112].
[39] *Alleged Violations of the 1955 Treaty of Amity, Economic Relations, and Consular Rights (Iran v US)* (March 30, 2023) ICJ Rep [107]–[108].
[40] Ibid [109].

not preclude international review of specific legal and factual questions invoked in the case. Thus, it can be concluded that the jurisprudence of the ICJ supports the conclusion that Security Exceptions, even if drafted in a self-judging manner, do not constitute a bar to jurisdiction and do not prevent the justiciability of a dispute but can modify the standard of review that an international court applies.

5.1.2 *Security Exceptions under WTO law*

Security Exceptions under the WTO agreements constitute a primarily substantive exception rather than a procedural exception.[41] The text of Security Exceptions does not explicitly mandate that a WTO panel be denied competence in cases involving the application of exceptions.[42] Once a panel is formed, it has the authority to consider a complaint and address all the legal issues related to the dispute, including when a respondent invokes Security Exceptions.[43]

Even assuming that Security Exceptions do not constitute the bar to WTO panel jurisdiction, the question arises whether the panel can make any findings regarding the interpretation of Security Exceptions, apart from stating that the exception has been invoked. To illustrate, for the US, the "self-judging" nature of Article XXI(b)(iii) means that its invocation by a member shall be considered "nonjusticiable" and "is therefore not capable of findings by a panel," meaning that the panel cannot make recommendations under Article 19.1 DSU in the dispute.[44] The US bases its arguments on the customary rules of treaty interpretation under the VCLT and refers to the overall grammatical structure of Article XXI(b) that is affected by the self-judging language "it considers."

The political nature of Article XXI disputes might help explain the drafters' decision to include the self-judging language "it considers" in the exception.[45] Yet, there are few grounds to believe that the effect of such discretionary language is not unlimited. It can be argued that if it were otherwise, the term "essential" security interests would become meaningless, as would the language that refers to the action "relating to fissionable

[41] *Russia – Measures Concerning Traffic in Transit* (April 5, 2019) WTO Panel Report WT/DS512/R [7.56].

[42] Ibid.

[43] Ibid [7.102]–[7.103].

[44] Ibid [7.52].

[45] Peter Lindsay, 'The Ambiguity of GATT Article XXI: Subtle Success or Rampant Failure' (2003) 52 Duke LJ 1277, 1295.

materials" or "taken in time of war or other emergency in international relations" in the subparagraphs of Article XXI(b). If Article XXI(b) was meant to be unbridled, the drafters could have simply limited the language to "nothing in this Agreement shall be construed to prevent any contracting party from taking any action which it considers necessary for the protection of its security interests,"[46] as this is the case in some IIAs, in particular, the ones concluded by and with the US. Furthermore, to construe Article XXI(b) as entirely self-judging would, in effect, mean that a WTO member is entitled to determine the scope and existence of its obligations under the GATT (1994), as it would be up to the member to unilaterally determine when it was obliged to comply with GATT obligations and when national security interests precluded such obligations. Since it is clear that the GATT was intended to create legal obligations, it can be argued that one must not interpret Article XXI in such an entirely self-judging way that would vitiate the legal effect of the WTO agreements.[47]

In 2019, similar to the ICJ practice, the panel in the *Russia – Traffic in Transit* dispute rejected the argument of Russia, supported by the US, that the Security Exception clause "is totally self-judging or non-justiciable."[48] The panel highlighted that it has "inherent jurisdiction" over the dispute due to its "adjudicative function"[49] and the fact that the DSU contains no special or additional rules for Article XXI disputes.[50] Interpreting Article XXI(b) according to its ordinary meaning, the context, and the goals of the GATT (1994) and the Marrakesh Agreement, the panel concluded that the phrase "it considers" does not pertain to assessing the situations listed in the subparagraphs of Article XXI(b). Rather, such circumstances are subject to objective determination meaning that it is not solely for Russia to determine that its action is taken in time of war or another emergency in international relations.[51] The panel also confirmed this interpretation based on the negotiating history of Article XXI(b).[52] Apart from the requirements of the subparagraphs of Article XXI(b), the panel regarded whether Russia

[46] Wesley A Cann, 'Creating Standards and Accountability for the Use of the WTO Security Exception: Reducing the Role of Power-Based Relations and Establishing a New Balance between Sovereignty and Multilateralism' (2001) 26 Yale J Intl L 413, 432.

[47] Dapo Akande and Sope Williams, 'International Adjudication on National Security Issues: What Role for the WTO?' (2003) 43 Virginia J Intl L 365, 384.

[48] *Russia – Measures Concerning Traffic in Transit* (April 5, 2019) WTO Panel Report WT/DS512/R [7.102].

[49] Ibid [7.53].

[50] Ibid [7.56].

[51] Ibid [7.82].

[52] Ibid [7.83]–[7.101].

defined its "essential security interests" in good faith[53] and whether the challenged measures were not "implausible as measures protective of these interests."[54] The panel in *Saudi Arabia – IPRs* adhered to the approach established in *Russia – Traffic in Transit.*[55]

The panels in *US – Steel and Aluminium Products* also reiterated their "function and duty under Article 11 of the DSU to make an objective assessment of the matter before [them]" and "the role of WTO dispute settlement, as recognized in Article 3.2 of the DSU, to preserve the rights and obligations of Members under the covered agreements."[56] In view of this, all four panels found that they are "required under the DSU to assess … disputed issues in an objective manner and to make findings on the basis of that assessment that will assist the DSB in making the recommendations or rulings provided for in the covered agreements."[57] The panel in *US – Steel and Aluminium Products (China)* disagreed with the US that Article XXI GATT (1994) imposes on a WTO member the sole requirement to indicate that it determined that it "consider[s] one or more of the circumstances set forth in Article XXI(b) to be present."[58] Instead, the panel reiterated that neither Article XXI(b) is "self-judging" or "non-justiciable," nor "its provision contains a 'single relative clause' that wholly reserves the conditions and circumstances of the subparagraphs to the judgment of the invoking Member."[59] The panel clarified that "Article XXI(b) is to be given meaning as a complete sentence with the enumerated subparagraphs (i) to (iii) representing alternative endings."[60] These alternative endings "qualify and describe the 'action' referred to in Article XXI(b)," meaning that Article XXI(b) applies to the actions that a state "considers necessary for the protection of its essential security interests" and that are either "relating to" the "materials" and "traffic" described in

[53] Ibid [7.132]–[7.133].
[54] Ibid [7.138].
[55] *Saudi Arabia – Measures Concerning the Protection of Intellectual Property Rights* (June 16, 2020) WTO Panel Report WT/DS567/R [7.230].
[56] *US – Certain Measures on Steel and Aluminium Products (China)* (December 9, 2022) WTO Panel Report WT/DS544/R [7.4]; *US – Certain Measures on Steel and Aluminium Products (Norway)* (December 9, 2022) WTO Panel Report WT/DS552/R [7.4]; *US – Certain Measures on Steel and Aluminium Products (Switzerland)* (December 9, 2022) WTO Panel Report WT/DS556/R [7.4]; *US – Certain Measures on Steel and Aluminium Products (Turkey)* (December 9, 2022) WTO Panel Report WT/DS564/R [7.4].
[57] Ibid [7.6], in each panel report respectively.
[58] See eg *US – Certain Measures on Steel and Aluminium Products (China)* (December 9, 2022) WTO Panel Report WT/DS544/R [7.105].
[59] Ibid [7.128].
[60] Ibid [7.111].

subparagraphs (i) and (ii), respectively, or "taken in time of" the circumstances referred to in subparagraph (iii).[61] While the panel acknowledged that Article XXI(b) grants WTO members broad discretion in determining what they "consider necessary for the protection of their essential security interests," it stated that the self-judging language does not qualify the subparagraphs (i) to (iii) to render them "self-judging" or "nonjusticiable." Such enumerating circumstances and conditions under subparagraphs (i) to (iii) determine when the member's discretion may be exercised and "must be given meaning and effect according to the ordinary meaning of their terms."[62] The other panels in *US – Steel and Aluminium Products* disputes based their finding on the same grounds.[63] Regrettably, none of the panels in *US – Steel and Aluminium Products* elaborated on the scope of the deferential or subjective review of other preconditions for the justification of Security Measures under Article XXI(b), such as the necessity of the measures and the existence of essential security interests, even though all of them implied the degree of deference to an invoking member.

The panel in *US – Origin Marking (Hong Kong, China)* confirmed that "the political nature of essential security interests does not in itself warrant the exclusion of any evaluation thereof by a panel."[64] To this end, it explained that "the WTO was entrusted with providing the multilateral framework on international trade."[65] Accordingly, other provisions of WTO agreements (such as Article 2.2 of the TBT Agreement referring to "national security requirements") demonstrate that the WTO members raise trade-related concerns with respect to Security Measures within the WTO institutional framework on different occasions.[66] While acknowledging that "the WTO should not become a forum to discuss security issues generally," the panel stated that the WTO agreements nevertheless "set forth the limited circumstances under which the WTO and its DSS have been tasked with addressing security matters linked to international trade."[67] Similar to the findings by

[61] Ibid [7.113].

[62] Ibid [7.122].

[63] *US – Certain Measures on Steel and Aluminium Products (Norway)* (December 9, 2022) WTO Panel Report WT/DS552/R [7.116]; *US – Certain Measures on Steel and Aluminium Products (Switzerland)* (December 9, 2022) WTO Panel Report WT/DS556/R [7.146]; *US – Certain Measures on Steel and Aluminium Products (Turkey)* (December 9, 2022) WTO Panel Report WT/DS564/R [7.143].

[64] *US – Origin Marking Requirements* (December 21, 2022) WTO Panel Report WT/DS597/R [7.147].

[65] Ibid.

[66] Ibid.

[67] Ibid [7.149].

previous panels, this panel saw no basis in the text of Article XXI(b) GATT (1994) for its reading as a "single relative clause" and for the phrase "which it considers" to qualify both the main part of Article XXI(b) (the chapeau) and its subparagraphs.[68] It confirmed that the subparagraphs of Article XXI(b) directly relate to the "action" portrayed by an invoking state as a Security Measure and that such subparagraphs are not affected by self-judging language.[69] The panel also reaffirmed that such a reading of Security Exceptions is in conformity with the object and purpose of the GATT (1994) since it "serves the security and predictability of the multilateral trading system by allowing for sufficient flexibility for Members to adopt the measures they consider necessary for the protection of their security interests, while at the same time ensuring that this flexibility is exercised within limits intended by the drafters."[70]

Thus, similar to the ICJ jurisprudence, the practice of WTO panels suggests that WTO-style Security Exceptions do not constitute a bar to jurisdiction and do not prevent the justiciability of a dispute but only affect the standard of review of Security Measures.

5.1.3 *Security Exceptions under International Investment Law*

The tribunals in the Argentine economic crisis cases have highlighted the importance of an express language to consider a Security Exception self-judging. To illustrate, in *Continental Casualty v Argentina*, the tribunal emphasized that "caution must be exercised in allowing a party unilaterally to escape from its treaty obligations without clear textual or contextual indications."[71]

In *Devas v India* and *Deutsche Telekom v India*, the tribunals interpreted the Security Exception clauses under India–Mauritius BIT and India–Germany BIT, respectively. Neither of the clauses uses self-judging language. The arbitrators concluded that the Security Exception clauses drafted in these treaties do not constitute the basis for dismissing the cases by merely asserting that the impugned measure concerned national security.[72] According to the arbitrators in *Devas v India*, "unless a treaty contains

[68] Ibid [7.69], [7.87].

[69] Ibid Part 7.3.3.2.2.2.

[70] Ibid [7.148].

[71] *Continental Casualty Co v Argentine Republic* (September 5, 2008) ICSID Case No Arb/03/9 Award [187].

[72] *CC/Devas (Mauritius) Ltd v Republic of India* (July 25, 2016) PCA Case No 2013-09 Award on Jurisdiction and Merits [219].

specific wording granting full discretion to the State to determine what it considers necessary for the protection of its security interests, national security clauses are not self-judging."[73] The arbitrators noted that "[s]elf-judging "essential security interests" provisions are far from being unknown in international law" and referred to Article XXI GATT (1994) and the phrase "it considers" as an example of a self-judging clause.[74] Since Article 11(3) of the India–Mauritius BIT (1998) does not include any explicit language to that effect, the *Devas* tribunal determined that it was not self-judging.[75] India subsequently tried to seek the annulment of the awards in *Deutsche Telekom v India*[76] and *Devas v India,*[77] arguing, among others, that the Security Exception clause under the respective treaty carved out essential security matters from the scope of the treaty and that the tribunal was therefore not competent to rule on the matter.[78] The District Court of the Hague in *Devas v India*[79] and the Swiss Federal Court in *Deutsche Telekom v India*[80] rejected such arguments. The Swiss Federal Court determined that the arbitral tribunal itself had characterized the issue to be one of the merits rather than jurisdiction, that international judicial practice weighs in favor of considering such exception clauses as a matter of merits, and that jurisdictional objectives relating to the nonjusticiability of security matters require clear textual expression as present in the recent Indian Model BIT (2015)[81] but as absent in India–Germany BIT (1995).[82]

[73] Ibid.

[74] Ibid.

[75] Mantilla Blanco Sebastián and Alexander Pehl, *National Security Exceptions in International Trade and Investment Agreements: Justiciability and Standards of Review* (Springer 2020) 47.

[76] Bundesgericht 4A 65-2018 – Deutsche Telekom AG v The Republic of India (December 11, 2018) PCA Case No 2014-10 [C].

[77] Case No C-09-529140-HA ZA 17-315 (November 14, 2018) Rechtbank Den Haag ECLI:NL:RBDHA:2018:15532 [3.1] https://uitspraken.rechtspraak.nl/inziendocument?id=ECLI:NL:RBDHA:2018:15532.

[78] Mantilla Blanco Sebastián and Alexander Pehl, *National Security Exceptions in International Trade and Investment Agreements: Justiciability and Standards of Review* (Springer 2020) 43.

[79] Case No C-09-529140-HA ZA 17-315 (November 14, 2018) Rechtbank Den Haag ECLI:NL:RBDHA:2018:15532 [4.42] https://uitspraken.rechtspraak.nl/inziendocument?id=ECLI:NL:RBDHA:2018:15532.

[80] Bundesgericht 4A 65-2018 – Deutsche Telekom AG v The Republic of India (December 11, 2018) PCA Case No 2014-10 [3.2.3.3.4].

[81] Chapter 4, section 4.2.5.

[82] Wolfgang Alschner and Kun Hui, 'Missing in Action: General Public Policy Exceptions in Investment Treaties' in Lisa Sachs, Jesse Coleman, and Lise Johnson (eds.), *Yearbook on International Investment Law and Policy* (OUP 2018) 387.

As the practice of the US, the EU, and BRICS confirms,[83] over time, more states have started including a "non-justiciable" language of Security Exceptions into their IIAs, arguably seeking to prevent any international scrutiny, including of the measures that affect existing investments. In particular, the IIAs concluded by the US and India, but also the Brazil CFIA and SADC Model BIT, expressly remove the measures adopted for national security reasons from the scope of the dispute settlement mechanism under the respective IIAs.[84] For example, Article 22.2(b) of the US–Colombia TPA (2006) clarifies in its footnote that if a party invokes a Security Exception, "the tribunal or panel hearing the matter shall find that the exception applies."[85]

In 2022, Colombia invoked the Security Exception under Article 22.2(b).[86] This is the first known case where an investment tribunal had to interpret a Security Exception that included the self-judging language "it considers necessary." The tribunal rejected Colombia's argument, ruling that the Security Exception is neither "non-justiciable" nor does it "operate to exclude a tribunal's jurisdiction."[87] The tribunal differentiated between a nonjusticiable and self-judging language of exception clauses. An example of the former is the Security Exception under India–Singapore CECA (2005), which expressly stipulates that "any decision of the disputing Party taken on such security considerations shall be non-justiciable." An example of the latter is Article XXI(b) GATT. The tribunal determined that neither Article 22.2(b) nor its accompanying footnote explicitly contained "non-justiciable" language.[88] The tribunal also acknowledged that interpreting the Security Exception as nonjusticiable "would be an omnipotent tool at a State's disposal, which could potentially undermine legal certainty and predictability for the investors."[89] Instead, considering the US treaty practice and the ordinary meaning of the agreement's terms, the tribunal concluded that the Security Exception is a self-judging provision, enabling Colombia to determine and invoke measures it deems essential for its security in good faith.[90]

[83] See chapter 4.
[84] See more chapter 4, section 4.2.
[85] Article 22 of US–Colombia TPA (2006).
[86] *Angel Samuel Seda and others v Republic of Colombia* (February 16, 2022) ICSID Case No ARB/19/6 Respondent's Rejoinder [6]–[18].
[87] *Angel Samuel Seda and others v Republic of Colombia* (June 27, 2024) ICSID Case No ARB/19/6 Award [711]–[725].
[88] Ibid [713].
[89] Ibid [720].
[90] Ibid [662].

Thus, even though the practice of investment tribunals on Security Exceptions is inconsistent, the tribunals generally reject the notion that a state's invocation of national security or national emergency ipso facto deprives any arbitral tribunal of jurisdiction, even if the language of the agreement indirectly implies otherwise.

5.2 Adjudicating Security Exceptions

Even assuming that the invocation of Security Exceptions does not affect the adjudicator's mandate to review the Security Measure at issue, it can affect the adjudicator's choice of the standard of review. In particular, the invocation of Security Exceptions can require an adjudicator to accept the determinations made by domestic authorities and to adjust the burden and standard of proof. Thus, this section investigates how the invocation of Security Exceptions affects the assessment made by an international court or tribunal and attempts to qualify the deference under the Security Exceptions in more precise terms.

5.2.1 Exception or Limitation?

The recent use of Security Exceptions has sparked a significant debate about their nature: whether they should be treated as a substantive rule limiting the treaty's scope or as an affirmative defense.[91]

In some cases, adjudicators characterize Security Exceptions as limiting the scope of the treaty obligations.[92] In other words, they treat the exception as confirming the drafters' intention that the treaty obligations will not capture the measures that meet the requirements of the exception.[93] In this case, adjudicators should determine whether the exception applies before reviewing whether the measure complies with the treaty's substantive norms.[94]

[91] Caroline Henckels, 'Permission to Act: The Legal Character of General and Security Exceptions in International Trade and Investment Law' (2020) 69(3) ICLQ 557, 561.

[92] Caroline Henckels, 'The Purpose and Role of Investment Treaty Exception Clauses' in Lorand Bartels and Federica Paddeu (eds.), *Exceptions in International Law* (OUP 2020) 372.

[93] Ibid 364.

[94] Caroline Henckels, 'Investment Treaty Security Exceptions, Necessity and Self-Defence in the Context of Armed Conflict' in Katia Fach Gómez, Anastasios Gourgourinis, and Catharine Titi (eds.), *European Yearbook of International Economic Law. Special Issue: International Investment Law and the Law of Armed Conflict* (Springer International Publishing 2019) 338.

To illustrate, the WTO panel's reasoning in *Russia – Traffic in Transit* suggests that the panel viewed the Security Exceptions in the GATT (1994) as a substantive limitation.[95] The annulment committee in *CMS v Argentina* also adopted a similar view stating that where the requirements of the exception are met, the "substantive obligations under the Treaty do not apply" (whereas customary defense of necessity "is only relevant once it has been decided that there has otherwise been a breach of those substantive obligations").[96] Further, the tribunal in *El Paso v Argentina* suggested that measures necessary to protect essential security interests "are not in breach of the relevant BIT."[97] In *Devas v India*, the tribunal quoted the CMS annulment committee decision stating that the application of the Security Exception "excluded the operation of the substantive provisions of the BIT," and the *Continental Casualty v Argentina* decision reaffirming that the treaty did not apply to the measures falling under the exception.[98] Likewise, in *Deutsche Telekom v India*, India argued that the Security Exception in India–Germany BIT (1995) excludes the application of the substantive obligations of the treaty.[99] Since the exception was found inapplicable, the tribunal concluded that "the BIT's substantive standards apply to . . . investment."[100]

In *Seda v Colombia*, the tribunal reaffirmed that given that the other exceptions within the Chapter "Exceptions" under the US–Colombia TPA (2006) serve as carve-outs from the TPA's covered matters, it was illogical to interpret the Security Exception as having a distinct, implicit, and narrower purpose.[101] The tribunal also differentiated between the Security Exception in the US–Colombia TPA (2006) and the necessity defense under Article 25 of ARSIWA. Accordingly, unlike Article 25 of

95 Momchil Milanov, 'A Lauterpachtian Affair: Security Exceptions as 'Self-Judging Obligations' in the Case Law of the International Court of Justice and beyond' (2021) 22(4) J World Investment & Trade 509, 555.

96 *CMS Gas Transmission Co v Argentine Republic* (September 25, 2007) ICSID Case No ARB/01/8 Decision of the ad hoc Committee on the Application for Annulment of Argentine Republic [129].

97 *El Paso Energy International Company v Argentine Republic* (October 31, 2011) ICSID Case No ARB/03/15 Award [553].

98 *CMS Gas Transmission Co v Argentine Republic* (September 25, 2007) ICSID Case No ARB/01/8 Decision of the ad hoc Committee on the Application for Annulment of Argentine Republic [146].

99 *Deutsche Telekom AG v Republic of India* (December 13, 2017) PCA Case No 2014–10 Interim Award [190].

100 Caroline Henckels, 'Permission to Act: The Legal Character of General and Security Exceptions in International Trade and Investment Law' (2020) 69(3) ICLQ 557, 573.

101 *Angel Samuel Seda and others v Republic of Colombia* (June 27, 2024) ICSID Case No ARB/19/6 Award [668]–[672], [682].

ARSIWA, which assumes that a wrongful act has been committed in violation of a State's international obligations, the Security Exception prevents certain measures from being deemed incompatible with the agreement in the first place.[102] Notably, the tribunal noted that Article XXI GATT (1994) operates in a similar manner – not by justifying a breach of international commitments but by ensuring that the measures in question are not considered a breach at all.[103]

Considering Security Exceptions as limiting the scope of a treaty arguably means that the claimant should bear the burden of proof to establish that a measure falls within the treaty's scope rather than the exception.[104] Also, as long as a state's measure falls within the exception, meaning falls outside the scope of the treaty, there is no breach of treaty commitments, and consequently, the question of compensation or state responsibility does not arise.[105]

The alternative approach is to regard Security Exceptions as an affirmative defense, which implies that a state relying on the exception would not deny the breach but would seek to avoid the consequences of such a breach by establishing that it was acting to protect its security interests permitted by the exception.[106] In other words, the action coming within the scope of the exception would justify the conduct that the treaty would otherwise prohibit.[107] To illustrate, in *Argentina – Import Measures*, the Appellate Body does not differentiate between Security Exceptions and other exception clauses under Article XXI GATT (1994). In particular, it acknowledges that "certain provisions of GATT (1994), such as Articles XII, XIV, XV, XVIII, XX, and XXI, permit a Member, in certain specified circumstances, to be excused from its obligations under Article XI:1 of GATT (1994),"[108] which according to Henckels reinforces

[102] Ibid [682].

[103] Ibid [685].

[104] Wolfgang Alschner and Kun Hui, ' Missing in Action: General Public Policy Exceptions in Investment Treaties' in Lisa Sachs, Jesse Coleman, and Lise Johnson (eds.), *Yearbook on International Investment Law and Policy* (OUP 2018) 375.

[105] William W Burke-White and Andreas von Staden, 'Investment Protection in Extraordinary Times: The Interpretation and Application of Non-Precluded Measures Provisions in Bilateral Investment Treaties' (2008) 146 Faculty Scholarship at Penn Law 307, 387.

[106] Caroline Henckels, 'The Purpose and Role of Investment Treaty Exception Clauses' in Lorand Bartels and Federica Paddeu (eds.), *Exceptions in International Law* (OUP 2020) 365.

[107] Ibid.

[108] *Argentina – Measures Affecting the Importation of Goods* (January 15, 2015) Appellate Body Report WT/DS438/AB/R, WT/DS444/AB/R, WT/DS445/AB/R [5.220].

that the Security Exceptions under the GATT (1994) are regarded as an affirmative defense.[109] The same approach was adopted by the WTO panel in *Saudi Arabia – IPRs*. Different from *Russia – Traffic in Transit*, this panel reverted to the order of analysis "traditional" for WTO exceptions: it first established that it had jurisdiction to hear the dispute, then assessed whether the measures were inconsistent with the substantive treaty provisions, and finally examined whether the measures could be justified under the invoked Security Exception.[110] The panels in *US – Steel and Aluminium Products*[111] also assessed the breach of the WTO commitments by the US before reverting to the US security defense, thereby reiterating that Security Exceptions under WTO law should be viewed as an affirmative defense. The panel in *US – Origin Marking (Hong Kong, China)* expressly rejected the approach of the panel in *Russia – Traffic in Transit* to the order of analysis and claimed instead that "where there is no breach, there is nothing to justify."[112] The panel split the review of Security Exceptions into two parts.[113] The panel initially turned to the analysis of whether Article XXI(b) "excludes any review by a panel."[114] Having found that it did not, the panel engaged in the review of the measures at issue to find that they were in breach of WTO law.[115] Only then did the panel review whether such a breach could be justified under Article XXI(b), meaning whether it met the substantive preconditions of a successful security defense.[116]

[109] Caroline Henckels, 'Investment Treaty Security Exceptions, Necessity and Self-Defence in the Context of Armed Conflict' in Katia Fach Gómez, Anastasios Gourgourinis, and Catharine Titi (eds.), *European Yearbook of International Economic Law. Special Issue: International Investment Law and the Law of Armed Conflict* (Springer International Publishing 2019) 332.

[110] *Saudi Arabia – Measures Concerning the Protection of Intellectual Property Rights* (June 16, 2020) WTO Panel Report WT/DS567/R [7.4]–[7.6].

[111] *US – Certain Measures on Steel and Aluminium Products (China)* (December 9, 2022) WTO Panel Report WT/DS544/R [7.7]–[7.10]; *US – Certain Measures on Steel and Aluminium Products (Norway)* (December 9, 2022) WTO Panel Report WT/DS552/R [7.7]–[7.10]; *US – Certain Measures on Steel and Aluminium Products (Switzerland)* (December 9, 2022) WTO Panel Report WT/DS556/R [7.7]–[7.10]; *US – Certain Measures on Steel and Aluminium Products (Turkey)* (December 9, 2022) WTO Panel Report WT/DS564/R [7.7]–[7.10].

[112] *US – Origin Marking Requirements* (December 21, 2022) WTO Panel Report WT/DS597/R [7.189].

[113] Ibid [7.17]–[7.21].

[114] Ibid Part 7.3.

[115] Ibid Part 7.4.

[116] Ibid Part 7.5.

This discussion touches upon the broader debate about the duality of exceptions and limitations under EU law, for example, in the copyright context. While an "exception" can be generally understood as a "divergence from the scope of a generally worded provision," a "limitation" is referred to as "the definition of the substance of the provision as such."[117] Yet, in some cases, the EU directives and the CJEU use these terms in a seemingly interchangeable manner, providing little guidance as to their clear scope.[118]

Whichever conceptual approach is adopted will, in the end, depend on the language of the specific treaty.[119] For example, Article XI:2 GATT (1994) provides that the general elimination of quantitative restrictions shall not extend to the items listed under subparagraphs (a)–(c). Such language suggests that subparagraphs (a)–(c) limit the scope of the obligation under Article XI not to impose quantitative restrictions.[120] No obligation exists when the requirements of one of the subparagraphs of Article XI:2 are met.[121] Different from XI:2, general exceptions under Articles XX GATT (1994) are drafted in a manner that preserves fairly broad policy space for future exigencies but also requires greater scrutiny of the purpose, design, and application of the measure when determining whether the exception applies. This suggests that rather than limiting the scope of the GATT obligations, they operate as affirmative defenses to justify measures that would otherwise be inconsistent with GATT obligations.[122] In this sense, Security Exceptions under Article XXI(b) GATT (1994) are drafted similarly to general exceptions.

At the same time, the preference of a responding state to present Security Exceptions as either the limitation on the scope of a treaty or as a defense against an apparent breach of the treaty may depend, among others, on the scope of the treaty at issue (whether a treaty refers to the importance of

[117] Thomas Dreier, 'Thoughts on Revising the Limitations on Copyright under Directive 2001/29' (2015) 11(2) JIPLP 138, 139.

[118] See more Tito Rendas, 'Are Copyright-Permitted Uses 'Exceptions', 'Limitations' or 'User Rights'? The Special Case of Article 17 Cdsm Directive' (2022) 17(1) JIPLP 54, 55–60.

[119] Wolfgang Alschner and Kun Hui, 'Missing in Action: General Public Policy Exceptions in Investment Treaties' in Lisa Sachs, Jesse Coleman, and Lise Johnson (eds.), *Yearbook on International Investment Law and Policy* (OUP 2018) 376.

[120] *China – Measures Related to the Exportation of Various Raw Materials* (January 30, 2012) Appellate Body Report WT/DS394/16 WT/DS395/15 WT/DS398/14 [334].

[121] Ibid.

[122] Caroline Henckels, 'Permission to Act: The Legal Character of General and Security Exceptions in International Trade and Investment Law' (2020) 69(3) Intl & Comp LQ 557, 563.

nontrade or noninvestment objectives which suggests the parties' intent to exclude from the scope of the treaty protections the measures coming within an exception), and the wording of the Security Exception itself.[123] The fact that many Security Exception clauses under international agreements follow the model of Article XXI(b) GATT (1994) weighs in favor of following the WTO's jurisprudence on this matter. The most crucial issue remains whether, in every case, an international court or tribunal does the best possible job of identifying in their rulings whether or not an exception constitutes an affirmative defense or limits the scope of a treaty at issue by applying basic interpretative principles under the VCLT.[124]

5.2.2 *Choice of Standard of Review*

Most statutes of international courts do not use or define the term "standard of review."[125] Judges determine the standard of review to be applied in a specific case by interpreting the rules and procedures applicable to the settlement of the dispute before them. Not all international courts explicitly recognize the concept of standard of review. While some of them address the issue directly (i.e. WTO panels and the Appellate Body[126] and some investment tribunals in their decisions), others do so only implicitly by simply showing various degrees of deference to domestic authorities (i.e. the ICJ). Nevertheless, the rationale behind the self-restraint of international judicial institutions and the way it is used is strikingly similar, irrespective of whether a particular body addresses the concept of standard of review or not in its analysis.[127]

[123] Caroline Henckels, 'Investment Treaty Security Exceptions, Necessity and Self-Defence in the Context of Armed Conflict' in Katia Fach Gómez, Anastasios Gourgourinis, and Catharine Titi (eds.), *European Yearbook of International Economic Law. Special Issue: International Investment Law and the Law of Armed Conflict* (Springer International Publishing 2019) 335.

[124] Caroline E Foster, 'Burden of Proof in International Courts and tribunals' (2010) 29(1) Aust YBIL Online 27, 72.

[125] Article 38 of the Statute of the ICJ.

[126] The DSU describes the "function of panels" (Article 11), the Appellate Body (Article 17), DSB (Articles 16, 17, 20), arbitration proceedings (Articles 21, 22, 25), and "expert review groups" (DSU Appendix 4) without using the term "standard of review." See Ernst-Ulrich Petersmann, 'Judicial Standards of Review and Administration of Justice in Trade and Investment Law and Adjudication' in Lukasz Gruszczynski and Wouter Werner (eds.), *Deference in International Courts and Tribunals: Standard of Review and Margin of Appreciation* (OUP 2014) 26–27.

[127] Lukasz Gruszczynski and Wouter Werner, 'Introduction' in Lukasz Gruszczynski and Wouter Werner (eds.), *Deference in International Courts and Tribunals: Standard of Review and Margin of Appreciation* (OUP 2014) 2.

Investment treaties typically do not address the relationship between the standards of investment protection and states' powers to regulate or the question of the applicable standard of review.[128] So far, no investment tribunal has established a clear and consistent framework for determining the appropriate standard of review in national security disputes. However, several tribunals have referred to the desirability of deference to domestic authorities.[129] The degree of such deference might differ depending on the obligation in question and the institutional setting.

The standard of review under WTO law defines the intensity of the review of the national measure by WTO adjudicators and thereby determines "the margin of discretion and vertical power allocation" that WTO members have.[130] Article 11 DSU is the starting point for the panel and Appellate Body's standard of review analysis. It requires that WTO adjudicatory bodies conduct an objective examination of the matter before them. The relevant part of Article 11 DSU stipulates that, in its entirety, "a panel should make an objective assessment of the matter before it, including an objective assessment of the facts of the case and the applicability of and conformity with the relevant covered agreements." However, on its face, the provision does not address when a WTO adjudicatory body should review a matter de novo or when a more deferential attitude is acceptable.[131]

The Anti-Dumping Agreement is the only WTO agreement that expressly specifies the standard of review. Article 17.6(i) is designed to preclude de novo review of facts. It provides, among others, that "if the establishment of the facts was proper and the evaluation was unbiased and objective, even though the panel might have reached a different conclusion, the evaluation shall not be overturned." The panel in *Colombia – Frozen Fries* clarified with this respect that "a panel examining an investigating authority's determination should not conduct a de novo review of the evidence, nor substitute its own judgment for that of the investigating authority."[132] Instead, it should consider whether "an

[128] Caroline Henckels, 'The Role of the Standard of Review and the Importance of Deference in Investor-State Arbitration' in Lukasz Gruszczynski and Wouter Werner (eds.), *Deference in International Courts and Tribunals: Standard of Review and Margin of Appreciation* (OUP 2014) 116–117.

[129] Ibid 117.

[130] Tsai-Fang Chen, 'To Judge the "Self-Judging" Security Exception Under GATT (1994): a Systematic Approach' (2017) 12(2) Asian J WTO and Aust YBIL Health Law and Policy 311, 323.

[131] Ibid 328.

[132] *Colombia – Anti-Dumping Duties on Frozen Fries from Belgium, Germany and the Netherlands* (December 21, 2022) Art 25 Arbitration Report WT/DS591/ARB25 [4.9].

unbiased and objective investigating authority" could have determined that it had "sufficient" evidence ("based upon an examination of the 'accuracy' and 'adequacy' of the evidence") to justify a decision of domestic authorities, such as the initiation of an anti-dumping investigation.[133] The arbitrators deciding the appeal from the panel report, in this case, confirm such an interpretation.[134]

In addition, Article 17.6(ii) of the Anti-Dumping Agreement provides that where a panel finds that a relevant provision admits of more than one "permissible" interpretation, it should find the authority's measure to be in conformity with the Anti-Dumping Agreement "if it rests upon one of those permissible interpretations." Different from the reports of the Appellate Body, the arbitrators in *Colombia – Frozen Fries* suggested that this provision does not invite an adjudicator to engage in de novo review "so as to arrive at what we consider to be the 'final' or 'correct' application" of customary rules of treaty interpretation envisaged under Articles 31 and 32 of VCLT.[135] They considered "that different treaty interpreters applying the same tools of the [VCLT] may, in good faith and with solid arguments in support, reach different conclusions on the 'correct' interpretation of a treaty provision."[136] Accordingly, the task of adjudicators is to review whether a treaty interpreter could have reached the interpretation advanced by an arguing party based on Articles 31 and 32 of VCLT, even if, as de novo treaty interpreters, they might have reached a different conclusion.[137]

A systematic interpretation and different wording of Article 17.6 of the Anti-Dumping Agreement and Article 11 DSU lead to the conclusion that the former prescribes a more deferential standard of review than that deemed appropriate for disputes outside the anti-dumping context.[138] This means that panels and the Appellate Body are expected to accord a higher degree of deference to national determinations in anti-dumping matters than under any other WTO agreement. Given that the WTO agreements, similar to other Regional Agreements, are concerned with pursuing integration through deregulation rather than harmonization of

[133] Ibid.

[134] In the first appeal under the Multi-Party Interim Appeal Arbitration Arrangement (MPIA), a framework created by a group of WTO members to overcome the challenges posed by the nonoperational Appellate Body.

[135] *Colombia – Anti-Dumping Duties on Frozen Fries from Belgium, Germany and the Netherlands* (December 21, 2022) Art 25 Arbitration Report WT/DS591/ARB25 [4.13].

[136] Ibid [4.14].

[137] Ibid [4.13].

[138] Matthias Oesch, *Standards of Review in WTO Dispute Resolution* (OUP 2003) 88–101.

state laws, it would seem appropriate to preserve the right of contracting parties to pass national regulations in certain instances without being second-guessed by an adjudicator.[139]

5.2.3 *Allocation of Burden of Proof and Standard of Proof*

The party making an assertion must generally prove that assertion.[140] Thus, if a state alleges a breach and the other state invokes an exception, the state alleging the breach must establish the breach, and the state invoking the exception must prove that the exception applies.[141]

The disputing parties' burden of proof is not explicitly set in the DSU.[142] The Appellate Body has ruled that the party asserting a claim or defense "adduces evidence sufficient to raise a presumption that what is claimed is true."[143] Concerning exception clauses, the Appellate Body in *US – Wool Shirts and Blouses* stated that the contents of general exceptions under Article XX GATT (1994) are "in the nature of affirmative defences," and "the burden of establishing such a defence should rest on the party asserting it."[144] However, "how much and precisely what kind of evidence . . . will necessarily vary from . . . provision to provision, and case to case."[145] Moreover, the Appellate Body has emphasized that "a panel is vested with ample and extensive discretionary authority to determine when it needs information to resolve a dispute and what information it needs."[146] To illustrate, in *Russia – Traffic in Transit*, faced with Russia's refusal to provide evidence of its affirmative defense, the panel did not expressly assign the burden of proof to Russia.[147] The panel seemed to avoid saying

139 Filippo Fontanelli, 'Whose Margin is It? State Discretion and Judges' Appreciation in the Necessity Quicksand' in Filippo Fontanelli and others (eds.), *Shaping Rule of Law Through Dialogue* (Europa Law Publishing 2010) 382.

140 Caroline Henckels, 'Should Investment Treaties Contain Public Policy Exceptions' (2018) 59 BC L Rev 2825, 2842, fn 71.

141 Stephan Schill and Robyn Briese, '"If the State Considers": Self-Judging Clauses in International Dispute Settlement' (2009) 13(1) Max Planck YB UN L Online 61, 124.

142 Pramila Crivelli and Mona Paulsen, 'Ṣeparating the Political from the Economic: The Russia – Traffic in Transit Panel Report' (2021) 20(4) World Trade Rev 582, 587.

143 Ibid.

144 *US – Measures Affecting Imports of Woven Wool Shirts and Blouses from India* (April 25, 1997) Appellate Body Report WT/DS33/AB/R [16].

145 Pramila Crivelli and Mona Paulsen, 'Separating the Political from the Economic: The Russia – Traffic in Transit Panel Report' (2021) 20(4) World Trade Rev 582, 587.

146 Ibid.

147 Ben Heath, 'Trade, Security and Stewardship (Part III): WTO panels as Factfinders under Article XXI' (*IELP Blog*, May 7, 2019) https://ielp.worldtradelaw.net/2019/05/

anything at all about respective burdens deliberately.[148] The same applies to the panel's findings in *Saudi Arabia – IPRs*. While the panels in *US – Steel and Aluminium Products* and *US – Origin Marking (Hong Kong, China)* did not discuss the allocation of the burden of proof directly, they seemed to act under the assumption that the US was supposed to provide enough evidence and information to prove that one of the subparagraphs under Article XXI(b) GATT (1994) applied to the challenged measures.[149]

Investment tribunals have considered the burden of proof to be a fundamental issue of determining "which party has to prove what, in order for its case to prevail."[150] Yet, the issue of the burden of proof has not been explicitly addressed by investment tribunals in relation to Security Exceptions.[151] The annulment committee in *Continental v Argentina* noted that "the ICSID Convention and the Arbitration Rules contain no provisions concerning the burden of proof or standard of proof. Accordingly, there cannot be any requirement that a tribunal expressly applies a particular burden of proof or standard of proof in determining the dispute before it."[152]

Tribunals have referred to the WTO law to get guidance on the rules concerning the burden of proof in international law.[153] In *Marvin Feldman v Mexico*, for example, the tribunal referred to the statement

guest-post-trade-security-and-stewardship-part-iii-wto-panels-as-factfinders-under-article-xxi.html.

148 Ibid.

149 *US – Certain Measures on Steel and Aluminium Products (China)* (December 9, 2022) WTO Panel Report WT/DS544/R [7.148]; *US – Certain Measures on Steel and Aluminium Products (Norway)* (December 9, 2022) WTO Panel Report WT/DS552/R [7.136]; *US – Certain Measures on Steel and Aluminium Products (Switzerland)* (December 9, 2022) WTO Panel Report WT/DS556/R [7.166]; *US – Certain Measures on Steel and Aluminium Products (Turkey)* (December 9, 2022) WTO Panel Report WT/DS564/R [7.163]; *US – Origin Marking Requirements* (December 21, 2022) WTO Panel Report WT/DS597/R [7.360].

150 Kabir Duggal and Wendy W Cai, 'Principles of Evidence in Public International Law as Applied by Investor-State Tribunals: Burden and Standards of Proof' (2019) 2 Brill Research Perspectives in Intl Investment Law and Arbitration 5–6.

151 Caroline Henckels, 'Investment Treaty Security Exceptions, Necessity and Self-Defence in the Context of Armed Conflict' in Katia Fach Gómez, Anastasios Gourgourinis, and Catharine Titi (eds.), *European Yearbook of International Economic Law. Special Issue: International Investment Law and the Law of Armed Conflict* (Springer International Publishing 2019) 337.

152 *Continental Casualty Co v Argentine Republic* (September 16, 2011) ICSID Case No Arb/03/9 Decision on the Application for Partial Annulment of Continental Casualty [135].

153 Greg Tereposky and Morgan Maguire, 'Utilizing WTO Law In Investor-State Arbitration' in Arthur W Rovine (ed.), *Contemporary Issues in International Arbitration and Mediation: The Fordham Papers (2010)* (Brill Nijhoff 2011) 282.

of the Appellate Body that "various international tribunals, including the International Court of Justice, have generally and consistently accepted and applied the rule that the party who asserts a fact, whether the claimant or respondent, is responsible for providing proof thereof."[154] In *Canfor v US*, the arbitrators also mentioned that the rules concerning the burden of proof in international law are well established, referring to the statements of the Appellate Body.[155] Thus, similar to the WTO practice, if a respondent raises a defense in investment arbitration, it must prove the facts on which that defense is based.[156]

As a practical matter, the main question is often not the one of the burden of proof but the one relating to the standard of proof. In *Rompetrol v Romania*, the tribunal set out the difference between the terms as follows: "the burden of proof defines which party has to prove what, in order for its case to prevail; the standard of proof defines how much evidence is needed to establish either an individual issue or the party's case as a whole."[157] The standard of proof refers to "[t]he amount, level, or quantum of proof that the party having the burden of proof must provide to prevail on its claim."[158] Thus, different from the standard of review, the standard of proof does not identify the degree of deference that domestic authorities should be granted, nor does it determine a broader or more restrictive approach to treaty interpretation.[159]

While the burden of proof rests on the asserting party, the burden to produce evidence may shift to the other party under certain circumstances.[160] To illustrate, under Article XX GATT (1994), it is, first, for the respondent to establish a prima facie case that its measure is "necessary" to protect, for example, the health of its population; however, it

[154] *Marvin Feldman v Mexico* (December 16, 2002) NAFTA Tribunal ARB(ȦF)/99/1 [177] referring to *US – Measures Affecting Imports of Woven Wool Shirts and Blouses from India* (May 23, 1997) Appellate Body Report WT/DS33/AB/R [14].

[155] *Canfor et al v US* (Consolidated) (September 7, 2005) NAFTA Tribunal Order of the Consolidation [93], fn 42.

[156] Daniele Favalli andMladen Stojiljkovic, 'Burden and Standard of Proof in Investment Arbitration' (VISCHER AG Lexology, 2020) www.lexology.com/library/detail.aspx?g=37bcab98-af79-4e83-b71a-0bdde3a02de9.

[157] *Rompetrol Group NY v Romania* (May 6, 2013) ICSID Case No ARB/06/3 Award [178].

[158] Joost Pauwelyn, 'Defences and the Burden of Proof in International Law' in Lorand Bartels and Federica Paddeu (eds.), *Exceptions in International Law* (OUP 2020) 89.

[159] Ibid.

[160] Daniele Favalli andMladen Stojiljkovic, 'Burden and Standard of Proof in Investment Arbitration' (VISCHER AG Lexology, 2020) www.lexology.com/library/detail.aspx?g=37bcab98-af79-4e83-b71a-0bdde3a02de9.

is up to the claimant to raise a possible alternative measure; and then it is for the respondent to demonstrate that the alternative proposed the claimant is not reasonably available.[161] Nevertheless, the real burden of proof under Article XX exceptions remains with the respondent.[162]

In the Corfu Channel case, the PCIJ/ICJ noted that the standard of proof depends on the context of a particular issue before the adjudicator.[163] In her separate opinion in *Oil Platforms*, Judge Higgins stated that the ICJ had not generally explained the standard of proof to be met in its decisions.[164]

According to investment tribunals, a party is generally considered to fail to meet the standard of proof when the tribunal cannot develop a view of the facts, for example, as it happened in *Plasma Consortium v Bulgaria*.[165] Notably, dispute settlement within the WTO is reserved for states, while investment arbitration deals with the standing of foreign investors (of a home state) against a host state. Foreign investors cannot be expected to have access to security-related information regarding the challenged measures, especially if such information is subject to the privilege of secrecy. Due to their size and financial constraints, they might also have difficulties collecting the factual evidence to prove a bad faith behavior of a host state or the availability of less restrictive alternatives. Such informational asymmetry may inform the different understanding of issues of burden and standard of proof in international trade and investment jurisprudence,[166] as will be further discussed.

5.2.4 *Refusal to Disclose Security-Sensitive Information*

The Security Exception under Article XXI(a) GATT (1994) states that "[n]othing in this Agreement shall be construed ... to require any

161 Joost Pauwelyn, 'Defences and the Burden of Proof in International Law' in Lorand Bartels and Federica Paddeu (eds.), *Exceptions in International Law* (OUP 2020) 101.

162 Ibid.

163 Corfu Channel (United Kingdom of Great Britain and Northern Ireland v Albania) (April 9, 1949) ICJ Rep Merits 16–17.

164 *Oil Platforms* (*Iran v US*) (November 6, 2003) ICJ Rep Separate Opinion of Judge Higgins 233.

165 Daniele Favalli andMladen Stojiljkovic, 'Burden and Standard of Proof in Investment Arbitration' (VISCHER AG Lexology, 2020) www.lexology.com/library/detail.aspx?g=37bcab98-af79-4e83-b71a-0bdde3a02de9.

166 Jürgen Kurtz, 'The Use and Abuse of WTO Law in Investor-State Arbitration: Competition and Its Discontents' (2009) 20(3) EJIL 749, 757.

contracting party to furnish any information the disclosure of which it considers contrary to its essential security interests" (the nondisclosure exception). Thus, it protects members' right to refuse the disclosure of information that could influence their essential security interests.[167] The initial reason for including this paragraph of the Security Exception clause in the ITO Charter was the US representatives' concern that the US government would be obliged to reveal classified or sensitive information, such as details that could disclose the identities of intelligence sources.[168] Many Regional Agreements incorporate similarly drafted exceptions for disclosing information that can jeopardize the essential security interests of a party concerned.[169]

Looking at Article XXI GATT (1994) from a systematic perspective, it seems that while paragraph (b) establishes specific additional requirements, paragraph (a) of Article XXI does not demand more than a threat to an essential security interest. Without formally interpreting Article XXI, the decision of the Ministerial Meeting concerning Article XXI GATT (1947) (hereafter the Article XXI Decision) provides in its first paragraph that "[s]ubject to the exception in Article XXI(a), [members] should be informed to the fullest extent possible of trade measures taken under Article XXI."[170] By including the wording "to the fullest extent possible," the contracting parties reiterate their understanding that Article XXI(a) limits the disclosure of sensitive information by the party concerned. Thus, the contextual reading of Article XXI(a) suggests that if a respondent bona fide refuses to disclose information needed for the application of Article XXI(b)(i)–(iii), the exercise of this legitimate right should not be held against the party in the subsequent decision on the merits.

The US takes the position that that Article XXI(a) explicitly states that a member is not required to disclose any information – whether to a WTO panel or to other WTO members – about its Security Measures or its

[167] Mantilla Blanco Sebastián and Alexander Pehl, *National Security Exceptions in International Trade and Investment Agreements: Justiciability and Standards of Review* (Springer 2020) 7.

[168] Ibid.

[169] For example, Article 4.8 of EU–Vietnam Investment Protection Agreement provides that "[n]othing in this Agreement shall be construed as: (a) requiring a Party to furnish information, the disclosure of which it considers contrary to its essential security interests;" Article 18 of US Model BIT (2004) provides that "[n]othing in this Treaty shall be construed: 1. to require a Party to furnish or allow access to any information the disclosure of which it determines to be contrary to its essential security interests."

[170] GATT, Decision Concerning Article XXI of the General Agreement (December 2, 1982) L/5426 www.wto.org/gatt_docs/english/SULPDF/91000212.pdf.

underlying security interests.[171] Accordingly, this provision recognizes the highly sensitive nature of a member's essential security interests and reveals the deference the drafters intended to give to members when exercising their rights under Article XXI.[172] As in the case of Article XXI(b), the US argues that Article XXI(a) is not intended to be reviewable against any legal standard.[173] Notably, in *US – Steel and Aluminium Products (China)*[174] and *US – Origin Marking (Hong Kong, China)*,[175] the US also initially maintained that it was not required to provide any information to prove its national security defense; nevertheless, it subsequently elaborated on its arguments and provided certain evidence with respect to the existence of an "other emergency in international relations."

Conversely, the EU believes that Article XXI(a) does not stipulate that information regarding Security Measures or the member's security interests does not have to be provided.[176] Accordingly, the invocation of Article XXI(a) is subject to adjudicative review, similar to Article XXI(b).[177] The respondent in a dispute "is expected at a minimum to explain in sufficient detail why such information cannot be shared with the panel."[178] When disclosed, confidential information must be treated as such by the WTO panels but also by any member having access to it. To this end, the panel might adopt, if necessary, appropriate procedures to deal with sensitive information to ensure that the disclosure of the information necessary for fact-finding in the dispute does not impede the respondent's essential security interests.[179] Such a position is also supported by several other WTO members involved in recent WTO proceedings where Security Exceptions have been invoked.[180]

171 *US – Origin Marking Requirements* (July 2, 2021) First Written Submission of the US in DS597 [50] https://ustr.gov/sites/default/files/enforcement/DS/DS597/US.Sub1.fin.pdf.
172 Ibid [52].
173 Ibid [226], [227].
174 *US – Certain Measures on Steel and Aluminium Products (China)* (December 9, 2022) WTO Panel Report WT/DS544/R [7.132]–[7.133].
175 *US – Origin Marking Requirements* (December 21, 2022) WTO Panel Report WT/DS597/R [7.258].
176 *Russia – Traffic in Transit* (January 25, 2018) Third-Party Oral Statement by the EU in DS512 [28] https://trade.ec.europa.eu/doclib/docs/2018/february/tradoc_156603.pdf.
177 Ibid.
178 Ibid [29].
179 Ibid.
180 See eg *US – Origin Marking Requirements* (December 21, 2022) Annex C-6 to WTO Panel Report Integrated Executive Summary of the Arguments of Norway WT/DS597/R/Add.1 [23].

A broad reading of Article XXI(a) proposed by the US may provide a respondent with a jurisdictional defense in the sense that it would allow it to withhold active participation in the proceedings.[181] To illustrate, facts and empirical evidence demonstrating the relevance of Security Measures and their potential to mitigate the consequences of armed conflict or other security threats can be deemed necessary to prevent possible abuse and disguised protectionism.[182] A state might invoke Article XXI(a) as its reason for failing to produce such evidence.[183] Accepting that invocation of Article XXI(a) is enough to satisfy the burden of proof under Article XXI(b)(i)–(iii) and (c) "would considerably undermine a complainant's right of defense."[184] Furthermore, it might prevent adjudicators from having access to the necessary evidence to be able to make the findings and decide on the legitimacy of challenged Security Measures.

The panel in *US – Origin Marking (Hong Kong, China)* also clarified that the existence of Article XXI(a) does not imply that the determination of the situations of war or other emergencies in international relations is self-judging but rather suggests "at most" that "if a case ever came up where the party invoking Article XXI(b) could not disclose any information relating to the existence of such situations because it would be contrary to its essential security interests, then it could potentially invoke Article XXI(a) as an explanation not to provide certain sensitive information to a panel."[185] Such an approach suggests that a WTO member can legally refuse to provide the requested information only under certain conditions and should not be allowed to invoke Article XXI(a) as a justification for providing no evidence necessary for making the findings in a dispute.

While it remains to be seen what WTO panels will decide on the standard of review of Article XXI(a) GATT (1994) in future disputes, it can be argued that adjudicators should at least be allowed to examine

[181] Hannes L Schloemann and Stefan Ohlhoff, 'Constitutionalization and Dispute Settlement in the WTO: National Security as an Issue of Competence' (1999) 93 Am J Intl L 424, 448.

[182] Pramila Crivelli and Mona Paulsen, 'Separating the Political from the Economic: The Russia: Traffic in Transit Panel Report' (2021) 20(4) World Trade Rev 582, 602.

[183] Dapo Akande and Sope Williams, 'International Adjudication on National Security Issues: What Role for the WTO?' (2003) 43 Virginia J Intl L 365, 394.

[184] *Russia – Measures Concerning Traffic in Transit* (April 5, 2019) WTO Panel Report WT/DS512/R [7.118].

[185] *US – Origin Marking Requirements* (December 21, 2022) WTO Panel Report WT/DS597/R [7.102].

whether this exception or an analogous clause under another agreement is "invoked in good faith and, in particular, whether there is at least procedural fairness in determining the information" the disclosure of which is arguably considered contrary to a respondent's essential security interest.[186] Admittedly, a good faith review under Article XXI(a) and analogous clauses under other trade and investment agreements, if adopted, might invoke similar problems as the review of Security Measures under existing Article XXI(b), either undermining the authority of international adjudicators to decide foreign and security matters or significantly lowering the standard of proof required from an invoking state that refuses to substantiate its security defense.[187] It might be especially problematic in disputes where adjudicators cannot draw evidence from the UN documents recognizing the situation as an emergency or a serious concern with security implications that call upon the UN members to take action.[188]

Several scholars have discussed the possibility of breaking down the concept of security into different categories to offer different views on access to security information (e.g. military knowledge versus other expert knowledge)[189] and the possible limitations to the right of a WTO member to refuse the disclosure of security-related information (e.g. imminent threats versus sustained economic security policies).[190] To this end, WTO members can agree to differentiate the types of evidence they can be expected to provide to the WTO based on the category of security interests invoked. While such a proposal might, in theory, ensure a more coherent approach to collecting evidence in national security disputes, it would doubtfully help overcome the uncertainties arising from the application of Article XXI(a) as long as there is no clear agreement among all WTO members on the interpretation and application of Article XXI(b). Merely specifying in which cases which types of information an adjudicator might require would give the WTO members refusing to share necessary information because of opportunistic considerations few incentives to comply with a more specific

[186] Peter Van den Bossche and Sarah Akpofure, 'The Use and Abuse of the National Security Exception under Article XXI(b)(iii) of GATT (1994)' in Chia-Jui Cheng (ed.), *A New Global Economic Order: New Challenges to International Trade Law* (Brill Nijhoff 2021) 157.

[187] See more chapter 5, section 5.1 and chapter 6, sections 6.2 and 6.3.

[188] See more chapter 6, sections 6.2 and 6.3.

[189] See eg J Benton Heath, 'Making Sense of Security' (2022) 116(2) AJIL 289, 313–314.

[190] See eg Mona Paulsen, 'Let's Agree to Disagree: A Strategy for Trade-Security' (2022) 24(4) J Intl Econ L 527, 544.

procedure. Furthermore, reaching an agreement ex ante on clear limitations and guidance as to the situations where a WTO member can legitimately refuse to disclose information might be difficult in practice.

Alternatively, to prevent the abuse of Article XXI(a), WTO members might agree to empower the WTO DSS with additional tools that allow panels and potentially the Appellate Body to make the necessary findings in national security disputes without requiring an invoking member to provide the extensive evidence on the design and application of a challenged Security Measure.[191] WTO members can also elaborate on procedural requirements that ensure that the disclosure of sensitive information during the WTO proceedings would not undermine members' security interests.[192] Boosting the trust of WTO members in that international adjudicators can make findings on national security matters without undermining their national interests might provide disputing parties with additional incentives to comply with the WTO process and discourage the overreliance on Article XXI(a), where it is not necessary. The same premises can apply to the adjudication of Security Measures under Regional Agreements.

5.3 Balancing State Sovereignty and International Responsibilities

International adjudicators can provide important guidance on applying international rules and principles to balance the legality of unilateral actions by an individual state with its commitments under international law. Good faith and necessity can be potentially used as tools to perform such a balancing exercise. They can allow for some deference in the adjudicator's decision-making process when it comes to dealing with a national security dispute while ensuring the minimum level of control over the application of Security Measures. As concepts that hover above the law, they may have a corrective and harmonizing role that is essential for a review of national security matters, especially given the inconsistencies that abound in the law because of different approaches to interpreting Security Exceptions.

[191] See more chapter 7.

[192] See more Panos Delimatsis and Olga Hrynkiv, ' Article XIVbis: Security Exceptions' in Stoll PT and H Hestermeyer (eds.), *Commentaries on World Trade Law – Volume 5: Trade in Services* (Brill 2023) [36]–[38].

5.3.1 *Principle of Good Faith*

The duty to fulfill one's obligations in good faith is most prominently found in Article 2(2) of UN Charter. For treaty relations specifically, Articles 18, 26, and 31 of VCLT prescribe various overarching good faith-related obligations, such as the obligation not to defeat the object and purpose of a treaty that has not yet been ratified, the rule of *pacta sunt servanda*, and the obligation to interpret a treaty provision in good faith.

As for the legal notion of good faith, scholars agree that in the absence of further particularization, the principle remains an abstract and value-oriented notion that combines moral elements such as trust, honesty, fairness, loyalty, or reasonableness with more precise legal contents, for example, the principle of reciprocity.[193] The principle of good faith also finds manifestation in related principles or concepts such as legitimate expectations, estoppel, acquiescence, equity, abuse of rights (*abus de droit*), and others, some of which may overlap with codified expressions and/or mutually reinforce each other.[194] Case law confirms that international courts and tribunals frequently engage in good faith review to establish a breach of an international obligation.[195] Furthermore, when a standard is ambiguous, parties and tribunals rely more readily on a good faith review.[196]

Adjudicators might exercise the principle of good faith in the interpretation of a legal provision, in the application of a given provision by a state while adopting a challenged measure but also in the conduct of the dispute.[197] The use of good faith as a principle of treaty interpretation must be distinguished from its application to the performance of a treaty.[198] While such conceptual distinctions can be made in concrete circumstances, drawing the dividing line between using good faith for

[193] Andreas R Ziegler and Jorun Baumgartner, 'Good Faith as a General Principle of (International) Law' in Andrew D Mitchell, M Sornarajah, and Tania Voon (eds.), *Good Faith and International Economic Law* (OUP 2015) 11.

[194] Ibid 12.

[195] Andrei Mamolea, 'Good Faith Review' in Lukasz Gruszczynski and Wouter Werner (eds.), *Deference in International Courts and Tribunals: Standard of Review and Margin of Appreciation* (OUP 2014) 88.

[196] Emily Sipiorski, *Good Faith in International Investment Arbitration* (OUP 2019) [5.60].

[197] Marion Panizzon, *Good Faith in the Jurisprudence of the WTO: The Protection of Legitimate Expectations, Good Faith Interpretation and Fair Dispute Settlement* (Bloomsbury Publishing Plc 2006) 277.

[198] Eric De Brabandere and Isabelle Van Damme, 'Good Faith in Treaty Interpretation' in Andrew D Mitchell, M Sornarajah, and Tania Voon (eds.), *Good Faith and International Economic Law* (OUP 2015) 38.

interpretation or application is challenging because the application of the principle of good faith results from both interpreting treaty provisions and supplementing them with the application of good faith as a general principle of law.[199]

5.3.1.1 Presumption of Good Faith

Good faith is not for the state to self-judge.[200] At the same time, states benefit from a historic presumption against bad faith that manifests itself as a high standard of proof for the claimant.[201] In 1926, the PCIJ stated in *Germany v Poland* that bad faith is never presumed but always has to be proven.[202] The Court of Arbitration in *France v Spain* also stated that it is a general and well-established principle of law according to which bad faith is not presumed.[203]

WTO panels and the Appellate Body have inferred from the principle of *pacta sunt servanda*, as outlined in Article 26 of the VCLT, a presumption that WTO members fulfill their WTO obligations in good faith.[204] In *US – Continued Suspension* and *Canada – Continued Suspension*, the Appellate Body, however, clarified that "the presumption of good faith attaches to the actor, but not to the action itself. Thus, whilst the presumption of good faith concerns the reasons for which a Member acts, such a presumption does not answer the question of whether the measure taken by the implementing Member has indeed brought about substantive compliance."[205] In other words, the presumption of good faith means that a WTO panel or Appellate Body will assume that the member acted consistently with its obligations under the WTO agreements "without clear evidence to the contrary."[206] In this sense, the option to invoke a presumption of good faith allows a party to discharge

[199] Ibid 55.

[200] Andrei Mamolea, 'Good Faith Review' in Lukasz Gruszczynski and Wouter Werner (eds.), *Deference in International Courts and Tribunals: Standard of Review and Margin of Appreciation* (OUP 2014) 75.

[201] See eg *Affaire du Lac Lanoux (France v Espagne)* (1957) Arbitral Tribunal 12 RIAA 313.

[202] *Case concerning certain German Interests in Polish Upper Silesia (Germany v Poland)* (1926) PCIJ Merits 42.

[203] *Affaire du Lac Lanoux (France v Espagne)* (1957) Arbitral Tribunal 12 RIAA 313.

[204] Julien Chaisse, 'Deconstructing the WTO Conformity Obligation: A Theory of Compliance as a Process' (2015) 38(1) Fordham Intl LJ 57, 68–69.

[205] *Canada – Continued Suspension of Obligations in the EC – Hormones Dispute* (October 16, 2008) Appellate Body Report WT/DS321/AB/R [315].

[206] Helge Elisabeth Zeitler, 'Good Faith in the WTO Jurisprudence: Necessary Balancing Element or an Open Door to Judicial Activism' (2005) 8 J Intl Econ L 721, 725.

its burden of proof without presenting a prima facia case, that is, without adducing enough evidence.[207]

WTO panels and the Appellate Body generally refrain from challenging the presumption of good faith in light of the circumstances before them.[208] In particular, concerning Article 3.7 DSU, WTO panels "must presume, whenever a Member submits a request for the establishment of a panel, that such a Member does so in good faith, having duly exercised its judgment as to whether recourse to that panel would be 'fruitful.'"[209] In *Mexico – Corn Syrup*, the Appellate Body held that the panel was not obliged to consider, on its own initiative, whether the complainant had exercised its judgment as required by Article 3.7 DSU.[210] In *US – Offset Act (Byrd Amendment)*, though seemingly finding in general that "there [was] a basis for a dispute settlement panel to determine, in an appropriate case, whether a Member has not acted in good faith," the Appellate Body rejected the panel's finding that the US had acted in bad faith on the evidence, holding that "[n]othing . . . in the covered agreements supports the conclusion that simply because a WTO Member is found to have violated a substantive treaty provision, it has therefore not acted in good faith. In our view, it would be necessary to prove more than mere violation to support such a conclusion."[211] In the *Chile – Alcoholic Beverages* case, the Appellate Body also clarified that "Members of the WTO should not be assumed, in any way, to have continued previous protection or discrimination through the adoption of a new measure. This would come close to a presumption of bad faith."[212] In general, the Appellate Body has been reluctant to find an absence of good faith – or bad faith – on the part of any WTO member, going so far as to state repeatedly that a presumption exists that WTO members are acting in good faith in disputes and in carrying out their treaty obligations.[213]

207 See more on the use of presumptions and prima facie evidence in Joost Pauwelyn, 'Evidence, Proof and Persuasion in WTO Dispute Settlement: Who Bears the Burden' (1998) 1 J Int'l Econ L 227.

208 Andrew D Mitchell, 'Good Faith in WTO Dispute Settlement' (2006) 7 Melb J Intl L 339, 362.

209 *Mexico – Anti-Dumping Investigation of High Fructose Corn Syrup (HFCS) from the US* (October 22, 2001) Appellate Body Report WT/DS132/AB/RW [74].

210 Ibid [90].

211 *US – Continued Dumping and Subsidy Offset Act of 2000* (January 16, 2003) Appellate Body Report WT/DS217/AB/R WT/DS234/AB/R [297].

212 *Chile – Taxes on Alcoholic Beverages* (December 13, 1999) Appellate Body Report WT/DS87/AB/R WT/DS110/AB/R [74].

213 Helge Elisabeth Zeitler, 'Good Faith In The WTO Jurisprudence: Necessary Balancing Element Or An Open Door To Judicial Activism' (2005) 8 J Intl Econ L 721, 724.

Parties are also generally presumed to have acted in good faith in investment arbitration.[214] Consequently, a high standard is required to establish a breach of the good faith principle.

5.3.1.2 Burden and Standard of Proof and Good Faith

In light of the presumption that states act in good faith, it can be argued that if an international adjudicator is only entitled to review the invocation of the exception clause for good faith, the state alleging the breach should establish a lack of good faith on the part of the invoking state, rather than for the invoking state to establish the existence of good faith.[215] In *Devas v India*, for example, the tribunal emphasized that an investor seeking to contest a state's decision on national security issues must meet a substantial burden of proof, including demonstrating bad faith, lack of authority, or that the measures in question do not pertain to essential security interests.[216] In *Chevron Corp v Ecuador*, the tribunal also stated that burden of proving abuse falls firmly on the party alleging it.[217] "The nature of these defenses as exceptions to a general rule that leads to the reversal of the burden of proof stems from, among other factors, the presumption of good faith. A claimant is not required to prove that their claim is asserted in a non-abusive manner; it is for the respondent to raise and prove abuse as a defense."[218]

At the same time, showing that a government invoked the exception in bad faith might be next to impossible when the information to be disclosed is known only by the state concerned.[219] In the trade realm, it is close to impossible for the complaining state alleging the breach to provide security-related evidence in foreign jurisdictions to demonstrate that the "motive" of the host state that invokes Security Exceptions was purely commercial.[220] In addition, it is even more difficult for the complaining state to articulate the

[214] See eg *Novenergia II – Energy & Environment (SCA), SICAR v Kingdom Of Spain* (February 15, 2018) SCC Case No V2015/063 Final Award [521].

[215] Stephan Schill And Robyn Briese, '"If The State Considers": Self-Judging Clauses In International Dispute Settlement' (2009) 13(1) Max Planck YB UN L Online 61, 123.

[216] *CC/Devas (Mauritius) Ltd v Republic of India* (July 25, 2016) PCA Case No 2013–09 Award on Jurisdiction and Merits [245].

[217] *Chevron Corp v Ecuador* (December 1, 2008) PCA Case No 34877 Interim Award [139].

[218] Ibid.

[219] Hannes L Schloemann and Stefan Ohlhoff, 'Constitutionalization and Dispute Settlement in the WTO: National Security as an Issue of Competence' (1999) 93 Am J Intl L 424, 445.

[220] Shin-yi Peng, 'Cybersecurity Threats and the WTO National Security Exceptions' (2015) 18 J Intl Econ L 449, 477.

elements of "bad faith" if the measures have mixed motives.[221] Even a far higher likelihood of informational asymmetry exists in investor-state arbitration.[222] An investor cannot reasonably be expected to bear the full burden of proving that there was no crisis or that the measures are not sufficiently linked to protecting essential security interests.[223] Especially small investors can face the most significant disadvantage in their ability to collate the factual evidence necessary to bring and prove a claim.[224] Furthermore, as mentioned by Alvarez in his separate opinion in *Sempra v Argentina*, "it would be extraordinary if those who rely on their international law rights, particularly private parties such as foreign investors . . . would be themselves expected to prove that the governments who violate their rights had no other recourse but to violate their rights."[225] This explains, for example, why the burden of proving whether the exception applies generally lies with the state invoking the exception. By the same token, it can be argued that in the case of a good faith review of a Security Exception by an adjudicator, the burden of proof that the requirements of the Security Exception are met should rest on an invoking party (as a better-informed party).

5.3.1.3 Implications for Security Exceptions

International courts and tribunals seem to use a good faith review to limit the full discretion of the states invoking the exception but also to balance competing policies and interests. In *Djibouti v France*, good faith was used in order to limit the state's discretion rather than the source of a legal obligation.[226] The majority found that to demonstrate that France had relied on Article 2(c) in good faith, it had to prove that one of the reasons provided by the instructing judge for refusing to execute the letter rogatory (relating to the presence of declassified "defense secret" documents) fell under Article 2(c).[227] According to Schill and Briese, in

221 Ibid.

222 Jürgen Kurtz, 'The Use and Abuse of WTO Law in Investor-State Arbitration: Competition and Its Discontents' (2009) 20(3) EJIL 749, 758.

223 Jorge E Viñuales, 'Defence Arguments in Investment Arbitration' (2020) 18 ICSID Rep 9, 29.

224 Jürgen Kurtz, 'The Use and Abuse of WTO Law in Investor-State' Arbitration: Competition and Its Discontents' (2009) 20(3) EJIL 749, 758.

225 *Sempra Energy International v Argentine Republic* (September 18, 2007) ICSID Case No ARB/02/16 Award [55].

226 Robyn Briese, 'Djibouti v France: Self– Judging Clauses before the International Court of Justice' (2009) 10 Melb J Intl L 308, 817, fn 47.

227 Stephan Schill and Robyn Briese, '"If the State Considers": Self-Judging Clauses in International Dispute Settlement' (2009) 13(1) Max Planck YB UN L Online 61, 116.

this sense, the test applied resembles a "touch and feel" type test which, without further concretization, poses the risk that decisions of international courts or tribunals will remain unpredictable.[228]

In contrast to the majority judgment in *Djibouti v France*, Judge Keith suggests some concrete questions that may be asked to assess a breach of the good faith requirement. Accordingly, the principle of good faith requires the responsible state agency "to exercise power for the purposes for which it was conferred and without regard to improper purposes or irrelevant factors."[229] In this context, he cited the Court's statement in the *Gabčíkovo – Nagymaros Project* case that the good faith obligation "obliges the Parties [to a treaty] to apply it in a reasonable way and in such a manner that its purpose can be realized."[230] According to Briese, Judge Keith's analysis resembles the judicial review of administrative decision-making in many domestic systems.[231]

While reviewing the measures that Russia attempted to justify under Article XXI(b) GATT (1994), the panel in *Russia – Traffic in Transit* found that the obligation of good faith produces for an invoking member two legal requirements: to demonstrate that a Member has an essential security interest arising from the claimed emergency in international relations and to demonstrate that there is a plausible connection between such an interest and the measures adopted for their protection.

First, the panel states that the obligation of good faith prevents members from using the exceptions to circumvent their obligations under the GATT (1994), for example, by relabeling trade interests that they had agreed to protect as "essential security interests" falling outside the reach of that system.[232] Therefore, the member must articulate its essential security interests "sufficiently enough to demonstrate their veracity," which implies that the further removed from armed conflict or other "hard core" emergency the emergency at issue is, the greater the level of specificity is required.[233] In taking this approach, adjudicative bodies could exclude security interests that undermine the entire treaty regime,

228 Ibid 118.

229 *Case Concerning Certain Questions on Mutual Assistance in Criminal Matters (Djibouti v France)* (June 4, 2008) ICJ Rep Declaration of Judge Keith [6].

230 Ibid.

231 Robyn Briese, 'Djibouti v France: Self-Judging Clauses before the International Court of Justice' (2009) 10 Melb J Intl L 308, 323.

232 *Russia – Measures Concerning Traffic in Transit* (April 5, 2019) WTO Panel Report WT/DS512/R [7.133].

233 Ibid [7.134].

such as when a state claims that the need to protect domestic industries constitutes an essential security interest under a treaty.

Second, the panel states that the obligation of good faith is also applicable to the connection between essential security interests and the contested measure. The panel explains that, in this case, good faith means "that the measures at issue meet a minimum requirement of plausibility in relation to the proffered essential security interests, ie that they are not implausible as measures protective of these interests."[234] Specifically, a panel must assess "whether the measures are so remote from, or unrelated to, the . . . emergency that it is implausible that [the respondent] implemented the measures for the protection of its essential security interests arising out of the emergency."[235]

While conducting a good faith review of Russia's articulation of its essential security interests, the panel attempted to balance the already established emergency in international relations and essential security interests claimed by Russia. As the emergency at issue was close to "the 'hard core' of war or armed conflict," the panel required less specificity regarding the articulation of Russia's essential security interests.[236] Russia has articulated its security interests by referring to "certain characteristics of the 2014 emergency that concern the security of Ukraine–Russia border."[237] The panel found that based on Russia's domestic laws, "common knowledge," as well as the recognition by the UN General Assembly of the character of the 2014 emergency as involving armed conflict, it had no grounds for considering Russia's articulation of its security interests as "obscure or indeterminate."[238] Since "nothing in Russia's articulation suggested a means to circumvent its obligations under the GATT (1994)," it was found to be minimally satisfactory.[239]

As to the good faith review of the connection between essential security interests and the measure at issue, the panel found that the measures restricting the transit of goods across Russia were in the backdrop of an emergency in Russia's relations with Ukraine, and one which was directly related to the security of the Russia–Ukraine border.[240] Consequently, the panel found that the measures at issue could not be "regarded as so

234 Ibid [7.138].
235 Ibid [7.139].
236 Ibid [7.136].
237 Ibid.
238 Ibid [7.137].
239 Ibid.
240 Ibid [7.140].

remote from, or unrelated to, the 2014 emergency that it was implausible that Russia implemented the measures to protect its essential security interests arising out of that emergency."[241]

In *LG&E v Argentina*, the tribunal suggested that good faith review would "not significantly differ from the substantive analysis [the tribunal] presented"[242] in the context of the non-self-judging Security Exception under the US–Argentina BIT (1991). This statement does not exclude that the tribunal would nevertheless provide Argentina with a certain amount of deference or margin of appreciation while conducting a good faith review.[243]

In *Seda v Colombia*, Columbia claimed that the tribunal's scope for review of the self-judging Security Exception laid down in Article 22.2(b) of the US–Colombia TPA (2006) was strictly circumscribed to examining whether the exception has been invoked in good faith by Colombia, which "is, obviously, the case."[244] This suggests that Colombia referred to the presumption that it acted in good faith. The US challenged Colombia's belated invocation of the Security Exceptions on good faith grounds, but the tribunal nevertheless decided to accept the rejoinder's objections to jurisdiction as admissible.[245] In the end, the tribunal found that a good faith review, as supported by jurisprudence and legal scholarship, could ensure the proper application of Article 22.2(b) without undermining its self-judging nature.[246] It saw no evidence of bad faith in Colombia's identification of its essential security interests.[247] Additionally, the tribunal adopted a plausibility analysis, aligning with recent WTO panel reports, to assess the connection between Colombia's measures and its security interests.[248] It ruled that to be justified under a self-judging Security Exception, a measure needed not to be the primary or sole means of

241 Ibid [7.145].

242 *LG&E Energy Corp, LG&E Capital Corp, and LG&E International, Inc v Argentine Republic* (October 3, 2007) ICSID Case No ARB/02/1 Decision on Liability [214].

243 Stephan Schill and Robyn Briese, '"If the State Considers": Self-Judging Clauses in International Dispute Settlement' (2009) 13(1) Max Planck YB UN L Online 61, 124.

244 *Angel Samuel Seda and others v Republic of Colombia* (February 16, 2022) ICSID Case No ARB/19/6 Respondent's Rejoinder [43].

245 *Angel Samuel Seda and others v Republic of Colombia* (March 28, 2022) Procedural Order No 9 [11].

246 *Angel Samuel Seda and others v Republic of Colombia* (June 27, 2024) ICSID Case No ARB/19/6 Award [748].

247 Ibid [782].

248 Ibid [787].

addressing the issue – only that it was not so remote from the stated objective as to render the link implausible.[249]

5.3.2 · *Necessity under Treaty Exceptions and Customary Defense of Necessity*

In many legal systems, determining necessity would involve a balancing test that weighs the importance of the underlying regulatory objective with interest being protected.[250] International law uses the concept of necessity in two different senses. First, states may raise as a defense to their international obligations the doctrine of necessity included in the ARSIWA as one of the circumstances precluding the wrongfulness of the act. It is generally recognized as a part of customary international law (customary defense of necessity).[251] Second, the concept of necessity in several treaty-based regimes determines whether authorities can legally adopt a measure that restricts or limits a right or interest protected by the legal regime.[252]

Pelc traces the development of the concept of necessity, its origin and application in politics, interstate relations, and just war theory to conclude that the justification of the escape because of necessity is short of abuse because it is designed to be contingent on the nature of the circumstances leading up to it.[253] The necessity component of the treaty exception examines how well the chosen means align with the regulatory goal of the measure.[254] In many regimes, the necessity criterion focuses solely on the means and requires an adjudicative body to address a factual question: could the goal have been achieved through a less restrictive approach?[255]

[249] Ibid.

[250] Andrew D Mitchell and Caroline Henckels, 'Variations on a Theme: Comparing the Concept of "Necessity" in International Investment Law and WTO Law' (2013) 14(1) Chicago J Intl L 93, 100.

[251] Andrea K Bjorklund, 'Emergency Exceptions: State of Necessity and Force Majeure' in Peter Muchlinski, Federico Ortino, and Christoph Schreuer (eds.), *The Oxford Handbook of International Investment Law* (OUP 2008) 12.

[252] Andrew D Mitchell and Caroline Henckels, 'Variations on a Theme: Comparing the Concept of "Necessity" in International Investment Law and WTO Law' (2013) 14(1) Chicago J Intl L 93, 97–98.

[253] Krzysztof J Pelc, *Making and Bending International Rules: The Design of Exceptions and Escape Clauses in Trade Law* (CUP 2016) 45–75.

[254] Jürgen Kurtz, 'Adjudging the Exceptional at International Law: Security, Public Order and Financial Crisis (2010) 59 ICLQ 325, 365.

[255] See more Mark Elliott, 'Proportionality and Deference: The Importance of a Structured Approach' in Mark Elliot and others (eds.), *Effective Judicial Review: A Cornerstone of Good Governance* (OUP 2010).

Conversely, a different interpretation of the necessity requirement might apply if the necessity link is influenced by deference, that is it refers to the measures "[a state] considers necessary." The distinction between different meanings and functions of necessity must be further considered to understand how customary defense of necessity and the treaty-based exception that includes a "necessity" nexus might be applied by adjudicative bodies in international trade and investment contexts.

5.3.2.1 Necessity under ARSIWA

All tribunals to date have agreed that circumstances precluding wrongfulness under the ARSIWA are not self-judging.[256] Article 25 of ARSIWA prescribes strict limitations for the reliance on the customary defense of necessity.[257] First, "necessity" under the ARSIWA may only be invoked to safeguard an essential interest, such as "political or economic survival, the continued functioning of its essential services, the maintenance of internal peace, the survival of a sector of its population, the preservation of the environment of its territory or a part thereof, etc."[258] Such a vital interest must be protected from grave and imminent peril. The ICJ in *Gabčíkovo – Nagymaros Project* clarified that"[t]hat does not exclude ... that a 'peril' appearing in the long term might be held to be 'imminent' as soon as it is established, at the relevant point in time, that the realisation of the peril, however far off it might be, is not thereby any less certain and inevitable."[259]

Second, the measure should not seriously harm an essential interest of the other state or states concerned or the interests of the international community as a whole, "not merely from the point of view of the acting State but on a reasonable assessment of the competing interests, whether these are individual or collective."[260] Moreover,

[256] Andrea K Bjorklund, 'Emergency Exceptions: State of Necessity and Force Majeure' in Peter Muchlinski, Federico Ortino, and Christoph Schreuer (eds.), *The Oxford Handbook of International Investment Law* (OUP 2008) 46.

[257] Katia Yannaca-Small, 'Essential Security Interests under International Investment Law' in *International Investment Perspectives: Freedom of Investment in a Changing World* (OECD 2007) 100 www.oecd.org/daf/inv/investment–policy/40243411.pdf. See more Federica Paddeu and Michael Waibel, 'Necessity 20 Years On: The Limits of Article 25' (2022) 37 ICSID Review – Foreign Investment LJ 160, 162–184.

[258] Zena Prodromou, *The Public Order Exception in International Trade, Investment, Human Rights and Commercial Disputes* (Kluwer Law International BV 2020) 5 www– kluwerarbi tration– com.tilburguniversity.idm.oclc.org/document/KLI-KA-Prodromou- 2020-Ch04.

[259] *Gabčíkovo – Nagymaros Project (Hungary/Slovakia)* (September 25, 1997) ICJ Rep [54].

[260] Katia Yannaca-Small, 'Essential Security Interests under International Investment Law' in *International Investment Perspectives: Freedom of Investment in a Changing World* (OECD 2007) 101 www.oecd.org/daf/inv/investment–policy/40243411.pdf.

the taken course of action must be "the only way" available to safeguard the state's interest.[261]

Finally, necessity may not be used as an excuse if the responsible state "has contributed to the situation of necessity."[262] In the *Gabčíkovo – Nagymaros Project* case, the ICJ determined that Hungary had itself contributed to the situation of necessity since it, with full knowledge that the project at issue would have certain environmental consequences, had entered into the treaty it later sought to repeal. The ICJ thus concluded that Hungary could not have been permitted to rely on the necessity defense because it had helped, by act or omission, to bring the state of necessity relied upon.[263]

These features of Article 25 of ARSIWA confirm that the customary defense of necessity is only rarely available.[264] Treaty regimes generally incorporate additional exceptions that justify non-performance in a more extensive range of situations which takes due account of the particularities of the relevant treaty.[265] Different from Article 25 of ARSIWA, they specify in advance the interests for which they are available and generally grant governments more regulatory space.[266] When a particular treaty is silent on the relationship between the customary defense of necessity and the treaty-based exception, the question arises whether the very fact of incorporation of a treaty-based exception has consequences per se for the applicability of the customary defense of necessity. Notably, investment tribunals and annulment committees, while analyzing the same emergency measures concerning Argentina's financial crisis that took place at the end of the 1990s, adopted inconsistent approaches to the distinction between the customary defense of necessity and the Security Exception under US–Argentina BIT (1991) which resulted in different outcomes of the cases and created even more

[261] Ibid.

[262] Ibid.

[263] Andrea K Bjorklund, 'Emergency Exceptions: State of Necessity and Force Majeure' in Peter Muchlinski, Federico Ortino, and Christoph Schreuer (eds.), *The Oxford Handbook of International Investment Law* (OUP 2008) 24.

[264] Katia Yannaca-Small, 'Essential Security Interests under International Investment Law' in OECD, *International Investment Perspectives: Freedom of Investment in a Changing World* (2007 OECD) 99–100 www.oecd.org/daf/inv/investment- policy/40243411.pdf.

[265] Christina Binder, 'Non-Performance of Treaty Obligations in Cases of Necessity – From "Necessity Knows No Law" via the "Law(s) of Necessity" to Interfaces Between Different "Laws of Necessity"' (2011) 13(1) ARIEL Online 34 https://doi.org/10.1163/15736512-90000027.

[266] Federica Paddeu and Michael Waibel, 'Necessity 20 Years On: The Limits of Article 25' (2022) 37 ICSID Rev – Foreign Investment LJ 160, 191.

uncertainties about the role of Security Exceptions in international agreements.[267] Such outcomes of the Argentine crisis have pushed some states to reconsider how they draft treaty exceptions, thereby contributing to "making international investment law."[268] Yet, the question remains whether there is a legal basis for building a bridge between the customary defense of necessity and Security Exceptions under international agreements, particularly for elaborating on objective nexus requirements for reviewing Security Measures.[269]

5.3.2.2 Necessity Analysis under WTO law

WTO agreements do not specify whether reliance on the customary defense of necessity is possible. Yet, general international law remains in the background of states' interaction also after entering into the WTO agreements, which is even more so when the obligations breached concern legal interests owed either to the international community as a whole or to a group of states.[270] The power of the WTO panels to refer to other sources of international law for an objective application of the WTO agreements is safeguarded under both Articles 11 and 7.2 DSU. In the absence of an express provision to the contrary, the DSB, the WTO panels, and the Appellate Body can resort to and rely on all sources of international law in determining the cases brought before them. In addition, WTO panels and the Appellate Body have often referred to the general principles of international law and customary international law in their rulings.[271]

However, the reliance on other sources of international law is conditioned under WTO law on the requirement that reliance on general international rules does not add or diminish the rights and obligations provided in the WTO agreements. Thus, according to the WTO law, priority should be given to the interpretation in line with the WTO agreement as establishing a regime *lex specialis*.[272]

[267] See more chapter 5, section 5.3.2.3.

[268] Federica Paddeu and Michael Waibel, 'Necessity 20 Years On: The Limits of Article 25' (2022) 37 ICSID Rev – Foreign Investment LJ 160, 190–191.

[269] Mantilla Blanco Sebastián and Alexander Pehl, *National Security Exceptions in International Trade and Investment Agreements: Justiciability and Standards of Review* (Springer 2020) 51.

[270] Elena Katselli Proukaki, *The Problem of Enforcement in International Law: Countermeasures, the Non-Injured State and the Idea of International Community* (Taylor & Francis Group 2010) 237.

[271] Ibid.

[272] Ibid 230–231.

The concept of necessity is used in the WTO agreements, in particular as a component of the general exceptions under Article XX GATT (1994) and Article XIV GATS and Security Exceptions under Article XXI GATT (1994) and Article XIV*bis* GATS. In 2019, the panel in the *Russia – Traffic in Transit* dispute made the first attempt to answer some of the questions related to the interpretation of the "necessity" nexus in Security Exceptions under Article XXI GATT (1994). Among others, the panel determined that the adjectival clause "which it considers necessary" meant that "it is for [an invoking state] to determine the 'necessity' of the measures for the protection of its essential security interests."[273] Accordingly, "there is no need to determine the extent of the deviation of the challenged measure from the prescribed norm in order to evaluate the necessity of the measure, ie that there is no reasonably available alternative."[274] While analyzing Article XXI in light of the general rules of treaty interpretation under the VCLT, the panel did not refer to customary defense of necessity and did not discuss its relationship with Security Exceptions under the GATT (1994).

Notably, in the other cases discussing general exceptions under the WTO agreements, WTO panels and the Appellate Body also decided on the "necessity" nexus under treaty-based exceptions based on the provisions of a specific agreement without any reference to the customary defense of necessity.[275] One of the reasons for the lack of reference to the customary defense of necessity in the practice of the WTO dispute settlement bodies is that the exceptions under the WTO agreements are broader than the customary defense of necessity in the sense that they cover a more comprehensive range of emergencies which has arguably made the question about the relationship between the treaty-based exceptions and the customary law defense a subsidiary one.[276] While the ultimate reasons for the WTO panels and the Appellate Body's preference not to refer to the customary defense of necessity is subject to a sophisticated discussion that goes beyond the purview of this book, the practice of the WTO dispute settlement bodies suggests that the

[273] *Russia – Measures Concerning Traffic in Transit* (April 5, 2019) WTO Panel Report WT/DS512/R [146].

[274] Ibid [108].

[275] Christina Binder, 'Non-Performance of Treaty Obligations in Cases of Necessity: From "Necessity Knows No Law" via the "Law(s) of Necessity" to Interfaces Between Different "Laws of Necessity"' (2011) 13(1) ARIEL Online 20–21 https://doi.org/10.1163/15736512-90000027.

[276] Ibid 21.

mere use of the term "necessary" in the exception does not imply the adoption of the customary defense of necessity by reference and does not inherently alter the self-judging nature of a Security Exception clause.

5.3.2.3 Necessity Analysis under International Investment Law

The hybrid nature of investor-state disputes creates an even more uneasy relationship between the customary defense of necessity and the obligations that states have undertaken in their investment treaties, given that the exception clauses are supposed to be able to balance the investor's interests and the interests of a host state rather than the interests of state parties only. The relationship between the treaty-based exceptions and customary defense of necessity was considered in Argentine economic crisis cases. The tribunals followed two distinct approaches: first, treating a Security Exception as intertwined with customary defense of necessity and thus assimilating the two legal tests (in *CMS v Argentina*, *Enron v Argentina*, and *Sempra v Argentina*); second, treating the two norms as distinct, or the "separation" approach.[277] In particular, the CMS annulment committee observed that although there could be "some analogy" between the Security Exception under US–Argentina BIT (1991) and the customary defense of necessity, the two norms had "a different operation and content."[278] Similarly, the *Continental Casualty* tribunal stressed the differences between the treaty defense and customary defense of necessity available under Article 25 of ARSIWA.[279] Yet, it ultimately used the concept of necessity under the ARSIWA as a supplementary means of interpreting Article XI.[280]

The inconsistent approaches of investment tribunals concerning the relationship between Security Exception under US–Argentina BIT (1991) and customary defense of necessity invokes many questions while the different outcomes of the decisions in the discussed cases warrant analysis

[277] See more Panos Delimatsis and Olga Hrynkiv, 'Sovereign Investors and National Security Exceptions in WTO and Investment Law' in P Delimatsis, G Dimitropoulos, and A Gourgourinis (eds.), State Capitalism and International Investment Law (Hart Publishing 2023) 236.

[278] *CMS Gas Transmission Co v Argentine Republic* (September 25, 2007) ICSID Case No ARB/01/8 Decision of the Ad Hoc Committee on the Application for Annulment of Argentine Republic [131].

[279] *Continental Casualty Co v Argentine Republic* (September 5, 2008) ICSID Case No Arb/ 03/9 Award [166]–[167].

[280] Ibid [168].

as to their appropriateness and legitimacy.[281] As codified in Articles 31–32 of VCLT, the rules of treaty interpretation are the first possibility for incorporating the elements of customary defense of necessity into the respective treaty-based exception. In particular, Binder suggests that Article 25 of ARSIWA may be viewed as a "relevant rule" which is "applicable in the relations between the parties" within the meaning of Article 31(3)(c) of VCLT and thus should be taken into account, together with the context, while interpreting Security Exception.[282] At the same time, Binder warns that such an approach cannot change the ordinary meaning of the terms of the respective treaty exception.[283] Such an interpretation cannot read to the Security Exception additional requirements (that an essential interest is threatened by a grave and imminent peril or that the means chosen has to be the "only way" to protect such an essential interest) if the exception only demands that the measure is "necessary." Thus, the treatment of a Security Exception as intertwined with customary defense of necessity proposed by the tribunals in *CMS v Argentina*, *Enron v Argentina*, and *Sempra v Argentina* does not derive from the ordinary meaning of the term "necessary" in the Security Exception clause under the US–Argentina BIT (1991), as required by Article 31 of VCLT.

The customary defense of necessity cannot be readily used as a supplementary means of interpretation under Article 32 of VCLT either. Recourse may be had to supplementary means of interpretation to confirm the meaning of the application of Article 31 of VCLT or to establish the meaning when its interpretation remains ambiguous, obscure or leads to a manifestly absurd or unreasonable result – none of these circumstances seem to be identified by investment tribunals in the case of Article XI of US–Argentina BIT (1991).[284]

Consequently, the customary defense of necessity should not have been read into the interpretation of the Security Exception under Article XI of the US–Argentina BIT (1991). It is for the parties to the

281 Christina Binder, 'Non-Performance of Treaty Obligations in Cases of Necessity: From "Necessity Knows No Law" via the "Law(s) of Necessity" to Interfaces Between Different "Laws of Necessity"' (2011) 13(1) ARIEL Online 27 https://doi.org/10.1163/15736512-90000027.

282 Ibid 28.

283 Ibid 29.

284 See more Panos Delimatsis and Olga Hrynkiv, 'Sovereign Investors and National Security Exceptions in WTO and Investment Law' in P Delimatsis, G Dimitropoulos, and A Gourgourinis (eds.), State Capitalism and International Investment Law (Hart Publishing 2023) 236.

treaty rather than for adjudicators to negotiate and provide for these specific legal consequences.[285]

Investment tribunals have increasingly embraced the "separation" approach when examining the relationship between Security Exceptions and the customary defense of necessity. In *Deutsche Telekom v India*, the tribunal determined that Article 12 of the India–Germany BIT (1995) should be interpreted based on its own terms, without importing requirements from the customary defense of necessity not explicitly mentioned in the treaty.[286] The tribunal did not impose constraints such as limiting Article 12 to emergency situations, requiring the state to prove that the measure was the "only one" available, or proving that it did not contribute to the necessity situation.[287] Likewise, in *Devas v India*, the tribunal rejected the claimant's argument that the Security Exception under Article 11(3) of the India–Mauritius BIT (1998) should adhere to the stricter standards of Article 25 of ARSIWA, including that the respondent must demonstrate that "the wrongful act was the only way to safeguard (India's) essential interest under Article 25."[288] According to the tribunal, the respondent in the present case did not invoke a state of necessity defense under customary international law but, instead, the Security Exception of India–Mauritius BIT (1998), and therefore, it is the analysis of the Security Exception which shall guide the tribunal in determining whether or not the respondent is in breach of the India–Mauritius BIT (1998).[289] The tribunal stated that in light of the precise wording of Article 11(3) of the India–Mauritius BIT (1998), it would be strange to give the customary defense of necessity preponderance over it.[290] Thus, in its current application, the mere use of the term "necessary" is not sufficient to build the bridge between the customary defense of necessity and a Security Exception.

Yet, recent case law shows that the confusion persists. In *Michael Lee-Chin v Dominican Republic*, the respondent argued that it adopted the contested Security Measures in response to a health and environmental

[285] Diane A Desierto, 'Necessity and "Supplementary Means of Interpretation" for Non-Precluded Measures in Bilateral Investment Treaties' (2010) 31(3) U Pennsylvania J Intl Econ L 827, 934.

[286] *Deutsche Telekom AG v Republic of India* (December 13, 2017) PCA Case No 2014–10 Interim Award [229].

[287] Ibid [229].

[288] *CC/Devas (Mauritius) Ltd v Republic of India* (July 25, 2016) PCA Case No 2013–09 Award on Jurisdiction and Merits [249].

[289] Ibid [252].

[290] Ibid [253].

crisis at the Duquesa Landfill and that they were "necessary for the protection of its own national security interest."[291] The tribunal ruled that while the situation was serious and required urgent measures, the respondent failed to prove it constituted a national security emergency.[292] In particular, it found no evidence that the crisis had a national impact or that the country's security was at risk.[293] A dissenting opinion of Marcelo G. Kohen criticized this approach for again confusing a more lenient standard of review of Security Exceptions with a stricter standard of review of the customary defense of necessity.[294]

5.3.2.4 Noncontribution Requirement

As discussed before, Article 25 of ARSIWA also provides that a state cannot invoke the customary defense of necessity as a ground for precluding wrongfulness if it "has contributed to the situation of necessity." Yet, it is contentious whether international law should always prevent a state from taking steps essential to deal with existing emergencies and avoid domestic disasters because of its political officials' mistakes in the past.[295] While such an approach might be justified under Article 25 of ARSIWA aimed to disincentivize systematically irresponsible behavior of states under international law, a more nuanced approach might be required under international economic agreements where the contracting parties are expected to negotiate an optimal contract and agree on the allocation of risks ex ante. From the economic point of view, if the parties do not expressly agree ex ante that the contribution to the situation of emergency should preclude a state from invoking a security defense, there is no reason to reallocate the risk of every emergency to another party ex post. It can be argued that the rigidity of Article 25 of ARSIWA actually nudged states to include more lenient treaty exceptions with different preconditions for their invocation to leave states more regulatory space than the customary defense of necessity does.[296]

In the 1980s, in *US – Trade Measures Affecting Nicaragua*, Nicaragua raised an argument that a country could not be allowed to rely on the

291 *Michael Anthony Lee-Chin v Dominican Republic* (October 6, 2023) ICSID Case No UNCT/18/3 Award [217].

292 Ibid [248].

293 Ibid [251], [263].

294 Dissenting Opinion of Marcelo G Kohen (October 6, 2023) [44].

295 Alan O Sykes, 'Economic "Necessity" in International Law' (2015) 109(2) Am J Intl L 296, 318.

296 Federica Paddeu and Michael Waibel, 'Necessity 20 Years On: The Limits of Article 25' (2022) 37 ICSID Rev – Foreign Investment LJ 160, 191.

existence of an emergency that it had created itself.[297] In that respect, Nicaragua perceived the Security Exception under the GATT (1947) as analogous to the right of self-defense in international law. While the right to self-defense and Security Exceptions might be considered similar in their functions, there are no grounds for believing that the drafters of the GATT (1947) meant to limit the scope of Security Exceptions to self-defense.[298] To illustrate, Bhala supposes that if the drafters of the GATT (1947) wanted to limit Article XXI(b)(iii) to self-defense cases, then they would have expressly mentioned this and, perhaps, would even refer to the language of Article 51 of UN Charter.[299] Although Hahn agrees that the underlying concept of the "inherent right" to self-defense is similar to the theory underlying the notion of essential interests, he differentiates between the two concepts specifying that "the use of force is a substantially tamed instrument of sovereignty and takes due notice of the inherent limitations sovereignty faces in a way that the vital interests clause [e.g. Security Exception clause] does not."[300]

The current practice of WTO panels and investment tribunals sheds little light on the noncontribution requirement. The panel in *Russia – Traffic in Transit* noted that the determination of an emergency in international relations or necessity does not ask whether a respondent bears international responsibility for the existence of an emergency or how such an emergency is characterized under international law in general.[301] The facts to be assessed for the existence of an emergency in international relations do not originate necessarily from trade and economic matters but rather from the fields of international relations, diplomacy, and foreign and security policy, in which WTO adjudicators are generally not expected to have specific expertise.[302]

297 *US – Trade Measures Affecting Nicaragua* (October 13, 1986) GATT Panel Report L/6053 [4.5].

298 Raj Bhala, 'National Security and International Trade Law: What GATT Says, and what the United States Does Symposium on Linkage as Phenomenon: An Interdisciplinary Approach' (1998) 19 U Pa J Intl L 263, 274.

299 Ibid.

300 Michael J Hahn, 'Vital Interests and the Law of GATT: An Analysis of GATT's Security Exception' (1991) 12 Mich J Intl L 558, 563.

301 *Russia – Measures Concerning Traffic in Transit* (April 5, 2019) WTO Panel Report WT/DS512/R [7.121].

302 Wolfgang Weiß, 'Interpreting Essential Security Exceptions in WTO Law in View of Economic Security Interests' in Wolfgang Weiß and Cornelia Furculita (eds.), *Global Politics and EU Trade Policy* (Springer International Publishing 2020) 279.

To illustrate, in *Russia – Traffic in Transit*, the panel had to deal with the question of whether "the annexation of the Autonomous Republic of Crimea and the military conflict in the east" of Ukraine constituted an "emergency in international relations" in the sense of Article XXI(b)(iii).[303] Notably, a key priority of Russia seemed to be that the panel report contains no legal characterization of the invasion of Ukraine.[304] The panel never directly addressed the "situation" between Russia and Ukraine as the annexation of the Autonomous Republic of Crimea; moreover, it remained careful to "not take a position on Russia's involvement in any armed conflict with Ukraine."[305] The panel did not even attempt to discuss whether a state, by its conduct, might create or contribute significantly to a situation of war or other emergency and then successfully invoke Article XXI GATT (1994), thereby treating trade and emergency as analytically separate from one another.[306] The panel in *US – Origin Marking (Hong Kong, China)* similarly stated that it would not review the merits or the veracity of underlying circumstances or alleged circumstances that might have given rise to the situation that could constitute an emergency in international relations within the meaning of Article XXI(b)(iii).[307] Yet, the panel did not properly explain the reasons for such a decision.

The decisions of WTO panels to examine only the alleged violations of the WTO law imply that they can declare trade measures lawful even if a state takes them in a broader dispute on, for instance, territorial annexation and/or use of force.[308] This makes the question of the legality of specific Security Measures adopted, for example, in response to the war in Ukraine, particularly acute, given that both the measures adopted by

[303] Pramila Crivelli and Mona Paulsen, 'Separating the Political from the Economic: The Russia: Traffic in Transit Panel Report' (2021) 20(4) World Trade Rev 582, 589.

[304] Mona Paulsen, 'Characterizing War in a Trade Context' (*Opinio Juris*, March 10, 2022) http://opiniojuris.org/2022/03/10/characterizing-war-in-a-trade-context/.

[305] Pramila Crivelli and Mona Paulsen, 'Separating the Political from the Economic: The Russia: Traffic in Transit Panel Report' (2021) 20(4) World Trade Rev 582, 589.

[306] See more Panos Delimatsis and Olga Hrynkiv, ' Article XIVbis: Security Exceptions' in Stoll PT and H Hestermeyer (eds.), *Commentaries on World Trade Law – Volume 5: Trade in Services* (Brill 2023). See also Mona Paulsen, 'Characterizing War in a Trade Context' (*Opinio Juris*, March 10, 2022) http://opiniojuris.org/2022/03/10/characterizing-war-in-a-trade-context/.

[307] *US – Origin Marking Requirement* (December 21, 2022) WTO Panel Report WT/DS597/R [7.308].

[308] Momchil Milanov, 'A Lauterpachtian Affair: Security Exceptions as "Self-Judging Obligations" in the Case Law of the International Court of Justice and Beyond' (2021) 22(4) J World Investment & Trade 509, 557.

Western countries against Russia to prevent an imminent threat to human life and health in Ukraine and the measures adopted by Russia prohibiting the export of raw materials to Western countries are taken in the time of the Russia–Ukraine war.

Several investment tribunals in Argentine economic crisis cases took the non-contribution requirement into account while assimilating the conditions of the Security Exception under US–Argentina BIT (1991) and the customary defense of necessity under Article 25 of ARSIWA (without providing the proper legal grounds for such an interpretation).[309] To illustrate, in addition to focusing on the availability of less restrictive alternatives, the El Paso tribunal held that the requirement of "necessity" under Article XI of US–Argentina BIT (1991) "presupposes that the State has not contributed, by acts or omissions, to creating the situation which it relies on when claiming the lawfulness of its measures" (the non-contribution requirement).[310] Similarly, the Mobil Exploration tribunal held that the ordinary meaning of "necessary" under Article XI of US–Argentina BIT (1991) implies that the state invoking necessity did not create the situation of necessity.[311] Yet, as discussed before, in more recent cases, the tribunals separate the treaty-based Security Exceptions and customary defense of necessity and do not apply the non-contribution requirement as one of the preconditions for the successful invocation of a Security Exception.[312]

All this considered, it cannot be excluded that WTO panels and investment tribunals dealing with Security Exceptions in the future would also prefer to leave the question of non-contribution requirement open. WTO adjudicators seem to remain reluctant to act outside their traditional areas of trade and economics when evaluating facts requires "too specific expertise beyond a general familiarity with the foundations of international law and relations."[313] This is not to say that adjudicators cannot objectively review whether there are grounds for believing that an emergency in international relations exists and that the invoking state

309 See also chapter 5, section 5.3.2.3.

310 *El Paso Energy International Company v Argentine Republic* (October 31, 2011) ICSID Case No ARB/03/15 Award [613].

311 *Mobil Exploration and Development Inc Suc Argentina and Mobil Argentina SA v Argentine Republic* (April 10, 2013) ICSID Case No ARB/04/16 Decision on Jurisdiction and Liability [1063].

312 See more chapter 5, section 5.3.2.3.

313 Wolfgang Weiß, 'Interpreting Essential Security Exceptions in WTO Law in View of Economic Security Interests' in Wolfgang Weiß and Cornelia Furculita (eds.), *Global Politics and EU Trade Policy* (Springer International Publishing 2020) 279.

undertook Security Measures in time of such an emergency. It, however, should not be expected that WTO panels or investment tribunals dealing with Security Exceptions would rule on the questions related to the legal use of force in international relations.

It can be argued that such self-restraint exercised by WTO panels and investment tribunals can open a door for potential abuses, where a state would attempt to create an emergency and then justify the suspension of its trade commitments because of such an emergency. Yet, states are expected to adopt Security Measures in good faith. A good faith review of Security Measures should allow adjudicators to delimit the cases of apparent abuses of exceptions without resorting to the questions of public international law that are meant to be resolved by other institutions.[314] At the very least, adjudicators could continue to rely on the evidence and findings provided by the UN General Assembly, as the panel in *Russia – Traffic in Transit* did, or the ICJ practice. Alternatively, as suggested by the *Continental Casualty* tribunal, if a contracting party has contributed to endangering its essential security interest, its Security Measures "may fail to qualify as 'necessary' since that Party could have pursued some other policy that would have rendered them unnecessary."[315]

5.4 Conclusion

No treaty subject matter is categorically immune from judicial review in international law because of an inherent lack of jurisdiction for courts or tribunals to hear security-related disputes or because of the "nonjusticiable doctrine." In fact, when seized with the question of national security, international courts and tribunals, including the ICJ, WTO panels, and investment tribunals, have accepted jurisdiction in disputes where Security Exceptions were invoked in order to assess whether national security concerns were involved and to determine whether the measures that diverged from the state's international legal obligations were justified. In particular, the findings of WTO panels confirm that the invocation of Security Exceptions that use "it considers" language should not per se preclude the jurisdiction of an adjudicator or limit the justiciability of the dispute. WTO-style Security Exceptions are not totally "self-judging" in the sense that the "judgment" of the state invoking the

[314] See more chapter 6, sections 6.2 and 6.3.

[315] *Continental Casualty Co v Argentine Republic* (September 5, 2008) ICSID Case No Arb/03/9 Award [234].

exception is still subject to judicial review, even if it is a lenient one. Yet, as the practice of WTO panels demonstrates, as long as respondents continue to claim that Security Exceptions are nonreviewable or non-justiciable and until such an issue is not clarified by WTO members collectively or by the Appellate Body, it cannot be said with certainty that the discussion over the review of Security Exceptions under WTO law has completely shifted from questioning the jurisdiction of the judicial body over a national security dispute and its justiciability to the actual standard of review.

International adjudicators are expected to provide a coherent interpretation of legal rules and establish clear-cut limits of state sovereignty. The coherent approach to the review of Security Exceptions should ensure that international adjudicators strive for uniformity and clarity in interpreting Security Exceptions rather than deferring to the interpretation advanced by a particular state. This does not mean that deference to the decisions of domestic authorities in security matters is not possible or desirable. On the contrary, developing a coherent approach to reviewing different types of Security Exceptions might require a more lenient review of the self-judging elements of Security Exceptions while preserving a stricter review of its objective elements.

On the one hand, the comparative analysis provided in this Chapter has revealed that international adjudicators consider a deferential standard of review to be appropriate where the text, objects, and purposes of a particular treaty provision, or an established rule of international law, affirmatively provide that deference should be given to the decisions of national authorities. Adjudicators consider whether deference should be given to domestic authorities under different conditions, referring to the open-ended character of specific rules, the margin of appreciation doctrine, and the police power doctrine. For example, adjudicative bodies usually refrain from second-guessing decisions adopted by domestic authorities when it comes to dealing with public policy-related disputes or other disputes that comprise discretionary or standard-type norms, such as Security Exceptions.[316]

On the other hand, a common approach of international adjudicators is that the right of a state to determine the most appropriate standard of protection for its security interests should ensure, at the minimum, the avoidance of potential abuses of treaty commitments. The concept of

[316] Valentina Vadi, *Proportionality, Reasonableness and Standards of Review in International Investment Law and Arbitration* (Edward Elgar Publishing 2018) 237.

good faith can be seen as a valuable tool to differentiate between permissible actions dealing with unforeseen contingencies and a state's opportunistic behavior, allowing for a balance between a state's sovereignty and international control over the appropriateness of the means employed to achieve legitimate purposes.[317] As has transpired from cases of international courts and tribunals, the role of good faith is not to establish a specific rule of conduct but to act as an interpretative principle crucial for the interpretation and application of relevant procedural and substantive rules.[318] The measures that strike a clearly unreasonable balance between the protection of the national security interests of an invoking party and the rights or interests of another state may signal a lack of good faith. The good faith review could also focus on procedural issues and the factual basis of domestic decisions, whether they were adequately investigated, and/or whether the agency abided by the proper procedure.[319]

At the same time, an objective necessity test (not limited by a self-judging language) authorizes an adjudicator to assess whether the means chosen to achieve the policy objective of a state were "necessary" (rather than whether an invoking state considered them necessary). It should be differentiated from the customary defense of necessity under the ARSIWA. The consensus emerging from the current adjudicatory practice is that the necessity test under Security Exceptions should not borrow from parameters of the customary defense of necessity unless the contracting parties have expressly agreed on this. Ultimately, even an objective necessity test does not imply a de novo review of whether an adjudicator would have pursued the same policy objective under the circumstances or the review of whether the chosen measure was "the only way" to protect the state's interest, leaving at least some deference to domestic decisions.

The specific nature of Security Exceptions, and having a more deferential standard for their review, does not necessarily affect the substantive content of treaty obligations. It thus does not affect the approach to treaty interpretation. In particular, even though the practice of international courts and tribunals on this issue is not certain, there are no grounds for believing that (unlike other treaty exceptions) Security Exceptions, as

[317] Enzo Cannizzaro, 'Proportionality and Margin of Appreciation in the Whaling Case: Reconciling Antithetical Doctrines?' (2016) 27(4) EJIL 1061, 1068.

[318] Andrea Gattini, Attila Tanzi, and Filippo Fontanelli (eds.), *General Principles of Law and International Investment Arbitration* (Brill 2018) 218.

[319] Stephan Schill and Robyn Briese, '"If the State Considers": Self-Judging Clauses in International Dispute Settlement' (2009) 13(1) Max Planck YB UN L Online 61, 124.

they are drafted under Article XXI(b) GATT (1994), are not an affirmative defense. However, this may differ in the context of investment treaties, where investment tribunals see some Security Exceptions framed more as limitations on the treaty's scope rather than as justifications for a breach.

The distinction between treating Security Exceptions as an affirmative defense or treating it as a substantive rule limiting the scope of a treaty is not a purely theoretical issue or an issue relevant only to deciding on the order of analysis. The true analytical need for maintaining distinct subcategories may have some practical value, given the crucial powers that lie in the hands of international courts and tribunals to allocate the burden of proof and apply customary rules and principles while choosing the approach to take to the interpretation of Security Exceptions. For example, viewing Security Exceptions as an affirmative defense implies that a state invoking a Security Exception should bear the burden of proof and that the treaty rules on compensation or the law on state responsibility might apply to the dispute.

6

Achieving Coherence in the Interpretation and Application of Security Exceptions

Despite their early common origins in FCN treaties, trade and investment remain legally separate regimes.[1] The international norms reflected in the WTO agreements and BITs differ.[2] The WTO agreements are concerned with trade liberalization and include norms that address tariffs, nontariff barriers, and unilateral trade remedies that have no analogy in BITs.[3] At the same time, BITs are concerned with investment protection against unlawful expropriation, the denial of justice, and guarantees of full protection and security, which have no analogy in the WTO agreements.[4] At least in some cases, these protections might reflect constitutional assurances against violations of due process and the uncompensated taking of property and thus require financial compensation to injured investors even when a government is responding to emergencies.[5] As a result, the remedial contexts of the trade and investment regimes also differ. Under WTO agreements, the losing party is expected to bring its measures into compliance in the future, whereas under investment treaties, the losing state is often expected to compensate for its past actions.[6]

At the same time, the trade and investment regimes are increasingly converging. They promote similar objectives of globalization, economic integration, trade promotion, and investment protection.[7] They

[1] Nicholas DiMascio and Joost Pauwelyn, 'Nondiscrimination in Trade and Investment Treaties: Worlds Apart or Two Sides of the Same Coin' (2008) 102 Am J Intl L 48, 51.

[2] Roger P Alford, 'The Convergence of International Trade and Investment Arbitration' (2013) 12 Santa Clara J Intl L 35, 40.

[3] Ibid.

[4] Ibid.

[5] José E Alvarez, 'Sovereign Concerns and the International Investment Regime' in Karl P Sauvant and others (eds.), *Sovereign Investment: Concerns and Policy Reactions* (OUP 2012) 279–280.

[6] J Benton Heath, 'Eco Oro and the Twilight of Policy Exceptionalism' (*IISD*, December 20, 2021) www.iisd.org/itn/en/2021/12/20/eco-oro-and-the-twilight-of-policy-exceptionalism/.

[7] Roger P Alford, 'The Convergence of International Trade and Investment Arbitration' (2013) 12 Santa Clara J Intl L 35, 37.

incorporate several similar substantive protections, particularly the rules against discrimination and protectionism.[8] Albeit in different ways, they both use international adjudicators to ensure judicial review of sovereign state violations of international law.[9] Furthermore, both systems had to overcome a structural prioritization of trade and investment liberalization vis-à-vis conflicting regulatory concerns.[10] The GATT model of "embedded liberalism" granted countries the possibility to politically adjust their engagement with the system in times of pressure by invoking treaty exceptions.[11] Similarly, as a matter of newer treaty practice, parties prioritize the insertion of exceptions in IIAs often modeled on the WTO law.[12] Yet, as the practice of the US, the EU, and BRICS demonstrates,[13] some states have different approaches to drafting Security Exceptions under trade agreements and investment treaties, underpinning the differences in the types of commitments and the political economy of the two regimes.

Acknowledging that each Security Exception clause should be analyzed in relation to commitments under the specific regime and its context, this chapter explores the possibility of converging the approaches to interpreting Security Exceptions under international trade and investment agreements (section 6.1). As a technical matter, the adjudicative review of Security Exceptions under both regimes can enforce primary and secondary safeguards for applying Security Measures.[14] Primary safeguards perform a gatekeeping function, labeling certain types of purported "essential security interests" or certain declared "emergencies in international relations" as outside the Security Exception clause. Secondary safeguards do not deal with the existence of a security interest or an international emergency as such but rather examine the nexus between the security interest and the particular measure adopted.[15] This might include considering the necessity of the

[8] Ibid.

[9] Ibid.

[10] Sungjoon Cho and Jürgen Kurtz, 'Convergence and Divergence in International Economic Law and Politics' (2018) 29(1) EJIL 169, 170.

[11] Ibid.

[12] Ibid 189; Wolfgang Alschner and Kun Hui, 'Missing in Action: General Public Policy Exceptions in Investment Treaties' in Lisa Sachs, Jesse Coleman, and Lise Johnson (eds.), *Yearbook on International Investment Law and Policy* (OUP 2018) [21:02].

[13] Chapter 4.

[14] J Benton Heath, 'The New National Security Challenge to the Economic Order' (2020) 129 Yale LJ 1020, 1064.

[15] Ibid.

Security Measure or its relevance for the protection of invoked security interests. This chapter thus discusses the approach of the emerging jurisprudence to the interpretation of primary and secondary safeguards for the application of Security Measures and the directions in which it can further develop (section 6.4.

6.1 Convergence of Approaches

The investment treaty regime has been gradually moving toward multilateral agreements, which presupposes more "issue linkages" between trade and investment across multiple WTO members.[16] Although there is nothing inherently natural or inevitable about the absence of exception clauses in earlier BITs,[17] the transfer of the exceptions drafted for WTO agreements to investment treaties remains contentious.

The exceptions under trade law are designed to apply in the dispute between governments over the measure of general application, such as tariffs or regulatory schemes.[18] They are not necessarily well-equipped to deal with a dispute with a specific investor arising in a complex factual context.[19] To illustrate, the question arises as to whether compensation measures should follow the successful invocation of the exception under the investment treaty.[20]

On the one hand, exception clauses under trade law are generally designed to justify the breach.[21] If the breach is justified, the treaty remedies do not apply. On the other hand, in the investment treaty context, a state is generally liable to compensate an investor in the case

[16] Jonathan Bonnitcha, Lauge N Skovgaard Poulsen, and Michael Waibel, *The Political Economy of the Investment Treaty Regime* (OUP 2017) 4.

[17] Jürgen Kurtz, *The WTO and International Investment Law: Converging Systems* (CUP 2016) 172, 227.

[18] J Benton Heath, 'Eco Oro and the Twilight of Policy Exceptionalism' (*IISD*, December 20, 2021) www.iisd.org/itn/en/2021/12/20/eco-oro-and-the-twilight-of-policy-exceptionalism/.

[19] Ibid.

[20] CUI Fan, Catherine Hoeffler, and Stephanie C Hofmann, 'National Security and Other Non-trade Objectives under WTO Law' in Bernard Hoekman, Xinquan Tu, and Dong Wang (eds), *Rebooting Multilateral Trade Cooperation: Perspectives from China and Europe* (CEPR Press 2021) 109 http://respect.eui.eu/wp-content/uploads/sites/6/2021/07/Chapter_5.pdf.

[21] J Benton Heath, 'Eco Oro and the Twilight of Policy Exceptionalism' (*IISD*, December 20, 2021) www.iisd.org/itn/en/2021/12/20/eco-oro-and-the-twilight-of-policy-exceptionalism/.

of direct or indirect expropriation.[22] The exception to this rule is the police power doctrine under customary international law. If a measure falls within the police power based on customary international law (or the modified version included in some treaties), no compensation is due to the investor even though a deprivation of property has occurred.[23] The relationship between states' defenses under treaty exception clauses modeled on trade law and the police power doctrine remains unclear. It can be argued that treaty exceptions do not limit the police power doctrine and thus do not prevent the relief of a host state from the obligation to compensate in the case of expropriation when the police power doctrine applies.[24] At the same time, the tribunal in *Bear Creek v Peru* applied treaty exceptions as *lex specialis* to exclude any other defenses under international law, including police powers.[25] As a result, it found that, even if the exception makes states' measures lawful, this does not prevent an investor from claiming the compensation.[26] In *Eco Oro v Colombia*, the tribunal came to a similar conclusion and held that if the parties intended to eliminate compensatory liability when the exceptions apply, they would expressly stipulate this in the text of the treaty.[27]

Such conflicting approaches demonstrate some of the challenges of interpreting IIAs with many potentially overlapping exceptions.[28] If states want to balance investor protection and essential policies based on the trade agreements model, they might consider adjusting the borrowed exception clauses to the underlying structure of investment treaties,[29] for example, by clarifying the provisions on compensation or including more specific compensation requirements.[30]

22 Ibid.

23 Céline Lévesque, 'The Inclusion of GATT Article XX Exceptions in IIAs: A Potentially Risky Policy?' in Roberto Echandi and Sauvé Pierre (eds.), *Prospects in International Investment Law and Policy: World Trade Forum* (CUP 2013) 370.

24 Ibid 367–370.

25 *Bear Creek Mining Corporation v Republic of Peru* (November 30, 2017) ICSID Case No ARB/14/21 Award [473], [474].

26 Ibid [473], [477].

27 *Eco Oro Minerals Corp v Republic of Colombia* (September 9, 2021) ICSID Case No ARB/16/41 Decision on Jurisdiction, Liability, and Quantum [830].

28 Catharine Titi, 'The Right to Regulate in International Investment Law (Revisited)' (2022) International and Comparative Law Research Center 53.

29 J Benton Heath, 'Eco Oro and the Twilight of Policy Exceptionalism' (*IISD*, December 20, 2021) www.iisd.org/itn/en/2021/12/20/eco-oro-and-the-twilight-of-policy-exceptionalism/.

30 See more chapter 7, section 7.2.5.

The convergence of interpretive approaches to international trade and investment law also raises practical concerns. It has to be acknowledged that, as noted by the International Tribunal for the Law of the Sea in the MOX Plant case, "the application of international law rules on interpretation of treaties to identical or similar provisions of different treaties may not yield the same results, having regard to, inter alia, differences in the respective contexts, objects and purposes, subsequent practice of parties and travaux preparatoires."[31] Abi-Saab has also noted that "each of [treaty regimes] constitutes a legal universe quite different from the others. The difference can be explained not only by the disparity in the structure, mandate, and composition, but also, and perhaps mainly, by the 'judicial policy' of each forum, which is also a function of its environment."[32] Although different fora are all supposed to exercise the judicial function, including the treaty interpretation, each of them is a separate legal universe on its own. Thus, a significant difference between the WTO system and the international investment law regime is that the former has specific institutional characteristics such as a common treaty, an institutional structure, and a multilateral dispute settlement system with an appellate mechanism.[33] The international investment law regime does not possess any of these institutional characteristics and thus is arguably not the right forum to make findings on sensitive issues, for example, how the benefit of the state regulatory objective would balance against the restrictive effect on investment.[34] It follows that the investment regime might find it appropriate to borrow from the trade regime only in limited cases.[35]

On the flip side, as a recent practice demonstrates, some voluntary convergence in international trade and investment law is unavoidable and normatively required due to the increasing global interdependency

[31] Christoph Schreuer, 'Diversity and Harmonization of Treaty Interpretation in Investment Arbitration' in Malgosia Fitzmaurice, Olufemi Elias, and Panos Merkouris (eds.), *Treaty Interpretation and the Vienna Convention on the Law of Treaties: 30 Years On* (Martinus Nijhoff 2010) 136.

[32] Isabelle Van Damme, 'Jurisdiction, Applicable Law, and Interpretation' in Daniel Bethlehem and others (eds.), *The Oxford Handbook of International Trade Law* (Oxford Handbooks Online 2012) 28.

[33] Prabhash Ranjan, '"Necessary" in Non-Precluded Measures Provisions in Bilateral Investment Treaties: The Indian Contribution' (2020) 67(3) Netherlands Intl LR 473, 493.

[34] Ibid.

[35] See more Mark Wu, 'The Scope and Limits of Trade's Influence in Shaping the Evolving International Investment Regime' in Zachary Douglas, Joost Pauwelyn, and Jorge E Viñuales (eds.), *The Foundations of International Investment Law: Bringing Theory into Practice* (OUP 2014) 195–209.

and intensifying interactions among adjudicators. In both legal and institutional terms, the overlap between the trade and the investment regimes is driven by economic logic and the reality of the twenty-first century.[36] Linked by global value chains,[37] the two regimes represent two sides of the same coin for businesses and many policymakers.[38] Any abstract commitment to trade liberalization requires corresponding effective protection of investors' rights to operate in the receiving state and the other way around.[39] Given the economic nature of international trade and investment, WTO adjudicators and investment tribunals are unlikely to decide on economic issues entrenched in trade and investment disputes merely based on legal analysis.[40] With the mutually reinforcing nature of trade and investment and the aim of both regimes to prevent discrimination and protectionism, the solutions proposed for revitalizing trade remedies, in certain cases, might also become helpful in reinforcing investment guarantees.[41] In light of such developments, a modeling strategy whereby states take the best attributes of the WTO law and then tailor them in light of the distinct institutional context of investment law seems to be a reasonable and sustainable pathway for the future.[42]

Investment tribunals have occasionally relied on WTO jurisprudence while dealing with similar legal provisions and concepts under international investment law.[43] The continuance of such a tendency might reaffirm the similarity of concerns under both trade and investment law, thereby tying the two regimes together and making the commonality of certain interpretations possible.

[36] Sungjoon Cho and Jürgen Kurtz, 'Convergence and Divergence in International Economic Law and Politics' (2018) 29(1) EJIL 169, 181.

[37] Ibid.

[38] Debra Steger, 'International Trade and Investment: Towards a Common Regime?' in Roberto Echandi and Sauvé Pierre (eds.), *Prospects in International Investment Law and Policy: World Trade Forum* (CUP 2013) 165.

[39] Sungjoon Cho and Jürgen Kurtz, 'Convergence and Divergence in International Economic Law and Politics' (2018) 29(1) EJIL 169, 183.

[40] Fenghua Li, 'The Driving Forces of the Convergence of WTO Dispute Settlement Mechanism and International Investment Arbitration' (2018) 52(3) JWT 479, 485.

[41] Roger P Alford, 'The Convergence of International Trade and Investment Arbitration' (2013) 12 Santa Clara J Intl L 35, 61.

[42] Jürgen Kurtz, *The WTO and International Investment Law: Converging Systems* (CUP 2016) 227–28.

[43] Roger P Alford, 'The Convergence of International Trade and Investment Arbitration' (2013) 12 Santa Clara J Intl L 35, 62.

6.2 Primary Safeguards for Security Measures

Similar to WTO agreements, Regional Agreements generally refer in their Security Exception clauses to "essential security interests."[44] Therefore, the concept of "essential security interests" is key to interpreting Security Exceptions under international trade and investment law. Further, many Security Exception clauses are limited in their scope *ratione materiae*, applying only to certain goods or situations.[45] To illustrate, by invoking Article XXI(b) GATT (1994), a WTO member can justify trade restrictions that are aimed at the protection of its essential national security interests but only if such restrictions are: (i) relating to fissionable materials; (ii) relating to the traffic in arms, ammunition and implements of war or other similar goods; and/or (iii) adopted in time of war or other emergency in international relations. Thus, whereas the concept of national security can be deemed to encompass many areas of domestic interest, Article XXI(b) attempts to narrow down the scope of permissible policies aimed at protecting such security interests.[46] A similar approach has been adopted in the Regional Agreements incorporating WTO-style Security Exceptions.[47]

Difficulties have recently emerged under Article XXI(b)(iii) and similarly drafted provisions, particularly regarding the interpretation of the phrase "other emergency in international relations." The panel in *US – Origin Marking (Hong Kong, China)* confirmed that "the subject matters covered in subparagraphs (i) and (ii) are clearly related to the defence and military sector."[48] In contrast to subparagraphs (i) and (ii), subparagraph (iii) is not defined by reference to a particular type of product but instead by reference to events of certain gravity that have implications for international relations. Thus, the measures taken under this exception

[44] Only some agreements refer to "national security interests" or "national security" omitting the term "essential." For example, Article 14 of SAFTA (2004) provides for a separate broadly drafted Security Exception clause stipulating that: "[n]othing in this Agreement shall be construed to prevent any Contracting State from taking action and adopting measures which it considers necessary for the protection of its national security." See more chapter 4, sections 4.1 and 4.2.

[45] Dominik Eisenhut, 'Sovereignty, National Security and International Treaty Law the Standard of Review of International Courts and Tribunals with regard to "Security Exceptions"' (2010) 48(4) Archiv des V 431, 433.

[46] Willard L Thorp, 'Trade Barriers and National Security' (1960) 50 American Economic Rev 433, 434.

[47] Chapter 4, sections 4.1 and 4.2.

[48] *US – Origin Marking Requirements* (December 21, 2022) WTO Panel Report WT/DS597/R [7.301].

are not limited to certain activities but can cover any products traded between the respective countries as long as the other legal preconditions are fulfilled.[49] This increases the risk that in the case of a dispute over emerging security concerns that might not readily fit within the scope of Article XXI(b)(i) or (ii), states might attempt to squeeze their trade restrictions under the exception dealing with wartime or another emergency in international relations. As a result, Article XXI(b)(iii) is the most likely to be pushed to cover other goods, materials, services, and technologies that have no connection to the state's military and defense capacities or where the existence of such a connection remains disputable.

All this considered, this section focuses on the type of interests that WTO members can potentially protect under the evolving concept of "essential security interests" within international trade and investment agreements and the type of situations that could be understood as the "other emergency in international relations" within the meaning of WTO-style Security Exceptions, allowing WTO members to take necessary measures "in time of" such emergencies.

6.2.1 Evolving Concept of "Essential Security Interests"

Different from the original security agenda (which focused on military threats), contemporary national security strategies aim to address a wider array of security risks, including climate change, cyber threats, and pandemics, as well as vital industry concerns and potential weakening of the domestic economy. Nevertheless, the drafters of the GATT (1947) acknowledged a great danger in a Security Exception having too broad wording because it would "permit anything under the sun."[50] Therefore they aimed to "draft provisions which would take care of real essential security interests and, at the same time . . . to limit the exception so as to prevent the adoption of protection for maintaining industries under every conceivable circumstance."[51] Such an aim was achieved by

[49] George-Dian Balan, 'On Fissionable Cows and the Limits to the WTO Security Exceptions' (2019) 14(1) Global Trade and Customs Journal 2, 8.

[50] UN – Economic and Social Council, Preparatory Committee of the UN Conference on Trade and Employment – Second Session of the Preparatory Committee of the UN Conference on Trade and Employment – [Commission A] – Verbatim Report – Thirty-Third Meeting of Commission Held on Thursday, July 24, 1947, at 2.30 pm in the Palais des Nations, Geneva (July 24, 1947) E/PC/T/A/PV/33 20 https://docs.wto.org/gattdocs/q/UN/EPCT/W236.PDF.

[51] Ibid.

including the word "essential."[52] Irrespective of the approach of WTO members on the scope of their national security, the term "essential" has an ordinary meaning. Among others, the definition of "essential" includes "[t]hat is such in the absolute or highest sense" and "[a]ffecting the essence of anything; significant, important."[53] Therefore, the Security Exceptions using such language require a qualified security interest, in the absence of which Security Measures cannot be imposed.

Although not extensive enough, the practice of the ICJ, WTO panels, and investment tribunals indicate that, although military security is typically considered essential, nonmilitary security can also be viewed as crucial because of emerging threats and challenges in our interconnected world. In *Nicaragua v US*, the ICJ mentioned that "[i]t is difficult to deny that self-defence against an armed attack corresponds to measures necessary to protect essential security interests. But the concept of essential security interests certainly extends beyond the concept of an armed attack, and has been subject to very broad interpretations in the past."[54] For example, in the *Oil Platforms* case, the ICJ endorsed the view that "the uninterrupted flow of maritime commerce in the Persian Gulf" constituted a "reasonable" security interest of the US.[55]

Yet, the threshold for invocation of the essential security defense is high. In *Russia – Traffic in Transit*, the WTO panel highlighted that "'[e]ssential security interests,' which is a narrower concept than 'security interests,' may generally be understood to refer to those interests relating to the quintessential functions of the state, namely, the protection of its territory and its population from external threats, and the maintenance of law and public order internally."[56] The designation of essential

[52] UN – Economic and Social Council, Preparatory Committee of the UN Conference on Trade and Employment – Second Session of the Preparatory Committee of the UN Conference on Trade and Employment – [Commission A] – Verbatim Report – Thirty-Third Meeting of Commission Held on Thursday, July 24, 1947, at 2.30 pm in the Palais des Nations, Geneva (July 24, 1947) E/PC/T/A/PV/33 20 https://docs.wto.org/gattdocs/q/UN/EPCT/W236.PDF.

[53] The New Shorter Oxford English Dictionary (L Brown ed, 4th ed., Clarendon Press 1993) (excerpts) referred to by the US in *US – Origin Marking Requirements* (July 2, 2021) First Written Submission of the US in DS597 [39] https://ustr.gov/sites/default/files/enforcement/DS/DS597/US.Sub1.fin.pdf.

[54] *Case Concerning Military and Paramilitary Activities in and against Nicaragua (Nicaragua v US)* (June 27, 1986) ICJ Rep Merits [224].

[55] *Oil Platforms (Iran v US)* Judgment (November 6, 2003) ICJ Rep Merits [73].

[56] *Russia – Measures Concerning Traffic in Transit* (April 5, 2019) WTO Panel Report WT/DS512/R [7.130].

security interests is left, in general, to the WTO member[57] since "[t]he specific interests that are considered directly relevant to the protection of a state from such external or internal threats will depend on the particular situation and perceptions of the state in question, and can be expected to vary with changing circumstances."[58] In the panel's view, the WTO member should articulate its "essential security interests" "sufficiently enough" to check their veracity.[59] Following this logic, the panel reported that the 2014 Crimea emergency was very close to the "hard core" of war or armed conflict and accepted the accuracy of Russia's designation of its essential security interests.[60]

The panel in *Saudi Arabia – IPRs* also reaffirmed that in that case, Saudi Arabia's articulation of its essential security interest, that is protecting the country from the "dangers of terrorism and extremism," was sufficiently precise and related to the "quintessential functions of the state."[61] Although Qatar argued that such formulations are vague or imprecise, the panel saw no basis in the text of Article 73(b)(iii) or otherwise for demanding greater precision than to articulate its "essential security interests" sufficiently enough to allow an assessment of whether the Security Measures were related to those interests.[62] Thus, the existence of an "essential security interest" to be protected is not enough. An invoking state should articulate its "essential security interests" sufficiently enough to establish that the challenged trade restrictions are related to such interests, which is more difficult to prove in practice.

The above cases suggest that a line must be drawn between the security interests and other vital interests of a state; however, they provide little explanation as to how to draw this line or why military and defense functions should be considered on the one side and other matters, like emerging threats to national security in response to new geopolitical developments and economic instability, should be on the other.

[57] Ibid [7.131].

[58] Ibid.

[59] *Saudi Arabia – Measures Concerning the Protection of Intellectual Property Rights* (June 16, 2020) WTO Panel Report WT/DS567/R [7.250].

[60] *Russia – Measures Concerning Traffic in Transit* (April 5, 2019) WTO Panel Report WT/DS512/R [7.136].

[61] *Saudi Arabia – Measures Concerning the Protection of Intellectual Property Rights* (June 16, 2020) WTO Panel Report WT/DS567/R [7.280]–[7.281].

[62] Ibid [7.281].

6.2.1.1 National Security and Economic Security Under WTO Law

Driven by economic interdependence, the race to develop transformational technologies, and the ubiquity of cyberspace, certain states use economic tools to advance geopolitical objectives, thereby creating a new reality of the international trade order where national security and economics are converging.[63] This convergence opens the door to a wide range of state interventions into the economy justified on security grounds (e.g. industrial policies, such as subsidies and tariffs, or economic sanctions), where trade itself is seen as a threat to national security.[64]

To illustrate, China's overriding drivers for industrial policies addressing the development of next-generation internet technologies and infrastructure, namely regulatory standard setting, procurement, and public investment, are dominated by national security and related techno-nationalist concerns.[65] The US's measures also signal the attempts to ensure US national security through the support of domestic industries. To take just one obvious example, President Trump relied on Section 232 of the Trade Expansion Act (1962) to apply additional tariffs to steel and aluminum imports.[66] The US claimed, among others, that "the term 'national security' can be interpreted more broadly to include the general security and welfare of certain industries, beyond those necessary to satisfy national defence requirements that are critical to the minimum operations of the economy and government."[67] The US maintained that "the continued rising levels of imports of foreign steel threaten to impair the national security by placing the US steel industry at substantial risk of displacing the basic oxygen furnace and other steelmaking capacity, and the related supply chain needed to produce steel for critical infrastructure and national defence."[68] It also referred to "excess production and

[63] David H McCormick, Charles E Luftig, and James M Cunningham, 'Economic Might, National Security, and the Future of American Statecraft' (May 6, 2020) 3(3) Texas National Security Rev 50, 52.

[64] J Benton Heath, 'Trade and Security among the Ruins' (2020) 30 Duke J Comparative & Intl L 223, 229.

[65] See more Tai Ming Cheung, 'The Rise of China as a Cybersecurity Industrial Power: Balancing National Security, Geopolitical, and Development Priorities' (2018) 3(3) J Cyber Policy 306.

[66] US Presidential Proclamation 9705 on Adjusting Imports of Steel into the US 83 FR 11625 (March 8, 2018).

[67] *US – Certain Measures on Steel and Aluminium Products (China)* (December 9, 2022) WTO Panel Report WT/DS544/R [2.12], [2.22].

[68] Ibid [2.13].

capacity in China as a major factor contributing to the decline in US domestic aluminum production and loss of domestic production capacity" and thus threatening to impair its national security as defined in Section 232.[69] In a similar vein, the US adopted unilateral tariffs on certain imports from China under Section 301 of the Trade Act (1974), motivated, at least in part, to suppress the rise of China as a dominant technological power.[70]

The legitimacy of certain US tariffs and other related measures was challenged before the WTO in *US – Tariff Measures* and the *US – Steel and Aluminium Products* disputes, where the US invoked a public morals exception and a Security Exception, respectively. The panel in *US – Tariff Measures* confirmed that the general exceptions (such as a public morals exception) aimed to protect noneconomic public interests might "involve, directly or indirectly, a clear economic dimension."[71] It referred to the practice of prior panels recognizing that the "measures targeting money laundering, bridging the digital divide or promoting social inclusion and fraud prevention were measures related to public morals."[72] Notably, the panel also reiterated that a measure might fall within the scope of the public morals exception of Article XX(a), even if the legal instruments implementing the measure did not expressly mention the protection of public morals as its objective.[73] To this end, the panel relied on "the assessment of the design of the measure, its content, structure, and expected operation."[74]

In the *US – Steel and Aluminium Products* disputes, complainants denounced US tariffs on steel and aluminum as safeguard measures disguised as Security Measures. To illustrate, China contested before the WTO that the purpose of US tariffs "is not to protect so-called 'national security' of the US, but rather it serves to protect the commercial interests of the domestic industries. As such, such measures should be considered as safeguard measures under the Agreement on Safeguards."[75] Yet, the panel in *US – Steel and Aluminium Products*

69 Ibid [2.23].

70 See more Yong-Shik Lee, 'Weaponizing International Trade in Political Disputes: Issues Under International Economic Law and Systemic Risks' (2022) 56(3) JWT 405.

71 *US – Tariff Measures on Certain Goods from China* (September 15, 2020) WTO Panel Report WT/DS543/R [7.136].

72 Ibid [7.137].

73 Ibid [7.125].

74 Ibid.

75 *US – Certain Measures on Steel and Aluminium Products* (May 18, 2018) Statement by HE Ambassador Dr Zhang Xiangchen at the WTO General Council Meeting http://wto.mofcom.gov.cn/article/newsupdates/201805/20180502741686.shtml.

(China) took the position that according to Article 11.1(c) of the Agreement on Safeguards, the Agreement on Safeguards does not apply to the measures "sought, taken or maintained . . . pursuant to provisions of GATT 1994 other than Article XIX."[76] The panel clarified that the term "pursuant to" in Article 11.1(c) asks whether the provisions of the GATT (1994) "other than" Article XIX apply to the measures at issue, leaving "as a separate inquiry whether a measure is consistent with the requirements of such other provision."[77] To address this concern, the panel identified the relevant aspects of the design and application of the US tariffs with specific reference to their legal characterization by the US. It highlighted that the US tariffs were adopted under Section 232, which concerned actions taken for "[s]afeguarding [US] national security;" that the Presidential Proclamations imposing such measures referred to the US national security objectives; and that the US referred to its national security considerations in various notifications and statements before the WTO.[78] Having relied on such evidence at both the domestic and multilateral levels and the US reference to Article XXI GATT (1994) as the legal basis for the adoption of the US tariffs, the panel found that the challenged measures did not fall under Article XIX since "a central aspect of the design and application of the measures at issue is their relation to the United States' determination of a threat to its national security under the relevant domestic laws."[79] Such considerations allowed the panel to find that, in this dispute, the relevant provision of the GATT (1994) "other than" Article XIX is Article XXI GATT (1994), which excludes the application of the Agreement on Safeguards.[80] The WTO panels made identical findings in other disputes regarding the US tariffs.[81]

[76] *US – Certain Measures on Steel and Aluminium Products (China)* (December 9, 2022) WTO Panel Report WT/DS544/R [7.69]–[7.70]; *US – Certain Measures on Steel and Aluminium Products (Norway)* (December 9, 2022) WTO Panel Report WT/DS552/R [7.57]–[7.58]; *US – Certain Measures on Steel and Aluminium Products (Switzerland)* (December 9, 2022) WTO Panel Report WT/DS556/R [7.87]–[7.88]; *US – Certain Measures on Steel and Aluminium Products (Turkey)* (December 9, 2022) WTO Panel Report WT/DS564/R [7.85]–[7.86].

[77] *US – Certain Measures on Steel and Aluminium Products (China)* (December 9, 2022) WTO Panel Report WT/DS544/R [7.79].

[78] Ibid [7.87]–[7.99].

[79] Ibid [7.96].

[80] Ibid [8.1].

[81] *US – Certain Measures on Steel and Aluminium Products (Norway)* (December 9, 2022) WTO Panel Report WT/DS552/R [8.1]; *US – Certain Measures on Steel and Aluminium Products (Switzerland)* (December 9, 2022) WTO Panel Report WT/DS556/R [8.1]; *US –*

Such an approach of WTO panels suggests that the qualification of a measure by domestic authorities is enough to distill that the protection of a state's national security interest is "a central aspect" of its design and application, which enables the further review of such measures under Security Exceptions, rather than other exceptions. The panel finding in *US – Tariff Measures* with respect to a public morals exception also suggests that future panels can potentially find a measure to be related to a state's national security interest even if the objective of the protection of national security is not expressly mentioned in the legal mechanism implementing such a measure. Such a finding has not given the green light to the US tariffs in *US – Tariff Measures* since the invoked Article XX(a) GATT (1994) prescribes a stringent necessity test that the US tariff measures failed to satisfy.[82] Yet, given a more deferential standard of review of Security Exceptions,[83] following such an approach in future national security disputes might open the door to a range of domestic measures that are adopted to protect domestic interests that are far remote from states' military and defense concerns. Broadening the traditional approach to national security to include any matter that a state considers to be related to its security and to be "essential" under domestic law means accepting the risk that any measure could be remotely and creatively linked to national security issues, as exemplified by *Sweden – Import Restrictions on Certain Footwear*, where Sweden intended to label the interests of its shoe industry as an issue of national security.[84]

At the same time, there is a general understanding that WTO Security Exceptions were not designed to encompass the socioeconomic consequences resulting from the application of GATT principles, provide safeguards for vital industries, or justify the use of other protectionist measures in the name of economic or political welfare.[85] The object and purpose of the GATT (1994) are set out in the agreement's preamble, providing, among others, that the GATT (1994) sets forth "reciprocal and mutually advantageous arrangements directed to the substantial

Certain Measures on Steel and Aluminium Products (Turkey) (December 9, 2022) WTO Panel Report WT/DS564/R [8.1].

82 *US – Tariff Measures on Certain Goods from China* (September 15, 2020) WTO Panel Report WT/DS543/R [7.238].

83 See more chapter 6, section 6.3.

84 Angshuman Hazarika and Pieter Van Vaerenbergh, 'Climate Change as a Security Risk: Too Hot to Handle?' (2020) 54(3) JWT 417, 425.

85 Wesley A Cann, 'Creating Standards and Accountability for the Use of the WTO Security Exception: Reducing the Role of Power-Based Relations and Establishing a New Balance between Sovereignty and Multilateralism' (2001) 26 Yale J Intl L 413, 425.

reduction of tariffs and other barriers to trade." The exceptions under Articles XIX, XX, and XXI constitute derogations from this goal. Yet, in light of the obligation of good faith, WTO members are expected to use such exceptions only in order to achieve legitimate, nontrade policy objectives and not as a means to circumvent their obligations under the WTO agreements, for example, by relabeling their trade interests as "essential security interests."[86]

The context established by other GATT provisions favors a narrower interpretation of "essential security interests" to exclude economic security concerns in general.[87] General exceptions under WTO law (Article XX GATT (1994)) carve out permissible economic exceptions from the GATT (1994) in the case of the importation or exportation of gold or silver, price stabilization efforts, and resource scarcity. In addition, Article XIX GATT (1994) deals with economic distress, allowing WTO members to suspend their trade obligations when increased imports "cause or threaten serious injury to domestic producers" of competing products "to the extent and for such time as may be necessary to prevent or remedy such injury." It would be flawed reasoning to apply Security Exceptions to those situations already covered by other provisions, such as economic emergencies, and thereby neglect the distinct purpose the Security Exceptions are supposed to serve.[88]

All this considered, instead of following the approach of WTO panels in the *US – Steel and Aluminium Products* disputes, international adjudicators in future disputes could adopt a different approach that regards the inclusion of other exceptions under the treaty as restricting the scope of Security Exceptions. Based on the treaty context and the principle of integration, treaties can be expected to be interpreted as a whole,[89] which means that the other treaty obligations and exceptions affect the interpretation of Security Exceptions. It follows that the presence in the agreement of safeguard exceptions or the exception related to the

[86] *Russia – Measures Concerning Traffic in Transit* (April 5, 2019) WTO Panel Report WT/DS512/R [7.133].

[87] See more Panos Delimatsis and Olga Hrynkiv, 'Sovereign Investors and National Security Exceptions in WTO and Investment Law' in P Delimatsis, G Dimitropoulos, and A Gourgourinis (eds.), *State Capitalism and International Investment Law* (Hart Publishing 2023) 236.

[88] Stephan Hobe and Jörn Griebel, 'New Protectionism: How Binding Are International Economic Legal Obligations During a Global Economic Crisis?' (2010) 2 Goettingen J Intl L 423, 425.

[89] Malgosia Fitzmaurice and Olufemi Elias, *Contemporary Issues in the Law of Treaties* (Eleven International Publishing 2005) 219.

protection of exhaustible resources delimits and limits the scope of Security Exceptions. The underlying idea behind such a "division of labor in trade agreements" is that different exceptions are calibrated to respond to different political and economic pressures on international trade.[90] While, in principle, nothing prevents a respondent from invoking the justification under several treaty exceptions in the alternative,[91] adjudicators should ensure that the government does not channel its measure to a specific treaty exception for opportunistic purposes, such as profiting from its overbreadth or the uncertainty in its application. Adopting such an approach could, in principle, limit the invocation of Security Exceptions to the measures that pursue objectives different from the ones covered by other treaty exceptions and thus would discourage unnecessary securitization of states' policies in those areas.

6.2.1.2 National Security and Economic Security Under International Investment Law

States are also using the rhetoric of the criticality of certain industries for their national security to justify investment policies aimed at protecting emerging or declining industries and enabling their competitiveness on the international level.[92] In some instances, investment screening measures adopted to this end can violate the protection for foreign investors granted under BITs. Should the host state confronted with such a claim rely on Security Exceptions, the investment tribunal will have to decide whether such a Security Measure falls within the scope of Security Exceptions under the respective agreement. The primary question remains whether the concept of "criticality" covers not only industries essential for the functioning of the state but also the measures contributing to the competition of its economy.

Different from trade agreements, earlier BITs generally did not contain exceptions of the kind prescribed under WTO law.[93] The absence of other treaty exceptions suggests that "essential security interests" in these agreements can more naturally embrace economic dimensions in

[90] J Benton Heath, 'Trade and Security among the Ruins' (2020) 30 Duke J Comparative & Intl Law 223, 253.

[91] See eg *US – Import Prohibition of Certain Shrimp and Shrimp Products* (October 12, 1998) Appellate Body Report WT/DS58/AB/R [24].

[92] Chapter 3.

[93] Lizzie Knight and Tania Voon, 'The Evolution of National Security at the Interface between Domestic and International Investment Law and Policy: The Role of China' (2020) 21(1) J World Investment & Trade 104, 108.

addition to traditional security purposes.[94] To illustrate, US–Argentina BIT (1991) does not contain general exceptions or Security Exceptions of the kind prescribed in Articles XX and XXI GATT (1994).[95] Article XI of US–Argentina BIT (1991) allows contracting parties to adopt "measures necessary for the maintenance of public order, the fulfillment of its obligations with respect to the maintenance or restoration of international peace or security, or the protection of its own essential security interests." This BIT does not contain any reference to other possible exceptions, particularly related to situations of economic crisis. In several cases arising from the claims against Argentina following its response to the economic crisis in 2001–02,[96] Argentina invoked the only treaty-based exception clause under Article XI of US–Argentina BIT (1991).[97] Almost all tribunals examining Argentina's regulatory actions to address the crisis concurred that an economic crisis could impact a state's "essential security interests," even in the absence of a military threat. The CMS tribunal expressly stated that "if the concept of essential security interests were to be limited to immediate political and national security concerns, particularly of an international character, and were to exclude other interests, for example, major economic emergencies, it could well result in an unbalanced understanding of article XI."[98] However, it can be argued that a different conclusion could have been reached had the US–Argentina BIT (1991) incorporated other exceptions, such as ones dealing with the consequences of economic crisis or other economic distress.

Notably, it is not enough to determine that economic crises may constitute a security interest; the former must also be grave enough to trigger the application of the exception.[99] The tribunals handling

[94] William J Moon, 'Essential Security Interests in International Investment Agreements' (2012) 15(2) Intl Econ L 481, 492.

[95] Lizzie Knight and Tania Voon, 'The Evolution of National Security at the Interface between Domestic and International Investment Law and Policy: The Role of China' (2020) 21(1) J World Investment & Trade 104, 109.

[96] See eg *Sempra Energy International v Argentine Republic* (September 18, 2007) ICSID Case No ARB/02/16 Award; or *Enron Corporation v Argentine Republic* (May 22, 2007) ICSID Case No ARB/01/3 Award.

[97] Article XI of US–Argentina BIT (1991).

[98] *CMS Gas Transmission Co v Argentine Republic* (May 12, 2005) ICSID Case No ARB/01/8 Award [360].

[99] Catharine Titi, 'The Right to Regulate in International Investment Law (Revisited)' (2022) International and Comparative Law Research Center 67–68. See also Anne van Aaken and Jurgen Kurtz, 'Prudence or Discrimination? Emergency Measures, the Global Financial Crisis and International Economic Law' (2009) 12 J Int'l Econ L 859, 892.

Argentine economic crisis cases had differing opinions on how severe the crisis needed to be to successfully invoke the Security Exception under US–Argentina BIT (1991). The tribunals in *CMS v Argentina*,[100] *Enron v Argentina*,[101] and *Sempra v Argentina*[102] found that the economic crisis in Argentina was not severe enough to threaten Argentina's essential interests. Specifically, the CMS tribunal mentioned that "the Argentine crisis was severe but did not result in total economic and social collapse."[103] Conversely, the tribunal in *LG&E v Argentina* found that the crisis in Argentina was severe enough to jeopardize Argentina's essential interests: "[a]s evidence demonstrates, economic, financial or those interests related to the protection of the State against any danger seriously compromising its internal or external situation, are also considered essential interests."[104] The *Continental Casualty* tribunal also stated that the invocation of the Security Exception "does not require that the situation has already generated into one that calls for the suspension of constitutional guarantees and fundamental liberties."[105] Regrettably, a degree of ambiguity shrouds the findings of these tribunals, given that some of their deliberations were based on the treaty-based Security Exception, some on the customary defense of necessity, and others, while relying on the treaty-based exception, referred to both.[106] The *LG&E* tribunal, while interpreting Article XI of US–Argentina BIT (1991), does not even clearly distinguish between security and public order exceptions.[107]

In *CC/Devas v India*, India contended that it directed the Indian state-owned company Antrix to end the lease agreement for an S-band electromagnetic spectrum on two satellites with Devas, the claimant in the

[100] *CMS Gas Transmission Co v Argentine Republic* (May 12, 2005) ICSID Case No ARB/01/8 Award [344]–[352].

[101] *Enron Corporation v Argentine Republic* (May 22, 2007) ICSID Case No ARB/01/3 Award [324]–[326].

[102] *Sempra Energy International v Argentine Republic* (September 18, 2007) ICSID Case No ARB/02/16 Award [367].

[103] *CMS Gas Transmission Co v Argentine Republic* (May 12, 2005) ICSID Case No ARB/01/8 Award [355].

[104] *LG&E Energy Corp LG&E Capital Corp and LG&E International, Inc v Argentine Republic* (October 3, 2007) ICSID Case No ARB/02/1 Decision on Liability [251].

[105] *Continental Casualty Co v Argentine Republic* (September 5, 2008) ICSID Case No Arb/03/9 Award [180].

[106] Catharine Titi, 'The Right to Regulate in International Investment Law (Revisited)' (2022) International and Comparative Law Research Center 145–146.

[107] *LG&E Energy Corp LG&E Capital Corp and LG&E International, Inc v Argentine Republic* (October 3, 2007) ICSID Case No ARB/02/1 Decision on Liability [226].

dispute, due to concerns related to its "essential security interests."[108] The tribunal emphasized that national security issues should "relate to the existential core of a State"[109] and that India's actions did not qualify for the Security Exception under the India–Mauritius BIT (1998) because they addressed concerns beyond just military issues.[110] Specifically, according to the tribunal, the inclusion of "other public utility services and for societal needs" and "the country's strategic needs" or "strategic requirements" covers a whole range of government activities (such as economic strategies, public health strategies, and energy strategies) "which went far beyond the military or paramilitary sectors or the 'essential security interests' of [India]."[111] In *Deutsche Telekom v India*, the tribunal also found that no reasonable reading of Security Exceptions under India–Germany BIT (1995) could include other societal needs, including train tracking, disaster management, tele-education, tele-health, and rural communication, as falling within the natural meaning of the term "essential security interests."[112]

Notably, neither India–Mauritius BIT (1998) nor India–Germany BIT (1995) differentiates between general exceptions and Security Exceptions, and they include one provision that, in addition to essential security interests, addresses the exceptions for sanitary and phytosanitary measures – the prevention of diseases in pests and animals or plants.[113] India–Mauritius BIT (1998) also incorporates an exception directed to the protection of public health.[114] Furthermore, both BITs allow for expropriation or nationalization in the public interest/for public purposes, authorized by the laws of the respective party, on a nondiscriminatory basis and against compensation that shall be equivalent to the value of the expropriated or nationalized investment.[115] Thus, given that another exception already covered the situations when the public interest has to be protected for the prohibition of expropriation or nationalization, it seems to be

[108] *CC/Devas (Mauritius) Ltd v Republic of India* (July 25, 2016) PCA Case No 2013-09 Award on Jurisdiction and Merits [5]–[7].

[109] Ibid [245].

[110] Ibid [358].

[111] Ibid [315].

[112] *Deutsche Telekom AG v Republic of India* (December 13, 2017) PCA Case No 2014-10 Interim Award [281].

[113] Article 11 of India–Mauritius BIT (1998) and Article 12 of Germany–India BIT (1995) respectively.

[114] Article 11 of India–Mauritius BIT (1998).

[115] Article 5 of Germany–India BIT (1995) and Article 6 of India–Mauritius BIT (1998) respectively.

logical that the tribunal in *Deutsche Telekom v India* concluded that the "essential security interests" required for a successful invocation of Security Exceptions "must protect something of higher value than any 'public interest.'"[116]

Taking all these into account, although the need to protect strategic industries may reasonably invoke national security concerns, it is clear that they will not always suffice to trigger the application of a relevant Security Exception. The recent move toward the inclusion of separate general and Security Exception clauses modeled on the WTO law in IIAs illustrates the changes in the intended scope of investment protection and the exceptions to it.[117] Thus, unlike the Argentine economic crisis cases and the cases invoking other BITs that incorporate only Security Exceptions, the presence of a general exception clause in the new generation of investment treaties might limit the understanding of "essential security interests" potentially covered by their Security Exceptions.

Unlike previous tribunals that required emergency measures to exceed a certain threshold or involve presumed military objectives, the *Seda* tribunal asserted that a case centered on domestic asset forfeiture proceedings related to organized crime and drug trafficking could be enough for a Security Exception to apply. The tribunal found Colombia's justifications compelling, emphasizing that its efforts "to fight against organized crime, money laundering, and drug trafficking, thus ultimately protecting its population from the threats of paramilitary and marginalized groups that have been ravaging the country for years" were directly tied to public safety, national security, and the country's socioeconomic stability and thus, these interests could be considered "essential security interests."[118] This suggests that different from the WTO-style Security Exceptions, broadly drafted Security Exceptions in investment treaties can more readily apply to local challenges, extending beyond traditional military-related concerns or crises of a certain magnitude (even if the TPA additionally incorporates the WTO-like general exceptions).

[116] *Deutsche Telekom AG v Republic of India* (December 13, 2017) PCA Case No 2014–10 Interim Award [236].

[117] Armand de Mestral and Lukas Vanhonnaeker, 'Exception Clauses in Mega-Regionals (International Investment Protection and Trade Agreements)' in Thilo Rensmann (ed.), *Mega-Regional Trade Agreements* (Springer International Publishing 2017) 83 https://link-springer-com.tilburguniversity.idm.oclc.org/chapter/10.1007/978-3-319-56663-4_5.

[118] *Angel Samuel Seda and others v Republic of Colombia* (June 27, 2024) ICSID Case No ARB/19/6 Award [765].

6.2.1.3 Revisiting "Essential Security Interests"

The case law of the ICJ, WTO panels, and investment tribunals confirms that, whether strictly or loosely drafted, Security Exception clauses can potentially cover threats to a state's national security unconnected to situations of war and armed conflict or national defense capabilities. In light of this, the measures aimed to deal with the consequences of climate change, pandemics, economic crisis, protection of strategic industries, and cybersecurity vulnerabilities might, in principle, be regarded as matters related to the very existence of a nation, which is a matter of national security.[119] Yet, governments and international adjudicators have to be careful with justifying any economic concerns under existing Security Exceptions since it might exempt large portions of national economies from the jurisdiction of trade law, thereby rejecting multilateralism and international commitments in general.[120] On this view, it seems to be reasonable to require the invoking state, which relies on novel security interests (not related to a "traditional" security threat like a war or armed conflict), "to articulate its essential security interests with greater specificity."[121]

In principle, it would be difficult to prove that any state's geo-economic interest or the interest of its industry is "relating to the quintessential functions of the state, namely, the protection of its territory and its population from external threats, and the maintenance of law and public order internally," as defined by the *Russia – Traffic in Transit* panel.[122] Yet, the position of subsequent panels on this issue is unclear. By grounding the qualification of a Security Measure based on domestic law and practice alone, the WTO panels in the *US – Steel and Aluminium Products* disputes seem to take the position that the channeling of trade restrictions to different policy exceptions can be made only by the governments and not by adjudicators. Such an approach can potentially allow adjudicators to reveal the cases of apparent abuse, for example, where a state invoked a Security Exception to justify the measure that has not been qualified on a domestic level as necessary

[119] George-Dian Balan, 'On Fissionable Cows and the Limits to the WTO Security Exceptions' (2019) 14(1) Global Trade and Customs Journal 2, 6.

[120] Rachel Brewster, 'The Struggle for International Economic Law' in Chia-Jui Cheng (ed.), *A New Global Economic Order: New Challenges to International Trade Law* (Brill Nijhoff 2021) 236.

[121] *Russia – Measures Concerning Traffic in Transit* (April 5, 2019) WTO Panel Report WT/DS512/R [7.135].

[122] Ibid [7.130].

to protect national security.[123] Yet, it suggests that any measure portrayed as a Security Measure under domestic law should be regarded as potentially falling under a broadly drafted Security Exception, which might encourage states to push the application and interpretation of their "essential security interests" even further. Furthermore, none of the panels deciding on the scope of Security Exceptions discussed the relationship between Article XXI(b)(iii) and the subparagraphs of Article XX GATT (1994). The panel in *US – Origin Marking (Hong Kong, China)* considered Article XX as a relevant contextual provision for Security Exceptions "insofar as it is, like Article XXI, an exception."[124] However, it did not elaborate on the correlation between the general exceptions and Security Exceptions under WTO law. It can be argued that Article XX GATT (1994) covers nontrade legitimate objectives during peacetime, thereby confirming the distinct purpose the Security Exceptions are supposed to serve – to justify trade restrictions in exceptional situations.[125] Granting the governments full discretion to channel their measures to one of the treaty exceptions disregarding the above considerations might allow states to profit from a more lenient standard of review prescribed for Security Measures and thus lead to further securitization of states' policy objectives.

The problem with "second-guessing" states' security interests by adjudicators becomes even more acute when an invoking state adopts a Security Measure with mixed motives: not only to address a genuine security concern but also to protect the domestic economy or gain the bargain in trade negotiations. To illustrate, domestic industrial policies might be protectionist in nature but be phrased in terms of military procurement or defense readiness, or be aimed to shape a state's cybersecurity or green energy program, or ensure self-sufficiency in medical

[123] This is illustrated in *Devas v India* and *Deutsche Telekom v India*. Having analysed the nature and design of India's measures, the investment tribunals were able to differentiate between military-related concerns plausibly addressing India's national security interests and other public policy concerns, subject to a separate treaty exception. In those cases, however, the invoked Security Exception was not drafted in a self-judging manner. See more chapter 6, section 6.2.1.2.

[124] *US – Origin Marking Requirements* (December 21, 2022) WTO Panel Report WT/DS597/R Section 7.3.4.3.

[125] See more Panos Delimatsis and Olga Hrynkiv, 'Sovereign Investors and National Security Exceptions in WTO and Investment Law' in P Delimatsis, G Dimitropoulos, and A Gourgourinis (eds.), *State Capitalism and International Investment Law* (Hart Publishing 2023) 229.

goods. Such measures, however, do not lose their protectionist character because they also have a security component.[126]

Meyer proposes to approach the review of the measures with potentially mixed motives by establishing whether they are "predominantly" related to a state's security interest.[127] Such a predominant objective test reminds one of the components of the test developed in the WTO jurisprudence regarding the "relating to" component of Article XX (g) GATT (1994), which requires a panel or the Appellate Body to examine whether the chosen measure was "primarily aimed at" the declared policy goal.[128]

The ECJ expressly notes that the fact that the measures can achieve, in addition to the public security objectives, other objectives of an economic nature does not per se exclude the application of a public security exception under the EU law.[129] On other occasions unrelated to the review of Security Measures, the ECJ employs the "center of gravity" approach to establish the predominant object and purpose of the measure to determine its legal basis.[130] According to the CJEU case law, the main objective of the measure can be identified, with all the others being incidental, by examining the aim and the content of the measure based on the "objective factors which are amenable to judicial review."[131] More specifically, the ECJ can determine the aim of the measure through textual examination of its wording and the content of the measure by examining its effect on the aim.[132]

Adopting a "predominant motive" test for reviewing Security Exceptions or drawing upon the existing tests in the EU case law and WTO case law on general exceptions raises some analytical and factual hurdles. For one, it remains unclear how a "predominant motive" test would apply to the review of Security Measures where states might rely on the nondisclosure exception during litigation to withhold information necessary to analyze the true objective of their Security

[126] David D Knoll, 'The Impact of Security Concerns upon International Economic Law' (1984) 11(3) Intl Econ L 567, 573.

[127] Timothy Meyer, 'The Political Economy of WTO Exceptions' (2022) 99 Washington U L Rev 1299, 1325.

[128] *US – Standards for Reformulated and Conventional Gasoline* (April 29, 1996) Appellate Body Report WT/DS2/AB/R 14–19.

[129] Case C-72/83 *Campus Oil Limited and others v Minister for Industry and Energy and others* [1984] EU:C:1984:256 [36].

[130] Bart Van Vooren and Ramses A Wessel, *EU External Relations Law* (CUP 2017) 159–160; 179; see also Case C-155/07 *Parliament v Council* (EIB Guarantees) [2008] EU:C:2008:605 [34]–[35].

[131] Case C-176/03 *Commission v Council* [2005] EU:C:2005:542 [45].

[132] Bart Van Vooren and Ramses A Wessel, *EU External Relations Law* (CUP 2017) 160–178.

Measures.[133] Also, given the level of securitization of different policy objectives of the US, the EU, and BRICS and pro-security bias, it might almost always be possible for the adjudicators to find that the measure was predominantly aimed at protecting the state's security interests.

As mentioned before, the regional incentives to include specific exceptions addressing states' emerging concerns, such as cybersecurity, or clarify the scope of existing general exceptions, such as those related to environmental protection, already exist.[134] While not excluding all the risks of opportunism, granting contracting parties a possibility to address their policy concerns by relying on the treaty exceptions drafted explicitly for this purpose might discourage them from pushing the boundaries of loosely drafted Security Exceptions. Such an approach could be further reinforced by international adjudicators who can qualify a measure under international law based on the structural and contextual reading of relevant exceptions rather than completely deferring to the characterization of such a measure under domestic law.

Ultimately, until these issues are clarified by WTO members collectively, or until international adjudicators adopt a consistent approach to the relationship between Security Exceptions and other treaty exceptions in their decisions (preferably by the Appellate Body), future WTO panels and trade and investment tribunals dealing with the potential overlap between Security Exceptions and other treaty exceptions or the measures with mixed motives might continue to admit that the measures qualified as Security Measures under domestic law or the measures with mixed motives can potentially constitute states' "essential security interests." Yet, they might attempt to eliminate potential abuse of such a broad concept by relying on other safeguards for the invocation of Security Exceptions, as further discussed in the following sections.

6.2.2 *Emergency in International Relations*

Not all Security Exceptions further limit the scope of their application, applying only to certain goods or situations.[135] Certain Regional

133 See eg *US – Origin Marking Requirements* (July 2, 2021) First Written Submission of the US in DS597 [50] https://ustr.gov/sites/default/files/enforcement/DS/DS597/US.Sub1.fin.pdf.

134 See eg Article 25.1(2) and (3) of EU–New Zealand FTA (2022); Chapter 12 of RCEP (2020).

135 Dominik Eisenhut, 'Sovereignty, National Security and International Treaty Law the Standard of Review of International Courts and Tribunals with regard to "Security Exceptions"' (2010) 48(4) Archiv des V 431, 433.

Agreements allow for the measures that are necessary or that a party considers necessary for the protection of its essential security interests without prescribing additional preconditions.[136] The primary safeguards for a good faith invocation of such exceptions would thus be only the existence of a threat to an essential security interest of a state.[137] However, Article XXI(b) GATT (1994) and other WTO-style Security Exceptions prescribe additional preconditions for the recourse to security defense. Thus, even if a state may attempt to argue that the protection of its economy, of the rights and liberties of its citizens while processing their personal data, or mitigations of the potential consequences of future pandemics and climate change are part of the quintessential functions of the state, as it is seeking the maintenance of law and public order internally, the measures adopted to this end need also to fall under one of the subparagraphs of Article XXI(b) GATT (1994), such as to be undertaken "in time of war or other emergency in international relations."

In particular, to fall under the exception allowing for the measures taken "in time of . . . other emergency in international relations," the following criteria have to be met. To begin with, the term "emergency" excludes ordinary strained relations between states from its scope. The panel in *US – Steel and Aluminium Products (China)* referred to the dictionary definitions of the term "emergency" that includes "'[a] situation, esp. of danger or conflict, that arises unexpectedly and requires urgent attention,' 'a condition requiring immediate treatment,' or a 'pressing need.'"[138] Thus, a preliminary interpretation reveals that "emergency" encompasses some extreme conflict between states, for example, involving the use of force.[139] Read more liberally, the text of Article XXI(b)(iii) might reserve another option: the term "emergency" could have a meaning catching those hostilities that go beyond the situations comparable to wars, making any malfunction or problem in international relations a reason to escape GATT obligations.[140] Such a reading suggests that "emergency" might cover other situations not

136 Chapter 4.

137 Chapter 6, section 6.2.1.

138 *US – Certain Measures on Steel and Aluminium Products (China)* (December 9, 2022) WTO Panel Report WT/DS544/R [7.137].

139 *Russia – Measures Concerning Traffic in Transit* (April 5, 2019) WTO Panel Report WT/DS512/R [7.74].

140 Michael J Hahn, 'Vital Interests and the Law of GATT: An Analysis of GATT's Security Exception' (1991) 12 Mich J Intl L 558, 588.

necessarily involving the use of force.[141] The panel in *US – Origin Marking (Hong Kong, China)* expressly stated that each situation of emergency needs "to be considered on its individual merits," and it must not necessarily involve a state's defense and military interests.[142]

Yet, the existence of an emergency itself is not sufficient.[143] It should be an emergency "in international relations." The term "international relations" was interpreted by the panel in *Russia – Traffic in Transit* as "world politics" and "global political interaction, primarily among sovereign states."[144] Thus, the emergency in "international relations" cannot be purely domestic but should involve an international dimension, such as a conflict between two or more countries.[145] Finally, to be justified under WTO-style Security Exceptions, the measures must be taken "in time of" emergency in international relations. Each of these preconditions is further analyzed in detail.

6.2.2.1 Beyond War and Armed Conflict

The negotiation history of the ITO Charter and the GATT (1947) sheds some light on drafters' understanding of the scope of "emergency in international relations." In response to a question from the delegate for the Netherlands as to the meaning of the term "emergency in international relations," the delegate for the US gave the example of the situation of war affecting the activities of the invoking party even though this party does not directly participate in the war at the time of the adoption of the measures.[146] Thus, in principle, the unilateral economic sanctions imposed outside the UN by a country that does not participate

[141] Ibid 589.

[142] *US – Origin Marking Requirements* (December 21, 2022) WTO Panel Report WT/DS597/R [7.301].

[143] Olga Hrynkiv and Saskia Lavrijssen, 'Not Trading with the Enemy: the Case of Computer Chips' (2024) 58(1) JWT 61, 77–79.

[144] *Russia – Measures Concerning Traffic in Transit* (April 5, 2019) WTO Panel Report WT/DS512/R [7.73].

[145] *US – Certain Measures on Steel and Aluminium Products (China)* (December 9, 2022) WTO Panel Report WT/DS544/R [7.137]. See also George-Dian Balan, 'On Fissionable Cows and the Limits to the WTO Security Exceptions' (2019) 14(1) Global Trade and Customs Journal 2, 8.

[146] UN – Economic and Social Council, Preparatory Committee of the UN Conference on Trade and Employment – Second Session of the Preparatory Committee of the UN Conference on Trade and Employment – [Commission A] – Verbatim Report – Thirty-Third Meeting of Commission Held on Thursday, July 24, 1947, at 2.30 pm in the Palais des Nations, Geneva (July 24, 1947) E/PC/T/A/PV/33 20 https://docs.wto.org/gattdocs/q/UN/EPCT/W236.PDF.

in the ongoing war can be qualified as taken during the "emergency in international relations."

In *Russia – Traffic in Transit*, the panel asserts that: "[a]n emergency in international relations would . . . appear to refer generally to (1) a situation of armed conflict, or (2) of latent armed conflict, or (3) of heightened tension or crisis, or (4) of general instability engulfing or surrounding a state."[147] Subsequent panels in the *US – Steel and Aluminium Products* disputes reiterate that an "emergency in international relations" in subparagraph (iii) refers to "circumstances of a certain gravity or severity in terms of their impact on the conduct of international relations, as part of the balance of rights and obligations reflected in the ordinary meaning of the terms of Article XXI(b), interpreted in their context and in light of the object and purpose of the GATT 1994 and WTO Agreement."[148] Such situations give rise to particular types of interests for the WTO member in question, that is, "defence or military interests, or maintenance of law and public order interests."[149] A war is one example of the larger category of emergency in international relations.[150] The panel in *US – Steel and Aluminium Products (China)* explains that "the reference to 'war' informs the meaning of 'emergency in international relations' as part of the circumstances 'in time of' which a Member may act under Article XXI(b) for the protection of its essential security interests," which, according to the panel, is also supported by the French and Spanish language versions of Article XXI(b)(iii) GATT (1994).[151]

Based on the ordinary meaning of its terms and the contextual role of the concept "war" under Article XXI(b)(iii), the panel in *US – Origin Marking (Hong Kong, China)* provided a slightly different definition of an "emergency in international relations" to refer "to a state of affairs that occurs in relations between states or participants in international

[147] *Russia – Measures Concerning Traffic in Transit* (April 5, 2019) WTO Panel Report WT/DS512/R [7.76].

[148] *US – Certain Measures on Steel and Aluminium Products (China)* (December 9, 2022) WTO Panel Report WT/DS544/R [7.141]; *US – Certain Measures on Steel and Aluminium Products (Norway)* (December 9, 2022) WTO Panel Report WT/DS552/R [7.129]; *US – Certain Measures on Steel and Aluminium Products (Switzerland)* (December 9, 2022) WTO Panel Report WT/DS556/R [7.159]; *US – Certain Measures on Steel and Aluminium Products (Turkey)* (December 9, 2022) WTO Panel Report WT/DS564/R [7.156].

[149] *Russia – Measures Concerning Traffic in Transit* (April 5, 2019) WTO Panel Report WT/DS512/R [7.74].

[150] Ibid [7.72].

[151] *US – Certain Measures on Steel and Aluminium Products (China)* (December 9, 2022) WTO Panel Report WT/DS544/R [7.139].

relations that is of the utmost gravity, in effect, a situation representing a breakdown or near-breakdown in those relations."[152] The panel relied on the "spectrum covering friendly and peaceful interaction between Members, at one end, and the breakdown of relations between two or more countries, or Members, at the other end" and uses the analogy of a thermometer to illustrate how this spectrum works.[153] Accordingly, even such subjective human experiences, such as whether it is warm or cold, can be measured based on certain parameters with the help of a thermometer.[154] By the same token, an emergency in international relations is subject to certain parameters and should be situated at the spectrum closer to the extreme of a breakdown in relations rather than friendly and peaceful interaction between WTO members.[155] Such an approach arguably leads to a more narrow interpretation of the scope of Article XXI(b)(iii) compared to the approach adopted by the previous panels in *Russia – Traffic in Transit* and *Saudi Arabia – IPRs* and leaves no room for the appreciation of the situation by an invoking member.

All panels that have interpreted the scope of Article XXI(b)(iii) to date have decided that the subparagraphs of Article XXI(b) GATT (1994) should be subject to a full, objective judicial review based on the factual foundation rather than the subjective assessments of an invoking state.[156] This suggests that if a state invokes any subparagraph of Article XXI(b), the panel should attempt to obtain a suitable factual basis from the invoking party or via other sources.[157]

The panel in *Russia – Traffic in Transit* had no difficulties finding that "the annexation of the Autonomous Republic of Crimea and the military conflict in the east" of Ukraine constituted an "emergency in international relations" in the sense of Article XXI(b)(iii).[158] Russia did not provide substantial evidence of the "emergency in international relations." Nevertheless, the panel drew enough evidence from the facts submitted

152 *US – Origin Marking Requirements* (December 21, 2022) WTO Panel Report WT/DS597/R [7.290], [7.296].

153 Ibid [7.310].

154 Ibid.

155 Ibid [7.311].

156 See eg *Russia – Measures Concerning Traffic in Transit* (April 5, 2019) WTO Panel Report WT/DS512/R [7.101]; *US – Certain Measures on Steel and Aluminium Products (China)* (December 9, 2022) WTO Panel Report WT/DS544/R [7.136].

157 Michael J Hahn, 'Vital Interests and the Law of GATT: An Analysis of GATT's Security Exception' (1991) 12 Mich J Intl L 558, 616.

158 *Russia – Measures Concerning Traffic in Transit* (April 5, 2019) WTO Panel Report WT/DS512/R [7.115].

to it by both parties and from common knowledge. The panel relied on Ukraine's Trade Policy Review (TPR) report to identify further the factual situation, so long as it was not using them to determine legal liability.[159] Furthermore, the panel relied on the 2016 Resolution of the UN General Assembly, which described the situation between Ukraine and Russia as armed conflict, and on the fact that several countries had imposed economic sanctions against Russia in connection with the conflict.[160] The panel's conclusion followed that, at least as of March 2014, the relations between Ukraine and Russia had worsened to the extent that it had become a significant issue for the international community.[161] It can be argued that such a low threshold for the standard of proof required by the panel in this dispute practically empowers an invoking member to escape its obligation to provide evidence. For example, Ukraine expressed disappointment at the final DSB meeting that "the panel improperly bore the burden of proof and made a case for the respondent."[162]

The panel in *Saudi Arabia – IPRs* did not reflect on whether the *Russia – Traffic in Transit* panel made its findings with an "insufficient basis" of factual evidence.[163] In *Saudi Arabia – IPRs*, the panel also agreed with Saudi Arabia that one member's severance of "all diplomatic and economic ties" with another member could be regarded as "the ultimate State expression of the existence of an emergency in international relations."[164] It cited Article 41 of the UN Charter in this regard.[165] Referring to several third-party submissions, the panel concluded that "'a situation . . . of heightened tension or crisis' exists in the circumstances in this dispute, and is related to Saudi Arabia's 'defence or military interests, or maintenance of law and public order interests' (i.e. essential security interests), sufficient to establish the existence of an 'emergency in international relations' that has persisted since at least June 5, 2017."[166] In the panel's view, when states repeatedly accuse one another of supporting terrorism and extremism, that in

[159] Ibid [7.118].
[160] Ibid [7.122].
[161] Ibid.
[162] WTO, 'DS512: Russia – Measures Concerning Traffic in Transit' (WTO News Item, April 26, 2019) www.wto.org/english/news_e/news19_e/dsb_26apr19_e.htm.
[163] Pramila Crivelli and Mona Paulsen, 'Separating the Political from the Economic: The Russia – Traffic in Transit Panel Report' (2021) 20(4) World Trade Rev 582, 590.
[164] *Saudi Arabia – Measures Concerning the Protection of Intellectual Property Rights* (June 16, 2020) WTO Panel Report WT/DS567/R [7.259].
[165] Ibid [7.261].
[166] Ibid [7.269].

and of itself reflects and contributes to a "situation . . . of heightened tension or crisis."[167]

Subsequent panels in the *US – Steel and Aluminium Products* dispute found that the evidence and arguments submitted by the US were not enough to establish the existence of an "emergency in international relations" within the meaning of Article XXI(b)(iii), "particularly regarding the impact on international relations of situations falling under that provision."[168] To illustrate, in *US – Steel and Aluminium Products (China)*, the US initially maintained its interpretive view that it was not required to identify the relevant subparagraph under Article XXI(b) GATT (1994) that it considered most relevant.[169] Yet, subsequently, it elaborated its arguments based on its interpretation of an "other emergency in international relations" and relied on the extensive findings in its steel and aluminum reports which were "relating to the threatened impairment of national security by steel and aluminum imports, and the global crisis circumstances under which such importations were occurring."[170]

The panel in *US – Steel and Aluminium Products (China)* highlighted that the domestic reports provided by the US identify three factors as the basis for finding a threat to the US national security, including (i) "displacement of domestic steel/aluminium by excessive imports;" (ii) "the consequent adverse impact on the economic welfare of the domestic steel/aluminium industry;" and (iii) "the global excess capacity in steel and aluminium."[171] While the US referred to such factors "cumulatively," based on an objective ascertainment of relevant evidence and arguments, the panel noted that "the first two factors focus predominantly on developments relating to the domestic situation of steel and aluminium industries in the United States."[172] In view of this, the panel

[167] Ibid [7.263].

[168] *US – Certain Measures on Steel and Aluminium Products (China)* (December 9, 2022) WTO Panel Report WT/DS544/R [7.148]; *US – Certain Measures on Steel and Aluminium Products (Norway)* (December 9, 2022) WTO Panel Report WT/DS552/R [7.136]; *US – Certain Measures on Steel and Aluminium Products (Switzerland)* (December 9, 2022) WTO Panel Report WT/DS556/R [7.166]; *US – Certain Measures on Steel and Aluminium Products (Turkey)* (December 9, 2022) WTO Panel Report WT/DS564/R [7.163].

[169] *US – Certain Measures on Steel and Aluminium Products (China)* (December 9, 2022) WTO Panel Report WT/DS544/R [7.132]–[7.133].

[170] Ibid [7.132].

[171] Ibid [7.142].

[172] Ibid.

considered that only the third factor "reflects international concern expressed in the context of cooperative efforts to address excess capacity in a specific sector" and thus has a connection with the existence of an "emergency in international relations" under Article XXI(b)(iii).[173] The panel found that the relevant evidence and arguments submitted by the US in relation to global excess capacity did not establish that the situation in which the US had decided to adopt its Security Measures "rises to the gravity or severity of tensions on the international plane so as to constitute an 'emergency in international relations.'"[174] The identical finding was made by the panels in other cases regarding the *US – Steel and Aluminium Products* disputes.[175]

In a different dispute against the US, the panel in *US – Origin Marking (Hong Kong, China)* examined the US domestic instruments, the statements by other governments, and press reports to conclude that even though such evidence confirmed that the US and some other countries "expressed high levels of concern about the events in Hong Kong, China, especially on how such events affect the human rights of its residents and its democratic system, and adopted certain measures in response," such the situation did not meet the level of gravity required from an "emergency in international relations."[176] Notably, while the panels in the *US – Steel and Aluminium Products* dispute did not refer to the findings of previous panels on Security Exceptions, the panel in *US – Origin Marking (Hong Kong, China)* compared the situation portrayed by the US as an "emergency in international relations" in this case with the previous cases where the situations were found to constitute an emergency in international relations under Article XXI(b)(iii) GATT (1994).[177] Specifically, the panel highlighted that different from the situation with Hong Kong, China, the dispute in *Russia – Traffic in Transit* involved a significant breakdown in relations between the two disputing members, which was confirmed in a resolution of the UN General Assembly as related to

[173] Ibid [7.143], [7.148].

[174] Ibid [7.148].

[175] *US – Certain Measures on Steel and Aluminium Products (Norway)* (December 9, 2022) WTO Panel Report WT/DS552/R [7.136]; *US – Certain Measures on Steel and Aluminium Products (Switzerland)* (December 9, 2022) WTO Panel Report WT/DS556/R [7.166]; *US – Certain Measures on Steel and Aluminium Products (Turkey)* (December 9, 2022) WTO Panel Report WT/DS564/R [7.163].

[176] *US – Origin Marking Requirements* (December 21, 2022) WTO Panel Report WT/DS597/R [7.354].

[177] Ibid [7.355].

armed conflict.[178] In a similar vein, the US did not sever all "diplomatic, consular, or economic relations with China or Hong Kong, China," as was the case between the disputing parties in *Saudi Arabia – IPRs.*[179] In the panel's view, the lack of such considerations in the dispute between the US and Hong Kong, China was enough to conclude that the situation in Hong Kong, China, "has not escalated to a threshold of requisite gravity to constitute an emergency in international relations."[180]

Notably, in all cases where the panels found that there was no emergency in international relations to justify the invocation of Article XXI(b)(iii) GATT (1994), the US took the position that since WTO-style Security Exceptions, in its view, are totally self-judging, it should not provide a panel with specific evidence demonstrating the existence of such an emergency and its gravity. It cannot be excluded that if the US had changed its strategy and better substantiated its arguments on this matter, panels would have come to a different conclusion. Even in this case, however, the US would additionally have to prove that its measures were taken "in time" of such an emergency and satisfy the other prerequisites for the successful invocation of Article XXI(b).

6.2.2.2 "In Time of"

A WTO-style Security Exception, as prescribed in Article XXI(b)(iii), only applies to Security Measures "taken in time of" war or emergency in international relations, thereby referring to a specific period of time. In assessing whether the challenged measures were "taken in time of war or other emergency in international relations" within the meaning of Article XXI(b)(iii), the panel in *Russia – Traffic in Transit* explained that the phrase "taken in time of" refers to the temporal connection between the measure and war or other emergency in international relations in that subparagraph.[181] The panel in *US – Steel and Aluminium Products (China)* also considers that "in time of" requires a temporal coincidence between the action taken and a given situation.[182] At the same time, while

178 Ibid [7.356].
179 Ibid [7.357].
180 Ibid [7.358].
181 *Russia – Measures Concerning Traffic in Transit* (April 5, 2019) WTO Panel Report WT/DS512/R [7.70].
182 *US – Certain Measures on Steel and Aluminium Products (China)* (December 9, 2022) WTO Panel Report WT/DS544/R [7.140].

focusing the analysis of subparagraph iii of Article XXI(b) on the existence of the breakdown in the relations between the parties, the panel in *US – Origin Marking (Hong Kong, China)* did not address the durability or longevity of such breakdown.[183]

While discussing the measures "in the event of war" under the EU law in the *Sirdar* case, Advocate General La Pergola pointed out that such measures do not cover the actions undertaken in the preparation and organization of the armed forces, in other words, in a situation of normality, even if they are inspired by the preoccupation to ensure combat effectiveness.[184] In its submission as a third party in *Russia – Traffic in Transit*, the EU argued that without establishing specific time limits for "war" or "emergency in international relations," there could be continuous disruptions to WTO nondiscrimination rules.[185] Instead, the interpretation of the measures taken "in time of" war or emergency implies an expectation that the time of war or emergency eventually ends.[186]

Restraining the possibility of relying on Security Exceptions only for the duration of the emergency can be deemed necessary to prevent the justification of a measure retroactively based on a past emergency in international relations but also proactively based on a potential emergency. Thus, such a temporal requirement also significantly limits the scope of Article XXI(b)(iii) GATT (1994) by excluding the justification of any measures adopted to address future emergencies.

6.2.2.3 Revisiting "Emergency in International Relations"

In *Russia – Traffic in Transit* and *Saudi Arabia – IPRs*, the WTO panels interpreting whether the measures in question were taken "in time of emergency in international relations" left many questions open in part because of the lack of authority to deal with the questions related to the use of force under international law, and the unwillingness to discuss the sensitive issues related to a state's sovereignty and armed conflict, and in

[183] See more Mona Paulsen, 'The Beginning, End, and Imminence of Invoking Essential Security at the WTO' (*IELP Blog*, January 6, 2023) https://ielp.worldtradelaw.net/2023/01/if-i-were-an-appellate-body-post-1.html.

[184] Case C-273/97 *Angela Maria Sirdar v The Army Board and Secretary of State for Defence*, Opinion of Mr Advocate General La Pergola (May 18, 1999) EU:C:1999:246 [20].

[185] *Russia – Measures Concerning Traffic in Transit* Annex D-5 to WTO Panel Report WT/DS512/R/Add.1 [18].

[186] Mona Paulsen, 'If I were an Appellate Body. Post 1' (*IELP Blog*, July 24, 2021) https://ielp.worldtradelaw.net/2021/07/the-beginning-end-and-imminence-of-invoking-essential-security-at-the-wto.html.

another part because of the circumstances of having to decide on the measures adopted during the armed conflict and heightened tension that was taking place between the parties to the disputes. As will be further discussed, the minimal legal and factual evidence required by the panels from respondents in these cases to properly articulate the emergency seems to be tethered to the panels' overarching finding that the disputes touched the "hard core" of war or armed conflict, which was also recognized at the UN level.

In the *US – Steel and Aluminium Products* disputes and in *US – Origin Marking (Hong Kong, China)*, the WTO panels examined the existence of an emergency in international relations more closely, not least because the situation invoked by the US as an "emergency" was not related to an armed conflict between the parties or the crisis of the international gravity. Notably, these cases confirm that a state's qualification of the gravity or severity of the situation in which it adopted Security Measures is not enough to demonstrate the international character of the claimed emergency, which significantly limits the scope of WTO-style Security Exceptions and might have implications for the future disputes, where states attempt to portray a threat to their national security based solely on domestic law and domestic perspective.

It remains uncertain whether investment tribunals dealing with the WTO-style Security Exceptions under investment treaties in the future would adopt a similar interpretation of the term "emergency in international relations" and use a similar evidential basis as WTO panels. There is no reason to believe that investment tribunals are prevented from relying on UN General Assembly resolutions on a case-by-case basis where the merits of the dispute require it. Similar to the trade regime, most difficulties would arise when a tribunal decides on a matter that the international community has not addressed at the international level.

The question remains to what extent adjudicators in future disputes would be flexible in interpreting WTO-style Security Exceptions to cover situations that go beyond severance of "all diplomatic and economic ties" amounting to armed conflicts to include severance of diplomatic and economic ties for other reasons, such as strategic competition (e.g. the US–China conflict) or the response to cyber attacks, the consequences of economic crisis, pandemics, or climate change. Notably, the panel in *Russia – Traffic in Transit* observed that merely political or economic differences between members do not suffice to be an emergency in international relations.[187] The panel in *US – Origin Marking (Hong Kong, China)* also confirmed that "most political tensions and differences among countries, even those that may appear to be of a quite serious nature," would typically be situated close enough to the end of the spectrum encompassing friendly and peaceful interaction between states rather the other end covering the breakdown of relations between two or more countries.[188]

Furthermore, an "emergency in international relations" under Article XXI(b)(iii) refers "to situations of a certain gravity or severity and international tensions that are of a critical or serious nature in terms of their impact on the conduct of international relations."[189] Thus, even assuming that the economic crisis can, in principle, constitute an emergency in the sense of Article XXI(b)(iii), it appears that it would need to be severe enough, not least because the emergency under the Security Exception clause is mentioned alongside "war," which sets the benchmark of a supposed disturbance at a relatively high level, but also because it needs to be recognized on the international level and to involve and/or affect multiple states before it could be considered an emergency "in international relations."[190] By the same token, for cyberattacks and the consequences of pandemics or climate change to qualify under Article XXI(b)(iii), the "international" dimension of the emergency must also be demonstrated. Thus, commercial or economic threats between two states, including systematic theft of trade secrets of digital companies, or cyber threats to individual privacy, are unlikely to give rise to an emergency in international relations.[191]

Finally, the Security Exception under Article XXI(b)(iii) is limited to the measures that respond to a current crisis rather than measures adopted to prevent a future crisis or deal with an imminent or permanent threat.[192] Such a requirement can significantly limit the scope of WTO-style Security Exceptions. For example, cyber-related emergencies are not always temporary/time-bound, given that they can originate anywhere, at any time,

[187] *Russia – Measures Concerning Traffic in Transit* (April 5, 2019) WTO Panel Report WT/DS512/R [7.75].

[188] *US – Origin Marking Requirements* (December 21, 2022) WTO Panel Report WT/DS597/R [7.311].

[189] *US – Certain Measures on Steel and Aluminium Products (China)* (December 9, 2022) WTO Panel Report WT/DS544/R [7.147].

[190] Sergey Ripinsky, 'Global Economic Crisis and the Danger of Protectionism: Does International Law Help?' (2009) 1(3) Amsterdam LF 3, 7.

[191] Neha Mishra, 'The Trade: (Cyber)Security Dilemma and Its Impact on Global Cybersecurity Governance' (2020) 54(4) JWT 567, 582.

[192] Timothy Meyer, 'Trade Law and Supply Chain Regulation in a Post-Covid-19 World' (2020) 114(4) Am J Intl L 637, 645.

and cause instantaneous damage.[193] The same applies to the measures aimed at preventing potential consequences of climate change and new pandemics. It remains contentious whether WTO-style Security Exceptions can be read as available to WTO members that decide to impose Security Measures as long as they perceive a risk of a future cyber war or a highly sophisticated cyber attack, or an existential danger of climate change or a highly infectious disease. Based on the existing approach to drafting WTO-style Security Exceptions, allowing for such a broad defense covering all cybersecurity, environmental or health-related measures necessary to avert imminent threats appears counterproductive, given that it can easily be misused and result in the systematic overreliance on the exceptions, thereby excluding a significant portion of transactions from the international trading regime. Nonetheless, ignoring the pitfalls of future threats from cyber weapons and catastrophic events sets an equally dangerous precedent for the international trade community.[194]

Assessing in each case whether imminent threats can result in a state of emergency in international relations is difficult in practice.[195] Where cyber threats are imminent in nature, the adjudicator could require substantial evidence to conclude that the said threats are likely to result in a war or emergency in international relations in the future. By the same token, facts and empirical evidence clearly demonstrating the imminent threats posed by climate change or future pandemics might be necessary to prevent possible abuse and disguised protectionism while adopting national "green policies" and mitigation measures to protect the health of the population from new diseases and their consequences.[196] In some cases, respondents might lawfully refuse to provide such information and evidence relying on Article XXI(a) GATT (1994) or similarly drafted provisions,[197] which makes the imminent threats extremely difficult to assess and thus to fit into the scope of existing WTO-like Security Exceptions. The same logic applies to the measures aimed at protecting

193 Neha Mishra, 'The Trade: (Cyber)Security Dilemma and Its Impact on Global Cybersecurity Governance' (2020) 54(4) JWT 567, 584.

194 Ibid.

195 Ibid 582–584.

196 Pramila Crivelli and Mona Paulsen, 'Separating the Political from the Economic: The Russia – Traffic in Transit Panel Report' (2021) 20(4) World Trade Rev 582, 602. See more Daniel Kang Wei-En, 'Adapting GATT Article XXI(B)(III) to Climate Change Threats: An Overdue Rethinking of Security Blues for an Urgent Green Way Forward?' (2020) 27 Austl Intl LJ 103.

197 See more chapter 5, section 5.2.4.

critical domestic infrastructure to prevent a future emergency rather than to deal with the consequences of an existing emergency.

Ultimately, a broader reading of Security Exceptions that do not limit Security Measures to wartime or another time of emergency encompasses the positive duty of states to preserve the life, health, and general well-being of their citizens, for example, by addressing imminent cyber threats or threats to state's critical infrastructure, as well as threats posed by climate change and future pandemics. Yet, the approach to drafting WTO-style Security Exceptions and their interpretation by WTO panels suggest that Article XXI(b) do not readily cover the measures adopted to deal with such emerging national security issues, particularly when they are related to future emergencies rather than current ones or domestic emergencies rather than emergencies in international relations. Where WTO members want to ensure that they can rely on WTO-style Security Exceptions to justify their response to insidious, nonimmediate, yet severe national security concerns, they might consider changing their course in drafting such exceptions.

6.3 Secondary Safeguards for Security Measures

Once it has been determined that a Security Measure passes the primary safeguards discussed above and falls under the Security Exception clause as such, the question then is whether it can meet the requirements of the secondary safeguards. In particular, secondary safeguards deal with the nexus requirement between the measure and the protection of a state's essential security interest. Exception clauses differ in the requirement as to the nexus between a measure and its objective, including "necessary to" achieve the objective and "appropriate to," "related to," "directed to," or "for" that objective. The UN Conference on Trade and Development (UNCTAD) study identifies four basic approaches to such a nexus requirement in Security Exceptions under international investment agreements: (1) necessity as an objective precondition; (2) no reference to necessity; (3) self-judging clauses; and (4) exclusion of judicial review.[198] The same classification applies to Regional Agreements.[199]

[198] *CC/Devas (Mauritius) Ltd v Republic of India* (July 25, 2016) PCA Case No 2013–09 Award on Jurisdiction and Merits [239] referring to UNCTAD, 'The Protection of National Security in IIAs' (2009) UNCTAD Series on International Investment Policies for Development 91–96 https://unctad.org/webflyer/protection-national-security-iias.

[199] Chapter 4, sections 4.1 and 4.2.

This section focuses on the standard of review and thus discusses only the three first approaches highlighted in the study, applicable to both IIAs and RTAs.

The first approach, using necessity as an objective precondition, considerably reduces the regulatory discretion of WTO members.[200] It is found in some IIAs and less often in RTAs. To assess the necessity of the measures for safeguarding the state's essential security interests, adjudicators could determine "whether the measure was principally targeted to protect the essential security interests at stake and was objectively required to achieve that protection," considering the possibility of adopting reasonable alternatives, less in conflict or more compliant with its international obligations.[201] Such an approach could be compatible with the necessity test under Article XX GATT (1994) and other similarly drafted provisions.

The second approach is to omit the requirement of necessity and to consider it sufficient that the taken measure has another connection (instead of being "necessary") or is otherwise relevant to the protection of national security interests. It can be found in some IIAs. For example, Article 11(3) of the India–Mauritius BIT (1998) allows for any action "which is directed to the protection of [a party's] essential security interests." This approach grants more regulatory freedom to contracting parties to decide on the type of measure they consider appropriate, given that it is directed toward protecting national security.[202] It does not require the measure to be objectively necessary. Still, it allows the adjudicators to verify whether there is a definite nexus between the Security Measure and the protection of a state's essential security interest.

The third approach is to leave it entirely to the discretion of a WTO member to decide on the type of measure it considers necessary to respond to a security threat. For example, in *Russia – Traffic in Transit*, the panel concluded that it was for Russia to determine the "necessity" of the measures to protect its essential security interests. This conclusion is inevitable if the clause "which it considers" under Article XXI GATT

[200] UNCTAD, 'The Protection of National Security in IIAs' (2009) UNCTAD Series on International Investment Policies for Development 93 https://unctad.org/webflyer/protection-national-security-iias.

[201] Mantilla Blanco Sebastián and Alexander Pehl, *National Security Exceptions in International Trade and Investment Agreements: Justiciability and Standards of Review* (Springer 2020) 60.

[202] UNCTAD, 'The Protection of National Security in IIAs' (2009) UNCTAD Series on International Investment Policies for Development 94 https://unctad.org/webflyer/protection-national-security-iias.

(1994) is to be given legal effect.[203] However, in addition to the necessity nexus, the panels in *Russia – Traffic in Transit* and *Saudi Arabia – IPRs* concluded from the WTO-style Security Exceptions that the challenged measures have to be adopted "for" the protection of the claimed essential security interests of an invoking state. In the panels' view, this nexus is not completely self-judging in the sense that it is subject to a good faith review. Apart from WTO agreements, this approach to drafting Security Exceptions has been used in many recent RTAs modeling their exception clauses on the WTO law, as well as some IIAs that prefer to keep the scope of exceptions broad.[204] This section will further discuss each of these types in turn.

6.3.1 *Necessity of Security Measures*

Security Exceptions under Regional Agreements using the necessity nexus as an objective precondition for their invocation generally remain silent as to how to determine that the measure adopted by the state to achieve a security-related objective is "necessary." Thus, states delegate this task to adjudicators. Courts and tribunals have developed different criteria to determine whether a measure at issue is necessary. In contrast to the relatively fragmented practice in investment arbitration, WTO adjudicators have developed a relatively sophisticated jurisprudence regarding the interpretation of the concept of necessity related to general exceptions under WTO agreements,[205] as further discussed.

6.3.1.1 Necessity Test Under WTO Law

Unlike WTO-style Security Exceptions allowing a state to adopt the measure "it considers necessary," Article XX(a), (b), and (d) GATT (1994) refers to the necessity as an objective precondition for the invocation of the exceptions. The Appellate Body interpreted for the first time the word "necessary" in Article XX(d) GATT (1994) in *Korea – Various Measures on Beef*, suggesting a cost-benefit balancing test (or a sort of proportionality test)[206] that weighs and balances the benefits from the

[203] *Russia – Measures Concerning Traffic in Transit* (April 5, 2019) WTO Panel Report WT/DS512/R [7.146].

[204] See more chapter 4.

[205] Suzanne A Spears, 'The Quest for Policy Space in a New Generation of International Investment Agreements' (2010) 13 J Intl Econ L 1037, 1062.

[206] Joel P Trachtman, 'A Map of the World Trade Organization Law of Domestic Regulation of Goods: The Technical Barriers to Trade Agreement, the Sanitary and Phytosanitary

measure in the achievement of claimed goal against the cost of the measure in restricting trade.[207] At the same time, it has also emphasized the principle that an invoking state is entitled to choose for itself the level of achievement of the claimed goal,[208] which according to Regan, contradicts a standard cost-benefit balancing test.[209]

In *China – Publications and Audiovisual Products*, the Appellate Body reinforces the balancing test for determining the "necessity" under Article XX GATT (1994), which involves "'weighing and balancing' a number of distinct factors relating both to the measure . . . and to possible alternative measures that may be reasonably available."[210] Such factors might include the relative importance of the interests or values pursued, the degree of contribution, and the degree of trade-restrictiveness.[211] In *Brazil – Retreaded Tyres*, for instance, the Appellate Body found that the measure was "apt to produce a material contribution to the achievement of its objective."[212] In *EC – Seal Products*, however, the Appellate Body clarified that there is no "generally applicable standard requiring the use of a predetermined threshold of contribution in analysing the necessity of a measure."[213] This threshold will depend on the relative trade-restrictiveness of the contested measure: the more trade-restrictive the measure is, the high threshold of contribution might be required to prove its necessity.[214] Furthermore, whether a measure is necessary should be determined not only by the level of contribution but also based on other factors, including "the nature, quantity, and quality of evidence and whether a panel's analysis is performed in quantitative or qualitative terms."[215] In *US – Tariff Measures*, the US was found to fail to demonstrate

Measures Agreement, and the General Agreement on Tariffs and Trade' (2014) 48(2) JWT 351, 374.

207 *Korea – Measures Affecting Imports of Fresh, Chilled and Frozen Beef* (December 11, 2000) Appellate Body Report WT/DS161/AB/R WT/DS169/AB/R [162]–[164].

208 Ibid [176], [178].

209 Donald H Regan, 'The Meaning of "Necessary" in GATT Article XX and GATS Article XIV: The Myth of Cost-Benefit Balancing' (2007) 6(3) World Trade Rev 347, 348.

210 *China – Measures Affecting Trading Rights and Distribution Services for Certain Publications and Audiovisual Entertainment Products* (December 21, 2009) Appellate Body Report WT/DS363/AB/R [239].

211 *Colombia – Measures Relating to the Importation of Textiles, Apparel and Footwear* (June 7, 2016) Appellate Body Report WT/DS461/AB/R [5.77].

212 *Brazil – Measures Affecting Imports of Retreaded Tyres* (December 3, 2007) Appellate Body Report WT/DS332/AB/R [151].

213 *EC – Measures Prohibiting the Importation and Marketing of Seal Products* (May 22, 2014) Appellate Body Report WT/DS400/AB/R WT/DS401/AB/R [5.213].

214 Ibid.

215 Ibid [5.215].

the existence of the contribution by not providing an explanation that proves "a genuine relationship of ends and means" between the imposition of contested duties and the invoked public morals objective,[216] which reminds a suitability test.

Finally, *EC – Asbestos* and later WTO cases[217] require that a preliminary conclusion that the measure is necessary based on the tests discussed above must be further validated by evaluating whether there are less trade-restrictive alternatives that still effectively achieve the same objective.[218] Notably, panels and the Appellate Body generally take the approach that a measure will not fail the necessity test merely because they can contemplate a less restrictive alternative.[219]

Similar to Security Exceptions, the application of the necessity test by the WTO adjudicatory bodies under general exceptions has raised concerns over the degree of deference afforded to a state's legitimate policy objectives.[220] In particular, while the term "necessary" requires the level of connection between the policy goal and the achievement of the policy goal, the above-discussed balancing tests, least trade-restrictive alternative tests, and suitability tests used in the context of "necessity" seem to enable a closer analysis of measures than what certain governments believe is appropriate.[221]

6.3.1.2 Necessity Test in the Practice of Investment Tribunals

An example of a Security Exception using the necessity nexus as an objective precondition for invocation is Article XI of the US–Argentina BIT (1991). The decided cases in international investment law regarding the interpretation of this clause demonstrate a high degree of variance with respect to this nexus requirement: from a strict one to a more

216 *US – Tariff Measures on Certain Goods from China* (September 15, 2020) WTO Panel Report WT/DS543/R [7.215].

217 See eg *Brazil – Measures Affecting Imports of Retreaded Tyres* (December 3, 2007) Appellate Body Report WT/DS332/AB/R [406].

218 Joel P Trachtman, 'A Map of the World Trade Organization Law of Domestic Regulation of Goods: The Technical Barriers to Trade Agreement, the Sanitary and Phytosanitary Measures Agreement, and the General Agreement on Tariffs and Trade' (2014) 48(2) JWT 351, 374.

219 Andrew D Mitchell and Caroline Henckels, 'Variations on a Theme: Comparing the Concept of "Necessity" in International Investment Law and WTO Law' (2013) 14(1) Chicago J Intl L 93, 102.

220 Gisele Kapterian, 'A Critique of the WTO Jurisprudence on "Necessity"' (2010) 59(1) ICLQ 89, 89.

221 Ibid 125–127.

deferential approach to the necessity test.[222] As discussed above, the early tribunals' decisions on the Argentine economic crisis assimilated the conditions of the Security Exception under US–Argentina BIT (1991) and the customary defense of necessity under Article 25 of ARSIWA.[223] The tribunals in *CMS v Argentina*, *Enron v Argentina*, and *Sempra v Argentina* determined that an alternative measure was available for Argentina under the circumstances with little or no consideration of whether it was feasible, given that they applied the "only way" requirement under the customary defense of necessity, which precludes the invocation of necessity even where other means are "more costly or less convenient."[224] The *LG&E* tribunal accepted that, at least in the case of an economic crisis, states should be granted discretion in determining whether the measures are necessary, provided that such measures are legitimate and reasonable in the circumstances.[225]

As discussed above, the mere use of the term "necessary" should not be seen as involving the incorporation by reference of the customary defense of necessity either to WTO agreements or investment treaties unless it is evident from the treaty's wording, context, subsequent agreements or practices, or relevant international law provisions outlined in the treaty.[226] In this vein, the *Continental Casualty* and *Deutsche Telekom* tribunals do not intertwine the customary defense of necessity with the necessity test under Security Exceptions. Instead, the *Continental Casualty* tribunal, led by an arbitrator who had previously served on the Appellate Body, was guided by the WTO's approach under Article XX GATT (1994).[227] It clarified that:

> [s]ince the text of Art. XI derives from the parallel model clause of the U.S. FCN treaties and these treaties in turn reflect the formulation of Art. XX

222 Andrew D Mitchell and Caroline Henckels, 'Variations on a Theme: Comparing the Concept of "Necessity" in International Investment Law and WTO Law' (2013) 14(1) Chicago J Intl L 93, 104.

223 Chapter 5, section 5.3.2.3.

224 See more José E Alvarez and Tegan Brink, 'Revisiting the Necessity Defense: Continental Casualty v Argentina' in Karl P Saùvant (ed.), *Yearbook on International Investment Law & Policy* (OUP 2012).

225 Andrew D Mitchell and Caroline Henckels, 'Variations on a Theme: Comparing the Concept of "Necessity" in International Investment Law and WTO Law' (2013) 14(1) Chicago J Intl L 93, 160.

226 Diane A Desierto, 'Necessity and "Supplementary Means of Interpretation" for Non-Precluded Measures in Bilateral Investment Treaties' (2010) 31(3) U Pennsylvania J Intl Econ L 827, 934. See more chapter 5, section 5.3.2.

227 *Continental Casualty Co v Argentine Republic* (September 5, 2008) ICSID Case No Arb/03/9 Award, fns 280, 294–296, 299.

> of GATT (1947), the Tribunal finds it more appropriate to refer to GATT and WTO case law which has extensively dealt with the concept and requirements of necessity in the context of economic measures derogating to the obligations contained in GATT, rather than to refer to the requirement of necessity under customary international law.[228]

The *Continental Casualty* tribunal laid down a two-prong test to determine whether a measure is "necessary" or not: first, it examined whether the measure contributed materially to the realization of the regulatory objective, and second, whether reasonably available alternative measures existed, "which were least in conflict or more compliant with its international obligations while providing an equivalent contribution to the achievement of the objective pursued."[229] The term "material contribution," as enunciated by the *Continental Casualty* tribunal, implies the actual or the real contribution of the measure in attaining the regulatory objective.[230] The tribunal found that the Argentine measures were "in part inevitable," "in part indispensable," "and in any case material or decisive in order to react positively to the crisis, to prevent the complete breakdown of the financial system," which confirms "a genuine relationship of end and means in this respect."[231]

Further, citing the Appellate Body's ruling in *Korea – Various Measures on Beef*, the *Continental Casualty* tribunal applied a variation of the least restrictive means test by reviewing whether there is a reasonable alternative measure available to the state that achieves the same level of protection, and if so, whether it results in less restrictive effects on foreign investment.[232] The *Continental Casualty* tribunal held that an alternative measure could be reasonably available only if it is not impracticable for the host country to adopt it or if its effects are not speculative.[233]

While not referring to WTO jurisprudence, the *Deutsche Telekom* tribunal also laid down a two-prong test to interpret the "necessity" in

[228] Ibid [192].

[229] Ibid [198].

[230] Prabhash Ranjan, '"Necessary" in Non-Precluded Measures Provisions in Bilateral Investment Treaties: The Indian Contribution' (2020) 67(3) Netherlands Intl L Rev 473, 492.

[231] *Continental Casualty Co v Argentine Republic* (September 5, 2008) ICSID Case No Arb/03/9 Award [197].

[232] Jürgen Kurtz, *The WTO and International Investment Law: Converging Systems* (CUP 2016) 222–223.

[233] *Continental Casualty Co v Argentine Republic* (September 5, 2008) ICSID Case No Arb/03/9 Award [198].

the meaning of the Security Exception in India–Germany BIT (1995), which resembles the test proposed in *Continental Casualty v Argentina.*[234] Different from the *Continental Casualty* tribunal that referred to the measure as making a "material or a decisive contribution" to the objective,[235] the *Deutsche Telekom* tribunal held that the measure must be "principally targeted" to address the issue at stake.[236] The term "principally targeted" used by the *Deutsche Telekom* tribunal suggests that a measure should be able to contribute to the objective rather than have an actual contribution.[237] According to the tribunal, whether a measure is "principally targeted" at the protection of essential security interests mainly stems from the measure's importance and intended effect and subsequent events.[238] Ultimately, the tribunal still analyzed the design and architecture of the challenged measures and the events surrounding their adoption,[239] which is similar to what the *Continental Casualty* tribunal did while examining the material contribution of the measure.[240]

The *Deutsche Telekom* tribunal adopted a similar approach to examining alternative measures as the *Continental Casualty* tribunal.[241] However, since the *Deutsche Telekom* tribunal found that the measure was not principally targeted at the protection of essential security interests of India, it did not examine whether the alternative measures were reasonably available. The tribunal summarily held that India did not consider the "reasonable, least restrictive alternative measures, although they were clearly available."[242]

234 *Deutsche Telekom AG v Republic of India* (December 13, 2017) PCA Case No 2014–10 Interim Award [239].
235 *Continental Casualty Co v Argentine Republic* (September 5, 2008) ICSID Case No Arb/03/9 Award [196].
236 *Deutsche Telekom AG v Republic of India* (December 13, 2017) PCA Case No 2014–10 Interim Award [239].
237 Prabhash Ranjan, '"Necessary" in Non-Precluded Measures Provisions in Bilateral Investment Treaties: The Indian Contribution' (2020) 67(3) Netherlands Intl L Rev 473, 492.
238 *Deutsche Telekom AG v Republic of India* (December 13, 2017) PCA Case No 2014–10 Interim Award [285].
239 Ibid [285]–[291].
240 *Continental Casualty Co v Argentine Republic* (September 5, 2008) ICSID Case No Arb/03/9 Award [196]–[197].
241 *Deutsche Telekom AG v Republic of India* (December 13, 2017) PCA Case No 2014–10 Interim Award [239].
242 Ibid [290].

More recently, in *Seda v Colombia*, the tribunal took recourse to the plausibility review of Security Exceptions established in recent WTO panel reports. Accordingly,

> [p]lausible – or, for that matter, prima facie or rational – connection does not require the Tribunal to establish that the measures enacted by Respondent were the main avenue to combatting organized crime, let alone a sole instrument. It suffices that the measures could serve such purpose on their face, i.e., are not 'so remote from, or unrelated to' the stated objective as to render the connection implausible.[243]

The tribunal was also mindful of the systemic differences between international trade and investment law, noting that international trade law principles do not directly apply to investment disputes.[244] While Article XXI(b) GATT differs in key aspects from the Security Exception at hand, the tribunal found its wording and related case law useful for interpretation, though not decisive.[245] It remains to be seen whether future investment tribunals will continue this approach.

6.3.1.3 Problematic Questions

Relying on the WTO jurisprudence under Article XX in the context of BIT's Security Exceptions invokes several questions, some of them touched upon before.[246] Focusing on the textual discrepancies between BITs and WTO rules and the different objects and purposes of the two regimes, Alvarez and Brink critique the *Continental Casualty* decision to extrapolate from the WTO jurisprudence on the necessity under the BIT's Security Exception.[247] They claim that the *Continental Casualty* tribunal failed to consider that the word "necessary" in Article XI of US–Argentina BIT (1991) needs to be read in light of a particular treaty whose object and purpose is to guarantee to the investors the safety of their investments, particularly in the case of an unstable economy.[248] Another criticism of the *Continental Casualty* decision is that while referring to a weighing and balancing test similar to the WTO approach under Article

243 Ibid [787].

244 *Angel Samuel Seda and others v Republic of Colombia* (June 27, 2024) ICSID Case No ARB/19/6 Award [687].

245 Ibid.

246 Chapter 6, section 6.1. See more Kathleen Claussen, 'The Casualty of Investor Protection in Times of Economic Crisis' (2009) 118 Yale L J 1545.

247 See more José E Alvarez and Tegan Brink, 'Revisiting the Necessity Defense: Continental Casualty v Argentina' in Karl P Sauvant (ed.), *Yearbook on International Investment Law & Policy* (OUP 2012).

248 Ibid.

XX GATT (1994), the tribunal did not undertake any balancing by considering the importance of the measures' objective and the measures' effectiveness versus their impact on the investment.[249]

While not clarifying all the questions arising from the application of the necessity test, the *Continental Casualty* and *Deutsche Telekom* cases have provided a more sophisticated analysis of the Security Exceptions than the earlier awards of investment tribunals. There is nothing inherent about the necessity analysis under IIAs that makes it incompatible with the similarly drafted necessity nexus under the WTO agreements. It is indisputable that investor-state arbitrators need to apply the specific treaty before them, even at the expense of advancing harmonious international investment law. Yet, this should not preclude investment tribunals from applying, where relevant, certain aspects of WTO necessity analysis as helpful guidance. In particular, investment tribunals can view international trade law and its jurisprudence as a "relevant rule" that is "applicable in the relations between the parties" within the meaning of Article 31(3)(c) of VCLT.[250] Recognizing the public law context of international investment arbitration can provide a necessary direction for future tribunals in rebalancing investor protections with state sovereignty.

Few investment arbitrators have experience in both trade and investment, which may explain why so few WTO analogies are employed in the investment sphere.[251] At the same time, it can be argued that based on recent treaty-drafting practice, negotiators may well have adopted the specific language of exceptions modeled on WTO agreements, at least in part, due to the assumption that the interpretation of the exceptions would be based on the Appellate Body's established jurisprudence.[252] Thus, the convergence between WTO jurisprudence and investment awards concerning the concept

[249] Andrew D Mitchell and Caroline Henckels, 'Variations on a Theme: Comparing the Concept of Necessity in International Investment Law and WTO Law' (2013) 14(1) Chicago J Intl L 93, 116–117.

[250] Tobias Ackermann, 'Exception Clauses in International Investment Agreements: A Case for Systemic Integration?' (2019) International Challenges in Investment Arbitration 37, 49–53.

[251] Amelia Keene, 'The Incorporation and Interpretation of WTO-Style Environmental Exceptions in International Investment Agreements' (2017) 18 J World Investment & Trade 62, 82.

[252] Ibid 72.

of necessity may be further enhanced by the inclusion of WTO-style exception clauses in IIAs.[253]

6.3.2 Nexus between Security Measures and Security Interests Other Than Necessity

Different from the US–Argentina BIT (1991), which refers to the measures "necessary for . . . the protection of [state's] own essential security interests," the word "necessity" or any reference thereof is absent in some Security Exception clauses.

The UNCTAD study concludes that Security Exceptions referring to the measures that are "directed to" or taken "for" the protection of essential security interests have a lower threshold for review than the measures that are "necessary" and could even have the practical effect that is very close to a self-judging clause since only in extreme cases can a tribunal be expected to conclude that the measure has no relation to national security interests.[254] The tribunal in *Devas v India* has not agreed with this latter statement. The tribunal considered the condition laid down in Article 11(3) of the India–Mauritius BIT (1998) concerning the nexus between the measures and the state's essential security interests, embodied in the phrase "directed to."[255] Relying on the VCLT, the tribunal rejected the claimant's assertion that a measure has to be "necessary," in the sense of being the only means available, to benefit from the exception, and instead concluded that it merely has to be shown that a measure is "related to" one of the specific objectives stated to meet the nexus requirement.[256] In particular, the tribunal emphasized that "[i]n the case of self-judging clauses, it suffices for the State to declare, in its discretion, that it considers the adopted measure necessary for the protection of its security interests."[257] However, "[i]n situations like the

[253] Andrew D Mitchell and Elizabeth Sheargold, 'Necessity Testing' in Andrew D Mitchell and Elizabeth Sheargold (eds.), *Principles of International Trade and Investment Law* (Edward Elgar Publishing 2021) 122. See more on the repercussions of this trend in chapter 6, section 6.1.

[254] UNCTAD, 'The Protection of National Security in IIAs' (2009) UNCTAD Series on International Investment Policies for Development 95 https://unctad.org/webflyer/protection-national-security-iias.

[255] *CC/Devas (Mauritius) Ltd v Republic of India* (July 25, 2016) PCA Case No 2013–09 Award on Jurisdiction and Merits [211].

[256] Wolfgang Alschner and Kun Hui, 'Missing in Action: General Public Policy Exceptions in Investment Treaties' in Lisa Sachs, Jesse Coleman, and Lise Johnson (eds.), *Yearbook on International Investment Law and Policy* (OUP 2018) [21:63].

[257] *CC/Devas (Mauritius) Ltd v Republic of India* (July 25, 2016) PCA Case No 2013–09 Award on Jurisdiction and Merits [242].

one in this case or those mentioned in the UNCTAD study, a tribunal is called upon to assess whether the measure adopted by the State is not only directed to the protection of its security but that it must also be for the protection of its essential security interests."[258]

The tribunal in *Devas v India* found out that while India did not have to demonstrate the necessity in that the measure adopted was the "only one," it still had to establish that the measure was related to its essential security interests.[259] Applying this construction of the clause to the facts, the tribunal found out that not all interests of India at issue were its essential security interests.[260] In particular, the tribunal, by the majority, concluded that India's decision to annul the Devas Agreement on the S-band spectrum (Annulment Decision) appears to have "a mix of objectives" and has been only in part "directed to the protection of its essential security interests."[261] Several other objectives were included in that decision, which had nothing to do with national security, for example, related to the protection of "strategic needs" or "strategic requirements" that covered a range of activities that "went far beyond the military or paramilitary sectors or the 'essential security interests' of India."[262]

In a dissenting opinion, Haigh argued for a more restrictive interpretation of a "directed to" nexus requirement.[263] Accordingly, India was required to show by a preponderance of the evidence that its decision to annul the Devas Agreement on the supply of S-band spectrum "was directed fundamentally and absolutely to protecting" essential security interests.[264] Since it failed to do so, it failed to prove any connection between its measures and the protection of its essential security interests.[265] Haigh observed that the term "essential security interests" itself requires the tribunal to determine whether the objective of the Annulment Decision was directed to protecting an essential security interest.[266] He highlighted that not only the objectives of the annulling of the Devas Agreement were mixed, but the wording of the announcement

258 Ibid.
259 Ibid [243].
260 Ibid [245].
261 Ibid [354].
262 Ibid [356]. See more chapter 6, section 6.2.1.2.
263 *CC/Devas (Mauritius) Ltd v Republic of India* (July 25, 2016) PCA Case No 2013-09 Dissenting Opinion of Arbitrator David R Haigh.
264 Ibid [108].
265 Ibid.
266 Ibid [98].

of the Annulment Decision was plain that India did not decide to reserve the S-band for the military or paramilitary forces but instead referred to the determination of that issue on a later stage.[267] In these circumstances, it is impossible to say that the Annulment Decision was directed toward the essential security interests of India since, at the time of its announcement, the question of S-band spectrum allocation remained open.[268] It could have been used for military purposes and disaster management or railway tracking that the tribunal has not considered as falling within the scope of a state's essential security interest.[269] Thus, until the final use of the goods was determined, no action was directed at protecting essential security or military interests, no matter what India's authority might have requested or wished for.[270] With this regard, Blanco and Pehl consider that such an analysis proposed by Haigh places an excessive and unprecedented burden on a responding state where a Security Exception requires a measure to be merely "directed at" the protection of national security.[271]

Even though Haigh's understanding of the measure being "directed to" comes close to the idea of the material contribution of the Security Measure, in the sense of an "unavoidable" or "indispensable requisite," Haigh did not mention the need to demonstrate the actual contribution of the measure. Neither Haigh further discussed the need to examine whether there were any other less trade-restrictive alternatives reasonably available, thus differentiating between the necessity analysis and the nexus that merely requires a measure to be directed to the protection of the state's essential security interest. Requiring the measure to be directed fundamentally and absolutely to the protection of essential security interests can allow for differentiating between the protection of national security, on the one hand, and the protection of commercial or other opportunistic interests of a state, on the other hand, and thus prevent potential abuses.

Article XX GATT (1994) also distinguishes between the measures "necessary for" and the measures merely "relating to." While interpreting the term "relating to" under Article XX(g), the Appellate Body in *US – Gasoline* noted that this term was equivalent to "primarily aimed at."[272] In *US – Shrimp*, the

[267] Ibid [100].
[268] Ibid [96].
[269] Ibid.
[270] Ibid.
[271] Mantilla Blanco Sebastián and Alexander Pehl, *National Security Exceptions in International Trade and Investment Agreements: Justiciability and Standards of Review* (Springer 2020) 58.
[272] *US – Standards for Reformulated and Conventional Gasoline* (April 29, 1996) Appellate Body Report WT/DS2/AB/R 18.

Appellate Body appears to have abandoned the "primarily aimed at" test and rather focused on a reasonable "means and ends relationship" between the measure and the natural resource conservation.[273] In *China – Rare Earths*, the Appellate Body also held that a GATT-inconsistent measure that is merely incidentally or inadvertently aimed at a conservation objective would not satisfy the "relating to" condition.[274] Such analysis of the Appellate Body seems to require a lower threshold than what Haigh argued for including in the "directed to" nexus requirement.

It is important to mention that in the second investment treaty dispute arising out of the same facts initiated by Deutsche Telekom, a German investor with an ownership stake in Devas, the tribunal adopted a different test for the essential security defense.[275] The case turned on Article 12 of India–Mauritius BIT (1998), less restrictively drafted than its above-discussed counterpart, the Security Exception clause under the India–Germany BIT (1995). The tribunal distinguished the provision "to the extent necessary for" of the India–Germany BIT (1995) from the "is directed to" language of the India–Mauritius BIT (1998), finding that the former implies a more stringent nexus between ends and means.[276] Inspired by the WTO's GATT Article XX necessity test, it applied a variation of the reasonable alternative test. Ultimately, the two cases arising from similar facts were subject to divergent standards of review, which illustrates the importance of differences in the treaty wording.[277]

6.3.3 *Self-Judging Clauses and Nexus Requirements*

As the practice of the ICJ, WTO panels, and investment tribunals demonstrates, even if the Security Exception clause includes self-judging wording, such as "it considers," it is up to the adjudicator to decide to which parts of the clause the self-judging language applies.[278]

[273] *US – Import Prohibition of Certain Shrimp and Shrimp Products* (October 12, 1998) Appellate Body Report WT/DS58/AB/R [141].

[274] *China – Measures Related to the Exportation of Rare Earths, Tungsten and Molybdenum* (August 7, 2014) Appellate Body Report WT/DS431/AB/R WT/DS432/AB/R WT/DS433/AB/R [5.112].

[275] *CC/Devas (Mauritius) Ltd v Republic of India* (July 25, 2016) PCA Case No 2013-09 Award on Jurisdiction and Merits [467].

[276] Ibid [240].

[277] Wolfgang Alschner and Kun Hui, 'Missing in Action: General Public Policy Exceptions in Investment Treaties' in Lisa Sachs, Jesse Coleman, and Lise Johnson (eds.), *Yearbook on International Investment Law and Policy* (OUP 2018) [21:70].

[278] Chapter 5, section 5.1.

Concerning the WTO-style Security Exceptions, the panel in *Russia – Traffic in Transit* had to decide whether the adjectival clause "which it considers" in the chapeau of Article XXI(b) can be interpreted to apply solely to the "necessity" of the measures, or if it also qualifies the assessment of "essential security interests," or even the evaluation of the circumstances outlined in each subparagraph of Article XXI(b).[279] Given the heightened sensitivity of national security, applying a strict interpretation of "necessary" from other provisions to WTO Security Exceptions – such as requiring indispensability of the measures or the absence of less restrictive alternatives – sets an unreasonably high standard. This approach overlooks the delicate nature of security issues and the states' responsibility to protect their security when they consider it necessary.[280] Taking such concerns into account, the panel in *Russia – Traffic in Transit* determined that the clause "which it considers necessary" under Article XXI GATT (1994) meant that "it is for Russia to determine the 'necessity' of the measures for the protection of its essential security interests."[281] At the same time, the panel acknowledged that based on the wording of Security Exceptions, the measures have not only to be considered necessary but also to be adopted "for" the protection of the essential security interests of an invoking state. This link between the protection of "essential security interests" and the measure in question is subject to a good faith assessment.[282]

The approach of the WTO panels in *Russia – Traffic in Transit* and *Saudi Arabia – IPRs* confirms that a good faith test is loose and not easy to apply or administer but acknowledges that the exercise of a right for the sole purpose of evading an obligation or of causing injury is unlawful. According to the panel in *Russia – Traffic in Transit*, the threshold for a good faith review is lower than the review of the objective nexus between the measures and security interests, such as "directed to" or "necessary," given that it is enough for an invoking state to demonstrate that there is "a minimum requirement of plausibility in relation to the proffered essential security interests" without demonstrating the

[279] *Russia – Measures Concerning Traffic in Transit* (April 5, 2019) WTO Panel Report WT/DS512/R [7.63].

[280] Dapo Akande and Sope Williams, 'International Adjudication on National Security Issues: What Role for the WTO?' (2003) 43 Virginia J Intl L 365, 395.

[281] *Russia – Measures Concerning Traffic in Transit* (April 5, 2019) WTO Panel Report WT/DS512/R [7.146].

[282] See more chapter 5, section 5.3.1.

objectives of the measure or providing any evidence that the measure is capable of contributing to such an objective.[283]

Such a test seems to be sufficient to differentiate between the measures that are potentially related to the protection of the state's essential security interests and those that are not, as demonstrated in *Saudi Arabia – IPRs*.[284] Yet, it might not be sufficient to eliminate all possibilities for abuse.

To illustrate, the panel in *Russia – Traffic in Transit* seemed to be guided by the idea that the burden of proof in respect of Article XXI(b) "cannot be understood in isolation from the overarching logic of that provision, and the function which it is designed to serve."[285] The panel did not require Russia to define its essential security interests clearly or provide any factual foundation for the empirical assessment of the relationship between the measures and the claimed security interests, which would be indispensable to demonstrate the real motivation behind the measures.[286] Instead, the panel carefully avoided consideration of the motivations of Russia altogether.[287] The preliminary economic analysis conducted by Paulsen and Crivelli confirms obvious economic and geopolitical considerations for the imposition of Russia's measures, directly questioning their plausibility and their good faith application.[288] The panel, for example, did not consider the fact that Russia had not adopted a complete embargo but instead applied specific restrictive measures.[289] With this respect, Paulsen and Pramila argue that it is implausible that only dutiable goods in transit from Ukraine, subject to Russia's measures, threatened Russia's essential security interests.[290] Accordingly, the protection of essential security interests cannot depend on the duty status of goods and thus would require a horizontal ban on all imported goods or a ban on particular goods selected based on security criteria.[291] In addition, it remains unclear whether such measures could

[283] *Russia – Measures Concerning Traffic in Transit* (April 5, 2019) WTO Panel Report WT/DS512/R [7.136].

[284] *Saudi Arabia – Measures Concerning the Protection of Intellectual Property Rights* (June 16, 2020) WTO Panel Report WT/DS567/R [7.288]–[7.289].

[285] Shin-yi Peng, 'Cybersecurity Threats and the WTO National Security Exceptions' (2015) 18 J Intl Econ L 449, 478.

[286] Pramila Crivelli and Mona Paulsen, 'Separating the Political from the Economic: The Russia – Traffic in Transit Panel Report' (2021) 20(4) World Trade Rev 582, 603.

[287] Ibid 592.

[288] Ibid 602.

[289] Ibid 593.

[290] Ibid 601–602.

[291] Ibid 602.

be considered retaliatory and, if so, whether retaliatory economic measures could be used to protect national security by weakening the "enemy" in an international conflict.[292]

The controversies in the panels' findings can be attributed to the flaws in the chosen analytical approach to Security Exceptions but also to a gap between theory and practice. Particularly, it can be argued that the theoretical test for examining Security Exceptions proposed by the panels in *Russia – Traffic in Transit* and *Saudi Arabia – IPRs* was far more stringent than the test the panels eventually applied in practice.[293]

The panels in *US – Steel and Aluminium Products* disputes and the panel in *US – Origin Marking (Hong Kong, China)* also imply the degree of deference in the state's determination of the action that "it considers necessary for the protection of its essential security interests" (excluding the subparagraphs). Yet, regrettably, none of these panels have elaborated on the scope of such a deferential review. After having established that Article XXI(b)(iii) is not "non-justiciable," the panels in *US – Steel and Aluminium Products* disputes proceeded to the analysis of subparagraph iii, making an ambiguous statement that they would use the evidence and arguments submitted by the parties to assess whether the "'action[s] which [the United States] considers necessary for the protection of its essential security interests' were taken under the circumstances described in the subparagraphs of Article XXI(b)(iii)."[294] It remains unclear whether the findings and recommendations of the panels in these cases would have been different should they found that the US took its measures in time of the "emergency in international relations" as required by subparagraph iii. In particular, should the US prove the existence of the emergency in international relations, the question remains whether the panels would have assumed that the US measures were considered by the US "necessary for the protection of its essential security interests" and thus justified under the GATT's Security Exceptions or whether (and if so, to what extent) the panels would have still reviewed a good faith

292 Ibid.

293 Jacob Gladysz, 'The National Security Exception in WTO Law: Emerging Jurisprudence and Future Direction' (2021) 52 Geo J Intl L 835, 852–854.

294 *US – Certain Measures on Steel and Aluminium Products (China)* (December 9, 2022) WTO Panel Report WT/DS544/R [7.136]; *US – Certain Measures on Steel and Aluminium Products (Norway)* (December 9, 2022) WTO Panel Report WT/DS552/R [7.124]; *US – Certain Measures on Steel and Aluminium Products (Switzerland)* (December 9, 2022) WTO Panel Report WT/DS556/R [7.154]; *US – Certain Measures on Steel and Aluminium Products (Turkey)* (December 9, 2022) WTO Panel Report WT/DS564/R [7.151].

invocation of essential security interests by the US and a plausible connection between the measures and the US security interests (as the previous panes did). Thus, the existing WTO case law maintains a zone of ambiguity in the application of Security Exceptions that still needs to be navigated by future panels and potentially the Appellate Body.

Notably, exception clauses in other systems often allow states to act based on what they consider or deem necessary, rather than requiring strict necessity. An example of a self-judging Security Exception can be found in Article 2(c) of the Convention concerning Judicial Assistance in Criminal Matters between Djibouti and France discussed in *Djibouti v France*, where it was found that the appropriate standard of review of a self-judging clause was that of good faith that focuses on the review of the legitimacy of the reasons for taking the alleged actions.[295]

Under Article 99(1)(d) of the EU–Russia Partnership Agreement (1994), the ECJ in *Rosneft* had to review whether the measure that Russia "considers necessary for the protection of its essential security interests" was taken "in time of war or serious international tension constituting threat of war."[296] The ECJ decided that taking into consideration the broad discretion enjoyed by the Council in this area, it "could take the view that the adoption of the restrictive measures at issue in the main proceedings was necessary for the protection of essential European Union security interests and for the maintenance of peace and international security."[297] The ECJ reached such a conclusion relying on the facts that the Council concluded that the situation with respect to Ukraine remained grave, as well as that it was apparent from the statements of the Council that the aim of the restrictive measures prescribed by the contested acts was to promote a peaceful settlement of the crisis in Ukraine, which is consistent with the objective of maintaining peace and international security under the EU law.[298] This approach aligns with the ECJ rulings on the necessity nexus in general.[299] The degree of scrutiny that it applies to a measure depends on the circumstances: the ECJ is more likely to accept a government's assertions as to the necessity of a measure where the measure is in a sensitive policy area, one in which

295 *Case Concerning Certain Questions on Mutual Assistance in Criminal Matters (Djibouti v France)* (June 4, 2008) ICJ Rep [145]. See more chapter 5, section 5.1.

296 Case C-72/15 *PJSC Rosneft Oil Company v Her Majesty's Treasury and Others* [2017] EU:C:2017:236 [10].

297 Ibid [116].

298 Ibid [115].

299 See more chapter 5, section 5.4.

there is no European consensus or one where national authorities have exclusive competence.[300]

Ultimately, while agreement exists that self-judging language affects the standard of review of the nexus between a Security Measure and the protection of essential security interests, suggestions about the applicable standard of review differ. First, according to the ICJ, the invocation of the self-judging elements in Security Exceptions is subject to only a very limited good faith review. The ICJ does not clarify how to operationalize such review or its specific limits.[301] Second, in light of the "it considers necessary" language, the WTO panels in *Russia – Traffic in Transit* and *Saudi Arabia – IPRs* have left it entirely to the discretion of invoking states to determine whether their measures are necessary to protect their essential security interests. Accordingly, an adjudicator should only review whether there is a plausible connection between the measure and the protected security interest to establish whether an invoking state acted in good faith. Third, the ECJ seems to focus the review of a self-judging "necessity" on the procedural aspects of the Council's decisions and the claimed objectives of the challenged measures. The only investment tribunal dealing with a self-judging Security Exception adopted a limited good faith review of Security Exceptions, drawing from the WTO case law.[302]

6.3.4 *Revisiting Nexus Requirements*

Standard of review of either self-judging or nonself-judging Security Exception clauses might require adjudicators, at least to a certain extent, to consider the assessment of the invoking state about the definition of its essential security interests and the choice of a concrete measure to protect those interests in the case that several comparable policy options are available.[303] A self-judging clause would simply formalize the margin of discretion that would otherwise be a matter of judicial deference.[304]

[300] Caroline Henckels, *Proportionality and Deference in Investor-State Arbitration: Balancing Investment Protection and Regulatory Autonomy* (CUP 2015) 58.

[301] Stephan Schill and Robyn Briese, '"If the State Considers": Self-Judging Clauses in International Dispute Settlement' (2009) 13(1) Max Planck YB UN L Online 61, 116.

[302] See more chapter 4.

[303] UNCTAD, 'The Protection of National Security in IIAs' (2009) UNCTAD Series on International Investment Policies for Development 129 https://unctad.org/webflyer/protection-national-security-iias.

[304] Stephan Schill And Robyn Briese, '"If The State Considers": Self-Judging Clauses in International Dispute Settlement' (2009) 13(1) Max Planck YB UN L Online 61, 124.

However, it does not imply that the same standard of review should apply to both types of exceptions since it would mean disregarding the intent of the contracting parties to retain different levels of discretion for themselves under a self-judging clause and a nonself-judging clause. States would not adopt the trend of incorporating self-judging clauses in the first place if there was no difference between the nature of nonself-judging clauses and self-judging clauses.[305] If international courts and tribunals could decide on the sensitive national security area and review the self-judging clause without deference to an invoking state, there would be no meaning for the state parties to make particular self-judging clauses literally.[306]

While it seems to be an agreement that Security Exceptions under international treaties using a self-judging nexus requirement are at least subject to a good faith review, it remains unclear what this review should imply. As the case of *Russia – Traffic in Transit* demonstrates, even a fairly sophisticated test for the review of Security Exceptions can be undermined by a low standard of proof that does not allow an adjudicator to differentiate between the economic and security motives of the measure.[307] It can be argued that a plausibility test should require adjudicators to investigate the factual basis of the state's decision, including the measures' economic effects, the consistency of the state's actions, and the connection between the measure and the claimed security interests. The standard of review should still be limited to establishing whether a member genuinely considers that its measure is related to the objective of protection of its essential security interests and whether it considers that there are serious reasons to take the measures that would make it proportionate to the protection of those interests.[308]

Furthermore, similar to the position taken by Judge Keith in his Declaration in *Djibouti v France*, international courts and tribunals could review self-judging clauses on the grounds used for judicial review for misuse of discretion under domestic administrative law regimes.[309] Such an approach would allow a review of, among others, whether the factual

305 Ji Ma, 'International Investment and National Security Review' (2019) 52 Vand J Transnatl L 899, 937.
306 Ibid.
307 Chapter 6, section 6.3.3.
308 Stephan Schill and Robyn Briese, '"If the State Considers": Self-Judging Clauses in International Dispute Settlement' (2009) 13(1) Max Planck YB UN L Online 61, 109.
309 Stephan Schill and Robyn Briese, '"If the State Considers": Self-Judging Clauses in International Dispute Settlement' (2009) 13(1) Max Planck YB UN L Online 61, 140.

basis of the state's decision was adequately investigated and whether the proper procedure for the decision was met.[310] Adjudicators could also assess the MFN principle's requirement for equal treatment when determining if multiple states pose a comparable threat to a state's essential security interests. They would need to evaluate whether similar measures have been applied to all such states.[311] If similar measures have not been imposed, resulting in discrimination among states with similar threats, this would suggest a lack of good faith.[312] To illustrate, some of India's RTAs and Model BIT (2015) expressly prescribe that Security Measures should be imposed on a nondiscriminatory basis.[313]

Notably, the general obligation to exercise good faith also has a procedural dimension. It demands that a member relying on Security Exceptions not only participate in panel proceedings but also provide the information necessary for the panel to make the findings within its competence.[314] As discussed before, the burden of proof should rest on the party invoking the Security Exceptions.[315] Combined with a requirement to the invoking party to provide a reasoned explanation of the magnitude of the risk to its essential security interests, a review of plausibility nexus can enable the detection of the cases where a state had no grounds for adopting the Security Measure of a kind since such a measure is not connected to the protection of the claimed interests and/or has been adopted for a different purpose.

At the same time, where the treaty refers to the necessity as an objective precondition for the invocation of Security Exceptions, future courts and tribunals can be expected to continue to rely on a two-tier test to review the nexus between a Security Measure and the protection of a state's essential security interest. In particular, as proposed by the *Deutsche Telekom* tribunal, an invoking state should be able to prove that the measure was at least aimed at and could potentially contribute to the realization of its legitimate aim of protecting the state's essential security interests and that a state did not have reasonably available alternatives that were less conflicting or more aligned with its international

[310] Ibid.
[311] Ibid 108.
[312] Ibid.
[313] Chapter 4, section 4.2.5.
[314] Hannes L Schloemann and Stefan Ohlhoff, 'Constitutionalization and Dispute Settlement in the WTO: National Security as an Issue of Competence' (1999) 93 Am J Intl L 424, 448.
[315] Chapter 5, section 5.3.1.

obligations.[316] While these criteria cannot be readily imported from different treaty frameworks, the WTO law can provide helpful guidance for the future development and application of the necessity test for Security Exceptions.

In the trade realm, WTO adjudicators balance the degree of the measure's contribution to the objective versus the extent to which the measure restricts international trade, which by itself is a politically sensitive exercise. It would be unreasonable to expect ad hoc trade and investment tribunals to embark on such a mission while reviewing Security Measures under IIAs, allowing them to consider the importance of the measures' objective and the measures' effectiveness versus their impact on the investment. Requiring a potential contribution of the measure and focusing on the intention of an invoking party confirmed by the submitted evidence enables to establish "a genuine relationship of ends and means" between the imposition of the measure and the protection of states' security interests without necessarily proving a material contribution of the measure or determining its restrictiveness on trade or investment. Notably, the degree of the potential contribution required should be more than just what an invoking state considers necessary, allowing for the differentiation between the necessity and self-judging necessity nexus.

Furthermore, the consideration of alternatives requires adjudicators to evaluate hypothetical situations and foresee whether contracting parties under these situations could effectively achieve the claimed objective.[317] It would draw the distinction between the measures that have to be "relating to" the pursuance of national security objectives as discussed above[318] and the measures that have to be "necessary for" the achievement of such an objective. Kurtz and Ranjan agree that the critical part of the necessity test in the investment context is determining whether the least restrictive investment measure is reasonably available and would achieve the same objective.[319] Due to the sensitivity of the state's security

[316] UNCTAD, 'The Protection of National Security in IIAs' (2009) UNCTAD Series on International Investment Policies for Development 127 https://unctad.org/webflyer/protection-national-security-iias.

[317] Andrew D Mitchell and Caroline Henckels, 'Variations on a Theme: Comparing the Concept of "Necessity" in International Investment Law and WTO Law' (2013) 14(1) Chicago J Intl L 93, 101.

[318] Chapter 6, section 6.3.2.

[319] Jürgen Kurtz, *The WTO and International Investment Law: Converging Systems* (CUP 2016) 222; Prabhash Ranjan, '"Necessary" in Non-Precluded Measures Provisions in Bilateral Investment Treaties: The Indian Contribution' (2020) 67(3) Netherlands Intl L Rev 473, 490.

policies, adjudicators should not be expected to weigh directly and balance the measure's benefits with the cost of investment or trade restriction and judge the relative importance of the regulatory objective that the invoking state wishes to pursue.[320] Adjudicators, however, have to ensure that the proposed alternative measure is available in the sense that it should be within the means of the invoking state. By analogy with the claim about reducing the level of scientific involvement of courts and giving an operational meaning to what "minimum science" is,[321] the dialectic interdisciplinary dialogue between adjudicators and state authorities might be useful in deciding on the questions of the availability of alternative measures in the national security domain. Some due deference should be granted to the invoking state's decision about the level of benefit or the regulatory objective, considering its technical and administrative capacity to implement the alternative measure. The WTO case law on less restrictive measures under general exceptions can serve as helpful guidance for other adjudicators performing this delicate exercise.

6.4 Conclusion

The existing case law suggests that the presence of self-judging language does not amend the standard of review for other preconditions for the invocation of Security Exceptions but the secondary safeguards, such as the nexus requirement between the measure and the need to protect the state's essential security interests. Objective language of the nexus requirement, such as "necessary," "directed to," and "related to," allows an adjudicator to require the invoking state to present more evidence proving the nature and the motives of the measure, their potential contribution to the protection of essential security interests, and, in case of the availability of other alternatives, to show that they were not reasonably available under the circumstances. An adjudicator is not expected to ask the invoking state to provide the same evidence, nor should it second-guess the efficiency in the application of the measure when Security Exceptions allow for the actions that a state "considers necessary for the protection of its essential security interests."

[320] Prabhash Ranjan, '"Necessary" in Non-Precluded Measures Provisions in Bilateral Investment Treaties: The Indian Contribution' (2020) 67(3) Netherlands Intl L Rev 473, 497.

[321] Alberto Alemanno, 'The Dialogue between Judges & Experts in the EU and WTO' in Filippo Fontanelli and others (eds.), *Shaping Rule of Law Through Dialogue* (Europa Law Publishing 2010) 374.

Such a nexus requirement should be only subject to deferential good faith review, which, in theory, allows an adjudicator to distinguish between the cases when the state adopts the measure to protect its essential security interests and where it pursues clearly protectionist objectives. In practice, such a review presents challenges to adjudicators who have to delimit the cases of opportunism while applying a low standard of proof. To prevent its potential abuse, this book recommends that a good faith review of a self-judging clause (or its component) should include not only a requirement of plausibility, as advanced by WTO panels, but also a reasoned explanation of the magnitude of the risk to the essential security interests of an invoking state and its motives. Notably, applying such a test can be difficult in cases where an invoking state relies on the nondisclosure exception during litigation to withhold information necessary to analyze the true objective of its Security Measures.[322]

Analysis of the case law of WTO panels and investment tribunals on Security Exceptions under international economic agreements also leads to the conclusion that where "essential security interests" are not limited to specific factual scenarios, fact-finding in security matters remains illusory because of the lack of an established baseline and subjectivity in constructing the terms.[323] It follows that states can never be entirely sure about the exact margin of discretion they are accorded to keep their Security Measures legal where the text of the agreement includes a broad concept of "essential security interests" without limiting it to specific goods or situations. The subsequent rulings of the adjudicators cannot clarify the exact boundaries of the regulatory powers that still belong to the WTO members in defining such a concept. Thus, what can be understood as a threat to the essential security interest of a state can vary from agreement to agreement depending on the determination of the invoking party, language, and context of a treaty, as well as the treaty's object and purpose. In conjunction with self-judging language in international economic agreements, the exception with the broad, open-ended term "essential security interests" gives the maximum discretion to WTO members.

States' discretion to invoke Security Exceptions can be significantly reduced if the exception contains other conditions for recourse to national security, limiting the actions adopted to protect the state's

[322] See more chapter 5, section 5.2.4.

[323] Harlan Grant Cohen, 'Waiting for Gundy' (*Just Security*, July 17, 2019) www.justsecurity.org/64946/the-national-security-delegation-conundrum/?s=03.

"essential security interests" to the cases of arms trafficking or the responses to wars and other emergencies as provided in WTO-style Security Exceptions. Since WTO-style Security Exceptions relate to "emergencies in international relations" rather than domestic emergencies, it can be assumed that the determination of whether there was an emergency would be, at least to a certain extent, confirmed by the UN or by the actions and declarations of the international community in general or of the bloc of states affected, thus leaving no grounds that it would be approached differently from the perspective of different agreements.

In particular, the approach of WTO panels to the interpretation of the security defense under WTO law suggests that the successful invocation of Article XXI(b)(iii) GATT (1994) is possible only in case of "a breakdown or near-breakdown in the relations between states" which is proved by the recognition of the international gravity of such a situation on the UN level, the introduction of sanctions by multiple members, and the existence of the evidence of the severance of "diplomatic, consular, or economic relations" between an invoking state and affected parties.[324] Such an interpretation potentially leaves a door open for justifying Security Measures required to protect the population from pandemics, the consequences of climate change, or other global security threats. Nevertheless, it prevents the justification of measures aimed at addressing emerging national security concerns that have not led to a breakdown in the relationships between an invoking state and affected parties, even if such measures are necessary to ensure the security of such sensitive areas of national concern as cyberspace or the health of the population. Furthermore, if interpreted narrowly, WTO Security Exceptions seem to be inadequate in allowing for mitigation and adaptation measures required to protect the population from future emergencies, even if such measures are adopted in good faith.

The WTO panels in *Russia – Traffic in Transit* and *Saudi Arabia – IPRs* have developed a sophisticated analytical framework for the interpretation of WTO-style Security Exceptions, which is based on the principle of good faith and the need to balance the security interests of invoking state and the trade interests of other WTO members. Yet, these panels have not answered all the questions arising from the application of such a framework in practice.

[324] *US – Origin Marking Requirements* (December 21, 2022) WTO Panel Report WT/DS597/R [7.356].

Furthermore, the other WTO panels reviewing the invocation of WTO Security Exceptions by the US have taken a more technical approach to the interpretation of an "emergency in international relations" that significantly limits a member's security defense under WTO law and, consequently, might further escalate the tension between the supporters and opponents of nonjusticiability arguments. Notably, the panels in these cases have refused to accept the US security defense merely because of the US failure to demonstrate the existence of an emergency in international relations. The panels have not addressed the other components of a Security Exceptions test developed in *Russia – Traffic in Transit* and *Saudi Arabia – IPRs*. In particular, the panels have not discussed whether the US "sufficiently articulated" its essential security interests at stake and whether the US measures met a minimum requirement of plausibility in relation to the invoked essential security interests. It can be argued that the lack of such an analysis has prevented the panels from considering the impact on the US interests of the existing situations resulting in the application of Security Measures and, thus, from performing a true balancing exercise that takes into account the security interests of an invoking member and the trade interests of other states.

It stems from this analysis that, in theory, existing WTO-like Security Exceptions and the exceptions that use no self-judging language allow adjudicators to differentiate cases of genuine national security concerns and of opportunistic behavior. Yet, they do not necessarily fully encompass the threats to national security that states might have to deal with in the globalized and technologized world, leaving this question to be determined by adjudicators on a case-by-case basis. At the same time, broader drafted and nonreviewable Security Exceptions provide excessive latitude for WTO members to use pretextual claims of security concerns to avoid their obligations. Both approaches could be unsustainable for the future of the international trade and investment regimes given that they might either cancel the benefits of free trade and investment liberalization or unjustifiably limit the pressing need of WTO members to take efficient security actions, as further discussed.

7

Legal and Policy Responses to Security Measures

Using the current geo-economic developments as a launching pad for long-needed reform, this chapter concludes the discussion on the portrayed clash between trade and security by taking a more transformative vision of Security Exceptions.[1] First, it discusses the prospects and challenges of existing Security Exceptions in international economic law through the lenses of realism, institutionalism, constructivism, and economic contract theory (section 7.1). Second, this chapter reconsiders the role of the WTO, the UN, and domestic policymakers in managing international economic relations and national security (section 7.2). Third, this chapter recaps critical claims about how combining legal and policy responses at the international level can help reformulate the balance between treaty-based commitments and states' sovereignty to take security actions under WTO agreements, RTAs, and IIAs (section 7.3).

7.1 From Insecurity to Security

As things stand now, WTO agreements incorporate Security Exception clauses that use self-judging language yet limit permissible Security Measures to military and defense-related goods and the situations of war or other emergency in international relations. The wording of such exceptions has remained the same since 1947. Such Security Exceptions arguably lack the flexibility to justify responses to imminent cybersecurity concerns or to emerging concerns arising from the need to protect critical infrastructure or prevent the consequences of climate change and pandemics, since it would be difficult to prove that they meet the requirements of one of the subparagraphs of current Article XXI(b) GATT (1994).[2]

[1] See also Olga Hrynkiv, 'Legal and Policy Responses to Security Measures under International Economic Law' (2024) 54(2) Georgetown J Intl L 165.

[2] See more chapter 6, section 6.2.2.

The approach to drafting Security Exceptions in Regional Agreements depends on the contracting parties at issue and has been changing over time.[3] The EU prefers to follow the approach used in WTO agreements. In most cases, BRICS also incorporate in their RTAs the Security Exceptions modeled on the WTO law. Conversely, the recent tendency of the US is to include a broad self-judging Security Exception concerning trade matters and a non-reviewable Security Exception concerning investment matters. Other countries, such as Brazil, India, and South Africa, take the direction of completely excluding the adjudicatory review of investment disputes when Security Exceptions are invoked. In the aftermath of the Argentine crisis and the inconsistent decisions of investment tribunals trying to embody the stricter conditions of the customary defense of necessity in the treaty exceptions, states might see the possibility that exhaustively drafted exceptions and their inconsistent treatment by tribunals could undermine national regulatory priorities, making investment-related Security Exceptions that are drafted in broad terms a more appealing option. Such Security Exceptions might, though, provide insufficient control over states' behavior and grant excessive scope for permissible action in dimensions other than national security.

It follows that existing Security Exception clauses are either drafted too broadly, making it difficult to control the good faith application of Security Measures (such as "self-judging" or nonreviewable exceptions),[4] or too narrowly, arguably excluding the novel and emerging security threats from their scope (such as WTO-like Security Exceptions).[5] There is a risk that both approaches might undermine the balance between states' sovereignty and international economic law by either unjustifiably limiting the ability of WTO members to take security actions or nullifying the benefits of free trade and investment liberalization by allowing any measure that a state considers necessary.

Looking at the approaches of major schools of thought on the power or strategically invoked economic discourses lends support to this argument.

From the perspective of realism, power politics always prevails over legalism.[6] The rise in conventional and emerging security threats, protectionism, the securitization of different policy areas, and the lack of trust among contracting parties seem to nourish one another. Competing

[3] Chapter 4, section 4.1 and 4.2.
[4] Chapter 6.
[5] Ibid.
[6] Chapter 2, section 2.5.2.

narratives and strategic politics signal not only the pursuit of relative power and security by individual states but also the significance of relative economic competitiveness within the current global order and its impact on interstate cooperation. In particular, politically and economically powerful states might seek to rebalance the international trade order to better reflect their current perceived interests and reinforce their sense of security. By doing so, they can be expected to push the boundaries of Security Exceptions under WTO and other trade agreements if it is necessary to achieve their national objectives. They are also more likely to claim that security matters are overwhelmingly political in nature and thus nonjusticiable, advocating for a broader scope of national security defense under international law. The US–China strategic rivalry that justifies the use of economic institutions and rules at the service of US foreign policy is a good example of such realistic premises. On the flip side, politically and economically "weaker" states might view Security Exceptions as a shield from the economic coercion used against them by "stronger" states, preferring to limit their scope to specific situations.

In the realist scenario, it might be in the interests of the international trade regime to permit the most powerful states to temporarily modify their commitments for the duration of situations they consider to be extreme and dangerous for their existence while maintaining their continued participation in treaties. It is not to say that Security Exceptions should be transformed into an open escape clause that has no limits. Security defenses should continue to be available in extremely rare situations with the idea that the concerned states would return to compliance as soon as possible and other governments would continue to perceive a security defense as an exception rather than a rule. Yet, while looking at international trade and investment agreements through enforcement lenses can help establish who is more convincing in proving the urgency to protect national interests, it would doubtfully encourage compliance by or affect the opportunistic tendencies of certain governments.

Since states define their national security interests differently and their approach to the determination of a threat to national interests cannot be set in stone, the exact limits of Security Exceptions should rather be clarified ex post through a dialogue between interested parties rather than adjudication. For example, the US seems to follow such an approach. It claims that it has complete discretion to take any measures it considers necessary to protect its national security interests, yet, it is ready to negotiate and, where required, lift such measures with like-minded partners. It might be, however, close to impossible to start a dialogue and reach an agreement on Security Measures imposed against strategic rivals, such as in the US–China relations. Thus, the dialogue alone should not be seen as a way to tame certain states' "national security" interests without any additional guidance on the limits of Security Exceptions agreed upon ex ante.

Distinct from realism, institutionalism turns attention away from the power narrative to the global legal, political, and economic architecture that shapes states' behavior. From the institutionalism lens, the preference for multilateralism or unilateralism will always remain a political choice of governments, biased due to WTO members' economic and political structures and the multi-government construction of international politics.[7]

Allowing any WTO member to escape its trade commitments based on false security concerns will undermine the credibility of this member before other members and the incentive to cooperate with it. Yet, states can be expected to violate treaties when their interests are strong enough to outweigh their sense of obligation and where they do not perceive their reputational costs and the risk of noncooperation as the more significant threat. It follows that should all legitimate security concerns be adequately accommodated under international agreements, states would have less incentive to push the boundaries of existing Security Exceptions and be more careful with advancing clearly illegitimate claims. Reputational costs might not be enough to preclude a state from adopting effective Security Measures in breach of its treaty commitments where it has no other legitimate way to protect its interests. However, where other legitimate options exist, a state might be more reluctant to securitize its policy objectives or undermine the legitimacy of international organizations and dispute resolution from which it also profits. Thus, optimal Security Exceptions should be broad enough to allow states to address their essential concerns, where there is no other legitimate way to protect national interests, but narrow enough not to undermine the existing international trade regime.

In some cases, providing credible information might be enough to encourage states to adopt measures more in line with their international commitments.[8] To illustrate, reforming the regulation of Security Measures under WTO law by creating a WTO committee on national

[7] Chapter 2, section 2.5.3.

[8] Timothy Meyer, 'Cooperating without Sanctions: Epistemic Institutions versus Credible Commitments Regimes in International Law' in Harlan Grant Cohen and Timothy Meyer (eds.), *International Law as Behavior* (CUP 2021) 61.

security measures (hereafter the Committee on Security Measures) and/or cooperating more closely with the UN can provide states with better guidance and space to exchange information and views, develop best practices, and improve the framework for better cooperation when addressing national security concerns and the possibility of invoking Security Exceptions under different circumstances.

From the perspective of constructivism, beyond the substantive, procedural, and evidential controls over the application of Security Measures, there appears to be an additional form of control operating besides mere textual interpretation of a treaty – the development of common or shared interests as a method of setting boundaries on unilateral state discretion.[9] Shared ideas and norms shape expectations about the appropriate behavior of actors and give a structure to the international order. When shared norms become internalized in actor beliefs and identities, they go unchallenged.

The proliferation of economic statecraft and national security rhetoric, resulting in the more frequent use of Security Exceptions under international law, suggests a fracturing of the global economic order partly due to conflicting norms and interests. Different governments seem to adopt different discursive strategies. While some continue to package trade and investment liberalization as a necessary response to external economic imperatives (e.g. the EU), others present economic interdependence as a threat to their national security (e.g. the US). Choosing one of these strategies plays a key role in shaping domestic political processes and has implications for a state's interaction with other actors, including its approach to drafting Security Exceptions under Regional Agreements and the invocation of Security Exceptions under WTO law.

If a state perceives that others share its values, it is more likely to cooperate on the boundaries of Security Measures. If, however, a state perceives the values of other actors as too different, even alien, it is more likely to portray their actions as an existential threat to its place in the international system and to use extreme responses to defend its interests. To take just one obvious example, notwithstanding the concerns raised at the WTO level, the US continues to securitize trade with China and to put significant effort into restraining China's development of technologies

[9] Ilona Cheyne, 'Deference and the Use of the Public Policy Exception in International Courts and Tribunals' in Lukasz Gruszczynski and Wouter Werner (eds.), *Deference in International Courts and Tribunals: Standard of Review and Margin of Appreciation* (OUP 2014) 56.

that are critical for its technological and military advancement.[10] On this view, existing linkages between trade and the security of cyberspace, the environment, health, or domestic stability can be portrayed as either a security issue or normal state policy, depending on a state's perception of other actors and the reliability of the international trading system as a whole.

As advanced by the concept of securitization, where an issue becomes a part of a domestic security discourse, extreme responses by the government become more credible to its citizens at the domestic level.[11] In this case, governments might also be more eager to portray such an issue as necessary for its national security interests at an international level and invoke a Security Exception. Security Exceptions subject to international review can provide some necessary guidance on the restraint of unnecessary securitization by embodying the rules of a just securitization theory. Such rules could differentiate between an objectively existing and a perceived existential threat to national security and establish the moral legitimacy of domestic interests to be protected by the measure and its appropriateness.[12] Such a test can be embodied in treaties by allowing adjudicators to review the existence of security threats subject to objective determination and the appropriateness of the response to them. Yet, where the objective determination of the threat by an adjudicator is impossible or not desired by the parties, Security Exceptions would not be able to separate the extraordinary circumstances when emergency actions should be allowed from the normal times when states should rely on ordinary policy measures. In this case, states might defer to power politics.

From the economic contract theory perspective, being unable to predict all future emergencies and their effects on interstate cooperation, contracting parties will always be reluctant to accept Security Exceptions that are governed by specific ex ante rules, leaving no or little room for maneuver. States choose to cooperate in their interest, but if circumstances change (costs and benefits), states may prefer to renegotiate or

[10] See eg 'Commerce Implements New Export Controls on Advanced Computing and Semiconductor Manufacturing Items to the People's Republic of China (PRC)' (Press Release of Bureau of Industry and Security, October 7, 2022) www.bis.doc.gov/index.php/documents/about-bis/newsroom/press-releases/3158-2022-10-07-bis-press-release-advanced-computing-and-semiconductor-manufacturing-controls-final/file.

[11] Chapter 2, section 2.5.5.

[12] Ibid.

deviate from their obligations.[13] Developments in the national security policies and trade agendas of different WTO members and a new geo-economic reality contribute to the changes in the costs and benefits of the performance of states' trade and investment commitments under international law. Such developments might require states to renegotiate their commitments or use more flexibility to deviate from them. In practice, when the core values of a state are at stake, such as national security, the costs of nonperformance outweigh the benefits of trade.[14] In this case, the best international law can do is to allow a state to suspend its obligations for the period of any such extraordinary situation, encouraging it to return to its performance as soon as the situation normalizes.

Existing Security Exceptions generally permit WTO members to use trade restrictions to protect their national security without bearing direct monetary costs while putting the burden of reduced market access on the members affected by such restrictions. If adopting a Security Measure were, however, made more costly for an invoking state, it would be more likely to avoid fostering the excessive securitization of domestic policies and, even in the case the international obligations were suspended because of the necessity to address security threats, it will still have the incentive to continue performing such obligations as soon as it becomes feasible. Thus, focusing on the costs of Security Measures, instead of establishing the "correct" balance between national security interests and commitments under international law, could encourage WTO members to estimate in advance the price they would need to pay for adopting Security Measures and thus behave more efficiently.[15]

Asking different theories to share common assumptions about the role of Security Exceptions in international law and politics is unrealistic. Yet, looking at their approaches to power, interstate relations, and global order, one can see a common view that it might be practically impossible to completely segregate the approaches toward, on the one hand, the scope of a national security defense under international economic law and, on the other, developments in national security policies and the international trading system. The securitization of additional policy areas, the changes in the costs and benefits of performance under treaties due to emerging concerns and the instability of the international trade order, and the erosion of the norms of self-restraint confirm that states'

[13] Chapter 2, section 2.5.1.

[14] David D Knoll, 'The Impact of Security Concerns upon International Economic Law' (1984) 11(3) Intl Econ L 567, 569.

[15] Harlan Grant Cohen, 'Nations and Markets' (2020) 23(4) J Intl Econ L 793, 812.

perception of threats to their national security has broadened and most likely will continue to change. States might appreciate policy space to respond to novel technological, social, and geopolitical changes or the rising importance of new actors in the global economy, including the non-state actors that act entirely in cyberspace.[16] Yet, Security Exceptions under WTO law do not reflect the portrayed developments in states' understanding of national security and the transitions that have happened in geopolitical and geo-economic contexts since 1947.

Even in the absence of a formal exception justifying its action, where a state genuinely perceives that a threat to its national security exists, there is no ground to believe that it would choose to comply with its international commitments rather than address a pressing domestic concern. In a similar vein, a state should not be expected to withdraw its Security Measure in compliance with the court's or tribunal's ruling. It would thus be counterproductive to ignore emerging security concerns by not recognizing their validity under international economic law, thereby putting the Security Measures adopted to address such concerns outside the international treaty regime. Instead, it can be suggested that international economic law should be flexible enough to encompass a broad set of rationales for unilateral measures aimed at protecting states' security interests, while discouraging opportunism and maintaining a sustainable balance between reciprocal commitments and states' unilateral interests.

Establishing such a balance based on the existing approaches to drafting Security Exceptions might be difficult in practice for the following reasons. In the 1940s, Security Exceptions under the GATT (1947) were designed both to ensure a balance between national autonomy and states' international responsibilities and to diminish possible abuse by giving each contracting party flexibility to determine when their Security Measures were necessary while limiting ex ante the specific situations in which such measures could be justified. The incorporation of such exceptions encouraged the parties to invest in the contractual relationship in the first place. The GATT and earlier WTO practices also reaffirm that such narrowly tailored exceptions could function reasonably well, despite their self-judging language, as long as they reflected the most prominent security concerns faced by GATT contracting parties/WTO members.

[16] Geraldo Vidigal and Stephan W Schill, 'International Economic Law and the Securitization of Policy Objectives: Risks of a Schmittean Exception' (2021) 48(2) Legal Issues of Economic Integration 109, 116.

Yet, WTO-style Security Exceptions were narrowly tailored ex ante (at the time of treaty conclusion) to address legitimate national security concerns only with respect to a limited number of situations where all contracting parties were ready to justify emergency actions at the time of negotiations. Such an agreement is not prepared to address all future contingencies, or, as the current practice reaffirms, is impossible to adhere to because of the ever-evolving threats to national security and different perceptions of their urgency by different WTO members, which is fostered nowadays by the emergence of new technologies and diverse risks that novel global concerns pose to different states. When the scope of Security Exceptions cannot be reasonably limited ex ante, the cost-benefit analysis informed by the economic contract theory favors the creation of broader standards that would leave contracting parties with more space to define their security concerns ex post (at the time of the adoption of a Security Measure).

However, the inclusion of broadly drafted Security Exceptions not limited ex ante to specific goods or situations creates more opportunities for nonperformance. Furthermore, the problem with adjudicators demarcating the scope of states' legitimate security concerns ex post is that the standard of review of the measures adopted in response to such concerns and the standard of their proof would invoke additional hurdles inherent in the interpretation of highly volatile concepts that can be subject, at least to a certain extent, to the nondisclosure exception.[17] International adjudicators would not always have access to the information necessary to verify the true motives or the effectiveness of Security Measures aimed to deal with such concerns or the availability of less trade-restrictive alternatives. It follows that traditional mechanisms used to balance national interests and binding law, such as a necessity test, might be of little help for adjudicators dealing with such cases. At the same time, requiring a responding state to only demonstrate a good faith invocation of Security Exceptions or making Security Measures non-reviewable increases the chances of states' opportunistic behavior. Such an open escape clause would be especially challenging to control when a state invokes emerging security concerns that are more difficult to define and verify with precision than the objective conditions of the emergency associated with ongoing wars or arms trafficking. The result could be vague standards

[17] Chapter 6.

that create unclear expectations for contracting parties and verification problems for adjudicators.

Drawing on the discussed theories and the portrayed problems arising from the application and adjudication of existing Security Exceptions, this research suggests that international rules should seek to distinguish the validity of security concerns on the basis of context. On the one hand, threats to national security produced by unforeseen externalities or other developments that are reasonably clearly defined in the agreement, such as the situation of war under Article XXI(b) GATT (1994) subject to objective review, allow an adjudicator to verify their genuine invocation and thus leave less room for abuse. The virtue of such an approach is that it preserves a broad degree of policy space for states to pursue their security interests under well-defined and observable circumstances while ensuring that they do not deliberately impose high costs on other contracting parties. On the other hand, this book argues that international law should also address other situations of unforeseen extraordinary contingencies that would compel government officials to deviate from their international commitments even in the absence of a formal exception. The virtue of incorporating the exception for such other situations is that it would permit temporary deviation from the commitments to preserve long-term cooperation. Yet, incentivizing politically efficient policy choices in the presence of an open-ended exception clause drafted for any externalities, not clearly defined by the contracting parties, might be more challenging if such an exception is left completely unconstrained. In this case, it would make an international treaty too expensive to enforce.

All this considered, the dialogue between states over a revised approach toward Security Exceptions might start with the proposal to draw a line between conventional security matters (hereafter the Conventional Security Measures), for which there is an ex ante agreement among all WTO members to justify extreme responses, and other security matters that might arise in the future or that are of concern for some contracting parties but where the agreement between all contracting parties over their urgency has not yet been reached (hereafter the Novel Security Measures). Given the evolving character of security concerns and the discussed difficulties of enforcing strict limits on their scope by adjudicators ex post, states might consider introducing new mechanisms to rebalance the right of a contracting party to adopt a Novel Security Measure and the substantive rights of other contracting parties in trade and investment liberalization.

7.2 Enhanced Control over the Application of Security Measures

This research adopts a comprehensive view of governance over Security Measures, which addresses the role of domestic and international institutions that can be potentially involved in revisiting the scope of Security Exceptions under international economic law. First, in light of the rise of emerging issues potentially related to the national security of at least some states, WTO members might choose to clarify at the WTO level the list of policy areas and activities that can fall within the scope of their "essential security interests" within the meaning of the WTO Security Exceptions. Such an approach would reassure members that Security Exceptions will be legitimately relied on when a threat is posed to the areas that WTO members agree to view as essential for their national security while concurrently decreasing unnecessary securitization of states' policies in other areas. Second, WTO members could ensure better transparency and accountability in the application and maintenance of Security Measures by adopting additional procedural safeguards for Security Exceptions. Third, the oversight of Security Measures might draw upon centralized security governance at the UN level. Fourth, the abusive use of Security Exceptions might be tamed through domestic policies and diplomacy that address the non-cooperative behavior of specific states. Finally, drawing on the economic contract theory, additional rebalancing mechanisms might incentivize WTO members to use Security Measures more efficiently.

7.2.1 Role of the WTO Ministerial Conference and the General Council

Given the lack of convergence among WTO members on the scope of some concepts used in existing Security Exceptions and the fear that the judicialization of national security matters could compromise the credibility of international adjudicators and undermine the treaty regime, it can be suggested that it would be better for the scope of Security Exceptions to be clarified by WTO members collectively rather than through litigation.[18] To illustrate, the Ministerial Conference or the General Council can adopt an official interpretation of Article XXI(b)

[18] Ernst-Ulrich Petersmann, 'WTO Negotiators and Academics Analyse the Doha Development Round of the WTO' in Ernst-Ulrich Petersmann and James Harrison (eds.), *Reforming the World Trading System: Legitimacy, Efficiency, and Democratic Governance* (International Economic Law Series OUP 2005) 35.

GATT (1994) pursuant to Article XI of the Marrakesh Agreement, which would include an illustrative list of policy areas that would naturally come within the ambit of Security Exceptions.[19] WTO members might also agree to clarify whether such Security Measures have to meet a certain degree of urgency (immediate threat from Russia's military actions in Ukraine versus potential concerns from the rising power of China) or whether they can be proactive or only defensive measures (aimed at preventing a new pandemic versus responding to terrorist actions).[20]

Such a proposal would encourage WTO members to seek a common understanding of the scope of Security Exceptions and ensure that national or regional regulatory objectives and practices in terms of the application of Security Measures are as transparent and detailed as possible.[21] When a state invokes a Security Exception to protect one of the areas from the list, it is more easily to be found to have acted in good faith. In this sense, the adoption of the list could help address several flaws of existing Security Exceptions: it would discourage the abuse of Security Exceptions and the invocation of Security Exceptions where the measure is covered by another more specific exception (such as by one of the subparagraphs of Article XX or Article XIX GATT (1994)), while also recognizing that certain other areas whose coverage by the existing exceptions remains questionable (such as activities in cyberspace or activities aimed to protect states' critical infrastructure) could receive legitimate protection in certain cases.

Yet, such a consensus might be difficult to reach in practice among all WTO members. First, a problem with this approach is the constant emergence of new threats to national security. Any decision of the Ministerial Conference or the General Council could only temporarily satisfy the legitimate need of WTO members to address their security concerns.

Second, establishing the list means recognizing that national security threats differ in magnitude and only particular concerns can reach the threshold to be justified under Security Exceptions. While this argument is entirely correct from the analytical perspective, as the practice of WTO members demonstrates, national security might mean different things to

[19] Article IX(2) of Marrakesh Agreement.

[20] See more eg Daniel W Drezner, 'How Everything Became National Security and National Security Became Everything' (2024) 103 Foreign Affairs 122.

[21] UNCTAD, 'The Protection of National Security in IIAs' (2009) UNCTAD Series on International Investment Policies for Development 24–25 https://unctad.org/webflyer/protection-national-security-iias.

different countries.[22] This also implies that the magnitude of a threat to national security posed by the same type of concern might be seen differently by different governments. Cybersecurity might be considered a primary security concern for developed countries, such as the US and EU member states, but be less relevant for some developing and least-developed countries.

Finally, the decision to adopt an interpretation of Article XXI GATT (1994) shall be taken by consensus, meaning that no WTO member present at the meeting where the decision is taken formally opposes the decision. If consensus cannot be achieved, the decision will then be determined by a majority vote.[23] In practice, the decisions in GATT/WTO have been taken mostly through consensus.[24] Thus, to reach a convergence of minds on the security areas would mean drafting a list that includes security concerns that all WTO members acknowledge. Consensus decisions better reflect the views of different WTO members and ensure that decisions and agreements are reached after careful discussions, which is appreciated by democracy theory.[25] At the same time, it allows a few uncooperative members to block any progress for long periods. Given that certain WTO members prefer to keep the scope of Security Exceptions narrower than others, the probability of reaching a consensus on the more concrete limits of national security defenses in the current geopolitical environment seems relatively low. To illustrate, in December 2024, at the close of Biden's administration, the US put out a formal proposal for the authoritative interpretation of Security Exceptions, reaffirming the US arguments that Article XXI is self-judging and that, if it is invoked, WTO Members shall have only recourse to a nonviolation nullification or impairment claim.[26] It isn't very likely that many other Members will endorse the proposed interpretation of Security Exceptions.

While reaching a consensus at the WTO level over the exact scope of all Security Exceptions ex ante might be close to impossible, WTO members might be more willing to cooperate on the clarification of the scope of the exception for Conventional Security Measures. *Russia – Traffic in Transit*

[22] Chapter 3.

[23] Article IX(2) of Marrakesh Agreement.

[24] Claus-Dieter Ehlermann and Lothar Ehring, 'Decision-making in the World Trade Organization' (2005) 8(1) J Intl Econ L 51, 51.

[25] Bashar Malkavi, 'Guest Post: Consensus as the Hallmark of the WTO: Time to Change' (*IELP Blog*, June 23, 2022) https://ielp.worldtradelaw.net/.

[26] Communication from the US, 'Reflections from the United States on the Handling of Disputes Involving Essential Security Measures' (December 11, 2024) JOB/DSB/10. See more chapter 7, section 7.2.5.1.

and *Saudi Arabia – IPRs* lend support to the assumption that disputes over security matters that are related to armed conflict or heightened tension or crisis that fall under narrowly drafted Security Exceptions can be resolved through traditional adjudicative mechanisms, which are used to balance national interests and binding law. The approach of WTO panels to interpreting Security Exceptions in these cases can be a basis for dialogue between WTO members on further clarification of the scope of Conventional Security Measures. The adoption of the list could be an attractive option for those WTO members that want to ensure greater certainty and predictability in the application of existing Article XXI(b) GATT (1994) by limiting it to specific areas, such as military and defense-related matters. But it could also be in the interests of those members that would prefer to expand its scope to additional areas, such as activities in cyberspace and areas related to critical infrastructure. The compromise between the two approaches seems more probable when, in addition to the narrowly drafted and interpreted Article XXI(b), the WTO law granted members other exceptions, such as those covering Novel Security Measures.

If adopted, the decision of the Ministerial Conference or the General Council on the clarification of the scope of Article XXI(b) GATT (1994) might also guide other trade and investment tribunals dealing with Security Exceptions modeled on WTO law.

7.2.2 *Role of Transparency and Accountability Rules*

WTO members might help normalize the extensive use of Security Measures by agreeing on general procedural requirements that make Article XXI(b) GATT (1994) and Security Exceptions under other trade and investment agreements more difficult to invoke if the measure does not have a clear national security nexus. Procedural requirements might also control the timely lifting of Security Measures, thereby offering an alternative mode for unilateralism based on transparency and peer monitoring.

7.2.2.1 Existing Notification Requirements

WTO members have not subjected the adoption of Security Measures under WTO agreements to specific procedural steps.[27] Nor does the

[27] Wolfgang Alschner and Kun Hui, 'Missing in Action: General Public Policy Exceptions in Investment Treaties' in Lisa Sachs, Jesse Coleman, and Lise Johnson (eds.), *Yearbook on International Investment Law and Policy* (OUP 2018) [21:63].

WTO judiciary have the authority to enforce such procedural guidelines. To illustrate, Article XXI GATT (1994) contains no procedural requirements. In 1982, the GATT Ministerial Meeting adopted the Article XXI Decision, which requires that contracting parties be informed as fully as possible of trade measures adopted under Article XXI of GATT.[28] Furthermore, the duty to notify is subject to Article XXI(a) GATT (1994), allowing the WTO members not to "furnish any information the disclosure of which it considers contrary to its essential security interests."[29]

By contrast, the parallel Security Exception in Article XIV*bis* GATS incorporates a binding notification requirement.[30] Accordingly, WTO members must notify the Council for Trade in Services (CTS) of those measures that fall within Article XIV*bis* to the fullest extent possible. The obligation inherently operates based on ad hoc notification of measures taken.

Furthermore, it can be argued that notwithstanding the lack of clear procedural rules, the notification of contracting parties is a strict duty mandated by the general duty of good faith and the practicalities of a treaty system as large and complex as WTO agreements.[31] In particular, WTO panels can divine the nature and scope of procedural requirements from the implied principle of good faith, including reason-giving, public participation, and transparency in the decision-making process.[32] At the national level (and similarly at the EU level), courts might encourage governments to improve procedures for implementing trade and investment restrictions, promoting mutual learning and experimentation with what constitutes legitimate procedures.[33] However, without explicit treaty standards, it is less clear how international courts or tribunals, acting independently, could effectively contribute to developing appropriate procedures for reviewing states' Security Measures.

As things stand now, WTO members continue to follow existing notification requirements under the GATS and Article XXI Decision

[28] GATT, Decision Concerning Article XXI of the General Agreement (December 2, 1982) L/5426 www.wto.org/gatt_docs/english/SULPDF/91000212.pdf.

[29] See more chapter 5, section 5.2.4.

[30] Andrew D Mitchell, 'Sanctions and the World Trade Organization' in Larissa Van den Herik (ed.), *Research Handbook on UN Sanctions and International Law* (Edward Elgar Publishing 2017) 302.

[31] Ibid.

[32] J Benton Heath, 'The New National Security Challenge to the Economic Order' (2020) 129 Yale LJ 1020, 1074.

[33] Ibid 1079.

selectively,[34] not at least because of the lack of clarity regarding how Article XXI(a) GATT (1994) or equivalent provisions under the other agreements limit the scope of such notification.

The situation is not more straightforward under Regional Agreements. Not all of them require contracting parties to notify about the adoption of Security Measures.[35] Even if they do, parties might rely on the nondisclosure exception to circumvent the disclosure of any information related to their national security.[36] It follows that, in the case of broadly drafted Security Exceptions, states can impose trade restrictions for protectionist purposes or mixed motives but later invoke Security Exceptions during adjudication, labeling the restriction as a Security Measure[37] (even if there is no evidence that any national security concerns were invoked to adopt the measure at the first place).

7.2.2.2 Way Forward

WTO agreements already provide a sophisticated infrastructure for transparency and peer review concerning specific trade-restrictive measures. For example, the SPS Agreement was adopted to encourage reliance on and participation in international standards, guidelines, and recommendations developed by relevant international organizations,[38] thereby reducing unilateral incentives and promoting the harmonization of SPS measures. One of its control mechanisms is to ensure transparency through the notification procedure that requires a member to give advance notice before adopting a standard.[39] "Where urgent problems of health protection arise or threaten to arise for a Member," such

[34] For example, Ukraine informed the WTO and its members about a complete economic embargo on Russia pursuant to Article XXI GATT, Article XXI Decision, Article XIVbis, paragraph 2, GATS, and Article 73 of the TRIPs Agreement. See Ukraine's Letter No 80/017 from March 2, 2022 to the WTO General Council.

Similarly, the US related to import and export prohibitions against Russia on the ground of national security pursuant to the Decision on notification procedures for quantitative restrictions. See US' Notification G/MA/QR/N/USA/5/Add.3 from March 21, 2022 to the Committee on Market Access. Yet, not all Security Measures are notified to the WTO.

[35] See eg US–Colombia TPA (2006).

[36] See eg Article 32.2(a) of USMSA (2018) allowing not to disclose certain information.

[37] See eg *Angel Samuel Seda and others v Republic of Colombia* (February 16, 2022) ICSID Case No ARB/19/6 Respondent's Rejoinder.

[38] Joel P Trachtman, 'A Map of the World Trade Organization Law of Domestic Regulation of Goods: The Technical Barriers to Trade Agreement, the Sanitary and Phytosanitary Measures Agreement, and the General Agreement on Tariffs and Trade' (2014) 48(2) JWT 351, 366.

[39] Article 7 of SPS Agreement.

a notification can be made after the particular regulation is adopted.[40] Annex B of the SPS Agreement clarifies, inter alia, that a member has to publish a notice introducing SPS regulation, identifying the products to be covered by the regulation, and including a brief indication of its objective and rationale, thereby providing a basis for debate with other members.

The TBT Agreement also specifies the notification procedure for technical barriers, including those taken to address national security concerns.[41] As in the case of the SPS Agreement, the information about TBT measures shall be published ex ante before their adoption.[42] Yet, "[w]here urgent problems of safety, health, environmental protection or national security arise or threaten to arise for a Member," that state is only required to give notice about the adoption of the TBT measure at a later stage after the measure has been adopted.[43] Such notification should contain a brief indication of the objective of and rationale for the measure.[44] Notably, the presence of the equivalent of Article XXI(a) GATT (1994) under the TBT Agreement might also impede the effectiveness of such a procedure.[45]

Finally, the Agreement on Safeguards also imposes obligations on members to notify the WTO Committee on Safeguards about an intent to apply a safeguard measure and to enter consultations with other members, allowing them to, among others, review the provided information and exchange views on the measure.[46]

To ensure more transparency in the application of Security Measures and avoid the perpetual struggle of drawing the line between Security Measures and other public policy measures or protectionist measures, WTO agreements and Regional Agreements might subject the invocation of Security Exceptions to more specific notification requirements drawn on the principles prescribed for TBT, SPS, and safeguard measures, taking into account the sensitivity of the information related to states' security concerns. Notifying trading partners of a Security Measure is a starting point for interactions between WTO members. Governments

[40] Ibid Annex B, para. 6.

[41] Articles 2.2, 2.9, and 5.6 of TBT Agreement.

[42] Ibid Articles 2.11, 2.12, 5.8, 5.9.

[43] Ibid Articles 2.10, 5.7.

[44] Ibid Article 2.10.1.

[45] Ibid Article 10.8.3. See more Mona Paulsen, 'Let's Agree to Disagree: A Strategy for Trade-Security' (2022) 24(4) J Intl Econ L 527.

[46] Article 12 of the Agreement on Safeguards.

could be required to give notice about the intent to adopt a Security Measure. Yet, where urgent problems of national security arise or threaten to arise for a member, it should be allowed to submit a notification after the adoption of the Security Measure, though as soon as practically possible.

Similar to safeguard measures, it could be required that in order to fall under Article XXI GATT (1994), "a measure must present certain constituent features," absent which it could not be considered a Security Measure.[47] For one, domestic authorities could be allowed to invoke Security Exceptions only if the measure were characterized as a Security Measure under domestic law; namely, the domestic procedures that led to its adoption were related to dealing with national security threats, and the measure had been notified to the WTO. There might be some additional specific requirements to the form of notifications; for example, a state might have to substantiate that it had specific security purposes for the application of such measures or to reveal such factual elements as may be required to show that it either was at war or had another emergency.[48] Unlike in the case of safeguard, TBT, or SPS measures, domestic authorities should not be expected to make publicly available an investigation report or a report explaining the conclusion reached before applying the Security Measure. Instead, they should be able to refer to the domestic regulations and procedures according to which the measure was established and their relevance to national security considerations. In case of a dispute, a WTO panel could review all these aspects of the measure in order to determine whether a WTO member could justify it under Security Exceptions.

Admittedly, the suggestion to prescribe specific notification rules for the invocation of Security Exceptions comes with some carve-outs.

First, the practice of the application of other trade measures reveals the problem with the "chronic low level of compliance with existing notification requirements" under many WTO agreements.[49] A proposal to strengthen WTO notification requirements is not new. For example,

[47] For example, with respect to safeguard measures *Indonesia – Safeguard on Certain Iron or Steel Products* (August 15, 2018) Appellate Body Report WT/DS490/AB/R; WT/DS496/AB/R [5.60].

[48] Michael J Hahn, 'Vital Interests and the Law of GATT: An Analysis of GATT's Security Exception' (1991) 12 Mich J Intl L 558, 618–619.

[49] Council for Trade in Goods, Procedures To Enhance Transparency And Strengthen Notification Requirements Under WTO Agreements (June 25, 2021) JOB/GC/204/Rev5 JOB/CTG/14/Rev5, Preamble.

eleven WTO members, including the EU and the US, have suggested strengthening notification requirements under WTO agreements by moving the supervision over compliance with such requirements away from formal dispute settlement.[50] Among others, the proposal advances the reform based on which the failure to notify within prescribed time periods is identified automatically rather than by adjudicators, and such a failure can automatically lead to certain administrative measures.[51] Adopting a similar proposal in the future could boost the advantages of prescribing a mandatory notification requirement in the case of the use of Security Measures. In particular, WTO members could agree on the conditions under which a WTO member can be deemed to have failed to notify its Security Measure to the WTO, without waiting for the decision of a WTO adjudicator, and to preclude such a member from invoking Security Exceptions to justify such a measure.

Second, the reliance on the member's notification on the adoption of Security Measures implies that states are expected to design the domestic process of adopting Security Measures in a way that ensures that such measures are directed at genuine and pressing national security concerns. This, of course, requires economic measures to have clearly articulated security goals and procedures for their adoption – a questionable proposition in many cases.

As domestic law and practice demonstrate,[52] the US, the EU, and BRICS consider some threats to their national security to be more compelling than others, which can affect their choice of the type of response to the threat and the strategy to justify it when taken to an international court. More policy objectives are securitized in single-minded WTO members, such as the US, than in a multilateral entity,

[50] General Council, Draft Decision on Procedures to Enhance Transparency and Strengthen Notification Requirements under WTO Agreements (June 25, 2021) JOB/GC/204/Rev.5 JOB/CTG/14/Rev.5. See also comments of Joost Pauwelyn on earlier draft in Joost Pauwelyn, 'New Proposal to Strengthen WTO Notification Requirements: From Dispute Settlement to Compliance Regime?' (*IELP Blog*, April 3, 2019) https://ielp.worldtradelaw.net/2019/04/new-proposal-to-strengthen-wto-notification-requirements-from-dispute-settlement-to-compliance-regim.html. This proposal was eventually revisited and amended in General Council, Draft Decision on Procedures to Enhance Transparency and Strengthen Notification Requirements under WTO Agreements (April 28, 2022) JOB/GC/204/Rev.9 JOB/CTG/14/Rev.9.

[51] General Council, Draft Decision on Procedures to Enhance Transparency and Strengthen Notification Requirements under WTO Agreements (June 25, 2021) JOB/GC/204/Rev.5 JOB/CTG/14/Rev.5 [11].

[52] Chapter 3.

such as the EU. Notably, while the US is specific about the cases when its trade and investment restrictions can be adopted for national security purposes, other states, such as Russia, China, and India, draft their regulations very broadly, leaving vast discretion to domestic authorities to decide on a case-by-case basis when the application of economic restrictions in the interest of national security is justifiable.

The lack of articulated or achievable security goals questions the good faith application of Security Measures. The nontransparent decision-making process of some governments, the exclusion of national security issues from the review of domestic courts, and past examples of controversial Security Measures adopted to satisfy the interests of domestic political elites also signal little incentive to elaborate on domestic procedural safeguards that would prevent the abuse of security discourse. Finally, when states see economic warfare as a way to gain a competitive advantage in technological, agricultural, or vital industries, they care about the immediate costs and benefits of such measures rather than their moral value. It follows from such realists' premises that domestic control over Security Measures is not an idealistic postulate that could tame states' growing appetite to escape from their obligations under international economic agreements.

Nevertheless, requiring an ex ante notification for Security Measures would make WTO members think more carefully about the scope of Security Exceptions and the design of their regulations and would incentivize them to consider the nature of potentially illegal measures before actually adopting them. Even a retrospective disclosure following the adoption of a Security Measure, as is the case for urgent TBT or SPS measures, can encourage proper debate and discussion before litigation and opens the door for more dialogue. The practice of the application of SPS measures confirms such a view.[53]

The WTO could also improve the interaction among WTO members by facilitating periodic reviews and consultations concerning the need to adopt and maintain Security Measures.[54] Based on the examples of safeguard, TBT, and SPS measures, the Committee on Security Measures

[53] See more Henrik Horn, Petros C Mavroidis, and Erik N Wijkström, 'In the Shadow of the DSU: Addressing Specific Trade Concerns in the WTO SPS and TBT Committees' (2013) 47(4) JWT 729, 753.

[54] UNCTAD, 'The Protection of National Security in IIAs' (2009) UNCTAD Series on International Investment Policies for Development 132–135 https://unctad.org/webflyer/protection-national-security-iias.

could help oversee the discussions.[55] Similar periodic reviews and consultations could occur among the contracting parties of Regional Agreements, supervised by the security committees created under the respective agreements. For instance, in the case of an economic crisis, contracting parties could agree to regularly assess during committee meetings whether the crisis was still severe enough to justify applied trade or investment restrictions.[56]

Taking all this together, strengthening the procedural safeguards for invoking Security Exceptions and ensuring transparency in the identification of the objectives of both Conventional and Novel Security Measures and their qualification under domestic law could be an acceptable compromise – albeit, no doubt, imperfect – between oversight and policy discretion in national security disputes for two reasons. First, it would ensure the basis for dialogue between all WTO members about the nature of Security Measures and their impact before any litigation process starts. Second, it would allow international courts and tribunals to focus on procedural judicial review, thereby resolving the most striking problems related to the lack of adjudicator expertise to decide foreign and security matters, restricted access to classified material, and the shortage of necessary personnel to assess specific questions. The turn to procedural limitations on the invocation of Security Exceptions thus could be seen as a method of assuring the good faith behind the application of Security Measures.

7.2.3 Role of the UN

The negotiation and drafting history of the ITO confirms that economic measures undertaken directly in connection with political matters were intended to be left within the UN's competence. Australian, Belgian, and Swedish delegates considered that the ITO should not be left without the capacity to act upon economic measures taken for political reasons where the UN did not or would not involve itself.[57] The delegates of the UK, Greece, the US, South Africa, Iraq, and India argued that a technical,

[55] Simon Lester and Inu Manak, 'A Proposal for a Committee on National Security at the WTO' (2020) 30 Duke J Comparative & Intl Law 267, 267–281.

[56] UNCTAD, 'The Protection of National Security in IIAs' (2009) UNCTAD Series on International Investment Policies for Development 132 https://unctad.org/webflyer/protection-national-security-iias.

[57] David D Knoll, 'The Impact of Security Concerns upon International Economic Law' (1984) 11(3) Intl Econ L 567, 605.

economic organization had to decline jurisdiction over political matters.[58] Mr. Paiva of Brazil suggested that "declining jurisdiction for the ITO provided a pragmatic and generally acceptable solution for states most concerned with the problem ... [t]hese nations could not be coerced to submit to a jurisdiction upon whose parameters agreement could not be reached."[59] The record of the Havana Sub-Committee meeting demonstrates that the delegates eventually concluded that the measures regarding political matters or matters related to the essential interests of members "should be made in connection with an article on 'Relations with the United Nations,' since the question of the proper allocation of responsibility as between the [ITO] and the United Nations was involved."[60]

To address the allocation of responsibility between the ITO and the UN, Article 94(1)(c) was eventually moved to the new Article 86 related to "Relations with the United Nations," while Article 94 became Article 99 of the Havana Draft of the ITO Charter.[61] Article 86 of the Havana Draft dealt with various institutional questions. It stated in paragraph 3:

> The Members recognize that the Organization should not attempt to take action which would involve passing judgment in any way on essentially political matters ... any measure taken by a Member directly in connection with a political matter brought before the United Nations in accordance with the provisions of Chapters IV or VI of the United Nations Charter shall be deemed to fall within the scope of the United Nations, and shall not be subject to the provisions of this Charter.[62]

The interpretative notes to paragraph 3 provided that:

> If any Member raises the question whether a measure is in fact taken directly in connection with a political matter brought before the United Nations in accordance with the provisions of Chapters IV or VI of the United Nations Charter, the responsibility for making a determination on the question shall rest with the Organization. If, however, political issues beyond the competence of the Organization

58 Ibid.
59 Ibid 605–606.
60 US Committee on Interior and Insular Affairs, Hearings, Reports and Prints of the Senate Committee on Interior and Insular Affairs (US Government Printing Office 1954) 929.
61 UN – Economic and Social Council, Preparatory Committee of the UN Conference on Trade and Employment, Final Act of the UN Conference on Trade and Employment and Related Documents (April 1948) 85 www.wto.org/english/docs_e/legal_e/havana_e.pdf.
62 Ibid.

> are involved in making such a determination, the question shall be deemed to fall within the scope of the United Nations.[63]

The purpose of these provisions was explained by the Sixth Committee as follows:

> The Committee was of the opinion that the important thing was to maintain the jurisdiction of the United Nations over political matters and over economic measures of this sort taken directly in connection with such a political matter, and nothing in Article [86] could be held to prejudice the freedom of action of the United Nations to settle such matters and to take steps to deal with such economic measures in accordance with the provisions of the Charter of the United Nations if they see fit to do so.[64]

Thus, it can be understood that the initial purpose of permitting Security Exceptions in the early multilateral trade agreement was to provide flexibility to each contracting party to diverge from the agreed obligations under exceptional emergency situations which deserved political consensus under the UN umbrella.

It can be argued that with its focus on international trade, the WTO can use the expertise of the UN, authorized to deal with questions of international security, to make more sensible decisions on national-security-related matters. For example, instead of or in addition to international trade and investment courts, the oversight of Security Measures can be conducted by the UN or joint UN–WTO committee or mediated settlement supervised by the UN.[65] Thereby, improved interaction between the WTO and the UN can also help retain control over the use of Security Measures without undermining the legitimacy of the international trade regime and its dispute resolution function.

Proposals for enhanced cooperation between the UN and the WTO on security matters are not new. To ensure the proper use of Article XXI(b) GATT (1994), Bhala has suggested increasing coordination between the WTO and the UN Security Council by establishing a joint WTO–Security Council committee on security measures, which could render at least a nonbinding, nonprecedential opinion in each case that addresses the security-related questions.[66] The WTO and the UN pursue similar

[63] Ibid 114.

[64] Ibid.

[65] J Benton Heath, 'The New National Security Challenge to the Economic Order' (2020) 129 Yale LJ 1020, 1080.

[66] In particular, the questions of whether the use of Security Measures comply with the terms of Article XXI(b), and whether such Security Measures are reasonable in relation to the threat or actual danger posed. See Raj Bhala, 'National Security and International

objectives, and nothing precludes stronger ties between the two organizations on security matters in the future.[67] To this end, Perez has argued that the WTO legal order should look to the practices of the UN to ascertain the circumstances under which a state could legitimately invoke Security Exceptions, in particular, whether the UN Security Council has ever found a similar situation to warrant international enforcement action.[68] The other more ambitious proposal is to encourage the use of Security Measures only after an appropriate resolution of the UN Security Council.[69]

At the same time, the international trading system has undergone substantial transformations since the ITO negotiations, where the UN was considered the only right forum to decide on security matters. WTO panels and the Appellate Body are regularly asked to review WTO members' non-economic concerns, which are political in nature. The dichotomy between "political" and "legal" disputes is not reflected in the text of current trade and investment agreements.[70]

Furthermore, one prominent flaw of allowing the UN to have a final word on states' security issues is the concerns over the UN Security Council voting system and the possibility of five permanent members (comprising China, France, Russia, the UK, and the US) vetoing substantial resolutions.[71] The permanent members have almost always been divided into geopolitical blocs, which led to one of them, mostly the Soviet Union – now Russia – or the US, exercising its veto on the most crucial decisions.[72] A recent example is the UN Security Council voting on a draft resolution that condemned the Russian occupation of four regions of Ukraine in September 2022. The resolution was not adopted because of the veto by Russia.[73] In addition, greater involvement by the

Trade Law: What GATT Says, and what the United States Does Symposium on Linkage as Phenomenon: An Interdisciplinary Approach' (1998) 19 U Pa J Intl L 263, 276.

67 Chapter 2, section 2.3.

68 Antonio F Perez, 'WTO and UN Law: Institutional Comity in National Security' (1998) 23 Yale J Intl L 301, 306.

69 Raj Bhala, 'National Security and International Trade Law: What GATT Says, and what the United States Does Symposium on Linkage as Phenomenon: An Interdisciplinary Approach' (1998) 19 U Pa J Intl L 263, 276.

70 Chapter 5, section 5.1.

71 Loraine Sievers and Sam Daws, *The Procedure of the UN Security Council* (OUP 2015) 296–364.

72 See more UN Security Council Meetings and Outcomes Tables maintained by Dag Hammarskjöld Library https://research.un.org/en/docs/sc/quick/meetings/2022.

73 Edith M Lederer, 'Russia Vetoes UN Resolution Calling its Referendums Illegal' *The Washington Post* (September 30, 2022) www.washingtontimes.com/news/2022/sep/30/russia-vetoes-un-resolution-calling-its-referendum/.

UN in questions at the intersection of national security and economic law might require the broadening of the definition of force or aggression to capture extensive unilateral sanctions so as to bring Security Measures more clearly within the UN Security Council's ambit.[74]

Nevertheless, the UN might take the lead in coordinating states' responses to security threats by facilitating the flow of information, coordinating efforts according to the nature of the crises, and collecting and preserving valuable data during and after the emergency. In particular, the existence of a resolution of the UN General Assembly that recognizes a specific situation as an emergency and calls states to urgent actions could also make a good faith invocation of the Security Exceptions with respect to novel and emerging security threats more credible.[75]

The UN and the WTO have agreed on cooperation, which, among others, includes the provision and exchange of relevant information.[76] The General Assembly has the power to "discuss any questions relating to the maintenance of international peace and security" and to "recommend measures for the peaceful adjustment" of various situations.[77] It has to be acknowledged that UN members might have divergent views on novel security threats. Yet, as the practice demonstrates, the debates in the UN mostly focus on the perceived aims of new policy directions rather than on whether or not climate change, energy, or other emerging concerns have security implications.[78] On multiple occasions, the decisions of the UN General Assembly have invited its members and/or relevant international organizations to adopt policies or take certain actions with

[74] Alain Pellet, 'Unilateral Sanctions and International Law' in *Yearbook of Institute of International Law* (Pedone 2015) 734.

[75] A resolution of the UN General Assembly has always some political effect, particularly, when, being addressed to a certain member or members of the UN. Not taking the course recommended in such a resolution presents a risk of losing the political friendship and understanding of those members who voted for it. See more DHN Johnson, 'The Effect of Resolutions of the General Assembly of the United Nations' (1955–56) 32 Brit YB Intl L 97.

[76] Arrangements for Effective Cooperation with Other Intergovernmental Organizations: Relations between the WTO and the United Nations (November 15, 1995) WT/GC/W/10 2.

[77] Articles 11 and 14 of the UN Charter. See more Cóman Kenny, 'Responsibility to Recommend: The Role of the UN General Assembly in the Maintenance of International Peace and Security' (2016) 3(1) J on the Use of Force and International Law 3.

[78] See more Lyn Jaggard, 'Climate Change Politics, the UN and National Interests' (2008) 38 Envtl Policy & L 230.

respect to the protection of the environment,[79] human life and health,[80] cybersecurity and critical information infrastructures,[81] or to consider and address possible security implications of climate change.[82] Different from the resolutions of the UN Security Council that can be blocked by the veto of one of the permanent members, decisions of the UN General Assembly on important questions, such as recommendations with respect to the maintenance of international peace and security, shall be made by a two-thirds majority of the members present and voting.[83] The General Assembly is expressly authorized to make recommendations (up to and including collective measures) in the face of a threat to international peace and security, even when the UN Security Council is unable to act because of the lack of unanimity of the permanent members.[84] This leaves more room for addressing security concerns and emergency situations where one of the most powerful UN members opposes the decision for political reasons.

The world is only at the beginning of the learning curve when it comes to dealing with emerging security threats, other than wars or armed conflicts, such as threats posed by cyberattacks or climate change. Given the representative value of the UN General Assembly, its resolutions on international emergencies and regional crises might potentially discourage certain countries from sabotaging their trade commitments in "normal" times when there is no recognized state of emergency or the probability of such an emergency in the future. It can also assist international adjudicators in deciding on the lawful invocation of Security Exceptions by releasing them from the need to characterize the situation as either rising to the level of emergency or not. The reliance of a WTO panel in *Russia – Traffic in Transit* on the evidence and findings provided

[79] UN General Assembly, The Human Right to a Clean, Healthy and Sustainable Environment, Resolution Adopted by the General Assembly (August 1, 2022) A/RES/76/300.

[80] UN General Assembly, Declaration of Solidarity of the United Nations in the Face of the Challenges posed by the Coronavirus Disease 2019 (COVID-19), Resolution Adopted by the General Assembly (March 27, 2020) A/74/L.51.

[81] UN General Assembly, Creation of a Global Culture of Cybersecurity and the Protection of Critical Information Infrastructures, Resolution Adopted by the General Assembly (December 23, 2003) A/RES/58/199.

[82] UN General Assembly, Climate Change and Its Possible Security Implications, Resolution adopted by the General Assembly (September 11, 2009) A/64/350.

[83] Article 18(2) of the UN Charter.

[84] UN General Assembly, Resolution 377 (V) Uniting for Peace adopted at the 294th Plenary Meeting of the UN General Assembly (November 3, 1950).

by the UN General Assembly[85] can be viewed as the first step to such growing cooperation and coordination between the WTO and the UN. While the question remains of whether the UN resolutions can be considered "subsequent agreement" or "subsequent practice" in the sense of Article 31 of VCLT, adjudicators might use them as "supplementary means of interpretation" within the meaning of Article 32 of VCLT.[86]

7.2.4 *Role of Domestic Policies and Diplomacy*

The vulnerabilities of the international trading system when dealing with national security matters and the securitization of states' economic policies might require an alternative approach to considering Security Exceptions that excludes the involvement of international trade and investment courts and tribunals or the WTO altogether. One possible advantage of solving any controversies involving national security matters through diplomatic routes is that it opens the door to a broader set of mutually beneficial solutions. This can partially explain why most cases to date where Security Exceptions were invoked before GATT/WTO were eventually settled by the parties without the final decision of a panel or the Appellate Body. Yet, the existence of the WTO and the costs of litigation and enforcement under the WTO agreements can be assumed to also contribute to such final settlements. Thus, the question remains of whether leaving disputes over Security Measures to domestic politics and diplomacy alone would benefit the international trade and investment regimes or contribute to further uncertainty and lack of predictability about the market access of foreign importers and investors.

Individual governments or blocs of governments can attempt to discipline an uncooperative counterparty that pushes the scope of Security Exceptions too far by using tools of soft balancing, such as concerted diplomacy via limited, informal ententes or economic statecraft.[87]

[85] Chapter 6, section 6.2.2.

[86] Eg the ICJ recognized that the UN General Assembly resolutions could be "factually relevant." See *Case Concerning Military and Paramilitary Activities in and against Nicaragua (Nicaragua v US)* (1986) ICJ [72]. The Appellate Body referred to the World Customs Organization's decisions (introduced by the US as "subsequent practice") as "relevant" for interpreting the tariff concessions. See *EC – Customs Classification of Certain Computer Equipment* (June 5, 1998) Appellate Body Report WT/DS62/AB/R [90]. See more Maria Foltea, *International Organizations in WTO Dispute Settlement: How Much Institutional Sensitivity?* (CUP 2012) 282–85.

[87] Anders Wivel and TV Paul, 'Soft Balancing, Institutions, and Peaceful Change' (2020) 34(4) Ethics & Intl Affairs 473, 474.

States, particularly great powers, can resort to institutional soft balancing to bolster the legitimacy of their own policies and to deny the legitimacy of the actions of their opponent, making their strategic goals more difficult to obtain.[88] Examples of institutional soft balancing include attempts by France, Germany, Russia, and China to use the UN to restrain the US before the invasion of Iraq,[89] or the alliance of China and India at the WTO, enabling them to increase their bargaining power and to successfully balance against the US and other Western powers in the Doha Round, as well as in the post-Doha negotiations on both agriculture and fisheries.[90]

Institutional soft balancing on the national security discourse within the international trading system can be challenging for several reasons. For one, different national security cultures pose a barrier to effective cooperation on security matters.[91] Even among the US, the EU, and BRICS, there is no clear uniformity on the desirable limits and scope of national security defenses. While the practice demonstrates that the US remains the most eager to push the boundaries of existing Security Exceptions, other WTO members don't seem to steadily oppose it beyond a relatively short-lived phase of joint rhetoric over the importance of free trade and multilateralism on the global stage. On the contrary, the invasion of Ukraine by Russia and the unrest in Taiwan because of China brought the EU and the US closer due to their peacemaking goals,[92] despite their disagreement over the permissible limits of economic coercion in other cases. This was also confirmed by the ability of the EU and the US to reach an agreement that ended the dispute between the two regions regarding the US tariffs on steel and aluminum portrayed as Security Measures.[93]

Soft balancing usually works for straightforward foe–foe or friend–friend constellations rather than mixed soft balancing coalitions in which

[88] Ibid.

[89] Ibid 483.

[90] See more Kristen Hopewell, 'Balancing, Threats & Wedges in International Political Economy: The Origins and Impact of the Sino-Indian Alliance at the WTO' (2022) J Contemporary China 1–17 https://doi.org/10.1080/10670564.2022.2090074.

[91] Sonia Lucarelli, Luk Van Langenhove, and Jan Wouters, *The EU and Multilateral Security Governance* (Routledge 2013) 36.

[92] See eg European Commission, 'EU–US Joint Statement of the Trade and Technology Council' (Press Release, December 5, 2022) https://ec.europa.eu/commission/presscorner/detail/en/STATEMENT_22_7516.

[93] *US – Certain Measures on Steel and Aluminium Products (EU)* DS548 (settled in 2022).

both a foe and a friend of the counterpart are engaged.[94] As things stand now, there is little evidence of the prospects for creating a coalition against the US because of its securitization discourse, at least by the EU and BRICS. Even if such a coalition is, in principle, created, soft balancing against the US at the WTO has already backfired, prompting the US to favor bilateral negotiations and to undermine the WTO enforcement mechanism by paralyzing the Appellate Body. Further escalation could prompt the US to abandon the WTO altogether, a move that would have irreparable consequences for the rules-based multilateral trading system.

Another way to deal with a noncooperative counterparty is economic statecraft. For example, states can adopt domestic regulations that neutralize the effect of trade restrictions imposed by such a counterparty in the interests of national security, such as blocking statutes, or countermeasures, or other actions in retaliation outside international rules. However, as current practice demonstrates, such measures are rarely effective and are generally available only to more politically and economically powerful states. To illustrate, the EU blocking statute has largely failed to prevent EU persons from escaping sanctions for violating its terms.[95] It remains to be seen whether and how the EU might use its new anti-coercion instrument to respond to the US aggressive tariffs imposed during President Trump's second term. The Chinese authorities are cautious about taking measures against foreign companies complying with the US sanctions to avoid collateral damage by making them choose between access to the Chinese markets and the US infrastructure.[96] Neither countersanctions adopted by Russia or China against Western countries nor retaliation in response to the US tariffs on steel and aluminum by China have incentivized the governments that have adopted controversial Security Measures to lift such measures or to change the policy on their implementation.[97] While the detailed analysis of the impact of other states' responses to the behavior of an uncooperative counterparty is outside the purview of this research, the above examples suggest that, at least with respect to Security Measures, such responses might not be enough to change the policy of a non-cooperative

[94] Sebastian Biba, 'Ganging up on Trump? Sino-German Relations and the Problem with Soft Balancing against the USA' (2020) 25(4) Chinese J Political Science 531, 545–546.

[95] Patrick CR Terry, 'Secondary Sanctions: Why the US Approach Is Unlawful and the EU's Response Is Ineffective' (2022) 17(9) Global Trade and Customs Journal 370, 378.

[96] Alexandr Svetlicinii, 'China's Defense against Secondary Sanctions: Lessons from the EU Blocking Statute' (2022) 21 (3) J Intl Trade Law and Policy 217, 230–231.

[97] Chapter 3.

government without additional institutional control and sophisticated economic incentives and domestic lobbying.

Finally, even if strengthening domestic control and attempts at soft rebalancing can temporarily tame certain security-rooted practices, they might also cause side effects. Unilateral incentives and/or diplomatic talks with like-minded governments bypassing the WTO might help in the short run to settle a dispute, as in the case of *US – Steel and Aluminium Products (EU)*,[98] or to prevent a blockage in trade negotiations, as in the case of USMCA (2018).[99] Nevertheless, such ad hoc settlements circumvent the discussion and an objective assessment of the measures under the WTO framework leading to more uncertainty and unpredictability about market access in the long run and the lack of trust in the coordination of matters affecting trade in the WTO. Furthermore, recent developments surrounding the USMCA highlight that even reaching a consensus on the wording of Security Exceptions does not necessarily prevent a contracting party from launching a "tariff war" against its other trade partners under the pretext of national security.

7.2.5 *Role of Economic Incentives*

In principle, trade-restrictive measures of a WTO member reduce market access or otherwise restrict trade with certain partners, making the latter bear the costs of such measures. As things stand now, when the WTO exception applies, the costs of the breach remain with the affected party.[100]

Compensation under IIAs is a key protection for foreign investors and might be available even if a treaty exception applies.[101] Yet, the availability of compensation for investors in the case of the adoption of Security Measures by a host state depends on the exact treaty language. To illustrate, the tribunal in *Copper Mesa v Ecuador* confirmed, referring to the *Methanex v US* and *Tecmed v Mexico* awards, that nondiscriminatory bona fide public purpose regulations are noncompensable.[102]

98 *US – Certain Measures on Steel and Aluminium Products (EU)* DS548 (settled in 2022).

99 Mexico and Canada were exempted from the US national security tariffs under Section 232 of the Trade Expansion Act. As a result, the disputes in DS550 and DS551 were settled. See more chapter 7, section 7.3.3.

100 See more chapters 3 and 4.

101 J Benton Heath, 'The New National Security Challenge to the Economic Order' (2020) 129 Yale LJ 1020, 1045.

102 *Copper Mesa Mining Corporation v Republic of Ecuador* (March 15, 2016) PCA No 2012-2 Award [6.60].

Such a conclusion is in line with the police power doctrine as a justification for nonpayment of compensation in cases of expropriation of investments for public purposes.[103] The *Devas* tribunal also referred to the CMS annulment committee decision and the award in *Continental v Argentina* to confirm that if a state properly invokes a Security Exception under an IIA, it cannot be liable for compensation of damages.[104] Given that the relationship between the police power doctrine and Security Exceptions remains undecisive,[105] as a practical matter, the lack of just compensation for foreign investors in the case of any emergencies, either objectively defined or perceived as such by a host state, might discourage investors from investing in host states, especially the ones with unstable economies.

Thus, both international trade and investment regimes provide little incentive for the responding state to reduce the costs of Security Measures and their possible adverse effect on the other party.

Economic contract theory assumes a commensurability between the damage suffered from the breach and a monetary payment or other forms of compensation.[106] Nothing under international law precludes compensation when the breach by a state is justified under one of the exceptions or a circumstance precluding wrongfulness under international law. It can be argued that a successful necessity defense imposes costs on a party other than the party acting under necessity because the party in breach protects a vital interest of higher value than the interest in the performance of its international commitments.[107] Yet, Article 27 of ARSIWA expressly states that the invocation of a circumstance precluding wrongfulness under international law, such as the customary defense of necessity, does not preclude the possibility of compensation for the aggrieved state. The commentary to this Article clarifies that compensation might be required in certain cases to discourage a state seeking "to shift the burden of the defence of its own interests or concerns onto an innocent third state."[108] The provisions of ARSIWA on compensation

[103] Chapter 6, section 6.1.

[104] *CC/Devas (Mauritius) Ltd v Republic of India* (July 25, 2016) PCA Case No 2013–09 Award on Jurisdiction and Merits [293].

[105] Chapter 6, section 6.1.

[106] Joel P Trachtman, *The Economic Structure of International Law* (HUP 2008) 143.

[107] Cynthia C Galvez, 'Necessity, Investor Rights, and State Sovereignty for NAFTA Investment Arbitration' (2013) 46 Cornell Intl LJ 143, 146.

[108] Report of the International Law Commission on the Work of its Fifty-Third Session, Commentary to Article 27 of ARSIWA (2008) 86.

might supplement otherwise applicable treaty provisions unless contracting parties have agreed to a different legal rule as a matter of *lex specialis*.

In a similar vein, several academic commentators support the view that international trade agreements can be reviewed to at least partially shift the costs of Security Measures from the affected party to the invoking state.[109] Such a proposal could also be tailored to the particularities of the international investment regime.[110] This section further discusses the challenges and prospects of the implementation of a compensation mechanism for Security Measures under WTO law, RTAs, and IIAs separately.

7.2.5.1 Rebalancing under WTO law

Since the legal consequences of a breach of WTO law are regulated by the DSU, the provisions of ARSIWA on compensation for damages do not regulate the breach of WTO law.[111] As things stand now, nothing in the DSU provides that a WTO member shall either comply with its obligations under the WTO agreements or pay damages.[112] Trade compensation under WTO law is allowed but only under specific conditions: first, in case of noncompliance with the WTO ruling to withdraw or modify a WTO-inconsistent measure (compensation for noncompliance); second, for disputes concerning a claim that a measure nullifies or impairs the benefits that a member was expecting to receive (nonviolation complaints);[113] and third, where trade liberalization causes or threatens to cause serious injury to domestic producers (safeguard measures).[114] In all these cases, trade compensation becomes the preferred option, or if such compensation cannot be agreed upon, trade retaliation. Pauwelyn discusses the variable nature of the goal of GATT/WTO retaliation, concluding that in addition to inducing compliance, such retaliation might pursue other objectives, such as temporary

[109] See eg Simon Lester and Huan Zhu, 'A Proposal for Rebalancing to Deal with National Security Trade Restrictions' (2019) 42 Fordham Intl LJ 1451.

[110] See eg Ala n O Sykes, 'Economic "Necessity" in International Law' (2015) 109(2) Am J Intl L 296.

[111] As a matter of *lex specialis*. See more Peter Van den Bossche and Werner Zdouc, *The Law and Policy of the World Trade Organization. Text, Cases, and Materials* (5th ed., CUP 2022) 223.

[112] Michelle Limenta, *WTO Retaliation: Effectiveness and Purposes* (Bloomsbury Publishing 2017) 14.

[113] Article XXIII GATT (1994).

[114] Ibid Article XIX.

rebalancing of trade concessions, some form of political or economic compensation, or the deterrence of possible future violations.[115]

Several commentators argue against the analogy between WTO agreements and private contracts prescribing compensation in case of non-performance since it can lead to a misunderstanding of the identity of the WTO.[116] A two-part objection may reasonably be put forward to the suggestion of introducing a monetary compensation or a more efficient trade compensation mechanism into the WTO system. First, it can be argued that the lack of an interstate system of expectation damages has forced states to design their agreements ex ante to balance the expected gains from breaches that can be prevented with the expected losses from undeterrable breaches.[117] Second, the compensation mechanism ignores domestic political factors.[118] Requiring a member to pay either monetary or trade compensation does not address a free-rider problem or the possibility that domestic authorities would manipulate the mechanism to serve interests other than preserving a treaty balance.[119] Nor does it incentivize a violating state to punish the groups that instigated the trade violation or an affected state to benefit the groups that suffer from such a violation.[120] Instead, the option to violate an agreement and pay the compensation might encourage domestic lobbies to put more pressure on their governments,[121] leading to even more inefficient and politically charged decisions when enforcing WTO obligations.

On the flip side, in the case of legitimate security threats (either objective or genuinely perceived ones), the compensation for the harm caused by Security Measures would happen under the circumstances

[115] See more Joost Pauwelyn, 'The Calculation and Design of Trade Retaliation in Context: What is the Goal of Suspending WTO Obligations?' in Joost Pauwelyn and Chad P Bown (eds.), *The Law, Economics and Politics of Retaliation in WTO Dispute Settlement* (CUP 2010).

[116] Michelle Limenta, *WTO Retaliation: Effectiveness and Purposes* (Bloomsbury Publishing 2017) 14.

[117] Timothy Meyer, 'The Political Economy of WTO Exceptions' (2022) 99 Washington U LR 1299, 1325.

[118] Jide Nzelibe, 'The Case against Reforming the WTO Enforcement Mechanism' (2008) 2008 U Ill L Rev 319, 340–345. See more Krzysztof J Pelc, *Making and Bending International Rules: The Design of Exceptions and Escape Clauses in Trade Law* (CUP 2016).

[119] Jide Nzelibe, 'The Case against Reforming the WTO Enforcement Mechanism' (2008) 2008 U Ill L Rev 319, 323–324.

[120] Ibid 323.

[121] Krzysztof J Pelc, *Making and Bending International Rules: The Design of Exceptions and Escape Clauses in Trade Law* (CUP 2016) 33–39.

where there is little ground to believe that a member would withdraw its WTO-inconsistent measures in compliance with the court's or tribunal's ruling until it perceives that a threat to its national security no longer exists and/or reaches agreement with the affected counterparties. In this situation, compensation does not replace the performance of WTO obligations. Instead, it attempts to re-establish the balance under the agreement for the period of a security threat by inducing a violating party to comply with its commitments when it can, offering a way of compensating the affected parties (at least partially), and deterring possible future violations where WTO members might otherwise attempt to abuse the overbreadth of Security Exceptions. Furthermore, a compensation requirement might reduce the incentive of certain WTO members to carry out irresponsible policies and accept the remote risk of WTO litigation in the future by making them consider the effect of Security Measures on their counterparties and the costs they would have to compensate for before actually adopting such measures.

This section further explores the possibility of introducing rebalancing mechanisms for Security Measures drawing upon the existing compensatory and retaliatory mechanisms under WTO law. Compensation or retaliation under Article 22 DSU might attempt to restore the contractual balance initially negotiated by the parties under the agreement but distorted by the breach.[122] Furthermore, both nonviolation complaints[123] and safeguard measures[124] represent an attempt to solve the contractual incompleteness of WTO agreements by allowing WTO members to adjust their legal commitments when unforeseen contingencies upset the contractual balance. It thus might provide insights valuable for restoring the balance between trade and security concerns of WTO members without focusing on the legitimacy of their national interests. Each of these rebalancing mechanisms will be further discussed in turn.

Rebalancing under Article 22 DSU in Case of Violation Complaints In principle, where a WTO panel (and potentially the Appellate Body) find that the measure of a WTO member is in breach of WTO law and is not satisfied under the invoked treaty exception (if invoked), such a breach

[122] Simon Lester and Huan Zhu, 'A Proposal for Rebalancing to Deal with National Security Trade Restrictions' (2019) 42 Fordham Intl LJ 1451, 1469.

[123] Robert W Staiger and Alan O Sykes, 'How Important Can the Non-Violation Clause Be for GATT/WTO?' (2017) 9(2) American Economic Journal: Microeconomics 149, 149.

[124] Alan O Sykes, 'Economic "Necessity" in International Law' (2015) 109(2) Am J Intl L 296, 304–306.

must be remedied by restoring compliance: either withdrawing or modifying the inconsistent measure. If the responding member refuses to restore compliance, the WTO law allows the parties to negotiate compensatory trade concessions or authorizes the complainant to retaliate by suspending "equivalent" trade concessions vis-à-vis the respondent in accordance with Article 22 DSU.[125] The DSU clarifies that performance is the preferred remedy, while trade compensation or retaliation are only temporary measures.[126]

Several issues arise from such rebalancing under the WTO agreements after Security Measures are found in breach of international commitments and where a violating member refuses to comply with a WTO's ruling. First, because of the sensitivity and the political nature of national security concerns, the disputes regarding the legitimacy of Security Measures put a higher burden on WTO adjudicators.[127] Second, as the outcomes of the *US – Steel and Aluminium Products* disputes confirm, compliance with adverse findings over national security matters remains questionable. If a WTO panel, or potentially the Appellate Body, rules that the Security Measures of a WTO member are not justified under Article XXI(b), it is unlikely that this member would comply with the ruling as long as the conditions triggering it to adopt such Security Measures remain, or unless the parties settle the dispute through diplomatic means. In this case, trade compensation or retaliation remains the only remedy. Third, Article 22 DSU can be invoked only if the DSB adopts a panel ruling (or an Appellate Body ruling) against a WTO member and such a member fails to bring its inconsistent measure in compliance with WTO law "within the reasonable period of time."[128] It is not available in cases where the panel report is unadopted, for example, because of the absence of a functioning Appellate Body to hear the appeal and where the expedited arbitration under Article 25 DSU is not available.[129]

In order to sharpen, and reify, the issues, this section further presents the example of the US refusing to comply with the adverse WTO panel

[125] Article 22.4 DSU.
[126] Ibid Article 22.1.
[127] See more chapters 6 and 7.
[128] Article 22.1 DSU.
[129] Arbitration under Article 25 DSU is available if both parties agree. Several WTO members set up an interim appeal arbitration arrangement pursuant to Article 25. Yet, the US does not participate in it. See more WTO, Multi-Party Interim Appeal Arbitration Arrangement Pursuant to Article 25 of the DSU (April 30, 2020) Job/DSB/1/Add.12.

rulings on its national security in the *US – Steel and Aluminium Products* disputes and in *US – Origin Marking (Hong Kong, China)*. The US has further appealed such rulings "into the void." It means that the panel reports against the US cannot be adopted because of the lack of a functioning Appellate Body to hear such appeals. Consequently, the DSB will not be able to allow complainants to retaliate should the US fail to negotiate "mutually acceptable compensation" with them.

Notably, several WTO members, including China, Turkey, and Russia, have already retaliated against the US in response to the US measures without waiting for the panel recommendations and the DSB's authorization.[130] The US has further challenged such retaliatory measures before the WTO.[131] It remains to be seen how the findings in the *US – Steel and Aluminium Products* cases will affect the outcomes of such disputes brought by the US. It also remains unclear how China, Norway, Switzerland, and Turkey will react to the US refusal to comply with the panel rulings and their appeal "into the void."

The refusal to comply with the adverse WTO rulings on national security issues, the lack of a functioning Appellate Body, and retaliation outside the WTO procedures can have far-reaching consequences for the stability and integrity of the WTO DSS, leading to further proliferation of national security defenses and de facto leaving an essential part of international trade outside the control of the WTO regime. One of the ways to mitigate such consequences is to allow WTO members to use the trade compensation and retaliation mechanisms under Article 22 DSU in national security disputes without waiting for the adoption of a WTO panel report by the DSB and the refusal by such a WTO member to comply with its ruling (immediate rebalancing).

In the past, WTO members have been willing to offer compensation instead of compliance with DSB rulings,[132] implying that, at least in some instances, violating members might prefer immediate compensation for the use of Security Measures to the burdensome litigation that undermines their security concerns and the legitimacy of the WTO

[130] See more International Trade Administration of US Department of Commerce, 'Foreign Retaliations Timeline' (last updated March 29, 2022) www.trade.gov/feature-article/foreign-retaliations-timeline.

[131] See eg *Turkey – Additional Duties on Certain Products from the US* (pending) DS561; *China – Additional Duties on Certain Products from the US* (pending) DS558; *Russia – Additional Duties on Certain Products from the US* (pending) DS566.

[132] Nicolas Lamp, 'At the Vanishing Point of Law: Rebalancing, Non-Violation Claims, and the Role of the Multilateral Trade Regime in the Trade Wars' (2019) 22 J Intl Econ L 721, 731.

dispute settlement function. Domestic legislation of WTO members also introduces new tools that enable their governments to retaliate in response to the trade and security policies of other governments without waiting for a definite WTO DSB resolution. The most recent example is the new legislation in Brazil allowing the government to unilaterally suspend concessions under the WTO agreements if a responding state appeals the WTO panel report "into the void" because of the lack of a functioning Appellate Body.[133] Such practices suggest that even though prescribing immediate rebalancing rules for Security Exceptions would doubtfully help overcome all concerns related to the invocation of a security defense, it might, nevertheless, keep governments at the bargaining table, save time and costs of burdensome litigation, and channel the responses of other WTO members to Security Measures into legal processes to limit the abuse.

Rebalancing under Article XXIII of GATT in Case of Nonviolation Complaints Article XXIII(1)(b) GATT (1994) allows for a nonviolation complaint where a WTO member considers that "any benefit accruing to it directly or indirectly under this Agreement is being nullified or impaired or that the attainment of any objective of the Agreement is being impeded as the result of . . . the application by another Member of any measure, whether or not it conflicts with the provisions of this Agreement."[134] The drafters of the GATT (1947) borrowed the concept of a non-violation complaint from various earlier bilateral treaties, keeping in mind the concerns that the US economy might return to the depression conditions preceding World War II or other unforeseen circumstances.[135] When the conditions of Article XXIII(1)(b) are met, there is no need for a panel to determine that a respondent has breached WTO law or to require a respondent to withdraw the measure. Instead, WTO members have an opportunity to negotiate for compensatory adjustments, withdraw their own concessions if negotiations fail, or withdraw from the agreement.[136]

In *EC – Asbestos*, the Appellate Body rejected the argument that non-violation complaints are limited to matters not explicitly addressed

[133] Provisional Measure No 1098 (2022) (Breach of Obligations by WTO Member), www.planalto.gov.br/ccivil_03/_ato2019-2022/2022/lei/L14353.htm referred to by Mona Paulsen in 'Let's Agree to Disagree: A Strategy for Trade-Security' (2022) 24(4) J Intl Econ L 527.

[134] Article XXIII(1)(b) GATT (1994).

[135] Robert W Staiger and Alan O Sykes, 'Non-Violations' (2013) 16 J Intl Econ L 741, 744.

[136] Ibid.

elsewhere in the GATT (1994),[137] suggesting that claims for compensation for nonviolation nullification or impairment are allowed even in cases where a measure is permissible under the Article XX(b) exception for protection of human health.[138] By the same token, a nonviolation complaint followed by compensation or retaliation should not be prevented when a member can rely on Security Exceptions under Article XXI(b). To support this view, the panel in *US – Steel and Aluminium Products* has reviewed the negotiating history of the ITO, which confirms "the shared understanding among negotiators that ITO members affected by security measures could submit non-violation complaints."[139] The EU, Switzerland, Turkey, and even the US, being the most vigorous proponent of the "self-judging" Security Exceptions, also seem to believe that Article XXI does not prevent or limit non-violation complaints (to the exclusion of claims of a breach).[140] According to the US, if a Member is impacted by a Security Measure and needs the WTO assistance with rebalancing, the only appropriate response is a nonviolation nullification or impairment claim.[141]

Pursuing nonviolation complaints under Article XXIII(1)(b) instead of challenging a measure proclaimed to be justified under Security Exceptions allows for circumvention of discussions about the breach of WTO commitments and the compliance of the measure with the Security Exceptions test together with the political problems arising from that. Such an approach could recognize the nullification or impairment caused to other members by Security Measures and allow for appropriate compensation, which would restore the balance of concessions that existed before the Security Measures were imposed while respecting the respondent's discretion in national security matters.[142] Furthermore, Lamp argues in favor of nonviolation complaints because, "almost by definition," Security Measures will nullify or impair benefits under the GATT (1994), making it faster for claims to be adjudicated.[143]

137 *EC – Measures Affecting Asbestos and Asbestos-Containing Products* (March 12, 2001) Appellate Body Report WT/DS135/AB/R [187].

138 Robert W Staiger and Alan O Sykes, 'Non-Violations' (2013) 16 J Intl Econ L 741, 750.

139 *US – Certain Measures on Steel and Aluminium Products (China)* (December 9, 2022) Appendices to the WTO Panel Report WT/DS544/R/Suppl.1 [2.42]; [3.30]–[3.37].

140 Ibid [2.22], [2.42].

141 Communication from the US, 'Reflections from the United States on the Handling of Disputes Involving Essential Security Measures' (December 11, 2024) JOB/DSB/10.

142 Tatiana Lacerda Prazeres, 'Trade and National Security: Rising Risks for the WTO' (2020) 19 World Trade Rev 137, 145.

143 Nicolas Lamp, 'Guest Post: Why WTO Members Should Bring Pure Non-Violation Claims Against National Security Measures' (*IELP Blog*, October 15, 2018) https://ielp

The discussion over the application of nonviolation complaints to Security Measures was raised in *US – Trade Measures Affecting Nicaragua*. Both Nicaragua and the US claimed that an invocation of a Security Exception under Article XXI GATT (1947) did not prevent recourse to XXIII(1)(b) GATT (1947).[144] Yet, given that the challenged embargo prohibited not only imports from Nicaragua into the US but also exports from the US to Nicaragua, the panel found that no decision under Article XXIII could re-establish the balance of advantages that had accrued to Nicaragua under the GATT (1947) before the US embargo, and thus proposed no ruling on the inquiry of whether actions under Article XXI could nullify or impair GATT benefits,[145] leaving many questions arising from its application open.

Notably, pursuing nonviolation complaints under Article XXIII(1)(b) instead of challenging a measure proclaimed to be justified under Security Exceptions poses its own set of challenges.[146] The US in *US – Trade Measures Affecting Nicaragua*, for example, argued that nullification or impairment could not be presumed in cases in which Security Exceptions were invoked but should be "made dependent on the facts and circumstances of the particular case."[147] Even though nonviolation complaints do not require WTO adjudicators to establish a breach of WTO commitments or follow the test of Article XXI, they do not necessarily prevent a need to consider the facts of the case.[148] The difficulty of meeting the burden of proof by a complainant when a nonviolation complaint is invoked is confirmed by the fact that, throughout GATT and now WTO practice, non-violation complaints have been infrequent and often not adjudicated, and those adjudicated were not often successful.[149] By December 2018, in seven out of eight cases, panels

.worldtradelaw.net/2018/10/guest-post-why-wto-members-should-bring-pure-non-violation-claims-against-national-security-measures.html.

144 *US – Trade Measures Affecting Nicaragua* (October 13, 1986) GATT Panel Report L/6053 [4.8]–[4.9].

145 Ibid [5.11].

146 Simon Lester, 'Non-Violation Claims Against National Security Measures' (*IELP Blog*, October 31, 2019 https://ielp.worldtradelaw.net/2019/10/non-violation-claims-against-national-security-measures.html.)

147 *US – Trade Measures Affecting Nicaragua* (October 13, 1986) GATT Panel Report L/6053 [4.9].

148 Tania Voon, 'The Security Exception in WTO Law: Entering a New Era' (2019) 113 AJIL Unbound 45, 49.

149 Robert W Staiger and Alan O Sykes, 'Non-Violations' (2013) 16 J Intl Econ L 741, 775.

concluded that complainants failed to meet the burden of proof.[150] Given fewer incentives on the side of complainants to resort to non-violation complaints in the case of Security Measures, it remains questionable whether nonviolation complaints would help to circumvent the need to resort to specific violations.

Rebalancing Based on Safeguards Model Different from other exceptions under WTO law, the safeguard exceptions allow for measures that are not motivated by public interest but by a domestic economic interest. Article XIX GATT (1994), as implemented by the Agreement on Safeguards, requires an invoking member to compensate the losses of an affected member from nonperformance, as agreed by the parties, or allows the affected member to retaliate even in the absence of a WTO panel or Appellate Body ruling on the breach.[151] As a matter of practice, perhaps in part because of the strict substantive and procedural conditions for the invocation, WTO members use safeguard measures infrequently.[152]

The idea of rebalancing in response to the safeguard measures was born in the reciprocal trade agreements negotiated by the US and other countries in the 1930s and further transferred to GATT negotiations.[153] It resembles the standard US remedy for most contract breaches – expectation damages – that facilitates efficient breach where the contractual performance is not in the interests of the party due to unforeseen contingencies.[154] The conditions for deviating from undertaken trade commitments under the safeguard mechanism – such as the existence of "unforeseen development" or "serious injury" – are vague and imprecise, making it difficult to observe and verify a genuine economic emergency.[155] This problem has been addressed by introducing the compensation requirement and making safeguard measures subject to specific procedural rules aimed at limiting and discouraging

[150] Tatiana Lacerda Prazeres, 'Trade and National Security: Rising Risks for the WTO' (2020) 19 World Trade Rev 137, 146.

[151] Peter Van den Bossche and Werner Zdouec, *The Law and Policy of the World Trade Organization* (5th ed., CUP 2022) 694, 715.

[152] WTO, Statistics on Safeguard Measures www.wto.org/english/tratop_e/safeg_e/safeg_e.htm#statistics.

[153] Simon Lester and Huan Zhu, 'A Proposal for Rebalancing to Deal with National Security Trade Restrictions' (2019) 42 Fordham Intl LJ 1451, 1466.

[154] Alan O Sykes, 'Economic "Necessity" in International Law' (2015) 109(2) Am J Intl L 296, 300.

[155] Ibid 305–306.

opportunism. When the contracting party prefers to compensate the affected state for the lost performance value rather than perform the contract, the contract should allow for an efficient breach.[156] In the same vein, safeguard measures under WTO law represent an attempt to encourage an efficient breach under WTO agreements in specific cases by allowing a WTO member to disregard some of its commitments for a limited period of time as long as it compensates or is willing to bear the costs of retaliation.[157]

It can be argued that different from compensation/retaliation under Article 22 DSU, the safeguards rebalancing is "the 'price' to be paid for breach" rather than "a 'sanction' to induce compliance."[158] Such a distinction can explain, for example, why the country imposing the safeguards is subjected to "substantially equivalent" suspensions of concessions, while the country that does not comply with the WTO ruling in accordance with Article 22 DSU is subjected to "equivalent" suspensions of concessions.[159]

As a current practice demonstrates, certain domestic measures aimed at protecting national security pose similar challenges to the international community as safeguard measures.[160] First, they are adopted in circumstances where there is little or no hope of achieving compliance with treaty commitments as long as a perceived security threat continues to exist. Second, they rely on imprecise standards that are difficult to verify in practice. There are no grounds to expand the existing safeguards' rebalancing rules under Article XIX GATT (1994) and the Agreement on Safeguards beyond their scope to include all types of Security Measures. Furthermore, this research does not attempt to put Security Measures and safeguard measures into the same category. Yet, it can be

156 Eric A Posner and Alan O Sykes, 'Efficient Breach of International Law: Optimal Remedies, "Legalized Noncompliance" and Related Issues' (2011) 110(2) Mich L Rev 243, 258.

157 Alan O Sykes, 'Economic "Necessity" in International Law' (2015) 109(2) Am J Intl L 296, 304–306.

158 Joost Pauwelyn, 'The Calculation and Design of Trade Retaliation in Context: What is the Goal of Suspending WTO Obligations?' in Joost Pauwelyn and Chad P Bown (eds.), *The Law, Economics and Politics of Retaliation in WTO Dispute Settlement* (CUP 2010) 60.

159 See more Joost Pauwelyn, 'The Calculation and Design of Trade Retaliation in Context: What is the Goal of Suspending WTO Obligations?' in Joost Pauwelyn and Chad P Bown (eds.), *The Law, Economics and Politics of Retaliation in WTO Dispute Settlement* (CUP 2010).

160 Chapter 3.

argued that the revised Security Exceptions can accept the logic of efficient breach while discouraging opportunism by including a new rebalancing mechanism, explicitly designed for Security Measures, that allows WTO members to adopt temporary measures when they consider it necessary to protect their national security, subject to a trade compensation (retaliation) requirement. To this end, Security Exceptions can draw on principles from the safeguard measures.

Such a proposal has apparent flaws. Security Measures can either be protectionist in nature and address temporal economic emergencies rather than protecting genuine and pressing national security concerns. Yet, the rebalancing based on a safeguards model does not consider the motives of the state's actions and thus does not differentiate between genuine national security measures and measures that are protectionist in nature, which in combination with domestic political pressure, might, in some cases, result in less efficient use of Security Exceptions.

Furthermore, the difference between the emergency actions allowed under Article XIX GATT (1994) as safeguard measures and the measures adopted in response to the emergencies in the sense of the narrowly interpreted Article XXI(b) GATT (1994) is that the former aims to address regulatory challenges arising from the long-term economic effects of temporal irregularities of the international trading system, while the latter was designed to deal with the need to protect states' noneconomic legitimate concerns. Where the long-term economic effects of the application of WTO agreements are difficult to foresee, contracting parties can reasonably anticipate that their counterparty affected by war or other comparable emergencies might not be able to meet its trade commitments. In this sense, narrowly tailored Security Exceptions under Article XXI(b) GATT (1994) aimed to address states' traditional security concerns are more similar to the measures allowed under the general exceptions of Article XX than Article XIX GATT (1994).

All this suggests that, in certain situations, rebalancing drawn upon safeguard measures could limit the overbreadth of broadly drafted Security Exceptions. Specifically, it might be considered a valuable tool to ensure an efficient invocation of Security Exceptions where there is no clear agreement over the exact scope of such a defense ex ante and where the adjudication of the legality of Security Measures ex post might create more tension between governments and undermine the credibility of the WTO DSS, as will be further explored.

7.2.5.2 Rebalancing under RTAs

In the international trade regime, safeguard measures are incorporated in many RTAs, providing an escape mechanism for parties seeking a temporary excuse from their trade concessions to address the adjustment needs of the domestic industry harmed by trade liberalization.[161] Some RTAs provide additional rebalancing mechanisms for specific exceptions. For example, the exception regarding cultural industries in Article 32.6 USMCA (2018) allows the parties to adopt measures to protect cultural industries but to agree that the other parties may "take a measure of equivalent commercial effect in response."[162] However, such a mechanism is not subject to any procedural requirements or control apart from general dispute settlement provisions under the agreement.[163] As under WTO law, the incorporation of similar rebalancing mechanisms for Novel Security Measures, authorizing either compensation or retaliation and prescribing clear procedural safeguards and institutional control over their implementation, might be the first step toward revitalizing the role of national security in bilateral and regional trade negotiations.

7.2.5.3 Compensation to Foreign Investors under IIAs

Similar to trade agreements, by focusing on the costs of Security Measures, a compensation requirement in investment treaties could encourage a host state to use a security defense as the last resort and look for alternatives to respond to national concerns rather than immediately limiting FDI. It could ensure that a potential host state would prohibit FDI only when compensating an investor for the damage caused by such a measure.

Admittedly, trade and investment agreements differ in many aspects.[164] For one, reputational effects mitigating the moral hazard problem under IIAs might be even less effective than under the WTO agreements and RTAs. Trade agreements regulate interstate relations and aim to increase trade liberalization and maximize absolute gains. A state

[161] Chad P Bown and Mark Wu, 'Safeguards and the Perils of Preferential Trade Agreements: Dominican Republic–Safeguard Measures' (2014) 13(2) World Trade Rev 179, 181–182.

[162] Article 32.6 USMCA (2018).

[163] Nicolas Lamp, 'At the Vanishing Point of Law: Rebalancing, Non-Violation Claims, and the Role of the Multilateral Trade Regime in the Trade Wars' (2019) 22 J Intl Econ L 721, 734.

[164] Chapter 6, section 6.1.

that disregards its trade commitments because of an emergency situation can be generally presumed to be willing to continue to profit from the international trade regime and thus have the incentive to return to compliance in the future under normal circumstances. In other words, the costs of potential compensation for the violation are offset by the prospect of future cooperation.

The state's primary goal in signing an investment treaty is to attract foreign investment by providing the assurance that these investments will receive at least a minimum level of protection enforced through international arbitration or domestic courts. If any changes in the state's policy lead to a breach of the investment treaty, an affected investor expects monetary compensation for the damage caused by the state's actions rather than the restoration of compliance. However, problems with compliance with tribunal rulings on compensation due to investors have been raised on multiple occasions. To take just one obvious example, the review of the necessity of the Security Measures in *Devas v India* allowed the tribunal to differentiate between India's security interests and other public interests. Based on the evidence submitted by the parties, the tribunal found that "a reasonable allocation of spectrum directed to the protection of the [India's] essential security interests would not exceed 60% of the S-band spectrum allocated to the [investors]," while the remaining 40 percent was allocated for other public interest and was subjected to expropriation conditions under Article 6 of India–Mauritius BIT (1998).[165] Different from *Eco Oro v Colombia*, where the tribunal awarded investors compensation even though the challenged measures were justified under the general exceptions,[166] the tribunal in *Devas v India* found that 60 percent of the value of the Devas' investment covered by Security Exceptions was not subject to compensation.[167] At the same time, India was required to compensate Devas for 40 percent of the value of its investment expropriated for other public purposes.[168]

While the complicated questions arising from the methodology used by tribunals to calculate the damages owed to investors and the

[165] *CC/Devas (Mauritius) Ltd v Republic of India* (July 25, 2016) PCA Case No 2013-09 Award on Jurisdiction and Merits [245], [373].

[166] See more *Eco Oro Minerals Corp v Republic of Colombia* (September 9, 2021) ICSID Case No ARB/16/41 Decision on Jurisdiction, Liability, and Quantum [822]–[830].

[167] *CC/Devas (Mauritius) Ltd v Republic of India* (July 25, 2016) PCA Case No 2013-09 Award on Jurisdiction and Merits [450].

[168] *CC/Devas (Mauritius) Ltd v Republic of India* (October 30, 2020) PCA Case No 2013-09 Award on Quantum [663].

compliance with the compensation requirement under international investment law are outside the purview of this research, it can be argued that the problem might become even more acute if a tribunal requires a host state to pay compensation where a Security Exception applies to a challenged measure and where such a measure is taken in time of war or another emergency that affects the payment capacity of a host state. All these challenges will be further addressed while suggesting the directions for drafting Security Exceptions in future IIAs.

7.3 Security Exceptions Revisited

All in all, it seems that none of the policy and legal options raised above can individually or conclusively revitalize the role of Security Exceptions under international law. Yet, considering the different implications they might have for Conventional and Novel Security Measures and tailoring such options to the particularities of international trade and investment regimes might be helpful for framing the directions for future reforms of Article XXI GATT (1994) and an alternative approach to drafting Security Exceptions in new RTAs and IIAs.

This research does not attempt to advance a reform of Security Exceptions that best fits all conceivable situations. Nor does it attempt to suggest the model clause of Security Exceptions that would fit under all WTO agreements and Regional Agreements. The respective political economies of trade and investment differ, as do the security concerns of different WTO members. The text of Security Exceptions under different treaty regimes and between different members might also continue to differ in certain respects. Instead of suggesting one correct approach to balancing trade and security in state practice and adjudicatory decisions, this book makes a contribution by suggesting the grounds for further dialogue among WTO members over the improvement of the constructed balance between trade normalities and Security Exceptions under trade and investment treaty regimes.

7.3.1 Directions for Reforming Article XXI GATT (1994)

Rather than attempting to fit all national security concerns under the current Article XXI(b) GATT (1994), which was not designed to deal with all emerging security threats and geopolitical uncertainties, WTO members are advised to renegotiate Article XXI GATT (1994) to permit a range of measures that address emerging national security threats while incentivizing governments to decrease the sweeping application of the national security defense, or at least ensuring that such securitization occurs in a more calibrated and proportionate manner.

Drawing upon the discussed policy and legal options for reconsidering Security Exceptions under international economic law,[169] this book suggests to differentiate between Conventional Security Measures (drafted based on existing Article XXI(b)) and Novel Security Measures (drafted as a separate paragraph of Article XXI) and attempts to bring more transparency and predictability in their adoption. Such a proposal can also be seen as a basis for reforming other Security Exceptions under WTO law tailored to the particularities of each WTO agreement.

For greater certainty, this book suggests that a WTO member should be able to invoke any Security Exception under WTO agreements only if it notifies all WTO members and potentially the newly created Committee on Security Measures about the need to adopt such security actions and explains its security concerns.[170] Such notification could serve as a primary document to channel the measure into the category of Conventional Security Measures or Novel Security Measures.

7.3.1.1 Conventional Security Measures

This research proposes to preserve the current approach to drafting Article XXI(b) GATT (1994) for Conventional Security Measures. The adjective "conventional" is used here not only to refer to the measures that are related to states' military and defense concerns as negotiated at the time of GATT adoption but also to encompass the additional measures that states expressly agree to include under Article XXI(b) as reflected in the text of the clause, or in the subsequent practice of WTO members. To this end, WTO members might agree to incorporate new alternative preconditions for the invocation of Article XXI(b) in addition to the existing subparagraphs to ensure that, for example, the measures adopted to deal with certain imminent cybersecurity threats or threats posed to members' critical infrastructure[171] are treated as Conventional rather than Novel Security Measures under WTO law.

Alternatively, the Ministerial Conference or the General Council is recommended to adopt the decision on the interpretation of current Article XXI(b) GATT (1994) to establish the list of recognized security

169 Chapter 7, section 7.2.

170 Ibid.

171 As the practice of several RTAs suggests. See more chapter 4, section 4.1.

areas (hereafter Article XXI Decision II).[172] This research does not attempt to second-guess the exact scope of security areas under the revisited Article XXI(b) GATT (1994). WTO members might agree to limit them to military and defense-related matters (as it stands now) or to expressly acknowledge that, for example, the measures aimed to protect cyberspace or critical infrastructure might also, in certain cases, be considered as Conventional Security Measures. In both scenarios, the reliance on Article XXI Decision II, together with the notification requirement encouraging transparency and peer review, would aid in the WTO panels' adaptation toward establishing a better balance between trade liberalization and members' security policies, even when applying a looser standard of review and proof because of the self-judging language of Article XXI(b) GATT (1994).

Notably, the authoritative interpretations of the Ministerial Conference and the General Council can "clarify but not modify" the rights and obligations of WTO members.[173] This implies that Article XXI Decision II would not be able to expand the scope of current Article XXI(b) to justify the measures that are aimed to address insidious, nonimmediate threats to cyberspace or energy security and that are not adopted "in the time" of existing "emergency in international relations." Should WTO members prefer to broaden the scope of Conventional Security Measures to embrace such concerns, they are recommended to modify the text of current Article XXI(b).

Finally, this book does not suggest that the category of Conventional Security Measures should be set in stone. It cannot be excluded that some emerging security threats will become of systematic concern for more governments in the future (e.g. the measures aimed to deal with cybersecurity threats). In this case, even if WTO members initially agreed to see the responses to such threats as Novel Security Measures, over time, they might reach a consensus on viewing such measures as Conventional Security Measures. At the same time, certain measures aimed at dealing with emerging security threats, such as CBA measures, could also be portrayed by certain WTO members as a threat to their economic security. Reaching an agreement on viewing them as Conventional Security Measures might be more challenging in practice. In any case, any changes

172 Chapter 7, section 7.2.1.

173 See more Tarcisio Gazzini, 'Can Authoritative Interpretation under Article IX:2 of the Agreement Establishing the WTO Modify the Rights and Obligations of Members?' (2008) 57 Intl & Comp LQ 169.

to the framework of Conventional and Novel Security Measures should be based on dialogue and cooperation between WTO members.

7.3.1.2 Novel Security Measures

This research recommends the exception for Novel Security Measures to be drafted in a broader manner in the sense that, different from existing Article XXI(b), it would not limit national security interests ex ante to specific goods or situations (similar to "self-judging" exceptions under several existing Regional Agreements). Yet, to ensure the balance of rights and obligations between the right of a member to invoke such a security defense and its substantive obligation to the other WTO members, additional treaty tools should be incorporated to prevent states' opportunistic behavior.

The challenge of deciding whether a trade-restrictive measure falls within the scope of an open-ended exception under WTO law is not unique to Security Measures. To illustrate, Article XX(a) GATT (1994) also preserves a fairly broad policy space for policies related to public morals. This exception is not restrained to specific goods or situations and cannot be adjudicated based on commonly accepted objective evidence. To limit the potential overbreadth of such an exception, Article XX(a) prescribes two doctrinal constraints: a trade restriction should be necessary to protect the interest at stake (e.g. the necessity requirement under subparagraph (a)), and it should be applied in good faith (the chapeau requirements). The WTO jurisprudence confirms that determining the legality of the application of general exceptions requires a great level of scrutiny of the purpose, design, and application of the measure.[174]

The most significant contrast between the exceptions for national security and other public values in this respect is that a general exception (such as prescribed under Article XX of GATT 1994)) could apply in ordinary times, whereas a Security Exception is expected to be invoked in extraordinary circumstances.[175] This distinction can potentially justify the disproportionate responses to a national security threat and the

[174] See eg *US – Measures Affecting the Cross-Border Supply of Gambling and Betting Services* (April 7, 2005) Appellate Body Report WT/DS285/AB/R [296]–[298]. See more Jeremy C Marwell, 'Trade and Morality: the WTO Public Morals Exception after Gambling' (2006) 81 New York U L Rev 802.

[175] Caroline Henckels, 'Permission to Act: The Legal Character of General and Security Exceptions in International Trade and Investment Law' (2020) 69(3) Intl & Comp LQ 557, 564.

refusal of an invoking state to provide information necessary to analyze the nature of its Security Measures. It is reinforced by the fact that existing Security Exceptions under WTO law expressly limit the intensity of adjudicatory review of the necessity of Security Measures.[176] Following the same line, this research suggests that to limit the potential overuse of a broadly drafted exception for Novel Security Measures, the mentioned doctrinal constraints established for the general exceptions could be tailored to the particularities of the extraordinary situations in which Security Exceptions should be invoked. This section discusses each of such proposed constraints in turn.

Ensuring a Good Faith Application of Novel Security Measures A WTO member should be allowed to invoke a Security Exception in order to justify a Novel Security Measure only if such a measure is "not applied in a manner which would constitute a means of arbitrary or unjustifiable discrimination between countries where the same conditions prevail, or a disguised restriction on international trade" – a requirement that draws upon the chapeau of Article XX GATT (1994).

The Appellate Body has reiterated on multiple occasions that the chapeau of Article XX GATT (1994) embodies the principle of good faith,[177] or "a line of equilibrium between the right of a Member to invoke an exception under Article XX and the rights of the other Members under varying substantive provisions ... of the GATT 1994."[178] Interpreting existing Security Exceptions under Article XXI(b)(iii) GATT (1994), the WTO panels have also noted that while deciding on the impact on international relations of situations falling under an "emergency in international relations" within the meaning of Article XXI(b)(iii), they were mindful of their mandate under the DSU, "as well as the balance of rights and obligations reflected in the terms of Article XXI of the GATT 1994."[179] The panel's statement suggests that the existing Security Exceptions under Article XXI(b)(iii) GATT (1994) preserve such a balance by granting states broad discretion to decide on the necessity of their actions while ex ante limiting the scope of the situations in which

[176] Chapter 6, section 6.3.3.

[177] *US – Standards for Reformulated and Conventional Gasoline* (April 29, 1996) Appellate Body Report WT/DS2/AB/R 22.

[178] *US – Import Prohibition of Certain Shrimp and Shrimp Products* (October 12, 1998) Appellate Body Report WT/DS58/AB/R [159].

[179] See eg *US – Certain Measures on Steel and Aluminium Products (China)* (December 9, 2022) WTO Panel Report WT/DS544/R [7.148].

a WTO member can justify such actions. In a similar vein, this book proposes to ensure the balance of rights and obligations under WTO law in the case of the invocation of broadly drafted Security Exceptions for Novel Security Measures (not limited to certain situations ex ante) by prescribing additional preconditions for the manner in which such measures should be adopted, similar to Article XX GATT (1994).

While analyzing whether the challenged measures meet the requirements of the chapeau of Article XX, the Appellate Body considers the efforts of respondents to establish international coordination and cooperation. In *US – Gasoline*, for example, the Appellate Body, in finding that the US measures constituted "unjustifiable discrimination" and a "disguised restriction on international trade," took into account the fact that the US had not sufficiently pursued the possibility of entering into cooperative arrangements with affected governments in order to mitigate the administrative problems that it raised in justification of its measures.[180] The Appellate Body in *US – Shrimp* also found that the appraisal of justifiable or unjustifiable discrimination depends on the respondent's attempts to engage in "across-the-board negotiations with the objective of concluding bilateral or multilateral agreements" regarding the concern at hand.[181] Thus, for example, the existence of an agreement between all or several WTO members on the specific concern may support the argument that a unilateral trade restriction is neither arbitrary nor unjustifiable.[182]

"Arbitrary discrimination," "unjustifiable discrimination," and "disguised restriction" on international trade may, according to the Appellate Body, "be read side-by-side"; "they impart meaning to one another."[183] The fundamental theme in the analysis of these concepts is "the purpose and object of avoiding abuse or illegitimate use of the exceptions."[184] By the same token, the inclusion of an express good faith requirement for Novel Security Measures under the renegotiated Security Exceptions for Novel Security Measures could focus on the legitimacy of the objectives

[180] *US – Standards for Reformulated and Conventional Gasoline* (April 29, 1996) Appellate Body Report WT/DS2/AB/R 27.

[181] *US – Import Prohibition of Certain Shrimp and Shrimp Products* (October 12, 1998) Appellate Body Report WT/DS58/AB/R [166].

[182] Joel P Trachtman, 'WTO Law Constraints on Border Tax Adjustment and Tax Credit Mechanisms to Reduce the Competitive Effects of Carbon Taxes' (2017) 70(2) National Tax Journal 469, 481.

[183] *US – Standards for Reformulated and Conventional Gasoline* (April 29, 1996) Appellate Body Report WT/DS2/AB/R 25.

[184] Ibid.

of such measures and on avoiding abuse. To this end, a member could be assumed to act in good faith when it adopts a measure in response to the situation recognized in the resolution of the UN General Assembly as a threat to international, regional, or national security. Such a qualification of the situation on the UN level would also assist the governments and WTO adjudicators in categorizing the Security Measures into Conventional or Novel Security Measures and differentiating between Security Exceptions and other treaty exceptions.

Different from essentially unilateral measures, the unilateral measures that have emerged from the multilateral consensus are more likely to have no protectionist character. The proposal for different regulations of these types of measures under WTO law is not new. According to Article 3.2 of the SPS Agreement, "[s]anitary or phytosanitary measures which conform to international standards, guidelines or recommendations shall be deemed to be necessary to protect human, animal or plant life or health, and presumed to be consistent with the relevant provisions of this Agreement and of GATT 1994." Likewise, the TBT Agreement generally requires WTO members to use relevant international standards as a basis for their technical regulations to diminish the trade-restrictive effect of technical barriers.[185] By the same token, this research suggests that WTO members can be allowed to adopt Novel Security Measures where the raised national security concern is recognized by the UN General Assembly.

The UN General Assembly may adopt the resolution that recognizes the security implications of a specific situation ex post or portrays certain events or the activities of certain actors as a threat to international, regional, or national security ex ante and call on UN members to take urgent action.[186] Different from the resolutions of the UN Security Council, the resolutions of the UN General Assembly on important questions, such as regarding the maintenance of international peace and security, shall be made by a two-thirds majority of the members present and voting.[187] Thus, a WTO member that does not accept the

185 Article 2.4 of TBT Agreement. See more Peter Van den Bossche and Werner Zdouc, *The Law and Policy of the World Trade Organization. Text, Cases, and Materials* (5th ed., CUP 2022) 1007.

186 Rebecca Barber, 'The Powers of the UN General Assembly to Prevent and Respond to Atrocity Crimes: A Guidance Document' (April 29, 2021) Asia-Pacific Centre for the Responsibility to Protect 7–8 https://r2pasiapacific.org/files/7091/2021_UNGA_GuidanceDocument4.pdf.

187 Article 18(2) of the UN Charter. See more chapter 7, section 7.2.3.

security-related concerns of other members will be unable to block the decision that recognizes a specific situation as an emergency or security threat to prevent other members from legally adopting Novel Security Measures to address such a situation.

The ICJ notes that even though the UN General Assembly resolutions are not binding, they "may sometimes have normative value."[188] To avoid any doubts, WTO members might expressly agree to recognize the relevant resolutions of the UN General Assembly as proof that the members that adopt Novel Security Measures in response to such resolutions and in line with their objectives act in good faith. In this case, even if a WTO member does not accept the security-related concerns of other members recognized by the resolution of the UN General Assembly, it cannot expect the WTO DSB to recommend other members to lift their Novel Security Measures based on such a resolution, yet it can still claim the compensation for the harm caused by such measures or retaliate, as further discussed.

Such an approach implies that the responses to emergencies and international, regional, or national security challenges recognized by multiple states are thoroughly incorporated into the larger texture of international law. It also incentivizes states to cooperate on their national security matters and, to the greatest extent possible, seek solutions at the multilateral level.

Rebalancing through Compensation or Retaliation Additionally, a WTO member should be allowed to invoke a Security Exception to justify a Novel Security Measure provided that it compensates for the harm caused to affected states by the measure or suffers the consequences of retaliatory measures. The compensation (retaliation) requirement would encourage a WTO member to identify other means of protecting its national security interests before adopting a Novel Security Measure. It would also incentivize a member to design such a measure in the least trade-restrictive way. In this sense, the readiness to pay the compensation would serve as proof – admittedly imperfect – that a WTO member genuinely considered its measure to be necessary to protect its national security interest.

Even if WTO members agree to incorporate rebalancing rules for Novel Security Measures, the question is how to calculate such compensation and supervise the potential retaliation.

[188] ICJ, Legality of the Threat or Use of Nuclear Weapons, Advisory Opinion (1996) ICJ Rep 226 [70].

As a practical matter, compensation should ensure that the costs of violation make it beneficial to suspend performance temporarily when necessary but expensive enough to avoid abuse. In other words, it should provide for the "optimal levels of compensation."[189] Under WTO law, the traditional form of compensation is trade compensation, either in case of nonviolation complaints, safeguard measures, or noncompliance with a DSB recommendation to lift or amend an illegal measure. It follows that a member that has a duty to compensate must, for example, reduce the tariff barrier equivalent to the amount of harm suffered by other members because of its measure. Yet, the concept of monetary compensation has often been raised throughout the history of GATT/WTO.[190] In practice, monetary compensation was used to resolve the dispute in *US – Section 110(5) Copyright Act*, where the EC and the US jointly agreed to suspend the arbitration proceedings under Article 22 DSU, provided that the US financially compensated the EC in exchange for allowing the continuance of the infringing practices.[191]

The introduction of monetary compensation under WTO law has been criticized for many reasons, not least because of the complications arising from its calculation.[192] Bronckers and Van den Broek propose alleviating the problems arising from the calculation of monetary compensation through the establishment of liquidated damages, a proven technique in contract law.[193] Similarly, it can be suggested that to incentivize the efficient use of Security Exceptions, WTO members can predetermine under the agreement the liquidated damages by which a member adopting a Novel Security Measure has to compensate affected members.

[189] Krzysztof J Pelc, 'Seeking Escape: The Use of Escape Clauses in International Trade Agreement' (2009) 53 Intl Studies Q 349, 352.

[190] See more Nuno Limão and Kamal Saggi, 'Tariff Retaliation Versus Financial Compensation in the Enforcement of International Trade Agreements' (2008) 76(1) J Intl Economics 48.

[191] See more Bernard O'Connor and Margareta Djordjevic, 'Practical Aspects of Monetary Compensation: The US-Copyright Case' (2005) 8 J Intl Econ L 127.

[192] See more Mercurio Bryan, 'Why Compensation Cannot Replace Trade Retaliation in the WTO Dispute Settlement Understanding' (2009) 8 World Trade Rev 315.

[193] Marco Bronckers and Naboth Van den Broek, 'Financial Compensation in the WTO Improving the Remedies of WTO Dispute Settlement' (2005) 8(1) J Intl Econ L 101, 113.

Sykes also discusses a system of monetary compensation for aggrieved exporters (rather than WTO members) concluding that this mechanism has many disadvantages in the WTO context, not least because of the costs of measuring the economic losses of individual exporters and the cost and volume of possible litigation. See more Alan O Sykes, 'Optimal Sanctions in the WTO: the Case for Decoupling (and the Uneasy Case for the Status Quo)' in Chad P Bown and Joost Pauwelyn (eds.), *The Law, Economics and Politics of Retaliation in WTO Dispute Settlement* (CUP 2009) 350–354.

Such monetary compensation could be predetermined at a certain annual amount, being either one standard sum for all affected WTO members or a variable sum linked to the size of their economies.[194] The advantage of such a method is that if the damages are predetermined, a member adopting a Security Measure can calculate with more certainty the total costs of its actions before deciding to take them. While not always offsetting all the damage caused to affected WTO members, such an approach would offer them at least some financial compensation to rebalance the contracting performance and might save the cost of negotiations over the adequacy of trade compensation or trade retaliation. In this way, specifying the amount of monetary compensation in advance can create appropriate incentives for a member to adopt Security Measures only when protecting the security interest at stake is less costly than the amount of liquidated damage it would have to compensate for.

However, implementing a system of monetary compensation for whenever Novel Security Measures were applied would cause many challenges for both the WTO and state administrations. For one, monetary compensation does not motivate a member to adopt a Security Measure for a limited period of time and return to compliance as soon as possible. If a member pays the predetermined liquidated damages, it has no further incentive to remove the measure as soon as possible. It follows that such compensation could allow rich nations to "buy out" their obligations whenever convenient.[195] Furthermore, predetermining the amount of compensation in advance does not address cases where the price of the adoption of Security Exceptions is either too excessive or not high enough to prevent the sweeping application of Security Exceptions in the first place.

As an alternative to monetary compensation, China and the EU seem to support the idea that the invocation of the Security Exception should be followed by trade compensation or retaliation proportionate to the initial move.[196] Whether negotiating WTO agreements or responding to breaches of undertaken commitments, the WTO system relies on the

194 See Communication from China, China's Proposal on WTO Reform (May 13, 2019) WT/GC/W/773 and the EU responses to the US restrictions on steel and aluminium analysed in Marco Bronckers and Naboth Van den Broek, 'Financial Compensation in the WTO Improving the Remedies of WTO Dispute Settlement' (2005) 8(1) J Intl Econ L 101, 125.

195 Bryan Mercurio, 'Why Compensation Cannot Replace Trade Retaliation in the WTO Dispute Settlement Understanding' (2009) 8 World Trade Rev 315, 334.

196 Tatiana Lacerda Prazeres, 'Trade and National Security: Rising Risks for the WTO' (2020) 19 World Trade Rev 137, 146–147.

paradigm of reciprocal concessions.[197] To require a member that adopts a Novel Security Measure to offer adequate means of trade compensation or to allow an affected member to suspend "substantially equivalent" (based on safeguards model) or "equivalent" (based on the DSU retaliatory mechanism) concessions provides both an incentive for compliance and a mechanism for maintaining reciprocity under the WTO regime. Similar to the proposal of monetary compensation, such rebalancing of concessions cannot completely restore the status quo ante.[198] Yet, such rebalancing not only prevents a member from completely shifting its performance costs onto its trading partners but also incentivizes it to return to compliance as soon as possible and enables the maintenance of reciprocity in trade relations.

Given the similarities between safeguard measures and Novel Security Measures – in that they are both expected to deal with unforeseen contingencies that change the cost and benefits of performance under the GATT (1994) – and the discussed advantages of trade compensation over monetary compensation under WTO law, WTO members might adopt the rebalancing mechanism for Novel Security Measures drawn from the principles of safeguard measures. To this end, a member that adopts a Novel Security Measure (an invoking member) can be encouraged to engage in consultations with affected parties to agree on a mutually beneficial compensation bargain. Similar to the safeguard mechanism, the term "affected party" should be understood narrowly to include those WTO members that have a substantial interest in the trade of the product (service) restricted by a Security Measure, making such compensation available to only a subset of WTO members.[199] Forcing an invoking member to suggest possible compensation options could boost the negotiating process.

Where the compensation cannot be agreed upon, an affected member should be allowed to retaliate under the authorization of the newly created Committee on Security Measures. Such retaliatory measures should be aimed at compensating the members affected by Novel Security Measures for the adverse effects of such measures on their trade while also encouraging an invoking member to search for less trade-restrictive alternatives and to return to compliance as soon as

[197] Robert Z Lawrence, *Crimes & Punishments? Retaliation Under the WTO* (Institute for International Economics 2003) 14.

[198] Ibid 28.

[199] Petros C Mavroidis, *Trade in Goods: GATT and the Other WTO Agreements Regulating Trade in Goods* (2nd ed., OUP 2012) 652.

possible. Thus, even though the right of retaliation for safeguard measures shall generally not be exercised during the first three years, WTO members might agree to the suspension of "substantially equivalent concessions" starting from the first year that a Novel Security Measure is in effect.[200] The Committee on Security Measures can oversee the negotiations on such compensation and retaliation and review "whether proposals to suspend concessions or other obligations are 'substantially equivalent.'"[201] The Committee on Security Measures can also be designated to control a time-bound application of Security Measures and their periodical review.

It is important to acknowledge the difficulties in reaching an agreement between all WTO members on the creation of the Committee on Security Measures and the strategic interests of the members of such a committee that might affect its decision-making process.[202] All this considered, WTO members might opt for an alternative rebalancing mechanism for Novel Security Measures drawn upon the principles of compensation/retaliation in response to an established breach of the rules under Article 22 DSU.[203] Based on such a model, it can be suggested that, initially, a WTO Member adopting a Novel Security Measure should enter into negotiations with affected parties[204] "with a view to developing mutually acceptable compensation."[205] If no agreement on satisfactory compensation has been reached, any affected party may request authorization from the DSB "to suspend the application to the Member concerned of concessions or other obligations under the covered agreements."[206] The level of the suspension of concessions or other obligations authorized by the DSB should be "equivalent to the level of the nullification or impairment" suffered by the affected parties.[207] The DSB decides on the authorization to retaliate by reverse consensus, which

[200] See more on prospects and hurdles of such a mechanism for safeguard measures in Mitsuo Matsushita and others, *The World Trade Organization: Law, Practice, and Policy* (3rd ed., OUP 2015) 424–426.

[201] See by analogy with the Committee on Safeguards under Article 13 of the Agreement on Safeguards.

[202] The Committee on Safeguards follows the practice of consensus. See more Fernando Piérola-Castro, *WTO Agreement on Safeguards and Article XIX of GATT: A Detailed Commentary* (CUP 2022) 342–343.

[203] Article 22 DSU. See more chapter 7, section 7.2.5.1.

[204] The reference to "affected parties" here is drawn on the safeguards model, as discussed above.

[205] Article 22 DSU.

[206] Ibid.

[207] Ibid [4].

means that the DSB must approve the decision unless there is a consensus against it.[208] Unlike in the safeguards model, in case of any disputes over the level of suspension proposed under Article 22 DSU, the matter can be referred to arbitration (usually carried out by the original panel).[209]

7.3.2 Alternative Approaches to Drafting Security Exceptions under RTAs

As existing practice demonstrates, the introduction of new rules under the multilateral trade regime might start with bilateral or regional initiatives. Negotiations on e-commerce are an example. Many WTO members have started beyond the WTO multilateral framework and inserted e-commerce regulation chapters in their RTAs[210] before initiating exploratory work toward WTO negotiations on trade-related aspects of e-commerce.[211] Such RTA chapters revealed the prospects for potential compromise between WTO members on e-commerce regulations. Given that the US, the EU, China, and Japan are considered powerful digital behemoths, reconciling their positions on e-commerce is essential for the prospects of reaching a multilateral agreement on e-commerce at the WTO level.[212]

It can be argued that the prospects for integrating any new equilibrium into Security Exceptions might also start with RTAs. While discussing the introduction of novel clauses to a system of treaties, Pauwelyn and others point out that trade agreements are more likely to incorporate novelties when they involve parties with diverse legal and structural experiences in

208 Ibid [6].

209 Ibid [6]–[7].

210 Robert Wolfe, 'Learning about Digital Trade: Privacy and E-Commerce in CETA and TPP' (2019) 18 World Trade Rev 63, 63.

211 On July 26, 2024, participants managed to finalize a "stabilized" text for a WTO E-commerce Agreement. It incorporates Security Exceptions (Article 23) from the GATT (1994) and GATS. However, the US did not join this arrangement, citing the need for further work, particularly regarding language on Security Exceptions. See more Joint Statement Initiative on Electronic Commerce (July 26, 2024) INF/ECOM/87 https://docs.wto.org/dol2fe/Pages/SS/directdoc.aspx?filename=q:/INF/ECOM/87.pdf&Open=True; Statement by US Ambassador María L Pagán on the WTO E-Commerce Joint Statement Initiative (July 26, 2024) https://geneva.usmission.gov/2024/07/26/statement-by-ambassador-maria-l-pagan-on-the-wto-e-commerce-joint-statement-initiative/.

212 Simon Abendin and Pingfang Duan, 'Global E-Commerce Talks at the WTO: Positions on Selected Issues of the United States, European Union, China, and Japan' (2021) 20(5) World Trade Rev 707, 707–708.

the respective area.[213] Security Exception clauses under RTAs signal the differences in the approaches of major trading partners toward the scope of desirable security defenses. As this research demonstrates, the US and the EU have a specific preference for the type of Security Exceptions they incorporate in their RTAs and different understandings of the scope of Security Exceptions under WTO agreements.[214] Given the unprecedented attention paid to Security Measures over the last couple of years and their impact on the existing international trading system, these WTO members are also expected to pay more attention to drafting Security Exceptions under future RTAs. If the US (as the most vigorous proponent of the "self-judging" exceptions) and the EU (that follows the current WTO model for drafting Security Exceptions) decide to renew negotiations on Transatlantic Trade and Investment Partnership and compromise on the language of Security Exceptions, it could be seen as the first step toward reconciling the positions of different WTO members and reaching agreement on the clarification of the scope of Security Exceptions under WTO law. The future negotiations on the trade pillar within the Indo-Pacific Economic Framework for Prosperity (IPEF) (between the US, Australia, Brunei, India, Indonesia, Japan, the Republic of Korea, Malaysia, New Zealand, Philippines, Singapore, Thailand, and Vietnam) might also shed some light on the direction that WTO members are ready to take in the negotiation on security matters.[215]

When negotiating national security issues, governments are generally risk averse and reluctant to alter the status quo or take bold initiatives, yet they are more eager to compromise while negotiating trade agreements from which they also seek to profit.[216] This does not exclude states involved in RTA negotiations from using the security discourse to either delay the negotiations or shape the content of the resulting RTA. To

[213] James Hollway, Jean-Frédéric Morin, and Joost Pauwelyn, 'Structural Conditions for Novelty: The Introduction of New Environmental Clauses to the Trade Regime Complex' (2020) 20(1) International Environmental Agreements: Politics, Law and Economics 61, 77–78.

[214] See chapter 4, section 4.1.

[215] IPEF partner countries together represent over 40% of the global economy. See more Office of the US Trade Representative, 'United States and Indo-Pacific Economic Framework Partners Announce Negotiation Objectives' (Press Release, September 9, 2022) https://ustr.gov/about-us/policy-offices/press-office/press-releases/2022/september/united-states-and-indo-pacific-economic-framework-partners-announce-negotiation-objectives.

[216] Daniel Druckman, 'Turning Points in International Negotiation: A Comparative Analysis' (2001) 45(4) J Conflict Resolution 519, 521.

illustrate, the negotiations might become problematic when the negotiating states in symmetrical power positions are in opposition over the scope of Security Exceptions (such as in the potentially renewed negotiations between the US and the EU). Then negotiators will either face a deadlock or attempt to achieve a substantial compromise.[217]

The negotiation history of NAFTA's Security Exceptions is a good example of such a compromise. At the time of negotiations, the US's preferred approach was already to incorporate "self-judging" type Security Exceptions. Yet, Canada initially preferred a Security Exception clause that entailed a stricter adjudicatory review. As discussed earlier, the parties reached a compromise by incorporating a different type of Security Exception in each of the three areas: investment measures, energy-related restrictions, and other trade measures.[218]

The successor of NAFTA (USMCA) further confirms that the outcome of RTA negotiations may not last for subsequent negotiations. The USMCA (2018) does not incorporate the constraints on the exceptions prescribed in either WTO law or NAFTA with respect to trade matters, presumably to give the US – the only USMCA party that has invoked the Security Exceptions before the WTO – desirable flexibility in using Security Exceptions to maintain its economic security.[219] Notably, Mexico and Canada were exempted from the US national security tariffs under Section 232 of the Trade Expansion Act since both countries were refusing to move forward on ratifying the USMCA as long as the tariffs imposed by the US remained in place.[220]

The example of NAFTA illustrates that when negotiating parties have different preferences over the scope of Security Exceptions but are nevertheless interested in increased trade cooperation under an RTA, they might be ready to compromise by enhancing procedural control over the application of Security Measures and/or subjecting their Security Measures in different areas to different legal tests. In this way, negotiating states can ensure that each of them has enough policy space to take action in the areas most essential for their security interests while ensuring stricter legalism and compliance in other areas.

[217] Larry Crump and Don Moon, 'Precedents in Negotiated Decisions: Korea–Australia Free Trade Agreement Negotiations' (2017) 33(2) Negotiation Journal 101, 123.

[218] Chapter 4, sections 4.1.1 and 4.2.1.

[219] David A Gantz, *An Introduction to the United States-Mexico-Canada Agreement: Understanding the New NAFTA* (Edward Elgar Publishing Limited 2020) 214–215.

[220] Ibid. See also US Presidential Proclamation 9704 on Adjusting Imports of Aluminum into the US 83 FR 51 (February 1, 2021).

Following such an example, WTO members with different security concerns and views on the scope of national security defenses can attempt to reach a compromise on drafting Security Exceptions under future RTAs by differentiating between different Security Measures and prescribing different preconditions for their lawful application. The approach that puts Conventional Security Measures and Novel Security Measures into different buckets[221] can be seen as a middle path between the two extreme positions that either limit Security Exceptions to traditional military and defense matters or tolerate the securitization of any policy objective of the invoking state.

Similar to the proposal for the reform of Article XXI GATT (1994), Conventional Security Measures under RTAs can be considered those related to the products and areas that are expressly agreed upon by the parties and specified in the Security Exception clause. For example, the parties can agree that "conventional" measures are those measures that fall under the exceptions based on current Article XXI(b) GATT (1994) or additionally specify that Conventional Security Measures cover energy-related restrictions based on the example of NAFTA.

Concurrently, similar to the proposal for Novel Security Measures under WTO law, the parties can still be allowed to adopt other Security Measures, provided that they are taken in a timely manner and meet two requirements. First, such Novel Security Measures shall not be applied "in a manner which would constitute a means of arbitrary or unjustifiable discrimination" against the other party/parties "or a disguised restriction on international trade."[222] This requirement is already prescribed in the Security Exception clauses under certain RTAs concluded by Russia and India.[223] While the lack of adjudicatory practice does not shed light on possible hurdles and challenges arising from their application, the existing drafting practice suggests that, as of now, at least several WTO members view such a requirement as appropriate to control the legitimacy of Security Measures. Second, Novel Security Measures shall be subject to trade compensation or potential retaliation. Differentiating between Conventional Security Measures and Novel Security Measures would give contracting parties a reasonable expectation that their counterparties would shift onto them the costs of nonperformance of contractual obligations under RTAs only under certain conditions or with

[221] Chapter 7, section 7.3.1.

[222] Based on the chapeau of Article XX GATT (1994).

[223] See chapter 4, sections 4.1.4 and 4.1.5.

respect to a specified range of products expressly agreed upon. Should any contracting party be urged to protect its security interests in a broader range of areas and decide to adopt a Novel Security Measure, it should be ready to bear the costs of such a measure itself.

As in the case of WTO agreements, the parties under RTAs are also advised to agree on specific notification requirements and agree on which authority would supervise compliance with the compensation (retaliation) requirement. Some current RTAs already incorporate the notification requirement.[224] Clear procedural safeguards and institutional control ensuring transparency and predictability in enforcing such rebalancing mechanisms would be essential for the good faith invocation of such renegotiated Security Exceptions.

At the same time, it is important to acknowledge that bilateral and regional arrangements mostly occur between like-minded WTO members with fewer concerns about the application of Security Exceptions.[225] Contracting parties that have similar approaches toward drafting their Security Exceptions or have no strong preference for the type of Security Exceptions in their RTAs might not need to compromise and thus might decide not to differentiate between Conventional and Novel Security Measures but rather continue with existing Security Exception clauses in their future RTAs.

Alternatively, the contracting parties modeling their Security Exceptions on existing Article XXI GATT (1994) might agree on additional security objectives that would be justified under such treaty exceptions. Several RTAs adopted by the EU, China, and India already follow such an approach by incorporating additional grounds for the reliance on the need to protect their essential security interests, along with military and defense-related matters, such as the protection of critical infrastructure or the need to address a domestic emergency.[226]

7.3.3 Alternative Approaches to Drafting Security Exceptions under IIAs

The interests and bargaining power of negotiating parties also determine the credibility of commitments under the investment regime. Unlike the

[224] See chapter 4.

[225] Tania Voon, 'Multilateral Rules on Trade in Goods – Exceptions and Regulatory Autonomy' Pre-peer review draft forthcoming in Julien Chaisse and Christoph Hermann (eds.), *The International Law of Economic Integration* (OUP 2025).

[226] See more chapter 4, section 4.1.

trade regime, where the rights and obligations of the parties are based mainly on the mutual exchange of concessions, IIAs do not aim to equally allocate the rights between private investors from a home state and public authorities of a host state.[227] The primary function of IIAs is to constrain the political actions of a host state, thereby allowing foreign investors to construct a business plan on the expectation that the relevant legal environment of a host state will ensure investors' access to its market.[228] In this sense, it can be argued that power asymmetries imply pressures on host states (capital importers) to make concessions to powerful home states (capital exporters).[229]

At the same time, the parties negotiating current and potentially future IIAs often have a great national interest in the protection of inward investments but also outward investments, leaving more room for reciprocity.[230] Also, a growing number of investor-state disputes focus on the exercise of social and political responsibilities of host states' governments for which they are held accountable to their people.[231] This practice suggests that future IIAs may pay more attention to preserving enough flexibility for host states to address their regulatory concerns. In light of such developments, both a host state and a home state may be willing to and capable of bargaining with each other to establish the appropriate investment regime that balances investors' reasonable reliance on expectations of market access and the right of a host state to regulate.

As things stand now, Security Exceptions under the IIAs of the US, the EU, and BRICS can be divided into two categories: (i) the exceptions that are drafted in a broad manner ("self-judging" exceptions) or that exclude the adjudication of national security disputes; and (ii) the exceptions that are modeled on trade law and limit the invocation of Security Exceptions to specific situations or include an objective necessity requirement. The parties can be expected to opt for the first category when they want to ensure that they have enough policy space to restrict foreign investments whenever they are forced to undertake emergency actions. Should the

227 Beth A Simmons, 'Bargaining over BITs, Arbitrating Awards: The Regime for Protection and Promotion of International Investment' (2014) 66 World Politics 12, 41–42.

228 W Michael Reisman, 'Negotiating and Maintaining Investment Treaties: Mechanisms for Anticipating and Controlling Textual Drift' (2019) 6 J Intl & Comp L 75, 76.

229 Beth A Simmons, 'Bargaining over BITs, Arbitrating Awards: The Regime for Protection and Promotion of International Investment' (2014) 66 World Politics 12, 40.

230 See eg China and the US.

231 Beth A Simmons, 'Bargaining over BITs, Arbitrating Awards: The Regime for Protection and Promotion of International Investment' (2014) 66 World Politics 12, 42.

parties be willing to profit from the guidance and relative predictability of WTO law, they can be expected to choose the second category. Put this way, the proposed solutions to revisiting these two categories of Security Exceptions would also differ.

Regarding the first category, where a treaty provides no or fewer tools to differentiate between good faith actions to protect national security and opportunistic behavior toward investments, it would be unreasonable to expect investors to bear all the risks arising from the adoption of Security Measures. Placing the costs of Security Measures on an investor and its home state rather than the host state would give a host state little incentive to minimize the costs of investment restrictions and the possible detriment to an investor. Furthermore, given the lack of clarity about cases when a host state might proclaim a threat to its national security, it would disrupt a foreign investor's reasonable reliance on expectations of market access in a host state. Under such circumstances, investors would not be able to accurately estimate all the commercial and political risks of their investments, while host states would have to bear additional costs from frequent investor-state disputes.

Because of such implications, this section proposes to internalize the costs of Security Measures under IIAs and to incentivize host states to calibrate Security Measures as narrowly as possible by clarifying that a host state is required to provide just monetary compensation to a foreign investor whenever its measures cause damage, even if such measures are justified under the treaty-based Security Exceptions. For greater clarity and reliability, IIAs can also clarify that the court or tribunal can review the matters arising from the calculation and enforcement of the compensation. Several IIAs concluded by India already do this by specifying that a foreign investor who has suffered losses in the territory of a host state due to war, other armed conflict, or other extreme situation can claim compensation or any other settlement; and that the disputes over damages and/or compensation due to the application of Security Measures may be submitted to adjudication, even if a Security Measure is nonreviewable.[232]

Regarding the second category, the WTO members that prefer either to incorporate, in their IIAs, exception clauses modeled on current trade law or to impose a strict necessity requirement should accept the risk that their Novel Security Measures would potentially fail to meet the Security Exceptions test. Alternatively, they can ensure either that such measures

[232] Chapter 4, section 4.2.5.

fall under other exceptions specifically drafted for such situations or that they are allowed as Novel Security Measures subject to the compensation requirement, similar to the proposal for trade agreements discussed above.[233]

Reputational constraints aside, one might argue that such a proposal would create a situation where a host state would have to compensate a foreign investor for the damage caused by investment restrictions either when it is found in breach of its treaty commitments or when it invokes a Security Exception. Such an approach is problematic for several reasons. First, optimal investment treaties are not expected to shift all the risks from investors to a host state. Whenever possible, IIAs should give foreign investors the incentive to hedge against typical economic risks that are usually a part of business practice rather than shifting all the risks to a host state.[234] Second, an investor who makes investments in reliance on an IIA and who is guaranteed its expected return in the case of any breach will be induced to make excessive investments, even if a significant probability exists that future developments would justify the restriction of such investments for security reasons.[235] Third, demanding compensation from a host state in a time of war or other emergency might be unreasonable because of its limited payment capacity. All this considered, the alternative approach should only entitle foreign investors to partial compensation rather than full compensation when a host state violates its treaty commitments to protect its national security interests.

Tribunals have avoided addressing the issue of the limited payment capacity of a host state directly, though it can be implied that the paying capacity of a host state has been considered in assessing compensation. To illustrate, in *CMS v Argentina*, the tribunal held that it was unrealistic to believe that no adjustments would have been made to a pay-or-ship contract as a result of Argentina's financial difficulties.[236] Alternatively, some academic commentators argue for the desirability of postponing the payment until a host state is no

233 Chapter 7, sections 7.3.1 and 7.3.2.

234 Anne Van Aaken, 'On the Necessity of Necessity Measures: a Response to Alan O Sykes' (2016) 109 AJIL Unbound 181, 185.

235 Alan O Sykes, 'Economic "Necessity" in International Law' (2015) 109(2) Am J Intl L 296, 321.

236 *CMS Gas Transmission Co v Argentine Republic* (May 12, 2005) ICSID Case No ARB/01/8 Award [444].

longer in a state of emergency or until it has recovered from the emergency so as to be in a position to compensate.[237]

This book does not propose one correct approach to calculating compensation that would apply across treaties. Investment tribunals are generally granted broad discretion in deciding on the standards and methodologies used to determine monetary compensation to investors for a breach, which also presents challenges and hurdles.[238] The ultimate goal of such compensation should be to remedy the negative consequences of the nonperformance by a host state of its contractual obligations by compensating the actual damage suffered by an investor.[239] Given the discussed implications of Security Measures, IIAs can clarify that a host state is required to compensate for actual damage to a foreign investor caused by Security Measures but may mention that the amount of this compensation can be adjusted depending on a host state's payment capacity, the investor's behavior, the sector in question, and other relevant circumstances. For greater clarity and reliability, IIAs can draw upon the example of India's investment chapters in India–Singapore CECA (2005), India–South Korea FTA (2009), and India–Malaysia CECA (2011).[240] More specifically, future IIAs can specify that even if Security Exceptions apply, foreign investors are entitled to compensation or any other settlement which is "no less favourable than that which [a host state] accords to its own investors or to investors of any non-Party, whichever is more favourable to the investor."[241]

237 Alan O Sykes, 'Economic "Necessity" in International Law' (2015) 109(2) Am J Intl L 296, 320.

238 Gabrielle Kaufmann-Kohler, 'Compensation Assessments: Perspectives from Investment Arbitration' in Chad P Bown and Joost Pauwelyn (eds.), *The Law, Economics and Politics of Retaliation in WTO Dispute Settlement* (CUP 2009) 634–635.

239 Patrick Dumberry, 'Compensation for Moral Damages in Investor-State Arbitration Disputes' (2010) 27(3) J Intl Arbitration 247, 274.

240 Chapter 4, section 4.2.5.

241 See eg Article 10.13 of India–South Korea FTA (2009).

8

Conclusion and Future Directions

This book starts with the recognition that WTO members view Security Exceptions as a shield from international responsibility when they need to take efficient security actions. Yet, recent developments in national security policies and international economic law portrayed in the previous chapters confirm the increasing intertwinement between states' trade and investment agendas and national security. This intertwinement can further transform Security Exceptions into a weapon to facilitate protectionist or populist economic measures aimed at gaining an advantage in negotiations or competition with trading partners. Allowing governments to use security exceptionalism to change global trade governance presents unprecedented challenges to global security and the global economy. So do emerging threats to national security. All this considered, this book suggests that the problem with the existing Security Exceptions can be addressed by reinforcing the ability of international economic agreements to shield states from responsibility in extreme situations, but meanwhile requiring updated tools and mechanisms to prevent the weaponization of the security defense.

The contribution of this book is threefold. First, it provides a comprehensive doctrinal and empirical account of Security Exceptions under international trade and investment regimes and distills a direction in which the current practice and jurisprudence are heading. Second, it attempts to steer a middle path between discipline and flexibility in addressing states' security concerns, stressing the role of adjudicators, the WTO, and the UN, as well as governments and other domestic policy actors in fostering transformation and cooperation in dealing with emerging and re-emerging threats to national security and free trade. Third, it suggests institutional and legal restructuring to revitalize the role of Security Exceptions in international economic law. Expanding the rulebook on the application of Security Exceptions, improving cooperation between the WTO and the UN, incentivizing states to use Security Measures efficiently, and reinforcing procedural safeguards for invoking national security defense can facilitate economic cooperation and trade while permitting more policy space for calibrated responses to new externalities.

8.1 General Findings

First, the conducted analysis of the existing case law on Security Exceptions under trade and investment regimes highlights certain common features in the approaches of adjudicators that may be seen as a starting point for the formation of jurisprudence on Security Exceptions.[1] These common features can be deduced to viewing Security Exceptions as justiciable unless the treaty at issue expressly states otherwise and subjecting the components of the exception clause to an objective or deferential (good faith) standard of review depending on the exact treaty language. By accepting the jurisdiction in national security disputes and attempting to balance the essential security interests of WTO members and their treaty commitments, international courts and tribunals have established solid grounds for demarcating the scope of Security Exceptions by adjudicators while also highlighting potential hurdles of interpreting and applying self-judging and objectively drafted Security Exceptions in the future. In particular, this book discusses different checks on opportunism in international trade and investment law to conclude that the emerging jurisprudence on the interpretation of Security Exceptions permits adjudicators – albeit, no doubt, imperfectly – to differentiate cases of genuine national security concerns and of opportunistic behavior, where Security Measures are adopted to address traditional military or defense-related cases and/or where invoked Security Exceptions are narrowly drafted. Additional procedural and institutional safeguards, such as a notification requirement, can help discipline further the sweeping use of such Security Exceptions and reduce the burden of international adjudicators in cases of apparent abuse. Yet, the lack of consistency in the approaches of international trade and investment tribunals to the review of the substantive components of security defense and the inability to force coherence among WTO panel rulings because of a nonfunctional Appellate Body does not allow for establishing a solid framework for the review of different types of Security Measures in the future, particularly the ones involving nontraditional and emerging security concerns.

[1] Chapters 5 and 6.

Second, this book argues that WTO-style Security Exceptions are drafted too narrowly to encompass all emerging security issues,[2] leaving international adjudicators with an impossible task: to disregard states' legitimate security concerns, even if it means that compliance with such a ruling is doubtful, or to broaden the scope of acceptable behavior, which might open a Pandora's box of more opportunistic actions. Looking at how each major school of thought approaches power, interstate relations, and global order leaves no ground to believe that a stricter interpretation of Security Exceptions by adjudicators would enhance multilateralism.[3] International law has little capacity to affect the behavior of states in situations where they proclaim a threat to their essential interests, be it an objective or perceived one.[4] The best it can do is to allow a state to suspend its obligations for the period of such an extraordinary situation while encouraging it to take the least trade-restrictive measures and to return to its performance as soon as the situation normalizes. Yet, existing WTO-style Security Exceptions provide WTO members with no incentive to adopt Security Measures that are time-bound and efficient from an economic perspective.

Third, this book argues that different from WTO-style Security Exceptions, the inclusion of broadly drafted Security Exceptions not limited ex ante to specific goods or situations ("self-judging" exceptions)[5] creates unclear expectations for contracting parties to RTAs and potential verification problems for adjudicators, increasing the chances of states' opportunistic behavior and non-performance. Such open-ended exception clauses do not incentivize states to make economically and politically efficient policy choices or to cooperate in establishing the boundaries of Security Measures.[6]

Fourth, this book argues that, similar to trade agreements, existing IIAs provide inadequate incentives for optimal behavior by host states.[7] Either their Security Exceptions are drafted in a very broad manner which fosters protectionism or opportunism in connection with foreign investment (e.g. "self-judging" and nonreviewable exceptions), or they do not grant host states enough flexibility to act in response to emerging threats or future emergencies, such as the ones related to cybersecurity or

[2] Chapter 3.
[3] Chapter 7, section 7.1.
[4] Chapter 3.
[5] Chapter 4, section 4.1.
[6] Chapter 7, section 7.1.
[7] Ibid.

critical infrastructure (e.g. WTO-style exceptions and the exceptions that require the "objective" necessity of a measure).[8] Acknowledging the distinct political economy of trade and investment, this book tailors the proposals to address the portrayed problems with existing Security Exceptions to the particularities of the two regimes.[9]

8.2 Directions for Reforms under International Trade Law

The foregoing findings suggest that WTO members should consider reforming Article XXI GATT (1994) and might decide to change their approach to drafting Security Exceptions under regional and bilateral trade agreements. To this end, this research advances a proposal to bring more flexibility and predictability to the limits of permissible security actions by splitting Security Exceptions into two categories.[10] First, it is proposed to narrowly tailor the Security Exceptions for Conventional Security Measures, thereby strengthening the need to leave a broad policy space for WTO members to act in the case of well-defined and observable extraordinary circumstances. Second, it is proposed to recognize the right of each WTO member to respond to other national security concerns, not considered "conventional," provided that they are recognized at the UN level and that such a WTO member is ready to compensate for the harm it might cause to other WTO members with its measures. The introduced concept of Novel Security Measures would address such emerging security concerns and would further delimit the scope of Conventional Security Measures. Besides, this book recommends the specific procedural conditions for invoking the exception for such Novel Security Measures with the aim of incentivizing cooperation and dialogue among WTO members, thereby ensuring that such measures are adopted only in rare circumstances.

Based on such a proposal, the scope of Conventional Security Measures should be clarified at the WTO level ex ante. The idea behind including an exception for Conventional Security Measures remains the same as at the time of drafting Security Exceptions for the ITO Charter and the GATT (1947), namely that there is an agreement between all WTO members as to the situations in which they can use security defense as a shield from responsibility for the non-performance of their WTO

[8] Chapter 4, section 4.2.
[9] Chapter 7, sections 7.3.2 and 7.3.3.
[10] Chapter 7, section 7.3.1.

commitments. Such situations should be expressly specified in the existing and/or additional subparagraphs to Article XXI(b) GATT (1994). To this end, WTO members might agree to incorporate additional grounds for the invocation of existing Article XXI(b) GATT (1994) (e.g. to address the imminent threats posed to cyberspace that do not readily come under existing exceptions) or rely on its authoritative interpretation by the Ministerial Conference or the General Council – potential Article XXI Decision II.

The WTO jurisprudence (comprising only the reports of the panels because of a nonfunctional Appellate Body) is taking a direction where some parts of WTO-like Security Exceptions are capable of objective review and the other parts allowing for some subjectivity are subject to a good faith review that includes a requirement of a plausible relationship between the protection of national security and the measure at issue.[11] It also suggests that the standard of proof required from an invoking state would depend on the essential security interest at issue. The further the security interest is removed from national defense or military interests, the greater specificity and more evidence might be required from a state raising a security defense. This book additionally suggests that WTO adjudicators can bring more certainty to the interpretation and application of such Security Exceptions by clarifying the scope of a good faith review of their self-judging components and the standard of proof such a review entails.

Admittedly, the US backlash against the review of Security Measures by the WTO, the lack of a cohesive authority to review the panel reports because of the paralyzed Appellate Body, and the difficulties of fact-finding in security matters revealed in the discussed panel rulings also call for strengthening the procedural requirements encouraging transparency and peer review in the adoption of Conventional Security Measures. Such requirements might aid in the WTO adjudication of sensitive national security issues, even when applying a low standard of proof.

Additionally, this research proposes to introduce a category of Novel Security Measures under a new paragraph of Article XXI GATT (1994) that should be broad enough to include all other legitimate security concerns of each WTO member. Unlike the exception for Conventional Security Measures, an open-ended exception for Novel Security Measures that defers to states' determinations of essential

[11] Chapter 6.

security interests would require revised tools that could balance a member's interest in protecting national security against the interests of other members in trade liberalization. For one, the recognition of the security implications of a specific situation in the resolution of a UN General Assembly would lend support that such Security Measures are "not applied in a manner which would constitute a means of arbitrary or unjustifiable discrimination between countries where the same conditions prevail, or a disguised restriction on international trade" and thus are adopted in good faith.[12] Given that the adjudication of the necessity of such measures, including the availability of less trade-restrictive alternatives, would be difficult in practice, such an exception should preserve a self-judging language limiting the intensity of adjudicatory review of the necessity of Novel Security Measures. Yet, introducing a duty to compensate would incentivize a WTO member to identify less trade-restrictive alternatives first and adopt a Novel Security Measure only if its costs were lower than the costs of complying with its treaty commitments or the costs of less trade-restrictive alternatives. Combined with a threat of retaliation, such a compensation requirement could help deter possible abuses of Security Exceptions.

Notably, while acknowledging that the prospects for reaching a new consensus at the WTO level might emerge from the current regional and bilateral initiatives, this book suggests that a final agreement at the WTO level, if reached, could eventually serve as a way to encourage more WTO members to follow the revised approach to drafting Security Exceptions in future bilateral and regional trade arrangements. Thus it could also contribute to a greater degree of harmonization among trade agreements on the approach to Security Measures, thereby reducing market uncertainty and stumbling blocks to regional trade liberalization where contracting parties have different approaches to the scope of Security Exceptions.

Internalization of costs of Novel Security Measures in the political decisions of WTO members, coupled with institutional oversight over the time-bound adoption of such measures and the payment of trade compensation or retaliation, can restrain unnecessary securitization of policy objectives or at least ensure that such securitization occurs in a more calibrated and proportionate manner and for a specific period of time, rather than indefinitely. In this sense, it would incentivize governments to manage one another's expectations better and to pay

[12] The chapeau of Article XX GATT (1994).

more attention to the possible consequences of their Security Measures while negotiating or renegotiating Security Exceptions under WTO agreements and future RTAs. By taking a middle path and combining deference to a state's decision to apply a Novel Security Measure with international control that is procedure- and efficiency-oriented, such a proposal for trade agreements aims to prevent further aggravation of interstate tension and distrust and to reduce unproductive coercion in the international trading system.

The foregoing is not meant to suggest that legitimizing Novel Security Measures under international economic law will solve all challenges facing the WTO and its members. Yet, rather than leaving security responses to power politics alone, it would place evolving national security issues within the control of the treaty regime, incentivizing states to use trade restrictions transparently, temporarily, and efficiently.

The tax regime can be a good example of how peer review and diplomacy can diffuse global tension and build normative consensus by coordinating unilateralism through encouraging and managing compliance rather than strictly policing it through a judicialized mechanism.[13] This is also achieved to some extent in the practice of adopting TBT and SPS measures under WTO law by encouraging proper debate and discussion between WTO members before they litigate the legitimacy of such measures.[14] Similarly, shifting the task of controlling Security Measures from the adjudication alone back to governments, encouraging WTO members to cooperate under the UN ambit before reverting to unilateralism, and facilitating dialogues by establishing the Committee on Security Measures and/or by enforcing the notification requirement might help accommodate the diverse interests of different WTO members and keep them at the bargaining table.

Consequently, such reforms can strengthen the legitimacy of international economic law, contribute to rebuilding trust in the multilateral trading system and its dispute settlement function, and help overcome possible deadlocks in regional and bilateral negotiations.

[13] See more Wolfgang Alschner, 'Shifting Design Paradigms: Why Tomorrow's International Economic Law May Look More Like the Tax Regime than the WTO' (2020) 114 AJIL Unbound 270.

[14] See more Peter Van den Bossche and Werner Zdouc, *The Law and Policy of the World Trade Organization. Text, Cases, and Materials* (5th ed., CUP 2022) 1012–1014, 1066–1069.

8.3 Directions for Reforms under International Investment Law

By the same token, this book suggests that the approach to drafting Security Exceptions in IIAs can be revisited to provide more adequate incentives for optimal behavior by host states. This can be achieved, for example, by deferring to a host state's determination of its essential security interest at stake and the necessity of a security action but requiring it to compensate foreign investors for the actual damage caused to them due to the application of a Security Measure.[15]

Similar to trade agreements, the compensation requirement would incentivize host states to use Security Measures in a narrower range of situations and look for less restrictive options to protect their national interests. Where states prefer to incorporate broadly drafted or non-reviewable Security Exceptions in IIAs, they might agree on the compensation requirement to apply to any Security Measure. In other cases, states could continue to model their Security Exceptions on trade law and adopt the above proposal that differentiates between Conventional Security Measures and Novel Security Measures, while subjecting the latter to the compensation requirement. In both cases, states are advised to clarify in IIAs that a court or tribunal can decide over the amount of monetary compensation owed to foreign investors, potentially adjusting such an amount to the particularities of each case and the payment capacity of the host state affected by an emergency or another security threat.

8.4 Future Research Agenda

Future studies may examine in more detail how the proposed reforms could be implemented at international and domestic levels and how to ensure their compatibility and coherence with the UN regime. One of the apparent difficulties would be all WTO members reaching an agreement on the rebalancing rules under Article XXI GATT (1994) and the creation of the Committee on Security Measures. In particular, this book acknowledges the pros and cons of designing a proposed rebalancing mechanism for Security Exceptions based on the safeguards model or Article 22 DSU. Doubts about the prospects and hurdles of such reforms and their implications for interstate relations must be further weighed

[15] Chapter 7, section 7.3.3.

against potential political and economic challenges and the worldwide backlash against globalization.

Furthermore, this book focuses on how international law can manage trade and security clashes. The normative upshot of the possible solutions to limiting economic warfare and accepting international reforms at the domestic level is far more modest. Calls for tightening regulation of Security Measures in domestic legislation and the role of the private sector in advancing such incentives could be further explored as a way forward to tame the overuse of Security Exceptions and its creeping consequences and to assist the WTO's adaptation in reviewing politically sensitive issues.[16] Also, while introducing the rebalancing mechanism for Novel Security Measures, one must be attentive to the argument that the compensation requirement imposed on political systems with various agency problems can lead to different distortions unless implemented and administered with reasonable accuracy.[17] This requires additional research on the role of political, economic, cultural, and historical factors in incentivizing different WTO members (not only the US, the EU, and BRICS) to adopt Security Measures and invoke Security Exceptions under international agreements to justify them.

Going forward, we are still yet to see the consequences of ongoing traditional and trade wars, intensified by the recent US actions in the interest of national security, and re-emerging and emerging global concerns related to technological developments, climate change and the mitigation measures in response to it, and global supply shocks leading to food and energy insecurity. Among others, questions remain to which extent the present practices of regulating technology can be justified under existing Article XXI(b)(ii) GATT (1994) and to which extent computer microchips, so-called "the new oil" of the modern economy, can be considered novel implements of war the restrictions on which are justified under such a Security Exception.[18] While the profound analysis of the exact scope of Article XXI(b)(ii) and its analogs is outside the purview of this research, the legal and policy responses to Security Measures under international economic law examined in this book could also contribute to such ever-growing discussions.

16 For example, with respect to the US, Kathleen Claussen, 'Trade's Security Exceptionalism' (2020) 72 Stan L Rev 1097, 1156–1159.

17 See more Alan O Sykes, 'Economic "Necessity" in International Law' (2015) 109(2) Am J Intl L 296.

18 See more Olga Hrynkiv and Saskia Lavrijssen, 'Not Trading with the Enemy: The Case of Computer Chips' (2024) 58(1) JWT 61.

BIBLIOGRAPHY

Books and Edited Volumes

Alexander K, *Economic Sanctions: Law and Public Policy* (Palgrave Macmillan 2009).

Alperen MJ, *Foundations of Homeland Security: Law and Policy* (2nd ed., Wiley 2017).

Anguelov N, *Economic Sanctions v Soft Power: Lessons from North Korea, Myanmar, and the Middle East* (Palgrave Macmillan 2015).

Aydinli E, *Emerging Transnational (In)security Governance: A Statist-Transnationalist Approach* (Routledge 2010).

Bailliet CM (eds.), *Research Handbook on International Law and Peace* (Edward Elgar Publishing 2019).

Barnard C, *The Substantive Law of the EU: The Four Freedoms* (OUP 2007).

Barnett M and B Duvall (eds.), *Power in Global Governance* (CUP 2005).

Bartels L and F Paddeu (eds.), *Exceptions in International Law* (OUP 2020).

Bethlehem D and others (eds.), *The Oxford Handbook of International Trade Law* (Oxford Handbooks Online 2012).

Bianchi A, D Peat, and M Windsor (eds.), *Interpretation in International Law* (OUP 2015).

Bonnitcha J, LN Skovgaard Poulsen, and M Waibel, *The Political Economy of the Investment Treaty Regime* (OUP 2017).

Bown CP and J Pauwelyn (eds.), *The Law, Economics and Politics of Retaliation in WTO Dispute Settlement* (CUP 2009).

Brown L (ed.), *The New Shorter Oxford English Dictionary on Historical Principles* (OUP 1993).

Brown ME and others, *The Perils of Anarchy: Contemporary Realism and International Security International Security Readers* (MIT Press 1995).

Bungenberg M and others (eds.), *European Yearbook of International Economic Law* (Springer International Publishing 2016).

Cai C, H Chen and Y Wang (eds.), *The BRICS in the New International Legal Order on Investment* (Brill 2020).

Cardenas BM and ZR Berg, *Conditions for Foreign Direct Investments in India* (Nova Science Publishers 2010).

Cass DZ, *The Constitutionalization of the World Trade Organization: Legitimacy, Democracy, and Community* (OUP 2005).

Chaisse J and C Hermann (eds.), *The International Law of Economic Integration* (OUP 2025).

Chaisse J and others (eds.), *Handbook of International Investment Law and Policy* (Springer Nature Singapore Pte Ltd 2019).

Chayes A and AH Chayes, *The New Sovereignty: Compliance with International Regulatory Agreements* (HUP 1996).

Cheng CJ (ed.), *A New Global Economic Order: New Challenges to International Trade Law* (Brill Nijhoff 2021).

Chimni BS, *International Law and World Order: A Critique of Contemporary Approaches* (2nd ed., CUP 2017).

Cohen HG and T Meyer (eds.), *International Law as Behavior* (CUP 2021).

Conti J, *Between Law and Diplomacy: The Social Contexts of Disputing at the World Trade Organization* (SUP 2011).

Dawidowicz M, *Third-Party Countermeasures in International Law* (CUP 2017).

Dekker IF and E Hey, *Netherlands Yearbook of International Law* (Vol. 41, TMC Asser Press 2011).

Delimatsis P, G Dimitropoulos, and A Gourgourinis (eds.), *State Capitalism and International Investment Law* (Hart Publishing 2023).

Demchak CC, *Wars of Disruption and Resilience: Cybered Conflict, Power, and National Security* (UGA Press 2011).

De Mestral A and C Lévesque (eds.), *Improving International Investment Agreements* (Routledge 2013).

Dolzer R and C Schreuer, *Principles of International Investment Law* (OUP 2012).

Douglas IA, *Free Trade Under Fire* (4th ed., Princeton UP 2015).

Douglas Z, J Pauwelyn, and JE Viñuales (eds.), *The Foundations of International Investment Law: Bringing Theory into Practice* (OUP 2014).

Drury A, *Economic Sanctions and Presidential Decisions: Models of Political Rationality* (Palgrave Macmillan 2005).

Dunoff JL and MA Pollack (eds.), *Interdisciplinary Perspectives on International Law and International Relations: The State of the Art* (CUP 2013).

Echandi R and S Pierre (eds.), *Prospects in International Investment Law and Policy: World Trade Forum* (CUP 2013).

Eeckhout P, *EU External Relations Law* (2nd ed., OUP 2012).

Elliot M and others (eds.), *Effective Judicial Review: A Cornerstone of Good Governance* (OUP 2010).

Eventon R (ed.), *Reclaiming Public Interest in Europe's International Investment Policy. EU Investment Agreements in the Lisbon Treaty Era: A Reader* (Transnational Institute 2010).

Fahner JH, *Judicial Deference in International Adjudication: A Comparative Analysis* (Hart 2020).

Fichera M and J Kremer (eds.), *Law and Security in Europe: Reconsidering the Security Constitution* (Intersentia 2013).

Fitzmaurice M and O Elias, *Contemporary Issues in the Law of Treaties* (Eleven International Publishing 2005).

Fitzmaurice M, O Elias, and P Merkouris (eds.), *Treaty Interpretation and the Vienna Convention on the Law of Treaties: 30 Years On* (Martinus Nijhoff 2010).

Foltea M, *International Organizations in WTO Dispute Settlement: How Much Institutional Sensitivity?* (CUP 2012).

Fontanelli F and others (eds.), *Shaping Rule of Law through Dialogue* (Europa Law Publishing 2010).

Gantz DA, *An Introduction to the United States-Mexico-Canada Agreement: Understanding the New NAFTA* (Edward Elgar Publishing Limited 2020).

Gattini A, A Tanzi, and F Fontanelli (eds.), *General Principles of Law and International Investment Arbitration* (Brill 2018).

Geiß R and N Melzer (eds.), *The Oxford Handbook of the International Law of Global Security* (OUP 2021) http://opil.ouplaw.com/view/10.1093/law/9780198827276.001.0001/law-9780198827276.

Gómez KF, A Gourgourinis, and C Titi (eds.), *European Yearbook of International Economic Law. Special Issue: International Investment Law and the Law of Armed Conflict* (Springer International Publishing 2019).

Graham EM and D Marchick, *US National Security and Foreign Direct Investment* (Peterson Institute for International Economics 2006).

Gruszczynski L and W Werner (eds.), *Deference in International Courts and Tribunals: Standard of Review and Margin of Appreciation* (OUP 2014).

Henckels C, *Proportionality and Deference in Investor-State Arbitration: Balancing Investment Protection and Regulatory Autonomy* (CUP 2015).

Hindelang S and A Moberg (eds.), *YSEC Yearbook of Socio-Economic Constitutions 2020* (Springer 2020).

YSEC Yearbook of Socio-Economic Constitutions 2020: A Common European Law on Investment Screening (CELIS) (Springer International Publishing 2021).

Hirschauer S, *The Securitization of Rape: Women, War and Sexual Violence* (Palgrave Macmillan 2014).

Hobbes T, *Leviathan* (first published 1651, OUP 1998).

Hoekman B, X Tu, and D Wang (eds.), *Rebooting Multilateral Trade Cooperation: Perspectives from China and Europe* (CEPR Press 2021) http://respect.eui.eu/wp-content/uploads/sites/6/2021/07/Chapter_5.pdf.

Hosli MO and J Selleslaghs (eds.), *The Changing Global Order: Challenges and Prospects* (Springer International Publishing 2020).

Hudec RE, *GATT Legal System and World Trade Diplomacy* (2nd ed., Butterworth Legal 1990).

Hufbauer GC and others, *Economic Sanctions Reconsidered* (3rd ed., Peterson Institute for International Economics 2009).

Hurd I, *How to Do Things with International Law* (Princeton UP 2017).

Irwin DA, PC Mavroidis, and AO Sykes, *The Genesis of GATT* (CUP 2008).

Jackson JH, *Sovereignty, the WTO and Changing Fundamentals of International Law* (CUP 2006).

Karns MP and others, *International Organizations: The Politics and Processes of Global Governance* (3rd ed., Lynne Rienner Publishers 2015).

Kiggins RD (ed.), *The Political Economy of Rare Earth Elements: Rising Powers and Technological Change* (Palgrave Macmillan UK 2015).

Kirchner EJ and J Sperling (eds.), *National Security Cultures: Patterns of Global Governance* (Taylor & Francis Group 2010).

Kreijen G and others (eds.), *State, Sovereignty, and International Governance* (OUP 2002).

Kurtz J, *The WTO and International Investment Law: Converging Systems* (CUP 2016).

Lawrence RZ, *Crimes & Punishments? Retaliation under the WTO* (Institute for International Economics 2003).

Lenihan AT, *Balancing Power without Weapons: State Intervention into Cross-Border Mergers and Acquisitions* (CUP 2018).

Lessambo FI, *Mergers in the Global Markets: A Comparative Approach to the Competition and National Security Laws among the US, EU, and China* (Springer International Publishing 2020).

Lewis MK and others (eds.), *A Post-WTO International Legal Order: Utopian, Dystopian and Other Scenarios* (Springer International Publishing 2020).

Limenta M, *WTO Retaliation: Effectiveness and Purposes* (Bloomsbury Publishing 2017).

Long CX and G Hale, *Foreign Direct Investment in China: Winners and Losers* (World Scientific Publishing Company 2012).

Lucarelli S, LV Langenhove, and J Wouters, *The EU and Multilateral Security Governance* (Routledge 2013).

Macrory P, A Appleton, and M Plummer (eds.), *The World Trade Organization: Legal, Economic, and Political Analysis* (Springer Science Business Media Inc 2005).

Marceau G, *A History of Law and Lawyers in GATT/WTO: The Development of the Rule of Law in the Multilateral Trading System* (CUP 2015).

Marossi AZ and MR Bassett (eds.), *Economic Sanctions under International Law: Unilateralism, Multilateralism, Legitimacy, and Consequences* (Springer Asser Press 2015).

Matsushita M and others, *The World Trade Organization: Law, Practice, and Policy* (3rd ed., OUP 2015).

Mavroidis PC, *Trade in Goods: GATT and the Other WTO Agreements Regulating Trade in Goods* (2nd ed., OUP 2012).

Mavroidis PC, *The Regulation of International Trade: GATT and the WTO Agreements on Trade in Goods* (Vol 1, MIT Press 2016).

Max Planck Encyclopedia of Public International Law (OUP 2013).

Mitchell AD and E Sheargold (eds.), *Principles of International Trade and Investment Law* (Edward Elgar Publishing 2021).

Mitchell AD, M Sornarajah, and T Voon (eds.), *Good Faith and International Economic Law* (OUP 2015).

Moore GJ, *North Korean Nuclear Operationality:. Regional Security and Nonproliferation* (John Hopkins University 2013).

Moran T, *Three Threats: An Analytical Framework for the CFIUS Process* (Peterson Institute for International Economics 2009).

Morgenthau HJ, *Politics among Nations: The Struggle for Power and Peace* (Knopf 1948).

Morosini FC and MRS Badin (eds.), *Reconceptualizing International Investment Law from Global South* (CUP 2018).

Mota CE, *Foreign Investment, Strategic Assets and National Security* (Intersentia 2018).

Muchlinski P, F Ortino, and C Schreuer (eds.), *The Oxford Handbook of International Investment Law* (OUP 2008).

Oda H, *Law and Politics of West-East Technology Transfer* (Martinus Nijhoff Publishers 1991).

Oesch M, *Standards of Review in WTO Dispute Resolution* (OUP 2003).

Panizzon M, *Good Faith in the Jurisprudence of the WTO: The Protection of Legitimate Expectations, Good Faith Interpretation and Fair Dispute Settlement* (Bloomsbury Publishing Plc 2006).

Park TJ, *Incomplete International Investment Agreements* (Edward Elgar Publishing 2022).

Pauwelyn J and CP Bown (eds.), *The Law, Economics and Politics of Retaliation in WTO Dispute Settlement* (CUP 2010).

Peet R and others, *Unholy Trinity: The IMF, World Bank and WTO* (SIRD 2003).

Pelc KJ, *Making and Bending International Rules: The Design of Exceptions and Escape Clauses in Trade Law* (CUP 2016).

Peral L (ed.), *Global Security in a Multipolar World* (EUISS 2009).

Petersmann EU and J Harrison (eds.), *Reforming the World Trading System: Legitimacy, Efficiency, and Democratic Governance* (OUP 2005).

Piérola-Castro F, *WTO Agreement on Safeguards and Article XIX of GATT: A Detailed Commentary* (CUP 2022).

Poh A, *Sanctions with Chinese Characteristics: Rhetoric and Restraint in China's Diplomacy* (Amsterdam UP 2021).

Prévost D, I Alexovičová, and JH Pohl (eds.), *Restoring Trust in Trade: Liber Amicorum in Honour of Peter Van den Bossche* (Hart Publishing 2019).

Prodromou Z, *The Public Order Exception in International Trade, Investment, Human Rights and Commercial Disputes* (Kluwer Law International BV 2020).

Proukaki EK, *The Problem of Enforcement in International Law: Countermeasures, the Non-Injured State and the Idea of International Community* (Taylor & Francis Group 2010).

Rajput A, *Protection of Foreign Investment in India and Investment Treaty Arbitration* (Kluwer Law International 2017).

Rensmann T (ed.), *Mega-Regional Trade Agreements* (Springer International Publishing 2017).

Ribeiro GL (ed.), *Social, Political and Cultural Challenges of the BRICS* (Langaa RPCIG 2015).

Rigod B, *Optimal Regulation and the Law of International Trade: The Interface between the Right to Regulate and WTO Law* (CUP 2015).

Roeder RW, *Foreign Mining Investment Law: The Cases of Australia, South Africa and Colombia* (Springer 2016).

Ronzitti N (ed.), *Coercive Diplomacy, Sanctions and International Law* (Brill 2016).

Rovine AW (ed.), *Contemporary Issues in International Arbitration and Mediation: The Fordham Papers (2010)* (Brill Nijhoff 2011).

Sachs L, J Coleman, and L Johnson (eds.), *Yearbook on International Investment Law and Policy* (OUP 2018).

Sampson GP (ed.), *WTO and Global Governance: Future Directions* (UNUP 2008).

Sarooshi D (ed.), *International Organizations and their Exercise of Sovereign Powers* (OUP 2007).

Sauvant KP (ed.), *Yearbook on International Investment Law & Policy* (OUP 2012).

Sauvant KP and others (eds.), *Sovereign Investment: Concerns and Policy Reactions* (OUP 2012).

Schmitt C, *Political Theology: Four Chapters on the Concept of Sovereignty* (George Schwab tr., Halliday Lithograph 1988).

Scott RE and PB Stephan, *The Limits of Leviathan: Contract Theory and the Enforcement of International Law* (CUP 2006).

Sebastián MB and A Pehl, *National Security Exceptions in International Trade and Investment Agreements: Justiciability and Standards of Review* (Springer 2020).

Shaffer GC, *Emerging Powers and the World Trading System: The Past and Future of International Economic Law* (CUP 2021).

Shan W, P Simons, and D Singh (eds.), *Redefining Sovereignty in International Economic Law* (Hart Publishing 2008).

Sievers L and S Daws, *The Procedure of the UN Security Council* (OUP 2015).

Simons G, *Imposing Economic Sanctions: Legal Remedy or Genocidal Tool?* (Pluto Press 1999).

Singh K and B Ilge (eds.), *Rethinking Bilateral Investment Treaties. Critical Issues and Policy Choices* (Both ENDS, Madhyam, SOMO 2016).

Sipiorski E, *Good Faith in International Investment Arbitration* (OUP 2019).

Stolberg AG, *How Nation-States Craft National Security Strategy Documents* (Strategic Studies Institute US Army War College 2012).

Stoll PT and H Hestermeyer (eds.), *Commentaries on World Trade Law – Volume 5: Trade in Services* (Brill 2023).

Suttle O, *Distributive Justice and World Trade Law: A Political Theory of International Trade Regulation* (CUP 2017).

Suttle O, *The British Yearbook of International Law* (OUP 2020).

Titi C, *The Right to Regulate in International Investment Law* (Nomos 2014).

Trachtman JP, *The Economic Structure of International Law* (HUP 2008).

Trachtman JP, *The Future of International Law: Global Government* (CUP 2013).

Vadi V, *Proportionality, Reasonableness and Standards of Review in International Investment Law and Arbitration* (Edward Elgar Publishing 2018).

Van den Bossche P and W Zdouc, *The Law and Policy of the World Trade Organization: Text, Cases, and Materials* (5th ed., CUP 2022).

Van den Herik L (ed), *Research Handbook on UN Sanctions and International Law* (Edward Elgar Publishing 2017).

Van der Loo G, *The EU–Ukraine Association Agreement and Deep and Comprehensive Free Trade Area* (Brill 2016).

Van Vooren B and RA Wessel, *EU External Relations Law* (CUP 2017).

Vandevelde KJ, *The First Bilateral Investment Treaties: U.S. Postwar Friendship, Commerce, and Navigation Treaties* (OUP 2017).

Venzke I, *How Interpretation Makes International Law: On Semantic Change and Normative Twists* (OUP 2012).

Wakefield J, *Giovanni Gentile and the State of Contemporary Constructivism: A Study of Actual Idealist Moral Theory* (Andrews UK Ltd 2015).

Wallace H, N Koutsiaras, and G Pagoulatos (eds.), *Europe's Transformations: Essays in Honour of Loukas Tsoukalis* (OUP 2021).

Weiß W and C Furculita (eds.), *Global Politics and EU Trade Policy* (Springer International Publishing 2020).

White ND, *Advanced Introduction to International Conflict and Security Law* (Elgar 2014).

Wigell M, S Scholvin, and M, Aaltola (eds.), *Geo-Economics and Power Politics in the 21st Century: The Revival of Economic Statecraft* (Routledge 2018).

Yearbook of Institute of International Law (Pedone 2015).

Wolfrum R, PT Stoll, and H Hestermeyer (eds.), *WTO: Trade in Goods* (Max Planck Commentaries on World Trade Law, Martinus Nijhoff 2011).

Yerxa R and B Wilson (eds.), *Key Issues in WTO Dispute Settlement: The First Ten Years* (CUP 2005).

Yueh L, *The Law and Economics of Globalisation: New Challenges for a World in Flux* (Edward Elgar Publishing 2009).

Zarate JC, *Treasury's War: The Unleashing of a New Era of Financial Warfare* (1st ed., PublicAffairs 2013).

Journal Articles

Abbott KW and D Snidal, 'Why States Act through Formal International Organizations' (1998) 42(1) J Conflict Resolution 3.

Abbott KW and D Snidal, 'Hard & Soft Law in International Governance' (2000) 54 Intl Org 421.

Abendin S and P Duan, 'Global E-Commerce Talks at the WTO: Positions on Selected Issues of the United States, European Union, China, and Japan' (2021) 20(5) World Trade Rev 707.

Ackermann T, 'Exception Clauses in International Investment Agreements: A Case for Systemic Integration?' (2019) International Challenges in Investment Arbitration 37.

Akande D and S Williams, 'International Adjudication on National Security Issues: What Role for the WTO?' (2003) 43 Virginia J Intl L 365.

Alekseenko AP, 'New Russian Model BIT and the Practice of Investment Arbitration' (2019) 16 Manchester J Intl Econ L 79.

Alford RP, 'The Self-Judging WTO Security Exception' (2011) Utah L Rev 697.

Alford RP, 'The Convergence of International Trade and Investment Arbitration' (2013) 12 Santa Clara J Intl L 35.

Alschner W, 'Shifting Design Paradigms: Why Tomorrow's International Economic Law May Look More Like the Tax Regime than the WTO' (2020) 114 AJIL Unbound 270.

Ananyev B, 'Sanctions in IR: Understanding, Defining, Studying' (2019) 14(3) Intl Org Research J 136.

Andenas M and S Zleptnig, 'Proportionality and Balancing in WTO Law: A Comparative Perspective' (2007) 20(1) Cambridge Rev Intl Affairs 71.

Anderer CE, 'Bilateral Investment Treaties and the EU Legal Order: Implications of the Lisbon Treaty' (2010) 35(3) Brook J Intl L 851.

Anuradha RV, 'Petrificus Totalus: The Spell of National Security!' (2018) 13 Asian J WTO & BLI Health Law and Policy 311.

Armijo LE, 'The BRICs Countries (Brazil, Russia, India, and China) as Analytical Category: Mirage or Insight?' (2007) 31 Asian Perspective 7.

Azaria D, 'Trade Countermeasures for Breaches of International Law Outside the WTO' (2022) 1 ICLQ 389.

Bakhin SV and IK Beketova, 'Conclusion of Bilateral Investment Treaties: New Approaches of the Russian Federation' (2017) 61(5) Pravovedenie 160 (in Russian) https://pravovedenie.spbu.ru.

Balan GD, 'On Fissionable Cows and the Limits to the WTO Security Exceptions' (2019) 14(1) Global Trade and Customs Journal 2.

Baldwin DA, 'The Concept of Security' (1997) 23 Rev Intl Stud 5.

Balzacq T, 'The Three Faces of Securitization: Political Agency, Audience and Context' (2005) 11(2) European J of Intl Relations 171.

Balzacq T, S Léonard, and J Ruzicka, '"Securitization" Revisited: Theory and Cases' (2016) 30(4) Intl Relations 494.

Baroncini E, 'La Soluzione Delle Controversie Commerciali Tra Stati Tra Multilateralismo E Regionalismo by Laura Zoppo' (2014) 17(2) J of Intl Economic Law 473.

Baroncini E, 'The Relation between the Marrakesh System and Regional Trade Agreements in the WTO Case-Law' (2017) 2 Dialoghi Con Ugo Villani 835.

Barrington JR, 'CFIUS Reform: Fear and FIRRMA, an Inefficient and Insufficient Expansion of Foreign Direct Investment Oversight' (2019) 21 Transactions: Tenn J Bus L 77.

Bartels L, 'The Separation of Powers in the WTO: How to Avoid Judicial Activism' (2004) 53 Intl & Comp LQ 861.

Baum A, 'Investment Screening for Developing Asia' (June 10, 2020) Yale J Intl Affairs www.yalejournal.org/publications/investment-screening-for-developing-asia.

Bell DSA, 'Anarchy, Power and Death: Contemporary Political Realism as Ideology' (2002) 7 J Political Ideologies 221.

Bendor AL, 'Are There Any Limits to Justiciability: The Jurisprudential and Constitutional Controversy in Light of the Israeli and American Experience' (1997) 7 Ind Intl & Comp L Rev 311.

Bhala R, 'National Security and International Trade Law: What GATT Says, and what the United States Does Symposium on Linkage as Phenomenon: An Interdisciplinary Approach' (1998) 19 U Pa J Intl L 263.

Biba S, 'Ganging up on Trump? Sino-German Relations and the Problem with Soft Balancing against the USA' (2020) 25(4) Chinese J Political Science 531.

Binder C, 'Non-Performance of Treaty Obligations in Cases of Necessity: From "Necessity Knows No Law" via the "Law(s) of Necessity" to Interfaces Between Different "Laws of Necessity"' (2011) 13(1) ARIEL Online https://doi.org/10.1163/15736512–90000027.

Bown CP and M Wu, 'Safeguards and the Perils of Preferential Trade Agreements: Dominican Republic–Safeguard Measures' (2014) 13(2) World Trade Rev 179.

Boyd RH, 'FIRRMA: "Buy American" Products, or Bye American Progress?' (2019) 19(2) Wake Forest J Bus & IPL 103.

Briese R, 'Djibouti v France: Self-Judging Clauses before the International Court of Justice' (2009) 10 Melb J Intl L 308.

Bronckers M and N Van den Broek, 'Financial Compensation in the WTO Improving the Remedies of WTO Dispute Settlement' (2005) 8(1) J Intl Econ L 101.

Bryan M, 'Why Compensation Cannot Replace Trade Retaliation in the WTO Dispute Settlement Understanding' (2009) 8 World Trade Rev 315.

Bu Q, 'China's Blocking Mechanism: The Unreliable Entity List' (2020) 19(3) J Intl Trade Law and Policy 159.

Burke-White WW and A von Staden, 'Investment Protection in Extraordinary Times: The Interpretation and Application of Non-Precluded Measures Provisions in Bilateral Investment Treaties' (2008) 146 Faculty Scholarship at Penn Law 307.

Cable V, 'What Is International Economic Security?' (1995) 71(2) Intl Affairs 305.

Campion AS, 'From CNOOC to Huawei: Securitization, the China Threat, and Critical Infrastructure' (2020) 28(1) Asian J Political Science 47.

Canestaro NA, 'Realism and Transnationalism: Competing Visions for International Security' (2007) 25(1) Boston U Intl LJ 113.

Canes-Wrone B, Lauren Mattioli, and Sophie Meunier, 'Foreign Direct Investment Screening and Congressional Backlash Politics in the United States' (2020) 22(4) The British J Politics and Intl Relations 666.

Cann WA, 'Creating Standards and Accountability for the Use of the WTO Security Exception: Reducing the Role of Power-Based Relations and Establishing a New Balance between Sovereignty and Multilateralism' (2001) 26 Yale J Intl L 413.

Cannizzaro E, 'Proportionality and Margin of Appreciation in the Whaling Case: Reconciling Antithetical Doctrines?' (2016) 27(4) EJIL 1061.

Chachko E, 'Administrative National Security' (2020) 108 Geo LJ 1063.

Chachko E, 'Revisiting Judicial Review in Foreign Affairs' (2020) 43 Fordham Intl LJ 1273.

Chaisse J, 'Deconstructing the WTO Conformity Obligation: A Theory of Compliance as a Process' (2015) 38(1) Fordham Intl LJ 57.

Chen TF, 'To Judge the "Self-Judging" Security Exception Under GATT (1994): A Systematic Approach' (2017) 12(2) Asian J WTO and Aust YBIL Health Law and Policy 311.

Chen X and X Gao, 'Analysing the EU's Collective Securitisation Moves towards China' (2022) 20 Asia Eur J 195.

Cheung TM, 'The Rise of China as a Cybersecurity Industrial Power: Balancing National Security, Geopolitical, and Development Priorities' (2018) 3(3) J Cyber Policy 306.

Cho S and J Kurtz, 'Convergence and Divergence in International Economic Law and Politics' (2018) 29(1) EJIL 169.

Choer HM and F Hees, 'Breaking the BIT Mold: Brazil's Pioneering Approach to Investment Agreements' (2018) 112 Ajil Unbound 197.

Chow DKCh, 'United States Unilateralism and the World Trade Organization' (2019) 37 BU Int'l LJ 1.

Claussen K, 'The Casualty of Investor Protection in Times of Economic Crisis' (2009) 118 Yale L J 1545.

Claussen K, 'Trade's Security Exceptionalism' (2020) 72 Stan L Rev 1097.

Cody DA, 'The United States Bilateral Investment Treaties: Egypt and Panama' (1983) 13 Ga J Intl & Comp L 491.

Cohen AF and J Ravitch, 'Economic Sanctions, Domestic Deprivations, and the Just Compensation Clause: Enforcing the Fifth Amendment in the Foreign Affairs Context' (1988) 13 Yale J Intl L 146.

Condon BJ, 'Treaty Structure and Public Interest Regulation in International Economic Law' (2014) 17 J Int'l Econ L 333.

Cohen HG, 'Nations and Markets' (2020) 23(4) J Intl Econ L 793.

Cohen HG, 'Toward Best Practices for Trade-Security Measures' (2024) 27(1) J Intl Econ L 93.

Coyle JF, 'The Treaty of Friendship, Commerce and Navigation in the Modern Era' (2013) 51 Colum J Transnatl L 302.

Crivelli P and M Paulsen, 'Separating the Political from the Economic: The Russia – Traffic in Transit Panel Report' (2021) 20(4) World Trade Rev 582.

Crump L and D Moon, 'Precedents in Negotiated Decisions: Korea–Australia Free Trade Agreement Negotiations' (2017) 33(2) Negotiation Journal 101.

Dalby S, 'Security, Intelligence, the National Interest and the Global Environment' (1995) 10 Intelligence and National Security 175.

Davis L and S Engerman, 'History Lessons Sanctions: Neither War nor Peace' (2003) 17(2) J Economic Perspectives 187.

De LT Oliveira G, 'Chinese Land Grabs in Brazil? Sinophobia and Foreign Investments in Brazilian Soybean Agribusiness' (2018) 15(1) Globalizations 114.

Deane F, 'The WTO, the National Security Exception and Climate Change' (2012) 2 Carbon & Climate L Rev 149.

Desierto DA, 'Necessity and "Supplementary Means of Interpretation" for Non-Precluded Measures in Bilateral Investment Treaties' (2010) 31(3) U Pennsylvania J Intl Econ L 827.

DiMascio N and J Pauwelyn, 'Nondiscrimination in Trade and Investment Treaties: Worlds Apart or Two Sides of the Same Coin' (2008) 102 Am J Intl L 48.

Dreier T, 'Thoughts on Revising the Limitations on Copyright under Directive 2001/29' (2015) 11(2) JIPLP 138.

Drezner DW, 'How Everything Became National Security and National Security Became Everything' (2024) 103 Foreign Affairs 122.

Druckman D, 'Turning Points in International Negotiation: A Comparative Analysis' (2001) 45(4) J Conflict Resolution 519.

Duggal K and WW Cai, 'Principles of Evidence in Public International Law as Applied by Investor-State Tribunals: Burden and Standards of Proof' (2019) 2 Brill Research Perspectives in Intl Investment Law and Arbitration 1.

Dumberry P, 'Compensation for Moral Damages in Investor–State Arbitration Disputes' (2010) 27(3) J Intl Arbitration 247.

Ehlermann CD and L Ehring, 'Decision-making in the World Trade Organization' (2005) 8(1) J Intl Econ L 51.

Eilmansberger T, 'Bilateral Investment Treaties and EU Law' (2009) 46(2) CMLR 383.

Eisenhut D, 'Sovereignty, National Security and International Treaty Law the Standard of Review of International Courts and Tribunals with regard to "Security Exceptions"' (2010) 48(4) Archiv des V 431.

Emmerson A, 'Conceptualizing Security Exceptions: Legal Doctrine or Political Excuse' (2010) 11 J Intl Econ L 135.

Fahner JH, 'In Dubio Mitius: Advancing Clarity and Modesty in Treaty Interpretation' (2021) 32(3) EJIL 835.

Floyd R, 'Can Securitization Theory Be Used in Normative Analysis? Towards a Just Securitization Theory' (2011) 42(4–5) Security Dialogue 427.

Foster CE, 'Burden of Proof in International Courts and tribunals' (2010) 29(1) Aust YBIL Online 27.

Friis K and O Lysne, 'Huawei, 5 G and Security: Technological Limitations and Political Responses' (2021) 52(5) Development and Change 1174.

Galvez CC, 'Necessity, Investor Rights, and State Sovereignty for NAFTA Investment Arbitration' (2013) 46 Cornell Intl LJ 143.

Gao H, 'China's Changing Perspective on the WTO: From Aspiration, Assimilation to Alienation' (2022) 21 World Trade Rev 342.

Gazzini T, 'Can Authoritative Interpretation under Article IX:2 of the Agreement Establishing the WTO Modify the Rights and Obligations of Members?' (2008) 57 Intl & Comp LQ 169.

Giumelli F, F Hoffmann, and A Książczaková 'The When, What, Where and Why of European Union Sanctions' (2021) 30(1) Eur Security 1.

Gladysz J, 'The National Security Exception in WTO Law: Emerging Jurisprudence and Future Direction' (2021) 52 Geo J Intl L 835.

Glaser CL, 'A Flawed Framework: Why the Liberal International Order Concept Is Misguided' (2019) 43(4) Intl Security 51.

Golsong H, 'Russian Federation – United States: Treaty concerning the Encouragement and Reciprocal Protection of Investment' (1992) 31(4) ILM 794.

Gourgourinis A, 'General/Particular International Law and Primary/Secondary Rules: Unitary Terminology of a Fragmented System' (2011) 22(4) EJIL 993.

Guzzini S, 'Securitization as a Causal Mechanism' (2011) 42 Security Dialogue 329.

Hahn MJ, 'Vital Interests and the Law of GATT: An Analysis of GATT's Security Exception' (1991) 12 Mich J Intl L 558.

Hasnat B, 'US National Security and Foreign Direct Investment' (2015) 57(3) Thunderbird Intl Business Rev 185.

Hazarika A and P Van Vaerenbergh, 'Climate Change as a Security Risk: Too Hot to Handle?' (2020) 54(3) JWT 417.

Heath JB, 'The New National Security Challenge to the Economic Order' (2020) 129 Yale LJ 1020.

Heath JB, 'Trade and Security among the Ruins' (2020) 30 Duke J Comparative & Intl L 223.

Heath JB, 'Making Sense of Security' (2022) 116(2) AJIL 289.

Helmersen ST, 'Evolutive Treaty Interpretation: Legality, Semantics and Distinctions' (2013) 6(1) Eur J L Stud 127.

Henckels C, 'Should Investment Treaties Contain Public Policy Exceptions' (2018) 59 BC L Rev 2825.

Henckels C, 'Permission to Act: The Legal Character of General and Security Exceptions in International Trade and Investment Law' (2020) 69(3) International and Comparative Law Q 557.

Hobe S and J Griebel, 'New Protectionism: How Binding Are International Economic Legal Obligations During a Global Economic Crisis?' (2010) 2 Goettingen J Intl L 423.

Hofer A, 'All the World's a Stage, and Sanctions the Merely Props: An Interactional Account of Sender-Target Dynamics in the Ukrainian Crisis' (2021) 28 Intl Peacekeeping 259.

Hollway J, JF Morin, and J Pauwelyn, 'Structural Conditions for Novelty: The Introduction of New Environmental Clauses to the Trade Regime Complex' (2020) 20(1) International Environmental Agreements: Politics, Law and Economics 61.

Hopewell K, 'Trump & Trade: The Crisis in the Multilateral Trading System' (2020) 26(2) New Political Economy 271.

Hopewell K, 'Balancing, Threats & Wedges in International Political Economy: The Origins and Impact of the Sino-Indian Alliance at the WTO' (2022) 32(141) J Contemporary China 369.

Horn H, PC Mavroidis, and EN Wijkström, 'In the Shadow of the DSU: Addressing Specific Trade Concerns in the WTO SPS and TBT Committees' (2013) 47(4) JWT 729.

Hrynkiv O, 'Export Controls and Securitization of Economic Policy: Comparative Analysis of the Practice of the United States, the European Union, China, and Russia' (2022) 56(4) JWT 633.

Hrynkiv O, 'Legal and Policy Responses to Security Measures under International Economic Law' (2024) 54(2) Georgetown J Intl L 165.

Hrynkiv O and S Lavrijssen, 'Foreign Investments and Energy Transition in the Netherlands: Balancing Economic and Security Interests' (2024) 42(1) JLCOM 1.

Hrynkiv O, 'Not Trading with the Enemy: the Case of Computer Chips' (2024) 58(1) JWT 61.

Huang C, 'China's Take on National Security and its Implications for the Evolution of International Economic Law' (2021) 48(2) Legal Issues of Economic Integration 119.

Hurd I, 'Legitimacy and Authority in International Politics' (1999) 53 Intl Org 379.

Ikenberry JG, 'Why the Liberal World Order Will Survive' (2018) 32(1) Ethics & Intl Affairs 17.

Jacobs J, 'Tiptoeing the Line between National Security and Protectionism: A Comparative Approach to Foreign Direct Investment Screening in the United States and European Union' (2019) 47(2) IJLI 105.

Jaggard L, 'Climate Change Politics, the UN and National Interests' (2008) 38 Envtl Policy & L 230.

Jang-Jaccard J and S Nepal, 'A Survey of Emerging Threats in Cybersecurity' (2014) 80 Special Issue on Dependable and Secure Computing 973.

Jean CES, 'The Changing Nature of "International Security": the Need for an Integrated Definition' (2007) 8 Graduate J Intl Affairs 22.

John A, 'Inarticulate and Unconscious: Non-Justiciability before the International Court of Justice' (2021) 20 LPICT 77.

Johnson DHN, 'The Effect of Resolutions of the General Assembly of the United Nations' (1955–56) 32 Brit YB Intl L 97.

Kaplow L, 'Rules versus Standards: An Economic Analysis' (1992) 42 Duke LJ 557.

Kapterian G, 'A Critique of the WTO Jurisprudence on "Necessity"' (2010) 59(1) ICLQ 89.

Keene A, 'The Incorporation and Interpretation of WTO-Style Environmental Exceptions in International Investment Agreements' (2017) 18 J World Investment & Trade 62.

Kenny C, 'Responsibility to Recommend: the Role of the UN General Assembly in the Maintenance of International Peace and Security' (2016) 3(1) J on the Use of Force and International Law.

Keohane RO, 'International Institutions: Two Approaches' (1988) 32(4) Intl Studies Q 379.

Kirchner S, 'From "China Shock" to Deglobalisation Shock: China's WTO Accession and US Economic Engagement 20 Years on' (January 2022) US Studies Centre at the University of Sydney 19.

Knight L and T Voon, 'The Evolution of National Security at the Interface between Domestic and International Investment Law and Policy: The Role of China' (2020) 21(1) J World Investment & Trade 104.

Knoll DD, 'The Impact of Security Concerns upon International Economic Law' (1984) 11(3) Intl Econ L 567.

Kocs SA, 'Explaining the Strategic Behavior of States: International Law as System Structure' (1994) 38(4) Intl Studies Q 535.

Kokott J and C Sobotta, 'The Kadi Case – Constitutional Core Values and International Law – Finding the Balance' (2012) 23 Eur J Intl L 1015.

Korzun V, 'The Right to Regulate in Investor-State Arbitration: Slicing and Dicing Regulatory Carve-outs' (2017) 50 Vand J Transnatl L 355.

Koutrakos P, 'Judicial Review in the EU's Common Foreign and Security Policy' (2018) 67 ICLQ 1.

Kubota CJ, 'Closing the Open Door to Foreign Direct Investment' (1982) 15(1) Cornell Intl LJ 121.

Kuilwijk J, 'Castro's Cuba and the U.S. Helms-Burton Act: An Interpretation of GATT Security Exemption' (1997) 31(3) JWT 49.

Kurtz J, 'The Use and Abuse of WTO Law in Investor–State Arbitration: Competition and Its Discontents' (2009) 20(3) EJIL 749.

Kurtz J, 'Adjudging the Exceptional at International Law: Security, Public Order and Financial Crisis (2010) 59 ICLQ 325.

Lai C, 'Acting One Way and Talking Another: China's Coercive Economic Diplomacy in East Asia and Beyond' (2018) 31(2) The Pacific Rev 169.

Lai K, 'National Security and FDI Policy Ambiguity: A Commentary' (2021) 4(4) J Intl Business Policy.

Lamp N, 'At the Vanishing Point of Law: Rebalancing, Non-Violation Claims, and the Role of the Multilateral Trade Regime in the Trade Wars' (2019) 22 J Intl Econ L 721.

Lang A, 'Protectionism's Many Faces' (2020) 44 Yale J Intl L Online https://cpb-us-w2.wpmucdn.com/campuspress.yale.edu/dist/8/1581/files/2019/02/6_Lang_YJIL-Symposium_Protectionisms-Many-Faces_12.07.18-2nrcl0m.pdf.

Larson AP and DM Marchick, 'Foreign Investment and National Security: Getting the Balance Right' (2006) Council on Foreign Relations.

Lauterpacht H, 'Boycott in International Relations' (1933) 14 Brit YB Intl L 125.

Lauterpacht H, 'The Doctrine of Non-Justiciable Disputes in International Law' (1928) 24 Economica 277.

Lee YS, 'Weaponizing International Trade in Political Disputes: Issues Under International Economic Law and Systemic Risks' (2022) 56(3) JWT 405.

Lenaerts K, 'The Kadi Saga and the Rule of Law within the EU' (2014) 67 SMU L Rev 707.

Lester S and H Zhu, 'A Proposal for Rebalancing to Deal with National Security Trade Restrictions' (2019) 42 Fordham Intl LJ 1451.

Lester S and I Manak, 'A Proposal for a Committee on National Security at the WTO' (2020) 30 Duke J Comparative & Intl Law 267.

Li F, 'The Driving Forces of the Convergence of WTO Dispute Settlement Mechanism and International Investment Arbitration' (2018) 52(3) JWT 479.

Li X, 'National Security Review in Foreign Investments: A Comparative and Critical Assessment on China and U.S. Laws and Practices' (2016) 13(1) Berkeley Business LJ 255.

Liberman P, 'Trading with the Enemy: Security and Relative Economic Gains' (1996) 21(1) International Security 147.

Lim B and others, 'Impacts of Reverse Global Value Chain (GVC) Factors on Global Trade and Energy Market' (2021) 14 Energies 1.

Limão N and K Saggi, 'Tariff Retaliation Versus Financial Compensation in the Enforcement of International Trade Agreements' (2008) 76(1) J Intl Economics 48.

Lincicome S and AC Obregon, 'The (Updated) Case for Free Trade' (2022) Policy Analysis No 925 Cato Institute.

Lindsay P, 'The Ambiguity of GATT Article XXI: Subtle Success or Rampant Failure' (2003) 52 Duke LJ 1277.

Ma J, 'International Investment and National Security Review' (2019) 52 Vand J Transnatl L 899.

Mahoney CJ, 'Treaties as Contracts: Textualism, Contract Theory, and the Interpretation of Treaties' (2007) 116 Yale LJ 824.

Marceau G and J Wyatt, 'Dispute Settlement Regimes Intermingled: Regional Trade Agreements and the WTO' (2010) 1(1) JIDS 67.

Marwell JC, 'Trade and Morality: the WTO Public Morals Exception after Gambling' (2006) 81 New York U L Rev 802.

Mathews JT, 'Redefining Security' (1989) 68 Foreign Affairs 162.

McBride E, 'Treaties and Other International Agreements: The Role of the United States Senate' (1985) 12(1) Government Publications Rev 79.

McCormick DH, CE Luftig, and JM Cunningham, 'Economic Might, National Security, and the Future of American Statecraft' (May 6, 2020) 3(3) Texas National Security Rev 50.

McGoldrick D, 'The Boundaries of Justiciability' (2010) 59(4) ICLQ 981.

Meyer T, 'The Political Economy of WTO Exceptions' (2022) 99 Washington UL Rev 1299.

Meyer T, 'Trade Law and Supply Chain Regulation in a Post-Covid-19 World' (2020) 114(4) Am J Intl L 637.

Milanov M, 'A Lauterpachtian Affair: Security Exceptions as 'Self-Judging Obligations' in the Case Law of the International Court of Justice and beyond' (2021) 22(4) J World Investment & Trade 509.

Mishra N, 'The Trade: (Cyber)Security Dilemma and Its Impact on Global Cybersecurity Governance' (2020) 54(4) JWT 567.

Mitchell AD, 'Good Faith in WTO Dispute Settlement' (2006) 7 Melb J Intl L 339.

Mitchell AD and C Henckels, 'Variations on a Theme: Comparing the Concept of "Necessity" in International Investment Law and WTO Law' (2013) 14(1) Chicago J Intl L 93.

Moberg A and S Hindelang, 'The Art of Casting Political Dissent in Law: The EU's Framework for the Screening of Foreign Direct Investment' (2020) 57(5) CMLR 1427.

Mollaian SL, 'Does Trade Equal Peace? The Role of the WTO in International Peace' (2019) 46(1) Legal Issues of Economic Integration 77.

Monsees L and D Lambach, 'Digital Sovereignty, Geopolitical Imaginaries, and the Reproduction of European Identity' (2022) 31(3) European Security 377.

Moon WJ, 'Essential Security Interests in International Investment Agreements' (2012) 15(2) Intl Econ L 481.

Morrison R, 'Efficient Breach of International Agreements' (1997) 23 Denv J Intl L & Poly 183.

Mota CE, 'A More Targeted Approach to Foreign Direct Investment: The Establishment of Screening Systems on National Security Grounds' (2018) 15 Braz J Intl L 440.

Müller P and C Gebauer, 'Austria and the Global Compact on Migration: The "Populist Securitization" of Foreign Policy' (2021) 19 Comp Eur Polit 760.

Nagy CI, 'World Trade, Imperial Fantasies and Protectionism: Can You Really Have Your Cake and Eat It Too?' (2019) 26(1) Indiana J Global Legal Studies 87.

Nam J, 'Model BIT: An Ideal Prototype or a Tool for Efficient Breach' (2017) 48 Geo J Intl L 1275.

Nichols PM, 'Realism, Liberalism, Values, and the World Trade Organization' (2014) 17 U Pa. J Intl L 851.

Nzelibe J, 'The Case against Reforming the WTO Enforcement Mechanism' (2008) 2008 U Ill L Rev 319.

O'Connor B and M Djordjevic, 'Practical Aspects of Monetary Compensation: The US-Copyright Case' (2005) 8 J Intl Econ L 127.

Paddeu F and M Waibel, 'Necessity 20 Years On: The Limits of Article 25' (2022) 37 ICSID Rev – Foreign Investment LJ 160.

Paulsen M, 'Trade Multilateralism and U.S. National Security: The Making of GATT Security Exception' (2020) 41 Mich J Intl L 109.

Paulsen M, 'Let's Agree to Disagree: A Strategy for Trade-Security' (2022) 24(4) J Intl Econ L 527.

Paulsen M, 'The Past, Present, and Potential of Economic Security' (2025) 50 Yale J Intl L 222.

Paulsen M, Saggi K, and Mavroidis P, 'The National Security Exception at the WTO: Should It Just Be a Matter of When Members Can Avail of It? What About How?' (2024) 23(3) World Trade Review 271.

Pauwelyn J, 'Evidence, Proof and Persuasion in WTO Dispute Settlement: Who Bears the Burden' (1998) 1 J Int'l Econ L 227.

Pauwelyn J, 'The Re-Convergence of International Trade and Investment Law: Causes, Questions, and Reform' (2014) 108 Proceedings of the ASIL Annual Meeting 255.

Peng SY, 'Cybersecurity Threats and the WTO National Security Exceptions' (2015) 18 J Intl Econ L.

Perez AF, 'To Judge between the Nations: Post Cold War Transformations in National Security and Separation of Powers-Beating Nuclear Swords into Plowshares in an Imperfectly Competitive World' (1997) 20 Hastings Intl & Comp L Rev 331.

Perez AF, 'WTO and UN Law: Institutional Comity in National Security' (1998) 23 Yale J Intl L 301.

Piczak CT, 'The Helms-Burton Act: U.S. Foreign Policy Toward Cuba, the National Security Exception to GATT and the Political Question Doctrine' (1999) 61 U Pitt L Rev 287.

Portela C, 'Where and Why Does the EU Impose Sanctions?' (2005) 3(17) Politique Européenne 83.

Posner EA and AO Sykes, 'Efficient Breach of International Law: Optimal Remedies, "Legalized Noncompliance," and Related Issues' (2011) 110(2) Mich L Rev 243.

Pospieszna P, J Skrzypczyńska, and B Stępień, 'Hitting Two Birds with One Stone: How Russian Countersanctions Intertwined Political and Economic Goals' (2020) 53(2) PS: Political Science & Politics 243.

Powell R, 'Absolute and Relative Gains in International Relations Theory' (1991) 85(4) The American Political Science Rev 1303.

Powell R, 'Anarchy in International Relations Theory: The Neorealist-Neoliberal Debate' (1994) 48 Intl Org 313.

Prazeres TL, 'Trade and National Security: Rising Risks for the WTO' (2020) 19 World Trade Rev 137.

Rajavuori M and Huhta K, 'Investment Screening: Implications for the Energy Sector and Energy Security' (2020) 144 Energy Policy 1.

Ranjan P, 'Non-Precluded Measures in Indian International Investment Agreements and India's Regulatory Power as a Host Nation' (2012) 2 Asian J Intl L 21.

Ranjan P, 'Comparing Investment Provisions in India's FTAs with India's Stand-Alone BITs Contributing to the Evolution of New Indian BIT Practice' (2015) 16 J World Investment & Trade 899.

Ranjan P, '"Necessary" in Non-Precluded Measures Provisions in Bilateral Investment Treaties: The Indian Contribution' (2020) 67(3) Netherlands Intl L Rev 473.

Ranjan P, 'Investor-State Dispute Settlement (ISDS) Cases and India: Affronting Regulatory Autonomy or Indicting Capricious State Behaviour?' (2022) 21(1) J Intl Trade Law and Policy 42.

Ravikumar S, 'GATT Security Exception: Systemic Safeguards Against its Misuse' (2016) 9 NUJS L Rev 322.

Regan DH, 'The Meaning of "Necessary" in GATT Article XX and GATS Article XIV: The Myth of Cost-Benefit Balancing' (2007) 6(3) World Trade Rev 347.

Reisman WM, 'Negotiating and Maintaining Investment Treaties: Mechanisms for Anticipating and Controlling Textual Drift' (2019) 6 J Intl & Comp L 75.

Rendas T, 'Are Copyright-Permitted Uses "Exceptions," "Limitations" or "User Rights"? The Special Case of Article 17 CDSM Directive' (2022) 17(1) JIPLP 54.

Riffel C, 'The Chapeau: Stringent Threshold or Good Faith Requirement' (2018) 45(2) Legal Issues of Economic Integration 141.

Ripinsky S, 'Global Economic Crisis and the Danger of Protectionism: Does International Law Help?' (2009) 1(3) Amsterdam LF 3.

Roberts A, HC Moraes, and V Ferguson, 'Toward a Geoeconomic Order in International Trade and Investment' (2019) 22(4) J Intl Econ L 655.

Rose-Ackerman S and B Billa, 'Treaties and National Security' (2008) 40(2) NYU J Intl L & Pol 437.

Rosendorff BP and HV Milner, 'The Optimal Design of International Trade Institutions: Uncertainty and Escape' (2001) 55(4) Intl Org 829.

Rubins N and A Nazarov, 'Investment Treaties and the Russian Federation Baiting the Bear?' (2008) 9(2) BLI 100.

Ruggie JG, 'International Regimes, Transactions, and Change: Embedded Liberalism in the Postwar Economic Order' (1982) 36 Intl Org 379.

Saggi K and HM Yildiz, 'Bilateralism, Multilateralism, and the Quest for Global Free Trade' (2010) 81 J Intl Econ 26.

Sahu AK and S Mohan, 'From Securitization to Security Complex: Climate Change, Water Security and the India–China Relations' (2022) 59(2) Intl Politics 320.

Salacuse JW, 'BIT by BIT: The Growth of Bilateral Investment Treaties and Their Impact on Foreign Investment in Developing Countries' (1990) 24 Intl L 655.

Schill S and R Briese, '"If the State Considers": Self-Judging Clauses in International Dispute Settlement' (2009) 13(1) Max Planck YB UN L Online 61.

Schloemann HL and S Ohlhoff, 'Constitutionalization and Dispute Settlement in the WTO: National Security as an Issue of Competence' (1999) 93 Am J Intl L 424.

Schüller R, 'The ITO Charter' (1948) 15(2) Social Research 135.

Schwartz A and RE Scott, 'Contract Theory and the Limits of Contract Law' (2003) 113(3) Yale LJ 541.

Scott SV, 'International Law as Ideology: Theorizing the Relationship between International Law and International Politics' (1994) 5 EJIL 313.

Shaffer G, 'Governing the Interface of U.S.–China Trade Relations' (2021) 115(4) Am J Intl L 622.

Shaffer G, 'Trade Law in a Data-Driven Economy: The Need for Modesty and Resilience' (2021) 20(3) World Trade Rev 259.

Shaffer G and G Henry, 'A New Chinese Economic Order?' (2020) 23(3) J Intl Econ L 607.

Simmons BA, 'Compliance with International Agreements' (1998) 1 Annual Rev of Political Science 75.

Simmons BA, 'Bargaining over BITs, Arbitrating Awards: The Regime for Protection and Promotion of International Investment' (2014) 66 World Politics 12.

Slaughter AM, 'International Law in a World of Liberal States' (1995) 6 Eur J Intl L 503.

Slaughter AM and others, 'International Law and International Relations Theory: A New Generation of Interdisciplinary Scholarship' (1998) 92(3) Am J Intl L 367.

Slepak V, 'National Security Clause: Law and Practice of European Union and Eurasia Economic Union' (2019) 1406 J Phys: Conf Ser 1.

Spears SA, 'The Quest for Policy Space in a New Generation of International Investment Agreements' (2010) 13 J Intl Econ L 1037.

Sperling J and M Webber, 'The European Union, Security Governance and Collective Securitization' (2019) 42(2) West Eur Politics 228.

Staiger RW and AO Sykes, 'Non-Violations' (2013) 16 J Intl Econ L 741.

Staiger RW and AO Sykes, 'How Important Can the Non-Violation Clause Be for GATT/WTO?' (2017) 9(2) American Economic Journal: Microeconomics 149.

Stritzel H, 'Towards a Theory of Securitization: Copenhagen and Beyond' (2007) 13(3) Eur J Intl Relations 357.

Suresh M, 'The Slow Erosion of Fundamental Rights: How Romila Thapar v Union of India Highlights what is Wrong with the UAPA' (2019) 3(2) Indian L Rev 212.

Svetlicinii A, 'China's Defense against Secondary Sanctions: Lessons from the EU Blocking Statute' (2022) 21 (3) J Intl Trade Law and Policy 217.

Swisa M, 'Future Stability in the European Union: Realism, Constructivism, and Institutionalism' (2011) Claremont-UC Undergraduate Research Conference on the European Union 125.

Sykes AO, 'Economic "Necessity" in International Law' (2015) 109(2) Am J Intl L 296.

Tella O, 'South Africa in BRICS: The Regional Power's Soft Power and Soft Balancing' (2017) 44(3) Politikon 387.

Terry PCR, 'Secondary Sanctions: Why the US Approach Is Unlawful and the EU's Response Is Ineffective' (2022) 17(9) Global Trade and Customs Journal 370.

Thorp WL, 'Trade Barriers and National Security' (1960) 50 American Economic Rev 433.

Toye R, 'Developing Multilateralism: The Havana Charter and the Fight for the International Trade Organization, 1947–1948' (2003) 25(2) The Intl History Rev 282.

Trachtman JP, 'A Map of the World Trade Organization Law of Domestic Regulation of Goods: The Technical Barriers to Trade Agreement, the Sanitary and Phytosanitary Measures Agreement, and the General Agreement on Tariffs and Trade' (2014) 48(2) JWT 351.

Trachtman JP, 'WTO Law Constraints on Border Tax Adjustment and Tax Credit Mechanisms to Reduce the Competitive Effects of Carbon Taxes' (2017) 70(2) National Tax Journal 469.

Ufimtseva A, 'The Rise of Foreign Direct Investment Regulation In Investment-Recipient Countries' (2020) 11(2) Global Policy 222.

Van Aaken A, 'International Investment Law between Commitment and Flexibility: A Contract Theory Analysis' (2009) 12 J Intl Econ L 507.

Van Aaken A, 'Smart Flexibility Clauses in International Investment Treaties and Sustainable Development: A Functional View' (2013) 15 J World Investment & Trade 827.

Van Aaken A, 'On the Necessity of Necessity Measures: a Response to Alan O Sykes' (2016) 109 AJIL Unbound 181.

Van Aaken A and J Kurtz, 'Prudence or Discrimination? Emergency Measures, the Global Financial Crisis and International Economic Law' (2009) 12 J Int'l Econ L 859.

Vandevelde KJ, 'The Political Economy of a Bilateral Investment Treaty' (1998) 92 Am J Intl L 621.

Van Langenhove L, T Felicio, and I Torta 'The EU's Preferences for Multilateralism: A SWOT Analysis of EU/UN Relations' (2006) O-2006/21 UNU-CRIS.

Vankovska B, 'Dealing with COVID-19 in the European Periphery: Between Securitization and "Gaslighting"' (2020) 7(1) J Global Faultlines 71.

Verellen T, 'When Integration by Stealth Meets Public Security: The EU Foreign Direct Investment Screening Regulation' (2021) 48(2) Legal Issues of Economic Integration 19.

Vidigal G, 'WTO Adjudication and the Security Exception: Something Old, Something New, Something Borrowed – Something Blue?' (2019) 46(3) Legal Issues of Economic Integration 203.

Vidigal G and SW Schill, 'International Economic Law and the Securitization of Policy Objectives: Risks of a Schmittean Exception' (2021) 48(2) Legal Issues of Economic Integration 109.

Viñuales JE, 'Defence Arguments in Investment Arbitration' (2020) 18 ICSID Rep 9.

Voon T, 'The Security Exception in WTO Law: Entering a New Era' (2019) 113 AJIL Unbound 45.

Voon T, 'Russia – Measures Concerning Traffic in Transit' (2020) 114(1) Am J Intl L 96.

Voon T and D Merriman, 'Incoming: How International Investment Law Constrains Foreign Investment Screening' (2023) 24 J World Investment & Trade 75.

Wagner RH, 'Economic Interdependence, Bargaining Power, and Political Influence' (1988) 42(3) Intl Organization 461.

Wang H, 'The RCEP and Its Investment Rules: Learning from Past Chinese FTAs' (2017) 3(2) The Chinese J Global Governance 160.

Wei-En DK, 'Adapting Gatt Article XXI(B)(III) to Climate Change Threats: An Overdue Rethinking of Security Blues for an Urgent Green Way Forward?' (2020) 27 Austl Intl LJ 103.

Weimer M, 'Reconciling Regulatory Space with External Accountability through WTO Adjudication: Trade, Environment and Development' (2017) 30 Leiden J Intl L 901.

Weiß W, 'Adjudicating Security Exceptions in WTO Law: Methodical and Procedural Preliminaries' (2020) 54(6) JWT 829.

Wells PJ, 'Unilateralism and Protectionism in the World Trade Organization: The Interpretation of the Chapeau within GATT Article XX' (2014) 13(3) J Intl Trade Law and Policy 222.

Wendt A, 'Anarchy Is What States Make of It: The Social Construction of Power Politics' (1992) 46 Intl Org 391.

Wilcox C, 'The London Draft of a Charter for an International Trade Organization' (1947) 37(2) The American Economic Rev 529.

Williams MC, 'Words, Images, Enemies: Securitization and International Politics' (2003) 47(4) Intl Studies Q 511.

Wivel A and TV Paul, 'Soft Balancing, Institutions, and Peaceful Change' (2020) 34(4) Ethics & Intl Affairs 473.

Wolfe R, 'Learning about Digital Trade: Privacy and E-Commerce in CETA and TPP' (2019) 18 World Trade Rev 63.

Wolfers A, '"National Security" as an Ambiguous Symbol' (1952) 67(4) Political Science Q 481.

Woolcock S, 'The Role of the European Union in the International Trade and Investment Order' (2019) 26(1) J of Constitutional Law in Eastern and Central Europe 1.

Wouters J and V Hegde, 'Reform of Global Trade Governance: The Role of the European Union' (2022) 44(5) J of European Integration 715.

Wu CH, 'The EU's Proposed Anti-coercion Instrument: Legality and Effectiveness' (2023) 57(2) JWT 297.

Wu M, 'Rethinking the Temporary Breach Puzzle: A Window on the Future of International Trade Conflicts' (2015) 40 Yale J Intl L 95.

Yin W, 'A Comparison of the US and EU Regulatory Responses to China's State Capitalism: Implication, Issue and Direction' (2020) 19(1) Asia Europe Journal: Studies on Common Policy Challenges 1.

Yoo JY and D Ahn, 'Security Exceptions in the WTO System: Bridge or Bottle-Neck for Trade and Security?' (2016) 19(2) J Intl Econ L 417.

Zangl B and others, 'Between Law and Politics: Explaining International Dispute Settlement Behavior' (2012) 18 Eur J Intl Relations 369.

Zarra G, 'The Issue of Incoherence in Investment Arbitration: Is There Need for a Systemic Reform?' (2018) 17(1) Chinese J Intl L 137.

Zeitler HE, 'Good Faith in the WTO Jurisprudence: Necessary Balancing Element or an Open Door to Judicial Activism' (2005) 8 J Intl Econ L 721.

Zhang H and D Van Den Bulcke, 'China's Direct Investment in the European Union: A New Regulatory Challenge?' (2014) 12 Asia Eur J 159.

Zhao T, 'Sanction Experience and Sanction Behavior: An Analysis of Chinese Perception and Behavior on Economic Sanctions' (2010) 16(3) Contemporary Politics 263.

Zhou W, H Jiang, and Z Chen, 'Trade v Security: Recent Developments of Global Trade Rules and China's Policy and Regulatory Responses from Defensive to Proactive'(2022) World Trade Rev 1.

Zillman DN, 'Energy Trade and the National Security Exception to GATT' (1994) 12(1) J Energy & Natural Resources Law 117.

Zwartkruis W and B de Jong, 'The EU Regulation on Screening of Foreign Direct Investment: A Game Changer?' (2020) 31(3) Eur Bus L Rev 447.

Working Papers and Unpublished Material

Meltzer JP, 'Cybersecurity, Digital Trade, and Data Flows: Re-thinking a Role for International Trade Rules' (2020) 132 Global Economy & Development Working Paper, Brookings 1.

Titi C, 'The Right to Regulate in International Investment Law (Revisited)' (2022) International and Comparative Law Research Center.

Wehrlé F and J Pohl, 'Investment Policies Related to National Security: A Survey of Country Practices' (2016) 2016/02 OECD Working Papers on International Investment, OECD Publishing.

Wolfe R, 'Is Using Trade Policy for Foreign Policy a "SNO Job"? On Linkage, Friend-Shoring and the Challenges for Multilateralism' (2022) Robert Schuman Centre for Advanced Studies Research Paper No RSC 2022/74 https://cadmus.eui.eu/bitstream/handle/1814/75067/RSC_WP_2022_74.pdf?sequence=1.

Reports and Studies

Barber R, 'The Powers of the UN General Assembly to Prevent and Respond to Atrocity Crimes: A Guidance Document' (April 29, 2021) Asia-Pacific Centre for the Responsibility to Protect https://r2pasiapacific.org/files/7091/2021_UNGA_GuidanceDocument4.pdf&#x003E.

Congressional Research Service, 'Committee on Foreign Investment in the United States (CFIUS)' (updated December 9, 2024) CRS Report https://crsreports.congress.gov/product/pdf/IF/IF10177.

Congressional Research Service, 'International Emergency Economic Powers Act: Origins, Evolution, and Use' (updated July 14, 2020) CRS Report https://sgp.fas.org/crs/natsec/R45618.pdf.

Council on Foreign Relations, 'Foreign Investment and U.S. National Security' (August 28, 2018) www.cfr.org/backgrounder/foreign-investment-and-us-national-security.

Draft Treasury Annex Composite Investment (July 22, 1992) www.international.gc.ca/trade-agreements-accords-commerciaux/assets/pdfs/chap11-neg-14.pdf.

Hoekman B, Mavroidis P, and Nelson DR, 'Non-Economic Objectives, Globalisation, and Multilateral Trade Cooperation' (CEPR, September 11, 2023) https://cepr.org/voxeu/columns/non-economic-objectives-globalisation-and-multilateral-trade-cooperation.

Gehrke T, 'Redefining the EU-China Economic Partnership: Beyond Reciprocity Lies Strategy' (Security Policy Brief, February 2019) www.egmontinstitute.be/content/uploads/2019/02/SPB-Gehrke-Final.pdf?type=pdf.

Hanemann T and others, 'National Committee on U.S. China Relations, An Outbound Investment Screening Regime for the United States?' (2022) Report by the US–China Investment Project https://rhg.com/wp-content/uploads/2022/01/RHG_TWS_2022_US-Outbound-Investment.pdf.

Morgott I, 'Strategic Security in the Digital Age: The EU's Deep Dive into Critical Technologies' (Inline, October 27, 2023) www.inlinepolicy.com/blog/eu_critical_technology.

National Academy of Engineering and others, 'Finding Common Ground: U.S. Export Controls in a Changed Global Environment' (National Academies Press, 1991).

OECD Secretariat, 'Acquisition- and Ownership-related Policies to Safeguard Essential Security Interests. Current and Emerging Trends, Observed Designs, and Policy Practice in 62 Economies (OECD, May 2020) www.oecd.org/investment/OECD-Acquisition-ownership-policies-security-May2020.pdf.

OECD Secretariat, 'Transparency, Predictability and Accountability for Investment Screening Mechanisms' (OECD, May 27, 2021) www.oecd

.org/daf/inv/investment-policy/2009-Guidelines-webinar-May-2021-background-note.pdf.

Office of Investment Security, Guidance Concerning the National Security Review Conducted by the Committee on Foreign Investment in the US Federal Register Vol 73 No 236 (December 8, 2008).OSCE Strategy to Address Threats to Security and Stability in the Twenty-First Century www.osce.org/mc/17504?download=true&#x003E.

Report of the International Law Commission on the Work of its Fifty-Third Session, Commentary to Article 27 of ARSIWA (2008).

Study Prepared for the Committee of Foreign Relations by the Congressional Research Service Library of Congress on Treaties and Other International Agreements: The Role of The United States Senate (2001) www.govinfo.gov/content/pkg/CPRT-106SPRT66922/html/CPRT-106SPRT66922.htm.

UN, Human Rights and World Trade Agreements: Using General Exception Clauses to Protect Human Rights (2015) Office of the UN High Commissioner for Human Rights www.ohchr.org/Documents/Publications/WTOen.pdf.

UNCTAD, 'Bilateral Investment Treaties 1995–06: Trends in Investment Rulemaking' (2007) www.unctad.org/en/docs/iteiia20065_en.pdf.

UNCTAD, 'The Protection of National Security in IIAs' (2009) UNCTAD Series on International Investment Policies for Development https://unctad.org/webflyer/protection-national-security-iias&#x003E.

UNCTAD, 'National Security-Related Screening Mechanisms for Foreign Investment. An Analysis of Recent Policy Developments' (December 2019) https://unctad.org/system/files/official-document/diaepcbinf2019d7_en.pdf.

Weiss MA, CRS Report for Congress, 'The U.S. Bilateral Investment Treaty Program: An Overview' (April 24, 2007) Congressional Research Service.

WTO, 'Legal Status of Adopted/Unadopted Reports in other Disputes' www.wto.org/english/tratop_e/dispu_e/disp_settlement_cbt_e/c7s2p1_e.htm.

WTO, 'Trade Policy Commitments and Contingency Measures' (2009) World Trade Report www.wto.org/english/res_e/publications_e/wtr09_e.htm.

WTO, Analytical Index DSU – Article 7 (Jurisprudence) www.wto.org/english/res_e/publications_e/ai17_e/dsu_art7_jur.pdf.

WTO, Statistics on Safeguard Measures www.wto.org/english/tratop_e/safeg_e/safeg_e.htm#statistics.

Newspaper Articles and Press Releases

'Anti-Foreign Sanction Law what MNCs Need to Know about' (Dentons, March 31, 2022) www.dentons.com.

'Could Business be Caught in the Crossfire of China's 'Legal Battle with the West?' *AP News* (June 9, 2021) https://apnews.com/article/china-933c947665ca463b85b4dd9375ceb18f.

'Government Imposes Restriction on Palm Oil Import after Malaysia's Criticism of PM Modi's Action on Kashmir, CAA' *Business Today* (January 9, 2020) www.businesstoday.in/current/economy-politics/govt-imposes-restriction-on-palm-oil-import-after-malaysia-criticism-of-pm-modi-action-on-kashmir-caa/story/393445.html.

'Investment Climate Statements: Brazil' (2020) www.state.gov/reports/2020-investment-climate-statements/brazil/.

'Pulwama Terror Attack: India withdraws Most Favoured Nation' *The Times of India* (February 15, 2019) https://timesofindia.indiatimes.com/india/pulwama-attack-india-withdraws-mnf-status-from-pakistan/articleshow/68004450.cms.

'VVD'er: Kabinet moet Overname Delfts Chipbedrijfje door Nexperia Blokkeren' *FD* (December 1, 2022) (in Dutch) https://fd.nl/tech-en-innovatie/1459876/vvd-er-kabinet-moet-overname-delfts-chipbedrijfje-door-nexperia-blokkeren.

Albert E, 'China Leans Into RCEP Conclusion as Win – The Diplomat' *The Diplomat* (November 19, 2020) https://thediplomat.com/2020/11/china-leans-into-rcep-conclusion-as-win/.

Albert E, 'Russian Import Ban on EU Products' https://ec.europa.eu/food/horizontal-topics/international-affairs/eu-russia-sps-issues/russian-import-ban-eu-products_en.

Albert E, 'EU–US Joint Statement of the Trade and Technology Council' (Press Release, December 5, 2022) https://ec.europa.eu/commission/presscorner/detail/en/STATEMENT_22_7516.

Anuradha RV, 'India. Evolving Regulations on National Security and How They Impact Investments' *Mondaq* (September 17, 2018) www.mondaq.com/india/international-trade-investment/737050/evolving-regulations-on-national-security-and-how-they-impact-investments.

Bhardwaj N and M Cyrill, 'Chinese Investment in India: Impact of New FDI Restrictions by New Delhi' *India Briefing News* (March 5, 2021) www.india-briefing.com/news/india-rethinking-its-fdi-policy-stance-with-china-what-we-know-21824.html/.

Brown L, S Hempel, and L Lu, 'China's National Security Screening for Foreign Acquisitions: Case Study of Blackstone and Carlyle' *Mondaq* (July 17, 2007) www.mondaq.com/china/compliance/50338/chinas-national-security-screening-for-foreign-acquisitions-case-study-of-blackstone-and-carlyle.

Bureau of Industry and Security, 'Commerce Implements New Export Controls on Advanced Computing and Semiconductor Manufacturing Items to the People's Republic of China (PRC)' (Press Release, October 7, 2022) www.bis.doc.gov/index.php/documents/about-bis/newsroom/press-releases/3158-2022-10-07-bis-press-release-advanced-computing-and-semiconductor-manufacturing-controls-final/file.

Council of the EU, 'Declaration by the High Representative Josep Borrell on behalf of the EU: European Union Response to Promote International Security and Stability in Cyberspace' (Press Release, July 30, 2020) www.consilium.europa.eu/en/press/press-releases/2020/07/30/declaration-by-the-high-representative-josep-borrell-on-behalf-of-the-eu-european-union-response-to-promote-international-security-and-stability-in-cyberspace/.

Datta P, 'India Needs National Security Screening of FDI' *The Indian Express* (March 13, 2021) https://indianexpress.com/article/opinion/columns/india-foreign-direct-investments-rules-china-7225979/.

Dwivedi A, 'India's Flawed Approach to Bilateral Investment Treaties' *The Diplomat* (December 4, 2020) https://thediplomat.com/2020/12/indias-flawed-approach-to-bilateral-investment-treaties/.

European Parliament, EU Framework for FDI Screening (Briefing, April 2019) www.europarl.europa.eu/RegData/etudes/BRIE/2018/614667/EPRS_BRI%282018%29614667_EN.pdf.

European Parliament, 'Proposed Anti-Coercion Instrument' (Briefing, June 16, 2022) www.europarl.europa.eu/thinktank/en/document/EPRS_BRI(2022)729299.

FAS, Constitutional Court of the Russian Federation recognized Oilfield Services in Subsoil Areas of Federal Significance as a Strategic Activity (FAS News, July 6, 2020) https://web.archive.org/web/20210814175503/http://fas.gov.ru/news/30069.

Government of India, Department of Industrial Policy and Promotion, Ministry of Commerce and Industry, 'Review of Foreign Direct Investment (FDI) Policy for Curbing Opportunistic Takeovers/Acquisitions of Indian Companies due to the current COVID-19 Pandemic' (Press Note 3, April 17, 2020).

Jiangyu W, 'An Offensive Defense: China's Anti-Foreign Sanctions Law' *Beijing Review* (June 18, 2021) www.bjreview.com/Opinion/Voice/202106/t20210618_800250032.html.

Khaitan N, 'The UAPA amendments: What it Really Means' *Hindustan Times* (August 9, 2019) www.hindustantimes.com/analysis/the-uapa-amendments-what-it-really-means/story-9gOsDNk1syqxyYd0iFeHDN.html.

Khanna A, 'Devising an Indian policy on Sanctions for Pakistan' *Gateway House* (April 30, 2020) www.gatewayhouse.in/indian-policy-sanctions-pakistan/&gt.

Kirchgaessner S and K Hille, 'Huawei in Challenge to US' *FT* (February 15, 2011) www.ft.com/content/f7d582f0-393a-11e0-97ca-00144feabdc0.

Layton R, 'Why Is U.S. Policy Tough On Huawei And TikTok But Not Lenovo?' *Forbes* (June 26, 2020) www.forbes.com/sites/roslynlayton/2020/06/26/why-is-us-policy-tough-on-huawei-and-tiktok-but-not-lenovo/.

Lederer EM, 'Russia Vetoes UN Resolution Calling its Referendums Illegal' *The Washington Post* (September 30, 2022) www.washingtontimes.com/news/2022/sep/30/russia-vetoes-un-resolution-calling-its-referendum/.

Lu D and C Flavelle, 'Rising Seas Will Erase More Cities by 2050, New Research Shows' *The New York Times* (October 29, 2019) www.nytimes.com/interactive/2019/10/29/climate/coastal-cities-underwater.html.

Manak I, 'Suspend Russia's Trade Benefits, For Now' (Council on Foreign Affairs, March 3, 2022) www.cfr.org/article/suspend-russias-trade-benefits-now.

Meeting on Improving the Sustainability of the Development of the Russian Economy (Government News, March 1, 2022) http://government.ru/news/44677/.

Ministry of Commerce and Industry, 'Buying of Palm Oil from Malaysia' (PIB Delhi, February 7, 2020) www.pib.gov.in/PressReleseDetailm.aspx?PRID=1602417.

Ministry of Communications, 'Telecom Department Gives go-ahead for 5 G Technology and Spectrum Trials' (Press Release, May 4, 2021) www.pib.gov.in/PressReleasePage.aspx?PRID=1715927.

Ministry of Electronics and IT, 'Government Bans 59 Mobile Apps which are Prejudicial to Sovereignty and Integrity of India, Defence of India, Security of State and Public Order' (PIB Delhi, June 29, 2020) https://pib.gov.in/PressReleasePage.aspx?PRID=1635206.

Ministry of the Foreign Affairs of the People's Republic of China, 'Foreign Ministry Spokesperson Wang Wenbin's Regular Press Conference' (February 21, 2022) www.fmprc.gov.cn/mfa_eng/xwfw_665399/s2510_665401/2511_665403/202202/t20220221_10644075.html.

Ministry of the Foreign Affairs of the People's Republic of China, 'Foreign Ministry Spokesperson Zhao Lijian's Regular Press Conference' (November 9, 2022) www.fmprc.gov.cn/mfa_eng/xwfw_665399/s2510_665401/2511_665403/202211/t20221109_10891661.html.

Office of the US Trade Representative, 'United States and Indo-Pacific Economic Framework Partners Announce Negotiation Objectives' (Press Release, September 9, 2022) https://ustr.gov/about-us/policy-offices/press-office/press-releases/2022/september/united-states-and-indo-pacific-economic-framework-partners-announce-negotiation-objectives.

Office of the US Trade Representative, Statement from USTR Spokesperson Adam Hodge (Press Release, December 9, 2022) https://ustr.gov/about-us/policy-offices/press-office/press-releases/2022/december/statement-ustr-spokesperson-adam-hodge?s=03.

Office of the US Trade Representative, Statement from USTR Spokesperson Adam Hodge (Press Release, December 21, 2022) https://mailchi.mp/394146669449/statement-from-ustr-spokesperson-adam-hodge?s=09.

Phartiyal S, 'India Holds up Wireless Approvals for China-Made Devices, Delaying Launches' *Reuters* (May 7, 2021) www.reuters.com/business/media-telecom/exclusive-india-holds-up-wireless-approvals-china-made-devices-delaying-launches-2021-05-07/.

Rennemo A, 'How China Joined the Sanctions Game' *The Diplomat* (February 8, 2021) https://thediplomat.com/2021/02/how-china-joined-the-sanctions-game/.

Reuters Staff, 'Russia Rejects Abbott Laboratories' Plan to Buy Petrovax' *Reuters* (April 19, 2013) www.reuters.com/article/us-abbott-russia-idINBRE93I0GJ20130419.

Sauer P, 'Russia Will Not Resume Gas Supplies to Europe until Sanctions Lifted, Says Moscow' *The Guardian* (September 5, 2022) www.theguardian.com/world/2022/sep/05/russia-will-not-resume-gas-supplies-to-europe-until-sanctions-lifted-says-moscow.

Sen N and A Nandy, 'What Ails India's Model BIT?' *BusinessLine* (June 28, 2020) www.thehindubusinessline.com/opinion/what-ails-indias-model-bit/article31939413.ece.

Sheng Y and W Qi, 'EU Needs to 'Cooperate with China' as Concerns of Trade War with US Rise' *Global Times* (December 5, 2022) www.globaltimes.cn/page/202212/1281181.shtml.

Statement by Secretary of the Treasury Janet L Yellen on President Biden's Executive Order on the Committee on Foreign Investment in the United States, US Department of the Treasury (September 15, 2022) https://home.treasury.gov/news/press-releases/jy0951.

The Associated Press, 'Argentina Seizes Falkland Islands; British Ships Move' *The New York Times* (April 3, 1982) www.nytimes.com/1982/04/03/world/argentina-seizes-falkland-islands-british-ships-move.html.

The Council of the EU, 'Cyber Attacks: EU Ready to Respond with a Range of Measures, including Sanctions' (Press Release, June 19, 2017) www.consilium.europa.eu/en/press/press-releases/2017/06/19/cyber-diplomacy-toolbox/.

The Council of the EU, 'Cyber-Attacks: Council is now Able to Impose Sanctions' (Press Release, May 17, 2019) www.consilium.europa.eu/en/press/press-releases/2019/05/17/cyber-attacks-council-is-now-able-to-impose-sanctions/.

The Council of the EU, 'EU imposes the First-Ever Sanctions against Cyber-Attacks' (Press Release, July 30, 2020) www.consilium.europa.eu/en/press/press-releases/2020/07/30/eu-imposes-the-first-ever-sanctions-against-cyber-attacks/.

Toh M, 'The US-China Chip War is Spilling over to Europe' *CNN* (November 25, 2022) https://edition.cnn.com/2022/11/25/tech/us-china-chip-war-spillover-europe-intl-hnk/index.html.

US Committee on Interior and Insular Affairs, Hearings, Reports and Prints of the Senate Committee on Interior and Insular Affairs (US Government Printing Office 1954).

US Congress House, Committee on Foreign Affairs, 'Sanctions and Financial Pressure: Major National Security Tools' Hearing Before the Committee on Foreign Affairs, House of Representatives, One Hundred Fifteenth Congress, Second Session (Publishing Office, January 10, 2018) www.govinfo.gov/content/pkg/CHRG-115hhrg28178/html/CHRG-115hhrg28178.htm.

Venkatesh M, 'India's Withdrawal of MFN Status for Pakistan Has More to Do with Diplomacy Than Trade' *The Print* (February 15, 2019) https://theprint.in/theprint-essential/indias-withdrawal-of-mfn-status-for-pakistan-has-more-to-do-with-diplomacy-than-trade/193442/.

Watts G, 'China Moves to Close the Door on Opening-up' *Asia Times* (August 28, 2019) https://asiatimes.com/2019/08/china-moves-to-close-the-door-on-opening-up/.

White E, D Sevastopulo, and E Olcott, 'China Hits back at US Chip Sanctions with WTO Dispute' *FT* (December 13, 2022) www.ft.com/content/4eaedee4-5267-4e3a-b9da-5d2bb6f356ee.

WTO, 'DS512: Russia – Measures Concerning Traffic in Transit' (WTO News Item, April 26, 2019) www.wto.org/english/news_e/news19_e/dsb_26apr19_e.htm.

WTO, 'DS590: Japan – Measures Related to the Exportation of Products and Technology to Korea' (WTO News, July 29, 2020) www.wto.org/english/news_e/news20_e/dsb_29jul20_e.htm.

Zhang L, 'China: Government Releases Provisions on Unreliable Entity List Regime' (Library of Congress, October 9, 2020) www.loc.gov/law/foreign-news/article/china-government-releases-provisions-on-unreliable-entity-list-regime/.

Zhihong W, 'Carlyle Abandons Xugong Dream' *China Daily* (July 24, 2008) www.chinadaily.com.cn/business/2008-07/24/content_6873004.htm.

Main Online Sources

EC/EU documents https://ec.europa.eu/growth/single-market/european-standards_en.

GATT/WTO documents www.wto.org/, www.wto.org/gatt_docs/.

Investment Policy Hub of the UNCTAD https://investmentpolicy.unctad.org/international-investment-agreements.

OECD, Foreign Direct Investment Statistics: Data, Analysis and Forecasts www.oecd.org/investment/statistics.htm#:~:text=Top%20recipients%20of%20FDI%20inflows,Kingdom%20(USD%2036%20billion).

RTA-IS database https://rtais.wto.org/UI/PublicMaintainRTAHome.aspx.

UN Security Council Meetings and Outcomes Tables maintained by Dag Hammarskjöld Library https://research.un.org/en/docs/sc/quick/meetings/2022.

Blogs & Other

'Federal Antimonopoly Service Strengthens Enforcement of Foreign Investments Legislation' (White & Case, December 3, 2020) www.jdsupra.com/legalnews/foreign-direct-investment-reviews-2020-82639/.

'Foreign Investment Control Heats Up: A Global Survey of Existing Regimes and Potential Significant Changes on the Horizon' (*Jonesday*, January 2018) www.jonesday.com/files/upload/Foreign%20Investment%20Control%20Heats%20Up.pdf.

'How Brazilian Restrictions on the Acquisition of Rural Land by Foreigners have an Impact on Corporate Transactions' (*Ibradim*, 2022) https://ibradim.org.br/how-brazilian-restrictions-on-the-acquisition-of-rural-land-by-foreigners-have-an-impact-on-corporate-transactions/.

'Legal Overview of Foreign Investment in Russia's Strategic Sectors' (Clifford Chance, May 2014) www.cliffordchance.com/content/dam/cliffordchance/briefings/2014/05/a-legal-overview-of-foreign-investment-in-russias-strategic-sectors.pdf.

'Russia Complies with WTO Requirements to Open Pork Imports from Europe' (*IZ.RU*, December 6, 2017) https://iz.ru/679773/2017-12-06/rf-podchinilas-trebovaniiam-vto-otkryt-import-svininy-iz-evropy.

Awasthi S, 'Concept of State – Article 12' (*ILMS Academy Blog*, June 23, 2021) www.ilms.academy/blog/concept-of-state.

Baetens F and M Bronckers, 'The EU's Anti-Coercion Instrument: A Big Stick for Big Targets' (*EJIL:Talk!*, January 19, 2022) www.ejiltalk.org/the-eus-anti-coercion-instrument-a-big-stick-for-big-targets/.

Bělín M and J Hanousek, 'Making Sanctions Bite: The EU–Russian Sanctions of 2014' (*VOX EU*, April 29, 2019) https://voxeu.org/article/making-sanctions-bite-eu-russian-sanctions-2014.

Bhandari D and D Pokhriyal, 'The Continuing Threat of India's Unlawful Activities Prevention Act to Free Speech' (*Jurist*, June 2, 2020) www.jurist.org/commentary/2020/06/bhandari-pokhriyal-uapa-free-speech/.

Biersteker T and C Portela, 'EU Sanctions in Context: Three Types' (EUISS, July 2015) www.iss.europa.eu/sites/default/files/EUISSFiles/Brief_26_EU_sanctions.pdf.

Bond I, 'Huawei, My Way or the Highway: Which Way Should the EU Turn?' (Center for European Reform, June 18, 2019) www.cer.eu/insights/huawei-my-way-or-highway-which-way-should-eu-turn.

Bonnitcha J, 'The Return of Investment Screening as a Policy Tool' (IISD, December 19, 2020) www.iisd.org/itn/en/2020/12/19/the-return-of-investment-screening-as-a-policy-tool-jonathan-bonnitcha/.

Buchanan K, 'FALQs: Article 370 and the Removal of Jammu and Kashmir's Special Status' (Library of Congress, October 3, 2019) https://blogs.loc.gov/law/2019/10/falqs-article-370-and-the-removal-of-jammu-and-kashmirs-special-status/.

Bush N and R Xu, 'China's Expanding Economic Sanctions Regime' (DLA Piper, March 31, 2021) www.dlapiper.com/en/romania/insights/publications/2021/03/chinas-expanding-economic-sanctions-regime/.

Carvajal BT, 'American Unilateralism v European Multilateralism: The World Is Watching' (*Vocal Europe*, July 26, 2018) www.vocaleurope.eu/american-unilateralism-vs-european-multilateralism-the-world-is-watching/.

Casey CA and others, 'The International Emergency Economic Powers Act: Origins, Evolution, and Use' (March 25, 2022) Congressional Research Service 45.

China Threatens US Firms with Sanctions over Taiwan Arms (*RIA Novostiat*, January 30, 2010) http://en.rian.ru/world/20100130/157723449.html.

Cohen HG, 'Waiting for Gundy' (*Just Security*, July 17, 2019) www.justsecurity.org/64946/the-national-security-delegation-conundrum/?s=03.

Da Motta Veiga P and SP Rios, 'China's FDI in Brazil: Recent Trends and Policy Debate' (Policy Center for the New South, June 25, 2019) www.policycenter.ma/publications/china%E2%80%99s-fdi-brazil-recent-trends-and-policy-debate.

Desierto D, 'Protean "National Security" in Global Trade Wars, Investment Walls, and Regulatory Controls: Can "National Security" Ever Be Unreviewable in International Economic Law?' (*EJIL:Talk!*, April 2, 2018) www.ejiltalk.org/national-security-defenses-in-trade-wars-and-investment-walls-us-v-china-and-eu-v-us/.

Desierto D, 'The Reviewability of the Security Exception in GATT Article XXI in *Russia – Traffic in Transit*: Implications for South China Sea Investment Disputes in GATT Article XXI-Type Clauses in ASEAN Regional Investment Treaties' (*EJIL:Talk!*, April 9, 2019) www.ejiltalk.org/wto-panel-in-russia-traffic-in-transit-declares-gatt-article-xxi-is-reviewable/.

Duchâtel M, 'The New Landscape of Investment Screening in Europe' (*Institut Montaigne*, June 21, 2021) www.institutmontaigne.org/en/blog/new-landscape-investment-screening-europe.

Elgueta GR and B Mauro, 'The Paradoxical Relationship between "Foreign Direct Investment Screening" and International Investment Law: What Role for Investor–State Arbitration?' (*Kluwer Arbitration Blog*, April 30, 2020) http://arbitrationblog.kluwerarbitration.com/2020/04/30/the-paradoxical-relationship-between-foreign-direct-investment-screening-and-international-investment-law-what-role-for-investor-state-arbitration/.

Favalli D and M Stojiljkovic, 'Burden and Standard of Proof in Investment Arbitration' (VISCHER AG Lexology, 2020) www.lexology.com/library/detail.aspx?g=37bcab98-af79-4e83-b71a-0bdde3a02de9.

Flicker SM and DM Parsons, 'Huawei – CFIUS Redux: Now It Gets Interesting' (*Paul Hastings*, March 31, 2011) https://webstorage.paulhastings.com/Documents/PDFs/1868.pdf.

Funakoshi M, H Lawson, and K Deka, 'Tracking Sanctions against Russia' *Reuters* (March 9, 2022, updated July 7, 2022) www.reuters.com/graphics/UKRAINE-CRISIS/SANCTIONS/byvrjenzmve.

Global Legal Group, 'International Comparative Legal Guides. Foreign Direct Investments Regimes. China' (November 15, 2024) https://iclg.com/practice-areas/foreign-direct-investment-regimes-laws-and-regulations/china.

Glöckle C, 'The Second Chapter on a National Security Exception in WTO Law: The Panel Report in Saudi Arabia – Protection of IPR' (*EJIL:Talk!*, July 22, 2020) www.ejiltalk.org/the-second-chapter-on-a-national-security-exception-in-wto-law-the-panel-report-in-saudi-arabia-protection-of-ipr/.

Goodman MP, M Reynolds, and J Fittipaldi, 'Economic Security in Emerging Markets' (*CSIS Briefs*, May 2022) https://csis-website-prod.s3.amazonaws.com/s3fs-public/publication/220517_Goodman_Economic_Security.pdf?5RvPqxIMcJNgIl0fb2V3rYd0MKL.HTr.

Hackenbroich J and P Zerka, 'Measured Response: How to Design a European Instrument against Economic Coercion' (ECFE, June 23, 2021) https://ecfr.eu/publication/measured-response-how-to-design-a-european-instrument-against-economic-coercion/.

Harrell P, E Rosenberg, and E Saravalle, 'China's Use of Coercive Economic Measures' (Center for a New American Security, June 2018) https://s3.us-east-1.amazonaws.com/files.cnas.org/documents/China_Use_FINAL-1.pdf?mtime=20180604161240&focal=none.

Heath B, 'Trade, Security and Stewardship (Part III): WTO panels as Factfinders under Article XXI' (*IELP Blog*, May 7, 2019) https://ielp.worldtradelaw.net/2019/05/guest–post–trade–security–and–stewardship–part–iii–wto–panels–as–factfinders–under–article–xxi.html.

Heath B, 'Trade, Security and Stewardship (Part III): WTO Panels as Factfinders under Article XXI' (*IELP Blog*, May 7, 2019) https://ielp.worldtradelaw.net/2019/05/guest-post-trade-security-and-stewardship-part-iii-wto-panels-as-factfinders-under-article-xxi.html.

Heath B, 'Eco Oro and the Twilight of Policy Exceptionalism' (*IISD*, December 20, 2021) www.iisd.org/itn/en/2021/12/20/eco-oro-and-the-twilight-of-policy-exceptionalism/.

Hett F and M Wien (eds.), Between Principles and Pragmatism Perspectives on the Ukraine Crisis from Brazil, India, China and South Africa (Friedrich Ebert Stiftung, May 2015) https://library.fes.de/pdf-files/id-moe/11354.pdf.

Huawei – Building a Fully Connected, Intelligent World www.huawei.com/en/.

International Trade Administration of US Department of Commerce, 'Foreign Retaliations Timeline' (last updated March 29, 2022) www.trade.gov/feature-article/foreign-retaliations-timeline.

Kennedy-Good S and others, 'COVID-19 Crisis Inspires Global Tightening of Foreign Investment Screening' Norton Rose Fulbright www.nortonrosefulbright.com/-/media/files/nrf/nrfweb/knowledge-pdfs/global-rules-on-foreign-direct-investment/global-rules-on-foreign-direct-investment—eu.pdf?la=en-mx.

Kuhn F, 'Offensive Realism and the Rise of China: A Useful Framework for Analysis?' (E-International Relations, July 9, 2021) www.e-ir.info/2021/07/09/offensive-realism-and-the-rise-of-china-a-useful-framework-for-analysis/.

Lamp N, 'Guest Post: Why WTO Members Should Bring Pure Non-Violation Claims Against National Security Measures' (*IELP Blog*, October 15, 2018) https://ielp.worldtradelaw.net/2018/10/guest-post-why-wto-members-should-bring-pure-non-violation-claims-against-national-security-measures.html.

Lester S, 'Non-Violation Claims Against National Security Measures' (*IELP Blog*, October 31, 2019) https://ielp.worldtradelaw.net/2019/10/non-violation-claims-against-national-security-measures.html.

Lobo CA and V Rozenthal, 'The New Protectionism Era: Its Effects on M&A Transactions Globally and in Brazil' (*IBA*, 2021) www.ibanet.org/article/7585c6ae-c97f-40d3-b2b5-6d0bd3efa653.

Lorber EB and JC Zarate, 'National Economic Security' (*FDD*, January 14, 2021) www.fdd.org/analysis/2021/01/14/national-economic-security/.

Malkavi B, 'Guest Post: Consensus as the Hallmark of the WTO: Time to Change' (*IELP Blog*, June 23, 2022) https://ielp.worldtradelaw.net/.

Mir H, 'Kashmir Situation Likely to Deteriorate in 2021: Report' (AA, February 23, 2021) www.aa.com.tr/en/asia-pacific/kashmir-situation-likely-to-deteriorate-in-2021-report/2153865 .

Mishra N, 'India: Leading or Thwarting Data Governance and Digital Trade?' (*Hinrich Foundation*, August 10, 2021) www.hinrichfoundation.com/research/article/digital/india-leading-or-thwarting-data-governance-and-digital-trade/.

Moreira NC, 'Cooperation and Facilitation Investment Agreements in Brazil: The Path for Host State Development' (*Kluwer Arbitration Blog*, September 13, 2018) http://arbitrationblog.kluwerarbitration.com/2018/09/13/cooperation-and-facilitation-investment-agreements-in-brazil-the-path-for-host-state-development/.

Mosia J, 'When is Foreign Direct Investment Beneficial to a Country and When Is It Not? The Case of South Africa' (2012) Economic Diplomacy Programme www.files.ethz.ch/isn/145917/saia_spb_44_mosia_20120223.pdf.

Mota CE, *Foreign Investment, Strategic Assets and National Security* (Intersentia 2018).

Naidu L and S Matsinhe, 'South Africa: The de-Globalizing Pandemic – FDI and Preparing for the Post-COVID Reality' (*Lexology*, July 15, 2020) www.lexology.com/library/detail.aspx?g=abb50576-cd28-45d9-bdf0-1e9959a2565d.

Nainar A, 'Building Indian States' Capacity in Monitoring FDI' (*CSIS*, November 5, 2020) www.csis.org/blogs/new-perspectives-asia/building-indian-states-capacity-monitoring-fdi.

O'Connor B, 'European Union: Is the EU Becoming More Unilateralist?' (NCTM Studio Legale, August 29, 2018) www.mondaq.com/export-controls-trade-investment-sanctions/731312/is-the-eu-becoming-more-unilateralist.

Olson S, 'US-EU Steel Agreement is no Victory for Free Trade – and That's Fine' (*Hinrich Foundation*, November 1, 2021) www.hinrichfoundation.com/research/article/protectionism/us-eu-steel-agreement-free-trade/.

Osisanya S, 'National Security versus Global Security' UN Chronicle www.un.org/en/chronicle/article/national-security-versus-global-security.

Paulsen M, 'The Beginning, End, and Imminence of Invoking Essential Security at the WTO' (*IELP Blog*, July 24, 2021) https://ielp.worldtradelaw.net/2021/07/the-beginning-end-and-imminence-of-invoking-essential-security-at-the-wto.html.

Paulsen M, 'Characterizing War in a Trade Context' (*Opinio Juris*, March 10, 2022) http://opiniojuris.org/2022/03/10/characterizing-war-in-a-trade-context/.

Paulsen M, 'The Beginning, End, and Imminence of Invoking Essential Security at the WTO' (*IELP Blog*, January 6, 2023) https://ielp.worldtradelaw.net/2023/01/if-i-were-an-appellate-body-post-1.html.

Pauwelyn J, 'New Proposal to Strengthen WTO Notification Requirements: From Dispute Settlement to Compliance Regime?' (*IELP Blog*, April 3, 2019) https://ielp.worldtradelaw.net/2019/04/new-proposal-to-strengthen-wto-notification-requirements-from-dispute-settlement-to-compliance-regim.html.

Protocol to the Agreement between the Federal Republic of Germany and the Union of Soviet Socialist Republics concerning the Promotion and Reciprocal Protection of Investments (1989) in relation to Article 3 https://investmentpolicy.unctad.org/international-investment-agreements/treaty-files/1398/download>.

Qiang CZ and others, 'Foreign Direct Investment and Global Value Chains in the Wake of COVID-19: Preparing for the New Normal' (*World Bank Blogs*, May 22, 2020) https://blogs.worldbank.org/psd/foreign-direct-investment-and-global-value-chains-wake-covid-19-preparing-new-normal.

Rahmetov A, 'Is WTO Reform Feasible? Lessons from Political Science Research', Summary of Professor Manfred Elsig's speech at the April 3, 2019 Trade

Lecture Sessions www.wti.org/institute/news/589/is-wto-reform-feasible-lessons-from-political-science-research/.

Reuter M, 'Responding to the China Challenge: The State of Play on Investment Screening in Europe' (*ECFR (blog)*, November 27, 2020) https://ecfr.eu/article/responding-to-the-china-challenge-the-state-of-play-on-investment-screening-in-europe/.

Rosenberg E, 'Assessing the Use of Sanctions in Addressing National Security and Foreign Policy Challenges. Testimony before the HFSC Subcommittee on National Security' (CHAS, May 15, 2019) www.cnas.org/publications/congressional-testimony/assessing-the-use-of-sanctions-in-addressing-national-security-and-foreign-policy-challenges.

Russell M, 'Sanctions over Ukraine. Impact on Russia' (Briefing EPRS, March 2016) www.europarl.europa.eu/EPRS/EPRS-Briefing-579084-Sanctions-over-Ukraine-impact-Russia-FINAL.pdf.

Sheng J and C Xu, 'China Publishes New Rules on National Security Review of Foreign Investment' (*JD Supra*, December 23, 2020) www.jdsupra.com/legalnews/china-publishes-new-rules-on-national-23076/.

Smith, T and G Beaumont-Smith, 'An Analysis of the United States–Mexico–Canada Agreement' (*The Heritage Foundation*, January 28, 2019) www.heritage.org/trade/report/analysis-the-united-states-mexico-canada-agreement.

Toshiya T, 'Three Things to Know About China's "Economic Security"' (*Nippon*, March 7, 2022) www.nippon.com/en/in-depth/a07902/.

Tran H, 'Decoupling/Reshoring Versus Dual Circulation: Competing Strategies for Security & Influence' (Atlantic Council Geoeconomics Center, April 2021) www.atlanticcouncil.org/wp-content/uploads/2021/04/Decoupling_Reshoring_versus_Dual_Circulation.pdf.

Walt SM and R Belfer, 'An International Relations Theory Guide to the War in Ukraine' (*Foreign Policy*, March 8, 2022) https://foreignpolicy.com/2022/03/08/an-international-relations-theory-guide-to-ukraines-war/.

Wesley M, 'Australia and the Rise of Geoeconomics' (*The Centre of Gravity Series*, November 2016) http://bellschool.anu.edu.au/sites/default/files/uploads/2017-05/australia_and_the_rise_of_geoeconomics.pdf.

Yannaca-Small K, 'Essential Security Interests under International Investment Law' in *International Investment Perspectives: Freedom of Investment in a Changing World* (OECD 2007) www.oecd.org/daf/inv/investment–policy/40243411.pdf.

Yi D, 'Yonghui Drops Plans to Increase Stake in Chinese Retailer After National Security Probe' (CX Tech, December 17, 2019) www.caixinglobal.com/2019-12-17/yonghui-drops-plans-to-increase-stake-in-chinese-retailer-after-national-security-probe-101495178.html.

INDEX

Printed by Integrated Books International,
United States of America